Inside Texas Politics

Power, Policy, and Personality of the Lone Star State

THIRD EDITION

Brandon Rottinghaus

Carefully scratch off the silver coating to see your personal redemption code.

OXFORD
UNIVERSITY PRESS

Directions for accessing

Oxford Insight Study Guide and Additional Digital Course Materials

Inside Texas Politics comes with a wealth of powerful tools to help you succeed in your course.

Follow these steps to access your resources:

Visit oup.com/he/rottinghaus3e

Select the edition you are using, then select student resources for that edition

Follow the on-screen instructions, entering your personal redemption code when prompted

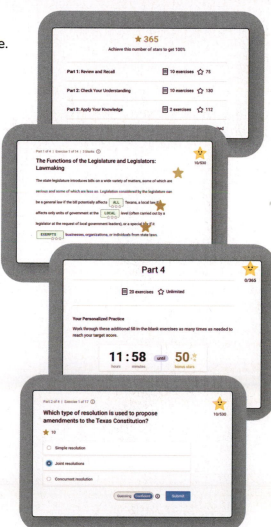

INSIDE TEXAS POLITICS

POWER, POLICY, AND PERSONALITY OF THE LONE STAR STATE THIRD EDITION

Brandon Rottinghaus

University of Houston

NEW YORK OXFORD
OXFORD UNIVERSITY PRESS

Oxford University Press is a department of the University of Oxford.
It furthers the University's objective of excellence in research, scholarship,
and education by publishing worldwide. Oxford is a registered trade mark of
Oxford University Press in the UK and certain other countries.

Published in the United States of America by Oxford University Press
198 Madison Avenue, New York, NY 10016, United States of America.

Library of Congress Cataloging-in-Publication Data
Names: Rottinghaus, Brandon, 1977- author.
Title: Inside Texas politics: power, policy, and personality of the Lone
    Star State / Brandon Rottinghaus.
Description: Third edition. | New York, NY: Oxford University Press, 2021. |
    Includes bibliographical references and index.
Identifiers: LCCN 2020032335 (print) | LCCN 2020032336 (ebook) | ISBN
    9780197545416 (paperback) | ISBN 9780197545454 (epub)
Subjects: LCSH: Texas—Politics and government.
Classification: LCC JK4816 .R67 2021 (print) | LCC JK4816 (ebook) | DDC
    320.4764—dc23
LC record available at https://lccn.loc.gov/2020032335
LC ebook record available at https://lccn.loc.gov/2020032336

9 8 7 6 5 4 3 2 1
Printed by Quad/Graphics, Inc., Mexico

To my family.

BRIEF CONTENTS

About the Author   xvii

Preface   xviii

Acknowledgments   xxvi

1   **The Struggle For Texas: Demographics, Culture, and Political Power   2**

2   **The Texas Constitution   34**

3   **Federalism   68**

4   **Voting and Elections   98**

5   **Political Parties: Texas in Blue And Red   136**

6   **Interest Groups   172**

7   **The Legislature   206**

8   **Governors of Texas   244**

9   **The Plural Executive and The Bureaucracy   278**

10   **The Texas Judiciary   316**

11   **Criminal Justice   352**

12   **Local Government   382**

13   **Budget, Finances, and Policy   416**

14   **Public Policy in Texas   440**

Glossary   G-477

Notes   N-483

Credits   C-515

Index   I-517

CONTENTS

About the Author   xvii

Preface   xviii

Acknowledgments   xxvi

CHAPTER 1   **The Struggle For Texas: Demographics, Culture, and Political Power   2**

1.1 The Origins of Texas   4

Native Americans   4
Spanish Settlers   6
Tejanos   7
Anglos   7
ANGLES OF POWER: The Benefits and Challenges of Diversity   8
African Americans   9

1.2 Continuity and Change in the Texas Economy   9

Food and Fiber   10
Fuel   10
King Cattle (And Other Four-Legged Friends)   12
Manufacturing   12
Military and Defense Industries   12
High Tech   14
Health Care   14
Recreation and Retirement   14
Assessing the Texas Economy   14

GREAT TEXAS POLITICAL DEBATES: Accent Marks on State Documents   15

1.3 Continuity and Change in Texas Demographics   16

State Population Growth   17
IS IT BIGGER IN TEXAS? U.S. States with the Largest Population Increases, 2000–2019   18
Challenges of Population Growth   19
Racial and Ethnic Trends in Texas   20
Challenges of Shifting Racial and Ethnic Trends   22
An Aging State   23
Challenges of an Aging Texas   23

1.4 Continuity and Change in Texas Political Culture   24

INSIDER INTERVIEW: Joe Holley, *Houston Chronicle* Writer   25
Individualistic Political Culture   26
Traditionalistic Political Culture   28
Culture Conflicts   29

CHAPTER 2   The Texas Constitution   34

2.1 Constitutional Government   36

2.2 The Roots of Rebellion and the Declaration of Independence   37

2.3 The 1836 Constitution of the Republic   40

2.4 The 1845 Constitution of the (New) State of Texas   42

2.5 Secession, Reconstruction, and the Constitutions of 1861, 1866, and 1869   44

The 1861 Constitution—"The Confederacy Constitution"   45
The 1866 Constitution—"The Readmission Constitution"   45

The 1869 Constitution—"The Reconstruction Constitution"   47

2.6 The Constitution of 1876—The Current Constitution   49

The Crafting of the 1876 Constitution   50
Principles of the Texas Constitution   50
INSIDER INTERVIEW: Former Chief Justice Tom Phillips   52
GREAT TEXAS POLITICAL DEBATES: Confederate Flag License Plates and the Battle over Free Speech   55

2.7 Amending the Constitution   56

Constitutional Amendments   56
Recent Major Reform Attempts   61
IS IT BIGGER IN TEXAS? Number of Words in State Constitutions   62
ANGLES OF POWER: Debates about Amending the Constitution   63

CHAPTER 3   Federalism   68

3.1 Organizing the Constitutional System   70

The Supremacy Clause   71
Enumerated and Implied Powers   71
Reserved Powers   74
Concurrent Powers   74
Full Faith And Credit   75

3.2 Advantages of Federalism   76

A Stronger Central Government   76
ANGLES OF POWER: Texas, the Military, and Jade Helm   77
Representation   77
Policy Innovation   78
Trust in Levels of Government   79

3.3 Texas and Federal Funding   80

IS IT BIGGER IN TEXAS? Federal Aid as a Percentage of General Revenue   81

3.4 Styles of Federalism   84

Dual Federalism   84
Cooperative Federalism   85
New Federalism   86
Coercive Federalism   87
INSIDER INTERVIEW: Michael C. Massengale, Appeals Court Judge   88

3.5 Texas and Conflicts over Federalism   89

Texas Versus Washington   89
Tidelands Controversy   90
Red River Border Dispute   91
Immigration   91
GREAT TEXAS POLITICAL DEBATES: Sanctuary Cities   92
Voter Identification at Election Places   93
Common Core Education Standards   94

CHAPTER 4 Voting and Elections 98

4.1 Voting in Texas 100
Registration 100
Types of Elections 102
Early Voting 103
Mobile Voting 105
Election Day 105
Administration 107

4.2 Suffrage Struggles and their Consequences 107
Literacy Tests 108
Poll Tax 108
White Primary 108
Hispanics 109
ANGLES OF POWER: Political Machines 110
INSIDER INTERVIEW: Victor Morales, U.S. Senatorial Candidate in 1996, U.S. House Candidate in 1998 111
African Americans 113
Women 114
Asian Americans 116

4.3 Voter Turnout in Texas 116
Why Texans don't Vote 117
Social Pressure and Political Socialization 118
IS IT BIGGER IN TEXAS? Voter Turnout by State, 2020 119
How can Voter Turnout be Increased? 120
Voter ID 121

4.4 How to Campaign, Texas Style 123
Building Campaign Infrastructure 123
Image, Limelight, and the Media 124
Negative Campaigning 124
Courting the Base 125
Microtargeting 125
Surfing National Trends 126
Funding Elections 126

4.5 Who Wins and Why 129
Money and Election Outcomes 129
Parties and Straight-Ticket Voting 131
Incumbents and Voter Turnout 131
GREAT TEXAS POLITICAL DEBATES: "No Excuse" Mail Voting 132
The Electoral System 132
Will Texas Turn Blue? 132

CHAPTER 5 Political Parties: Texas in Blue and Red 136

5.1 The Functions of Parties 138
Simplifying Electoral Choices 138
Recruiting Candidates 139
Mobilizing Voters 140
Articulating Interests 140
Organizing Government 141

5.2 Party Organization 141
Precinct Chairs 142
County Party Chairs 142
State Party Chair 143
Party Executive Committees 143
Party Conventions 144
State Party Platforms 144

5.3 Rise and Fall of Political Parties in Texas 146
Democratic Reign in the Postbellum Era 146
The Decline of the Democrats 147
The Rise of the Republicans 149
The Tea Party 151
Fissures in the Republican Party 153
Lessons from Texas Party Politics 155

5.4 Party Competition 156
INSIDER INTERVIEW: Jared Woodfill, Former Harris County Republican Party Chair 156
Apportionment 157
IS IT BIGGER IN TEXAS? Party Competition, 1972–2015 158

Legislative Redistricting   159
ANGLES OF POWER: The 2003 Redistricting Battle and the Killer Ds   161
Party Switching   163
GREAT TEXAS POLITICAL DEBATES: Switching Parties   164

5.5 Third Parties and Independents   165
La Raza Unida Party   166
Libertarian Party of Texas   167
Green Party of Texas   167
Independents   168

CHAPTER 6   Interest Groups   172

6.1 Interest Groups in the Political Process   175
Pluralist Theory   175
Elite Theory   176
Transactional Theory   176
Which Theory Fits Texas?   177

6.2 Why Join Interest Groups   177
The Free Rider Problem   177
Selective Benefits   178

6.3 Types of Interest Groups   179
Business Groups   179
Trade Associations and Professional Organizations   180
Labor Unions   180
Identity Groups   180
IS IT BIGGER IN TEXAS? Rates of Union Membership   181
Public Interest Groups   182
Single-Issue Groups   182
Government Interests   183

6.4 What Interest Groups Do   183
Education   184

Citizen Campaigns   184
Electioneering   185
Lobbying The Courts, the Legislature, and the Executive Branch   187

6.5 Lobbying: The Third House   187
The Role of Lobbyists   188
What Lobbyists Do   189
Iron Triangles in Texas   192
INSIDER INTERVIEW: Andrea McWilliams, co-founder of McWilliams Government Affairs Consultants   192
IS IT BIGGER IN TEXAS? Number of Years Elected Officials must Wait before Becoming Lobbyists   194

6.6 Scandals and Reforms   195
Sharpstown Scandal   196
The 1991 Reforms   197
Current Ethics Legislation   197

6.7 Oversight of Interest Groups   198
Texas Ethics Commission   198
Recusal   201
GREAT TEXAS POLITICAL DEBATES: Donations and Legal Defense Funds   201
Disclosure   202

CHAPTER 7   The Legislature   206

7.1 The Functions of the Legislature and Legislators   208
Lawmaking   208
Texas House Versus Senate   210
Casework   211
Winning Reelection   211

7.2 The Texas Legislature in Context   214
The Legislative Session   214
IS IT BIGGER IN TEXAS? Length of Legislative Session   216
Legislative Staff   217
Legislative Boards and Councils   217

Salary   217
GREAT TEXAS POLITICAL DEBATES: Should Texas have Annual
Legislative Sessions?   218
Incumbency and Turnover   218
Consequences of the Texas Legislative
Structure   218

(**⚡**) **7.3 How the Legislature is
Organized**   220
The Committee System   220
Speaker of the House   221
ANGLES OF POWER: Choosing a Speaker   223
The Lieutenant Governor   224

(**⚡**) **7.4 The Legislative Process**   224
In Committee   224
On the Floor   226

House and Senate Agreement   227
In Conference Committee   227
The Real Enemy: The Calendar   228
Rules Rule the Chambers   229

(**⚡**) **7.5 Working Together**   230
Slowing it Down   231
Speeding It Up   235
Increasing Partisanship   235

(**⚡**) **7.6 Demographic Representation**   237
Women Legislators   237
INSIDER INTERVIEW: Senfronia Thompson, State
Representative, Houston, Texas   239
African Americans   239
Hispanics   239
Religion and other Factors   240

CHAPTER 8   Governors of Texas   244

(**⚡**) **8.1 Rules of the Office**   246
Eligibility   246
Informal Qualifications   247
Terms   247
Removal from Office   247
Succession   249
Salary and Staff   249
IS IT BIGGER IN TEXAS? Governor Staff Size   250

(**⚡**) **8.2 Formal Powers of Texas
Governors**   251
Execution Of Laws   251
Appointment Powers   253
IS IT BIGGER IN TEXAS? Unilateral Executive Orders by
Governor in Select States   254
Legislative Powers   255
Military Powers   261
Judicial Powers: Pardon and Clemency   262

(**⚡**) **8.3 Informal Powers of Texas
Governors**   263
Legislative Bargaining   263
INSIDER INTERVIEW: Former Democratic Governor Mark
White   263
Agenda Setting   265
GREAT TEXAS POLITICAL DEBATES: Budget Powers of the
Governor   268

(**⚡**) **8.4 Weak And Strong Governor**   271
Sheer Length of Term   271
IS IT BIGGER IN TEXAS? Map of Gubernatorial
Power   272
Appointees   273
Party Power   273
ANGLES OF POWER: A "Power Grab" or Efficient
Executive?   273
Criticisms and Reforms   274

CHAPTER 9   The Plural Executive and the Bureaucracy   278

(**⚡**) **9.1 Bureaucracy in Texas**   280
The Size of the Texas Bureaucracy   281
What the Texas Bureaucracy Does   281

IS IT BIGGER IN TEXAS? State Employees per 10,000
Residents   282
The Structure of The Texas Bureaucracy   284

9.2 Independently Elected Officers 286

Lieutenant Governor 286
IS IT BIGGER IN TEXAS? Lieutenant Governor Power Index 287
ANGLES OF POWER: The Power of the Lieutenant Governor beyond Politics 290
INSIDER INTERVIEW: David Dewhurst, Former Democratic Lieutenant Governor of Texas 291
Attorney General 292
Comptroller of Public Accounts 294
Commissioner of the General Land Office 297
Agriculture Commissioner 297
Plural Executive Feuds 298

9.3 Governor-Appointed, Single-Headed Agencies 299

Secretary of State 299
Commissioner for Health and Human Services 299
Department of Insurance 300

9.4 Governor-Appointed, Multimember Agencies 301

Public Utility Commission 301
Department of Transportation 301
Texas Parks and Wildlife Department 301
Texas Commission on Environmental Quality 302

9.5 Multimember Elected Commissions and Hybrid Agencies 303

Texas Railroad Commission 303
Texas Ethics Commission 304
State Board of Education 304

9.6 Controlling The Bureaucracy 305

Selection of The Bureaucracy 305
Sluggish Policymaking 306
Oversight and Change 307
GREAT TEXAS POLITICAL DEBATES: Sunset Sunset? 311

CHAPTER 10   The Texas Judiciary   316

10.1 The Role of the Courts 318

Dispensing Justice 318
IS IT BIGGER IN TEXAS? Total Trial Courts 320
Interpreting The Law 321

10.2 Trial Courts 322

Local Courts 322
County Trial Courts 324
State District Courts 325

10.3 Appellate Courts 326

Intermediate Appellate Courts 328
Appellate Courts of Last Resort 328

10.4 Quality of Justice in Texas 330

ANGLES OF POWER: Two Supreme Courts? 331
Caseload: Overworked Judges? 331
Length of Court Cases 331
Salary: Underpaid Judges? 332
IS IT BIGGER IN TEXAS? Salaries of Judges in the Five Most Populous States 333
Turnover of Judges 334
Access to Justice 334

10.5 Judicial Selection and Removal 335

Judicial Selection in Texas 335
IS IT BIGGER IN TEXAS? Primary Judicial Selection Process at the State Supreme Court Level 336
INSIDER INTERVIEW: Justice Rebeca Aizpuru Huddle, Texas Supreme Court 337
Censure and Removal From Office 338
Judicial Qualifications 338
Problems With Partisan Elections 339

10.6 Who are the Justices? 342

Women 345
African Americans 346
Hispanics 346
Asians 346

10.7 Reforming the System 346

Nonpartisan Elections 347
Merit Selection 347
Public Financing of Elections 347
Limiting Fundraising Totals 347
GREAT TEXAS POLITICAL DEBATES: The "Geezer Amendment" and Age Limits 348

CHAPTER 11   **Criminal Justice**   352

ⓦ 11.1 Texan Justice   354
Rights of The Accused   355
Victim Rights   355

ⓦ 11.2 Types of Crimes   357
Misdemeanors   357
Felonies   357
Drug Crimes   358
Juvenile Crime   359

ⓦ 11.3 Criminal Justice Process in Texas   360
Pretrial   360
Trial   361
Punishment   362
ANGLES OF POWER: Race and Finances in the Texas Prison System   363
Incarceration   365
IS IT BIGGER IN TEXAS? State and Federal Prisoners under Jurisdiction of Correctional Authorities   366

GREAT TEXAS POLITICAL DEBATES: Prison Conditions in Texas   369
Death Penalty   369

ⓦ 11.4 Life After Prison   373
Restricted Licensing, Employment, And Access To Programs   373
Voting Rights   374
Parole   374
IS IT BIGGER IN TEXAS? Restrictions on Voting Post-Felony, by State   375

ⓦ 11.5 Reforms   376
Alternatives to Incarceration   376
Bail Reforms   376
Addressing Prison Suicides   377
Grand Jury Reform   377
Death Penalty Reform   377
INSIDER INTERVIEW: Former Court of Criminal Appeals Judge Cathy Cochran   378

CHAPTER 12   **Local Government**   382

ⓦ 12.1 The Powers and Functions of Local Government   384
Dillon's Rule   384
Local Regulation   385
GREAT TEXAS POLITICAL DEBATES: Paid Sick Leave   385

ⓦ 12.2 County Government   386
IS IT BIGGER IN TEXAS? Number of Local Governments   387
County Judge and Commissioner's Court   388
County Sheriff   389
County Prosecutors   389
County Administrators   390
County Finance Officials   390

ⓦ 12.3 City Governments   391
General Law Cities   391
Home Rule Cities   391

INSIDER INTERVIEW: Local activist Barry Klein, Texas Property Rights Association   393

ⓦ 12.4 Types Of City Government   394
Mayor–Council System   394
Commission Government   396
Council–Manager System   396

ⓦ 12.5 Special Districts   398
School Districts   398
IS IT BIGGER IN TEXAS? Special-Purpose Districts Nationwide   399
Special Improvement Districts   400
Junior/Community College Districts   400
Library Districts   401
Municipal Utility Districts   401
Hospital Districts   401
Homeowners' Associations   402

Ⓦ **12.6 Elections** 402

County Elections 403
City Elections 403
Minority Representation in Municipal
Governments 403
Low-Turnout in Municipal
Elections 404
Voting And Corruption 404

Ⓦ **12.7 Issues in Local Government** 406

Local Governments Short on Cash 406
Rising Debt 408
ANGLES OF POWER: The Stadiums that Ate Texas 408
Cooperation Across Governments 409
Sprawl 411
To Zone Or Not To Zone 412
Pensions 412

CHAPTER 13   Budget, Finances, and Policy 416

Ⓦ **13.1 Taxes and other Revenue
Sources** 418

Sales Tax 418
Property Tax 420
IS IT BIGGER IN TEXAS? State and Local Sales Taxes,
2019 421
INSIDER INTERVIEW: Dale Craymer, President of the
Texas Taxpayers and Research Association 422
Franchise (Business) Taxes 423
ANGLES OF POWER: Putting a Lid on Property
Taxes 423
Oil and Natural Gas Taxes 424
Car Taxes: Motor Fuel Tax ("Gas" Tax) and Motor
Vehicle Taxes 424
Sin Taxes 425

Ⓦ **13.2 Alternative Sources of
Funds** 425

Fees and Fines 425
The "Rainy Day" and other
Funds 426
GREAT TEXAS POLITICAL DEBATES: A "Poor
Tax"? 427
Why No Income Tax? 427
Debates Over Taxes 428

Ⓦ **13.3 The Budget** 430

Budget Cycle 430
Budget Limitations 430
Budget Players and Process 433
Budget Tricks 436

CHAPTER 14   Public Policy in Texas 440

Ⓦ **14.1 Public Policy Priorities
and Process** 442

Ⓦ **14.2 Health Care and Welfare** 444

Medicare 445
INSIDER INTERVIEW: Eva DeLuna Castro, State Budget
Analyst, Center for Public Policy Priorities 445
Medicaid 446
Children's Health Insurance Program 447
The Affordable Care Act 447
Social Security 448
Temporary Assistance to Needy Families 448

GREAT TEXAS POLITICAL DEBATES: Drug Testing for
Benefits 449
IS IT BIGGER IN TEXAS? Maximum TANF Benefit as a
Percentage of the Poverty Line 450
Unemployment Benefits 451
Workers' Compensation 451

Ⓦ **14.3 Immigration and Border
Security** 452

Economic Impact 452
Public Opinion and State Laws 453
Deportations and Border Security 454

(ω) 14.4 Education 455

Sources Of K–12 Funding 455
School Finance 456
Teacher, Student, and School Performance 457
ANGLES OF POWER: Standardized Tests and Education
Accountability 460
Diversity in Public Education 461
Vouchers 463
Special Education 464
Bullying 464

(ω) 14.5 Higher Education 465

Funding 465

Community Colleges 466
Standards 467
Affirmative Action 467

(ω) 14.6 Transportation 468

IS IT BIGGER IN TEXAS? Unmet Demand for
Transportation (Percentage of
Population) 469

(ω) 14.7 Energy and the Environment 470

Water 470
Water and Air Pollution 472
Energy Sources 473

Glossary G-477
Notes N-483
Credits C-515
Index I-517

ABOUT THE AUTHOR

BRANDON ROTTINGHAUS is Professor of Political Science at the University of Houston. He grew up in Dallas and has published on and taught American and Texas government for more than 20 years. He has also worked in Texas politics at every level. Dr. Rottinghaus regularly provides commentary on national and Texas politics in hundreds of media outlets.

His research interests include Texas politics, executive and legislative politics, and research methods. His work on these subjects has appeared in dozens of academic journals and multiple edited volumes. He is also the author of three other books: *The Provisional Pulpit: Modern Conditional Presidential Leadership of Public Opinion* (Texas A&M University Press, 2010), *The Institutional Effects of Executive Scandal* (Cambridge University Press, 2015), and *The Dual Executive: Unilateral Orders in Separated and Shared Powers System* (Stanford University Press, 2017).

Dr. Rottinghaus co-hosts a podcast on national and state politics called *Party Politics* through *Houston Public Media* (Houston's NPR/PBS). He is the creator and weekly contributor to *Monday Morning Politics* on Houston's Fox 26 that reviews the political events of the past week and previews the week to come.

His commentary on national and Texas politics has also appeared in the *Texas Tribune*, the *Houston Chronicle*, the *Dallas Morning News*, the *Austin-American Statesman*, the *Corpus Christi Caller*, the *Lubbock Avalanche Journal*, the *McAllen Monitor*, the *San Antonio Express-News,* the *El Paso Times*, CNN, *The Texas Standard*, National Public Radio, the *Guardian*, the *Washington Post,* and the *New York Times*.

PREFACE

THE LATE MOLLY IVINS once wrote, "Good thing we've got politics in Texas—finest form of free entertainment ever invented." Or, as she put it later in her career, "If Texas were a sane place, it wouldn't be nearly as much fun."

The characters in Texas politics are among the most interesting and influential in all levels of government. Three of the last ten presidents hailed from Texas. Incensed by a federal ban on Mirax, a Texas exterminator was elected to the U.S. House and became U.S. House majority leader, determined to exact revenge on the Environmental Protection Agency. One former state senator falsely claimed he was shot by Communists to make himself more attractive to voters. A state house member frequently sipped gin out of a 7Up bottle during floor debates. State officials frequently have come to blows over education, taxation, and smaller issues such as whether teachers should be allowed to shoot students on school buses in self-defense. The state legislature tries to ban cities from offering sanctuary to undocumented immigrants, while cities go to battle against state agencies that plan to store nuclear waste in their backyards.

Teaching Texas government and politics is exciting because the history of the state is rich with these stories of political struggles, and speculation about the future of Texas politics provides for intriguing learning opportunities.

⊌ THEME

True to the title—*Inside Texas Politics*—the book takes a unique tactic, describing and analyzing Texas politics from an insider's perspective. I wrote the text to make the material on Texas government and politics accessible and memorable for today's students, as well as to provide an insider's perspective on how power struggles have shaped Texas institutions and political processes. My goal is to bring Texas government to life by recounting how colorful characters and Texans from all walks of life have both influenced and been influenced by the governing process. The chapters are rich with historical accounts, engaging recent examples, and relevant (but accessible) statistical data.

The Texas Higher Education Coordinating Board (THECB) requirements have recently added additional fundamental component areas for social and personal responsibility, where students are asked to understand knowledge of civic responsibility, community engagement, and connecting actions and consequences to ethical decision making. The theme and data presentation developed in this text lends itself well to executing and assessing these requirements. Marginal questions query students to consider concepts from a social and personal responsibility perspective. Questions below every figure and table ask students to practice analyzing the data, to think critically about it, to evaluate trends, and to communicate them.

This book exploits use of original data (collected for this project by the author) and institutional data (from official government sources) to provide a whole picture of government and politics in Texas. Data literacy is a major component of how material is presented, and students will be able to build skills to serve as a foundation for future learning.

NEW TO THE THIRD EDITION

CHAPTER 1: THE STRUGGLE FOR TEXAS

- Expanded discussion about worker casualties and wage theft among undocumented immigrants.
- Updated population changes by rural, suburban, and rural counties.

CHAPTER 2: THE TEXAS CONSTITUTION

- New political cartoon highlighting liberty versus security debate.
- Updated constitutional changes from recent 2019 election.

CHAPTER 3: FEDERALISM

- Discussion of public support for federal, state and local handling of COVID-19.
- Updated exploration of federalism dynamics in immigration policy issue.

CHAPTER 4: VOTING AND ELECTIONS

- New evaluation of voting administration and right, including pros and cons of "mobile voting."
- New original data on school district compliance with state registration laws.

CHAPTER 5: POLITICAL PARTIES

- Expanded details and controversies about ballot access by minor parties.
- Will Texas turn blue? Enhanced conversation about political competition in Texas for 2020 and beyond.

CHAPTER 6: INTEREST GROUPS

- Added exchange on "temporary employees" (like Uber or PostMates) and interest group success.
- Expanded discussion about protest politics (covering protests for those against COVID-19 lockdown orders and Black Lives Matter)

CHAPTER 7: THE LEGISLATURE

- Further subsidiary discussion about controversy around retiring Speaker Dennis Bonnen.
- Renewed data on social media conversations and Texas legislature personality and policies.

CHAPTER 8: GOVERNORS OF TEXAS

- Revised information on governor legislative success rates over time.
- New data on comparative state use of gubernatorial executive orders.

CHAPTER 9: PLURAL EXECUTIVE AND BUREAUCRACY

- Updated review of how the bureaucracy affects laws on surprise medical billing.
- Expanded review of how politics and personalities affect legislature committee selection.

CHAPTER 10: JUDICIARY

- Expanded references to recent court cases, including surprise hospital bills, upskirt laws, and short term rental controversy.
- References to findings of Texas Commission on Judicial Selection.

CHAPTER 11: CRIMINAL JUSTICE

- Modernized evaluation of controversial criminal justice issues like police shootings of African Americans (such as the Botham Jean case in Dallas and more).
- Increased examination of significant changes to post-conviction voting laws around the nation.

CHAPTER 12: LOCAL GOVERNMENT

- Expanded discussion of local policy issues like game rooms and scooters and the role local government plays.
- Updated recent examples from friction between mayors and city managers.

CHAPTER 13: BUDGET, FINANCES, AND POLICY

- Expanded example of policy affects people and how Texans can change policy, such as "tampon tax" laws.
- Increased consideration of controversy surrounding millions of dollars in fines for the poor.

CHAPTER 14: PUBLIC POLICY IN TEXAS

- Updated evidence on impacts of financial crisis due to COVID-19, especially unemployment benefits and government social services.
- Amended and updated figures on major changes to elementary and secondary school spending.

FEATURES

The book is rich in features that draw students in and explore the important features and events from Texas politics from an insider's perspective. Opening vignettes explore a particular political struggle and how Texans shape and are shaped by government. A concluding section, The Insider View, provides a summary of each chapter's theme, emphasizing how the institutions and processes discussed in the chapter are evolving. In addition, each chapter has four boxed features.

Insider Interviews. Following the theme of an inside look at politics in Texas, each chapter has an "Insider Interview" with an individual who is a practitioner in the subject of the chapter. For example, in Chapter 8, Texas governor Mark White discusses the challenges he faced as governor and his insights into the office.

Great Texas Political Debates. These features tell the story behind a current event or issue, such as paid sick leave litigation and the controversy over "no excuse" mail voting. These features are organized around concepts, such as political culture and the formal powers of the Texas governor. After reading the context, students assess two or more perspectives.

Is it Bigger in Texas? Each chapter contains at least one "Is it Bigger in Texas" boxed feature that compares Texas with other states in the union. Like the figures and tables, each feature presents a question related to THECB goals and provides bulleted observations for students to consider.

Angles of Power. This feature investigates political and personal interactions between the politics or personality of individuals and groups that shape state politics or policy. The feature then asks students to explain or analyze the situation.

DIGITAL TEACHING AND LEARNING TOOLS TO ENRICH YOUR COURSE

Every new print and digital copy of *Inside Texas Politics: Power, Policy, and Personality of the Lone Star State,* **Third Edition** comes with a wealth of digital teaching and learning tools to ensure you and your students' success in the course. Visit oup.com/he/rottinghaus3e to explore the following resources:

ENHANCED E-BOOK

Oxford's enhanced e-Books combine high quality text content with a rich assortment of integrated multimedia and self-assessment activities to deliver a more engaging and interactive learning experience. The enhanced e-Book version of *Inside Texas Politics, 3e* is available via RedShelf, VitalSource, through Inclusive Access programs, and other leading higher education e-book vendors.

OXFORD INSIGHT STUDY GUIDE

This personalized and data-driven digital learning tool reinforces key concepts from the text and encourages effective reading and study habits. Developed with a learning-science-based design, Oxford Insight Study Guide engages students in an active review of chapter content—focused on the text's chapter learning objectives—empowering them to critically assess their own understanding of course material. Real-time data generated by student activity in the study guide helps instructors ensure that each student is supported along their unique learning path.

INSTRUCTOR LECTURE PLANNING AND ASSESSMENT TOOLS

Save time in course prep with valuable teaching tools that include an Instructor's Manual with Classroom Activities, Hand Outs, and Discussion Questions; a Test Item File with Multiple Choice, Short Answer and Essay questions; Lecture PowerPoint Slides; Art PowerPoint slides; and timely, topical videos to integrate into your lectures. Many of the student resources for this text allow instructors to assign digital homework that is automatically graded and reports to a learning management system (see below under **Assignable Student Activities** and **Flexible Delivery Options**).

ASSIGNABLE STUDENT ACTIVITIES

In addition to chapter-level study tools like Flashcards, Key Terms Quizzes, Chapter Quizzes and Exams, Web Activities and Web Links, students can access a suite of digital activities designed to show real world application of course materials, promote data literacy, encourage civil debate, and provide short tutorials on key concepts.

Media Tutorials: These animated videos are designed to teach key concepts in the course as well as address important contemporary issues. Each tutorial runs 2-4 minutes in length. When used in an LMS environment, assessments at the end of each tutorial report to a gradebook. Topics include:

Political Culture and Differences Across States

What Does the Constitution Do?

Incorporating the Bill of Rights

What Affects Voter Turnout?

How Does Gerrymandering Work?

How Political Parties are Organized

What is a Political Action Committee (PAC)

Data Explorers: These special activities present students with graphs and charts illustrating data on many important topics in Texas government and politics. By analyzing the data and answering corresponding quiz questions, students develop data literacy which they can use to better understand important contemporary politics issues—both in the classroom and in everyday life. Activity topics include:

Migration

Amendments to the Texas Constitution

Federal and State Funding

Campaign Contributions

Party Control

Interest Groups

The Texas Legislature

Power of the Texas Governor

Bureaucracy

State Judicial Systems

Criminal Convictions in Texas

Texas Government Debt

Immigration

In the News **weekly features:** Selected by the text author, each weekly feature will highlight a timely topic discussed in the news with commentary designed to help students make sense of real-world politics. Discussion questions and assessments are provided with each feature. Each semester will offer 15 new weekly features for course use.

Topical, timely videos: Each chapter's content includes several topical videos to show real world examples of the material discussed. When used in an LMS environment, these activities finish with assessment that reports to a gradebook.

FLEXIBLE DELIVERY OPTIONS

The Oxford Digital Difference gives you the flexibility to teach your course the way that YOU want to. At Oxford University Press, content comes first. Our high quality, engaging digital material is available in a variety of formats delivered it to you in the way that best suits the needs of you, your students, and your institution. You can choose to have your students access all of the activities and resources listed above in one of the following ways:

OXFORD LEARNING LINK DIRECT

Bring the digital teaching and learning tools for *Inside Texas Politics,* **3e** right to your local learning management system. Instructors and their LMS administrators simply download the Oxford Learning Link Direct cartridge from Oxford Learning Link, and with the turn of a digital key, incorporate engaging content from Oxford directly into their LMS for assigning and grading.

OXFORD LEARNING CLOUD

Developed for instructors who do not use a learning management system or prefer an easy-to-use alternative to their school's designated learning management system, Oxford Learning Cloud delivers engaging learning tools within an easy-to-use, mobile-friendly, cloud-based courseware platform. Learning Cloud offers pre-built courses that instructors can use "off the shelf" or customize to fit their needs. A built-in gradebook allows instructors to see quickly and easily how students are performing.

OXFORD LEARNING LINK

For self-study, students can access the digital materials for *Inside Texas Politics,* **3e**, including Oxford Insight Study Guide, directly through Oxford Learning Link, your central hub for a wealth of engaging digital teaching and learning tools.

For more information on all of the *Inside Texas Politics,* **3e** digital teaching and learning tools and how to integrate them into your course, contact your Oxford University Press representative or visit **oup.com/he/ rottinghaus3e.**

FORMAT CHOICES

Oxford University Press offers cost-saving alternatives to meet the needs of all students. This text is offered in a loose-leaf format at a 30 percent discount off the list price of the text. You can also customize our textbooks to create the course materials you want for your class. For more information, please contact your Oxford University Press representative or call 800.280.0280.

PACKAGING OPTIONS

Adopters of *Inside Texas Politics,* **3e** can package any Oxford University Press book with the text for a 20 percent savings off the total package price. See our many trade and scholarly offering at www.oup.com, then contact your OUP sales representative to request a package ISBN. Below are additional suggestions to package with the text:

STAY CURRENT

For an additional $10, package *Current Debates in the Lone Star State,* 1e.

WRITE AND RESEARCH BETTER

Package *Writing in Political Science* **for only $5** or *Research and Writing Guide for Political Science* for free!

KNOW YOUR RIGHTS

Package with *The United States Constitution: What it Says, What it Means* **for free!**

ACKNOWLEDGMENTS

Former House Speaker Gib Lewis misspoke in one of his famous "gibbisms:" "I cannot tell you how grateful I am—I am filled with humidity." As a Houstonian, I am always filled with humidity, but in writing this text, I am also filled with *humility* for all help from friends and colleagues along the way.

Special thanks to friends and colleagues in politics and journalism who kindly shared insights or observations about Texas politics, each shaping the content or coverage here in subtle or major ways.

Enormous thanks are due to those interviewed for the *Insider Interview* feature. Generous with their time and insightful in their comments, each was too modest to call himself or herself an "insider," but each has clearly left a mark on the state and indelibly on this book.

It is genuinely hard to imagine a better team to work with than Oxford University Press. Jen Carpenter, Executive Editor, was the architect of the project from the start of this trail drive and has been an excellent lead on this and other projects. Tony Mathias gave great advice on framing and big picture presentation. Naomi Friedman, Senior Development Editor, deserves her own section in the Acknowledgments for all the time she took to help this book find its voice from the start and for revising the third edition. No one has helped to bring the ideas in my head to fruition like Naomi, and she shares incomparably in whatever success this book finds. Meg Botteon, Senior Development Editor, continues to be a tremendous resource and helped bring the project home.

Finally, this book is dedicated to my family who has made this work both possible and worthwhile.

MANUSCRIPT REVIEWERS

We are greatly indebted to the many talented scholars and instructors who reviewed the manuscript of *Inside Texas Politics*. Their insight and suggestions helped shape the work.

Patrizio Amezcua
San Jacinto College

Lydia Andrade
University of the Incarnate Word

Kevin Bailey
Houston Community College

Brian Bearry
University of Texas at Dallas

Michelle Belco
Houston University

Madelyn Bowman
Tarrant County College

Jonathan Brown
Sam Houston State University

Rachel Bzostek
Collin College

John Carnes
Lone Star College—Kingwood

Tiffany Cartwright
Collin College

Dina D. Castillo
San Jacinto College

Mark A. Cichock
University of Texas at Arlington

Neal Coates
Abilene Christian University

Max Katz Crook
Texas A&M University, McAllen

Philip Crosby
Central Texas College

Jennifer Danley-Scott
Texas Women's University

Lena Denman
Blinn College

Matthew Eshbaugh-Soha
University of North Texas

Brandon Franke
Blinn College

Heidi Galito
Houston Community College

Shane A. Gleason
Texas A&M University, Corpus Christi

Craig Goodman
University of Houston, Victoria

Sylvia Gonzalez-Gorman
University of Texas, Rio Grande Valley

Matthew Gritter
Angelo State University

Jose Gutierrez
University of Texas at Arlington

Xaviera Haynes
Southwest Texas Junior College

Bruce Hunt
Angelo State University

Sonia Iwanek
Collin College

Alicja Jac-Kucharski
Lone Star College

Kevin Kearns
Texas A&M University, Corpus Christi

Milosz Kucharski
Lone Star College

Lanny S. Lambert
North East Lakeview College

Drew Landry
South Plains College

Mary M. Louis
Houston Community College

Darrell Lovell
Lone Star College, University Park

Sharon Manna
North Lake Community College

Michael McConachie
Collin College

Tom Miles
University of North Texas

Patrick Moore
Richland College

Sharon Navarro
University of Texas at San Antonio

John M. Osterman Jr.
University of Houston, Downtown

William Parent
San Jacinto College

Lisa Perez
Austin Community College

Sarah Perez
University of Texas, Rio Grande Valley

Sara Price
Odessa College and Portland Community College

Fiona Ross
Lone Star College—Montgomery

Andrew Sanders
Texas A&M University, San Antonio

Raymond Sandoval
Richland College

Maribel Santoyo
El Paso Community College

Les Stanaland
Collin College

Gabriel Ume
Palo Alto College

Rosalinda M. Valenzuela
Collin College

Corena White
Tarrant County College

Tyler Young
Lone Star College

1

THE STRUGGLE FOR TEXAS: DEMOGRAPHICS, CULTURE, AND POLITICAL POWER

1.1 Describe the settlement history of Texas.

1.2 Assess the impact industries have had on the Texas economy from 1860 to the present time.

1.3 Analyze how the changing demographics of the state affect government.

1.4 Examine the source and impact of political culture in Texas.

"Ben Franklin said the only two certainties in life are death and taxes," Governor Greg Abbott reminded Texans in his State-of-the-State Address in 2017, and then added, "As far as I'm concerned, the only good tax is a dead tax."[1] And yet even though the governor doesn't like taxes, Texans still have to pay them. Why? What do state and local governments do with our taxes? And why does it matter? Governments may seem to be disconnected from our everyday lives—and are unnecessarily expensive—but we don't even have to leave our homes to feel the consequences of their policies.

One day in early 2020, for example, 13-year-old Scott Neece came face to face with a 400-pound wild hog that was raiding the cattle feed on a ranch in Colorado County, Texas. Neece shot the beast with his AR-15.[2] Far from an isolated incident, the "hog apocalypse" is not only a physical threat, but it also costs Texans $52 million annually in damages to agriculture alone. Cities hire private contractors to trap the pigs, while county governments organize annual hog-hunting contests. As a result, the state government allows people to hunt feral hogs, even from helicopters and hot-air balloons.[3]

In 2016, most of the residents of Nordheim, Texas (population 316), descended on Austin. Wearing yellow "Concerned about Pollution" t-shirts, the residents were there to protest the state's decision to locate a 143-acre waste material facility in their community. Texas Railroad Commission experts had decided that the facility would not pollute the town's groundwater, but exasperated 80-year-old resident Kermit Koehler told reporters, "That's what you call a little town getting sh&% on."[4] All the same, construction of the facility was completed in early 2019.

● While popular movies and TV shows predict a zombie apocalypse, Texans face the real and increasingly perilous threat of wild hogs. Texas state and local governments intervene by attempting to eradicate the damaging species-even encouraging the hunting of the animals.

Texas's energy industry employs tens of thousands of workers, some of whom are undocumented. Undocumented workers are more vulnerable to wage fraud, but not all of them keep silent. For example, when 41-one-year-old Guillermo Perez's boss told him that he didn't have the $1,200 to pay him, Perez took action: "I told him that I'm going to the Texas Workforce Commission, which I did. Then after that, he came back two weeks later and paid me."

These anecdotes of wild hogs, the residents of Nordheim, and Perez show how ordinary Texans, as individuals and as groups, have reacted to and shaped Texas politics. Their values, visions, and goals often clash, however, and so Texas public policies—and even the structure of its institutions and the way they operate—are often the outcome of conflict.

In this chapter, we explore the interactions among the communities of natives, settlers, and immigrants. We discover who wins and who loses. We examine how the booms and busts in the Texas economy and the shifting demographics impact the politics of who gets what, when, and how. Finally, we examine political culture to see how Texans relate to government and politics. In doing so, we will witness the great battles that have sculpted the face of Texas today.

1.1 THE ORIGINS OF TEXAS

| 1.1 | Describe the settlement history of Texas. |

Power in Texas politics has been shaped by the people who settled and inhabited the state. Immigration is not a new political issue. Conflicts over territory and resources have transformed Texas for millennia. So, it is to this topic that we turn first.

NATIVE AMERICANS

Flint for knives and arrows drew Native Americans into the lands of Texas more than 10,000 years before the arrival of Europeans in the early sixteenth century.[5] Tribes in North America competed for land and violently displaced each other into new territory, eventually settling in lands throughout Texas (see Figure 1.1). The Caddo and Apache Indians, descendants of the first people to walk into North America, arrived early on. The Caddo enjoyed a more sedentary life because the region they lived in had plentiful game and

FIGURE 1.1 **Ethnolinguistic Distribution of Major Native American Tribes in Texas in 1776**

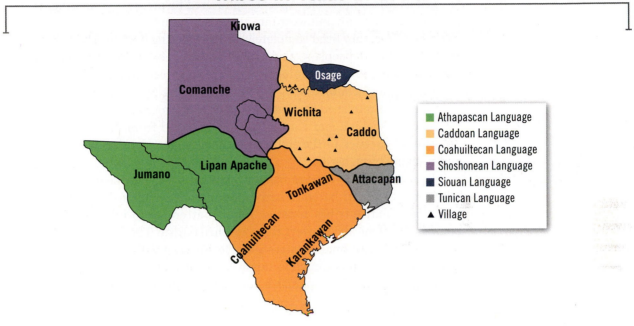

Source: University of Texas Libraries.

COMMUNICATION:

Where did the Native American tribes settle in Texas?

- The multiple tribes that settled Texas between 1500 and 1776 arrived there from the northern plains states.

- The Comanche and Apache resided in the north and west; the Tonkawa, Caddo, and Wichita settled in the northeast and east; and the Karankawa and Coahuiltecan lived along the coast.

CRITICAL THINKING:

What factors explain the settlement pattern?

- Some tribes settled in locations that suited their methods of sustaining themselves. For instance, the Comanche and Apache settled in drier areas where they hunted on horseback. The Karankawa settled along the marshy coast where they fished and moved north to hunt in the summer. The Caddo farmed, living off staples such as corn and squash in East Texas.

- Intertribal conflict also assisted in settlement patterns. Pressure from Comanche Indians pushed the Apaches farther to the south and west.

favorable conditions for growing crops. The settlements of Caddo Indians, primarily farmers, extended from the Trinity River to the Red River and as far east as Mississippi. The Apache, splintered by pressure from other tribes, pushed farther south and west into the area around Big Bend. Almost exclusively nomadic, they lived completely off the roaming buffalo. The Karankawa and Coahuiltecan people settled along the coast, coastal prairies, and brushy plains of South Texas beginning around the seventeenth century.[6]

Disease and conflict with the newly arriving Spanish and French settlers greatly diminished the numbers of Native Americans by the 1860s. The Comanche, Wichita, and Kiowa Indians migrated from the western United States on horseback in the eighteenth century, fleeing other warring groups and tracking bison herds.

The name *Texas* derives from a Spanish word that means "friendly" or "ally"—the term attributed to native populations by Spanish explorers. However, many native tribes resisted Spanish attempts to integrate them into Spanish missions and convert them to Christianity. The Caddo, for example, preferred to live in small clusters along fertile river valleys. They resented the unwillingness of the Spanish to supply them with firearms and bristled at the outrages committed by Spanish soldiers, including the molestation of Caddo women.[7] Following pitched battles, the Spanish burned native villages and seized Caddo to serve as guides.

Conflicts erupted further when Anglos (white settlers from the United States) streamed into Texas. Sam Houston, nicknamed "Big Drunk" by the leaders of the Cherokee tribe he lived with as a young man, tried to make peace and prevent Europeans from encroaching on Indian lands.[8] Houston negotiated a treaty in 1836 that recognized Cherokee land claims in exchange for a pledge of neutrality during the Texas Revolution. In the early days of the Republic, however, President Mirabeau B. Lamar relocated Native Americans to reservations. Today, only three reservations remain in Texas, homes to the Alabama-Coushatta, Tigua, and Kickapoo.

SPANISH SETTLERS

Searching for treasure, the legendary Fountain of Youth, and the fabled land of warlike Amazon women, Spanish explorers pursued romantic dreams in America. In November 1528, the Karankawa near Galveston Island encountered a shocking apparition—a starving, haggard, and half-naked stranger.[9] The man was Spanish explorer Álvar Núñez Cabeza de Vaca, whom the Karankawa rescued along with 80 survivors of his sunken ship. In the 1530s and 1540s, Francisco Vasquez de Coronado and Luis de Moscoso Alvarado explored North and East Texas.[10]

Over the next two centuries, the Spanish established missions and military outposts. The mission system in Texas operated as the political arm of "New Spain," which occupied what is now Mexico and southern Texas.[11] The expansion into Texas protected the interior of New Spain against the French settlers in Louisiana. "Glory, God, and Gold" was the phrase that summarized the Spanish colonists' approach to settlement. They established more than 50 missions and presidios (garrisons to guard the missions) in the area between 1680 and 1740.

Burdened with an economic downturn and rising debts from wars in Europe and South America, Spain increased taxes and cut expenses in its colonies. Resentment of autocratic Spanish rule, rigid class distinctions, and slavery prompted a revolutionary movement in New Spain. After a series of small revolts, New Spain—now known as the United Mexican States or Mexico—won its independence from Spain in 1821.

TEJANOS

In 1821, **Tejano**s (Mexican Texans) worked primarily in and around the ranching communities that had sprung up near military outposts along the northern frontier of Mexico, serving as a "buffer province" for New Spain.[12] Tejanos spread from what is now South Texas to the north to settle regions important for frontier defense. Tejanos had a profound effect on other settlers by transforming their lifestyle from agrarian to ranching and their culture from moccasin and "coonskin" caps to boots and "cowboy" hats.[13] Tejanos resisted centralized authority and embraced *ayuntamiento*, a form of local self-government. The Tejanos shaped local laws in Texas before the revolution and imbued the settlement with a desire for autonomy that planted the seed of independence well before many Anglos arrived. After the Texas Revolution, Tejanos who were in Texas in 1836 and did not aid Mexico were eligible for a "league and a labor" (25 square miles and 177 acres). However, they also found themselves a minority in their native land, and many lost family land to Anglo raiders.

Tejanos: Mexican Texans during the time of the Texas Revolution

ANGLOS

After gaining independence from Spain, Mexico sought to use Texas as a source of economic revenue, levying taxes on land. Rapid westward expansion of the land-hungry United States in the early 1800s threatened Spanish control over Texas. By the 1820s, however, the Mexican government aggressively promoted Anglo settlement of Texas, as we will see in Chapter 2, in order to promote commerce, spread religion, and provide a buffer against attacks by hostile Native Americans. Mexico inked deals with *empresarios*—individuals granted the right to help settle a new land and recruit new settlers—who then orchestrated the settlement of American citizens in Texas. Some settlers were fugitives on the run or wandering adventurers. Most, however, were subsistence farmers moving to Texas for cheap land and abundant space to support themselves and their families.

Tejanos soon began to view Anglo immigrants with hostility—as competitors for land and valuable resources. Friction between Anglo settlers and Tejanos erupted almost immediately. Cultured, Mexican aristocrats, like

Anglo settlers, first coming from neighboring southern states in the 1830s and 1840s, often cut "Gone to Texas" (or "GTT" in haste) into the wooden doors of their old homesteads. The phrase evoked hope for a better life that might be achieved through grit and toil. Today, the Texas flag has become a symbol of the rugged individualism these settlers brought with them.

Martin DeLeon, were openly scornful of the Anglo riff-raff streaming in. Anglo empresarios, like Green DeWitt from Victoria, often turned a blind eye when Anglos of their settlements smuggled in contraband tobacco and guns or stole livestock from Tejano ranchers. Indeed, when DeLeon traveled to Victoria swearing to "return with DeWitt's head,"[14] Stephen F. Austin quietly intervened to avert armed conflict, but ethnic tensions remained.

Laws decreed in 1830 to stop further immigration into Texas (and declare empresario contracts void) spurred Anglo illegal immigration. Rising tariff rates fanned the flames of rebellion, and eventually both Anglos and Tejanos demanded independence for Texas (which was then part of the Mexican state of Coahuila y Tejas [Coahuila and Texas]). Following the Texas Revolution, however, relations between Anglos and Tejanos soured. War heroes from the revolution and many of the original empresarios took over the reins of power, leaving the Tejanos without direct representation in the newly formed Texas government.

ANGLES OF POWER
The Benefits and Challenges of Diversity

Texas author Mary Laswell famously said, "I am forced to conclude that God made Texas on his day off, for pure entertainment, just to prove that all that diversity could be crammed into one section of earth." This diversity sometimes comes with a high cost. In 2019, a 21-year-old Plano Senior High School graduate drove hundreds of miles to a Walmart a few miles east of Eastwood High School in El Paso to "kill as many Mexicans as possible." He killed 23 people and injured 25 others. Twelve days later, Plano Independent School District (PISD) canceled the football game that was to take place between the two teams for security concerns. Texans in El Paso, in Plano, and elsewhere were outraged. Long-time sports anchor Dale Hansen blasted the decision saying, "when we cancel games because we're afraid to live, the bad guys win." PISD quickly reversed its decision. The players from Eastwood arrived in North Texas where Dallas Cowboys owner Jerry Jones welcomed them and local restaurants treated them to free meals. Wearing "El Paso Strong" t-shirts, some attended the Plano Senior High's pep rally in a display of unity. The members of both teams interspersed to stand shoulder to shoulder as the Star-Spangled Banner played before the players took the gridiron.[15]

PERSONAL RESPONSIBILITY: **Would you have objected to the school board's decision? Why or why not? Would you have known how to take action on this issue or on others important to you?**

AFRICAN AMERICANS

By 1823, Mexico had banned slavery, but beginning in 1829, Anglo settlers brought African American enslaved persons with them under the guise of "contract labor." At the time of the revolution in 1836, about 5,000 African Americans resided in Texas.[16] By 1847, after Texas gained its independence from Mexico and subsequently joined the United States, the number had risen to 38,753. The expansion of agriculture as an economic force prompted many settlers to import or purchase enslaved persons.

In the years before the Civil War, African Americans faced harsh slave codes that severely restricted their education, travel, public meetings, and possession of weapons. The Civil War and Reconstruction brought the promise of freedom, but the "Black Codes" passed by the legislature and several cities restricted their access to public facilities and largely relegated African Americans to rural areas for work as agricultural laborers.

Economic crises following the Civil War did little to provide independence to emancipated slaves. Policies of land redistribution, often referred to as "40 acres and a mule," initially offered African Americans economic opportunity, but by the 1890s, most African Americans worked as tenant farmers on former plantations. During this period, many African Americans moved from the state's rural areas to major urban areas, such as Dallas, Austin, Houston, and San Antonio. On the outskirts of cities, they established "freedman's towns," which became (and often continue to be) the heart of the African American community. City schools, public transportation, and other facilities remained segregated for over a century after the war.[17]

⭐ TEXAS TAKEAWAYS

1.1.1 Who settled Texas and why?

1.1.2 Why did the Texans rebel against Mexico?

1.2 CONTINUITY AND CHANGE IN THE TEXAS ECONOMY

If Texas were an independent nation, its economy would rank tenth in the world.[18] Texas is home to 6 of the top 50 companies on the Fortune 500 list. Its 2019 gross state product (the sum of all goods and services produced in a state) topped $1.8 trillion, the second highest in the United States. Although natural resources and energy production are still major economic assets, a balanced and diverse set of industries—including real

> **1.2** Assess the impact various industries have had on the Texas economy from 1860 to the present time.

estate, manufacturing, and technology—have contributed to Texas's economic success.

Until the 1980s, the Texas economy was heavily dependent on natural resources, especially oil and gas and agriculture. Many Texans got so rich so quickly in the oil boom of the 1970s that they were called the "Big Rich"; "better nouveau than never" was their rallying cry as they donned lynx fur coats and 17-carat diamonds to arrive at the grocery store in white Rolls-Royces.[19] However, when the price of oil dropped 24 percent between 1981 and 1986, personal bankruptcies, large oil manufacturing layoffs, and bank foreclosures rippled through the teetering Texas economy.

Texas responded by promoting economic diversity. The Texas economy today relies on a mix of agriculture and ranching, oil and natural gas, military and defense, information technology, electric power, and manufacturing (see Figure 1.2). It now has a balanced system, so that souring in one sector, like a drastic drop in oil prices, will not topple the whole economy.

FOOD AND FIBER

In antebellum Texas, three-quarters of all families drew their living from the state's plentiful farmland. Agricultural interests dominated the politics of the day. Settlers spread across Texas planting new crops: corn in the east, sorghum in the west, wheat in the northern high plains, citrus in South Texas, and rice in the coastal prairies. However, "King Cotton" was the most prominent crop. Slave-owning planters produced 90 percent of all the cotton grown in the state until the Civil War. Since the early 1900s, Texas has been the leading cotton-producing state in the nation.[20]

Timber production, located in the dense forests of East Texas, also played a major role in the state's economy between 1880 and 1910. In the 1920s, the price of lumber fell dramatically, hurting many Texas farm families and putting the lumber industry on tenterhooks. The industry did not recover until World War II, as wartime demand forced prices higher and mechanization made farming more productive.

After World War II, large commercial farms eclipsed small family homesteads. The farm population dropped from 1.52 million to about 245,000 between 1945 and 1990.[21] Today, Texas leads the nation in the production of several agricultural staples, generates more than $115 billion annually, and ranks fourth overall in the value of agricultural cash receipts.[22]

FUEL

"It roared, I'm tellin' you, it roared. . . ." exclaimed a Beaumont resident upon hearing a particularly massive oil gusher in Southeast Texas.[23] The discovery of a major oil deposit beneath the marshy soil at Spindletop Hill in Beaumont, Texas, in 1901 ushered in a new economic era—and one that continues to drive

FIGURE 1.2 **Booms in the Texas Economy**

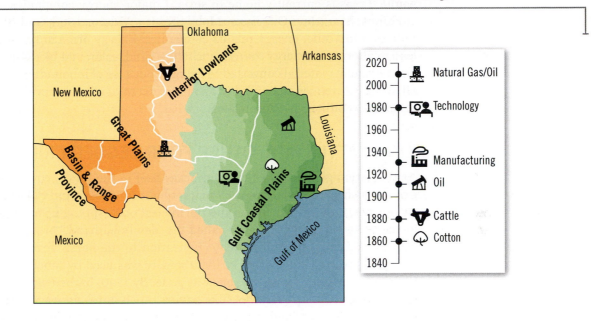

 COMMUNICATION:

What industries have spurred the Texas economy?

- Texas has experienced six major economic booms since becoming a state: cotton, beginning in the 1860s; cattle, beginning in about the 1880s; oil in the 1910s; manufacturing in the 1930s; high tech in the 1990s; and oil and natural gas from about 2005.

 CRITICAL THINKING:

Why have these industries grown?

- The state's abundant natural resources provide opportunity to meet national and international demand for these products.
- Hard work and luck fueled this growth.
- Government matters, too, both by staying out of the way in some instances and by offering incentives to invest in others.

the state's financial booms and busts despite the state's current more balanced economy. By 1940, Texas was the leading oil-producing state in the United States and would soon be central to the war effort.

The new industry also expanded state government. The discovery of the East Texas field by Columbus Marion "Dad" Joiner in 1930 near Kilgore prompted the newly created Texas Railroad Commission to limit pumping and production. The commission continues to regulate the industry today.

Today, Texas's energy industry is a leader not just in the state but in the world. Texas is currently home to several major energy companies—ConocoPhilips, Marathon Oil, ExxonMobil, Tesoro, Valero, Total, and Shell—as well as 5,000 other energy-related companies. Energy firms in the state also lead in alternative energy sources, including wind, solar, and biomass (animal and vegetable material converted to energy). Because of rebounding oil prices, oil and gas revenues amounted to about 3 percent of all state revenue in 2018 (topping $3 billion, up 60 percent from 2017).[24]

KING CATTLE (AND OTHER FOUR-LEGGED FRIENDS)

As the nation gained an appetite for Texas beef in the 1860s, cowboys began driving their herds north to reach market hubs in Kansas and Colorado. Cattle ranches, both the enormous and the modest ones, sprang up all over Texas in the 1870s. Barbed wire, once called the "devil's hatband," brought controversy, bloodshed, and (ultimately) civilization to the harsh Texas frontier.[25] Cheap to produce and easy to string, the wire was used by ranchers to fence their property, and the open range was gone. By 1890, barbed wire, a shift to corporate ownership practices (like paying ranch hands in wages instead of cattle), drought, and better access to rail lines ended cattle drives. Although cattle no longer roam freely, today Texas leads the nation in the production of cattle, sheep, and goats, which generates annual cash receipts of more than $12 billion.[26]

MANUFACTURING

After World War II, Texas experienced rapid industrial growth, doubling the number of manufacturing facilities in the period from 1930 to 1947. Wartime industries ballooned throughout Texas: steel mills in Houston; tin smelting in Texas City; aircraft factories in Garland, Grand Prairie, and Fort Worth; shipyards along the coast; and revitalized paper and wood pulp in East Texas.[27] Today, manufacturing amounts to approximately 13 percent of the state's gross domestic product, and the number of manufacturing jobs in Texas ranks second only to California.[28]

MILITARY AND DEFENSE INDUSTRIES

Texas has been home to an active military presence since World War II, when it served as the largest training ground in the world for soldiers and sailors.[29] Texas currently has 15 military bases, with all branches of the armed services represented except the Marines and Coast Guard. These posts are spread across the state but are concentrated in and around San Antonio (see Figure 1.3).

Defense contracting (a business that provides products or services to the military) is also a major part of the Texas economy, especially as a

FIGURE 1.3 Texas Military Installations

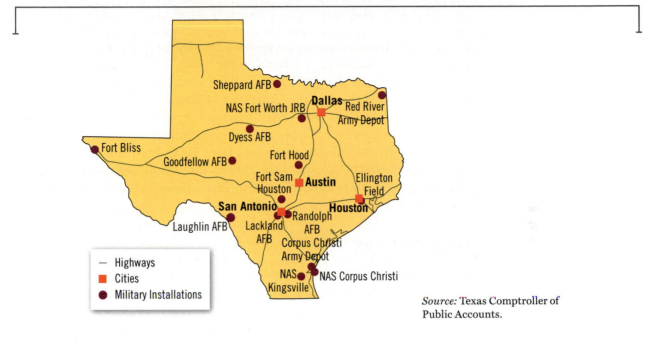

Source: Texas Comptroller of Public Accounts.

 COMMUNICATION:

How big is the U.S. military presence in Texas?

- Texas is currently home to 15 military bases, if we count the San Antonio joint base as three separate ones. These bases are primarily located in or outside of urban areas, especially around San Antonio and El Paso.

- The total military personnel stationed in Texas is approximately 195,000.

 CRITICAL THINKING:

Why are there so many bases in Texas?

- Texas has historically been an outpost for western expansion, and many of the military bases remain from the state's frontier days.

- Texas has a vast supply of cheap land and diverse geography for bases on both sea and land.

- Texas politicians have fought to keep these bases open, as bases bring in tens of thousands of jobs and millions of dollars in revenue.

significant employer. Major corporations such as Lockheed Martin, Boeing, KBR (formerly Kellogg Brown & Root, a Halliburton subsidiary), DXC Technology (formerly Ross Perot's Electronic Data Systems), and many others furnish aircraft, weapons, and technical know-how to support the U.S. military.

HIGH TECH

As early as the mid-nineteenth century, technology has sparked economic growth in Texas. H. Ross Perot left IBM in 1962 to form Electronic Data Systems, which designed computer systems for Medicare and Medicaid. Technology went from rich to "Big Rich" in the 1980s, when Rod Canion formed Compaq and "technobrat" Michael Dell founded Dell Computers at the age of 23 in his dorm room at the University of Texas.[30] The tech boom, which extends to information technology, financial services, health care technology, and aeronautics, continues today. Several major national corporations are headquartered in Texas, including Dell, Texas Instruments, Perot Systems, and Hewlett-Packard. In addition, thousands of smaller, start-up technology companies have sprouted in Texas, many in the "Silicon Hills" in and around Austin.

HEALTH CARE

The health care industry is among the fastest growing industries in the state, and Texas boasts some of the largest hospitals and health systems in the country. The Texas Medical Center in Houston is the largest medical center in the world. The industry itself not only has a significant economic impact, but also brings in millions of dollars in grants for medical innovation.

RECREATION AND RETIREMENT

Stroll along the river walk in San Antonio or the beaches of South Padre Island. Hike in Big Bend National Park. Gaze at the incredible art in Houston's many museums. The state is teeming with recreational and entertainment options, and tourists flock to the state for leisure activities. Although many rural Texas counties have lost mainstay industries, such as oil and gas production and agriculture, many still find they are positioned for growth in recreation and as a haven for retirees. Among these local recourses are tourism, hunting and fishing, birding, and retirement communities. Travel spending in Texas for events like South by Southwest, the Texas Motor Speedway, or the International Goat Cookoff in Brady, Texas, tops $80 billion and supports almost 700,000 jobs.[31]

ASSESSING THE TEXAS ECONOMY

Texas Miracle: the economic good fortune the state experienced from 2001 to 2008

Bumper stickers in Texas following economic downturns ask for salvation: "Please, God, give me one more oil boom . . . this time, I promise not to piss it away." Although the state has minimized its dependency on oil and gas, its economic fortunes are still linked to these natural resources. Known as the **Texas Miracle**, the economy found itself riding a massive gusher during

GREAT TEXAS POLITICAL DEBATES
Accent Marks on State Documents

Despite making up 40 percent of the state's population, Hispanics are sometimes misidentified in state documents. Why? Texas does not allow accent marks or tildes (in Spanish or other languages) on driver's licenses, birth certificates, or other personal identification documents. In 2017, Texas State Representative Terry Canales introduced legislation to allow their use. As Canales argued, "Since Texas was Spanish-speaking before English-speaking, this is something that's concerning. The roots of the state are of Spanish descent." [32]

PERSONAL RESPONSIBILITY: **Should Texas allow "diacritical" marks on vital state records?**

NO: The transfer of documents from the state's current system to a new system could cause a procedural "hiccup" when transferring personal information. The cost of upgrading is not worth the potential disruption.

YES: Individuals of Spanish descent are incorrectly identified on state documents because of this omission. This is both a legal problem and a cultural omission.

and after the 2001–2008 oil boom as the price of a barrel climbed to $140. Strong job creation in diverse sectors like technology and health care, demand for new housing and strong construction numbers, and relatively high oil and gas prices kept Texas in high cotton and able to shake off most shocks through 2020.

Critics of the Texas Miracle point out that nearly all of the boom was concentrated in only four metropolitan areas: Houston, Dallas, Austin, and San Antonio. Meanwhile, the number of low-skilled, low-pay positions jumped, prompting some to claim that "McJobs" had created an illusion of growth.[33] Median family income has not increased much since then, in part because population growth has provided a steady supply of new workers to keep salaries low.[34]

Critics also point out that a large share of Texans live below the poverty line. The gap between the rich and poor is huge: In 2018, the richest 1 percent of households earned on average over $1,343,897 per year, roughly 24 times greater than the rest of families in the state who earned an average income of $55,614 and much higher than the bottom 20 percent earning $22,800 per year.[35] Urban areas have particularly high rates of inequality. Race is a factor, too—poverty rates for African Americans and Hispanics are three times higher than those for Anglos, and Hispanics earn approximately 75 percent of what Anglos make. Latinas make only 44 cents for every dollar made by non-Hispanic men.[36]

On the positive side, Texas's energy companies, with their increased wind energy output, along with its manufacturing, aviation, aerospace, defense, and biotechnology industries, have expanded. Austin ranks first in concentration of start-ups, and San Antonio is a cybersecurity hub, with 140

Texas is famous for its extremes of weather. It is also known for its extremes of wealth and poverty.

 PERSONAL RESPONSIBILITY: **Has the state left behind its most economically vulnerable populations at the expense of a strong statewide economy?**

firms in the city.[37] The state's proximity to the border encourages trade, immigration to fuel population growth, and job creation. In fact, border protection itself has been a boon to the Rio Grande Valley in terms of jobs, investment in infrastructure, and sales tax revenue.[38]

Then the COVID-19 virus came. "Stay-at-home" orders decreased demand for oil and coincided with an international trade war for oil, driving prices down. A spike in unemployment across several industries, especially service and retail jobs, chop blocked the Texas economy, trickling down to manufacturing, tourism, and education. By April 2020, the state's unemployment figures shot up to double digits, the highest in history, and retailers lost billions of dollars in sales tax revenue. The impact cratered state, county, and city budgets from El Paso to Beaumont and Harlingen to Texline. Texas is still struggling with the economic fallout from the pandemic.

TEXAS TAKEAWAYS

1.2.1 How large is the Texas economy? How does it compare to other states?

1.2.2 What Texas industries have experienced economic booms and in what sequence?

1.2.3 What is the Texas Miracle?

1.3 CONTINUITY AND CHANGE IN TEXAS DEMOGRAPHICS

1.3 Analyze how the changing demographics of the state affect government.

Power and politics in Texas hug the arc of demographic shifts. As the state has become more urban and industrialized, citizens have required additional government services—driver's licenses, garbage pick-up, and water and sewer systems. As foreign-born populations have grown, the state is confronting new demands for social services and access to schools. As the state has aged, debates are erupting about health care and pensions. Political power, meanwhile, has shifted from rural to urban to suburban communities with the movement of high-income echelons of Texas society to these areas. These demographic shifts have repercussions for Texas politics.

STATE POPULATION GROWTH

Since achieving statehood, Texas has grown rapidly. Once a lonely, inhospitable frontier fraught with danger, it has emerged as a major population center. The state's population was a mere 212,592 in 1850 but ballooned to more than 29 million by 2020.[39] In every census taken since 1850, Texas has grown faster than the United States as a whole. Population growth and economic expansion have often gone hand in hand in Texas, as first land, then oil, and finally industry drew newcomers.

Texas today is the fastest growing of the largest states in the United States (see Figure 1.4) as baby boomers (those born between 1946 and 1964) retire and move to the "Sun Belt" and as jobs move from the industrial Northeast and Midwest to the South. And with population growth comes greater sway in the presidential elections, more seats in Congress, and more power on the national level.

Urbanization. The population has not increased uniformly across the state. Much of the growth has occurred in major urban areas. In 1890, Texas had no urban areas with a population larger than 40,000, but by 1920, four cities—Dallas, Fort Worth, Houston, and San Antonio—boasted more than 100,000 residents each. Rural populations have declined, and urban (especially suburban) populations have skyrocketed. The mechanization of farm labor and job opportunities in urban areas led people to flock to cities between 1900 and 1920. This migration continues today and has amplified in recent years (see Table 1.1). Yet, over half of the state's counties (most of them rural) were smaller in 2019 than in 2010. Those who remain worry that their small towns will catch a hard wind and blow away.[40] About 78 percent of the population of Texas lives in the "urban triangle" between Houston, Dallas, and San Antonio, and 6 of the 10 counties in the United States with the largest population gains in the decade were in Texas.[41] *Texas Monthly*'s Paul Burka described modern Texas as an "urban state with a rural soul."[42]

Suburbanization. The most significant demographic change in Texas has been **suburbanization**, a process in which the population shifts from urban and rural areas to suburban areas adjacent to major cities. While the smaller metro cities have lost population, the suburbs in the state have swelled with new residents. Texas suburban counties made up 4 of the country's 10 fastest growing counties in 2018.[43]

suburbanization: population shifts from urban and rural areas to suburban areas adjacent to major cities

Implications of Population Shifts. As the state's population has shifted from rural to urban to suburban centers, so too has political power. State policy priorities follow growing populations and wealthier citizens. The institutions of Texas government—the legislature, the bureaucracy, the courts—tend to

IS IT BIGGER IN TEXAS?

FIGURE 1.4 **U.S. States with the Largest Population Increases, 2000–2019**

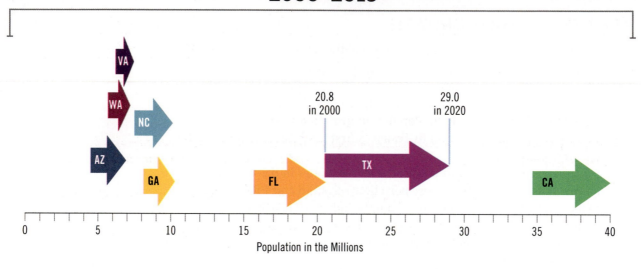

Source: U.S. Census Bureau. The arrows show the population growth of each state. The numeric growth shows the total increase in the number of individuals living in Texas.

COMMUNICATION:

How does the population growth of Texas compare to that of other large states?

- Texas had the largest increase in population growth.
- Southern states, like Georgia and Florida, are also large and growing.

CRITICAL THINKING:

Why has Texas grown so quickly?

- Hispanic population growth (in terms of both births and migration) has driven the population growth of Texas and California.
- Economic expansion brought many companies and thousands of jobs to the state, also boosting the population.
- Affordable real estate has made the state attractive for first-time home buyers and retirees, especially in urban and suburban areas.

address urban and suburban problems and focus less on rural issues. As the population rises in the cities and suburbs, so do their number of representatives in the Texas legislature. Consequently, greater resources and funding are streaming to these areas as state legislators bring projects and funds back to their electoral districts in the form of newer schools, highway funds, and other infrastructure projects. In addition, as like-minded individuals have settled

TABLE 1.1	Population by County Type, 1960–2020			
COUNTY TYPE	**1960**	**1990**	**2010**	**2020**
Big Six (Harris, Dallas, Tarrant, Bexar, Travis, El Paso)	41.2%	48.2%	47.0%	48.6%
Suburban	8.8%	14.1%	20.7%	17.5%
Other Metro	23.4%	19.4%	18.1%	23.2%
Small Town	26.6%	18.3%	14.2%	10.7%

Source: Red State, Thornburn (2014); Texas Demographer Office.

COMMUNICATION:

How have Texas's residential centers of populations changed over time?

- The "Big Six" counties accounted for almost half of the population of the state in 1990, 2010, and 2020. The population trend, however, has been flat in the past decade.
- Only 8 percent of the state lived in suburbs in 1960 while 17 percent did by 2020.
- Rural areas have seen the largest percentage drop in population.

CRITICAL THINKING:

Why are some areas growing and others are not?

- Suburban areas grew because of "white flight," during which Anglo residents of urban areas moved to areas that were cheaper, had better public schools, and were perceived to be safer.
- As urban and suburban areas expanded, rural areas began to shrink, since economic opportunities had moved to more populated areas. Agriculture declined as a family-run business.

into neatly urban and suburban pockets, political divisions have begun to develop between the conservative suburbs and the more liberal urban areas.

CHALLENGES OF POPULATION GROWTH

The state's population is expected to double by 2050 to 54.4 million people. Texas's urbanization and suburbanization are likely to continue through the middle of the century. How will these trends impact life in the coming decades?

Infrastructure. As the state grows, so do the demands on roads and other transportation systems. The state's transportation system is funded by state fuel taxes, vehicle registration fees, toll road revenues, bond proceeds, and federal transportation aid. As the state grows in population, some of this revenue will expand and some will not. The Texas Department of Transportation (TxDOT) estimates that road use in the state will grow 214 percent by 2033, but that road capacity will grow by only 6 percent.

Affordable Housing. High demand for properties and difficulties that local governments encounter in building affordable housing have burdened more than 2 million urban Texas households with housing costs that consume 30 percent or more of their income.[44] Today, San Antonio and Dallas top the charts for the highest rates of segregation by income.[45] In one report, 88 percent of private apartment complexes in the Dallas area did not accept housing vouchers which the federal government distributes to low-income Texans.[46] Poverty and wealth are likely to continue to concentrate in separate sectors of the city.

Water Use. The Texas Water Development Board's annual surveys show that the average residence consumes 86 gallons of water per day. Without planning for expected population increases, a drought in 2060 could mean that 85 percent of Texans would face water shortages.[47] An extended drought would also make agricultural irrigation (and therefore food) more expensive and the state susceptible to wildfires.

Health Care. In 2020, percent of Texans were reportedly without health insurance, which amounts to about 4.3 million Texans who did not have medical coverage during the spread of COVID-19.[48] Under federal law, hospitals must treat patients who show up in emergency rooms regardless of their ability to pay, placing a serious burden on hospitals that are not reimbursed for these costs. A growing number of residents without health insurance could increase this burden.

Energy Use. In 2017, Texas ranked sixth in the nation in per capita energy consumption, significantly above the national average in the United States. As the population surges, so will the demand for energy. The state has access to enough coal and natural gas to meet demands through 2030, but the state has been turning to alternative sources of energy, such as wind and nuclear energy, to meet growing market demand.

RACIAL AND ETHNIC TRENDS IN TEXAS

As important as *where* people live is *who* lives there. Both residential and demographic groups struggle for access to public resources, and so residential **segregation**, whether by income, racial, or ethnic group, can empower one group over another. Moreover, demographic groups have different needs to which governments must respond. For example, Latinos (sometimes called Hispanics) have higher poverty rates and greater health challenges than Anglos.[49] As a result, initially twice as many Texas Hispanics obtained health insurance through the Affordable Care Act (ACA) compared to whites.[50]

Although Anglos (whites) were a clear supermajority during the 1980s in Texas, the rapid rise of the Hispanic population has altered the social and political shape of the state and will continue to do so (see Figure 1.5). This growth puts Texas on a path to join New Mexico and California as states where Hispanics have become a plurality, comprising the largest racial or

segregation: enforced or de facto separation of different racial groups

FIGURE 1.5 **Projected Race Population Changes in Texas, 1980–2050**

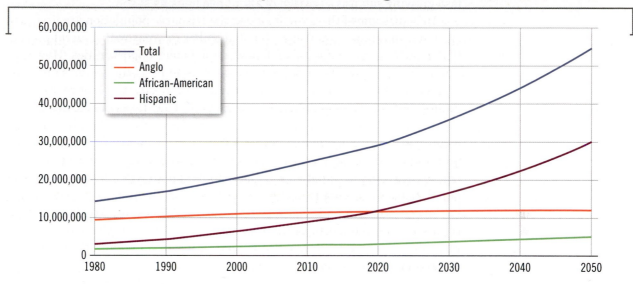

Source: U.S. Census; Office of the State Demographer, Population Projections.

 COMMUNICATION:

What will the state look like racially and ethnically in 40 years?

- The number of African American citizens is projected to increase slightly, and the number of Anglo citizens is predicted to remain steady.
- The number of Hispanic citizens is expected to rise from 10 million to almost 16 million by 2050.

 CRITICAL THINKING:

Why are some groups increasing but not others?

- Population replacement for African Americans and Anglos is only average: birth rates are low, and migration from other states or nations is modest.
- Most of the growth in the number of Hispanic families stems from the high birth rates of families already living in Texas.
- A healthy economy drew more immigrants from Latin and South American countries and kept many recent immigrants and their subsequent generations in Texas.

ethnic group.[51] Asian, Native Hawaiian, Pacific Islander, American Indian, and Alaska Native populations (which the census labels "other") have also experienced significant growth. The Census Bureau's estimates suggest that this trend is part of a long-term shift in the United States as the population becomes less white, older, and more Hispanic.

Residential segregation is prevalent in Texas: Most Anglos live in the suburbs, most African Americans in urban areas, and most Hispanics in smaller metropolitan areas. Hispanics make up a larger portion of the urban workforce in Texas than any other group, and they are moving into the state's fast-growing suburbs in search of affordable housing.[52]

Driving some of the growth among the Hispanic population are first-generation immigrants, a demographic that spikes in areas with general population growth because they often follow employment opportunities. How does the influx of foreign-born populations alter politics in the state? This trend impacts both the economy and government of Texas. The labor supply remains high, so wages are likely to stay low, allowing Texas businesses to continue to be competitive. Immigrants also pay about $1.6 billion in state and local taxes, and their unique cultures contribute to educational diversity.[53] Simultaneously, demand for public services and political representation increases in areas that experience higher population growth due to foreign-born populations. This demand, along with concern for job dislocation, particularly in the construction and food service industries where immigrants are over-represented, often alarms long-time residents.[54] Accordingly, many of these residents are pressing authorities to restrict immigration and the delivery of social services to immigrants.

CHALLENGES OF SHIFTING RACIAL AND ETHNIC TRENDS

Texas's population will likely continue to grow. What opportunities and challenges does this growth pose for Texans?

Education. Texas has more public school students than 28 states have residents. Texas public schools serve more than 5 million students, and that population is diversifying.[55] Racial and ethnic segregation has been a point of tension since the days when Texas was part of Spain and Mexico. In the 1950s, 90 percent of schools in South Texas were segregated—at least 122 districts had separate schools for Texans of Mexican descent.[56] Thousands of public schools are still as segregated now as they were 60 years ago: half of Texas students attend a school whose population is 80 percent one race or ethnicity.[57] Inequality in education outcomes also remains an issue. Texas has an overall graduation rate of 90 percent, but Anglos graduate at a rate of 94 percent, Hispanics at 88 percent, and African Americans at 86 percent.[58] Seventy percent of Anglos receive a bachelor's degree within 6 years of graduation compared to 54 percent of Hispanics and 44 percent of African Americans.[59]

Pressure on public schools to educate more students, especially more diverse students, will create a need for further teacher training and educational materials adapted to be inclusive of this diversity. In Chapter 14, we explore what Texas is doing to meet the challenges of a growing and increasingly diverse student body.

Income. Divergent levels of education across racial and ethnic groups contribute to differences in income. Despite rapid growth in the past 2 years, the median household income of Texan Hispanics lagged behind the state median income, at $51,450 versus $59,785. Black family income remained below $41,361, compared to $67,400 for non-Hispanic whites and $70,632 for Asians.[60] Many Hispanics are immigrants, contributing to lower wages because of their limited English proficiency and lack of legal status.[61]

Housing. Racial segregation in housing is also a major issue in Texas. Government-assisted housing is often located in areas that are not ethnically or racially diverse, perpetuating similar living conditions among residents. Vouchers for public housing may also encourage residents to live in areas that are less racially or ethnically diverse. Individual preferences play a role, too: Some groups, especially Anglos and Asians, respond in surveys that they would be less likely to buy a home in a neighborhood made up significantly of a different racial or ethnic group.[62]

AN AGING STATE

Texas is aging. Currently, the state has 3 million residents 65 years of age or older. Baby boomers, the nation's largest generation in the twentieth century, are now aging rapidly. By 2050, elderly Texans are expected to make up 17 percent of the state (up from 10 percent in 2010). The growth of younger Texans is not significant enough to replace those who are aging. The total projected population growth of individuals under the age of 18 will remain constant between now and 2050 despite the influx into Texas of 2.4 million foreign-born children who will be living with at least one parent who is an immigrant.[63] Much of the increase in young residents comes from Hispanics, while most of the rise in the older group is due to the expected aging of Anglo residents.

CHALLENGES OF AN AGING TEXAS

As Texas ages, there will be added pressure on the state's resources.

Income Security. Eleven percent of elderly citizens in Texas live below the poverty line, placing Texas among the 15 states with the highest poverty rate among older Americans.[64] Income insecurity may be particularly acute among Hispanics, who have a higher life expectancy than non-Hispanics and are less economically secure in their old age than other groups. Because only 31

"Juan Crow" laws that enforced discrimination against Latinos mirrored "Jim Crow" laws and used some of the same tactics. Signs reading "No Spanish or Mexicans" were common across Texas restaurants and other public accommodations.

SOCIAL RESPONSIBILITY: **Should Texas take governmental action to achieve ethnically and racially balanced residential areas and school systems? How?**

percent of non-Hispanics and only 8 percent of Hispanics have investment income, it is particularly important that both the U.S. and Texas governments keep Social Security solvent.[65]

Medicaid. Medicaid is an entitlement program through which qualified low-income individuals can receive medical care. Many elderly Texans qualify for access to Medicaid services, but budget cuts in 2015 and 2017 have restricted access and reduced the ability of elderly Texans on fixed incomes to receive ongoing medical care.[66]

Safety. Elderly Texans are often more vulnerable to crime, abuse, and natural disasters and thus require government assistance. The state's Department of Aging and Disability Services found that evacuating assisted living centers and nursing homes during natural disasters was slowed because of transportation complications and medical issues.[67] As a result, the state created a registry for disabled and elderly residents who would need help in an evacuation. Many elderly citizens are also vulnerable to unscrupulous individuals or outright criminals. Elder abuse in nursing homes and assisted living facilities is monitored by the Texas Adult Protective Services. The Texas Attorney General's Office runs programs to protect senior consumers against retirement planning or medical service scams.

 TEXAS TAKEAWAYS

1.3.1 How does the population growth in Texas compare to that of other states?

1.3.2 How would you characterize the demographics of the recent population growth in Texas?

1.3.3 What challenges does population pose for the state?

1.4 CONTINUITY AND CHANGE IN TEXAS POLITICAL CULTURE

1.4 Examine the source and impact of political culture in Texas.

Texas is a "state of mind," wrote American author John Steinbeck, and "a nation in every sense of the word."[68] The early pioneers infused Texas with a spirit of rugged individualism and a strong sense of fair play that continues to permeate the political environment today. Texans have always had an expansive and grandiose vision

Joe Holley, *Houston Chronicle* Writer

How would you describe the personality of Texas politics?

The dominant Texas political personality is conservative and suspicious of government intrusion into the lives of individuals. This political personality is the result of the state's origins. The Texas ethos is that of Scots-Irish borderlanders who migrated down from the Appalachians, people who brought with them a fierce independence, a suspicion of outsiders, and a willingness to resort to violence when provoked. Southerners who also settled Texas had similar characteristics.

PERSONAL RESPONSIBILITY: **Do you agree with this assessment of the impact of the Scots-Irish on Texas's political culture? What contributions have the Tejano, African American, German immigrant, and other groups made? How is your own experience of Texas political culture similar or different?**

of the state. President Mirabeau B. Lamar, who succeeded Sam Houston as the Republic's second president, envisioned a Texas nation that was large and powerful enough to rival the United States.

Although the issues may change and party labels may shift, Texans have retained their core political values. **Political culture** is a set of shared values and practices held by people that informs their expectations of government and their vision of a just society. These sentiments give meaning to the political process and help us explain political behavior.[69]

Why does a state's political culture matter? Political culture defines the relationship between a government and its people. Our political culture influences how we feel about the rights and responsibilities of citizens, the limits on government intervention in people's lives, and the obligations of government to the people. Do you expect government to solve problems, or do you want government to leave people alone? Do you expect to have constant input in making policy judgments, or should elected officials make decisions on their own? Your answers—and the answers of other Texans—to these questions determine the types of actions government takes, including what policies the legislature enacts, the types of executive actions governors take, how agencies in Austin enforce laws, how judges rule on cases, and how much power local governments have.

Political scientist Daniel Elazar argued that political cultures vary by state.[70] In fact, Elazar developed a classification of three basic political cultures that he says all states can fit into: individualistic, traditionalistic, and moralistic (see Table 1.2). Elazar placed Texas at the intersection of individualistic and traditionalistic political cultures. Those who settled Texas infused the state with the political cultures they brought with them.

political culture: a set of shared values and practices held by people that informs their expectations of government and their vision of a just society

COMMUNICATION:

How does political culture influence people's expectations of government?

TABLE 1.2	Elazar's Classification of Political Culture	
INDIVIDUALISTIC	TRADITIONALISTIC	MORALISTIC
The political arena is a clearinghouse for ideas. Government's role is limited. Government exists for utilitarian reasons only. Private concerns are more important than public concerns.	The goal of the political system is to maintain order. Political elites largely determine public policy. Government is a hierarchy, with a few elites in charge. Citizen participation is low.	The goal of the political system is to achieve the broadest good for the community. Government is a positive force designed to activate the public will, and citizens participate strenuously in government. Party competition is strong but not completely controlled by political elites.

These cultures have been reinforced by a collective ethos about what makes them Texans and the embrace of iconic figures that are passed from generation to generation—the ubiquitous Texas flag, reverence to Texas music, and larger-than-life historical figures. Stories—like that of Sam Houston bragging that his ragtag, starving army giving Mexican leader Santa Anna chase could march for 4 days with only one ear of corn for rations—inspire each succeeding generation of Texans. Scholarship finds that states with a longer frontier experience exhibit more prevalent individualism.[71] Texas shows elements of individualistic political culture through support for free enterprise, fierce opposition to big government (especially the federal government), and entrepreneurship. Traditionalistic political culture in Texas is seen in characteristics such as low voter participation, one-party dominance (first Democrats, then Republicans), and conservative social values as informed by strict religious beliefs.

INDIVIDUALISTIC POLITICAL CULTURE

individualistic political culture: emphasizes personal achievement, individual freedoms, individual enterprise, and loyalty to self instead of others

Texans embrace an **individualistic political culture** that emphasizes personal achievement, individual freedoms, individual enterprise, and loyalty to self instead of others. Individuals retain specific rights, and government does not alter or abridge those rights except in extreme circumstances. Individuals hold government accountable for protection of basic rights and little else. You're on your own in Texas to sink or swim, and Texans like it that way. As famed Texas folklorist and historian Frank Dobie wrote affectionately, an idealized Texan citizen was called a "Texan out of an Old Rock," a model of self-sufficiency and ingenuity.[72]

TABLE 1.3	Opinions on the Role of Government in Social Welfare

	Percent of Texans Who Strongly or Mildly Agree
Government should take a more active role in helping low-income individuals.	29%
Individuals should be responsible for improving their own situation.	52%
No strong opinion on whether governments or individuals should take a more active role.	16%

Source: Texas Politics Project/University of Texas Poll.

SOCIAL RESPONSIBILITY:

Does government have an obligation to help those in need, or are government's only obligations to maintain a level playing field and basic security?

Consider how these values spill over into state politics. People who embrace an individualistic political culture prefer **minimal government**. Government should only protect individuals from grave harm, maintain a functioning free market, provide a consistent legal system, and ensure that contracts are fairly upheld. They believe that the government should not interfere with free transactions among individuals or institutions. Von Ormy, Texas (population 1,300), with its motto "the freest little city in Texas," took these beliefs a step further by eliminating taxes and regulations and providing virtually no city services. The city imploded, however, after the police department shut down, stray dogs roamed streets, and businesses and residents fled after a needed sewer system was not installed.[73]

minimal government: a government that provides minimal services and interferes as little as possible in the transactions of individuals and institutions

This attitude shapes Texans' stance on a range of policy issues, such as health insurance, taxes, business regulation, and social welfare. Most Texans, for example, believe that the government should not take a more active role in providing assistance to low-income individuals (see Table 1.3). Hurricane Harvey in 2017 reawakened this debate when some looked to the state and federal government for recovery while others pointed to the "do-it-yourself" relief efforts of many Texans, which included an armada of boat owners, worried neighbors with laptops, and coders with mapping software who located fellow Texans in need.[74]

Texans are also protective of individual rights and prefer that government not meddle in their private lives. Texans generally oppose gun control, believing those rights are protected under the Second Amendment, but they do support background checks for those purchasing guns. Voters in Texas also approve of doctor-assisted suicide for terminally ill patients, allowing individuals to choose to end their lives with dignity.

Distrust of Government. Texans are generally distrustful of government at most levels. Fifty-eight percent of Texans believe that the state government can be trusted to do what is right some or none of the time.[75] Fifty percent of Texans also feel that the state "needs leaders from outside politics," compared to 19 percent who note that the state needs "leaders with experience in politics."[76]

Trust in the Free Market. Texans tend to believe that businesses should be allowed to operate with no or minimal government interference. The role of government should be to support economic growth by building infrastructure and a business-friendly environment.

TRADITIONALISTIC POLITICAL CULTURE

People who espouse a **traditionalistic political culture** expect government to maintain the existing social order. Consider how traditionalistic political culture shapes state policies on law and order as well as on social issues.

Law and Order. Traditionalistic political culture places a priority on the strict enforcement of **law and order**. Consistent with these values, Texans support harsh punishments. They strongly favor application of the death penalty in appropriate cases, with almost 75 percent of Texans supporting capital punishment.[77] At times, however, individualist values conflict with law and order concerns. Most Texans view high-tech scanners at airports, police "stop and frisk" procedures, and red light cameras at busy intersections with suspicion and must balance their desire for personal freedoms with the need for law and order.

Religion and Traditional Family Values. The traditionalistic character of Texas's political culture emphasizes rules and values that support existing institutions, such as church and traditional family structure. Texans attend church often (see Figure 1.6), more so than other Americans. More than 13 million people signaled that they were part of an organized religion in the state.[78] **Religiosity** shapes Texans' views of political issues and thus informs policy. Texas even passed the Merry Christmas Law that permits school holiday displays as long as more than one faith is represented.

Consider, for example, Texans' views on abortion. Opponents of abortion often take a religious stance, arguing that abortion ends a human life and thus constitutes murder. Advocates of abortion rights argue that unwanted pregnancies create burdens for the health or economic welfare of women. Today, most Texans temper their religious convictions and believe that abortion should be allowed (see Figure 1.7).

Many Texans also believe in a firm set of family values that include marital fidelity, close family ties, and adherence to faith-based principles. These values are contested, especially in politics. Republicans in Texas are more likely to define family values in conservative terms, such as supporting traditional roles for women and opposition to both same-sex relationships and legalization of drugs. Democrats are more likely to consider family values in

traditionalistic political culture: the goal of the political system is to maintain order, and a hierarchical set of political elites largely determines public policy

law and order: a dimension of Texas political culture that demands strict adherence to a fair and adequate criminal justice system and swift enforcement of laws

religiosity: the belief, practice, and activity of organized religion

FIGURE 1.6 **Role of Religion in Texas**

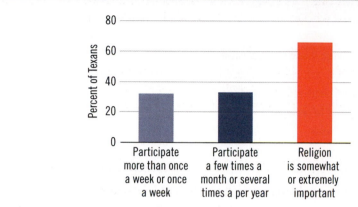

Source: Texas Politics Project/ University of Texas Poll, February 2020.

COMMUNICATION:

How religious are Texans?

- Religion is a major part of the lives of most Texans. Around 66 percent of respondents indicated that religion was extremely or somewhat important in their lives in 2020.

- About a third of Texans (32 percent) attend religious services weekly or more than once a week, and another third (33 percent) participate several times a year.

CRITICAL THINKING:

Why is religion such a major part of Texans' lives?

- Fear and uncertainty of frontier life promoted religion as a civil and social organization in early Texas history.

- Two major population segments in Texas—Latinos and African Americans—are very religious, increasing Texas's religiosity.

- Texas has built several of the largest, most influential, and nationally famous congregations—televised megachurches of all denominations that are each home to more than 20,000 members.

terms of providing for Texas families, including expanded health care, a living wage, and expanded social programs.

CULTURE CONFLICTS

The political culture of Texans, however, is far from stagnant. As Mary Lasswell writes in her book, *I'll Take Texas*, the state's "pioneer past" often clashes with its "urban present."[79] Consider how this conflict shapes Texans' view of three issues: college funding, gambling, marijuana.

College Funding. Texans generally expect their government to maintain an equal playing field. College education is critical to individual advancement

FIGURE 1.7   **Availability of Abortion**

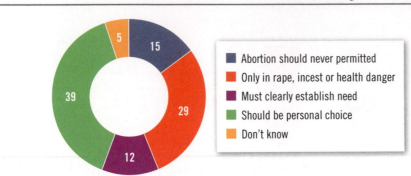

Legend:
- Abortion should never permitted
- Only in rape, incest or health danger
- Must clearly establish need
- Should be personal choice
- Don't know

Source: Texas Politics Project/
University of Texas Poll,
February 2019.

COMMUNICATION:

Where do Texans stand on abortion?

- A core of about 15 percent of Texans never approve of abortion in any circumstances, while about 39 percent approve of access to abortions for any reason.

- A large share of Texans occupy a middle position, approving of abortion when a need has been established and in specific cases, such as rape, ncest, or in the event of a health danger to the mother (41 percent).

CRITICAL THINKING:

Why?

- Abortion is legal and an established right as determined by the U.S. Supreme Court. Most Texans, even if they disagree with the procedure, desire that the law be followed.

- Abortion is both a moral and an individual issue. Texans split on the rights of women in pursing an abortion: Some are against the termination of a pregnancy, but others approve of an individual's right to choose.

and to development of a skilled in-state workforce, but it can be expensive. The state helps students pay for their education. However, when asked which individuals should receive state funds for higher education, most Texans (46 percent) respond that all groups should instead of "only the most needy Texans." Only a small segment of Texans (13 percent) favored expanding higher education funds to needy Texans. Underlying this approach is the sense that the state should not pick "winners and losers" but rather should provide opportunities for all individuals.

Yet Texans do believe in rewarding individuals for services rendered to the state. For example, most Texans do not generally support a "path to citizenship" for immigrants who come to the United States illegally. However, 57 percent of Texans support clearing a path for children of undocumented immigrants who join the military.

Morals and Money. Another clash occurs over the individualistic desire to keep taxes low and the traditionalistic belief that certain types of activities, such as gambling or use of illicit drugs, should be prohibited. In response to a budget crisis in 2011, Texans were asked if they approved of specific measures to raise revenue. They ranked gambling and legalization of marijuana lower on the list than increasing taxes on alcohol.

The scope and scale of government ultimately reflect the state's political culture. As a result, the struggle between groups with different values, and even the clash of different values within the same group, shape both public policy and government institutions themselves.

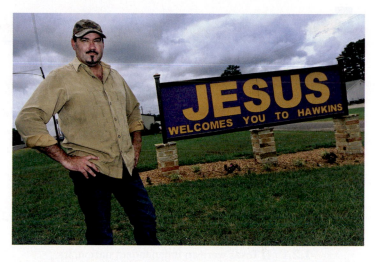

City officials in a small East Texas town dubbed the Pancake Capital of Texas tore down a prominent "Jesus Welcomes You to Hawkins" sign on private property in the middle of a summer night in 2019 after a year's long battle over the role of religion in the city's civic life. Supporters in other towns like Quitman and Mineola made similar signs, but organizations like the Freedom from Religion Foundation argued that it violated the separation of church and state.

 SOCIAL RESPONSIBILITY: **In the conflict between freedom and religion in this case, where do you draw the line?**

🏴 TEXAS TAKEAWAYS

1.4.1 How do we classify political culture in Texas?

1.4.2 What are the values that are derived from Texas's political culture?

THE INSIDER VIEW

Texas has always been a land of conflict—first with Native American tribes battling over territory, then with the Spanish settling the hostile land and converting the native tribes, and finally with the overthrow of Mexican rule by Tejano and Anglo settlers. Today, land is not the only resource Texans are fighting to control. Established groups are battling new and expanding groups for a greater share of public resources. Demographic shifts have also reoriented the scope and direction of public policy in Texas as the population has shifted from rural to urban centers. Throughout their history, Texans have always embraced individual rights, minimal government interference, and law and order. Issues may change and politicians come and go, but Texas government remains committed to these core political values even as they come into conflict and politicians make choices on difficult issues.

TEXAS TAKEAWAYS

1.1.1 Texas was first settled by Native Americans battling for territory, pushed by other tribes, and pulled by the roaming buffalo; next by the Spanish explorers looking for an expanded empire; and then by the Mexican government anxious to create a buffer between itself and the United States.

1.1.2 Texans revolted against Mexico because of anger over halted Anglo immigration, too few legal rights, higher taxation, and a general sense of self-sufficiency.

1.2.1 If Texas were an independent nation, its economy would be ranked tenth in the world. Its 2019 gross state product (the sum of all goods and service produced in a state) topped $1.8 trillion, the second highest in the United States.

1.2.2 The Texas economy has gone through several boom-and-bust cycles—first cotton and cattle, then energy (primarily oil), then manufacturing, and then energy again (natural gas especially).

1.2.3 The Texas Miracle is what some have called the state's economy from 2001 to 2008, which experienced a major boom during that period along with low unemployment, low inflation, and growing state coffers.

The economy was not rosy for everyone, however, as many jobs were low income and many residents lacked access to health care.

1.3.1 Between 2000 and 2010, Texas experienced the largest increase in population (more than 4 million people) of any state in the union. Even other large states like California and Florida did not add population as rapidly as Texas.

1.3.2 Texas's recent population growth is characterized as younger, more Hispanic, and more urban than in the past 10 years.

1.3.3 Pressure on the state to educate a diverse population, provide state health funds for aging Texans, protect equal opportunity housing, and ensure racial tolerance are all challenges the state faces as the demographics change.

1.4.1 Political culture in Texas, according to political scientist Daniel Elazar's analysis, involves two primary value dimensions: individualistic and traditionalistic.

1.4.2 Texans are religious, favor minimal government, approve of the free market, and embrace law and order. These values shape political beliefs on several issues like abortion, state spending, and illegal drugs.

KEY TERMS

individualistic political culture
law and order
minimal government
political culture
religiosity
segregation
suburbanization
Tejanos
Texas Miracle
traditionalistic political culture

PRACTICE QUIZ

1. What did early Spanish settlers call the territory of Texas?
   a. "The New World"
   b. "New Spain"
   c. "Tenochtitlan"
   d. "The West"

2. Where would the Texas economy rank in the world if it were an independent nation?
   a. Fifth
   b. Tenth

c. Twenty-third

d. Forty-fifth

3. The discovery of the East Texas oil field in 1930 near Kilgore prompted which agency to monitor pumping and production?

a. Oil Commission

b. Pumping and Natural Gas Commission

c. Fracking and Heavy Machinery Commission

d. Railroad Commission

4. What is the Texas Miracle?

a. The discovery of oil

b. The state's good economic fortune

c. The lack of scandals by Texas governors

d. The massive size of the state, claimed after the "Great War with Mexico"

5. Today, only three Native American reservations remain in Texas. Which of the following reservations is *not* included among the three currently occupied within the state?

a. Alabama-Coushatta

b. Tigua

c. Cheyenne

d. Kickapoo

6. By the 1820s, the Mexican government aggressively ...

a. Promoted Anglo settlement of Texas

b. Prohibited Anglo settlement of Texas

c. Promoted Spanish settlement of Texas

d. Prohibited Spanish settlement of Texas

7. By 1823, Mexico _____ slavery.

a. Permitted

b. Promoted

c. Turned a blind eye to

d. Banned

8. What was the rallying cry of the Big Rich?

a. "Black gold; Texas tea!"

b. "Don't tread on me!"

c. "Better nouveau than never!"

d. "Seize the oil!"

9. What notable event kick-started the struggling Texas economy in the wake of the Great Depression?

a. World War I

b. World War II

c. The Vietnam War

d. The Iran-Contra Scandal

10. Today, the cash receipts generated by the production of cattle, sheep, and goats in Texas totals more than ...

a. 10 billion dollars

b. 1 trillion dollars

c. 1 billion dollars

d. 50 million dollars

[Answer Key: B, B, D, B, C, A, D, C, B, A]

Learn more with this chapter's digital tools, including the Oxford Insight Study Guide, at www.oup.com/he/Rottinghaus3e.

2 THE TEXAS CONSTITUTION

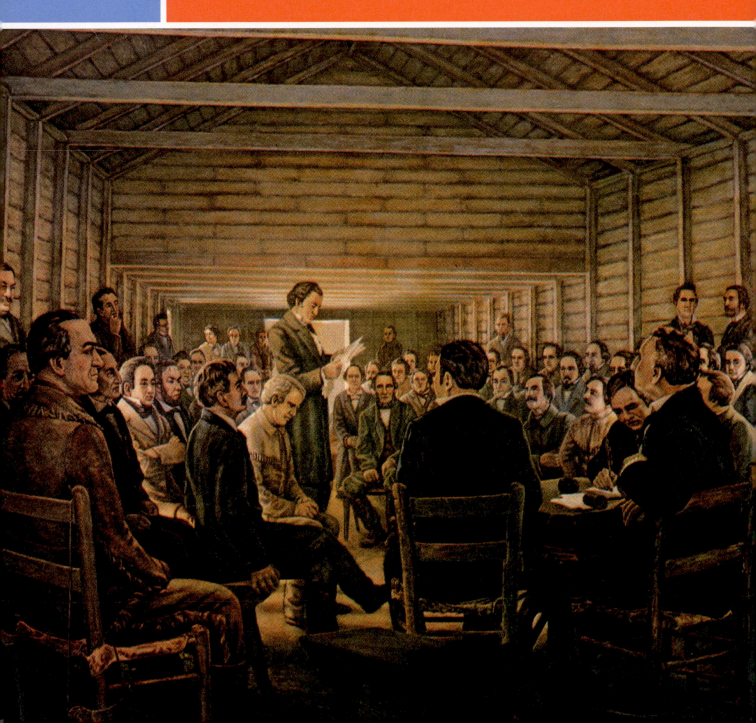

As the delegates to the young Texas government arrived in Washington-on-the-Brazos in 1836 to draft a declaration of independence and provisional constitution, they were less than inspired by their location. The town was a "disgusting place" of only "about a dozen wretched cabins or shanties" and only "one well-defined street," wrote one delegate. He concluded that it was "a rare place to hold a national convention in. They will have to leave it promptly to avoid starvation."[1]

As dawn broke on March 3, 1836, the delegates confronted cold weather from a Texas Norther that brought freezing rain and hail. The building where the delegates met had only one long wooden table, no doors in the doorways, and only a piece of cotton cloth stretched across the windows kept out the cold. Those who had been assigned to the drafting committee worked quickly to write a declaration of independence, but the first draft was found to have so many errors that it was returned to the committee for correction. Before supper, Lieutenant Colonel William Barret Travis's letter arrived from the Alamo pleading for reinforcements. After supper, to illustrate the fate of the new nation rising from the Battle of the Alamo, General Sam Houston positioned two men who had had too much drink and were half asleep shoulder to shoulder. He declared it was evident to all that "united they stand; divided they fall."[2]

This was the first birthday of the new Republic of Texas. Most of the delegates in that room would go on to shape the destiny of the state. The declaration of independence, though created when prospects for success seemed darkest, reflected an ardent desire for

LEARNING OBJECTIVES

2.1 Identify the function of constitutions.

2.2 Explain the events that led to the Texas Declaration of Independence.

2.3 Relate the goals of the 1836 Constitution to its outcome and reactions to it.

2.4 Differentiate between the 1845 Constitution and prior Texas constitutions.

2.5 Analyze the goals of the 1860s constitutions in the context of political and social developments.

2.6 Describe the principles of the modern Texas Constitution.

2.7 Outline the process for amending the Texas Constitution and attempts at constitutional change.

● The delegates to the Texas Independence Convention met in Washington-on-the-Brazos in 1836 to sign a declaration of independence from Mexico and forge a constitution for the new Republic.

democratic self-rule.[3] The constitution drafted in that session would be the first of many for Texas, but it would also outline the core principles of liberty, popular rule, and limited government that all Texas constitutions would guarantee. The struggle to establish and maintain the Texas Constitution would test these values as new issues and challenges emerged.

In this chapter, we look at the constitutions that have given Texas its basic structure. We first outline the roles of constitutional government in general and in Texas. We then examine the principles driving the Texas Revolution. We next observe the scope and functions of the government as set by the Republic, statehood, Confederacy, Reconstruction (after the Civil War), and post-Reconstruction (modern) constitutions. Finally, we examine the current constitution (passed in 1876) to assess the provisions, process, and prospects of amendment.

(U) 2.1 CONSTITUTIONAL GOVERNMENT

2.1 Identify the function of constitutions.

constitution: a document that establishes principles, powers, and responsibilities of government

bill of rights: a formal declaration of the rights of citizens

Constitutional government in Texas has shaped the rules and actors in governance since Texas was a province of Mexico. A **constitution** lays out the principles and responsibilities of government and specifies the powers of the branches of government and elected officials. The constitution structures the rules of the game and so shapes strategies used in political struggles. A major part of most constitutions, and of all constitutions in Texas, is the **bill of rights**, a formal declaration of the rights of the citizens. These may be rights that the government must provide, such as the right to a trial by jury, or rights that the government cannot restrict, such as freedom of speech.

The painstaking process of wording these rights in the state's first constitution led Thomas Rusk, the president of the 1836 Convention, to exclaim in exasperation, "We shall be here six weeks yet." But Texans were determined to get the wording right. Why? The answer lies in a revolution that had begun two centuries earlier. In the seventeenth and eighteenth centuries, Western political thinkers had proposed the idea that the legitimacy of government rested not on a "divine right" of kings but on the consent of the governed. The governed agree to give up some of the freedoms that they possess in the "state of nature" (an anarchical society with no government) in return for the government's commitment to providing their physical security and to safeguarding certain "natural rights." This agreement between the government and the governed is called a **social contract**, which—in republics—is often enshrined in a written constitution.

Early Texans valued rugged individualism and were not inclined to give up their freedoms to government rule lightly. Therefore, the challenge in crafting a constitution for Texas was to balance freedoms and government power. Throughout Texas history, the two themes woven into the many constitutions that have governed the Lone Star State have been a commitment to individual rights (for most) and a strict separation of powers among the three branches of government.

Constitutional government in Texas is older than the Republic itself. The story of how Texas constitutional principles were established starts when Texas was part of Mexico.

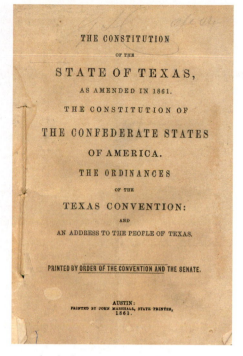

 TEXAS TAKEAWAYS

2.1.1 Explain what a constitution does.

2.1.2 What two themes run through the Texas constitutions?

Texas has had six constitutions beginning in 1836 that have been shaped by historical circumstances and political reactions to crises.

SOCIAL RESPONSIBILITY: **What key rights should a constitution protect?**

social contract: an agreement in which the governed give up certain freedoms in return for government protection

 **2.2 THE ROOTS OF REBELLION AND THE DECLARATION OF INDEPENDENCE**

The spirit of Texas government was forged in direct reaction to tyranny from multiple governments and several overbearing rulers. After the death of his father, Stephen F. Austin, the "father of Texas," traveled to Mexico City to request the continuation of his father's colony in Mexico. Arriving in 1822, Austin found himself in the middle of a debate in the Mexican Congress about whether to establish a **monarchy** or a **republic**. The debate mattered little in the short term as Augustín de Iturbide, who helped Mexico gain independence from Spain, abruptly seized power himself and replaced the democratically chosen Mexican Congress with

2.2 Explain the events that led to the Texas Declaration of Independence.

monarchy: a government run by a single individual, often a king or a queen, until death or abdication

republic: a form of government in which people rule indirectly through elected representatives

Stephen F. Austin was the first and most famous Texan empresario. His steady leadership helped to smooth over several delicate skirmishes between settlers and the Mexican government.

a loyal junta (a small group of leaders). In 1823, Iturbide was forced to abdicate after he lost support, and under the newly written Mexican Constitution of 1824, the Mexican Congress expanded settlement of the northern Mexico territory using empresarios and established a colonization law that future settlers were to obey. As mentioned in Chapter 1, empresarios were regional land distributors, serving as the local recruiters and leaders of a fixed area of land and the people who settled there. The empresarios (like Austin) would be in charge, but the Mexican government promised to protect the liberty, property, and civil rights of all "foreigners" who would in turn profess the Roman Catholic faith.

The Constitution of 1824 established a federal republic and specified that each state within the federation was to create its own constitution. In 1827, the Constitution of the State of Coahuila y Tejas (in 1824 the states of Coahuila and Texas had been combined) established separation of power among its three branches of government, not unlike the U.S. Constitution, and provided for basic freedom of speech, although it forbade the practice of any other religion except Catholicism, limited voting rights to those who could read and had employment, and restricted slavery. The Constitution of 1824 marked the high point of liberty granted to the Mexican colonists and would later be a rallying cry for the restitution of rights during the Texas Revolution. Most observers believed that if Mexico had agreed to reestablish the rights of Texans under the Constitution of 1824, the Texas Revolution would have lost momentum.

It didn't take long for new immigrants to Texas to populate much of the eastern part of the province, prompting the Mexican government to dispatch a surveyor to assess the situation. The unflattering report to the Mexican president stated that the "Mexican influence is disproportionately diminished" and that the "ratio of Mexicans to foreigners is one to ten." The newcomers were "fugitives from justice, vagabonds and criminals" who "travel with their pocket constitutions" and were "ready for war."[4] Following this assessment, the Mexican legislature passed the Law of April 6, 1830, which called for more Mexican soldiers to enforce a strict no-slavery policy. This law represented an alteration of Austin's contract to allow Mexico to take back the "coast leagues" (land granted to empresarios along the coast) and, most burdensome to the colonies, imposed a freeze on emigration of settlers from the United States.

In reaction to the new decrees and following disturbances at Anahuac, where Anglos took up arms to object to immigration limits and new tariffs, Texans met in October 1832 and April 1833 to draw up a formal petition to allow

sovereignty and independence for the Texas state and to repeal the Law of April 6, 1830. This petition, and the Turtle Bayou Resolutions that were written following the Anahuac disturbances, advocated for independence of Texas from Coahuila and reinstatement of the 1824 Constitution, which had been suspended. Austin was dispatched to Mexico City to deliver the petition to President Antonio Lopez de Santa Anna. In a moment of uncharacteristic impatience, Austin told Vice President Gomez Farias that if the situation were not remedied, "Texas would remedy them of themselves without waiting any longer." Gomez Farias interpreted this as a threat of rebellion and temporarily imprisoned Austin.[5]

Fanning the flames of rebellion by centralizing power in his own hands, Mexican President Santa Anna sent his vice president into exile, disbanded Congress, and dissolved the state legislatures in 1835. Santa Anna also dismissed the empresarios who organized local migration, including Austin, whereby Austin declared that the Mexican government could not "legally deprive Texans of these rights without the consent of the people.[6] On March 2, 1836, delegates from across Texas met and approved a declaration of independence that proclaimed Mexico had abandoned the constitutional principles expressed in the Constitution of 1824 (see Table 2.1) and had compromised the republican principles of self-government and representation.

Not all Texas residents embraced the cause of revolution. Benjamin Lundy, a New Jersey-born Quaker, had a religious and moral objection to slavery. Mexico had outlawed slavery in Texas, although a covert slave trade persisted. Lundy asserted that the Texas Revolution was being fought to further Texas as a slave state and eventually seek entry into the United States. Although derided at the time, Lundy's contention may have influenced Americans to delay annexation of Texas into the United States because of problems balancing slave and nonslave states in the Union.[7]

> **sovereignty:** authority over a political entity, such as a province or a state

TABLE 2.1 Grievances against the Mexican Government Expressed in the Declaration of Independence

Citizens forced to alter their religion by adopting Catholicism
Incarcerated Stephen F. Austin with no just cause
Refused right to trial by jury
Failed to establish public system of education
Dissolved Congress from Coahuila y Tejas
Commissioned foreign "desperados" for "piratical" attacks on commerce
Demanded collection of arms
Incited Native American attacks

Source: Texas Declaration of Independence.

SOCIAL RESPONSIBILITY:

In your opinion, are these grievances sufficient to justify rebellion? Or are these better remedied through political means?

Many Tejanos—Spanish-speaking Texans—were also divided between their loyalty to the young Mexican government and their growing dissatisfaction with its centralization of authority. Yet, many joined with the Anglos, providing invaluable intelligence and logistical support to the rebellion; indeed, three Hispanics (two of them Tejanos) signed the Texas Declaration of Independence: Jose Francisco Ruiz, his cousin Jose Antonio Navarro, and Lorenzo de Zavala.[8] Navarro, in his long career as *alcalde* (mayor) of San Antonio, Texan representative to the legislature in Coahuila and Texas, and state senator to the Mexican Congress, was a close associate of Austin and was instrumental in guaranteeing the growth of Anglo settlement and representation in Texas. During the Texas Republic, 4 Tejanos out of a total of 44 members served in the legislature. Juan Nepomuceno Seguin fought in the "runaway scrape" – the flight of south central Texans away from Santa Anna's marching army – and the final battle at San Jacinto and went on to serve as mayor of his native San Antonio, but conflicts with local Anglos led to death threats and prompted his move back to Mexico. Others like Plácido Benavides, the alcalde of Victoria, and Martín de León, the only Tejano empresario, fought for Texas sovereignty.

 TEXAS TAKEAWAYS

2.2.1 What events provoked Texans to rebel against Mexico?

2.2.2 What were the stated grievances of the Texas Declaration of Independence?

2.3 THE 1836 CONSTITUTION OF THE REPUBLIC

2.3 Relate the goals of the 1836 Constitution to its outcome and reactions to it.

Writing in haste and under fear of the approaching Mexican army, the delegates "scarcely put the finishing touches upon the Constitution" of 1836 before adjourning as news arrived of the fall of the Alamo.[9]

Yet the 1836 Constitution was more than a governing document. It aggressively voiced the ideals of frontier independence that would come to dominate the future political culture of the state. The Constitution of 1836 included a Declaration of Rights, outlining several unimpeachable liberties that "shall never be violated on any pretence whatever," and guarded "against the transgression of the high powers which we have delegated." Familiar liberties included freedom to worship, freedom of speech, freedom from unreasonable search and seizure, and the rights to bear arms, bail, legal counsel, and a speedy trial.

The Constitution of 1836 also provided for a strict **separation of powers** between the legislative, executive, and judicial branches. Under this system, each branch is selected by different procedures, serves different tenures in office, and is responsible for different obligations. Most of the authority was housed in the legislature, which had the power to collect taxes, levy tariffs, and pay debts. The president, head of the executive branch, was the commander-in-chief of the army, navy, and militia but was not to command the troops in the field unless ordered to by the legislature. Like the U.S. president, the president of Texas was able to make treaties and appointments with the approval of two-thirds of the Senate, fill vacancies, and "upon extraordinary occasions" convene the legislature.

separation of powers: a system that vests political, judicial, and policymaking authority across different branches of government

In the Constitution of 1836, we see hints of aversion to centralized power and an extreme distrust of executive authority. The president was not eligible to serve consecutive terms. All appointed offices were subject to the approval of the Senate, and if removal was necessary, the Senate had to approve that as well.

The 1836 Texas Constitution borrowed heavily from the U.S. Constitution. However, several differences between these constitutions are worth noting. First, no member of the clergy was eligible to serve in elected office in Texas, although the constitution required at least a "belief" in a higher power. Second, to separate the funding of government from those who serve it, the constitution established that persons "holding an office of profit under the government" or holders of "public monies" were not eligible to serve in the legislature. These passages provided the first framework for ethical government within the state. In addition, the 1836 Constitution recognized the right of free enterprise, unencumbered by government interference, while prohibiting monopolies. This capitalistic spirit, and the power provided to the organizations that promote it, has been a central feature of Texas politics ever since.

At the time the 1836 Constitution was drafted, many Texas residents presumed that the new Texas Republic would quickly join the United States. An overwhelming number of Texas citizens favored annexation only to find the United States cold to the idea. As suggested earlier, slavery was the issue. The 1836 Constitution did not allow government to prohibit the importation of slaves into Texas. In fact, slaveholders were barred from emancipating slaves without immediately removing them from Texas's borders. The state eventually went so far as to establish a

The current Texas Constitution outlaws a religious test for public office, but the constitution requires that a candidate "acknowledge the existence of a Supreme Being." Several groups have challenged this provision with little success, and a past Texas attorney general decision rendered it void. However, the provision remains.

PERSONAL RESPONSIBILITY: **Should the state require candidates to recognize the existence of a supreme being?**

law that required all free persons of color to leave the state by 1842 or be sold into slavery. The act sparked opposition among some Texas residents who in 1840 successfully petitioned the legislature to overturn the law through the Ashworth Act on behalf of friends or neighbors. The strong linkage to slavery prevented Texas's immediate entrance into the United States for more than a decade after the revolution ended.

⬛ TEXAS TAKEAWAYS

2.3.1 What was the structure of government established by the 1836 Texas Constitution?

2.3.2 What were the similarities and differences between the 1836 Constitution of the Republic and the U.S. Constitution with respect to the power of the president and the role of free enterprise?

2.4 THE 1845 CONSTITUTION OF THE (NEW) STATE OF TEXAS

| **2.4** | Differentiate between the 1845 Constitution and prior Texas constitutions. |

Both the internal struggle between slave and nonslave states and the threat of war with Mexico if the United States annexed Texas blocked the Republic's entrance into the Union. But in 1844, James Polk was elected to the U.S. presidency on a platform of Western expansion. In addition, due to its robust cotton trade, Texas grew closer to Great Britain, a rival of the United States, prompting a worried American government to initiate annexation talks. Texas, suffering from a drop in cotton prices that pinched the state's major revenue stream, welcomed the invitation. Texas formally entered the Union in December 1845.

Now a state, Texas needed a new state constitution. The task of writing it fell to an able group of individuals, including the president of the Republic, members of Congress, several members from the Convention of 1836, cabinet officers, and ministers.

The Constitution of 1845 (the "statehood constitution") was remarkably similar to the Constitution of 1836 in balancing government authority between the branches and outlining fundamental rights of citizens. The framers, however, erupted into a spirited debate about whether Tejanos should be allowed to vote. Some argued that voting rights should be limited to "free white males." The attempted exclusion failed due to the efforts of delegate Jose Antonio Navarro (the only native-born Texan at the convention) and 1836 convention president Rusk, who thought it wrong to insult the character of the state's heritage by excluding Tejanos.[10] Native Americans and African descendants, however, were excluded from voting. Navarro also fought, less successfully, in favor of land rights for Tejanos against "men, hungry for land" who attempted to use the "chicanery of the laws" to attack their property rights.[11]

At the same time, the Anglo framers introduced significant democratic reforms by extending **suffrage** to those not holding property. In the legislative branch, the doors of the building were to be physically kept open during the session—probably welcome in the days before air conditioning—and the legislators were to be paid the meager sum of $3 each month, not dissimilar to the current $600 per month (or roughly $20 per day) legislators are paid.

suffrage: the right to participate in the electoral process by voting

One significant innovation in the 1845 version of the constitution was its more muscular allowance for judicial authority. The state had a growing population, and the judicial system that had been modest and ineffective under Mexican rule was expanded to provide greater access to the court system for Texans. The framers granted the Texas Supreme Court appellate jurisdiction on legal matters, meaning that they could hear arguments from the lower courts. In addition to this authority, the Texas Supreme Court could "enforce its own jurisdiction" and compel a judge of a lower court to proceed to trial and judgment in a case.

We also see the introduction of a lieutenant governor for the first time in Texas history in the 1845 Constitution. Although today the Texas lieutenant governor is the most powerful statewide officer alongside the governor, the lieutenant governor in this version of the constitution was selected by the governor as a "running mate" instead of being elected separately, as would be the case later. The lieutenant governor was to be the president of the Senate and, like the vice president of the United States, have a tiebreaking vote in that chamber.

homestead law: a law that prevents Texans from losing their homes in the event of bankruptcy or other financial problems

The 1845 Constitution did not include provisions for popular election of many offices, such as judges or other executive officers, who instead were appointed by the governor. However, as a means of holding the state government accountable to the will of the people, Texans passed a constitutional amendment in 1850 to select these officials through popular election.

Two noteworthy provisions highlighted the state's concern about private property rights. The Constitution of 1845 gave birth to the **homestead law** in Texas, a rule that gives special protection to Texans' homes. Many of the early settlers came to Texas while fleeing creditors either in the United States or abroad. At the time, Stephen F. Austin worried that many

The first Texas Capitol building was constructed at Main Street and Texas Avenue in Houston before the capital moved to Austin in 1846. The Rice Hotel stands at this location today. The final president of the Republic, Anson Jones, distraught over not being selected to serve as U.S. senator, committed suicide here.

settlers would lose their homes or significant property if these debts were collected, and he successfully pushed the Mexican government for protection of the homestead. Although the Mexican legislature passed homestead protections for settlers during the pre-Republic days, they later repealed these laws. The threat of losing their homesteads and source of livelihood left a stamp of defiance in the minds of the ruggedly independent Texans. Subsequent constitutions broadened the exemption to limit the amount of property taxes collected on one's home and to allow local governments to give property tax reductions to older or disabled Texans. These laws allow only certain creditors, such as a mortgage holder or the government, to force the sale of a homestead. The 1845 Constitution was also innovative in its treatment of women's property rights. The framers extended property ownership to married women for property owned before marriage or acquired during marriage.

🚩 TEXAS TAKEAWAYS

2.4.1 Why did the 1845 Constitution extend popular control to state government?

2.4.2 In what ways was the 1845 Constitution different from the 1836 Constitution on property rights?

2.5 SECESSION, RECONSTRUCTION, AND THE CONSTITUTIONS OF 1861, 1866, AND 1869

2.5 Analyze the goals of the 1860s constitutions in the context of political and social developments.

The political battles over slavery, the turmoil of the Civil War, and the refashioning of political power in the South produced a rapid making and remaking of Texas government over the period of a decade. In the 1860s, the constitution was rewritten three times.

Largely in response to the election of Abraham Lincoln in 1860, Texas began the process of secession from the United States just 15 short years after joining. Citing failure of the federal government to protect its borders and the limitations of prosperity due to the likely abolition of slavery, anti-Union sentiment ran high in Texas. A series of mysterious fires in Denton and Dallas fueled rumors about a slave rebellion. In response, bands of Anglos lynched at least 30 enslaved African Americans and accused Union sympathizers. These "Texas Troubles" were used by advocates of secession to bolster public support for their cause. Many

Texans in favor of secession also believed that the Confederacy was more likely than the Union to open the route to Westward expansion.[12]

Sam Houston, the governor at the time, was against leaving the Union. The secessionist movement, however, forced him to call a special session of the legislature to consider the matter. In his office, Houston fumed at "the mob upstairs."[13] Ultimately, a convention in Austin issued a declaration of secession in February 1861, which was ratified by the majority of counties (see Figure 2.1). Sam Houston refused to sign an oath affirming his allegiance to the Confederacy and was removed from office.

THE 1861 CONSTITUTION—"THE CONFEDERACY CONSTITUTION"

In 1861, delegates to the Secession Convention wrote a constitution that was similar to the statehood constitution but certified Texas's membership in the Confederate States of America. Most prominently, the first passage added a clause granting supreme sovereign rights to the state, asserting that no "government or authority" can exercise power within the state without the consent of the people. The 1861 version also protected slavery and forbade slave owners from freeing their slaves without state permission.

THE 1866 CONSTITUTION—"THE READMISSION CONSTITUTION"

After the Civil War ended, Republicans, who held a strong majority in Congress after the elections of 1866, passed legislation that expanded military rule of southern states. Legislation also required former Confederate states to write new constitutions recognizing the U.S. Constitution and declaring allegiance to the Union.

Texas faced the threat of federal intervention if the state did not abide by the requirement to issue declarations against secession and demonstrate a "paramount allegiance" to the United States. Texans, however, were deeply divided in support for the Union. In order to present a pro-Union front toward the federal government, the Constitution of 1866 showed an unusual tendency toward centralized power, especially in the hands of the governor. The 1866 Constitution granted the governor greater powers to appoint public officials, an extended term in office, and higher pay.

The 1866 Constitutional Convention split into three factions: two aggressive factions of Unionists and Secessionists and a third group of moderate Unionists who held the balance of power. The Secessionists and moderate Unionists combined forces to elect James W. Throckmorton as president of the convention. Throckmorton had been an ardent opponent of secession (his was the only vote against secession in the legislature in 1861) but eventually joined the Confederate service and rose to the rank of brigadier general. This alliance steered the convention toward a few select goals. The convention

FIGURE 2.1 **1861 Texas Vote on Seceding from the Union**

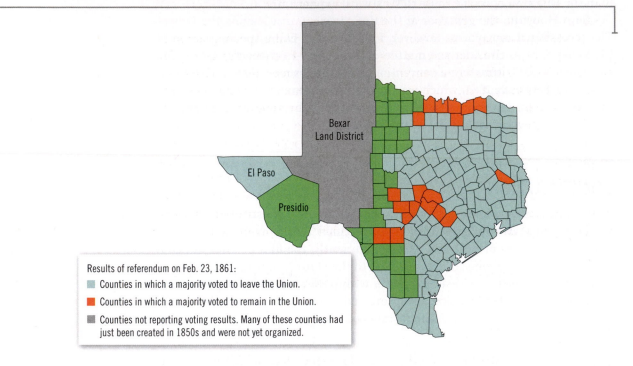

Results of referendum on Feb. 23, 1861:

■ Counties in which a majority voted to leave the Union.

■ Counties in which a majority voted to remain in the Union.

■ Counties not reporting voting results. Many of these counties had just been created in 1850s and were not yet organized.

Source: Texas Almanac.

 COMMUNICATION:

Did most counties in Texas support secession?

- By a vote of 166 to 8, Texas declared its secession in February 1861.
- Most counties voted to secede from the Union, although others chose to remain.

 CRITICAL THINKING:

Why were there such geographic differences?

- Much of northern Texas and the western border of the state voted in favor of staying in the Union due to safety concerns on the frontier and the fact that these settlers had migrated from neutral border states.
- Counties populated by immigrants from the southern United States voted to leave the Union primarily to preserve the practice of slavery.
- German settlers in counties of central Texas were opposed to secession because many did not have slaves. Counties where they held a majority voted in favor of staying in the Union.
- Sharing an agricultural need for the continuation of slavery, much of eastern Texas voted to secede from the Union.

agreed to the minimum demands for readmission to the Union, such as allegiance to the Union, repudiation of the state's war debt, and invalidation of all laws passed by the state government during the war.

While the provisional governor Andrew Jackson Hamilton, appointed by U.S. President Andrew Johnson, and other delegates believed in giving full voting and legal rights to former enslaved people, former Secessionists hindered progress toward the extension of rights to African Americans. The Constitution of 1866 reached a compromise. It gave African Americans the right to purchase and sell property, to sue and be sued, and to enter into legally binding agreements, but it deprived them of the right to vote, to stand for public office, and to serve on a jury. The legislature also passed "Black Codes," a move that many Texas Republicans and Unionists saw as a means of reinstituting slavery. Under these codes, African Americans could be fined or arrested for everything from curfew violations to displays of objectionable behavior and receive a punishment of forced labor with a "guardian" or prison labor.

THE 1869 CONSTITUTION—"THE RECONSTRUCTION CONSTITUTION"

Military rule over Texas was to continue until a "loyal sentiment" existed in at least a majority of inhabitants.[14] In addition, the U.S. Congress changed the terms of Reconstruction, forcing Texas state leaders to draft another constitution in 1869 in order to meet new objectives to end Reconstruction and formally return to the Union. All male citizens, regardless of race or color, were allowed to elect delegates to the convention. One prominent African American delegate, George Thompson Ruby from Galveston, helped to foster equality in the new constitution and later served in the Freedman's Bureau (a political organization to protect the rights of African Americans) and in the state senate.[15] The Reconstruction Constitution was required to grant equality to all persons before the law and recognize the supremacy of the U.S. Constitution, the "heresies" of secession, and the ratification of the Fourteenth Amendment.

As a result, the Reconstruction Constitution departed from the old political tradition by extending full voting rights to African Americans, who became a political power during this era. Between 1866 and 1896, African American politicians helped build the Republican Party in Texas, inform new voters on voting procedures, and push for action on issues like education and equal rights.[16] Nevertheless, the state remained highly segregated and racial violence continued.

The Constitution of 1869 also departed from past Texas constitutions in that it expanded the responsibilities assigned to the state government. For instance, the constitution expanded the duty of the legislature to make "suitable provisions for the support and maintenance of a system of public free schools." The constitution also outlined the power of the state to regulate the land belonging to railroads and affixed the power of the state to regulate and promote immigration.

The Reconstruction Constitution of 1869 additionally diverged from previous constitutions in that it further centralized authority. The powers of the governor under the Reconstruction Constitution were so far-reaching that the governor could appoint local officials, such as mayors, aldermen, and district attorneys. The constitution also granted the governor full control to appoint voter registrars in each county and school superintendents. These powers, combined with a short legislative session, instilled tremendous authority in the executive. Voters were also required to register and vote at the county seats, a hardship for many. State guard units, already despised by many, kept watch over the polling places.

As soon as it was drafted, the Reconstruction Constitution of 1869 drew ire from Texans for its centralization of power, especially in the hands of what some deemed the "radical" Republicans aligned with the national Republicans who had set the Reconstruction rules. In Texas, the 1869 elections placed Republican reformer Edmund J. Davis in the governor's office. However, Davis did not fare well politically amidst growing resentment.

A crime spree between 1865 and 1868, partially initiated by the Ku Klux Klan, targeted freedmen and federal soldiers. Motivated by racism and ill feelings over the outcome of the Civil War, roving gangs of "murderers and horse thieves" preyed on Texans in areas where Union sympathy was strong.[17] Governor Davis ordered state police and militia units to curb the violence and lawlessness and to aggressively seek criminals throughout the state. Families in central Texas resisted during the "Hill County Rebellion," jailing state police officials who were tracking the criminals responsible for local violence. The governor then imposed martial law in Hill, Walker, and Bastrop counties. Accustomed to minimal government oversight, many Texans charged that the governor had become the "Dictator of Texas" who took property or life at his own will, and they called the state police the "Governor's Hounds" and derided them as "snakes, wolves, and other undesirable things."[18] Texans accused the state police of tampering in local elections and murdering prisoners as a form of harsh retribution for criminal actions.[19]

The Davis administration also contributed to rampant corruption and cronyism in state politics. Observers reacted negatively to provisions in the 1869 Constitution that allowed the governor substantial authority to appoint offices made vacant after Texas was admitted to the Union, with those appointees to serve until the next general election. Many Texans complained that the candidates for the governor's appointees, the "henchmen of the governor," required no qualifications, as "no recommendation seemed to be needed other than that the incumbents were Democrats and that the aspirants were Republicans."[20]

In addition to the political problems, several social problems confronted the state at this time. The crime wave in the early 1870s had put pressure on the judicial system, and the "incompetence" of the judges appointed by Governor Davis elicited a desire for an elective judiciary with shorter terms.[21]

Substantial financial relief given to railroads, in the form of state subsidies, threatened to bankrupt the state. Local citizens complained that they had no control over their education system because the governor held the power to appoint school superintendents.

Governor Davis was defeated by 50,000 votes in 1873 but refused to leave office right away, barricading himself inside the State Capitol and noting that he was allowed to finish out his months as governor. The Texas Supreme Court agreed. But Democrats led by Richard Coke, the winner of the 1873 election, sneaked past the guards on the first floor of the Capitol, secured keys to the second floor, and took possession. The Travis Rifle Brigade, dispatched to protect Davis, refused to obey the order and instead insured the inauguration of Coke. U.S. President Ulysses S. Grant refused to send federal troops, and a compromise was reached in which Davis left office.

The Texas Declaration of Independence claimed that the Mexican government did not make provisions for adequate education. Subsequent state constitutions explicitly made quality public education a right for Texans.

SOCIAL RESPONSIBILITY: **Is it a basic right to have free, quality public schools? Should people who don't have children be taxed to support a public education system?**

TEXAS TAKEAWAYS

2.5.1 What was the position of the Constitution of 1861 on states' rights?

2.5.2 What prompted the Constitution of 1866 to be written, and what unique features did it contain as a result?

2.5.3 What are three important features of the Constitution of 1869?

2.6 THE CONSTITUTION OF 1876—THE CURRENT CONSTITUTION

Born from the Reconstruction Era resentment of the perceived overreaching power of Governor Davis, the Constitution of 1876 sought to return to a limited government approach. Factions fought over the role of the federal government and their growing concerns about the fate of

> **2.6** Describe the principles of the modern Texas Constitution.

liberty under a centralized state government. This fever continues to fuel debates about the constitution which is still in use today.

THE CRAFTING OF THE 1876 CONSTITUTION

The radical Republicans' rule was ending by the middle of 1870 as moderate Republicans joined the Democratic Party at the state and national levels. Under Governor Coke, Democrats began to call for a new constitution that would fix what they saw as the flaws in the Constitution of 1869: centralized executive power, an unwieldy judiciary, and duplicative state offices. In many ways, the framers fashioned the 1876 Constitution in direct reaction to the frustration with the strong, costly government imposed on Texas after the Civil War and the governorship of Edmund Davis. Delegates relied on the Constitution of 1845 as a model and generally favored a return to limited government and frugality.

Future governors and current Texas Rangers were delegates to the convention, along with many farmers from the Grange Movement who successfully pressed for economic reform to benefit agricultural interests. A total of 5 of the 15 Republican delegates were African American.[22]

Delegates demonstrated great enthusiasm for the new constitution. Upon final passage of the draft, one delegate voted "aye, with the Lord's blessing on it."[23] But passage by the voters proved challenging. Proponents of the new constitution argued that it gave too much authority to the people. Opponents of the proposed constitution took issue with the weakening role of the state in fostering immigration and consistent quality public education. After a grueling campaign, the new constitution was ratified by voters in the 1876 election, 136,606 votes to 56,652.

Consider whether the 1876 Constitution gave the people too much power.

PRINCIPLES OF THE TEXAS CONSTITUTION

The current Texas Constitution, organized into 17 articles (see Table 2.2), contains four key principles: popular sovereignty, limited state government through local control, separation of powers, and personal rights and liberties. These principles and their implementation within the 1876 Constitution strongly reflect Texas's political culture.

Popular Sovereignty. The 1876 Constitution recognizes the centrality of **popular sovereignty** to Texas's republican form of government: "political power is inherent in the people, and all free governments are founded on their authority, and instituted for their benefit" (Article 1, Section 2). The people rule through suffrage, the right to vote in elections, which today is extended to all citizens of the state except those under 18 years of age, those deemed mentally incompetent, and those convicted of certain crimes (including bribery, perjury, forgery, or other "high crimes"). Because all substantial policy

popular sovereignty: rule by the people.

TABLE 2.2 — Articles of the Texas Constitution

Article 1	Bill of Rights	Outlines rights and responsibilities
Articles 2–5, 9, 15, 16	Power of Government	Establishes powers of each branch of government; impeachment process
Article 6	Voting	Establishes right to vote and qualifications
Article 7	Education	Summarizes the right to education and local responsibility
Articles 8, 11, 12	Taxes, Revenue, and Corporations	Enumerates the types of and limits on taxes and revenue
Articles 10, 14	Public Lands, Railroads	Identifies the rights of state to control
Article 17	Amendments	Specifies how to amend the constitution

Source: Texas Constitution.

SOCIAL RESPONSIBILITY:

What possible political issues do the articles of the Texas Constitution address? What political issues should they address, if any?

changes must be approved by the voters, the role of the people in governing the state is critical. One prominent constitutional restriction is on income taxes—any attempt to establish a state income tax must be approved by a majority of voters who vote in an election.

National trends at the time of drafting that edged toward more inclusive, unrestricted suffrage for adult males also influenced the framers of the 1876 Constitution. Unlike today's version, the 1876 Constitution, however, did not immediately extend suffrage to all Texans. Women were excluded from voting.

The fight for ratification took on a racial overtone due to its universal sovereignty provisions. Anglos feared that the African American majority in some counties would "put whites completely under the control of their former slaves."[24] Republicans, who developed Union Leagues to encourage loyalty to the Union and voting, banded together to form a slate of all African American candidates to support the constitution in predominantly African American counties. As a result, several newspapers in those areas demanded that Anglos vote against the proposed constitution and its provisions for unrestricted suffrage. Texans, however, ratified the constitution with universal suffrage in place.

The framers of the 1876 Constitution appeased Anglo fears of universal male suffrage by adding a provision that voters must be taxpayers before voting on city finance elections. A poll tax of one dollar was also required to vote. Most Republican delegates in 1876 were opposed, primarily because African Americans were a major constituency and could not always afford to pay the tax. Some Democrats from the progressive Grange political movement also opposed the tax for poor farmers. A temporary partnership between

Republicans and the progressive Granger Movement, referred to as the "holy alliance," tried unsuccessfully to block the poll tax. The measure, in fact, remained unchallenged until passage of the Twenty-Fourth Amendment in 1964 and was not removed in Texas until 1966, when the U.S. Supreme Court ruled it unconstitutional.

limited government: a political system in which the government's functions and powers are restricted to protect individual liberty

Limited Government. Limited government is another central organizing feature of the Texas Constitution. Limited government implies that the impact of government is kept as small as possible, with few laws passed and as little intervention in the lives of citizens as possible. Experiences with overreaching executive power and with the "obnoxious acts" of the Twelfth Legislature under Governor Davis caused the authors of the 1876 Constitution to restrict government's power.

First, the framers fragmented the power of the executive branch, creating new offices, ripping the power to appoint established offices from the governor, and granting this power to the people, who now elect these officers. Under the current Texas Constitution, the powers of the executive branch rest not just in the governor's office but also in the offices of the lieutenant governor, secretary of state, comptroller of public accounts, commissioner of the General Land Office, and attorney general. Each office, except the secretary of state, is elected separately from the governor, diffusing the power of the executive into several offices and limiting executive authority. This structure is called a **plural executive**.

plural executive: diffusion of authority and power throughout several entities in the executive branch

Second, the framers took aim at the legislative branch. The new constitution shortened the terms of office and increased the number of representatives that had been established by previous constitutions. The Constitution of 1876 also stripped the legislature of its power to suspend laws that provide Texans access to courts.

INSIDER INTERVIEW

Former Chief Justice Tom Phillips

As a conservative judge on the Texas Supreme Court, what do you believe are the greatest strengths of the Texas Constitution?

The greatest strengths of the Texas Constitution, in my opinion, are negative ones. The limitation on legislative sessions makes our part-time legislators more aware of the effects of their laws than federal or other large state representatives. The constitution is too detailed, but at least it's easier to amend than those in some states. The constitution doesn't permit initiative and referendum.

 CRITICAL THINKING: **How does the Texas Constitution foster limited government?**

The framers also sought to limit the ability of the state legislature to encroach on the rights of local governments. The 1876 Constitution restricts the legislature from "regulating the affairs of counties, cities, towns, wards or school districts" and lists several specific things the state cannot do, including locating a county seat, laying out roads, granting divorces, and managing public schools. Whereas the legislature is required to create and fund public schools, the constitution gives full authority to local, independent school districts to use these funds. Local counties are also permitted to establish hospital districts.

Over time, however, Texans have voted to amend the Constitution of 1876 to modestly expand government's authority. Several amendments have given greater authority to the legislature to manage the economic and social affairs of the state, such as regulating railroads, administering state prisons, and monitoring local banks. Other amendments have restricted government's reach, such as those that established or increased term limits for judges.

Separation of Powers. The Texas Constitution of 1876 separates powers so that the legislative, executive, and judicial branches have the power to enact laws, implement laws, and interpret laws, respectively (see Figure 2.2). This

FIGURE 2.2 Separation of Powers

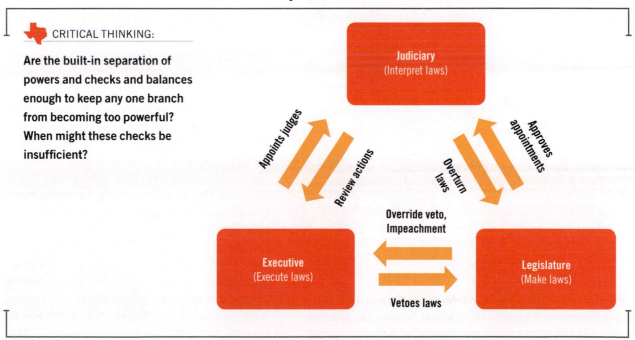

CRITICAL THINKING:

Are the built-in separation of powers and checks and balances enough to keep any one branch from becoming too powerful? When might these checks be insufficient?

Judiciary
(Interpret laws)

Appoints judges

Review actions

Approves appointments

Overturn laws

Override veto, Impeachment

Executive
(Execute laws)

Vetoes laws

Legislature
(Make laws)

separation prevents excessive concentration of power into any one branch and promotes effective government by encouraging each branch to specialize. As with past Texas constitutions, the framers endowed the legislative branch with the greatest authority.[25]

In 1876, however, concerns about overreaching government were tempered by worry about the crime wave that had afflicted the state during the early 1870s. Jails were full and thus expensive to maintain, and thousands of undecided cases sat before the Texas Supreme Court. An 1874 amendment to the 1869 Constitution to increase the number of Supreme Court judges from three to five had not solved the problem, and Texans bristled at the incompetence of judges appointed by Governor Davis. As a result, the framers agreed to an alternative means of selecting judges: Texas would elect judges.

Personal Rights and Liberties. The 1876 Constitution makes use of principles of liberty, equality, and freedom to guide the Texas Bill of Rights, which is contained in Article 1 of the Texas Constitution. The rights granted in this section are inviolate (forever protected by the state and safe from removal by government).

The Texas Bill of Rights is similar in many respects to the U.S. Constitution's Bill of Rights. Both contain references to equal rights, a republican form of government, freedom to worship, freedom of speech and the press, and the right to bear arms. Both bills of rights contain rights protecting against unreasonable searches and seizures, the rights of the accused, the right to trial by jury, the right to bail, and protections against "double jeopardy," whereby a defendant cannot be tried twice for the same crime.

The Texas Bill of Rights has been amended to encompass newer rights that evolved later. For example, the Texas Bill of Rights now includes the rights of crime victims (Article 1, Section 30), added to the constitution in 1989, which entitles a crime victim to reasonable protection from the accused throughout the criminal justice process and provides for restitution for the crimes committed. In 2009, voters also approved unrestricted access to public beaches (Article 1, Section 33), much to the delight of Texas spring breakers. Texans have extended the Texas Bill of Rights to provide for equal protection under the law

How does the constitution balance individual liberties on important issues such as abortion rights, criminal justice issues, or gun control?

SOCIAL RESPONSIBILITY: **Compare and contrast the state legal challenges to benefits for same-sex couples and abortion rights with the constitution's requirements of individual liberty.**

GREAT TEXAS POLITICAL DEBATES
Confederate Flag License Plates and the Battle over Free Speech

Texas has hundreds of specialty license plates that drivers can choose from, including "God Bless Texas," "Choose Life," and for the bold, dozens of out-of-state colleges that might be football enemies of one of Texas's universities. A major controversy erupted over the "Sons of Confederate Veterans" plate that prominently displayed the Confederate flag. A coalition of conservative and liberal Texas elected officials denounced the plates and banned their use, while the ACLU defended the plates as free speech. Joining Governor Rick Perry in disapproving of the plates, Democratic State Senator Royce West asked, "Why should we as Texans want to be reminded of a legalized system of involuntary servitude, dehumanization, rape, mass murder?"[26] In 2015, the U.S. Supreme Court ruled that Texas could refuse to issue the plates, ruling that the state had a right to restrict "government speech" that expresses disagreeable opinions.

PERSONAL RESPONSIBILITY: Should Texans be allowed to choose government-approved license plates to represent their beliefs?

YES: Texans have a right to advocate for their beliefs and, short of hurting another person, should have outlets to express these positions. There is no harm to other Texans when expressing views on a license plate.

NO: Some beliefs are too repugnant to be expressed, and Texas must regulate which groups are allowed to advocate on state-issued materials.

with respect to gender, as a means of reducing discrimination and extending the protections guaranteed by the U.S. Constitution.. An amendment also provides for denial of bail for individuals involved in family violence cases. As a result, the Texas Bill of Rights now contains many rights that the framers of the 1876 Constitution would not likely have even conceived of over 140 years ago.

The Texas Constitution provides for additional rights in other articles within it. Like earlier constitutions, the Texas Constitution stresses a "suitable provision" for the support and maintenance of an "efficient" system of public (K–12) free schools (Article 7). The legislature and the courts often interpret this language differently when it comes to funding, but in principle, the Texas Constitution provides for adequate and reasonably funded public schools throughout the state.

TEXAS TAKEAWAYS

2.6.1 What prompted the Constitution of 1876 to be written?

2.6.2 What are the four principles guiding the Texas Constitution?

2.6.3 Describe the Texas Bill of Rights and how it has evolved over time.

2.7 AMENDING THE CONSTITUTION

2.7	Outline the process for amending the Texas Constitution and attempts at constitutional change.

Texans have rejected any major reform efforts to overhaul the 1876 Constitution, preferring incremental change through constitutional amendments. In this section, we examine how the constitution changes incrementally and why reforms to modernize the constitution have failed.

CONSTITUTIONAL AMENDMENTS

Although the current basic structure of government is largely the same as the one established by the original 1876 Constitution, the document has grown significantly in length because it is frequently amended. Since 1876, the legislature has proposed 690 constitutional amendments: 687 have gone before Texas voters, and 507 have been approved (see Figure 2.3).[27] The most frequent amendments proposed deal with taxation, salary increases, and policy matters, such as prisons, pensions, and highways.

Why are there so many amendments to the Texas Constitution? As we've seen, the 1876 Constitution limited the role of government. Any change to state government that requires expansion of state authority must be approved by a constitutional amendment. Since 1876, the state's population and economy have grown significantly, and as a result, the state government has had to take on new responsibilities. For example, amendments have allowed expansion of the state university system and funding for public roads. Every little change in municipal taxation or local authority needs to be codified in the constitution. Even matters as minor as Proposition 10 in 2019, which allowed law enforcement officials to adopt retired law enforcement animals without a fee require an amendment. The frequently amended document is now thick with regulations, rules, and rights that have accrued over the decades.

The Texas Constitution can be amended through a four-step process. The process begins in the legislature, where two-thirds of both houses of the legislature propose an amendment. This does not require the governor to agree. The secretary of state and the attorney general approve the proposals, and the proposals are then advertised across the state. Voters have the final say in the process: a majority must approve each individual proposal in a general election or in a special election. Once the voters have spoken, the governor finalizes the new amendment by issuing a proclamation.

Since 1879, on average, 75 percent of amendments put to the voters have been enacted. Many of these amendments are "housekeeping" measures that concern outdated or unnecessary provisions, such as a series of deleted "deadwood amendments" in 1969 concerning prohibitions on dueling with deadly weapons and the use of manual labor as payment for those convicted of misdemeanors.

FIGURE 2.3 **Total Amendments Approved by Voters by Year**

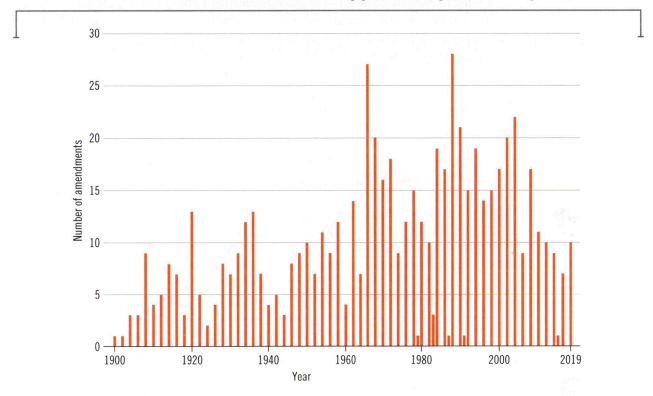

Source: Texas Legislative Council

 COMMUNICATION:

How many amendments are approved on average?

- In some years, only one proposed amendment was passed by the voters, such as in 1978, 1986, and 2014.
- In multiple years, 20 or more amendments were approved. For instance, in 2001, voters approved 20 amendments. These were primarily "constitutional cleanup" matters that moved specific provisions from one section to another or to a more appropriate section, or eliminated outdated or unnecessary language from the document.

 CRITICAL THINKING:

Why are there so many amendments in some years and so few in others?

- In some years, constitutional reform efforts become legislative priorities, often when the legislature faces fewer pressing policy issues.
- The legislature asks voters to approve measures that are controversial rather than create legislation and take possible blame for the result.
- In years when major issues are on the table (tax cuts, school reform), voters often must approve of changes.

When considering constitutional amendments, however, voters are more willing to approve some types of amendments than others (see Figure 2.4 and Table 2.3). For example, Texans tend to favor issuing bonds or tax relief. Since 1879, bond extension proposals (amendments to allow the issuance of bonds to borrow funds for specific purposes) have passed the voters' bar at a rate of 98 percent! When asked to cap, reduce, or eliminate several forms of taxes, voters approved of these measures on average at a rate of 85 percent. Voters were less willing to approve of constitutional cleanup measures, which pass by a rate of 79 percent. Historically, voters have been unwilling to alter the organization of a branch of government or to extend additional powers to politicians. These measures have only been approved 38 percent of the time by voters. Such propositions have included moving to an annual legislative session or altering the size of the Texas Supreme Court.

The benefit of the complicated amendment process is that it often allows legislators to require the voters to decide on controversial issues. For example, in 2019, in the midst of public outcry over the deteriorating quality of roads in the state, voters were asked in Proposition 8 whether they would divert some funds from the Rainy Day Fund, the state's reserve piggy bank for emergencies, to pay for flood infrastructure and drainage projects. The voters approved the amendment, but months passed before the funds were made available. Hence, the disadvantage of placing power more directly in the hands of voters is that lawmakers are often hamstrung by a lengthy process when they want to make substantive changes to the system or to public policy quickly.

Moreover, an ongoing weakness of the amendment process is low citizen participation. Voter interest in constitutional change has historically been

FIGURE 2.4 Highest and Lowest Percent Approval Rates of Proposed Amendments

 COMMUNICATION:

By how much do voters approve of amendments to the constitution? What might explain the variation in approval rates?

Property tax relief

93.8%

Mobile drilling equipment

50.1%

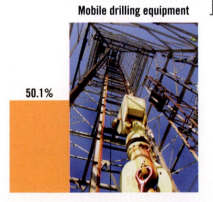

Source: Texas Legislative Council.

| TABLE 2.3 | **Proposed Amendments to the Texas Constitution** |

KEY PROPOSITIONS THAT PASSED	
AMENDMENT	YEAR ENACTED
Mandatory Judicial Retirement Age	1965
Elimination of Poll Tax	1965
Authorizing Bingo Games for Charitable Purposes	1979
Denial of Bail for Family Violence Cases	2007
KEY PROPOSITIONS THAT FAILED	
AMENDMENT	YEAR FAILED
Raise per Diem and Mileage Reimbursement for Legislators	1887, 1897, 1905, 1913
Provide for Annual Legislative Sessions	1958, 1969
Increase Size of the Texas Senate	1965
Increase Length of Term for House Members	1965

Source: Texas Legislative Council.

 COMMUNICATION:

What sorts of amendments pass? What sorts fail?

- Voters generally disapprove of changes to institutions, such as lengthening the terms of Texas House members or increasing the size of the Texas Senate.

- Voters tend to vote in favor of amendments that align with ideological or moral principles. For instance, voters chose to eliminate the poll tax and extend rights to crime victims.

 CRITICAL THINKING:

Why do some amendments pass but not others?

- Uncertainty about the impact of changes in government's design leads voters to reject institutional changes.

- Voters treat constitutional changes like a referendum on issues: They consider the personal impacts of policy and vote accordingly.

low, even on important matters (see Figure 2.5). Lack of voter interest is not terribly surprising because constitutional reform is often dense and legalistic. Yet the more citizens participate, the more the outcome is representative of the interests and values of the people.

Indeed, it is hard to blame the public for its lack of interest. Voters are often asked to vote on amendments in nonpresidential election years, which

FIGURE 2.5 Numbers and Percentages Voting for Amendments

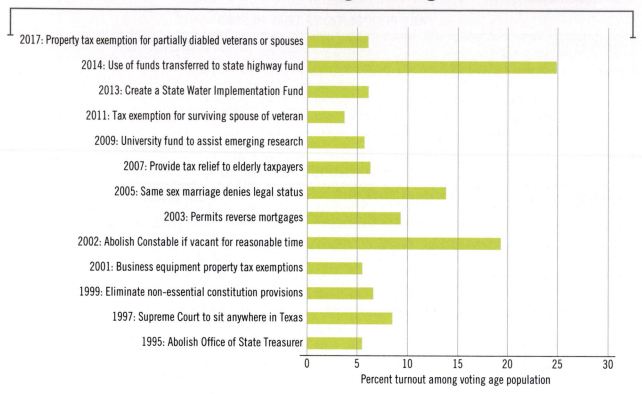

2017: Property tax exemption for partially diabled veterans or spouses

2014: Use of funds transferred to state highway fund

2013: Create a State Water Implementation Fund

2011: Tax exemption for surviving spouse of veteran

2009: University fund to assist emerging research

2007: Provide tax relief to elderly taxpayers

2005: Same sex marriage denies legal status

2003: Permits reverse mortgages

2002: Abolish Constable if vacant for reasonable time

2001: Business equipment property tax exemptions

1999: Eliminate non-essential constitution provisions

1997: Supreme Court to sit anywhere in Texas

1995: Abolish Office of State Treasurer

Percent turnout among voting age population

Source: Texas Secretary of State, Election Returns.

 COMMUNICATION:

For what years and what issues is voter turnout higher? Lower?

- Some issues spark voter interest, and some do not. For instance, turnout was only 3.7 percent in 2011 for the amendment allowing a tax exemption for the surviving spouse of a veteran, whereas the 2005 amendment to change the constitution's definition of marriage to one man and one woman drew 18 percent of the vote.

- Turnout in amendment elections tends to be higher when they coincide with a general election but lower otherwise.

 CRITICAL THINKING:

Why does turnout vary?

- Turnout in amendment elections tends to be lower when the issues are narrow or procedural, making them difficult for most voters to understand.

- Turnout tends to be higher when the issues in the amendment are of greater social or economic importance.

- Amendment elections also have no popular candidate to back or direct party involvement, and they are often held at times that don't correspond to other elections.

attract less interest. The amendments are always listed last on the ballot as well, so voters must often reach all the way to the end of the ballot—something they often do not do. Furthermore, the content and wording of the proposed amendments can be confusing. The information about the proposals is often minimal, and only habitual voters are likely to understand what the proposed amendment would do. For example, one 2019 amendment reads as follows:

> The constitutional amendment authorizing the legislature to provide for a temporary exemption from ad valorem taxation of a portion of the appraised value of certain property damaged by a disaster

In the layperson's terms, the amendment freezes property taxes for residents in counties after a natural disaster. After reading it, however, do you clearly understand it? Many Texans likely didn't.

RECENT MAJOR REFORM ATTEMPTS

Critics often claim that the Texas Constitution is too long, that it is often redundant because there are several outdated passages, that it reads more like a legal statute than a compact with citizens, and perhaps most important, that it hamstrings the ability of elected officials to efficiently manage public policy. The Texas Constitution's verbose 86,000 words both restrain government action and assign additional responsibilities. Whereas the constitutions in many other states have not grown significantly, the constitution in Texas has expanded greatly over time (see Figure 2.6). A 1929 editorial in the *Dallas Morning News* stated that the constitution was "like an overgrown boy in short pants."[28] Proponents for constitutional change also claim that the limitations on government authority are outdated and reflect a concern during the drafting in 1876 that the federal government would intervene should institutions be made too strong. Several attempts have been made to alter the document to remedy these shortcomings.

Most reform efforts have aimed to expand the tenure of elected officials, widen their political powers, or increase their pay. Voters have been less willing to allow this expansion of authority, holding steadfast to the original, basic design of the 1876 Constitution. The first attempt to change the constitution occurred in 1901 and was repeated in almost every legislative session for two decades. We highlight three recent attempts here: those in 1974, 1975, and 1999.

Constitutional conventions are the most thorough method of reforming the Texas Constitution. The most recent convention took place in 1974 after the Texas legislature established the Constitutional Revision Commission. The voters approved (by a margin of over half a million votes) a "limited convention" composed of members of the legislature who would not have the power to change the Bill of Rights. Following the recommendations from the commission, a Constitutional Convention (dubbed the "con-con") drafted a series of proposals to reform the 1876 Constitution.

As with so many legislative sessions, the focus of the convention quickly shifted to controversial issues, and reform efforts lost momentum. Two issues

IS IT BIGGER IN TEXAS?

FIGURE 2.6 Number of Words in State Constitutions

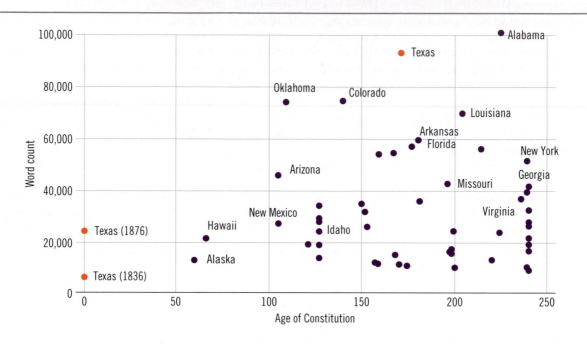

Source: Book of the States.

 COMMUNICATION:

How does the Texas Constitution compare to other state constitutions?

- Alabama's constitution is the longest. Texas's constitution trails far behind in second place but has also had many amendments.
- Newer, western, and smaller states, such as Hawaii, New Mexico, and Alaska, have shorter constitutions.

 CRITICAL THINKING:

Why is the Texas Constitution so long?

- The Texas Constitution is very restrictive. Minor issues such as tax exemptions for manufactured aircraft parts must be changed through the amendment process. As a result, the Texas Constitution's length increases consistently.
- Southern states have larger constitutions than others because they had to adapt restrictive constitutions after the Civil War. Alabama, Texas, Louisiana, and Virginia (and others not displayed) all have seen major changes.
- Western states, such as Hawaii, New Mexico, and Alaska, favor small government, and modest population growth has kept the number of changes in those states small.

ANGLES OF POWER
Debates about Amending the Constitution

The delegates to the 1876 Constitutional Convention spent a great deal of time on a great many issues. One critical issue about the method of amendment emerged during the convention: Would the legislature or the people have the final say?

As proposed, the amendment process would require two-thirds of the legislature to put an amendment to the voters, a majority of voters must approve, and the process would end when two-thirds of the members of each house in the next legislature agreed to the final amendments. Delegate Judge William Pitt Ballinger proposed eliminating the requirement of legislative acceptance after the voters had voted. Ballinger and his supporters held that the legislature should not have the power to defeat the will of the people. The idea that just over 100 legislators would overturn the will of the people "was utterly at war with the whole theory of our Government."[29] Ballinger's opponents asserted that this would prevent hasty amendments and safeguard against "injudicious" amendments. Delegate Judge West asserted that this prevented the constitution from being altered with "every change in the moon."[30] The Ballinger proposal passed, and the people have the final say in amending the constitution.

PERSONAL RESPONSIBILITY: **Who should have the final say in the amendment process? 1974 Constitutional Convention.**

of great concern to powerful interest groups stalled progress: a growing religious conservative movement opposed the expansion of racetrack gambling (parimutuel betting), and organized labor opposed the continuation of Texas as a "right to work" state, which would have prohibited union membership and agreements between unions and labor. Partisan conflict also erupted over proposed changes to public education funding. After 7 months, the convention closed without passing a slate of constitutional changes to submit to voters.

No Proposal Alive in 1975. Disappointment over the failure of the 1974 convention to produce any serious constitutional reform laid the groundwork for 10 proposals that were put to voters in 1975. The Texas Legislative Council cast the constitution as a used car that may "no longer be effectively patched and spot repaired, but must be overhauled."[31] Indeed, several of the proposals would have radically reshaped government authority across the branches. The executive branch would have established a new cabinet system of government that governors would appoint at the beginning of their term. The legislative branch would have been subject to term limits, and a special "veto session" would have allowed the legislature to respond to any gubernatorial veto. The court system would have been consolidated into fewer courts, including combining the two courts of last resort into a single supreme court. The proposals also required that Texas students have equal opportunity to public education and that petroleum tax revenue could be spent for any purpose, not just roads or the School Fund.

Some claimed that the proposals were "not controversial"—just housekeeping changes—but the voters rejected every single one. Some of these changes were minor, technical issues of little concern to most voters, including the modernization of county government through home rule and state debt-granting authority. Other changes were more significant and would have benefited voters, such as property tax relief and exempting goods like medicines and food from sales taxes. However, Texans—fearful of expanding government power—rejected the lot.

Junell–Ratliff Proposals (1999). In the 1999 legislative session, two major power players in government—Representative Rob Junell, the chair of the House Appropriations Committee, and Senator Bill Ratliff, the chair of the Senate Finance Committee—proposed several new constitutional amendments involving structural adjustments to the tenure or authority of the branches of Texas government. Many of these proposals were similar to past ones. For the legislative branch, the terms of the House and Senate members would be increased to 4 and 6 years, respectively. For the judicial branch, the court system would (again) be consolidated into fewer courts, and a merit system would replace the partisan reelection system of selecting judges. With no crisis to generate support for change, however, the proposals perished in committee and were eventually withdrawn by their supporters.

It has been difficult to convince the state's voters to significantly change the core design of the constitution, despite frequent amendments. Instead of fixing a flat tire, Texas voters have chosen not to fix it if the car can still run. Most observers agree, however, that the frequent need to change the constitution perpetuates an outdated system that better fits the small, agricultural state of the past rather than the megadiverse and massive state that Texas has become.

 TEXAS TAKEAWAYS

2.7.1 Why is the Texas Constitution amended so often?

2.7.2 What reforms have critics of the Texas Constitution tried to advance?

2.7.3 What percentage of amendments is approved by voters? What types of amendments do voters support, and what types do they reject?

 **THE INSIDER VIEW**

During its early history, Texas created and ratified six different constitutions as it transferred sovereignty from the Texas Republic to the United States to the Confederacy and back to the United States. Each constitution was written to challenge or embrace the political forces facing Texas. The constitution of the Republic constructed a system that expanded local authority, whereas the Reconstruction Constitution centralized power at the state level and demanded loyalty to the federal government. The current Texas Constitution was forged in reaction to a domineering governor, creating a plural executive and restoring the power of the legislative branch. Today, the independent spirit of Texas lives on in the Texas Constitution—and as a result, Texans have rejected major changes. Voters have, however, amended the constitution to reflect changing political circumstances, economic diversification, and social values. The present constitution is a lengthy document designed to limit power from amassing in any one political corridor and to promote popular control over government, in line with the political ethos of Texas.

TEXAS TAKEAWAYS

2.1.1 A constitution implements a social contract between people, spells out rights and responsibilities, and sets rules of government.

2.1.2 The two themes in Texas's constitutions have been a commitment to individual rights and a strict separation of powers.

2.2.1 The revoking of the Constitution of 1824, the high point of liberty granted to the colonists, became a rallying cry for the restitution of rights during the Texas Revolution.

2.2.2 The grievances contained in the Texas Declaration of Independence include forced Catholicism, no trial by jury, no education system, collection of weapons, and incitement of Native American attacks.

2.3.1 A separation of powers arranged responsibility between the legislative, executive, and judicial branches.

2.3.2 The 1836 Texas Constitution limited the role of the chief executive but enhanced the role of free enterprise.

2.4.1 The 1845 Constitution extended popular control to state government to provide more voter control over state officials.

2.4.2 The 1845 Constitution extended property rights to married women. It also included the homestead law.

2.5.1 The Constitution of 1861 took a strong position in favor of states' rights.

2.5.2 The Confederacy's loss in the Civil War brought federal government control, along with specific rules, to former Confederate states.

2.5.3 The Reconstruction Constitution was required to specify the equality of all persons before the law, ratify the Fourteenth Amendment, and decry the "heresies" of secession. The right to a public education was also first introduced, and the right to vote was extended to African Americans.

2.6.1 Distrust over centralized government, lack of local control of government, and a crime wave promoted a rewriting of the Texas Constitution in 1876.

2.6.2 The current Texas Constitution has four key principles: popular sovereignty, limited state government through local control, separation of powers, and personal rights and liberties.

2.6.3 The rights granted by the bill of rights are inviolate and certify the rights that Texans possess under the constitution. The bill of rights has also expanded to include specific individual rights, such as access to public lands and restitution for victims of crime.

2.7.1 The Texas Constitution is easy to amend—and is frequently amended because it inherently restricts state power to those provisions outlined in the constitution.

2.7.2 Critics of the constitution argue that it is too long, reads like a legal statute, and isn't flexible in allowing local governments to act efficiently. Proponents of change have been largely unsuccessful in altering these points.

2.7.3 Voters approve 74 percent of amendments and especially favor those that cut taxes. Voters reject amendments that change the structure of government.

KEY TERMS

bill of rights
constitution
homestead law
limited government
monarchy
plural executive
popular sovereignty
republic
separation of powers
social contract
sovereignty
suffrage

PRACTICE QUIZ

1. In 1823, when Emperor Iturbide was forced to abdicate, the new Mexican Congress ratified Austin's charter but established a colonization law that future settlers must obey. Regional land distributors served as the local recruiters and leaders of a fixed area of land and the people who settled there. What was the name of these distributors?

   a. Colonizers
   b. Luchadores
   c. Empresarios
   d. Coahuilans

2. The current Texas Constitution is also known as . . .

   a. The Constitution of 1876
   b. The Constitution of 1845
   c. The Constitution of 1869
   d. The Constitution of 1888

3. Most amendments put to Texas voters . . .

   a. Pass
   b. Fail
   c. Are referred to a "Special Session"
   d. Are debated by the governor and the legislature

4. The following individual was dispatched to Mexico City to deliver petitions, only to be imprisoned for inciting Texas to revolution by organizing a new state government without permission:

   a. Anastacio Bustamante
   b. Stephen F. Austin
   c. Sam Houston
   d. General Robert E. Lee

5. Which type of system vests political, legal, and policymaking authority across different branches of government?

   a. Gubernatorial system
   b. Constitutional monarchy
   c. Electoral College
   d. Separation of powers

6. In the single decade of the 1860s, how many times was the Texas Constitution rewritten?

   a. None
   b. One time
   c. Three times
   d. Eight times

7. In terms of state authority and power, the current Texas Constitution . . .

   a. Remains ambivalent on the matter
   b. Calls for a strong central governing body
   c. Is severely limiting
   d. Remains completely silent on the matter

8. All of the following concepts guided the creation of the Texas Constitution of 1876, EXCEPT . . .

    a. Popular sovereignty
    b. Limited government
    c. Self-government
    d. Capitalism

9. Former Chief Justice of the Texas Supreme Court Tom Phillips said which of the following regarding the level of detail included in the Texas Constitution?

    a. It is too detailed.
    b. It is not detailed enough.

    c. It has just the right amount of detail.
    d. He did not remark on this element of the Texas Constitution.

10. Voters have been willing to change the structure of government by constitutional amendment.

    a. True
    b. False

[Answers: C, A, A, B, D, C, C, D, A, A]

OXFORD insight study guide
Active Engagement, Deeper Understanding

Learn more with this chapter's digital tools, including the Oxford Insight Study Guide, at www.oup.com/he/Rottinghaus3e.

3 | FEDERALISM

Under the San Jacinto battle flag, Governor Abbott engaged in battle not with a foreign country, but with what he described in his 2019 State-of-the-State address as an overreaching government that has "become too oppressive." His proposed battleground is Texas where "so many people make life altering decisions to uproot their families and businesses and chart new paths." He continued: "They were fed up with big government policies increasingly running their lives and imposing burdensome regulations. They were taxed out of their states that some of their families had lived in for generations. They needed an escape. They longed for freedom. They wanted hope. They found it in Texas." Texas, he argued is the "governmental Holy Grail."[1]

Texas takes pride in its independent and ruggedly individualistic character. Politicians aggressively guard the state's rights from encroachment of the federal government. The trouble for Texas (and for every other state) is that the design of the American political system allows the federal government to set rules that must be followed by the state. The federal government also makes enticing financial offers that are too good to pass up, encouraging cash-strapped states to play by federal rules. In fact, more than a third of Texas's budget comes from the federal government. Even as Republican leaders in the state vilify oversight and regulations from Washington, the relationship between the state and federal government is hopelessly intertwined, creating a constant source

3.1 Identify the types of governmental systems and the sources of federal and state power.

3.2 Describe the advantages of federalism.

3.3 Evaluate how Texas uses the funding received from the federal government.

3.4 Assess how elements of cooperation and coercion within the federal system have changed over time.

3.5 Analyze examples of the conflicts over federalism.

● Governor Abbott boasts, "I didn't invent that phrase 'Don't Mess with Texas,' but I have applied it more than anyone else ever has."

of friction. The tension between state politics, national rules, and healthy budgets complicates power sharing between levels of government.

In this chapter, we explore the relationship between Texas and the federal government established by the U.S. Constitution. Then, we identify the alternative styles of federalism through which Texas and the federal government struggle for control on a range of public policy issues. Finally, we examine major controversies between Texas and the federal government.

3.1 ORGANIZING THE CONSTITUTIONAL SYSTEM

> **3.1** Identify the types of governmental systems and the sources of federal and state power.

unitary system: a central government that has complete authority over all levels of government

confederal system: a power-sharing arrangement in which a central government's authority is granted by the individual political units

There are three primary types of governmental systems: unitary, confederal, and federal. In a **unitary system**—a "top-down" style of government—the central government's authority is supreme and grants specific powers to state and local governments. Many European states adopted unitary systems, as did the Republic of Texas. The Republic's and later state constitutions established local governments as "creatures of the state," deriving their power and authority from the Texas Constitution and the state legislature. So, for example, the Republic of Texas's Constitution of 1836 established a right to public education, and the state set aside funds for public schools beginning in the Constitution of 1876. Texas's state government has since created specific performance standards that local school boards must endeavor to meet in their public schools.

In a **confederal system**, sovereign states or provinces delegate power to a central government for specific purposes only. The vast majority of power rests with the lower-level governments, whereas the central government has very little power. While in its infancy, the United States experimented with a confederal system. The Articles of Confederation were America's first constitution. This system amounted to little more than a "firm league of friendship," which limited central authority to overseeing matters of diplomacy, printing money, resolving controversies between states, coordinating war efforts, and running the post office. Within just a few years of its creation, however, the American confederation grew vulnerable to attack and rebellion and was on the verge of bankruptcy. As a result, the original 13 states ratified the U.S. Constitution of 1787, which established a federal system.

A **federal system** is a power-sharing arrangement between a central government and states or provinces. The federal government has authority over the states in some matters, the federal government and the states share authority in other matters, and the states have sole authority in still other matters. Let's take a look at how the U.S. Constitution lays out this power-sharing arrangement.

THE SUPREMACY CLAUSE

The U.S. Constitution outlines the specific provisions that establish the authority of the federal system in the United States. To assert that federal powers are superior to and above state powers, the **supremacy clause** specifies that the laws created under the authority of the United States "shall be the supreme law of the land" (Article VI, Section 2). Every article in a state constitution, every law passed by a state legislature, and every ruling made by a state judge that are interpreted to be in conflict with the U.S. Constitution or federal laws can be challenged and voided in federal court.

Rescue efforts during the aftermath of historic flooding after Hurricane Harvey, which battered and then drowned Houston. Disaster relief is conducted by local, state, and federal governments.

PERSONAL RESPONSIBILITY: **When you see problems around you (potholes, traffic congestion, crime), what level of government do you hold most accountable? What role should individual people or communities of interest play in addressing the problems around them?**

The supremacy clause puts the federal government and Texas on a collision course on several issues, especially the issue involving Texas's long border with Mexico. The federal government is responsible for controlling population flow across the border but does not always do so to the satisfaction of the state. Texas is also the largest emitter of carbon dioxide among the 50 states, and the federal government has created clean air standards that, for example, emissions-producing refineries along the coast must maintain. In these and other cases, federal rules often conflict with state goals.

ENUMERATED AND IMPLIED POWERS

How does the U.S. Constitution share powers between the central and state governments? First, the founders expressly identified actions that the federal government can take. These **enumerated powers** (sometimes called expressed or delegated powers) are specified in writing and retained by the federal government so that Congress has the exclusive province to act on them. Article I, Section 8, of the U.S. Constitution lists these powers—more than 30 in all. These include the power to collect taxes, to provide for the common defense, to borrow and print money, to protect patents, to raise and support

federal system: a power-sharing arrangement between the central governing authority and individual political units

supremacy clause: Article VI, Section 2, of the U.S. Constitution, which states that the U.S. Constitution and federal laws "shall be the supreme law of the land"

enumerated powers: powers that are expressly identified as those on which the federal government alone can act

the armed forces, and to organize militia as needed. Although grand in scope, the fact that these powers are specified demonstrates a limiting feature of the federal system. Those powers not specified are reserved to other actors in government, most prominently the states.

Realizing the need for flexibility in the growing nation, however, the framers of the U.S. Constitution also provided for **implied powers**. Implied powers are those that are not expressly identified but are referenced in the last part of Section 8 as follows:

> *Congress shall have the power . . . to make all laws which shall be necessary and proper for carrying into execution the foregoing powers, and all other powers vested by this Constitution in the government of the United States, or in any department or officer thereof.*

implied powers: powers that the federal government is not expressly granted but is assumed to possess so that Congress can carry out its duties

Referred to as the **necessary and proper clause**, this section has been interpreted to allow Congress to make laws in order to carry out the enumerated powers. Because the clause stretches the authority of Congress, it is often called the "elastic clause."

The federal government generally has an advantage when it comes to determining which level of government is in charge. Table 3.1 lists four key cases in which the federal government has been challenged in court by states and has won. These cases often involve either the necessary and proper clause, as in the case of *McCullough v. Maryland* in 1819, or the commerce clause. The **commerce clause** is one of the enumerated powers listed in the U.S. Constitution. It reads that Congress shall have the power "to regulate Commerce with foreign Nations, and among the several States, and with the Indian Tribes." Courts have generally taken a broad view of Congress's ability to control, regulate, and manipulate interstate commerce. Congress and the U.S. Supreme Court have used the commerce clause to extend the powers of the federal government.

necessary and proper clause: Article 1, Section 8, of the U.S. Constitution, which specifies that Congress is allowed to assume additional powers needed to carry out its function

commerce clause: the clause in the U.S. Constitution that gives Congress the power to regulate commerce with foreign nations and among the states

Ironically, the commerce clause has also been used to allow Congress to regulate noncommerce activities. In a 1942 case (*Wickard v. Filburn*), the U.S. Supreme Court dramatically expanded the permissible use of the commerce clause. The case involved Roscoe Filburn, an Ohio wheat farmer who grew more wheat than was allowed by Depression Era limits that were designed to keep prices low. Filburn argued that he had no intention of selling the wheat, but he was still ordered to pay a fine. The Court reasoned that production of the extra wheat reduced the amount of chicken feed on the open market, which is subject to interstate commerce. If many other farmers did the same, they could have a significant impact on chicken feed and thus should be regulated by the federal government. Critics of the expansive use of the commerce clause use examples like this to claim that Congress has overstepped its authority.

The federal government's regulations have their limits. In San Antonio in 1992, a 12th grader at Edison High School carried a concealed .38 pistol along with ammunition into his school. This violated the Gun-Free School Zone

TABLE 3.1	**Key Federalism Cases Decided by the U.S. Supreme Court**			
CASE (YEAR)	QUESTION	THE STATES SAY . . .	THE COURT SAYS . . .	IMPORTANCE TO FEDERALISM
McCullough v. Maryland (1819)	Can the federal government establish a national bank even though that power is not identified in the Constitution?	Maryland can tax the bank.	Maryland cannot tax the bank because it is federal property.	Congress could draw on "implied powers" to operate the national bank as they wished (Maryland could not tax it).
Gibbons v. Ogden (1824)	Who controls commerce between states?	New York can set import fees and regulate its own navigation privileges.	Only the U.S. Congress can set and alter rates for interstate commerce.	Interstate commerce set by Congress includes transportation of goods between states.
Baker v. Carr (1962)	Can the Supreme Court overrule state-drawn legislative districts?	Tennessee can draw its own boundaries for legislative districts.	Tennessee must consider the number of individuals in each district.	State decisions, even those regarding elections, can be overruled by the federal government.
Arizona v. United States (2012)	Do federal immigration laws supersede state law enforcement?	Arizona can establish laws allowing law enforcement to check the citizenship status of apprehended individuals.	Arizona may not implement its own immigration rules; only Congress can do this.	States may investigate immigration status but may not use race and ethnicity as a factor in apprehension.

Source: Oyez Project.

 COMMUNICATION:

Do states or the federal government generally get their way in federalism cases? Explain.

- Generally, the U.S. Supreme Court has ruled that when the state and federal governments clash, the federal government's view is paramount.

 CRITICAL THINKING:

Why has the Court ruled this way?

- Most early Court cases granted significant authority to the federal government.
- Recent cases, such as *Arizona v. United States*, have given states more latitude to implement policies as long as they are careful not to violate federal law.

Act that Congress had passed 2 years earlier. The case made its way to the U.S. Supreme Court (*United States v. Lopez* [1995]), which ruled that the federal government could not justify prohibiting firearms in state public schools based on the commerce clause because the possession of firearms isn't technically commerce. The federal government had the last say, though. The law was rewritten to include a provision that if the firearm in question affected interstate commerce in any way, it would be illegal.

RESERVED POWERS

reserve clause: the Tenth Amendment to the U.S. Constitution, which states that powers not delegated to the federal government are reserved for the states

Proponents of states' rights often point to the U.S. Constitution's Tenth Amendment as evidence that state sovereignty should be respected. The Tenth Amendment, often called the **reserve clause**, states that the listing of the powers not delegated in the U.S. Constitution are reserved for the states (or the people). It reads: "The powers not delegated to the United States by the Constitution, nor prohibited by it to the States, are reserved to the States respectively, or to the people." The states' reserved powers include policy matters such as public education, public health, and state elections. States also have the power to protect citizens and promote safety, welfare, and morals.

CONCURRENT POWERS

concurrent powers: powers shared between the state and federal governments

Federal and state governments share **concurrent powers** over a range of policy issues that affect both. In a way, federalism is a mixed recipe of unitary and confederal systems. The federal system in the United States requires the centrality of federal control on many issues, but it also limits this power. The federal system also provides expressed autonomy to the states by reserving specific power to the states. Concurrent powers allow both federal and state governments to establish courts and to tax citizens. Whereas Texas relies heavily on property taxes for revenue, other states rely more heavily on income taxes (Illinois), government service fees (New York), or a combination (California).

Enforcement of laws is an example of a concurrent power held by federal, state, and local governments. Both states and cities are responsibly for public safety. In 2019, Governor Greg Abbott presented an ultimatum to Austin Mayor Steve Adler: improve the Austin homelessness crisis or the state would step in. The city voted earlier in the year to allow for individuals to sit, lay, or camp in public places unless they presented a safety hazard or blocked a walkway. Abbott's office grew alarmed by reports of "violence, used needles, and feces littering the streets of Austin and endangering Texas residents." Republican officials and local business owners felt the situation constituted a threat to the local economy and to public health and safety. The mayor argued that the changes in the law had decriminalized homelessness. The governor charged the Texas Department of Transportation with clearing homeless camps from under Austin's highway underpasses. The mayor responded that unless the state had a "housing exit" for these individuals, such as a shelter, it would make the problem worse.[2]

FULL FAITH AND CREDIT

For federalism to work properly, the states must not only adhere to the federal government's policies but also respect the policies of the other states. The U.S. Constitution specifically directs that the rights and privileges of one state be extended to other states. The **full faith and credit clause** addresses the duties that all states have to respect "the public acts, records, and judicial proceedings of every other state" (Article 4, Section 1). Take the example of same-sex marriage. In the 1990s, same-sex marriage appeared to be on the horizon in several

El Cenizo, Texas, Mayor Paul Reyes helped pass a "safe haven" ordinance to prohibit city officials from inquiring about the legal status of residents. Lawyers for the tiny border city (population less than 4,000) have sued the state to block implementation of antisanctuary cities legislation that limits local control of immigration enforcement.

SOCIAL RESPONSIBILITY: **Which level of government should be in charge of immigration enforcement: local, state, or national? Should state or local officials be granted authority to deal with any immigration procedures?**

states, which raised the question of whether this right, if extended in one state, must be respected in another. In this case, the U.S. Congress passed the Defense of Marriage Act, which held that states did not need to recognize same-sex marriages as valid in their states, essentially waiving the full faith and credit clause in these instances. In addition, several states, including Texas in 2005, amended their state constitutions to prohibit marriage between couples of the same gender. Other states, however, allowed these marriages to take place. The U.S. Supreme Court's 2015 ruling in *Obergefell v. Hodges,* which held that same-sex marriage cannot be banned, mooted the argument and set a national standard to which all states were required to adhere.

full faith and credit clause: Article IV, Section 1, of the U.S. Constitution, which requires that each state respect the rights and proceedings of other states

TEXAS TAKEAWAYS

3.1.1 Name the three types of constitutional systems.

3.1.2 Explain the differences between enumerated and implied powers.

3.1.3 Describe an example of concurrent powers.

3.2 ADVANTAGES OF FEDERALISM

3.2 Describe the advantages of federalism.

Both prior to and following its establishment, the federal system served as a way to balance the needs of the states and the necessary authority of at least some centralized government. Because of this balancing power, federalism has several advantages.

A STRONGER CENTRAL GOVERNMENT

The U.S. Constitution established a federal government that was stronger and more centralized than that under the original Articles of Confederation. With no federal power to tax citizens or states to pay off debts, no provisions for independent leadership, and no mechanism for enforcement of laws under the Articles, the young U.S. government faltered in the face of several challenges—perhaps most notably Shays's Rebellion in 1786 and 1787. Fueled by economic inequity over taxation in western Massachusetts, frustration over the inflation of currency, and concerns about their inability to pay debts with worthless paper money, 4,000 rebels marched east behind Daniel Shays with the intention of capturing a weapons arsenal in Springfield, Massachusetts. The U.S. government had to raise a private militia led by George Washington, who came out of retirement to end the rebellion. Four rebels were killed and dozens wounded in the calamity. The rebellion vividly demonstrated the young nation's need for a stronger, more central government. In addition, a weak central government also contributed to the difficulty of raising an army, as states refused to pay soldiers promised wages, and to the inability to raise revenue, as miserly states refused to send funds to the capitol—both of which weakened the government.

Citizens in Bastrop protesting the federal government's Jade Helm 15 operation.

ANGLES OF POWER
Texas, the Military, and Jade Helm

Jade Helm 15 sounds like a science fiction movie, but it was actually the code name for the largest military training exercise of its kind, involving about 1,200 special operations troops across several states in 2015. Concerns from all over Texas poured in about the proposed operation, most stating that they "did not trust the president" on military matters, many claiming this was the beginning of psychological warfare, and a few making racist or xenophobic remarks.[3] Rumors circulated online, fed by anonymous online Russian "bots" spreading misinformation as claimed by a former CIA director, one suggesting Walmart locations might be turned into death camps.[4]

Relenting to public pressure, Governor Abbott directed the commander of the Texas State Guard to provide updates to the Governor's Office to "ensure that Texans' safety, constitutional rights, private property rights, and civil liberties will not be infringed."[5] While satisfying some, the governor's order antagonized others, as it looked like he was giving in to conspiracy theorists. One letter writer demanded a "hand written apology for your idiotic paranoid delusion that Texas was under attack by our federal government." Another noted that this was the "stupidest thing to come out of Texas in 20 years."[6] Politicians in both parties called out the governor for "pandering" to extremists' claims.

At the heart of the debate about Jade Helm is the suspicion that many Texans have of the federal government. In polling conducted after the operation, 39 percent supported the governor's decision and 28 percent opposed (32 percent responded they didn't know). Almost 50 percent of the public believed that the federal government would send troops to Texas to impose martial law, confiscate firearms, or violate property rights.[7] These attitudes may reflect Texas's long history of conflict with the federal government dating back to the Civil War.

SOCIAL RESPONSIBILITY: **Does the federal government have Texas's best interests at heart?**

REPRESENTATION

Unlike a unitary system, a federal system provides responsibility at many levels of government—local, state, and national, allowing much needed variations in public policy. A "one-size-fits-all" approach to creating public policy may make taxes too high in Wyoming and underfund education in Illinois. Who better to decide where and how to spend government resources than the individual states themselves? Federalism allows states and local governments to have a major say in how these funds are spent to meet their specific needs and goals. If you summed up the number of elected public officials who represent you at various levels of government in Texas, the number is more than two dozen, including state representatives, county officials, city council members, and judges. A federal system gives the responsibility of representation to these local officials and provides a wealth of opportunities for lower-level governments to craft policies that match the needs of Texans. Perhaps as a result, Texans often see these governments as more responsive (see Figure 3.1).

FIGURE 3.1 **Percentage of Texans Who Approved of Local, State, and Federal Governments**

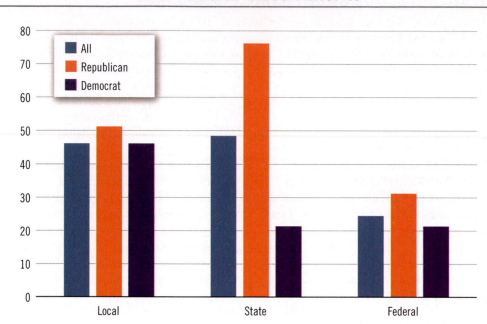

Source: UT/*Texas Tribune* Polling, June 2019.

 COMMUNICATION:

What level of government got the highest approval from Texans?

- State government received the highest approval (48 percent), with the local government close behind (46 percent). The federal government received the lowest approval (24 percent).

- Republicans were more likely to approve of the federal (31 percent) and state (76 percent) than the local government (51 percent). Democrats were generally likely to approve of local (46 percent) than state (21 percent) government or the federal (21 percent) government.

 CRITICAL THINKING:

Why?

- Republicans are happier with state government, run by Republicans rather than Democrats. This has been especially true during the COVID-19 outbreak as local control was minimized in some ways by the governor.

- Local government, often run by Democrats, is more favored by Democrats than the federal government. The federal government received poor marks from both parties.

POLICY INNOVATION

A federal system allows states to have autonomy over issues that are most critical to the people of that state and to innovate on matters of public policy. As a result, states are often called "laboratories of democracy." States experiment with policy solutions, and if these prove to be effective, other states and the federal government often adopt them. Two examples highlight state innovation.

During the 1990s, Texas grappled with an underperforming education system. Texas Governor George W. Bush promoted annual testing for students to improve school and teacher accountability. When Bush became president in 2001, he brought his solution to Washington, DC, and Congress passed his signature education policy "No Child Left Behind" in 2001, which he had developed in Texas to provide parental choice and local spending flexibility. A modified version of the Texas program garnered bipartisan support but also significant disagreement among President Bush's own party, many of whom felt education should be left fully to the states.

In the early 2000s, California, Texas, Florida, and other states suffered from overcrowded prisons. Texas experimented with different solutions to relieve overcrowding and introduced the "Texas Model." This policy increased the number of beds for outpatient substance abuse facilities for individuals on probation, increased in-prison treatment for drug abuse, and allowed more flexibility in sentencing. The state ultimately saved money but failed to reduce the number of incarcerated individuals or to decrease the racial or income disparity in prisons, calling the effectiveness of the model into question.[8] Bipartisan support for reforming bail practices, tackling a backlog of rape kits, and maintaining the death penalty continues.

TRUST IN LEVELS OF GOVERNMENT

Perhaps more than citizens in most states, Texans have historically been distrustful of national government. When asked about their views of the different levels of government, Texans express a much higher degree of trust in local and state government than they do in national government: 48 percent trusted state government while only 24 trusted the federal government.[9] In general, the American public tends to trust in lower levels of government—that is, in governments that are geographically closer to the people. In Texas, the legacy of federal intervention following the Civil War entrenched the value of state autonomy. Hence, Texans trust state and local government more than the federal government. This was especially true after the COVID-19 outbreak when as many Texans found the federal government's response in working with state and local governments "excellent" (27%) as "poor" (28%).[10] Not surprisingly, Texans feel like they have more of a say in state and local government.

Texans are also more likely to support the state government on economic or social policy matters rather than the national government. Texans don't trust any level of government on social issues but are more likely to trust the state over the federal government regarding economic issues.[11] There are several reasons why. First, the state's approach to regulation and oversight is more in line with the values of most Texans than the policies of the federal government. Texas government has historically viewed business regulation with reluctance, with many Texans seeing it as restricting business growth. Second, the state of Texas is perceived to provide more of the resources individuals and businesses need to succeed—in terms of fuel, food, fiber, or technology—than the federal government.

★ TEXAS TAKEAWAYS

3.2.1 What are the advantages of federalism?

3.2.2 On what issues do Texans support state government over the federal government?

♨ 3.3 TEXAS AND FEDERAL FUNDING

3.3 Evaluate how Texas uses the funding received from the federal government.

One important way that the federal government and states share power is through budget finance. More than 500 separate federal programs provide grants and funds to the states. In the 2020–2021 budget, Texas received $84 billion from the federal government.[12] Texas ranked 25th among states in per capita total federal funding—Texas received about $9,503 in federal spending per capita, while the national average was approximately $9,532.[13]

Texas relies on the federal government for just over a third of its total budget (see Figure 3.2). Texas's share of federal funds grew from 23 percent in 1989 to 33 percent by 2016. Driving the federal government's share of the state's budget up over this period were the American Recovery and Reinvestment Act of 2009 (also known as the "stimulus package") and the 2020 response to the outbreak of COVID-19; both increased the amount of federal money available to the states in several areas. Despite the antifederal government rhetoric from many politicians in Texas, the state needs federal funds to meet budget goals and maintain several of its policies.

How does Texas use the funds it receives from the federal government? Medicaid comprises most of the federal funds allocated to Texas (see Figure 3.3). Both the state and federal governments have an incentive to work together on Medicaid funding. The federal government has a responsibility to offer the entitlement to participants, and states have access to funding to cover needy and at-risk populations. Funds for business development is the second largest category of federal funds, whereas education falls in third place. The remaining funds include smaller amounts for transportation projects and other social programs.

One major way in which the states receive funds from the federal government is through disaster relief (see Figure 3.4). In fact, Texas relies on federal disaster funding more than any other state. The process is initiated by state governors who must formally declare a disaster and request federal assistance. Governors of Texas declared disasters over 230 times between 2001 and May of 2020. The president, if he or she chooses, then sanctifies the governor's disaster declaration by issuing a federal disaster declaration, which allows the state to tap into federal funds to deal with the disaster. Declaring a disaster

IS IT BIGGER IN TEXAS?

FIGURE 3.2 Federal Aid as a Percentage of General Revenue

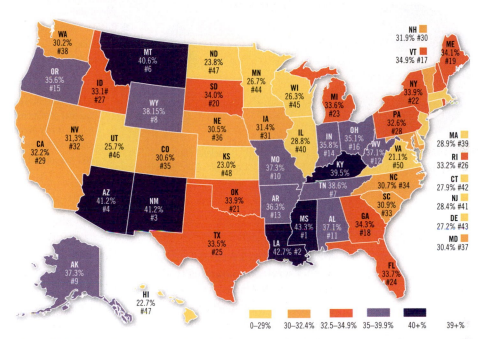

Source: U.S. Census Bureau and Tax Foundation.

 COMMUNICATION:

Which states accept more federal funding than others?

- Texas relies on the federal government for just over a third of its total budget.[14]
- States similarly situated (a third of their budget) include Oklahoma, Georgia, Florida, and Michigan. For comparison purposes, Mississippi and Louisiana rely on the federal government the most (43 percent), followed by Arizona, Kentucky, New Mexico, and Montana.

 CRITICAL THINKING:

Why do some states take more funds from the federal government than others?

- The biggest factor in a state accepting (or not accepting) federal funds is whether the state economy necessitates federal help.
- States that experience economic challenges or natural disasters, like Texas, receive more federal aid.
- States with a larger population of poor residents, like Texas and much of the southern and rural states, have greater need for federal assistance.

FIGURE 3.3 Federal Funds as a Percentage of All Texas Funds, 2020–2021 Biennium

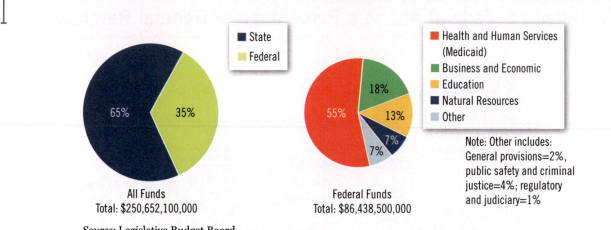

All Funds
Total: $250,652,100,000

Federal Funds
Total: $86,438,500,000

Note: Other includes: General provisions=2%, public safety and criminal justice=4%; regulatory and judiciary=1%

Source: Legislative Budget Board.

 COMMUNICATION:

What are federal funds used for in Texas?

- Most of the state's federal funds goes to agencies involved in health and human services, amounting to almost 55 percent of all federal funds allocated to the state.

- Education is the third largest category of federal funds in the 2020–2021 budget.

- Other pricey items that drive up health and human services and business and economic development costs include highway planning and construction, the national school lunch program, the Children's Health Insurance Program, and the Temporary Assistance to Needy Families program.

 CRITICAL THINKING:

Why?

- Texas has a large population and thousands of road miles, so it absorbs a significant share of federal transportation funds.

- Federal programs designed to help lower-income individuals funnel a significant amount of funds to Texas because the state has a large share of residents who qualify.

costs the governor and president nothing. The costs do not come out of the state coffers, and presidents have a fund already allocated from which to draw resources. Both governors and presidents can claim credit for solving a major problem, though presidents may get a better deal than governors: Research shows that presidents get a 1 percent bump in statewide votes for a single disaster declaration.[15] Disaster relief is an example of how the state and federal governments can work together to achieve both practical and political goals.

FIGURE 3.4 **Texas Disaster Declarations and Federal Emergency Management Administration Funds Spent**

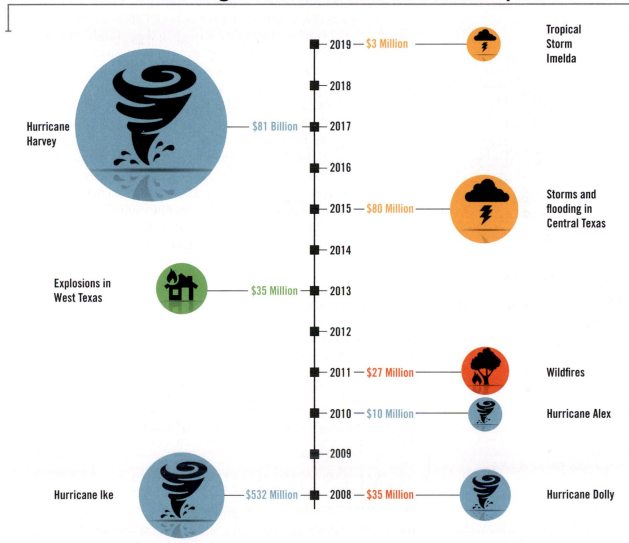

2019 — $3 Million — Tropical Storm Imelda

2018

Hurricane Harvey — $81 Billion — 2017

2016

2015 — $80 Million — Storms and flooding in Central Texas

2014

Explosions in West Texas — $35 Million — 2013

2012

2011 — $27 Million — Wildfires

2010 — $10 Million — Hurricane Alex

2009

Hurricane Ike — $532 Million — 2008 — $35 Million — Hurricane Dolly

Source: Federal Emergency Management Administration.

 COMMUNICATION:

How much in disaster funds does Texas receive and for what?

- Texas has received billions of dollars from the federal government since 2001, primarily in the aftermath of hurricanes.

 CRITICAL THINKING:

Why does Texas get so much disaster funding?

- Most disaster funds come in the wake of major hurricanes. Hurricane Harvey in 2017 involved almost $81 billion in federal funds.
- Severe storms and flooding also increase the disaster tab. Storms in central Texas in 2015 topped $80 million.

States can use disaster funds to replace public infrastructure, repair damaged water facilities, mend roads, and remove debris. States cannot use these funds to create new facilities beyond repair or replacement and cannot repair private homes or businesses (although individuals can apply for these funds). However, the federal government attaches strings to these funds: States must follow procedures to allow competitive procurement, an environmental review, payment of prevailing local wages, protection of worker civil rights, and annual audits.

Texas and the federal government also pool resources, share responsibility, and cooperate effectively on other issues. Texas and the U.S. Department of Agriculture partner to manage conservation efforts on public lands, such as the Sam Houston National Forest or the Caddo National Grasslands. After the offshore oil rig *Deepwater Horizon* exploded in the Gulf of Mexico in 2010, causing the largest oil spill in U.S. history in U.S. waters, the federal government partnered with Texas and other affected states to monitor the long-term environmental effects. The Texas Department of Public Safety also collaborates with federal agencies to combat human trafficking, share information, and fund programs.

⭐ TEXAS TAKEAWAYS

3.3.1 How much money and what percentage of the state budget does Texas receive from the federal government?

3.3.2 How does Texas spend the federal funds?

3.4 STYLES OF FEDERALISM

3.4 Assess how elements of cooperation and coercion within the federal system have changed over time.

The division of power between the federal, state, and local governments is not static, nor are the ways in which the federal and state governments work together to achieve their goals. The allocation of authority, channeling of funds, implementation of programs, and enforcement of rules are fluid and constantly changing. Let's look at how this cooperation and struggle for control over policy has changed over time.

dual federalism: a federalist system in which the government, whether federal, state, or local, has exclusive powers that are reserved to it alone

DUAL FEDERALISM

The simplest type of arrangement between a federal government and the individual states is referred to as **dual federalism**, whereby each level is coequal and sovereign. Under dual federalism, the government, whether federal, state, or local, has exclusive powers that are reserved to it alone. This is often referred to as "layer cake" federalism, in which each layer of government is distinct from the others and maintains its own power and authority. In the United States, the federal government is responsible for issues of trade, foreign policy, war and diplomacy, and immigration. States implement policies in the areas of education, criminal justice (prisons), police, elections, and pensions.

Dual federalism guided federal–state relations until the middle of the twentieth century and the onset of World War II. The battle over a pink worm illustrates the distinct, but hierarchical, levels of government under dual federalism. In 1919, the cotton crops in southern Texas were plagued by the pink bollworm, a small pest that burrows into the bolls of the cotton and feeds on the seeds. The federal government ordered Governor William P. Hobby to enact legislation to control the problem and threatened to quarantine Texas cotton should the state not act. This was one of the first incidents of direct intervention by the national government in the internal affairs of Texas since the establishment of martial law after the Civil War.[16] Agreeing to the federal government's demand, the state legislature passed legislation in 1920 to continue quarantine regulations and establish a board to oversee and limit future infestations.[17]

The intervention of the federal government in the pink bollworm epidemic sparked resentment across the state.

COMMUNICATION: **In a crisis that could affect a region or the nation, where do federal powers supersede state authority? Explain why.**

COOPERATIVE FEDERALISM

Cooperative federalism refers to a style of federalism in which each level of government has overlapping and intertwined authority over shared issues. Instead of the layer cake served for the dual federalism arrangement, cooperative federalism is better described as a "marble cake," where the layers (government) overlap and mix with each other and jurisdictions on policy and regulatory matters are not bound by cleanly set layers. The responsibilities of federal, state, and local governments became increasingly swirled together for issues like funding, rule-making, administration, and implementation. As the responsibilities of the federal government grew, for example, so did the interaction between the federal government and the states. And as the nation industrialized and the world globalized, the federal government took a larger role in the economy of the states.

The turning point that triggered this change was the economic disaster of the Great Depression, starting in 1929 when the stock market crashed. Americans were unable to find work, and states whose budgets were hit hard by the crisis were powerless to help their citizens. In Texas, farmers were particularly hard hit. Efforts by the federal government to funnel funds to the Reconstruction Finance Corporation aided many as crop prices fell. Federal efforts continued as the U.S. Congress passed the Federal Emergency Relief

cooperative federalism: a federalist system in which each level of government has overlapping and intertwined authority over shared issues

categorical grants: funds distributed to state or local governments for programs that require those governments to meet conditions established by the federal government

matching grants: funds the state adds to supplement specific federal government programs

new federalism: a federal system that returns greater responsibilities, duties, and funding to the states

block grants: fixed funds that are transferred to states for implementation of a policy or program

Act to distribute billions of dollars to Texas and other states. By August 1936, Texas had received more than $166 million in federal funds, putting Texans back to work.[18]

Cooperative federalism relies on grants-in-aid, which are payments made to state governments to implement social welfare, health care, educational, and other types of programs. **Categorical grants** are funds distributed to state or local governments for specific programs and policies requiring that states meet certain conditions. States must comply with any directive from the federal government, including eligibility criteria, outcomes reporting, and adherence to rules about discrimination or promotion of diversity. Financially, these grants require that Texas have "skin in the game"—namely, that the state provide matching funds. **Matching grants** make certain that the state is committed to the project and will be thrifty with the funds.

NEW FEDERALISM

In the 1970s, President Richard Nixon introduced **new federalism**, a system that returns greater responsibilities, duties, and funding to the states and reduces the size of the federal government. This transfer of power to states is often called devolution. At the center of devolution is a conservative philosophy, echoed by Republicans today, that states should have greater say in their own public policy than the federal government does. President Ronald Reagan called out what he considered federal intervention by saying, "What was once a federal helping hand has become a mailed fist."[19] The Reagan administration cemented the practice of new federalism, focusing on making the federal government smaller by returning much of the responsibility of social and economic assistance to the states. Part of the Republican Party of Texas's 2018 platform encouraged the state to "ignore, oppose, refuse, and nullify" federal legislation that infringes on the state's Tenth Amendment rights.[20]

Greater autonomy for states in new federalism does not mean that the federal government folds up its wallet and leaves the states on their own. The difference between funding arrangements in new federalism and other styles of federalism is that the funds are delivered to the states with fewer strings attached and with more flexibility for state use. Funding is often done through **block grants**—fixed funds that are transferred to states for application to a general issue such as Medicaid, which in Texas covers more than 4 million poor, disabled, and elderly people and costs roughly $40 billion a year, of which the federal government pays 60 percent.[21]

The major advantage of block grants is that they provide ultimate flexibility for states seeking to address specific problems. President Reagan called this a way for states to function as "laboratories of change in a creative democracy" by having the federal government cut the strings attached to funds.[22] Texas, like other states, prefers a block grant that allows it to make state-level changes to the program without receiving direct federal approval.[23] Block grants are not strictly an endless bag of cash left by the federal government at the states' doorstep, though: The federal government directs the state to solve a specific need but allows the state to choose the programs it will use to address that need.

One major example in the Lone Star State is the Texas Community Development Block Grant. The program is federally funded through a block grant of $8 million to the Texas Department of Agriculture to develop viable communities, provide decent housing, and expand economic opportunity for individuals of low-to-moderate income. These projects have included drainage improvements, housing rehabilitation, accessibility to public buildings, and building community centers. Power is again distributed across state and federal activities, tilting toward states in the case of block grants because states have more flexibility in determining spending priorities.

Critics of letting the states play mad scientist in the "laboratory" contend that shifting responsibility is a veiled way to cut liberal domestic programs. States looking to save money may ignore serious social problems without any federal oversight to ensure that the truly needy have adequate aid.

COERCIVE FEDERALISM

Beginning in the 1970s, states turned away from Washington, DC, for policy solutions, and economic troubles weakened the federal government's financial ability to encourage state–federal collaboration.[24] Even so, federal power was significant, as two decades of U.S. Supreme Court rulings centralized power in the federal government in the 1950s and 1960s. The federal government began using this authority to pressure states to achieve specific policy objectives, punishing the states for not participating in its programs in a system that became known as **coercive federalism**.

coercive federalism: a system in which the federal government establishes guidelines for the states and may punish the states for not participating

The Affordable Care Act (or "Obamacare") of 2010 expanded the Medicaid program for the states to cover up to 133 percent of the cost of the program. The original law punished states if they did not agree to the expansion of Medicaid by depriving them of their existing Medicaid benefits. Because a quarter of all state budget funds are composed of federal reimbursements for Medicaid, no state could afford not to join. The 2012 U.S. Supreme Court ruling found the Affordable Care Act to be constitutional but also held that coercion of the states in this manner was not permissible. Chief Justice Roberts said that the conditions on participation in the program would put a "gun to the head" of states, and he affirmed that participating in the expanded program should be voluntary.[25]

As a result of the ruling, many states chose not to participate in the program. Texas was one of those states. Most Republicans opposed the expansion of Medicaid and didn't believe the federal government would keep promises to cover the costs the state would incur if it chose to expand the program.[26] The federal government granted a temporary Medicaid waiver to Texas through 2022, giving the state a $25 billion shot in the arm.

Michael C. Massengale, Former Appeals Court Judge

What should the balance be between states' rights and federal autonomy?

Two distinct issues inform the balancing of federal and state regulation: constitutional limits on the scope of federal regulation, and the separate question of what level of government can most effectively and efficiently manage any particular policy area. Most issues don't need to be federalized, including many that tend to be the most divisive. If the national government were constrained to its limited powers as originally envisioned by the Framers, state and local governments would have more freedom to experiment and implement diverse policies that reflect local values and preferences.

SOCIAL RESPONSIBILITY: **Do you agree or disagree with this balance of state and federal responsibilities?**

unfunded mandate:
federal or state legislation that requires states to implement a policy but does not supply funding necessary for implementation

Unfunded Mandates. Congress routinely passes legislation, or rules are created at the federal level, that require states to implement policies without federal funding. This is an **unfunded mandate**. The federal government does not necessarily direct the state to spend money; rather, it sets rules to be followed or goals to be met that require the state to spend money in order to achieve these outcomes. In effect, states are getting a bill for a dinner they didn't order but have to eat. Often, local governments pick up the tab. Because the state also passes legislation that local governments must comply with, unfunded mandates are significant "cost drivers" for Texas county government.

For example, a rite of passage for Texas school kids is a medical examination for scoliosis, an abnormal curvature of the spine that can lead to permanent disabilities. School nurses all over Texas line up pupils in the sixth and ninth grades for the screenings, which most kids love because it gets them out of class. Local school districts, however, must foot the bill for the examinations. State-mandated assessment tests, gifted and talented programs, dropout prevention, and reporting requirements also wrench resources from local school districts. Counties must cover the cost of several social issues, including legal representation of indigent criminal defendants, health care in county jails, and appointments of counsel in cases involving child protective services.

The issue of unfunded mandates became so pronounced that in 2019, Governor Greg Abbott declared war on unfunded mandates claiming: "Texas must end unfunded mandates on cities and counties." The Texas Conference of Urban Counties calculated that indigent defense—lawyers for Texans who can't afford legal counsel but are required by law—was $260.5 million in 2018, only $37.2 million of which was reimbursed by the state.

Preemptions. Preemptions (sometimes called conditional preemptions) occur when the federal government grants states permission and funding to implement federal regulations in policy areas, but only if the states comply with a host of conditions. If states don't comply, the federal government preempts the states' policies and implements the program itself. Texas's long fight with the federal government over environmental regulations furnishes one example.

In 2010, the U.S. Environmental Protection Agency (EPA) began requiring companies that wanted to build new industrial plants to get "greenhouse gas permits" before beginning construction. When the Texas Commission on Environmental Quality (TCEQ; the Texas equivalent of the EPA) refused, the EPA took over responsibility for the permitting process, causing delays for some companies that lasted up to 2 years.[27] In 2013, to circumvent preemption, the Texas legislature passed a law authorizing the TCEQ to have control over the rule-making process with EPA approval. The EPA turned full permitting responsibility back to TCEQ in 2014.[28] The Texas Supreme Court backed TCEQ's preemption of local government in 2016 when it held that the city of Houston could not enforce more aggressive air quality standards than the state set.[29]

preemptions: when the federal government grants states permission and funding to implement federal regulations in policy areas, but only if the states comply with a host of conditions

 TEXAS TAKEAWAYS

3.4.1 Explain "layer cake" federalism and "marble cake" federalism.

3.4.2 Describe the differences between new federalism and coercive federalism.

3.4.3 Explain what an unfunded mandate is and why it is potentially harmful to local government.

 # 3.5 TEXAS AND CONFLICTS OVER FEDERALISM

Texas's distrust of the federal government, its individualistic culture, and its robust sense of states' sovereignty from the days of the Republic have prompted several intergovernmental squabbles over the years. These fights have been both political and substantive.

3.5 Analyze examples of the conflicts over federalism.

TEXAS VERSUS WASHINGTON

A resurgent Republican Party in Texas combined with the political opportunity to embrace states' rights led to conflicts between the state and the federal government. The legal system is often the arena for battle. Texas has sued the

Tension between Texas and the federal government peaks when policy goals conflict, and this friction is acute when the levels of government are controlled by different political parties. The city of El Paso adopted a resolution in 2017 to denounce President Trump's executive order to build a wall along the U.S.-Mexico border, projected to cost $20 billion.

SOCIAL RESPONSIBILITY: **How much flexibility should states be given to develop their own policies, and in what areas?**

federal government most frequently over environmental issues, including air quality, climate change, and natural resources, particularly during the Obama administration but also under the Trump administration as many of the same rules are still in place. The state's overall win–loss record is mixed in terms of success: The state received a favorable outcome (a win or dismissal of the case, or a withdrawal of the case that was in the state's favor) in only about a fourth of the cases. The state was somewhat more likely to succeed on issues related to voting rights. These victories are due in part to a U.S. Supreme Court ruling in *Shelby County v. Holder* (2013), which held that provisions of the Voting Rights Act of 1965 requiring certain southern states to obtain "preclearance" before altering voting laws or practices were unconstitutional. Preclearance was a tool the federal government used to examine and authorize any changes to voting laws in Texas or other southern states. The Court held that the provision requiring preclearance was outdated and a "drastic departure from basic principles of federalism" and that all states "enjoy equal sovereignty."

TIDELANDS CONTROVERSY

The tidelands controversy involved a question of the legal title to more than 2.5 million acres of submerged land in the Gulf of Mexico off the coast of Texas. Upon entering the Union in 1845, Texas was to keep all its land, including the boundary 3 leagues (about 10 miles) from shore. As important as the principle of ownership was to Texas, the financial stakes were even greater. The coastal area was rich in natural resources, which the state used to generate major revenue.

Before Texas entered the Union, the U.S. Supreme Court had already written two decisions holding that lands submerged under coastal waters within the boundaries of the original states "were not granted by the Constitution to the United States, but were reserved to the States respectively" and that "the new States have the same rights, sovereignty and jurisdiction over this subject as the original States."[30] The Annexation Agreement by which Texas became part of the United States on March 1, 1845, sealed the state's ownership of the tidelands.

Between 1845 and 1948, Texas made use of the tidelands to execute mineral rights for the School Land Board to fund public schools, selling the lands to private organizations and setting up lighthouses and fortifications. Yet several court cases initiated by the federal government challenged Texas's right to these lands. The U.S. Supreme Court held that although the state had owned tidelands and soil under navigable waters, the federal government should be responsible for them because oil and other property may be necessary for national defense purposes.

Politically, the tidelands issue split the Democratic Party, which was made up of conservative and liberal Democrats. The conservative Democrats urged support of General Dwight D. Eisenhower in the 1952 election in part because he promised to restore Texas's lands. The new Congress in 1953 made the restoration of the tidelands one of their first orders of business. The legislation, coauthored by Texas Senator Price Daniel, survived what was then the longest filibuster in U.S. Senate history (27 days) but finally won a majority in both houses of Congress.[31] The state ultimately prevailed on the issue, retaining title to its 3-league sunken land boundary, generating multiple billions of dollars in leases, rentals, and royalties.

RED RIVER BORDER DISPUTE

Texas has long had a rivalry with Oklahoma on the gridiron, but a legal battle for disputed territory around Texas's northern border with Oklahoma has taken the interstate Red River showdown to the courts. Texas Land Commissioner George P. Bush joined seven North Texas families in a lawsuit in 2017 against the Bureau of Land Management—the agency that administers public lands for the federal government—for an "arbitrary seizure" of land along a 116-mile strip of the Red River. This ribbon of land has shifted over the course of a century, allowing Mother Nature to redefine the border between the states. Federal courts ruled 30 years ago that this land belongs to the federal government, but Texans have long managed some of that land, hold deeds to it, and have diligently paid taxes on it.[32]

IMMIGRATION

Carlos, a 25-year-old construction worker who worked in the lawless "Wild East" of Honduras, was fed up with the violence and poverty in his native home and made the gut-wrenching decision to immigrate with his wife Claudia and 6-year-old daughter to America. Every year 100,000 refugee families like Carlos and Claudia cross the border, arriving in record numbers. In 2017, President Trump signed a "zero tolerance" order that criminally prosecuted illegal border crossers, and, after allegations of insensitivity to migrants, followed this policy with an executive order that would separate families crossing the border. But this remains more of a goal than a reality for many desperate families who flee violence, navigate drug cartels, dodge corrupt police and immigration agents, and avoid smugglers as they cross. Texas has the highest number of immigration detention centers, most of which are run by local governments.

Governor Abbott chastised the Texas congressional delegation for its failing immigration policies and called for an end to the broken system that rips "everybody's heart apart": "This disgraceful condition must end; and it can only end with action by Congress to reform the broken immigration system."[33] Overcrowding, unsanitary conditions, and shortage of supplies in cities like Carrizo Springs, McAllen, Clint, and El Paso spiked concerns. Cities like San Antonio have scrambled to meet the demand and have transformed an old Quiznos downtown into a Migrant Resource Center. The state spends $800 million on border security every year, but local governments, which collectively

GREAT TEXAS POLITICAL DEBATES
Sanctuary Cities

In 2015, an illegal immigrant who had been deported several times from the United States was charged with murder in San Francisco. The murder prompted outrage and reassessment of local immigration policies, especially in what some have called "sanctuary cities," cities that limit cooperation with federal immigration laws. Legislation passed by the U.S. House of Representatives in 2015 cuts off much needed federal funding to those cities, like San Francisco, that do not enforce federal immigration laws. This law represents a form of coercive federalism. The Texas legislature passed similar legislation in 2017, Senate Bill 4, which bans local government from not enforcing federal immigration law and levies civil penalties on police and law enforcement officers who violate the law. Many Republicans supported this legislation to ensure orderly adherence to state and federal laws and to promote public safety. Some business leaders, however, opposed the measures, fearing negative economic consequences. Many mayors, police chiefs, and immigrant rights groups who advocate for inclusion and reject racial profiling oppose the measures.[36] Local governments like Tarrant County in 2019 have signed agreements to work with the federal government to enforce federal immigration policy, while others like Dallas County have rejected these requests.

CRITICAL THINKING: **Should cities be required to enforce federal immigration policy?**

YES: We elect individuals to serve our needs in the federal government and to make choices on our behalf. The federal government helps Texas and other states reach clean air standards, provide health insurance to the elderly, create jobs, fund education, and achieve many important national goals. Sometimes these national goals conflict with state goals, but national interests outweigh state and local interests.

MAYBE: Texans' tax dollars pay for many of the basic services the federal government provides. Texans should expect some responsiveness from the federal government and flexibility in dealing with state issues.

NO: It is wrong for the federal government to impose rules and demand compliance when these solutions harm state interests. Texas should set its own immigration rules because it has the longest border with Mexico and bears the consequences of immigration policy—more so than any other state. Texas should not be forced to accept solutions that fit national interests but ignore state interests.

spent more than $2.5 million in 2019 transporting, sheltering, and feeding migrants upon their release from federal detention, are pushing back.[34] Williamson County, north of Austin, ended its contract with a local detention center. Houston, the city with the largest immigrant population in the country, applied pressure for a new facility. Houston's mayor, Sylvester Turner, said, "There comes a time when we must draw the line, and for me that line is with our children."[35]

The federal government challenged Texas's rigid voter identification law in court. Governor Abbott defended the law saying, "they are trying to deny Texas our sovereign rights." Ever the watchdog for voting fraud, Governor Abbott referenced cases of electoral fraud as justification for the voter ID law. Opponents counter that the instances of voter fraud are extremely rare.

VOTER IDENTIFICATION AT ELECTION PLACES

Voter identification laws require some form of formal identification to be presented at the polls prior to voting in an election. Depending on the state, identification can be a phone bill, a credit card bill, a student ID, or a state-issued photo ID. Texas has required state identification to vote since 1971. In 2011, the state legislature limited valid identification to include only a state-issued ID card, a driver's license, a military ID, a concealed handgun license issued by the Department of Public Safety, or a passport—documents that contain a photo of the holder.[37] Since the 2011 law was passed, there have been several legal challenges to it, primarily advancing the argument that the law discriminates against minority voters because they are less likely to have the proper identification.

The first step for Texas (and other southern states) in changing any election-related policy was to receive "preclearance" of the change in voting process by the Department of Justice, as required by the Voting Rights Act of 1965. However, as noted previously, in 2013 the U.S. Supreme Court struck down the automatic formula that is used to identify which state and local governments must comply with the preclearance provision in *Shelby County v. Holder*. With the need to clear Texas's voter ID law through the federal government removed, Texas implemented the voter ID law.

A federal court struck down the law in 2016, ruling that it discriminated against minority voters, but a federal appeals court upheld the revised version of the law in 2018. Trumpeting the importance of the legislation to preserve the secrecy and safety of the ballot, Governor Abbott has remained an advocate of the law. For example, he tweeted about a voter fraud case in Fort Worth where a candidate for a Democratic precinct chair position admitted to having her son vote on behalf of his father.[38] However, between 2004 and 2013, the Texas attorney general prosecuted only four cases that involved someone illegally casting a ballot at a polling place where a picture ID would have prevented the fraud. Most cases of voter fraud involve irregular mail-in ballots.[39]

COMMON CORE EDUCATION STANDARDS

One major policy arena in which states innovate is education. States are almost exclusively responsible for education policy, establishing both standards and funding. In 2010, the National Governors Association, working with organizations such as the Bill and Melinda Gates Foundation and the Council of State School Officers, developed education standards in math and literacy, known as Common Core, to prepare students for college or the workforce.[40] The U.S. Department of Education dispersed $5 million to states that adopted the Common Core standards, among other criteria such as teacher evaluations and data collection on student success.

In 2013, the Texas legislature passed a law prohibiting school districts from using Common Core in their lesson plans. Texas was not alone in this ban, although its allies were few in number. Oklahoma, Virginia, Alaska, Nebraska, North Carolina, South Carolina, and Indiana also did not adopt (or adopted and backed out of) the Common Core standards.[41] Critics of Common Core argued that it creates a "one size fits all" model for education and amounts to a federal takeover of education. Common Core may also incur unfunded mandate costs, such as purchasing corresponding textbooks, teacher training, testing, and assessment. Those in favor of Common Core counter that basic education standards are necessary for the states to prepare kids for higher education or occupational readiness. The merits mattered little to Republican leadership in Texas, however. In his inaugural speech as lieutenant governor, Dan Patrick proudly supported Texas's decision to reject Common Core, insisting, "We need to keep the federal government out of our schools." [42]

 TEXAS TAKEAWAYS

3.5.1 How often does Texas win in court against the federal government?

3.5.2 On what issues does Texas challenge the federal government?

3.5.3 What important Supreme Court case freed Texas from automatic federal oversight on voting and election issues?

 THE INSIDER VIEW

Principles and politics clash consistently over the practice of federalism. The Texas Constitution emphasizes the importance of preserving "local self-government."[43] Many Texans are still suspicious of the federal government, long after the Civil War. However, politics plays a major role in structuring Texans' response to federal intervention. Liberal Democrats welcome federal policies that forward goals such as Medicaid expansion, voting laws, or adoption of Common Core standards. Conservative Republicans actively challenge federal intervention, as Greg Abbott did as attorney general and now as governor. Still, such challenges steer attention away from the many ways in which Texas and the federal government work together on border control, in disaster relief, and in the implementation of social welfare, business growth, and other programs that impact many spheres of Texans' daily life. Relying on federal assistance to fund over one-third of the state budget, Texas is indeed thoroughly entrenched in our federalist system.

 # TEXAS TAKEAWAYS

3.1.1 The three types of constitutional systems are unitary, confederal, and federal.

3.1.2 Enumerated powers are specified in writing and retained by the federal government so that Congress has exclusive province to act on them. Implied powers are those that the federal government could possess but that are not expressly identified.

3.1.3 Examples of concurrent powers include the power of taxation and enforcement of immigration laws, which are shared at the state and federal levels.

3.2.1 The advantages of federalism are a stronger central government, representation of interests, policy innovation, and the ability to locate government closer to the people, which often result in a higher trust in government.

3.2.2 Texans support state government over the federal government on both economic and social issues.

3.3.1 The state received $68 billion in funding from the federal government. This amounted to about one-third of the state's budget.

3.3.2 Most of the federal funds the state spends goes toward social programs such as Medicare, followed by education. Other programs include transportation and other social welfare programs. Disaster funds are provided following a natural disaster.

3.4.1 "Layer cake" federalism is the model of dual federalism in which the arrangement of each layer of government is distinct from the other and each maintains its own power and authority. "Marble cake" federalism describes the style of cooperative federalism whereby the layers (of government) overlap and mix with each other, and jurisdictions on policy and regulatory matters are not bound by cleanly set layers.

3.4.2 New federalism gives more authority to the states, whereas coercive federalism makes demands on states to achieve specific objectives.

3.4.3 An unfunded mandate is a policy set by a higher level of government that requires spending but does not allocate funds for that purpose. In many cases, local governments may not have the funds to cover the policy.

3.5.1 Texas wins about 25 percent of the time in court against the federal government, although the number may be less important than the substance of the legal victory.

3.5.2 Texas challenges the federal government most on issues of immigration, education standards, environmental rules, election matters, medical care coverage, and business regulations.

3.5.3 *Shelby County v. Holder* (2013) was the U.S. Supreme Court case that released Texas from automatic federal oversight on voting and election issues.

KEY TERMS

block grants
categorical grants
coercive federalism
commerce clause
concurrent powers
confederal system
cooperative federalism
dual federalism
enumerated powers
federal system
full faith and credit clause
implied powers
matching grants
necessary and proper clause
new federalism
preemptions
reserve clause
supremacy clause
unfunded mandate
unitary system

PRACTICE QUIZ

1. _____ grants are provided by the federal government to states to offer flexibility to enact policies.
   a. Block
   b. Matching
   c. Formula
   d. Project
   Take the chapter quiz.

2. The transfer of federal power to the states is often called . . .
   a. Tea Party politics
   b. Revolution
   c. Devolution
   d. Delimiting powers

3. In _____ the U.S. Supreme Court struck down part of the Voting Rights Act, which cleared the way for Texas to pass _____.
   a. 2017; voter laws
   b. 2013; voter ID laws
   c. 2014; sanctuary cities laws
   d. 2013; vote fraud criminal penalties

4. What is the name of the power-sharing arrangement between a central governing authority and political units?
   a. Federalism
   b. Unionism
   c. Colonialism
   d. Texas reunification

5. What is the current (as of 2020) portion of the Texas budget that is received from the federal government?
   a. About 1/6
   b. About 1/5
   c. About 1/4
   d. About 1/3

6. Which of the following is NOT a type of federalism mentioned in this chapter?
   a. Cooperative federalism
   b. Regressive federalism
   c. Dual federalism
   d. New federalism

7. Dual federalism is often described as a layered cake.

   a. True
   b. False

8. Cooperative federalism is often described as a lemon cake.

   a. True
   b. False

9. Coercive federalism promotes good will between the states and the federal government.

   a. True
   b. False

10. Enumerated powers are those that are expressly identified as powers that the federal government has.

    a. True
    b. False

[Answers: A, C, B, A, D, B, A, B, B, A]

Learn more with this chapter's digital tools, including the Oxford Insight Study Guide, at www.oup.com/he/Rottinghaus3e.

4 VOTING AND ELECTIONS

Elections are often explosive affairs, pitting candidates against each other as races become heated. In 2019, incumbent Republican House Representative Rick Miller of Sugar Land dropped out of his primary after he claimed that his two primary opponents likely joined the race because they were Asian in a district with a sizeable Asian population. Both parties denounced Miller's comments, and prominent Republicans withdrew their support from his campaign.[1] The 2020 primary election for Precinct 2 constable in Harris County was a long, strange trip for two candidates named Jerry Garcia. The first was a lieutenant in the Harris County Constable's office; the second ran a vessel repair business on the Houston Ship Channel and had no political experience. The second Garcia also just happened to be a cousin of the incumbent Precinct 2 Constable, Chris Diaz, and was possibly put on the ballot in an effort to confuse voters and draw support away from his challenger who shared the famous name. Cousin Garcia withdrew from the race but his name remained on the ballot for the primary. Chris Diaz lost the primary; Jerry Garcia (the lieutenant) won by a few hundred votes.[2]

Texas campaigns can get so nasty that voters actually stay away from the polls. This makes it harder to achieve a goal that is important to most Texans: rule by the people. In this chapter, we look at how Texans vote and who votes. We explore how the struggle to broaden suffrage has changed Texas politics. We consider why voter turnout is so low, propose ways to improve on this, and show why participation is so important. We also examine campaigns and the role of money in the electoral process. Finally, we investigate factors that help determine who will win and who will lose elections.

4.1 Explain the process of registering and voting in Texas.

4.2 Assess how expanding voting rights has impacted Texas politics.

4.3 Evaluate how different factors affect voter turnout.

4.4 Describe how candidates campaign in Texas.

4.5 Analyze factors that influence election outcomes in Texas.

● There is a saying that "all politics are local." This is especially true when Texans vote in community centers, grocery stores, and, as shown here, public libraries.

4.1 VOTING IN TEXAS

4.1 Explain the process of registering and voting in Texas.

If voters and nonvoters looked alike, it wouldn't really matter who voted, as those who did vote would represent everyone else well. Unfortunately, this is not the case. Those with higher education and higher incomes are significantly more likely to cast a ballot—and therefore are more likely to influence policy.[3] The bottom line is that if you want your interests and values represented in state and local policy, you have to vote.

REGISTRATION

register: sign up to vote in elections

motor voter law: a statute mandating that state governments provide voter registration opportunities to individuals applying for or renewing their driver's license

Voters are required to **register** before the election as a way to ensure that only Texans eligible to vote actually do. In Texas, a prospective voter must register 30 days before an election and must be a U.S. citizen, a resident of the county where the individual intends to vote, at least 18 years old, not legally mentally incapacitated, and not a convicted felon (or if so, must have completed the sentence, probation, and parole or must have been pardoned for the crime).[4]

You can register to vote in person or by mail. You can acquire a registration form through the Texas secretary of state's website and mail it in, or you can go in person to the county's voter registrar's office, the county clerk, or elections administrator's office and fill out the form. Public high schools are required by state law to conduct registration drives twice a year. However, only 38 percent of schools have either required voter registration forms or conducted a voter drive with a local group, according to a report from the Texas Civil Rights Project (see Figure 4.1).[5] You can find registration forms in several locations, county offices, many university student centers, and even taco trucks around Houston. Are you currently registered to vote? Check out the state's online voter lookup (*www.votetexas.gov*) to see, and also find out where to vote and when.

In an effort to make voter registration easier—particularly for young people—the federal government passed the National Voter Registration Act of 1993, usually referred to as the **motor voter law**. This law required state governments to provide voter registration opportunities to individuals applying for or renewing their driver's license. The motor voter policy and registration drives have been shown to increase the proportion of registrants on the rolls, and these individuals are more likely to vote.[6]

Some states have experimented with Election Day (or "same-day") registration so that voters can register and vote then and there. Scholars have found that same-day registration does increase turnout by a small amount—mostly for Republican voters.[7]

Voter registration at gun shows? Several conservative political groups have set up shop at events where firearms and more are sold to identify nonregistered voters, hoping to funnel Second Amendment issue interest into voting.

FIGURE 4.1 **Compliance with High School Registration Requirement**

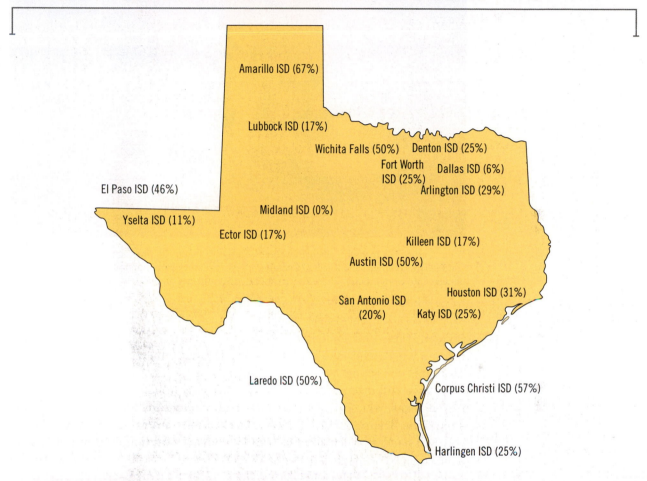

Amarillo ISD (67%)

Lubbock ISD (17%)

Wichita Falls (50%)   Denton ISD (25%)

Fort Worth   Dallas ISD (6%)
ISD (25%)   Arlington ISD (29%)

El Paso ISD (46%)

Midland ISD (0%)

Yselta ISD (11%)

Ector ISD (17%)   Killeen ISD (17%)

Austin ISD (50%)

Houston ISD (31%)

San Antonio ISD   Katy ISD (25%)
(20%)

Laredo ISD (50%)

Corpus Christi ISD (57%)

Harlingen ISD (25%)

Source: Texas Civil Rights Project. Data are recorded compliance by traditional high schools in 2017 or 2018.

 COMMUNICATION:

Where are school districts more compliant with registration laws?

- Large urban school districts (Houston, Dallas) have lower compliance than medium-sized districts (Corpus Christi, Laredo).
- Midsized metro areas with smaller public high schools (Amarillo, Wichita Falls) comply more with the law than other areas.

 CRITICAL THINKING:

Why are some districts more compliant than others?

- Areas with higher poverty rates or more at-risk students (Yselta, Harlingen) have lower compliance rates than other districts.
- Districts with frequent student turnover (Midland and Ector) find it hard to sustain a program of voter registration.
- Intervention by groups in areas like El Paso help school districts run voter registration drives.

Poder Quince is a Texas-based civic awareness initiative that hosts voter registration drives at Quinceñeras, known as "quinces," a coming-of-age ceremony commemorating a 15- year-old's passage into womanhood. There are an estimated 50,000 such ceremonies in America every year.

Sixteen states and the District of Columbia currently have automatic registration, where everyone is registered to vote automatically upon turning 18. Texas has neither option.

As we will discuss later, if you are a registered voter and you vote in person in Texas, you need some form of picture identification (a driver's license, a handgun license, a U.S. military identification, or a passport). Alternatively, you will need a sworn statement of citizenship and nonphoto proof of residency (a utility bill, paystub, or bank statement).

TYPES OF ELECTIONS

primary election: an election in which each party selects its nominees for office

open primary: an election in which any registered voter can vote for a party's candidates

closed primary: an election in which only voters registered with a party may vote for the party's candidates

Once you are registered, you can vote in several different types of elections. Although the general election—the races in which nominees from different parties square off against each other—gets more media attention, the **primary election** is often more important in Texas. Before the general election, each major party holds a primary election in which voters elect the party's nominee for governor, the state legislature, and other offices. A record number of candidates are running in primaries across the state because of increasing competition in several elections.[8]

There are two types of primary elections: open and closed. In an **open primary**, any qualified registered voter can vote in a party's primary. In a **closed primary,** only voters registered with a party may vote in that party's primary. Registered Democrats vote in the Democratic primaries, Republicans in the Republican primaries, and independents in neither. Texas technically has closed primaries because participants declare a party affiliation before voting—but this declaration is nonbinding for future elections. So, Texas primaries resemble open primaries, which encourage crossover voting in which someone might vote for candidates from the other party who are weaker or more ideologically extreme and thus give their own party's candidates a better chance of winning in the general election. Primary voters might also cross over to support the candidates they prefer from the opposing party. The 2008 Democratic primary turnout swelled to 2.8 million voters, more than three times the number in earlier primaries. Known as "Operation Chaos," approximately one-quarter of these voters tried to pack the Democratic primary elections with conservative nominees. They later voted Republican in the general election.[9]

In Texas, if no candidate gets a majority of the vote in the primary, a **runoff election** is held, which pits the top-two vote getters against each other, normally 6 weeks after the primary. Runoff elections are not held in the general elections, where a plurality suffices. The state also holds a **special election** to fill vacancies created by death, resignation, or removal from office. The governor calls for the special election and sets the day, which can be no later than 36 days before a scheduled election. Turnout in special elections is usually low because they take place off the cycle of normal elections and many voters are paying scant attention.

runoff election: an election in which, if no candidate receives a majority of the votes, the two-top vote getters run again

special election: an election held as needed to fill vacancies created by death, resignation, or removal from office

EARLY VOTING

In any election in Texas, you can vote early or on Election Day. **Early voting** traditionally starts on the Monday 2 weeks before the election and continues until the Friday before Election Day. Polls are normally open 12 hours on weekdays and on the weekend between the first and second weeks. You can avoid long voting lines on Election Day, and—in some counties—you can vote at any one of several locations, not just your assigned precinct.

In 2013, however, the Supreme Court struck down portions of the **Voting Rights Act of 1965**, which subjected Texas's voting procedures to federal oversight. Since then, more than 800 voting locations have closed, and counties with a growing share of Latino and African Americans closed the greatest percentage of polling places.[10]

Early voting has become very popular in Texas, increasing by 50 percent in many major counties since 2006 (see Figure 4.2). Early voting is argued to reduce the "cost" of voting because it gives people the flexibility to vote when convenient. In some counties, more than one-third of voters normally cast their ballots before Election Day. Early voters are typically older, more affluent, and long-term homeowners. Political science research has found that racial minorities are less likely to vote early, in part because the polling locations can be difficult to reach. Early voting reinforces the participation of already active and longer-term residents who know the process.

early voting: the ability to cast a ballot in Texas up to 2 weeks before Election Day

Voting Rights Act of 1965: landmark federal legislation that established practices to overcome racial discrimination in voting at the state and local levels

FIGURE 4.2 Percentage of Early Voters, 2012–2020

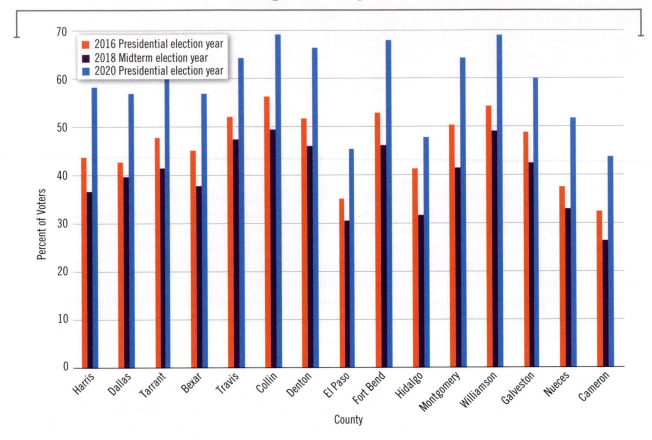

Legend:
- 2016 Presidential election year
- 2018 Midterm election year
- 2020 Presidential election year

Y-axis: Percent of Voters (0–70)

X-axis (County): Harris, Dallas, Tarrant, Bexar, Travis, Collin, Denton, El Paso, Fort Bend, Hidalgo, Montgomery, Williamson, Galveston, Nueces, Cameron

Source: Texas Secretary of State. Percentages are total voters out of total registered voters.

 COMMUNICATION:

How has early voting worked in Texas's most populous counties?

- Early voting in 2020 smashed all time early voting records. The biggest jumps from 2018 were in Montgomery County (23 percent increase), Fort Bend County (22 percent), and Harris County (21 percent).
- Suburban counties like Collin and Denton both rose by 20 percent between 2018 and 2020.
- Early voters as a percentage of total registered voters declined in the midterm elections of 2018, but the percentage was still higher in some counties than in the presidential election of 2012.

 CRITICAL THINKING:

Why is there variation in early voting?

- A competitive 2020 election and an extra week of early voting because of the pandemic drove massive turnout.
- Suburban areas tend to have larger turnout and more active voters, as seen in Collin, Fort Bend, and Denton counties.
- Voter turnout in midterm elections falls dramatically, but due to strong turnout in 2018, early voting only fell slightly.

MOBILE VOTING

Mobile voting (sometimes called "rolling polling") allows a polling place to be moved around to different locations. These places are popular because they enable individuals who would otherwise have difficulty getting to the polls, including rural residents, senior citizens, and the physically challenged, to vote.[11] These are especially popular on college campuses. Concerns that mobile voting has been used to tip the scales in favor of one candidate or party, however, caused lawmakers to reduce their use, requiring that a mobile polling location be transitioned to permanent ones or be shut down. Funding is the issue. According to one county clerk, because of lack of finances, "We won't be able to open polling places that some people have gotten used to."[12] State law is another issue – the legislature voted in 2019 to restrict the use of mobile voting.

ELECTION DAY

On Election Day in most counties, Texans fill out some of the longest ballots in the nation. Confronted with this long list of names and offices, what do you do? Many voters choose to vote straight ticket. **Straight-ticket voting** provides a good solution if you don't have the time or the interest to research candidates in the general election. You can just figure out which party's platform appeals most to you (see Chapter 5) and work your way through the ballot, selecting that party (Texas removed the "one-punch" straight-ticket voting option beginning in the 2020 election). If, however, you want to elect some candidates from one party and some candidates from another, you will be **split-ticket voting**.

straight-ticket voting: checking one box to vote for every candidate that a specific party has on the ballot

You can also "write in" names of candidate who are not party nominees. Like candidates appearing on the ballot, these write-in candidates must officially file with the state and have the signatures of 38 individuals who can serve as presidential electors (registered voters who can cast a ballot in the Electoral College). In recent presidential elections, several prominent politicians have received write-in votes, as have Jesus Christ, Willie Nelson, Big Bird, and Chuck Norris.[13] No write-in candidate, however, has ever won in Texas.

split-ticket voting: choosing candidates from different parties for different offices

Neighborhood Precincts. Each county designates neighborhood polling locations, which must be located within 25 miles from the home of each voter in the precinct on Election Day. The neighborhood precinct must be a public place—often a school or community center, but sometimes a grocery store, flea market, or even a barbecue joint is used.

Vote Centers. In 2005, the Texas legislature approved county-level decisions to move from traditional, neighborhood precinct polls to "vote centers." All voters in counties that allow it can vote at these centers in the general election, regardless of their address, so that they can choose the most convenient location and no longer need to panic at the last moment if they can't remember their assigned polling location. The hope is that vote centers might increase turnout, but research suggests that community connections encourage turnout and a loss of traditional neighborhood precincts could decrease it in some cases (see Figure 4.3).[14]

FIGURE 4.3   **Vote Centers and Vote Change**

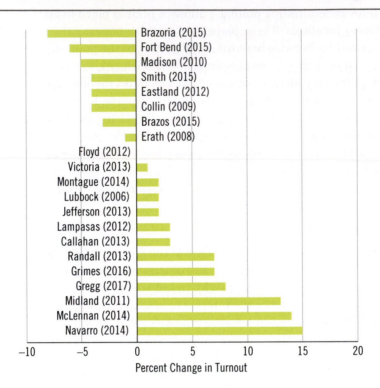

Percent Change in Turnout

Source: Texas Secretary of State website. Counties are those that adopted a vote center process and the election year they first adopted it. Percentages indicate increase or decrease in registered voter turnout from the year the switch was made to the next comparable election cycle.

COMMUNICATION:

What is the effect of the vote center?

- For most counties, the switch to vote centers resulted in a net positive in turnout in the next comparable election.
- Navarro, McLennan, and Midland counties had the largest change in the election after transitioning to vote centers.

CRITICAL THINKING:

Why do vote centers increase turnout in some counties but not others?

- Voter unfamiliarity with the (new) process may cause an early reduction in voter turnout since polling place location may be different than the past.
- As a new voting tradition sets in, voters may grow more comfortable with the process.
- Counties that switch during midterm elections have greater success in the next election than those counties that switch in other elections.
- Like real estate, it's all location, location, location. Counties who put polling locations in areas with voter density have higher turnout.

ADMINISTRATION

Voting in Texas, as in other states, is a patchwork effort from local officials from Beaumont to Floydada who tally votes and execute state laws in compliance with federal oversight. In 2018, more than 300,000 Texas voters were hindered by malfunctioning machines and other problems they encountered at voting locations.[15] Many Texas counties are hard pressed to find the money to replace an aging fleet of voting machines, which might cost $300,000 for annual maintenance and up to $1 million for complete upgrades in large counties—$350 million for the whole state.[16] As a result, local officials are outgunned in defending elections against hacking; "it's not a fair fight" according to one election security expert.[17]

 TEXAS TAKEAWAYS

4.1.1 How far in advance of an election must a Texas citizen be registered to vote?

4.1.2 What sort of identification do Texas voters need at the polls?

4.1.3 What are the differences between an open and a closed primary?

4.2 SUFFRAGE STRUGGLES AND THEIR CONSEQUENCES

For almost two centuries, Texans have engaged in riotous arguments about who gets to vote, how, and when. Scholar Alex Keyssar, author of *The Right to Vote*, argues that these decisions are made by those in power to maintain that power. Many practices keep the status quo firmly entrenched. Keyssar wrote, "Voting is like motherhood and apple pie, especially for 'my' people. If 'your' people want to vote, I'm not so sure."[18]

4.2 Assess how expanding voting rights has impacted Texas politics.

There is a practical reason behind this sentiment: Election results depend on the ability of a candidate or a party to build coalitions among groups. The struggle of groups to win the right to vote—and their success—has changed the makeup of these coalitions and has thus challenged the status quo. In this section, we explore the practices used to **disenfranchise** Texans, the struggle of groups to regain access to the polls, and how these groups shape election outcomes—and thus public policy by siding with one party or candidate over another.

disenfranchise: to deprive individuals of the right to vote

LITERACY TESTS

Beginning in the 1890s, southern states established "Jim Crow" laws and began to adopt literacy tests—an impromptu examination of an individual's ability to speak and pronounce specific legal passages or a short quiz pertaining to facts of state or U.S. government. Anglos were also subject to the requirements, but the grandfather clause exempted those who had already been eligible to vote before the Civil War. Because the tests were administered locally by voter registrars, Anglo voters were also often given easier passages to read than minorities. Literacy tests were upheld by federal courts in the 1950s but abolished in the South in the landmark 1965 Voting Rights Act. Texas never directly mandated literacy tests like other southern states did, but it did use other methods of disenfranchisement.

POLL TAX

poll tax: an unconstitutional tax that required those registering to vote to pay a fee

In 1902, Texans fearful of racial minorities "flooding the polls" and outvoting Anglos passed a constitutional amendment that restricted access to the ballot by instituting a **poll tax**, which required those desiring to register to vote to pay a fee. The fee ranged from $1.50 to $2.00.[19] Although all voters would have to pay the tax, Latinos and African Americans were less likely to be able to afford it.[20] The poll tax was meant to discriminate against racial and ethnic minorities, but it also disenfranchised Anglos who could not or chose not to pay it. When the flour salesman and frontman for the Light Crust Doughboys band, Pappy O'Daniel, ran for governor in 1938, his political rivals pointed out that he "hadn't been civic-minded" enough to pay his $1.75 poll tax. Pappy declared that "no politician in Texas is worth $1.75" and won the election.[21] Once elected, however, he did not eliminate the poll tax. The federal government outlawed the poll tax in federal elections in 1964, and the Supreme Court extended that to state elections in 1966.

WHITE PRIMARY

"I know you can't let me vote, but I've got to try." With this statement in 1924, Dr. Lawrence A. Nixon of El Paso issued the first challenge to the white primary.[22] With registration card and poll tax receipt in hand, Dr. Nixon—a charter member of the El Paso branch of the National Association for the Advancement of Colored People (NAACP) and a prominent physician—was turned away from the polling location.

Federal law prohibited discrimination in the general election, so Texas passed a law stipulating that only whites could participate in the *primary* election. In 1927, the U.S. Supreme Court ruled in Dr. Nixon's favor, finding that states could not hold white primaries. The Texas legislature then passed a law allocating responsibility for primary rules to the political parties, and the parties reestablished white primaries. Democrats who controlled the state government at the time wanted to ban African Americans from voting in part because of strong racial dislike and in part because they voted Republican and had sufficient numbers to politically dominate some districts.

The white primary was like an "iron curtain," for even if African Americans became literate, acquired property, and paid their poll taxes, they could not change the color of their skin.[23] Anglo Democrats would hold a "pre-election" to nominate a candidate through a political organization called the Jaybird Democratic Association. This early vote excluded African Americans from voting, and the winners of these "Jaybird primary" contests would inevitably win in the official primary. Latinos were also subject to exclusion in the white primary unless they were willing to go before an election committee and declare "I am a white person and a Democrat."[24]

Finally, in 1944, the case of Lonnie E. Smith, an African American dentist from Houston, came before the Supreme Court. In this case, *Smith v. Allwright*, the Court held that it was unconstitutional for the state to delegate all its authority on voting processes to the Democratic Party because it disenfranchised African Americans. This did away with the white primary once and for all.[25] Yet minority groups still had a long struggle ahead to overcome voting barriers during the twentieth century.

HISPANICS

Exclusion, bossism, corruption, and intimidation have impacted the electoral experiences of Hispanics in Texas. Although Tejano settlers arrived in Texas before Anglos, the Texas Constitution of 1836 revoked the citizenship of individuals who had left Texas during the revolution. This included many Tejanos who had sided with Mexico. Those who had sided with Texas were granted citizenship and voting rights. However, throughout the nineteenth century, intimidation—threats of being fired from work or physical harm—kept many from the polls. Outright bribery, like free food and alcohol on Election Day, pressured Hispanic Texans to vote in accordance with the Anglo majority.[26]

Throughout much of Texas history, Hispanics had an "ambiguous racial identity"—not Anglo but not African American. Hispanics were counted as "white" for purposes such as school integration but not for political inclusion.[27] After the 1923 white primary law passed, Hispanics were allowed to vote in some counties but not in others, depending on the needs of *"los jefes"* ("the bosses"), the Anglo political power brokers. Change was slow for Hispanics, but iconic Hispanic figures like Henry B. Gonzales (the first Hispanic elected to the Texas Senate) and Hector P. Garcia (the founder of the American GI Forum), along with other local leaders, emerged in the 1950s. Only a handful of Hispanics were elected to the legislature from 1900 to 1930, but by 1960, seven Hispanics represented their communities in the legislature.

Turnout rates remain low compared to other racial and ethnic minorities, and many lack confidence in the political system. But between 2014 and 2018 turnout spiked more than 128 percent in Hispanic precincts and more Latinos turned out to vote in 2020 than in 2018.[28]

ANGLES OF POWER
Political Machines

Political machines are organizations run by local bosses that engage in graft, bribery, and electoral fraud to collect and maintain political power. They gain the loyalty of groups of voters by delivering financial help or political favors. In the early 1900s, the *patrón* system in South Texas, a boss-run system with a wealthy, powerful leader, manipulated Hispanic voters caught in a feudal agrarian system into supporting a wealthy Anglo landowner's political stranglehold. Local Hispanics, who marked their allegiances with red or blue ribbons, exchanged their vote for household necessities, jobs, and even funeral expenses.

The most notorious *patrónes* were the members of the Parr family of Duval County. In 1914, on the night before a court-ordered investigation into his family's local finances, Archie Parr set fire to the courthouse to attempt to end the investigation.[29] Archie's son, George, known as the Duke of Duval after consolidating regional political power, is widely suspected of delivering the 87 infamous (some say manufactured) votes that won Lyndon Johnson a place in the U.S. Senate in 1948.[30] The Parr dynasty ended after the machine's primary guardian angel, Lyndon Johnson, left his Senate office in 1961 and when state and federal investigators returned hundreds of indictments against machine members.[31] In 1975, George Parr committed suicide on the day he was to be taken to prison after being convicted of income tax evasion. The boss system as a whole, however, ended gradually—not with a bang but a whimper—as bosses died or as voters organized to reject boss rule in favor of social activists or party leaders.

SOCIAL RESPONSIBILITY: **What rules should be in place to limit voter intimidation?**

Aggressive activism, demographic change, and the concentration of Hispanics into urban communities sparked a great political "awakening" of Hispanic voters in the late 1960s. Many Hispanics in Texas embraced the civil rights movement. Several groups protested discrimination, registered voters, and organized into PASSO (the Political Association of Spanish-Speaking Organizations).[32] The "Viva Kennedy" clubs in Texas supported John F. Kennedy's bid for the presidency in 1960 and yielded 91 percent of the Hispanic vote in Texas. Hispanic voters began winning local elections in Crystal City and Zavala County and elsewhere across South Texas.[33] As we see in Chapter 6, after the Democratic Party fended off a challenge from the Hispanic political party La Raza, a faction of liberal Democrats began to fight for the inclusion of Hispanic voters.

In 1965, Congress passed the Voting Rights Act, which prohibited discrimination against racial minorities, but this left the status of "language minorities" ambiguous.[34] In 1974, Willie Velasquez of San Antonio established the Southwest Voter Registration Education Project, which launched voter registration drives all over the state and became a vehicle of political influence for Latinos across the nation. The organization's efforts became synonymous with the phrase *"Su voto es su voz"* ("Your vote is your voice") and "lengthened the stride" of the Latino political power movement.[35] In 1975, the Voting Rights Act was finally amended to include language minorities and mandated the translation of voting materials. In 2020, Texas counties offered first-time-ever voter registrar training in Vietnamese and Chinese.[36]

Conflicts over voting power also worked their way into the court system. The Supreme Court rulings in *White v. Regester* (1972) and *Graves v. Barnes* (1974) declared that several Texas cities had diluted the Latino vote. The Court forced the redrawing of electoral district lines and the replacement of county-wide districts with **single-member districts**, opening the door to greater representation. The Mexican American Legal Defense and Education Fund—often called the law firm of the Latino community—also helped take the door off the hinges in 1990 when a federal court ruled in *Garza v. County of Los Angeles* that the city had discriminated against Latinos by diluting their influence across districts. The decision fractured the practice of drawing district lines to benefit Anglos at the expense of Latinos, and it forced the Texas legislature to draw districts that keep Latino communities intact.[37]

single-member districts: an electoral unit that elects only one member of a political body, such as a legislature, and through which smaller communities can gain representation on that body

The growth and concentration of the Hispanic population in geographic areas increased representation in certain quarters of the state. Between 1975 and 1994, the number of Hispanic elected officials exploded by 643 percent.[38]

By 2000, Hispanic candidates were a permanent fixture for elected office (see Figure 4.4). In 2002, the Democrats, seeking to claim some statewide and even national offices, nominated the "Dream Team"—a Hispanic gubernatorial candidate (millionaire businessman Tony Sanchez) and an African American U.S. Senate candidate (former Dallas Mayor Ron Kirk). The Democrats poured tremendous resources into the race, including $60 million of Sanchez's personal fortune. However, the strategy didn't work. The Democrats alienated the white vote and overestimated the strength of the Hispanic vote. Sanchez carried just seven of the counties north of Interstate 10.[39]

Today, the Hispanic vote is still smaller in Texas than in other states, either because many—as noncitizens—are not eligible to vote or because a

INSIDER INTERVIEW

Victor Morales, U.S. Senatorial Candidate in 1996, U.S. House Candidate in 1998

What lessons about the Hispanic vote in Texas did you learn from your campaigns?

I knew the Hispanic vote could be huge. I also felt that it could be energized. With the right candidate, and I felt like I could be that, that I would get a large turnout in the Hispanic vote. There is a hunger for a leader in the Hispanic population, a pride in seeing someone that looked like them for a big role. People were always telling me that they were so excited to see someone who looked like them who could share in their culture.

SOCIAL RESPONSIBILITY: **What impact do candidates who represent a demographic group have on the political efficacy and potential voter turnout of that group?**

FIGURE 4.4 **Support for Statewide Latino Candidates in Largely Hispanic Texas Counties, 2006–2018**

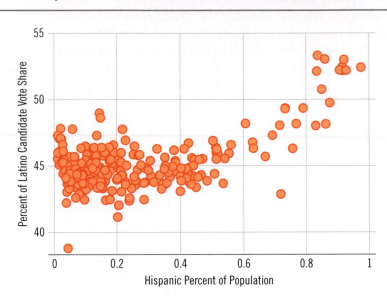

Source: Texas Secretary of State; U.S. Census. Data include candidates of both parties for lieutenant governor, governor, and U.S. Senate. Latino candidate percent is the percentage of the vote the Latino candidate won in the county. Hispanic percent is the percentage of total Hispanic population in the county.

 COMMUNICATION:

Do Latino candidates get more votes in counties with more Latinos?

 CRITICAL THINKING:

Why are Latino candidates overperforming in Latino-heavy counties?

- The scatterplot shows that candidates with Latino surnames get more votes in a county as the Latino population of that county increases.

- Sensing shared values and concerns, Latinos vote for Latino candidates, regardless of their party affiliation.[41]

- Latinos who self-identify more strongly as Latinos are more likely to vote for Latino candidates.

sizeable portion are either too young to vote or inattentive to politics. Yet Hispanics do place issues of importance to the community onto the state's political agenda. Issues like sanctuary cities, deportation halts, and birth certificate denials all have the potential to ignite the Hispanic base. However, the Republican majority in Texas does not depend on Hispanic voters to maintain their position.[40] Even so, Republicans have expanded their political reach and have searched for ways to embrace Hispanic causes to court these voters.

AFRICAN AMERICANS

The Texas Reconstruction Constitution extended full voting rights to African Americans, harnessing the legal authority of the **Fifteenth Amendment**. During Reconstruction, African Americans flocked to the Republican Party, the party of Lincoln. However, once the Union's military rule ended, Anglos were able to keep African Americans economically subservient and to reinforce discriminatory voting practices through intimidation. The Republican Party in Texas, champion of African American voting rights, found itself in the minority and relatively powerless to help. Moreover, the Republican Party leadership remained almost exclusively Anglo, making little room for African American participation. In 1906, African Americans were further alienated from the Republican Party when Republican President Theodore Roosevelt dishonorably dismissed 167 African American soldiers barracked in Brownsville for killing an Anglo bartender despite evidence that they were not involved. Many African Americans still voted Republican as the lesser of two evils, but some moved to the Democratic Party. Unease with African Americans voting led Democrats to press for the white primary.

Following World War II, African Americans migrated to large cities in significant numbers. African American veterans who had fought racism in Europe came home to find it unopposed in their own state. These veterans and other African Americans achieved a major victory in 1948, when Democratic President Harry Truman desegregated the U.S. military. The national and Texas branch of the NAACP also continued to bring court cases that challenged discriminatory voting practices. Many conservative Democrats in Texas held strong to segregation even in the wake of Supreme Court rulings, but liberal Democrats opposed them.

Then, in 1956, African American precincts in Fort Worth voted in great enough numbers to force a runoff in the U.S. Senate Democratic primary between liberal Ralph Yarborough and conservative Price Daniels.[42] Yarborough lost, but he later won the seat in a special election in 1957 with similar backing from African Americans. Liberal Democrats attempted to purge the party of segregationists from the 1950s to the 1960s with limited success. Those archconservatives who left the Democratic Party found a welcome home in the Republican Party in 1960, just at the time when conservative Barry Goldwater denounced the Civil Rights Act of 1957.[43] African Americans rallied to support Democrats who took a strong stand in favor of civil rights. This support may have made a difference in the 1960 presidential election that saw Democratic candidate John F. Kennedy win Texas by a slim margin.[44]

The national struggle for civil rights prompted the passage of the Voting Rights Act in 1965. Many voting restrictions in Texas law ran afoul of the act. The Voting Rights Act and other changes to federal law through the Supreme Court's intervention in the 1960s empowered African Americans, increasing voter turnout. Redistricting in 1970 helped elect many African Americans as districts were drawn to have more African American communities within the boundaries; from 1971 to 1992, the number of elected positions held by

Fifteenth Amendment: the 1870 amendment to the U.S. Constitution, which prohibited the denial of voting rights on the basis of race

African Americans in Texas rose from 45 to 472.[45] African American elected officials worked to desegregate public housing, improve inner-city education, and expand representation.

As the conservative exodus from the Democratic Party continued, more minorities began to vote. Before the Voting Rights Act of 1965, only 29 percent of eligible African Americans in Texas registered to vote, but this number increased dramatically by the 1970s. Today, African American turnout rivals Anglo turnout (see Figure 4.5), and African Americans are a powerful component of the Democratic Party. Approximately 85 percent of African Americans support the Democratic Party, the most loyal group to the party by far.[46]

WOMEN

Women were equal partners in the settlement of Texas but not always in politics. Politics, it was thought, would make women "coarse and crude," and their involvement would endanger the social order.[47] Through the progressive movement and women's suffrage organizations, however, women won the right to vote in primary elections in 1918 and were extended full voting rights in 1920 through ratification of the Nineteenth Amendment.

Women gradually became a force to be reckoned with, placing issues on the political agenda and serving as a catalyst during Texas's transition from a Democratic to a Republican state. In response to the New Deal, middle-and upper-class suburban women bolted from the Democratic Party due to their fear that their children would grow up in a "socialist nation." The "Minute Women" clubs of Houston and Dallas pledged to vote in every election, remove "every vestige of communism from federal and state governments," and focus on states' rights, fairer taxes, and the right to work.[48] Republican women's organizations sprang up all over the state from the 1950s to the 1970s, helping to elect Presidents Eisenhower (1956), Nixon (1972), and Reagan (1980) and re-elect John Tower to the Senate (1966).[49] Today, however, the tables have turned slightly in Texas: women are more likely to identify with the Democratic Party (36 percent) than with the Republican Party (33 percent).[50] All the same, this is lower than the national figure of 52 percent who identify as Democrats.[51]

The growth of Republican politics in Texas did not guarantee an emergence of women in leadership roles; women were often relegated to "housekeeping" chores that "earned male praise but not authority in the party hierarchy."[52] This has changed in recent decades as women have taken on prominent roles, particularly within conservative groups such as the Tea Party and the Texas Eagle Forum. The number of women serving in the Texas legislature also rose, from 2 in 1967 to 37 in 2015. Women have served in recent years as mayors of major cities (Anise Parker of Houston, Laura Miller of Dallas, and Ivy Taylor of San Antonio) and as governor (Ann Richards). Yet observers claim that some areas of Texas, such as the Rio Grande Valley, are still hostile to female candidates. However, voters in El Paso and Houston voted to send the first two Texan Latinas to Congress in 2018.[53]

FIGURE 4.5 **Voting Rates in Texas by Race**

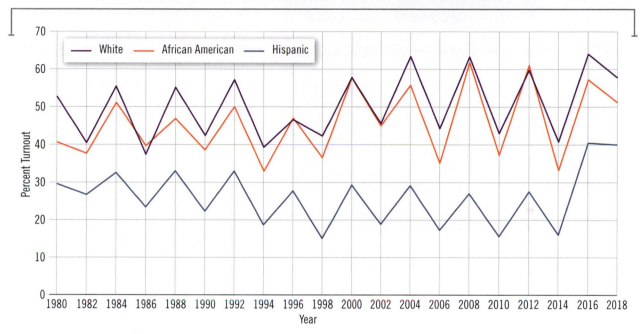

Source: U.S. Census. Pew Research Center.

 COMMUNICATION:

At what rate do racial groups turn out in Texas elections?

- The zig-zag pattern demonstrates that Texans are more likely to vote in presidential than in midterm elections.

- Anglos are the most likely to vote, followed closely by African Americans. In some elections, the percentage turnout of African Americans is equal to or higher than that of Anglos.

- Hispanics trend far behind both Anglos and African Americans in turnout, although Hispanic turnout spiked in 2016 and 2018.

 CRITICAL THINKING:

What causes the variation in participation?

- Anglos are more likely to vote for Republicans, who have dominated state politics for more than 20 years, so Republicans have an incentive to promote the turnout of Anglo voters.

- African Americans are historically the group most loyal to the Democratic Party. These numbers spike when African Americans embrace a presidential candidate like Barack Obama in 2008.

- Hispanic turnout is low because of their low assimilation into the politics of Texas, eligibility concerns, and a larger population of individuals under the age of 18.

In 2009, Texas State Representative Betty Brown took an insensitive position that Asians in Texas should adopt names that were "easier for Americans to deal with."

 SOCIAL RESPONSIBILITY: **Are voters who are racial minorities better represented by members of their own race?**

ASIAN AMERICANS

Asian Americans have often been treated as "outsiders" in politics.[54] The Chinese were the first Asian immigrants to arrive in Texas in the 1870s and the most numerous until an influx of Vietnamese 100 years later.[55] In 1882, Congress passed the Chinese Exclusion Act, which restricted immigration and classified Asian immigrants as "aliens," rendering them ineligible for citizenship and unable to vote. The act was not repealed until 1943.

Today, Asians are the fastest growing minority group in Texas. More than 50,000 immigrants from Asia arrived in Texas in 2013, double the number from 2005.[56] The Asian American community will see a 154% increase from 2010 to 2030.[57] Although geographically contained in several larger cities, Asians are an emerging force in Texas politics, and both parties court their votes. Like Hispanics, however, Asians are not a monolithic group—distinct ethnicities shape their voting behavior. As a group, however, they lean left, with 61 percent collectively supporting the Democratic Party in the 2020 presidential election.[58]

⬤ TEXAS TAKEAWAYS

4.2.1 What are some ways Texas has disenfranchised minority voters in the past?

4.2.2 What law passed in 1965 outlawed voter discrimination?

4.2.3 What percentage of African Americans support the Democratic Party?

4.3 VOTER TURNOUT IN TEXAS

4.3 Evaluate how different factors affect voter turnout.

Turnout shapes election outcomes and determines which groups' political values elected officials will represent. Yet voter turnout in Texas is very low (see Table 4.1). In this section, we explore why turnout is low and what Texans have done to increase—or repress—voter turnout.

TABLE 4.1	Most Texans Don't Vote, 2016, 2018, and 2020		
	2016	2018	2020
Voting-Age Population	20,832,609	19,307,355	22,058,260
Total Registered	15,015,700	15,793,257	16,955,519
General Turnout	8,878,152	8,323,954	11,231,799*
Republican Primary Turnout	2,836,488	1,549,573	2,008,385
Democratic Primary Turnout	1,435,895	1,068,463	2,076,046

Estimated turnout.

 COMMUNICATION:

What is voter turnout like in Texas?

- Many Texans don't vote, even in a presidential election year. More than 66 percent of registered voters turned out to vote in 2020, and that was only 50 percent of adults eligible to vote.

- Only 52 percent of registered voters turned out to vote in 2018, and that was only 43 percent of adults eligible to vote.

 CRITICAL THINKING:

Why are there significant differences between the parties?

- Only 1.5 million voted in the 2018 Republican primary, but this was significantly higher than the 1.1 million who voted in the Democratic primary that year.

- Turnout in presidential election years is higher than in other elections because competition is higher. In Texas, however, Republican candidates have an advantage, and the general election is often not competitive.

- Turnout was higher in 2018 than in most midterm elections because the U.S. Senate race was competitive as insurgent Democrat Congressman Beto O'Rourke challenged Senator Ted Cruz of Texas.

WHY TEXANS DON'T VOTE

Political scientists have identified several reasons why people decide not to vote in elections. Some of these reasons are linked to rational choices, while others emerge from the social environment and personal experiences.

The Rational Voter. Many scholars believe that voters weigh the costs and benefits of voting. While voting doesn't cost money, it does "cost" the time to get informed about the candidates, find the polling station, wait in line, and fill out the ballot. Approximately 36 percent of Americans say that they don't vote because they are "too busy," compared to 10 percent in Virginia and 5 percent in Florida.[59]

Others don't vote because they don't see a benefit from it. They lack **political efficacy;** that is, they don't believe that their vote will make a difference.

political efficacy: the belief that a person's participation can influence the political system

Although a single vote does not usually make a major difference, several recent elections have been decided by small margins. Indeed, the Texas House District 47 primary (west Austin) runoff matchup was decided by one vote in 2020; a city council race in Alamo Heights was decided by 4 votes in 2019; and a Texas House District in Grand Prairie was decided by 64 votes in 2016.

Some people abstain from voting because they don't see any differences between the parties or candidates. Political scientist Anthony Downs called this mindset the "expected vote differential"—voters judge the success of the current party in power and compare this to the past success of the other party. If voters believe that one party is more successful, they vote for that party. If they perceive no difference between the parties, they abstain from voting.

Some elections—like the 2020 presidential election—have a greater "wow" factor than others because they stir up controversy or feature candidates who are more entertaining to watch. Elections can be similar to horse races or sporting events, with the media supplying daily updates on opinion polls and analyses of what candidates have said or done. Competitive elections bring out more voters. Nonpresidential elections, such as midterm elections, special elections, and municipal elections, are critical to democracy, but voter turnout for these elections drops by about 20 percent.

SOCIAL PRESSURE AND POLITICAL SOCIALIZATION

Of course, a voter's sense of civic duty plays a role as well. If Texans feel a responsibility to participate in democratic governance or have a sense of pride, they will show up at the polls. Social pressure also enhances civic duty. In political science experiments, individuals who were informed about their neighbors' voting participation were more likely to vote because of the shame they would feel for not participating.[60] But where does this sense of civic duty spring from?

political socialization:
the process by which individuals acquire political values and behaviors that have a strong influence on future voting behavior

Political socialization is the process by which individuals acquire political values and behaviors that have a strong influence on future voting behavior. Family, friends, media, religion, region, and other sources of political socialization impact not only whether someone will vote, but also how they will vote. Family is often pointed to as the primary influence in the development of a young person's political orientation. These bonds are tight, but they do not always last forever. Texas Senator John Tower, who upset the Democrats' stranglehold on Texas in 1961 by winning a special election, described how he switched parties: "I decided in 1951 that being a Democrat because Granddaddy was a Democrat was foolish."[61]

School is another major agent of political socialization, and part of the reason that Texas seventh graders, high school students, and college students are required to take courses in civics and Texas government. Race and ethnicity also factor in. For example, experiences with local government, the role of democracy, and lack of English proficiency contribute to a lower turnout for Hispanic foreign-born voters and their children.[62] All these factors combine to produce lower voter turnout in Texas than in most other states (see Figure 4.6).

IS IT BIGGER IN TEXAS?

FIGURE 4.6 **Voter Turnout by State, 2020**

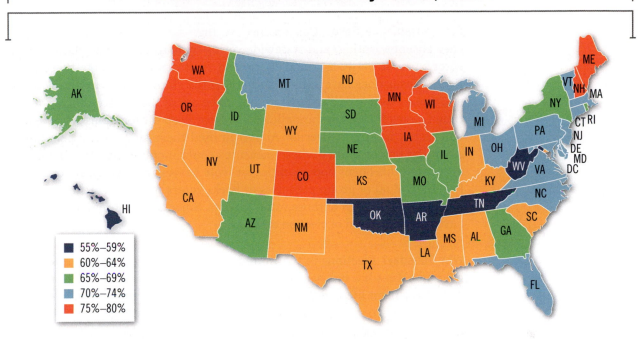

Source: U.S. Elections Project. Percentage voting estimates in each state out of total eligible voting population.

COMMUNICATION:

Which states have the highest percentage of voter turnout in a presidential election?

- Minnesota and Maine lead the nation, with almost 80 percent of their voting-age population voting.

- Texas is in the bottom ten of turnout, with approximately 61 percent of the voter-eligible population voting. Below Texas and rounding out the bottom are Tennessee, Hawaii, West Virginia, Arkansas, and Oklahoma.

CRITICAL THINKING:

Why do some states' citizens vote at higher rates?

- Several factors increase voter turnout. Some states make voting easier (Oregon allows voters to mail in their ballots), and some states make registering to vote easier (Minnesota and Maine allow voters to register and vote the same day).

- Texas, New Mexico, and California all have significant foreign-born populations and new emigrants from other states, and a recently arrived population may take time to register to vote and then turn out. These states also have significant younger and Hispanic populations who find barriers or choose not to register.

HOW CAN VOTER TURNOUT BE INCREASED?

Texas is a large, diverse, young, and mobile state long dominated by one party—today, the Republicans. These attributes produce poor turnout among registered voters. What might be done to increase turnout?

For Convenience Sake. "Convenience" voting—same-day registration, no-excuse absentee voting, and statewide voting by mail—has been shown to lift voter turnout between 2 and 10 percent in states that initiate these practices.[63] Texas does have mail-in voting, but the state limits it to disabled voters, those over 65, or Texans expecting to be out of the country during voting time frames.[64] Counties are allowed to have drop off locations for absentee ballots but in 2020 Governor Abbott limited these sites to one per county. Adopting one or more of these measures could increase turnout, but critics argue that this opens opportunities for "vote harvesting," where an unscrupulous individual or group pressures or tricks voters to vote a certain way then facilitates the return of those voters' ballots. Since 2018, more than 30 people have been convicted of election crimes.[65]

Why Tuesday? Elections in the United States have by law and tradition been held on a Tuesday, but because this is a weekday, getting off work or taking time away from life is difficult. Texas does have laws requiring employers to allow voters two paid hours off to vote. However, the vast majority of countries hold Election Day on a weekend or make the day a holiday from work. Such a change could increase turnout by 5 to 6 percent.[66]

Voter Targeting. Actively reminding and encouraging people to vote spurs turnout. Even in local municipal elections, research shows that effective local campaigns push voters to the polls.[67] Reminder phone calls and campaign mailers written in the language of the potential voter have been shown to successfully mobilize Asian Americas.[68] Targeting Millennial voters through banner ads on the Internet increased turnout of that group in competitive Dallas municipal elections.[69]

We're All in This Together. A sense of shared interests spurs voter turnout. For Latinos in California and Texas, appeals to ethnic group interests (called solidarity) can be especially effective for those who are less assimilated into the broader American culture or who more strongly identify with their Latino identity.[70]

I'm Asking for Your Vote. Research also shows that well-organized get-out-the-vote efforts by parties or organizations are effective if they rely on door-to-door visits or on phone calls from a volunteer. Repeated phone calls (at least two) are especially effective, and in-person persuasion produced major gains of up to 40 percent in increased turnout.[71] Live volunteer calling is critical because prerecorded "robo-calls" can annoy potential voters and reduce turnout.

Thanks for Voting. Political scientists have also shown that thanking individuals for voting in previous elections is effective in spurring turnout for the current election by about 3 percent.[72] Because social pressure works to activate voters' sense of civic duty, the "I voted" stickers may also be effective in encouraging others to vote.

Your Ballot Is Safe with Me. For first-time voters or those with lower awareness, voting can be intimidating. Scholars have shown that reminders from official sources (like the secretary of state) that the vote a person casts is kept secret helps to increase turnout.[73]

Viva Votación. Political science scholars have found that Spanish-language messages in a variety of mediums, including text messages, e-mails, mailed reminders, and radio advertisements, are effective in motivating Latinos to vote. The content of the message matters less than the language. The results are strongest with low-propensity voters and those whose primary language is Spanish.[74]

VOTER ID

In recent years, Texans waged a war in the legislature and the courts over whether to institute a voter ID requirement that might suppress voter turnout while reducing voter fraud, which has a long tradition in Texas. Lyndon Johnson is believed to have stolen the 1948 Democratic primary runoff for U.S. Senate when "Box 13" was "discovered" in an uncounted precinct.[75] In Texas today, many Republican politicians have expressed concerns about voter fraud. As attorney general, Greg Abbott identified 50 voter fraud cases and declared that they were just the "tip of the iceberg." The Texas attorney general's office opened a massive investigation into a vote-harvesting scheme in which individuals collected the mail-in ballots of other voters. These involved as many as 30,000 ballots in Tarrant County in 2016. In 2020, a candidate for mayor in Carrollton, Texas faced voter fraud charges.[76] Others argue, however, that voter fraud is extremely rare in Texas today.[77] In one case, the conservative Heritage Foundation identified only a dozen convictions in Texas between 2006 and 2015 for schemes ranging from vote buying to voter impersonation to falsely registering to vote without citizenship.[78] Another study found a "trickle, not a flood," with only three cases of fraud for every million votes cast.[79] Yet, four people were arrested in Starr County for illegally voting in elections in 2016, and investigators in Dallas County in 2018 impounded a "suspicious box" of mail-in ballots.[80] And a Fort Worth woman who was on probation for a tax fraud conviction was sentenced to 5 years imprisonment for voting illegally, based on new laws that prohibit felons on supervision from voting.

Whatever the true extent of the problem, the state legislature in 2011 passed a bill (SB 14) requiring that those Texans who vote in person show an official, government-issued photo identification (a driver's license, an election

Critics of the voter ID law argue that the measures unfairly target individuals who are new to the process, unfamiliar with voting, and less likely to have identification (individuals who are poor or racial minorities).

PERSONAL RESPONSIBILITY: **How would you design a voting system that protected the security of the ballot but also promoted fairness and access?**

identification certificate, or a passport). The law created immediate controversy and provoked a lawsuit. Opponents claimed that the law would disproportionately prevent African American, Hispanic, and older Texans from voting because these groups are less likely to have identification. A federal appeals court agreed and ruled that Texas's voter ID law was racially discriminatory and unconstitutional. The legislature then altered the original law in 2017 to allow those without a picture identification to show they were citizens by other means, such as a utility bill, as long as they swore an affidavit that they could not reasonably obtain a photo ID. A subsequent federal appeals court in 2018 found these changes to be legal. In a dissenting opinion, however, one judge wrote that "a hog in a silk waistcoat is still a hog" and that the revised law "merely carries forward the discriminatory strain of its predecessor."[81] Even so, Texas election officials acknowledged that at least 500 people who voted in 2016 (out of 13,500 who signed affidavits that they had an ID but not with them) did not have any photo ID.[82] Despite the legal controversy, 40 percent believed that laws should penalize the voter for not having a proper ID.[83]

 TEXAS TAKEAWAYS

4.3.1 Why do some Texans not vote?

4.3.2 How can voter turnout be increased?

4.4 HOW TO CAMPAIGN, TEXAS STYLE

Before launching his 1968 gubernatorial campaign, wealthy businessman and rancher Dolph Briscoe invited a dozen political players from around the state to his South Texas ranch for a weekend of hunting and fishing. Some committed right away to Briscoe's candidacy; others did not. Fort Worth businessman Jack Bean was one of the undecided. In the afternoon, a group including Bean went out to fish on the property. About the time the group started back to the house, the jeep suddenly quit. "Well, it's 20 miles back to the house," one of Briscoe's aides quipped with a straight face. "Do you want to sign up for Dolph—or walk back?" "I'll sign, I'll sign," panted Bean amid much laughter.[84] In the 1930s and 1940s, Texas politics was largely run by oil millionaires and other "Big Rich." Today, to win, a candidate needs to run a good campaign to connect with voters in addition to securing strong backing from political elites. In this section, we examine successful campaign strategies.

> **4.4** Describe how candidates campaign in Texas.

BUILDING CAMPAIGN INFRASTRUCTURE

Staffers are the engine that runs the machine of a campaign: political consultants who craft strategy, a campaign manager who executes the strategy, a fundraising director who raises funds from individuals and political action committees, a field director who coordinates the voter contact program, and volunteers who walk door to door. The main goal of the campaign is to get the candidate's message out to voters. Driving the strategy are two key components: persuading independents ("swing voters") and mobilizing the candidate's partisan base. Campaigns use **public opinion polling** to obtain information about what issues respondents support, what attributes of a candidate they like, and what factors would change their vote.

public opinion polling: a battery of survey questions asked of a representative sample of individuals

Candidates can pay for advertising via direct mail, radio, television, or the Internet. They can also access free media by staging an event, like a visit or a speech, and making themselves available for interviews. Here, Lieutenant Governor Dan Patrick visits the Texas border near McAllen in 2016.

🔺 SOCIAL RESPONSIBILITY: **Do these staged events take the place of real leadership on issues? Do they overshadow real problems?**

name identification: familiarity with a candidate's name

incumbents: candidates who are also the current officeholders

negative campaigning: a campaign that highlights the negative of the opponent over the positive of its own candidate

IMAGE, LIMELIGHT, AND THE MEDIA

A candidate's **name identification** is a benefit, as voters unfamiliar with the background of every candidate tend to pick those whose names they have heard. This is one great advantage of **incumbents**. In one campaign, to stoke his name identification, Governor John Connally (1963–1969) had his staff call airports in the state and have him urgently paged to make sure voters were thinking of him.[85] Today, candidates carefully craft their image by using the media to highlight their positions, record, and biography.

Candidates' actions may hurt them politically in the long run. In the 2014 governor's race, Republican supporters exploited Democratic nominee Wendy Davis's main claim to fame, a senate filibuster of a bill restricting abortion, to paint her as a flaming liberal. Ads derogatively referred to her as "abortion Barbie."[86] As a result, the Davis campaign was unable to persuade swing voters that she was more than a single-issue candidate.

NEGATIVE CAMPAIGNING

Politics can be a blood sport full of mudslinging. When progressive columnist Jim Hightower learned that conservative gubernatorial candidate Bill Clements was learning Spanish, he replied, "Oh good. Now he'll be bi-ignorant."[87] Quips like these are plentiful in Texas. But to get real traction with voters, candidates need to create a negative image of an opposing candidate that hits and sticks, a strategy called **negative campaigning**—which can at times backfire. During the 2014 Republican primary race for lieutenant governor, for example, Land Commissioner and candidate Jerry Patterson leaked documents revealing that candidate Dan Patrick had spent time in a mental health facility for depression and anxiety and had attempted suicide in 1984. In response, Texans rallied behind Patrick, who reported, "I have received a flood of new support and encouragement—much from those Texans who have suffered from depression or had it touch their families or loved ones."[88] Patrick won the primary runoff election by 30 percent.

Voters claim to dislike negative advertising, but it often works. Why? Political scientists have shown that negative advertising does not necessarily win votes overall, but it does demobilize the electorate by decreasing political efficacy and reducing support for the candidate who is the target of the negativity.[89] The rise both of external groups who fund campaigns and of political polarization has increased the amount of negative campaigning.[90]

COURTING THE BASE

When Bill Hobby was running for lieutenant governor in the 1970s, getting votes was a "one-stop shop" up to "the man" in about 20 counties in Texas. "The man" was usually a party boss who controlled the votes of a political party in a local area. Hobby recalled that "if 'the man' was for you, you would get about 75 percent of the vote." In Fayette County, that man was Sheriff Jim Flournoy, featured in the *Best Little Whorehouse in Texas*, who had the ladies (prostitutes) of the famous Texas Chicken Ranch addressing postcards for Hobby's election.[91] Courting the base, by whatever methods, has long been key to electoral success.

Wendy Davis's "Wheelchair" ad in 2014 accused Republican nominee for governor Greg Abbott, who was paralyzed after a tree fell on him in 1986, of profiting from his settlement while opposing large damage awards to other accident victims.

PERSONAL RESPONSIBILITY: **Should personal attacks be off-limits in campaign advertising?**

    In Texas politics today, candidates find it difficult to persuade members of the opposition party to side with them on policy matters. The electorate is too polarized to cross party boundaries, so campaigns spend more time courting those who are most likely to vote for them—the party base.[92] This practice is especially prominent during early voting, when candidates' **"get out the vote"** operations are designed to get friendly voters to the polls.[93] Both parties seek ways to maintain and widen their base. The Democrats have been losing Anglo voters, especially males, while the Republicans have been losing Hispanics.

> **"get out the vote":** a tactic to get friendly voters to the polls

MICROTARGETING

Political campaigns also try to court new voters through **microtargeting** to identify potential supporters online and in the real world. Your viewing, shopping, and eating habits tell campaigns much about you politically. Political marketers want to know whether you watch Fox News or read the *New York Times*. Do you shop at Neiman Marcus or hunt for bargains on eBay?[94] Based on this type of data, campaigns can figure out how to persuade you to vote for their candidate. Online advertisers track your Internet search history and browser cookies to determine your personal preferences as well as your racial, gender, and regional characteristics. Campaigns pay these online advertisers to display customized messages targeting those voters who are most likely to support their candidates. In the field, campaigns use neighborhood demographic characteristics along with household consumer behavior and past voting behavior to target individuals for door-to-door campaigning.

> **microtargeting:** identifying potential subgroups of supporters for customizable messages; also known as narrowcasting

SURFING NATIONAL TRENDS

National-level trends drive much of the state-level political changes we see in Texas. The popularity of the party in control of Congress or the occupant of the White House can shift voter sentiment in a faraway state. Dissatisfaction with the presidential administration of Jimmy Carter drew record numbers of conservatives to the polls in the historic 1978 election that brought Republican Bill Clements into the governor's seat. Donald Trump's inflammatory rhetoric on immigration in the 2020 presidential race increased turnout among Latino and Asian Democrats in Texas.

FUNDING ELECTIONS

A major component of getting a party's message out is fundraising. Money is often called the "mother's milk" of politics because it is essential to paying for a professional campaign staff, media, marketing, and research. Record amounts of money are raised and spent nationally in elections, especially during recent years. According to the Center for Responsive Politics, more than $6.8 billion was spent on the 2016 presidential campaign, making it the most expensive election in history.[95]

The same patterns hold in Texas. Candidates for all offices (both state and federal) raised over $512 million in 2020. This was up from $400 million in 2018. As campaigns become more contested, especially in the primary, the cost of campaigns rises. Open seats are usually more expensive, but in 2018 many incumbents were protecting their seats from challengers in a midterm election year with blockbuster turnout (see Table 4.2).[96]

These funds were driven up by contributions to high-profile statewide races for U.S. Senate between Ted Cruz and Beto O'Rourke and significant fundraising from Governor Greg Abbott and Lieutenant Governor Dan Patrick. But these high figures still fall short of the $95 million spent in the 2002 governor's race, where wealthy Democrat Tony Sanchez spent $67 million of his own money to Rick Perry's $28 million.[97]

PACS and Super PACs. Most candidates raise money from individuals, hosting events where donors are wined and dined, calling them on the phone (called "dialing for dollars"), or soliciting donors through e-mail or social media. Corporations, unions, and interest groups are barred from contributing directly to candidates for federal offices, but may form **political action committees** (**PACs**) to contribute to campaigns.

Some candidates themselves may also form PACs. High-profile incumbents or party leaders may form "leadership PACs" to donate funds to other like-minded candidates or causes. Outgoing Texas House Speaker Dennis Bonnen's PAC contributed more than $400,000 in 2020 to allies.[98] PACs are regulated by state or federal law.

In *Citizens United v. Federal Election Commission* (2010), the Supreme Court triggered a political earthquake when it ruled that it is unconstitutional to ban independent political spending by corporations and unions. **Super PACs**

political action committees (PACs): organizations that collect donations and use these funds to donate to candidates, parties, or other political causes

super PACs: independent expenditure committees that are legally permitted to raise and spend unlimited funds from individuals, corporations, unions, or other groups to advocate on behalf of their causes but are not permitted to give to candidates directly

TABLE 4.2   **Campaign Funds Raised for State Offices, 2019–2020**

FUNDS RAISED BY PARTY OF CANDIDATE	
Party	**Total Funds Raised**
Republican	$112,773,980
Democratic	$81,882,320
FUNDS RAISED BY INCUMBENCY STATUS OF CANDIDATE	
Open	$38,223,574
Challenger	$37,076,605
Incumbent	$81,232,318

Source: National Institute on Money in State Politics; *FollowTheMoney.org.*

 COMMUNICATION:

What type of candidate gets more funds?

- Republican candidates tend to beat Democrats in raising money.
- By incumbency status, incumbents (mostly led by Republicans in tough races) raised the most.

 CRITICAL THINKING:

What explains a plump war chest for some candidates?

- There are more Republican than Democratic incumbents in Texas, giving Republicans the fundraising edge because of resources and connections.
- Incumbents generally raise more money because they have an established donor base and ties to groups looking to donate to those in power.
- Open seats are the most competitive type of election and often draw a crowded and quality field. Fundraising can spike in these races as the campaigns battle for the seat.

are independent expenditure committees that are legally permitted to raise and spend unlimited funds from individuals, corporations, unions, or other groups to advocate on behalf of their causes, but they are not permitted to give to candidates directly. The Court ruling opened the door to massive spending from wealthy organizations in both parties and tied most major candidates, especially presidential candidates but also state and local candidates,

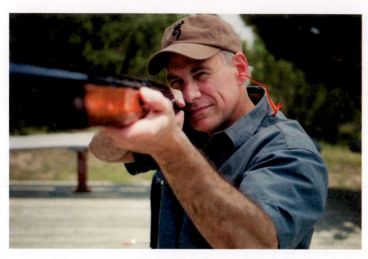

Donate and I'll Shoot. Candidates often find unusual ways to raise money. Governor Greg Abbott's 2014 campaign hosted a contest in which anyone who donated $25 could win a Texas-made shotgun. The campaign was quick to point out that the winner must be eligible to purchase the shotgun through a licensed gun dealer.

SOCIAL RESPONSIBILITY: **What limits should there be on how candidates raise funds?**

to a super PAC with whom they could not coordinate on strategy. Super PACs have prompted an explosion of money into electoral races. However, some candidates, like 2018 Senate candidate Beto O'Rourke, swear off Super PAC efforts on their behalf.

Rules and Limits. Federal election funding is regulated by the Federal Election Campaign Act, which requires candidates, party committees, and PACs to disclose the amount of campaign funds they raise and spend. Federal regulations on campaigns were originally designed to limit the lopsided influence of wealthy individuals and interest groups in federal elections. Individual candidates can accept $2,800 per person per election cycle (primary and general). PACs can accept $5,000 per person per election cycle and can donate $5,000 to candidates and other PACs and $15,000 to a political party. The national party committee for the Republicans or Democrats can accept up to $35,500 per person per cycle. Campaigns must identify the PACs that donate funds and any individual who contributes over $200.

State election funding for statewide and local candidates is regulated by the Texas Ethics Commission. Unlike federal rules that tightly limit campaign donations, there are few restrictions on Texas political giving. Texas has no contribution limits, except on judicial candidates (see Chapter 10), which makes it unique among the states. By contrast, the national average limit on donations in governors' races is $5,600, and in state legislative races, it is about $2,500.

Do these limits even out the playing field? Does money make a difference in elections? We'll explore these questions in the next section.

⬛ TEXAS TAKEAWAYS

4.4.1 What does negative advertising do to voters?

4.4.2 Why are there limits on campaign funding?

⦿ 4.5 WHO WINS AND WHY

Hoping to appeal to conservative voters in his district, an East Texas state representative had a cousin shoot him in the arm and falsely blamed it on a satanic and communistic cult "out to get him" because of his pro-family and pro-American stands in the legislature.[99] The ploy didn't work, and the candidate wound up in jail. However, candidates in Texas do try to game the process to their advantage. Let's look at some of the factors they should keep in mind.

> **4.5** Analyze factors that influence election outcomes in Texas.

MONEY AND ELECTION OUTCOMES

In Texas, as elsewhere, candidates need money to hire campaign staff, activate their base, and, most importantly, advertise. Not surprisingly, winning candidates raise more funds. This is not only because incumbents tend to attract more donors since they are more likely to win: Even in open primaries in Texas, 77 percent of candidates who raised the most money won or advanced to the runoff election.[100] However, money is not always the most significant factor in winning elections. In many races, particularly Texas judicial elections where there are strict limits on funds raised, party trumps fundraising as the key determinant of electoral success.[101] Why is this the case? To answer this question, we need to look at who contributes and how they contribute.

Who Contributes. A wide range of individuals and causes donate to candidates. Some donors have broad ideological agendas, while others have targeted, narrow objectives. Campaign funds are often more targeted when issues of concern to a group arise (see Figure 4.7). For instance, as the state ended a decade-long fight with Farmers Insurance Group, which Texas contended charged too much on homeowners' insurance rates for mold-damaged houses, the insurance group gave $50,000 in PAC funds to then Attorney General Greg Abbott's race for governor. Critics contended that as attorney general, Abbott gave Farmers a "sweetheart" deal while Abbott's office argued that the deal was fair.[102]

Not surprisingly, wealthy individuals give at higher rates than poorer individuals, and organizations with more resources give more than those with fewer resources. Scholars surveying the top 1 percent of earners found that 68 percent of their respondents made a political contribution (averaging $4,633) and that 21 percent had solicited or bundled contributions.[103] The political process, according to many observers, has evolved in ways that reinforce the advantages of wealth, especially as campaigns have become more expensive to run and organizations have raised spectacular amounts of campaign money.[104]

FIGURE 4.7 **Contributions by Group, 2020 Texas State Election**

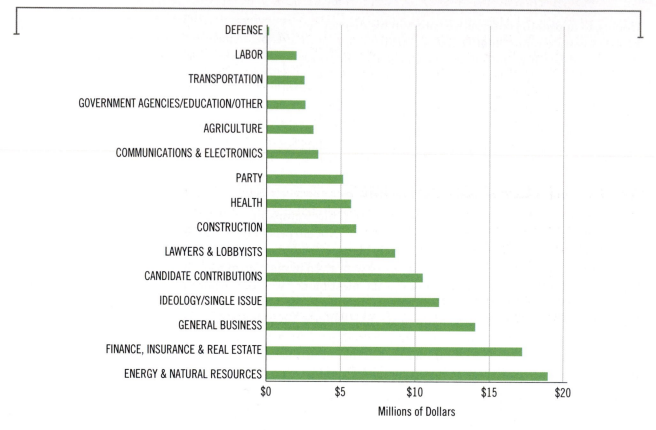

Source: National Institute on Money in State Politics.

 COMMUNICATION:

Who gives in Texas political races?

- Three big industry groups dominate the funds contributed in Texas: oil and gas, lawyers, and real estate professionals.

- Oil- and gas-related industry donors are by far the most generous, providing almost $19 million in 2020.

- Candidates themselves donated almost $6 million to their colleagues, shoring up support from within the party (or on occasion across parties).

 CRITICAL THINKING:

Why do some groups dominate political donations?

- The state has the greatest regulatory control over the location, refinement, and production of oil and gas, making state politicians a good target for access.

- Environmental regulations related to natural resources were at the top of the legislative agenda for 2019, making oil and gas industry donors particularly interested in election outcomes. Affordable housing concerns and infrastructure investment in many urban areas generate political interest from the real estate industry.

Who Donors Give To. Some donors contribute only to candidates who align with their own economic interests or political ideologies. Several wealthy donors, such as oilman Tim Dunn of Midland and Farris Wilks of Cisco, who have interests in natural gas, have given tens of millions of dollars to conservative candidates in the last few election cycles.[105] These individuals have business interests in the energy industry to protect in addition to political interests that match the conservative wing of the Republican Party. Steve and Amber Mostyn, two prominent attorneys who made a small fortune on hurricane-related litigation, have given more than $11 million to the Democratic Party. But on election night in 2014, those funds seemed wasted. As early votes rolled in, Steve Mostyn put it as bluntly as he could: "We're f&%ked."[106]

Does Money Buy Influence? Do these donations have an effect on elected officials? Political science research finds that the more time a candidate spends fundraising, the greater the influence of that fundraising on that candidate's political decisions.[107] Scholars have shown that political donations do not necessarily "buy" votes (by influencing the outcome of legislation), but they do buy access to an elected official's time.[108] Many interest groups and PACs donate funds to multiple candidates (even in the same race) in order to hedge their bets when it comes to having access to whichever party wins. In short, a politician to whom you donate may listen to you make your case about an issue but may not necessarily vote your way.

PARTIES AND STRAIGHT-TICKET VOTING

Straight-ticket voting helps both parties gain and maintain power, and parties exploit this advantage. In South Texas, where the Hispanic vote is often handled as a commodity by *politiqueras*— political workers who are paid to go door to door to get out the vote—Democrats target those who are likely to vote straight ticket.[109] In contrast, in major suburban counties, Republicans benefit from this practice, receiving three out of four straight-ticket votes.[110]

The number of Texans voting straight ticket was rising steadily through the 2018 elections. In 2017, however, Texas joined a dozen other states that have recently moved away from straight-ticket voting, passing legislation to end the practice in 2020. [111] Voters can still vote straight ticket, but the option for selecting one punch ended.

INCUMBENTS AND VOTER TURNOUT

Incumbency, the type of election, candidates, and voter turnout strongly influence who wins an election. Incumbents are more likely to win a general election with greater voter turnout because their name identification is higher, they are able to raise and spend more funds, and moderate voters participate more in these elections. This is known as the incumbent advantage. Challengers have a better chance of winning low-turnout primaries and runoffs— elections dominated by the most passionate voters.

When only 1.3 million primary voters cast ballots, for example, a candidate backed by conservative Tea Party groups can win with as few as

GREAT TEXAS POLITICAL DEBATES
"No Excuse" Mail Voting

Research shows that mail-in voting doesn't help any one party—even in states that have been using exclusively mail ballots for years—but partisan debates about using mail ballots remain.[113] Supporters of mail-in voting claim that it is safer, produces better informed voters, and leads voters to compete their ballots to the bottom at higher rates than in-person voting. Opponents argue that logistical problems like ballot counting and faulty addresses will lead to voter fraud or vote harvesting (a rare event), and that return rates for mail ballots are lower for younger, less affluent, and ethnic and racial minorities.

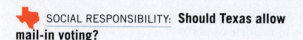 SOCIAL RESPONSIBILITY: **Should Texas allow mail-in voting?**

NO: In-person voting gives everyone the opportunity to vote and is a voting system that is easier to administer. As one Texas statewide official put it, if voters "can go to the grocery store, they can go to the polls."[114]

YES: Mail voting is easy for voters. Stated one college student: "If people are getting ballots at their homes, it's easier for them to vote without having to take time to get off work, go to the polls and brave some super-long line."[115]

MAYBE: Let voters choose: Counties can have mail and in-person options. Dual options are more expensive to run, but they do provide flexibility.

650,000 votes. As a result, the Republican Party power center has shifted to the ideological right.[112]

In the 2012 race for the U.S. Senate, Lieutenant Governor David Dewhurst, who had served for a decade in various statewide offices, was the favorite and received 45 percent of the vote in the primary. The runoff was a different story. Passionate conservatives were "in the mood to drop anvils on establishment folks" and put their support behind Ted Cruz, a relatively obscure candidate. Cruz, who went on to win the runoff with 57 percent of the vote, serves in the U.S. Senate and made a bid for the presidency in 2016.[116]

THE ELECTORAL SYSTEM

The type of electoral system (how votes are counted) also impacts the election outcome. Candidates who run locally are either elected from districts or **at-large** in a county, meaning that all citizens in a county can vote in the election. Federal court decisions in the early 1970s required Texas cities to have city council districts instead of at-large races because at-large districts dilute the power of minority voters.[117] Single-member districts, which are smaller, improve minority representation, as we will see in later chapters.

at-large: an electoral unit in which all citizens in a county can vote

WILL TEXAS TURN BLUE?

The prospect of increasing voter turnout among low-turnout groups as well as the growth of the Hispanic population have prompted many to wonder whether Texas could turn from a solid Republican "red" to a Democratic "blue"—or at least to a state with a more robust two-party system. Texas is already a majority–minority state. If the trends continue, Hispanics and Anglos will each account for around 40 percent of the state's population within the next decade. With more voter registration and robust turnout, Hispanics, who are not a monolithic group but lean Democratic, could tilt the state Democratic "blue." Swing constituencies in massive urban areas and growing suburbs like college-educated voters and women are supporting Democrats, whereas some of these votes would have gone to Republicans in the past.[118] Republicans are nervous about these trends: "The challenges we face in Texas are very real," says the party's state chairman.[119] National attention, especially fundraising, will aid Democrats in challenging (and beating) Republicans in more races.

There are several reasons to doubt this claim, however. First, while the Hispanic share of voters in gubernatorial elections rose from 11 percent in 1990 to 17 percent in 2010 to 26 percent in 2018, and in presidential elections from 20 percent in 2008 to 23 percent in 2020, the total number of Hispanic voters is still low in comparison to Anglo voters, primarily because many Hispanics are not citizens, are too young to vote, or have not been mobilized by either party.[120] Turnout among Hispanics lags significantly behind that among Anglos. This trend will change slowly as the Hispanic vote ages and organizations emerge to turn these voters out. Second, some demographic trends favor Republicans. The Democratic Party has a larger deficit with Anglo voters than the Republicans have with Hispanic voters, and, while younger voters favor Democrats, and their numbers are growing, older voters who vote Republican are more likely to vote than younger Texans.[121] All this said, the potential for the state to change exists, as other states with increasing Hispanic populations like California, Colorado, and Virginia have transitioned from red to blue.

 TEXAS TAKEAWAYS

4.5.1 Which groups were the top two donors to state candidates?

4.5.2 Does straight-ticket voting help or hurt incumbent parties?

 # THE INSIDER VIEW

Elites have always had a major say in recruiting and funding political candidates. Gone are the traditional "smoke-filled" rooms in Texas, only to be replaced by newer hangouts for politicians like the Austin Club. Today, however, Texas is no longer ruled by party bosses or one economic or demographic group. The road to voting rights has been long and difficult for women, African Americans, and Hispanics, with their struggle punctuated by demographic shifts, social changes, and favorable court rulings. The suffrage battles have given way to challenges in representation and opportunities to participate in parties and policymaking. Who runs and wins matters, but so do the tone of campaigns, the process of how Texans vote, and who votes—all shape the politics of the state. Change in Texas politics is slow, but it has and will result from battles over the electoral process and the collision of the political ideas of those who choose to vote.

TEXAS TAKEAWAYS

4.1.1 A Texas citizen must be registered to vote 30 days before an election.

4.1.2 Texas voters need to provide a photo identification or a sworn statement of citizenship with nonphoto proof of residency, such as a birth certificate, a utility bill, a paystub, or a bank statement.

4.1.3 In an open primary, any qualified registered voter can vote in the primary for any party. In a closed primary, only voters registered with a party may vote in that party's primary.

4.2.1 The poll tax, the white primary, and voter intimidation by certain people or groups are ways that Texas disenfranchised minority voters in the past.

4.2.2 In 1965, Congress passed the Voting Rights Act, which prohibited discrimination against racial minorities.

4.2.3 Approximately 85 percent of African Americans support the Democratic Party.

4.3.1 There are some who don't vote because voting is time consuming and difficult. There are others who don't vote because they don't see a benefit.

4.3.2 Voter turnout can be increased if the structure of voting is changed (having convenience voting) or if greater efforts are made to reach out to and educate voters.

4.4.1 Negative advertising often demobilizes the electorate by decreasing political efficacy and reducing support for the candidate who is the target of the negativity.

4.4.2 Federal regulations on campaigns were originally designed to limit the lopsided influence of wealthy individuals and interest groups in federal elections.

4.5.1 The top group was made up of oil- and gas-related donors. The second group included lawyers and lobbyists.

4.5.2 Straight-ticket voting generally helps parties gain and maintain power.

KEY TERMS

at-large
closed primary
disenfranchise
early voting
Fifteenth Amendment
"get out the vote"
incumbents
microtargeting
motor voter law

name identification
negative campaigning
open primary
political action committees (PACs)
political efficacy
political socialization
poll tax
primary election
public opinion polling
register

runoff election
single-member districts
special election
split-ticket voting
straight-ticket voting
super PACs
Voting Rights Act of 1965

PRACTICE QUIZ

1. The National Voter Registration Act of 1993, or the "motor voter law," provided for the opportunity to . . .
   a. Vote via "drive-thru" voting booths
   b. Register to vote when applying for a driver's license
   c. Register to vote when buying a car
   d. Vote when registering a car with the State Vehicle Inspection Office

2. Compared to all other states, where does Texas rank in the percentage of the state's registered voters turning out to vote?
   a. In the top five
   b. In the top half
   c. In the bottom half
   d. In the bottom five

3. The process whereby individuals acquire political values and behaviors, which have a strong influence on future voting, is called . . .
   a. Political socialization
   b. Sociology
   c. Political pandering
   d. Straight-ticket voting

4. Which of the following is/are NOT a type of primary election?
   a. Open
   b. Closed

   c. Neither A nor B is a primary election
   d. Both A and B are types of primary elections

5. In Texas, if no candidate wins the primary election (i.e., gets a majority of the vote), which of the following occurs?
   a. Special election
   b. General election
   c. Runoff election
   d. Plural election

6. For most counties in Texas that switched to vote centers, the impact on turnout was . . .
   a. Positive
   b. Negative
   c. No change
   d. None of the above

7. Suffrage refers to passing the age threshold to be eligible to vote.
   a. True
   b. False

8. Jim Crow laws mandating segregation and voting restrictions marginalized African Americans politically for almost a century.
   a. True
   b. False

9. Most Texans do not vote, even in a presidential election year.
   a. True
   b. False

10. In *Citizens United v. Federal Election Commission* (2010), the Supreme Court ruled that it was constitutional to ban independent political spending by corporations and unions.
    a. True
    b. False

[Answers: B, D, A, D, C, B, B, A, A, B]

Learn more with this chapter's digital tools, including the Oxford Insight Study Guide, at www.oup.com/he/Rottinghaus3e.

5

POLITICAL PARTIES: TEXAS IN BLUE AND RED

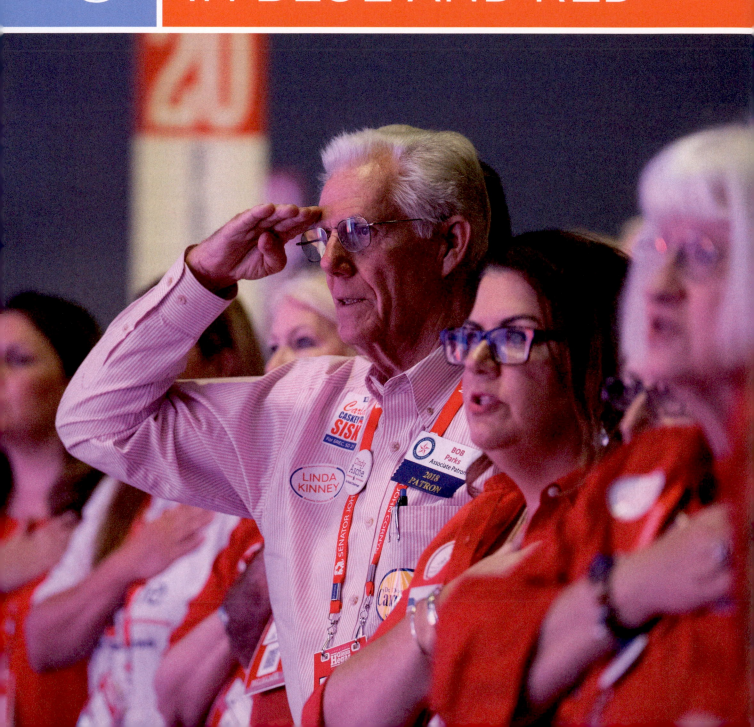

In a career-ending blunder, a Texas Republican Party staffer accidentally e-mailed the party's strategy for winning the 2020 elections to Democrats. The Republican Party planned to roll out websites with URLs that appeared to belong to Democratic candidates but provided negative information about those candidates. Although attack campaigns might be old hat, the vim and vigor of the 2020 elections ran high. For the first time since 2003, Democrats were hoping to take back the Texas House and push Texas back toward its Democratic roots.[1]

For a century after Reconstruction, the Democratic Party—an odd mixture of liberals and conservatives—dominated Texas politics. Texans saw the Republican Party, also known as the Grand Old Party (GOP) or the Party of Lincoln, as foreign occupiers who had declared military law and ruled Texas after the Civil War. Most Texans identified as "yellow dog" Democrats, a group that got their name because they would rather vote for a yellow dog than a Republican.

However, in the 1970s and 1980s, conservatives gravitated toward the Republican Party. The 1994 gubernatorial election marked a turning point. Democratic Governor Ann Richards had slung mud at Republican challenger George W. Bush every which way during the campaign. However, in his opening statement during the televised debate, Bush laid the whole matter to rest: "I'm the conservative candidate, and she's the liberal."[2] Richards lost in November by 8 percent. Her defeat demonstrated a fundamental shift within the state's party system. In offices at the top and bottom of the ballot, Democrats began to lose their seats as voters migrated to the Republican Party.

5.1	Describe the function of political parties in Texas.
5.2	Explain the levels of organization of political parties and their roles.
5.3	Outline the changes in party dominance since the Civil War.
5.4	Analyze the factors that affect party competition.
5.5	Evaluate the impact third parties have had on Texas party politics and the challenges they face.

● Delegates at the 2018 Texas Republican Party Convention in San Antonio.

How do parties change? How do they rise and fall? What political struggles erupt within parties to drive these transformations? The structure and function of different parties are often similar, but who makes up the parties—and the ideologies of their members—may shift dramatically over time. This chapter shows how individuals and factions within Texas parties have shaped their electoral prospects as well as their ability to govern. We also observe how the state party system shifted from one-party rule favoring the Democrats to one-party rule favoring the Republicans. The struggle over economic issues, growing concerns about federal intervention, and demographic changes ousted one dominant party—and may yet oust another.

5.1 THE FUNCTIONS OF PARTIES

5.1   Describe the function of political parties in Texas.

Nowhere does the U.S. Constitution mention parties, but it is hard to imagine how government would run without them. When most of us think of political parties, we think of their role in elections: parties organize political interests, form a shared platform or goals, and thus provide a way for citizens to choose candidates to represent them in government. But parties do much more than that.

Famous political scientist (as well as Austin native and University of Texas graduate) V. O. Key Jr. suggested that parties have three basic functions: assisting voters (parties-in-the-electorate) by simplifying electoral choice; facilitating party goals (parties-as-organizations) by performing tasks such as recruiting candidates, mobilizing voters, and articulating interests; and organizing government (parties-in-government). In this section, we look closely at these functions.

SIMPLIFYING ELECTORAL CHOICES

Politics can be a confusing mash of personality and policy—along with a lot of noise. Voters, especially less politically involved voters, may need assistance to understand the political process. Shortcuts, such as the party identity of a candidate or a party platform, are easy and convenient ways to summarize a great deal of information into understandable bites.

Party labels are often enough to tell people how they should vote. Voters can assume that Republican candidates in Texas are **conservative** and prefer

conservative: one who believes in a political philosophy that emphasizes limited government, free markets, and individual entrepreneurship

a smaller role for government, including fewer taxes, more support for business, and an adherence to socially conservative values. Voters can also trust that Democratic candidates in Texas will generally be **liberal**, thus favoring expanded government, working to improve economic equality and access to health care, and supporting the right to have an abortion.

Party labels are not perfect indicators of ideology, especially in a conservative state like Texas. Modern Democrats sometimes take conservative positions on fiscal and economic matters, and Republicans may take liberal positions on social issues. However, in recent years, as Republicans have shifted even more to the right toward more conservative positions and Democrats have increasingly shifted to the left, partisanship has increased.

RECRUITING CANDIDATES

Local and state party leaders evaluate potential candidates, often screening them for quality and party loyalty. Although parties have traditionally recruited for partisan races, the parties have expanded their base to include nonpartisan local races, such as school board and municipal races.[3] Parties also recruit candidates to widen the appeal of the party. Starting with the election of Governor Bush in 1994, Republicans have made concerted efforts to recruit Hispanics to run for office in order to make inroads into socially conservative segments within Texas's growing Hispanic population.[4] In 2020, 684 Hispanics ran as Republicans in local and statewide races compared to 233 who ran as Democrats.

How do parties recruit leaders and candidates for office? Until the early 1900s, party leaders at state conventions nominated candidates for state and local offices. Considerable power was centralized in the party elite and special interests. Not surprisingly, abuse was rampant. Friends of certain candidates would visit cattle roundups in West and Central Texas, persuade cowboys and their foremen to constitute themselves as "local conventions," and carry away enough commitments to sway the outcome at the state convention.[5] The progressive movement in the early twentieth century led to reforms to fight government corruption. In 1905, Texas passed legislation to hold public primaries to nominate candidates directly. This change weakened the party leadership's role in choosing candidates and opened up opportunities for attentive voters, large campaign donors, and interest groups to have a greater say in the electoral process.

Parties still play a role in recruitment, however. Once a good candidate is identified, parties offer that candidate support services, such as issue and logistical expertise, data on voters, campaign materials, and assistance with digital media strategies. They also use their considerable funds to finance the campaigns of their recruits (see Figure 5.1).

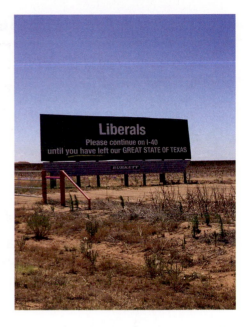

In 2018, when one Texan paid for a billboard in the tiny town of Vega urging liberals to leave the state, a resident of Amarillo launched a GOFUNDME campaign and raised funds for a billboard that read: "Texas is for everyone— not for bigotry. Welcome y'all."

PERSONAL RESPONSIBILITY: How tolerant are you of people with different ideological views? How tolerant are those around you are? What can you do to address this problem?

liberal: one who believes in a political philosophy that emphasizes social equality and a large role for government to protect liberties and alleviate social problems

FIGURE 5.1 Texas Party Political Spending

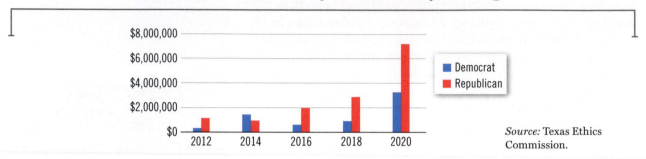

Source: Texas Ethics Commission.

COMMUNICATION:

How much do the parties spend?

- Both parties spend more money in presidential election years (2016, 2020) than in midterm election years (2014, 2018).
- The Democratic and Republican parties in Texas spend about the same overall, but Republicans spend more in competitive elections like 2016 and 2020.

CRITICAL THINKING:

Why are there differences?

- In 2018, Republicans spent more money to defend their seats as Democrats spent more to unseat them.
- Faith that demographic change favored Democrats in the 2020 election prompted Democratic-leaning donors to give funds. Major gains did not materialize.

MOBILIZING VOTERS

During elections, political parties fire up their turnout machines in order to get loyal voters to the polls to support party-endorsed candidates. Party activists often call other members to remind them to vote and even provide transportation to the polls. Turnout is critical to electoral victory. During the mayoral election in usually Democratic-leaning San Antonio in 2014, Leticia Van de Putte, who resigned her long-held state senate seat to run, lost to Republican Ivy Taylor, the interim mayor, by 3,331 votes. An exasperated consultant commented: "At the end of the day, we needed 3,000 Democrats to get off their asses and go vote, and they didn't." Taylor became the city's first African American mayor.[6]

ARTICULATING INTERESTS

Parties represent groups of citizens with shared values. Political scientists Robert Y. Shapiro and Joseph Bafumi found that since the 1980s, political ideology has become a stronger predictor of party identification.[7] Why?

During the civil rights battles in Texas of the 1960s and 1970s, conservatives concerned with states' rights flocked to the Republican Party, and liberals interested in pursuing voting rights and equal access to public facilities gravitated to the Democratic Party.

Parties also have an incentive to sharpen their differences: If voters perceive marked distinctions, parties can recruit candidates and passionate voters more effectively. These **partisans** tend to volunteer more of their time and money and are more likely to turn out to vote in party primaries and other elections. However, partisans do not necessarily represent Texan voters as a whole because they typically are more ideologically extreme.

partisans: strongly committed members of a party

Partisans play an oversized role in party politics by pushing the party to the extremes and exacerbating conflict.[8] Activists within a party may target a lawmaker and threaten party stability when representatives fail to deliver on promises or satisfy expectations. One Texas conservative activist growled "I'm going to be the skunk at the picnic" after Republican legislators failed to enact policies to his liking in 2015.[9]

ORGANIZING GOVERNMENT

Parties work to make sure that their candidates, once elected, toe the party line to deliver on electoral promises. Parties often organize legislators into forums where they work together to discuss and formulate policy. Party leaders then make sure that their members implement the party's plan. In this way, parties provide accountability to voters. This accountability is called responsible party government.

decentralization: the distribution of authority between national, state, and local party organizations so that each level exercises a degree of independent authority

⭐ TEXAS TAKEAWAYS

5.1.1 Name the three functions of political parties.

5.1.2 How are partisans important to parties?

5.2 PARTY ORGANIZATION

The backbone of the political party is the party organization: the group of individuals who volunteer or are paid minimally for positions at local and state levels. Parties are hierarchical, with authority flowing from the national to state to local level. However, due to the **decentralization** of party structure in the United States, state and local activists wield considerable influence over the future of the party—and often go to battle

5.2 Explain the levels of organization of political parties and their roles.

over policy and politics. Because these positions are influential, they are coveted and involve contentious elections.

PRECINCT CHAIRS

Counties are subdivided into smaller units called precincts. Precinct chairs are elected in the party's primary and serve for 2 years. As the most local party leaders, the precinct chairs recruit volunteers, coordinate campaign workers during elections, and participate in get-out-the-vote and voter registration drives.[10] Precinct chairs also serve on county executive committees where they choose state convention delegates and may be called on to replace a candidate on the ballot who resigns or otherwise can't stand for election. In 2016, Democratic precinct chairs worked overtime in Houston to replace a county commissioner who had died, the state senator who took his place, and the state representative who took her place.

Biennial elections for precinct chair positions are proxy wars for battles fought at the state level. In 2020, 80 of the 350 positions in Democratic precinct chair races in Bexar County were contested. Party infighting over finances, including charges of embezzlement, spurred opposing sides to try to win seats, with the fracture leading to two separate groups—one sanctioned by the state party and the other using the same name but conducting separate meetings and events.[11]

COUNTY PARTY CHAIRS

County party chairs recruit candidates to run for local or regional offices, act as spokespersons for local issues, and manage the funds of the local party. They also serve with precinct chairs on the county executive committee, which organizes party primaries and hosts county and senate district conventions.

Ideology rarely plays a role in these biennial elections, but they can sometimes become an issue. Four months after he staved off a Tea Party challenger, long-time Republican Party Chair Dr. Wally Wilkerson faced a coup that stripped him of several powers and established a seven-member steering committee. Affectionately known as "King Wally," Wilkerson had served as chair for 56 years, but this intraparty squabble pushed him out in 2020.[12] Other local county party

Robert Morrow was elected Travis County Republican chair despite making obscene comments about Texas politicians, advancing conspiracy theories, posting pictures of naked women on his Twitter account, and having a penchant for wearing a jester's hat. He was removed from his position after he filed to be a write-in candidate in the 2016 U.S. presidential election.

SOCIAL RESPONSIBILITY: **How might a party organization balance the need to include many voices with the need to maintain control and discipline of their message?**

organizations (like Travis and Galveston counties) also weakened their party chairs, claiming the need to decentralize power and increase transparency. The move alarmed party loyalists who saw it as a power grab by Tea Party activists.[13] "It's Republicans against Republicans," Wilkerson said.[14]

Party chairs aren't in the spotlight often, that is, unless they blunder. In 2020, Bexar County Republican Party chair Cynthia Brehm faced pressure from fellow Republicans to resign after she advanced a discredited conspiracy theory about the death of George Floyd in police custody in Minneapolis, Minnesota, an event that triggered outrage and protests across the country. She did not resign and she lost reelection in 2020.[15]

STATE PARTY CHAIR

The state party chair's primary responsibility is to develop and communicate the party's brand to voters and to raise and manage political funds for the party at the state level. State chairs also determine if a candidate is eligible to run for a party office. In 2019, Democratic Party chair Gilberto Hinojosa found Eagle Pass Mayor Ramsey Cantu ineligible to run for the legislature after another candidate for the seat provided documents suggesting that the mayor should be disqualified because he had not resigned his current office.[16] The race for party chair is largely conducted outside of the public eye. Party veterans communicate with each other to select a roster of candidates who then compete for the support of some 14,000 delegates across Texas. The Republican Party holds a caucus by state senate district while the Democrats have an open vote for all delegates.[17] Both parties mandate that one man and one woman serve as chair and vice chair.

Ideology does not always factor into the biennial elections for this office, primarily because candidates tend to be similarly situated ideologically. Rather, state chair campaigns zero in on management and leadership skills. In 2010, for example, the state Republican Party was half a million dollars in debt. During the heated battle for the Republican state chair, the two challengers attacked the incumbent on the issue of fiscal responsibility, something dear to the heart of Republican voters.[18] The incumbent lost his seat, and party finances rebounded. But when ideology is central to a contest, it can be a whopper, such as when Republicans ousted James Dickey who raised millions for the Party and elected former Florida Representative Allen West State Chair. His election signaled a new political direction for the Party—he said, "There are three words I hate to hear used. I hate 'big tent.' I hate 'inclusiveness.' And I hate 'outreach.'"[19]

PARTY EXECUTIVE COMMITTEES

Executive committee members are the center of party power as they govern the operations of the party and direct the overall message. Both the Republican and Democratic Party executive committees have 62 members (two members from each of 31 state senate districts) who are elected by the delegates to the party convention in each district. Democratic Party rules state that one man and one woman are selected from each district.

Because these groups have so much authority to direct the ideological trajectory of the parties, their actions are often controversial. In 2015, the Republican Party Executive Committee rejected a resolution to poll Republican primary voters about whether Texas should secede from the Union if "the federal government continues to disregard the constitution."[20] Opponents felt the resolution was frivolous, while supporters argued that it would show that the party was taking a strong stand against federal government intrusion into state matters.[21]

PARTY CONVENTIONS

Every 2 years, the party hosts conventions to decide how it functions and to set the political agenda. Precinct conventions elect delegates to county conventions. County conventions elect delegates to the state convention but also may submit resolutions that may become part of the **party platform**. In presidential election years, state conventions select delegates for the national convention and elect the slate of presidential electors to cast ballots for Texas in the Electoral College if their nominee wins the White House.

party platform: a list of values, beliefs, and policy issues that are endorsed and supported by a political party

STATE PARTY PLATFORMS

The planks of a party's platform range from providing concrete policy solutions to more general and ideological opinions (see Figure 5.2). For instance, the 2018 Texas Democratic platform called for curtailing the availability of military-style assault rifles, promoting marriage equality for all couples, repealing voter ID laws, as well as making ideological statements against capital punishment and border walls. The 2020 Republican platform (which did not change from 2018) called for the abolishment of multiple government agencies and the expansion of charter schools and private options using public school funds. The platform also contained a provision advocating strict adherence to the U.S. and Texas constitutions. These state platforms can differ significantly from the national party platforms, which have to appeal to a broader set of voters.[22]

Platforms are as much a political marketing tool as they are a guide to understanding party positions. Each state party's executive committee writes and revises the platform every 2 years (in even-numbered years, when the convention meets). The convention delegates approve the platform at the convention. In contrast to assertions that political parties desire to moderate their views to attract more swing voters, studies show that the ideological distance between the state party platforms of the two parties has been increasing.[23] State party competition also increases the ideological gap between the party platforms as each party attempts to shore up the more ideologically extreme voters who are more likely to vote in primary elections.

FIGURE 5.2   Word Clouds of Democratic and Republican Party Platforms, 2020

Democratic Platform

Republican Platform

Source: Republican Party of Texas and Texas Democratic Party.

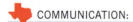

COMMUNICATION:

What are the most common words in each party platform?

- For Democrats, the most prominent words are "public," "health," "school," and "protect." Somewhat prominent words include "right," "care," "child," and "act."

- For Republicans, the most prominent words are "oppose," "united," and "state." Somewhat prominent words include "tax," "federal," "urge," "law," and "life."

CRITICAL THINKING:

Why are the party priorities different?

- The Democratic Party platform is issue-based but, without the Democrats being in power, amplifies what they believe and emphasizes education and health programs.

- The Republican Party platform takes a more negative posture, emphasizing opposition to the federal government but also adherence to rights and laws and protecting life.

★ **TEXAS TAKEAWAYS**

5.2.1 What does the state party chair do?

5.2.2 Why is the party platform important to the party?

🔄 5.3 RISE AND FALL OF POLITICAL PARTIES IN TEXAS

5.3 Outline the changes in party dominance since the Civil War.

For more than 130 years after the Civil War, Texas was dominated by the Democratic Party. The decline of the Democratic Party and the rise of the Republican Party tell a story about shifting political power, the people who made it happen, and the events that shaped it.

Strong, cohesive parties are able to use partisan endorsements and funding to control nominations and present a unified front in elections.[24] "Strong party" states also discipline legislators to uphold a governor's program and maintain a party "brand" that voters can understand. Because Texas has been dominated by one political party or another since the Civil War, as a result of which most of the policy fights have been internal to the majority party, Texas has traditionally been a "weak party" state, where party is not closely tied to a set of core principles.

DEMOCRATIC REIGN IN THE POSTBELLUM ERA

Republican representation in Texas was nearly uniform immediately following the Civil War. The Republican Party was the party of Abraham Lincoln, after all, and had waged the Civil War and spearheaded Reconstruction. But once the national government pulled its soldiers out of the state, many Texans rallied against the Republican Party, associating it with the scarcity that followed the Civil War and with unwanted military rule.[25]

The elections of 1871, 1872, and 1873 broke the Republican stranglehold on state politics. Moderate Republicans and Democrats unified against the "carpetbagger" Union (Republican) government and in their dislike of Republican Governor Edmund J. Davis. A "Taxpayer's Convention" that expressed frustration with increases in school taxes and wasted taxpayer funds pulled many voters into the Democratic Party. Democrats won all the congressional seats in 1871, took majority control of the state legislature in 1872, and captured the governorship in 1873. The Democratic Party then dominated Texas for the next hundred years.

THE DECLINE OF THE DEMOCRATS

In the 1930s, President Franklin Roosevelt pushed through the **New Deal**, which enabled Democrats to tie voters closer to the party through patronage. That is, participation in party politics meant contracts, jobs, and status. As is frequently the case, however, national politics also seeded a split between the liberal and conservative wings of the Democratic Party at the state level.

During President Roosevelt's first term, the Supreme Court declared much of the New Deal legislation unconstitutional. After a momentous re-election in 1936, Roosevelt pushed a plan in Congress to give the president the power to appoint a new justice to the Supreme Court whenever a sitting justice reached the age of 70 and failed to retire. In this way, Roosevelt could "pack" the Court with his supporters. The vice president, John Nance "Cactus Jack" Garner, was a Texas Democrat but came from the conservative, rural wing of the party. He and other conservative Democrats, known as the "Texas Regulars," quietly and privately began to drum up opposition to the Court-packing plan. Meanwhile, Texas House members Lyndon Johnson and Sam Rayburn backed President Roosevelt. Publicly accused of "sticking his knife into the president's back,"[26] Garner tried to smooth the matter over, but he could not regain Roosevelt's confidence. The president replaced Garner on the 1940 presidential ticket, a decision that sent tremors throughout the state party and produced the first crack between its wings.

In the 1952 presidential election, a permanent crack opened. The state Democratic convention divided along ideological lines, with some supporting national Democratic welfare programs and others supporting a more conservative economic approach. On one side were the conservative to middle-of-the road Democrats—the "Shivercrats" or, as already mentioned, "Texas Regulars"—led by Texas Governor Allan Shivers. In the other camp stood the "Loyalists," a liberal wing of the party. Both factions claimed to represent the "true" Democratic Party. Conservatives won the day, holding more statewide offices and capturing the party leadership, but a precedent was set: The factions held separate party conventions after the liberals walked out of the 1952 convention to support their preferred presidential candidate.[27] The Shivercrats favored Republican

New Deal: a federal economic recovery program in response to the Great Depression that stabilized the banking industry, created jobs, promoted fair labor standards, and produced a social welfare network

WHICH TWIN IS 'THE PHONY?

Texas Governor Allan Shivers was accused in 1954 of being a "Republican in Democratic clothing" by liberal-wing affiliate Ralph Yarborough. Many liberals in the Democratic Party hoped that the conservative Democrats leaving the party would allow them to take the party back. Instead, the shift strengthened the Republican Party.

CRITICAL THINKING: **How did the Shivercrats weaken the Democratic Party? Was this weakening inevitable?**

General Dwight Eisenhower, an ardent states' rights supporter, while the Loyalists favored Democratic Illinois Governor Adlai Stevenson. Although no Republican had won political office in Texas since Reconstruction, the Shivercrats' work on behalf of the Republican nominee led to Eisenhower's narrow victory in the state. This began the process of ideological sorting in Texas, with conservatives gravitating toward the Republican Party and liberals to the Democratic Party.

The 1970 primary for U.S. Senate increased tensions between the liberal and conservative wings of the Democratic Party. Lloyd Bentsen, a conservative, wealthy Democrat from Hidalgo County, challenged a leading liberal in the Democratic Party, Ralph Yarborough. Bentsen, with masterful timing, attacked Yarborough for endorsing Vietnam War moratorium demonstrations, missing votes in the Senate on school busing, and opposing voluntary school prayer.[28] Yarborough lost the primary race.

The rise of conservative, pro-Ronald Reagan Democrats, who favored cutting taxes, increasing military spending, and reducing social services, also widened the fissures in the party. Many conservative Democrats—so-called blue dog Democrats—supported Reagan. Liberal stalwart and Democratic state representative from Houston Mickey Leland sought to expel these traitorous "boll weevil" Democrats from the party in the 1980s.[29] This effort led to the further exodus of conservatives from the party.

Meanwhile, economic development and population growth weakened the Democratic Party further. Upper-class whites moved to the Republican Party. As cities boomed, rural areas, which had traditionally been havens of Democratic power, lost influence. And as migrants from other states poured into Texas to take jobs in rapidly expanding urban centers, the Democratic Party had trouble connecting with new voters unfamiliar with the customs and traditions of politics in the state. Texas voters had overlooked ideological differences and loyally voted the Democratic ticket, but new voters often rejected Democrats no matter their ideology.[30] Support for the Democratic Party declined (see Figure 5.3).

How did the Democrats maintain power? Party leaders, mostly from the conservative wing, served as gatekeepers for those seeking higher office. Taking advantage of rules called "cross filing," Democrats ran as both Republicans and Democrats in primaries (a practice no longer allowed). In this way, Texas conservatives stunted Republican Party ambitions and blocked liberals from securing party nominations because popular conservative Democrats could run in both primaries and win.[31] Moderates were systemically purged from the Democratic Party, and liberals found few friends.

The last hurrah for the Democrats occurred in 1982—the last election in which Democrats captured all statewide offices. But the party was hemorrhaging support, losing the votes of Anglos.[32] Observers point to December 2, 1997, as the day the Democratic Party in Texas collapsed, "not with a bang but a whimper." On this day, Democratic Attorney General Dan Morales, the last statewide elected Democrat, announced he would retire from politics.[33] For the first time since Reconstruction, the Democrats held no statewide office.

FIGURE 5.3 **State Party Affiliation**

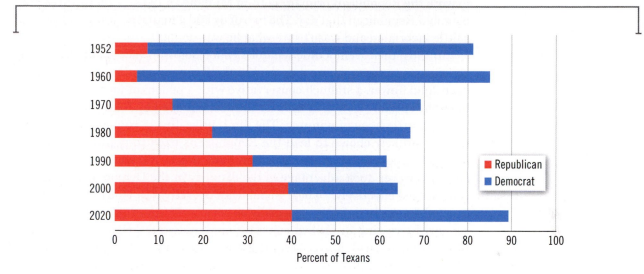

 COMMUNICATION:

How has party affiliation changed?

- In 1952 and 1960, nearly 80 percent of Texans identified with the Democratic Party.

- Today, only 48 percent of Texans identify with the Democratic Party, though fewer Texans (40 percent) identify with the Republican Party. "Independents," however, often vote with the Republicans.

 CRITICAL THINKING:

Why has political party affiliation changed over time?

- Attachment to Presidents Kennedy and Johnson and their policies initially spiked support for the Democrats, but conservative rejection of civil rights policies reduced support for the party.

- The sorting of the parties by ideology drove conservative Texans toward the Republican Party.

- Since 2000, the Democratic Party and allied organization efforts to reach out to latent and young new voters have increased support for the Democrats.

THE RISE OF THE REPUBLICANS

The Texas Republican Party was outflanked, dismissed, or outright ignored in electoral battles for the better part of a century. In some years, they didn't even hold primaries because not enough candidates were running.[34] To claim that the Democrats dominated state politics for much of the first half of the twentieth century would be an understatement. Future First Lady Barbara

Bush recalled when she and future president George H. W. Bush volunteered to work the Republican primary polls in Midland in 1958: "Exactly three people voted Republican that day. The two of us and a man who you could say was a little inebriated and wasn't sure what he was doing."[35]

In 1961, then-Democratic senator Lyndon Johnson vacated his seat in the U.S. Senate to serve as vice president in the Kennedy administration. Republican John Tower, a staunch conservative with a penchant for fancy suits, entered the special election in 1961 for the seat left open by Johnson's departure but with little hope of winning. The diminutive Tower, cool and often aloof, was an unlikely choice to lead the Republicans back to political relevance. As he often joked, "My name is Tower, but I don't."[36] Tower and the Republicans, however, took advantage of the disunity in the Democratic Party and campaigned effectively.[37] Local Republican operatives in Houston and Dallas courted donors in industry, especially oil services.[38] Tower solicited grassroots support by vowing to protect constitutional and states' rights. And the unthinkable happened: Tower became the first Republican to win statewide office since Reconstruction.

Tower's win established a bridgehead to legitimacy for other Republicans in the 1960s. Several future major Republican Party figures emerged in Texas at this time. A young George H. W. Bush won a position as Harris County Republican Party chair in 1962, which he used as a springboard for a challenge to incumbent Democratic senator Ralph Yarborough for the U.S. Senate in 1964.[39] Bush took up the mantle of the rising conservatism in the state by campaigning against the Civil Rights Act, claiming that states' rights should be paramount. The fortunes of Bush and the Republican Party were crushed, however, on the night in 1964 when Democratic presidential candidate Lyndon Johnson, incredibly popular after the assassination of John F. Kennedy, carried Texas by an overwhelming margin.

The subsequent Republican takeover at the national level in 1968 improved the fortunes of Texas Republicans. President Richard Nixon and, later, in 1975, President Gerald Ford were able to bring home the "big rock candy mountain" of federal patronage, including jobs and funding for projects.[40] Nixon in particular made use of what he called the "Southern strategy"—an emphasis on exposing divisions within the Democratic Party over racial integration and civil rights and in the general public on law and order issues. This approach was persuasive to the growing middle-class suburban electorate.[41] Republican strongholds in suburban and small-town areas from 1978 to 1994 made the state more competitive and grew the number of elected Republican officials.

By 1978, a deeply divided Democratic Party and a well-financed Republican Party cut a trail to the election of Bill Clements as governor and the re-election of John Tower to the U.S. Senate. As governor, Clements expanded the party's brand by putting a priority on reducing taxes and government bureaucracy and on expanding appointments of Republicans. By the 1980 presidential election, headlined by a very popular Ronald Reagan and hometown Republican favorite son George H. W. Bush, the Republicans had elected more than 150 county officials to complement substantial gains in the state legislature.[42] The 1998 state elections, a watershed for Republicans, saw the party sweep all statewide offices and win a majority on both supreme courts.[43]

As candidates began to see federal intervention as a primary cause of economic troubles in Texas during the 1970s and 1980s, more Republican candidates began to run for federal offices. Pathways to Washington also opened up as the first congressional districts were redrawn to favor Republican candidates.

Texas fire ants may be responsible for Republican success in congressional elections during the 1980s. Tom DeLay, Republican of Sugar Land, was an exterminator and a nondescript backbencher in the Texas House of Representatives when the federal government banned Mirex, the pesticide that was used to kill fire ants. The action radicalized DeLay, who decided that the U.S. Environmental Protection Agency (EPA) was an "evil empire" that had to be destroyed. He ran for the U.S. House of Representatives in 1984 and won. Reelected 10 times, DeLay rose to the ranks of majority leader. A beleaguered EPA official, hearing the story, would later mutter, "Christ, we could have lived with Mirex."[44]

Other Republicans ran for the U.S. House objecting to excessive regulation and wasteful spending by the federal government. By 2002, the Republican Party of Texas not only boasted strong representatives in the U.S. Congress, but also controlled every single statewide office and both chambers of the state legislature (see Figure 5.4).

THE TEA PARTY

The rise of the Republican Party led to the evolution of distinct wings within the party. Even in 1987, *Texas Monthly* observed that the party had moved "away from the genteel conservatism of John Tower toward the fierce ideological populism of Ronald Reagan." One wing consisted of traditional, business-minded conservatives who were often socially moderate and the other of a far-right-wing faction who were rabid anti-Communists. These ultraconservative Republicans were essential to the rise of the Republican Party both in Texas specifically and in the South more broadly. They courted anxious, middle-class, white suburban voters who embraced the values of individualism and "small government."[45]

Ideological divisions have produced a civil war within the Republican Party to gain control of the party and the government.

The 2006 primary elections brought a new breed of Republican voter to the polls. These voters were angry at the legislative session in 2005, which could not pass meaningful school voucher legislation, property tax relief, or budget restraints on local government. Influential donors, conservative activists, and leading political figures (like Governor Rick Perry) sought to purge the party of RINOs ("Republicans in Name Only").[46] One journalist concluded that "having devoured the Democrats, the Republicans have turned on one another."[47]

In the mid-2000s, the emergence of the groups that would eventually form the Tea Party deepened the fissure between economic conservatives and

SOCIAL RESPONSIBILITY:

Are divisions within a party healthy or disruptive to democratic government?

FIGURE 5.4 **Political Party Representation in the Texas Legislature**

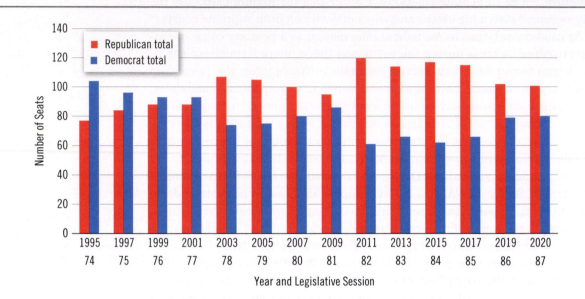

Source: Legislative Reference Library of Texas. Bars represent total party members for both House and Senate. The number below the year corresponds to the legislative session.

 COMMUNICATION:

What are the trends in party membership?

- Democrats maintained control of the legislature through the 1990s.
- Republicans gained a majority of the Texas House in the 2003 session for the first time since after the Civil War.
- Republicans possess supermajorities in both the Texas House and Senate in the most recent legislative session.

 CRITICAL THINKING:

Why did the number of Democrats decline?

- Redistricting (discussed later in this chapter) shaped seats with an even number of party voters into seats with a majority of one or the other party. Formerly strong Democratic districts were turned into weaker ones, and as Democrats switched parties to join the Republican Party, the advantage for Democrats began to shrink.
- Ideological changes pushed conservative Democrats out of the Democratic Party and into the Republican Party.

social conservatives. The Tea Party reached national prominence when it held a series of rallies in 2009 in response to the Obama administration's economic recovery plans and the Affordable Care Act (or Obamacare).[48] A coalition of grassroots conservative organizations rather than a separate "party," the Tea

Party originally pursued the goal of the original Boston Tea Party activists from the time of the American Revolution: relief from taxation. Over time, however, the Tea Party has adopted a wider agenda, embracing traditional family values, advocating for a smaller government that is more connected and accountable to the people, supporting gun rights, and opposing illegal immigration.

The movement has a national following but deep roots in Texas, sprouting from an organization formed by U.S. House Republican Texan Dick Armey.[49] Nationally, 18 percent of the public indicates support for the Tea Party.[50] The situation is different in conservative Texas, where support for the Tea Party is higher than it is nationally, especially within the Republican Party. Tea Party-backed candidates, such

Tea Party supporters at Dallas City Hall, with their dog Cookie, joined dozens of others with "Don't Tread on Me" flag t-shirts as Twisted Sister's "We're Not Gonna Take It" blasted from the loudspeaker, calling for smaller government, prudent spending, and personal responsibility.

as Senator Ted Cruz and Lieutenant Governor Dan Patrick, have expanded their influence, and local Tea Party activists continue to rally voters around conservative candidates.

The Tea Party in Texas sets the conservative litmus test for prospective nominees. Candidates who embrace the Tea Party in Republican primaries are often advantaged with a label that places them to the ideological right of their opponents and signals social conservatives, who make up a majority of the Republican primary electorate, to support them in the primary. A journalist noting these changes in Texas politics asked: "The question no longer is, 'Would Ann Richards be too liberal to be elected in Texas today?' but rather, 'Would George W. Bush?'"[51] This ideological party split makes it difficult to maintain party unity around legislative issues as more Tea Party-backed candidates are elected to the legislature. Some Republicans have voiced displeasure at the politics and tactics of these new Tea Party Republicans (see Figure 5.5). Michael Williams, the first Republican African American elected to statewide office, remarked, "Political parties are like milk. They do curdle and spoil over time."[52]

FISSURES IN THE REPUBLICAN PARTY

Conflicts are unavoidable in a "big tent" party that seeks to continue to win elections and govern, but the consequences of the rise of the Tea Party movement have been profound for Texas. Friction has developed between socially conservative voters who want their ideas of morality imposed on state policies and libertarians who want government out of just about everything. Skirmishes have also flared between fiscal conservatives who want a low-tax state with minimal spending on government services and business conservatives who see the

FIGURE 5.5 **Is the Texas Republican Party Welcoming?**

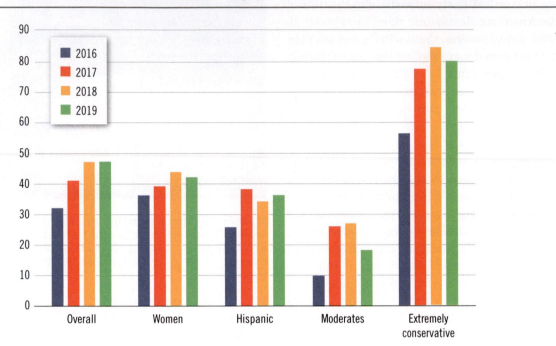

Source: Texas Politics Polling, 2016–2020. Question asked: "Is the Republican Party welcoming to people like you?"

 COMMUNICATION:

What percentage of the Texas electorate identifies with each party?

- Overall, about half of Texans feel the Republican Party is welcoming, but that has leveled off during the last few years.
- The most conservative Texans felt very welcome in the Republican Party, their numbers rising significantly from 2016.
- Hispanics, women, and moderates were less likely to claim the Republican Party was welcoming.

 CRITICAL THINKING:

Why have these percentages changed?

- Perceived racially based policies and aggressive language about women from some Republican leaders may have made these groups feel less welcome.
- As Republican leaders and activists move to more conservative policy positions, moderates feel less welcome.

need for increased spending on infrastructure, transportation, and education. More than 50 county Republican parties, including those of Bexar and Harris counties, and the State Republican Executive Committee rebuked or passed "no confidence" resolutions against moderate Republican Speaker of the House

Joe Straus in 2018 for not holding up to what they consider conservative principles.[53] In future, the growing political demands of the Tea Party may alienate moderate voters, causing them to leave the Republican Party. Outgoing Republican Party chair Tom Melcher noted that "[i]t is no secret that our party is divided into factions," and he offered a stern warning that the party should broaden its reach.[54]

LESSONS FROM TEXAS PARTY POLITICS

As with all party rises and falls, lessons can be learned from the events that preceded them. The power swings of party politics in the state demonstrate that history can, and often does, repeat itself in Texas politics.

Develop New Party Blood. The Democratic Party was criticized for embracing a "wait-your- turn" system of elections, where talented younger elected officials waited in line behind more senior members to have a shot at higher office. This system was argued to create "an ossified party rather than a dynamic one."[55] Candidates unwilling to wait either dropped out of politics or switched parties.

Offer a Bigger, Better Vision. Connecting with voters through issues that resonate with them is one of the most important ways that a party can win. While in office in the 1990s, Governor Ann Richards said that Democrats needed to "bring them[selves] into a new decade that requires new thinking and new resolutions."[56]

Give Goodies. Governor Bill Clements, the first Republican-elected governor since the Civil War, doled out dozens of appointments to Republicans, reshaping the landscape of the state's appointed officials. This tactic emphasizes both the governor's power of appointment as a tool of political power and the importance of these positions to government in Texas. Governor George W. Bush, elected in 1994, was able to take control of state agencies early in his term because of legislation that had allowed prior Governor Ann Richards to oust the previous governor's appointees.[57]

Co-Opt Emerging Ideologies. Incumbent party loyalists are often forced to adapt or reject new ideologies as they emerge within a party. The rise of the Tea Party movement from within the Republican Party changed the dynamics of Texas politics. In the 2010 Republican primary, Rick Perry, running for reelection as governor, smartly inoculated himself from a more robust Tea Party challenge by adopting the Tea Party's ideological platform early in the campaign and quelling any serious opposition.[58]

Build from the Bottom Up. Republicans in the 1960s changed Texas from a one-party to a two-party state by running candidates in every local election possible. As the old saying goes: In Texas politics, if you control the county

Jared Woodfill, Former Harris County Republican Party Chair

How can majority parties attract new members?

If we want to continue to grow our [Republican] party, we must be responsive to our grassroots base. We must embrace the principles identified in the Republican Party of Texas platform. We must embrace these principles and be loud and proud of our positions on issues. We must continue to support conservative social and fiscal policies. We must take our winning message to communities that have not traditionally voted Republican. People are looking for a party that stands for something.

 PERSONAL RESPONSIBILITY: **What tactics would you use to bring together a divided party?**

---

party competition: electoral conflict that signals how successful one party is over another

courthouse, you control the county. Following the momentum of Tower's 1961 victory and the party's first state senate win since 1927 in 1966, the Republicans fielded a full slate of candidates in the 1968 elections. Most did not win, but the Republicans were finally on the slow road to competitive politics.

🏴 TEXAS TAKEAWAYS

5.3.1 When did the Democrats begin their domination of state politics? Approximately when did it end?

5.3.2 How did the Republican Party rise to prominence in Texas politics?

5.3.3 When and on what issue did the Tea Party emerge as a major force in Texas elections?

 ## 5.4 PARTY COMPETITION

5.4	Analyze the factors that affect party competition.

Political parties at the state level have become better organized and more competitive. Political scientist Austin Ranney developed a widely used measure of **party competition**, referred to as the Ranney Index, based on the percentage of votes for the governor's office, the percentage of legislative seats held by each party, and other measures. A higher score indicates more competition. Figure 5.6 shows the Ranney Index. Overall, the most significant change across the past four decades is the increase in the level of two-party competition in the South as the dominant Democratic Party began to lose its grip on the region.

This growing party competition may be explained by a number of factors. A decline in traditional party loyalty means that more voters are willing to split their tickets in national and state elections.[59] The rise of "candidate-centered" campaigning channels voter loyalty toward the candidate rather than toward the party. Candidates can thus be competitive despite the partisan balance in a state or district. Today Texas is not fully competitive, but it is more competitive than in the past.

The change to Republican rule started in federal offices but gradually migrated to state offices as well. As former Texas Republican state party chair Wayne Thornburn noted in his book *Red State*, Republican candidates were first able to compete successfully in Texas federal elections, followed by gubernatorial elections, and then state legislative elections.[60] The best indicator of the shift in party power is the legislature, whose membership represents the partisan loyalties of the state's voters. District elections for state house and senate seats did not witness much competition between the two parties until the late twentieth century. Indeed, from 1900 to 1960, there were never more than three members of the Texas House and one state senator elected as a Republican.[61] Only later did Texas House and Senate districts become competitive. Today, Republicans have a supermajority in the Texas House and a majority in the Texas Senate. Republicans also hold all statewide elected positions and have majorities in both state supreme courts. Texas is not alone in Republican-run government. Republicans across the country in 2020 gained control of more seats than they have had since 1928, winning control of 54 of 99 state legislative chambers (Nebraska has only one chamber), their highest total in 58 years.[62]

What factors make one state more competitive than another? And is party competition likely to increase once again in Texas? To begin to answer those questions, we must look at apportionment, legislative redistricting, and party switching.

APPORTIONMENT

The U.S. Constitution mandates that representation in the U.S. House of Representatives be assigned based on state population after every census (which takes place every decade). Following the last two censuses, Texas gained seats in the U.S. House of Representatives because its population has been rising more sharply than that in other states. This process is called **reapportionment**. Each congressional district has an estimated 700,000 residents. For the state legislature, Texas House districts have approximately 167,000 residents, while Texas Senate districts have 811,000 residents.

reapportionment: redistribution of representation based on decennial recounting of residents

IS IT BIGGER IN TEXAS?

FIGURE 5.6 **Party Competition, 1972–2015**

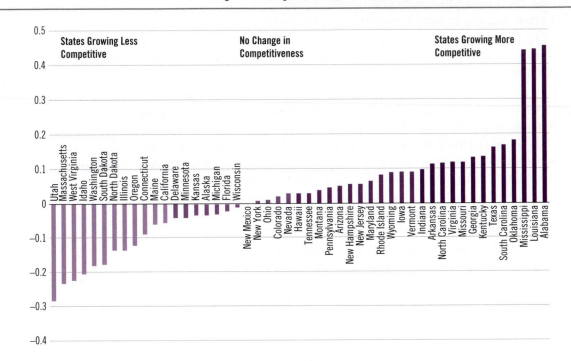

Source: Folded Ranney Index (representing a 4-year moving average, with the last year being used to compute the average being the year in question). A score closer to 0.5 indicates party domination in a state (one party or the other). Higher scores mean more party competition.

 CRITICAL THINKING:

How competitive is Texas?

- Most states have seen increased electoral competition, especially southern states. Texas has grown more competitive, but not as significantly as other southern states have.

- Some states have seen decreased competition as the party in power expands electoral influence. These states include Oregon (Democrats), South Dakota (Republicans), Massachusetts (Democrats), and Utah (Republicans).

 CRITICAL THINKING:

What factors explain the change in party competition in Texas?

- Gubernatorial elections became more competitive as Republicans began to win elections in the 1980s.

- In more recent years, partisan redistricting has made seats safe for each party, reducing party competition. Texas Democrats in particular have won districts drawn to favor Democrats and several swing districts in some elections.

LEGISLATIVE REDISTRICTING

State legislatures are responsible for redrawing the district lines to reflect population growth and to ensure that citizens have equal representation, making sure districts are of compact size, keeping communities together, and adhering to the geographic boundaries of local government. This redrawing process is called **redistricting**. Most states allow the state legislature to draw district lines, but a few have an independent commission to set the boundaries. The Texas Constitution requires the state legislature to redraw the district boundaries in the first regular session after the federal census.

Agreeing on legislative boundaries, which largely determine who will or will not get elected, is difficult because most members have some skin in the game. How these lines are drawn directly influences who is elected. In 1951, the Texas legislature developed a backup plan—a five-member board called the **Legislative Redistricting Board**, which draws the district lines when the legislature is not able to agree. The board is made up of most state-wide elected officials: the lieutenant governor, the speaker of the house, the attorney general, the state comptroller, and the land commissioner.

Even if the Legislative Redistricting Board can agree on a set of electoral maps, these maps may still be deemed unconstitutional by the U.S. Supreme Court. From the 1960s through the 1990s, the Court laid down detailed guidelines that enforced the one-person, one-vote rule established in *Baker v. Carr* (1962), which required electoral districts to encompass approximately the same number of people.[63] This ruling altered the balance of power in Texas by forcing the state to draw district lines to equalize populations, thus reducing the number of rural districts, increasing the number of urban districts, and shifting the power to legislators in urban districts. Explaining the Court's reasoning, Chief Justice Earl Warren wrote the famous line, "Legislators represent people, not trees or acres."[64]

A major point of legal contention has been the use of race to draw legislative lines. The Supreme Court ruled in *Gomillion v. Lightfoot* (1960) that districts drawn to discriminate against racial minorities violated the Fifteenth Amendment and that states could not draw districts to diminish the political power of minorities. As the Court found in *Shaw v. Reno* (1993), however, the state cannot **gerrymander** a district for race alone (a process of manipulating district boundaries to benefit a single group). It can do so, however, on the basis of a combined set of factors, including community cohesion and political subdivisions, or to keep together neighborhoods that historically have been in the same district.

redistricting: the redrawing of legislative districts to meet federal and state requirements

Legislative Redistricting Board: the group of officials who draw the district lines if the legislature is not able to agree

gerrymander: a process of manipulating district boundaries to benefit a single group

GONZALES
EL CAMPO
BAY CITY
CORPUS CHRISTI

TEXAS 27TH
"Glock Pistol"

Districts often take odd shapes as the architects attempt to include or exclude certain communities, geographic regions, or groups. The Texas Twenty-Seventh Congressional district resembles a gun pointed at a 45-degree angle. The gun's "handle" expanded to include more conservative areas in the 2010 redistricting, allowing a Republican to unseat a long-serving Democrat.

SOCIAL RESPONSIBILITY: **Would it be fair to have the party affiliation of the population be a factor in drawing district lines? What about race or ethnicity?**

Legislatures often draw seats with prospects for their party's electoral success in mind. This leads to districts that protect incumbent members or that make a seat held by the opposition party more vulnerable to challenge. Legally, however, redistricting may not purposively draw district lines to advantage one party over another. District lines drawn in this way over time lead to "safe" seats where one party or the other dominates because a significant majority of the voters in the district are loyal to that party.

Common gerrymandering tactics include "cracking" (spreading a population group across several districts to reduce influence), "packing" (stuffing a population group in a single district to reduce influence in neighboring districts), and "hijacking" (redrawing lines to pit two incumbents against each other). One legislator, who was unhappy about his district being redrawn in a way that included his house but excluded much of his core constituency, called his new district the "fickle finger" district because "it had a little finger that went down and got my house."[65]

The 2001 and 2003 Redistricting Battles: The Drama Begins. Following the 2000 census, Texas was slated to receive two additional congressional seats. Republican Governor Rick Perry controlled the governor's chair. However, the Democrats controlled the state house, and the state senate was split between the two major parties. As a result, the Texas legislature was unable to agree on new district lines in the 2001 session because both parties attempted to draw new district lines that would favor themselves. The task for redistricting then fell to the Legislative Redistricting Board. Since four of the five members of the board were Republican, the lines favored Republican candidates. The redistricting efforts shifted many safe Democratic districts to safe Republican districts. Not surprisingly, Republicans took a majority of the legislature in 2002 elections. With this new majority, Republicans, led by U.S. House Majority Leader Tom DeLay, proposed that the legislature draw new lines in the 2003 legislative session. This led to a contentious legislative session (see the next section, Angles of Power).

A legal challenge (*League of United Latin American Citizens v. Perry*) to the rare "mid-decade" redrawn lines ended in 2006 with the Supreme Court upholding the redrawn districts (except for one). Using these new boundaries, Republicans dominated the 2004 elections, taking more than two-thirds of the open seats in the state house (see Figure 5.7).

Texas Senate Democrats who took cover in New Mexico during a redistricting fight in 2003 hold a makeshift press conference from their Albuquerque hotel with the Texas flag behind them (see Angles of Power).

ANGLES OF POWER

The 2003 Redistricting Battle and the Killer Ds

Fearing a redistricting plan would pass in the legislature that would greatly reduce the number of Democrats, 52 Democrats from the Texas House and Senate fled Austin to a Holiday Inn in Ardmore, Oklahoma, for 11 days in 2003 to stall a vote. Without a sufficient number of senators, a vote in the chamber could not be held. The Texas Rangers have the authority in Texas to escort lawmakers home, but that jurisdiction ends at the state line. The Democrats were powerless as the minority party in the House. Representative Jim Dunnam of Waco bragged to a cheering crowd upon the return of the "Killer Ds" (as they were called), "I went to Ardmore, Oklahoma, and all I got was this hat from Denny's."[66]

The regular session ended with no redistricting bill, but Governor Perry called a special session to finish the job. This time, the Democrats bolted to Albuquerque, New Mexico, but one, Senator John Whitmire of Houston and the longest-serving member of the Texas Senate, broke ranks and returned to Austin to "preserve consensus in the state Senate instead of engaging in no-holds-barred partisan civil war."[67] For all of the delays, the redistricting bill eventually passed anyway.

SOCIAL RESPONSIBILITY: **Should parties use legislative majorities to engineer more electoral support for their party?**

Redistricting in 2011: Maps and More Maps. Texas's booming population registered in the 2010 census added four U.S. House seats to the Lone Star State. The growth was fueled by individuals moving to Texas from out of state and the rapidly rising population of racial minorities.[68] The Republican supermajorities in the Texas House and Senate recrafted the lines in 2011, only to be challenged in court for not taking the growth of the state's minority population into account. A panel of three San Antonio federal judges redrew the lines for use in the 2012 elections, only to have the Supreme Court order them to draw new lines based more closely on the maps designed by the state legislature. The awkward timing of this process forced the state to delay the scheduled 2012 primary elections from March to May.

Redistricting in 2013: Back to Court. Legislative redistricting in a special session in 2013 took place during the ongoing ping-pong match between the state legislature, the U.S. Justice Department, and the federal courts over the 2011 and 2012 maps. The legislature modestly doctored the maps used in the 2012 elections for the Texas House but left the Texas Senate and U.S. congressional maps in place. The new boundaries again generally favored Republicans—80 districts became more Republican-leaning. Democratic-held districts also solidified their advantage—65 districts swung to a more liberal

FIGURE 5.7 **Texas Representatives in the U.S. House**

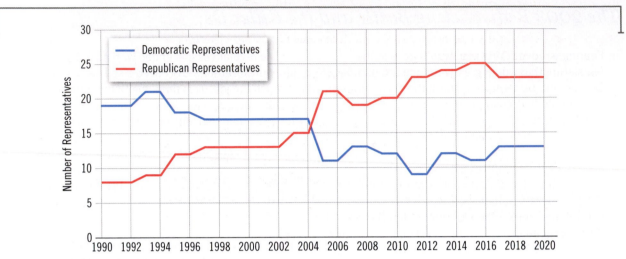

Source: Texas Legislative Reference Library.

 CRITICAL THINKING:

How has the partisan composition of the legislature changed?

- The largest increase in legislative representation of U.S. House Republicans in Washington, DC, came in the mid-2000s as the Texas delegation became a Republican majority.

- Despite tens of million of dollars spent in 2020, the partisan split of the delegation remained the same as 2018.

 CRITICAL THINKING:

Why has it changed?

- Republican wins in the 1960s and 1970s spurred an investment in party organization that made running for office as a Republican easier. Recruitment efforts paid off in the 1990s.

- Redistricting in 2000, aided by Republicans hungry to elect more of their own, drew district lines that favored Republican House candidates.

direction.[69] Latino organizations like the Texas Latino Redistricting Task Force proposed expanding the number of Latino seats, and the Texas legislative Black Caucus asked for nondiscriminatory lines to be drawn. A federal judge allowed the state to hold elections using these maps in 2014, claiming the courts didn't have adequate time to settle the legal dispute before those elections were to take place.[70] A three-judge federal panel in San Antonio ruled in 2015 that in order to avoid delay or confusion, the state should use the 2013 redrawn maps for the 2016 election. In 2018, the Supreme Court finally ruled Texas lawmakers did not intentionally discriminate in drawing district lines, arguing that the evidence was "plainly insufficient" that the original lines were drawn in "bad faith."[71] Except for one district in Fort Worth that did illegally use race to draw the lines, the Court sanctioned use of the maps in the 2018 election.

A separate legal challenge was brought, arguing that the boundaries were based on total population, not total voting population. The concern was that although most districts had a similar number of citizens, the number of voters was not equal because some racial groups, like Hispanics, are less likely to register to vote.[72] The Supreme Court ruled in *Evenwel v. Abbott* (2015), however, that the legislature was required to draw districts to equalize the total population of districts rather than the number of eligible voters. Using only registered voters, the Court reasoned, runs against the one-person, one-vote principle. The case demonstrates the importance of participation in the electoral system.

PARTY SWITCHING

One factor that reduces party competition within a district is party switching—when politicians of one party opt to switch to another, frequently to join the "winning team." National factors, such as Republican Party success in Congress beginning in the 1980s, pushed several incumbent southern legislators to switch from the Democratic to the Republican Party.[73] Between 2008 and 2013 in Texas alone, more than 200 Democrats at all levels of elected government switched to the Republican Party as the Democratic Party swung to the left and conservative Democrats felt left behind.[74] More recently, in 2018, Jefferson County judge Jeff Branick bolted to the Republican Party to run for his final term.[75]

Party switchers were mostly "WD-40s"—white Democrats over 40 years of age—who held onto their seats while fellow Democrats fell to Republican challengers.[76] Other officials found themselves in redrawn districts that would not elect a candidate from their party, prompting a switch. Corpus Christi Representative J. M. Lozano took the path of self-preservation by switching from the Democratic to the Republican Party in 2012 as his coastal district was redrawn to favor Republicans.[77] Happy to have another possible member, and a Hispanic lawmaker to boot, the Republican Party turned on the money spigot for Lozano, contributing more than $40,000 to his campaign.[78]

Does party switching change political voting habits? When Texas Representative Charlie Evans, who switched from the Democratic Party to the Republican Party in 1987, was asked about his party loyalty, he replied, "I'll probably be about as good a Republican as I was a Democrat."[79] Legislators often change their voting behavior to adhere to their new party's ideology, especially on votes on amendments and other procedural votes. Greater partisan

GREAT TEXAS POLITICAL DEBATES
Switching Parties

Switching parties, and the timing of it, can cause electoral problems, but it also poses ethical problems. In 1983, Phil Gramm, a former economics professor at Texas A&M University and Democratic member of the U.S. House, jumped from the donkey stables (Democrat) to the elephant pen (Republican). Observers noted that Gramm, who grew more unhappy with the Democrats' economic plans, "didn't quietly walk away from the Democratic Party in 1983; he gave it a kick in its smoldering ass and strutted into history." Gramm resigned his House seat and immediately re-filed to run as a Republican in the special election his resignation had created.[82]

Gramm's high-profile exit opened the door to more switching. Future governor Rick Perry turned Republican in 1989 as his views grew more conservative. Texas House Representative Allan Ritter joined the Republicans when he saw his district change: "I try to be what my district is," he explained as he gave Republicans a supermajority in 2010.[83] Texas House member Aaron Peña switched from the Democratic to the Republican Party immediately after his reelection in 2010, both because he felt that the Democratic Party had grown too liberal and for political survival. Peña remarked, "Somebody once told me that if you don't have a seat at the table, you may be on the menu."[84] Texas House Representative Bernard Erickson, hoping to avoid a primary challenge, switched to the Democratic Party. Erickson lost his reelection bid by 56 votes.[85] Judge Larry Meyers was a lifelong Republican but switched parties in 2013 citing the Republican Party's move too far to the right, only to be beaten in 2016.

SOCIAL RESPONSIBILITY: Is it ethical to switch parties?

YES: Politicians with credible and heartfelt core reasons to switch parties may be more able to survive political challenges than opportunistic politicians. Many officials legitimately gravitate to new issues, change their opinions on issues, or, as many claim, "the party leaves them" behind by taking on new, more extreme issues.

NO: Voters elect candidates because of their party label. The party platform tells a voter what that party (and candidate) stand for. Switching parties confuses voters and breaks the contract that elected officials have with the public.

MAYBE: The nature and timing of the switch matter. Candidates who get elected by one party and switch to another party hoodwink voters and leave the public with a fundamentally different elected official. Party switchers who switch before elections give voters an opportunity to reassess that candidate's qualities and value.

polarization increases pressure for new members to toe the party line, causing more extreme changes in their voting behavior.[80]

How does party switching impact electoral fortunes? Many of these party switchers do survive. Political scientists Christian Grose and Antoine Yoshinaka found that incumbents who switch parties receive a smaller share of the vote in the general election than before they switched, but that most switchers stay in office.[81]

🚩 TEXAS TAKEAWAYS

5.4.1 How do we define party competition?

5.4.2 What is the relationship between redistricting and party competition?

5.4.3 Since the 1980s, have more Democrats switched to the Republican Party or have more Republicans switched to the Democratic Party?

5.5 THIRD PARTIES AND INDEPENDENTS

Traditionally, the United States has had two major political parties. Why only two? Political scientists suggest that the structure of the electoral system is a major reason: a **winner-take-all election** in which the candidate who wins the most votes wins the seat. This is sometimes referred to as a "first past the post" system. In contrast, a proportional system elects several candidates—usually from a larger geographic area—based on the proportion of the vote won. So, if voters backed three parties equally in a geographic area represented by three elected officials, each party would have a representative in the government. Political scientist Maurice Duverger argued that winner-take-all systems generally lead to a two-party system because they encourage individuals and groups to band together to win that single seat. This is known as **Duverger's law**.

5.5 Evaluate the impact third parties have had on Texas party politics and the challenges they face.

winner-take-all election: whichever candidate wins the most votes wins the seat

Duverger's law: a winner-take-all electoral system generally leads to a two-party system

Several factors further obstruct the rise of independent and third-party candidates in Texas. Most voters are attached to the "name brand," or political platform, of one of the two major parties. They are less familiar with the names or platforms of the Christian Party, America's Party, or the None of the Above Party. The two major parties also have a significant head start on fundraising and can tap into a deep bench of donors. Furthermore, state laws set requirements that serve as obstacles for third parties and independent candidates. A new third party, for example, must create a state executive committee and establish procedures for governing the party meetings and selection of candidates. A new third party must also file a list of party participants with the secretary of state—and the number of participants must equal 1 percent of the total votes received by all candidates for governor in the most recent gubernatorial election. Furthermore, these participants must come from registered voters who did not vote in any other party's primary process, and that figure is currently 83,345. Once these requirements are met for the first time, a third party is then guaranteed an automatic slot on the ballot if the party received at least 2 percent of the vote in any statewide race, a threshold that reduced it from 5 percent, passed in 2019.[86] The Green Party will retroactively gain ballot access through 2026 because it obtained 2 percent in the statewide vote for Railroad Commissioner in 2016.

Still, though rare in Texas, third parties have upended state politics on occasion. These parties bring to light issues, such as underrepresentation of a minority, that have later been co-opted by major parties. Let's explore a few.

LA RAZA UNIDA PARTY

Unsettling the Democrats' hold on party politics in the 1970s was a social movement that grew into a political party called La Raza Unida (The People's Party). Reacting to a rule at Crystal City High School that mandated the homecoming queen be the daughter of a graduate (a transparent attempt to ensure the election of an Anglo), graduate student José Ángel Gutiérrez formed a group to protest. To capitalize on this organizational success, Gutiérrez and his allies formed La Raza Unida to break the Democrats' monopoly on local politics. The party gained control of the school board, the county court house, and the city council. As a separate political entity, La Raza Unida posed serious problems for Democrats as Mexican Americans began defecting to and voting for the new party.[87]

La Raza Unida candidate Ramsey Muñiz received more than 200,000 votes in the 1972 gubernatorial election, dangerously reducing Democrat Dolph Briscoe's margin to just under 100,000 votes. Although the La Raza Unida Party as a political power was in decline by the mid-1970s, the Democratic Party still viewed it as a threat. As Texas attorney general, Democrat John Hill led several investigations into the group's finances. The political payback was swift. La Raza Unida and allied groups partnered in the 1978 gubernatorial election to back Republican Bill Clements instead of the Democratic

Ramsey Muñiz ran again for governor in 1974, but as La Raza Unida waned in influence, he drew only half the votes (94,000) that he did in his historic 1972 run. His 1972 campaign for governor accelerated the inclusion of Latinos in Texas politics.

PERSONAL RESPONSIBILITY: **What role does your own race, ethnicity, religion, gender, or sexual orientation play in influencing which political party you support?**

nominee, John Hill. Clements ended up winning that race and became Texas's first Republican governor in 100 years.

The Democratic Party learned its lesson. In 1982, the liberal Democratic faction successfully courted the Hispanic vote and elected Democrat Mark White as governor. Inclusion of Mexican Americans in the Democratic Party did not occur on purpose; rather, it unfolded through "trench warfare" as former La Raza Unida members (running as Democrats) broke the Anglo hold on several counties.[88]

Women were also a key part of La Raza Unida's growth as a third party in the 1970s. Forming a caucus called Mujeres por La Raza Unida (Women for the People's Party), women served as organizers and often candidates when the men could not run for fear of retribution at work. Still, Latinas were excluded from the highest ranks of party leadership. At one meeting to express concern about the party's need to be inclusive of women's ideas, a young male shouted, "Why don't you go home to the dishes, where you belong?"[89] Over time, women like Virginia Múzquiz, who worked her way from county chair to state party chair, demonstrated that women could advance in the party.

LIBERTARIAN PARTY OF TEXAS

The Libertarian Party of Texas emphasizes liberty as its main philosophy, encouraging freedom of choice and emphasizing the importance of individual judgment. In practical terms, the party stands for a limited welfare state, free market economic principles, and small government, thus sharing the political values of fiscal conservatives within the Republican Party.

The Libertarian Party does not hold any state or federal offices at any level in Texas, but it does hold offices at the local level. Libertarians also peel off votes from other candidates, especially Republicans whose general philosophy they share. As a result, the Libertarian Party has played spoiler in swing districts.[90] In 2018, the impact of the Libertarian candidate was large enough to swing a State Board of Education race and a state representative race in west Houston to the Democrats.[91]

GREEN PARTY OF TEXAS

The Green Party of Texas emphasizes environmental justice, local control of communities, nonviolent resolution of disputes, and social justice. Specifically, the party supports public election financing in Texas, universal voter registration, universal health care, corporate income taxes in Texas, expanded use of medical marijuana, and abolishment of the death penalty. The Democratic Party—the major party ideologically closest to the Green Party—has been forced to adopt the main goals of its platform, including elements of the Green New Deal.

INDEPENDENTS

A Texan can run as an independent if he or she files a declaration to run. An independent candidate must then get signatures of registered voters that equal either 1 percent or 5 percent (depending on the office) of the total vote received by all candidates for governor in the most recent gubernatorial election in the district, county, or precinct sought. The signatures must also be from voters who did not vote in the primary of another party for that election cycle and can only be submitted between the end of major party primaries and the June deadline. Most independent candidates fail to gather enough signatures to be certified for the ballot. Electoral success is even more rare. In fact, until Laura Thompson from San Antonio won a 2016 special runoff election, no independent had won a statewide or legislative seat in Texas since 1936. In 2018, a total of 68 Texan independents ran for state and federal offices, up from 15 in 2016. Write-in candidates for statewide offices need 5,000 signatures, and state and federal legislative offices need the lesser of 500 signatures or 2 percent of the votes cast for governor in 2018.

Independent candidates can sap electoral support away from a majority party frontrunner. The wild 2006 gubernatorial race, for example, featured two independents, Carole "Grandma" Strayhorn and Richard "Kinky" Friedman, in addition to Democrat Chris Bell and incumbent Republican Governor Rick Perry. Strayhorn, a Republican and the state's comptroller of public accounts, was seen as a moderate alternative to Perry and styled herself "one tough grandma." Friedman was a cigar-chomping musician who quipped, "All I can say is thank God for bars and dance halls" where he found most of his signatures.[92] Perry won, but with only 39 percent of the electorate voting for him. These "kooky independents" revealed that populist candidates can pierce the one-party rule and even swing elections in some cases, often in local elections.[93]

 TEXAS TAKEAWAYS

5.5.1 What is the biggest impact of a winner-take-all election?

5.5.2 What requirements do third parties have to meet in order to be on the ballot?

⚘ THE INSIDER VIEW

The transition in Texas from a one-party Democratic state to a one-party Republican state involved a struggle over issues, ideology, and demographics. Republican Tom DeLay recalled that when he first ran for the Texas

House in 1978, a farmer was taken aback when informed that candidate DeLay was a Republican: "I want to tell you something, boy. It'll be a cold day in hell when a Republican wins this county."[94] DeLay not only won but went on to become Majority Leader in the U.S. House of Representatives, and Republicans dominate elected offices in the state today. What happened? National politics first shook the state party as the New Deal alienated economic conservatives, demographic change provided a foothold for the Republican Party, and then ideological division within the Democratic Party sent conservatives into the arms of the Republican Party. The Republican Party is as fragmented in the present, however, as the Democrats were in the past. Observers have argued that there are again three functional parties in Texas: the mainstream Republicans, the Democrats, and the Tea Party Republicans.

TEXAS TAKEAWAYS

5.1.1 Parties engage in three basic functions: assisting voters (parties-in-the-electorate), facilitating party goals (parties-as-organizations), and organizing government by structuring and controlling government (parties-in-government).

5.1.2 Partisans are the most strongly committed party loyalists and can be counted on to volunteer, donate money, and vote for the party's candidates.

5.2.1 The state party chair's primary responsibility is to develop and communicate the party's brand to the voters and to raise and manage political funds for the party at the state level.

5.2.2 A party platform is a list of values, beliefs, and policy issues that are endorsed and supported by a political party. It serves as a road map for the party during elections and in agenda setting.

5.3.1 Democrats won all the congressional seats in 1871, took majority control of the state legislature in 1872, and easily won the governorship in 1873. Observers point to December 2, 1997, as the day the Democratic Party in Texas collapsed.

5.3.2 The Democrats were divided along ideological grounds. Republicans began to see federal intervention as a primary cause of economic troubles. The growth of the suburbs gave rise to new conservatives. Residents arriving from other states did not have the same attachments to the Democratic Party as long-term Texans had.

5.3.3 The Tea Party reached national prominence when it held a series of rallies in 2009 in response to the Obama administration's economic recovery plans and the Affordable Care Act.

5.4.1 Party competition is defined as the relative electoral success between the parties.

5.4.2 Gerrymandered district lines drawn over time lead to "safe" seats where one party or the other dominates, given the voters stacked into a district. This tends to reduce party competition.

5.4.3 More Democrats have switched to the Republican Party since the 1980s.

5.5.1 One winner generally leads to a two-party system because individuals and groups band together to win that single available seat.

5.5.2 A third party must create a state executive committee, establish procedures for governing the party meetings and selection of candidates, and file a list of party participants with the secretary of state.

KEY TERMS

conservative
decentralization
Duverger's law
gerrymander
Legislative Redistricting Board
liberal
New Deal
partisans
party competition
party platform
reapportionment
redistricting
winner-take-all election

PRACTICE QUIZ

1. Strongly committed members of a political party are called . . .
   a. Polarizers
   b. Blue dog Democrats
   c. RINOs
   d. Partisans

2. Which of the following are not formal positions in the party organization?
   a. State representatives
   b. Precinct chairs
   c. State party chair
   d. Party executive committee members

3. Between the years 1952 and 2015, in what decade did the number of affiliated Republicans FIRST surpass the number of affiliated Democrats in Texas?
   a. 1960
   b. 1980

   c. 1990
   d. 2010

4. On average, what percentage of women believe the Republican Party is welcoming in 2019?
   a. 5–15 percent
   b. 20–30 percent
   c. 40–50 percent
   d. 80–90 percent

5. What percentage of votes are third parties required to achieve on a statewide election for their candidates to continue to appear on ballots?
   a. 2 percent
   b. 5 percent
   c. 7 percent
   d. 10 percent

6. Which of the following factors did NOT contribute to the declining power of the Democratic Party?
   a. Party switching
   b. Suburban growth
   c. Newcomers to the state
   d. Growth of the Green Party

7. Political parties are organizations of individuals who aggregate political and policy interests for their members.
   a. True
   b. False

8. Democrats currently dominate the Texas political landscape.
   a. True
   b. False

9. The term "WD-40" in the context of political party switchers refers to white Democrats over 40 years of age.

    a. True
    b. False

10. Third parties have a strong presence in Texas politics.

    a. True
    b. False

[Answer Key: D, A, C, B, A, D, A, B, A, B]

Learn more with this chapter's digital tools, including the Oxford Insight Study Guide, at www.oup.com/he/Rottinghaus3e.

6 INTEREST GROUPS

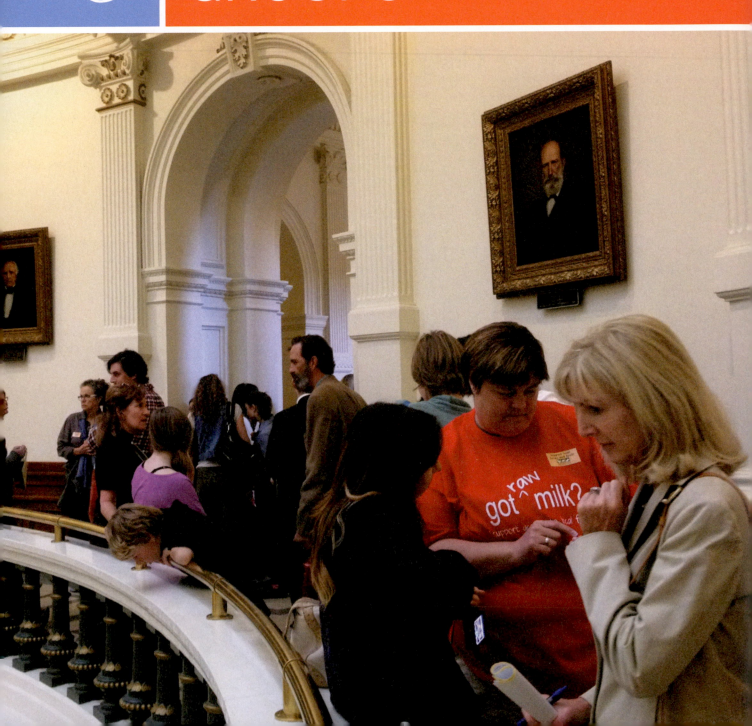

In 1989, Governor Bill Clements called a special session of the Texas legislature on workers' compensation. At issue was legislation that would force workers to negotiate with employers prior to accessing their right to a jury trial. This change to workers' compensation would limit the number of cases that went to a jury and save business interests millions of dollars each year.

The legislature was deadlocked. Early in the session, Lonnie "Bo" Pilgrim, a big Republican donor and the founder and chairman of the Pilgrim's Pride Corporation based in Pittsburg, Texas, roamed the floor of the Texas Senate. His chicken empire was the largest poultry processing firm in the nation at the time, and he had a keen interest in the outcome of the legislation: worker claims had cost his business millions of dollars annually. Pilgrim sidled up to several legislators, handing out $10,000 checks and bluntly explaining, "We need some help." Pilgrim left the payee's name blank on checks he gave to nine members in the two days before the state senate's vote on the workers' compensation bill. Several legislators quickly returned the checks, but one accepted because Pilgrim was a "long-time friend," one angrily refused and escorted Pilgrim out of his office, and several did not make up their minds.[1]

Word reached Lieutenant Governor Bill Hobby in his capitol office, and Hobby reported the incident to the Travis County district attorney. Calling the act "outrageous," the district attorney nevertheless indicated that "[i]n Texas, it's almost impossible to

LEARNING OBJECTIVES

6.1 Explain the theories that describe the role of interest groups in Texas.

6.2 Assess the incentives for individuals to join interest groups.

6.3 Identify the types of interest groups in Texas.

6.4 Describe the types of activities interest groups engage in to pursue their agendas.

6.5 Explain what lobbying is and how lobbyists serve the interests of those involved.

6.6 Illustrate the role of scandals in shaping interest group politics and reform efforts.

6.7 Outline the ways the state oversees the interactions of interest groups and state officials.

● Lobbyists at the State Capitol spend much of the legislative session monitoring the progress of legislation, reviewing proposed agency rules, talking to legislative staff, and educating members on the pros and cons of legislation. Large groups are thought to have the most sway, but grassroots lobbying from smaller organizations like the Farm and Ranch Alliance, which advocates for independent farmers, ranchers, and livestock owners, can find legislative success on the right issues.

interest groups: formal organizations of individuals or groups that seek to influence government to promote their common cause

bribe a public official as long as you report it." Pilgrim emphatically denied the checks were bribes: They were standard lobby practice, he claimed.[2] The bill failed to pass, as Pilgrim had wanted, but the incident hurt the credibility of the business interests.

The episode also spurred the legislature to pass a series of new campaign finance laws. One of these laws prohibits lawmakers from accepting campaign contributions while the legislature is in session, and another restricts accepting contributions inside the Capitol building.

The affair also highlights the role of **interest groups** in influencing the policy process. "For virtue," wrote journalist Molly Ivins, "try Minnesota."[3] Yet, one businessperson does not necessarily dominate the process, for interest groups do not always go unopposed in Texas. The scuffles between two or more interest groups shape both policy and the political process—as we just saw with the legislation that followed the Bo Pilgrim incident. Interest groups also serve important functions within Texas society and government. As a long-time Texas lobbyist once said, the negative attention on interest groups overshadows the positive role that they play in representing the public's interest—"[i]f you're a florist, you think, 'thank goodness for the Texas State Florists' Association's lobbyist.'"[4]

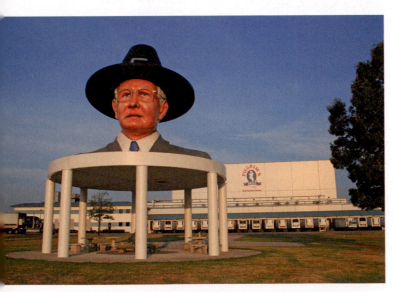

Bust of Bo Pilgrim a few miles down the road from his massive estate, Cluckingham Palace. Though famous for his chicken empire, Pilgrim's legacy will live on in the reforms that followed his lobbying efforts.

CRITICAL THINKING: How should Texas regulate the influx of money from business interests into the political system?

Interest groups attempt to influence government for the benefit of their members through legislation, rules, or actions that are aligned with their cause. A successful interest group has the ability both to get things done and to keep things from getting done. In this chapter, we explore the types of interest groups, the functions they serve, and the role they play in the policymaking process. We discover how interest groups sometimes become too influential, requiring oversight and regulation through various state agencies. Moments of crisis, as in the Bo Pilgrim example, reveal the ongoing struggle to police interest groups and ensure they play a role that strengthens, rather than weakens, democracy in Texas.

Ⓤ 6.1 INTEREST GROUPS IN THE POLITICAL PROCESS

At the birth of this country, the founders had a vision for the role that organized interests might play in the political process. In *Federalist Paper 10*, founding father James Madison referred to the undue influence of powerful interest groups as the "mischief of factions," but he argued that multiple competing interests would reduce this mischief. In other words, one group checks the influence of another. In practice, however, the imbalance of power may allow some groups to have greater influence.

6.1 Explain the theories that describe the role of interest groups in Texas.

Political scientists have advanced several theories to explore the role of interest groups in American democracy today, including the pluralist theory, elite theory, and transactional theory.

PLURALIST THEORY

Scholars writing in the 1950s and 1960s developed **pluralist theory**. Similar to Madison's vision, this theory views competition among many groups as keeping any one group from exercising too much control over policy.[5]

We can find examples of pluralism among the political struggles in Texas. The legislature created the Texas Windstorm Insurance Association (TWIA), a public–private agency, in 1971 to provide insurance for costal residents. TWIA was the only option many of these residents had to get necessary insurance for their properties, especially after several major hurricanes. In 2017, two powerhouse interest groups, Texans for Lawsuit Reform and the Texas Trial Lawyers Association, went to war against each other when the Texas legislature tried to change the way TWIA handled the claims process. The two groups battled over liability issues and "venue shopping." When the dust settled, the law that passed created a more difficult route to the courthouse for claimants: It made it harder to name adjusters and agents as defendants, and it lowered the penalty on companies that denied or underpaid a claim. However, the outcome was not all bad for the Texas Trial Lawyers Association. The law also allowed consumers to sue insurance companies if the firms did not settle a legitimate claim "fairly and timely."[6] This compromise suggests that the pluralist theory can be applied to understand the role of interest groups in policymaking.

Sometimes, however, even billionaires lose. In 2017, Warren Buffett, one of the wealthiest men on the planet, needed a regulatory fix (a "carve out") to alter Texas law and allow him to own both a vehicle manufacturer and auto dealerships inside the Lone Star State. Citizen activists got wind of the "Buffett Bill" and launched a phone campaign that killed the bill "dead as a hammer." Tea Party leader JoAnn Fleming said the bill pitted wealthy business interests against grassroots Texans and that "we won this one."[7]

pluralist theory: the theory that competition keeps powerful interest groups in check and that no single group dominates

ELITE THEORY

elite theory: groups with greater resources are in a better position to accomplish their goals

Not all scholars accept pluralist theory. Political scientist E. E. Schattschneider famously articulated that "[t]he flaw in the pluralist heaven is that the heavenly chorus sings with a strong upper-class accent."[8] According to the **elite theory** that he and others advanced, groups with greater resources are in a better position to accomplish their goals. Sociologist C. Wright Mills suggested that this power elite is drawn from high-ranking government officials and major corporate owners.

Examples of elite theory in Texas politics abound. In the 2011 legislative session, for instance, the legislature passed a bill requiring disclosure of the names of chemicals used to extract natural gas from the ground (fracking), but lobbying from industry groups postponed the disclosure for 2 years and allowed certain operators not to disclose certain chemicals by declaring them trade secrets.[9] Was it in the best interests of the people of Texas to protect these trade secrets? Or was this undue influence by the oil and gas industry? Former member of the Texas House of Representatives Mike Martin put it this way: "There's the Texas Chemical Council; there's the oil and gas interests; there's the electrical utility industry; there's the hazardous waste interests—that's four right there. The amount of money they have pumped into the legislature is phenomenal. And when those issues come up, straight up, those guys, the big guys, win all the time."[10]

transactional theory: the theory that public policy is bought and sold like a commodity to the highest bidder

Interest groups sometimes arise when major events call attention to an issue. The death of Houston native George Floyd while in police custody in Minneapolis, Minnesota, for example, sparked protests from multiple groups in many cities in Texas. Some of these groups are transitory, while others persist over time.

SOCIAL RESPONSIBILITY: **Do small interest groups have enough sway in Texas politics? Does protest politics change policy? What should be done to make sure the people have a voice in the democratic process?**

TRANSACTIONAL THEORY

An extension of the power elite theory is **transactional theory**. This theory proposes that public policy is bought and sold like a commodity to the highest bidder. For example, lobbyists for Handy, an app-based cleaning and maintenance company, leaned on the Texas Workforce Commission Chair to draft new marketplace contractor rules, specifying that temporary employees for businesses like Uber, Lyft, and PostMate should be exempted from payments into the states' unemployment insurance fund.[11] Of the nine rules the agency proposed to label employees "independent contractors," seven were lifted almost entirely verbatim from suggested language provided to the commission by the group's lobbyists.[12] State lobbying disclosures show that Handy began lobbying the workforce commission in 2017, which was not disclosed until the media exposed it, to classify workers who get hired for on-demand work as independent contractors.[13] The commission denied it was influenced by this lobbying and says the rule is in response to a changing workplace.

WHICH THEORY FITS TEXAS?

Which theory best explains how interest groups influence policy in Texas: pluralist, elite, or transactional theory? Perhaps all three. And it depends on the circumstances. For example, political scientists have found that transactional theory and elite theory might explain the policymaking process at the state level, where legislatures have significant authority and oversight is modest.[14] For cases in which two powerful interest groups vie for different policy outcomes, however, or for cases that enjoy a high degree of public attention, pluralist theory might provide a better explanation.

 TEXAS TAKEAWAYS

6.1.1 What do interest groups do?

6.1.2 Explain the differences between pluralist and elite theories.

6.1.3 What is transactional theory?

6.2 WHY JOIN INTEREST GROUPS

private interest groups: groups that advocate for the benefit of their members

For our democracy to move toward the pluralist ideal envisioned by James Madison and other founders, individuals and groups must be motivated to join interest groups. **Private interest groups**, like labor unions, advocate for the benefit of their members. **Public interest groups** benefit the public in general, such as all Gulf Coast residents, all Texans, or all Americans. However, interest groups, especially those devoted to solving shared problems, suffer from the **free rider problem**. Let's take a closer look at this problem and some solutions.

> **6.2** Assess the incentives for individuals to join interest groups.

public interest groups: groups that benefit the public in general

free rider problem: a situation in which individuals benefit from a publicly provided good or service without paying for it and actively supporting its acquisition

THE FREE RIDER PROBLEM

Many interest groups work to solve collective action problems—that is, problems that are shared by a large group of people. You want clean air, more efficient government, or expanded civil rights? Dozens of organizations are

The Texas National Rifle Association advocates for open carry laws, but it also provides members with discounts on car rentals, legal consultation, the opportunity to purchase rare firearms, and contributions to student scholarship funds.

PERSONAL RESPONSIBILITY: **What kinds of organizations have you joined because of the benefits you received? Would you have joined them without the offer of these benefits?**

working to ensure this goal. But why should you join if they'll do the work without your help? Free riders are people who receive the benefits without paying the cost. For example, the group Texas Campaign for the Environment advocates for curbside composting, battery recycling, firmer enforcement of oil and gas regulations, and other environmental protections. Do you enjoy a good environment with clean air and water? If so—and if you are not a member of this or a similar interest group that has worked for these policies—then you are a free rider.

Don't feel bad. You are not alone. Economist Mancur Olson famously argued in his book *The Logic of Collective Action* that it is rational for individuals to leave solving the problem to others and reap the benefit without having paid the cost of participation. The end result, however, is that interest groups pursuing altruistic, public goals often have a harder time acquiring the resources to be successful compared with interest groups that pursue narrower, more selfish goals. Interest groups thus provide incentives for participation that help overcome the free rider problem.

SELECTIVE BENEFITS

selective benefits: private goods made available to people who organize for a collective good

One way to solve the free rider problem is by providing **selective benefits** (or incentives) to people who organize for a collective good. These benefits can be material, solidary, or purposive.

Material benefits are tangible rewards, generally monetary, such as wages, fringe benefits, or patronage. For example, the Texas Public Employees Association is a nonpartisan organization that advocates for higher wages and better health and retirement benefits for state employees. Members also receive discounted tickets to Texas Rangers games and Six Flags Over Texas amusement parks.[15]

Solidary benefits are intangible rewards from joining a group, such as social status or social interactions with like-minded people. Do you live in a big city and sometimes feel like you are stuck in a giant concrete jungle? The Dallas Downriver Club or the Adventure Club of San Antonio gives you the opportunity to enjoy outdoor activities and to socialize with people with similar interests.

Often, Texans join an interest group to serve a cause. Groups like Texas Right to Life or Planned Parenthood Texas take opposing views of abortion, but both advance the cause their members care about. The satisfaction that members feel when working with a group to realize their political values is called a purposive benefit.

 TEXAS TAKEAWAYS

6.2.1 How is the free rider problem associated with interest groups?

6.2.2 What kinds of benefits might interest groups offer to encourage people to join?

6.3 TYPES OF INTEREST GROUPS

Are you a member of an interest group? You might be and not even realize it. If you are part of a business group, trade association, professional organization, or labor union, you are a member of an economic interest group. You might also be a member of a noneconomic group, such as a public interest group like the Sierra Club or a single-issue group like the San Antonio Humane Society. Let's take a closer look at some of your options.

> **6.3** Identify the types of interest groups in Texas.

BUSINESS GROUPS

If you are a small-business owner, you might be a member of the Chamber of Commerce. Individual businesses and organizations representing many businesses often advocate on behalf of their own interests—and sometimes battle each other. For example, ahead of the last three legislative sessions, Tesla Motors, a maker of electric cars, unleashed a powerful group of lobbyists in Texas. Their goal: to persuade lawmakers to allow Tesla to bypass auto dealerships and sell electric cars in Texas directly to the public. Unlike other automakers, Tesla sells its cars directly to consumers but is prohibited from doing so in Texas. A dealership can make between 400 and several thousand dollars per car sold, however, and auto dealerships in Texas are organized into an interest group. In fact, the Texas Automobile Dealers Association has gained serious political influence over the decades, and deep-pocketed car franchise owners are also often big campaign contributors.[16] So, despite spending almost $1.2 million in 5 years, Tesla failed. Governor Greg Abbott shut the garage door on Tesla, insisting that the state would not carve out a loophole to allow Tesla to sell cars directly to the public.[17]

Political scientists have found that business lobbies prevail mainly on issues that are important only to a single company or industry because these usually attract little media coverage.[18] Because they may consist of a small regulatory change, these victories can often be hidden from public view or ignored. Yet these changes may supply a significant financial benefit to industry groups.

TRADE ASSOCIATIONS AND PROFESSIONAL ORGANIZATIONS

You might also be a member of an interest group because of the job you have. Trade associations serve the interests of an industry, such as farmers, locksmiths, or realtors. Professional organizations are groups that represent a specific occupation. For example, among the most powerful groups in the state are the Texas Trial Lawyers Association, the Texas Medical Association, the Texas Association of Realtors, and the Texas State Teachers Association. These groups represent tens of thousands of industry professionals and millions of dollars in political contributions. Considering their strength, trade associations are frequently successful in the legislature.

LABOR UNIONS

Organized labor first entered Texas politics in the early 1900s as the oil and manufacturing boom drew new workers into the state. After World War II, organized labor emerged as a powerhouse, backing winning candidates in several Democratic primary races, including Senator Ralph Yarborough's successful races for the U.S. Senate in the 1950s and 1960s. An endorsement by labor unions meant not only funding but also "boots on the ground" to walk neighborhoods and get out the vote.

Organized labor's position has declined in the last few decades. Texas is a "right to work" state, which means an employee can decide whether or not to join a union. In other states, all employees in certain professions like electricians and construction workers are required to join unions when they get the job. Due to outsourcing, downsizing, and contracting out, union membership has tapered off. Fewer than 5 percent of workers in Texas are unionized today (see Figure 6.1).

Skilled labor is more organized than less skilled labor. Why? Skilled labor, like electricians organized by the International Brotherhood of Electrical Workers, has a well-defined constituency and specific interests on a range of policy issues. Groups dedicated to lower-wage workers, such as janitors, cleaners, or fast-food workers, are not often organized by occupation.[19]

IDENTITY GROUPS

Identity groups represent the interests of specific groups based on such aspects as race, ethnicity, religion, age, sexual orientation, gender, or income. These identity groups form in part because they have been ill served

IS IT BIGGER IN TEXAS?

FIGURE 6.1 Rates of Union Membership

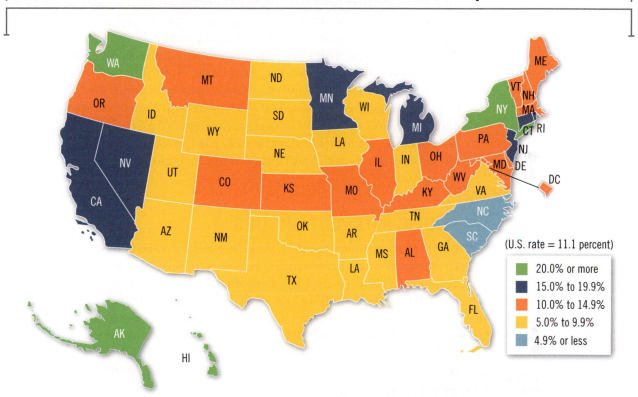

(U.S. rate = 11.1 percent)

- 20.0% or more
- 15.0% to 19.9%
- 10.0% to 14.9%
- 5.0% to 9.9%
- 4.9% or less

Source: U.S. Bureau of Labor Statistics, 2018 annual averages of union rates as a percentage of the employed population

 COMMUNICATION:

Which states have more union members?

- Southern states, like Texas, Arkansas, South Carolina, and North Carolina, have lower unionization rates than other states.
- States with stable agricultural economies, like California, Washington, and some of the upper plains states, have more union members.
- States whose economies rely on manufacturing, like Michigan, Ohio, and New Jersey, have more unionized workers.

 CRITICAL THINKING:

Why are union rates lower in some states than other states?

- Texas, like other southern states, allows workers to choose to join a union, while other states like New York require union membership.
- Recent employment gains in construction and agriculture in states like Michigan and Nevada have increased their union participation rates.
- Growth in hospitality and construction trades has boosted New York to the highest unionization rates in the country.

by the two major political parties or because they feel underrepresented by the electoral system.[20] The National Council of La Raza, the Texas National Association for the Advancement of Colored People (NAACP), the Bangladesh Association of North Texas, and other identity groups make up a small share of the total number of organized interest groups, but they can be influential in state politics. The most pronounced success of these organizations comes in following up on the victories of a social movement through lobbying, litigation, or government monitoring.[21] Building on the fight for bilingual education during the civil rights movements of the 1960s and 1970s, for example, Latino groups challenging the "No Spanish" in public schools rule successfully advocated for legislation at the federal and state levels to improve education among native Spanish speakers. Student groups, the Mexican American Legal Defense Fund, and the League of United Latin American Citizens continue to pursue their agendas in the courts today.[22]

PUBLIC INTEREST GROUPS

Public interest groups focus on providing quality collective goods, such as environmental protections, natural resource conservation, or consumer safety. Texans for Public Justice advocates for more efficient and transparent government. The group monitors and reports on campaign financing and has filed more than two dozen actions with the Texas Ethics Commission since the group's formation in 1997. Their complaints have led to indictments against former U.S. House Majority Leader Tom DeLay, Governor Rick Perry, and Attorney General Ken Paxton.[23]

SINGLE-ISSUE GROUPS

Are you a member of the National Rifle Association or an animal rights group? Single-issue groups like these are interest groups dedicated to one specific issue, often ideological. The issue of abortion, for example, remains a contentious political issue. Two single-issue groups on each side of the issue in Texas regularly go to battle. Pro-Choice Texas fights for policies that guarantee reproductive rights as well as short- and long-term contractive methods, whereas Texas Alliance for Life advocates for the rights of the unborn and the protection of life from the moment of conception until natural death. The groups clashed in the 2019 legislation session over a bill that would impose criminal penalties on doctors who fail to treat babies born alive

Run out of a basement office in Austin by Craig McDonald, Texans for Public Justice adopted a "no frills" approach that underscores their interest in good government and public disclosure of political financial information. Says McDonald of his office, which has three employees, one intern, and a budget of $250,000: "Once a year, I bring in cookies, but that's about it."[24]

after failed abortion attempts. This is a rare event and unnecessary according to pro-choice groups, but it is a "line in the sand" for pro-life groups.[25] The governor signed the measure into law.

GOVERNMENT INTERESTS

Local, state, or even national governments often seek the assistance of other governments to advance their goals. State government attempts to influence the federal government. Political scientist Kay Schlozman argues that because the national government often ties financial support to regulations, state and local governments have an incentive to organize to express their collective interest.[26] Texas has acted both alone and together with other states to persuade the U.S. Congress to enact policies such as expanding transportation funding or easing regulations on carbon emissions. Local government also tries to influence the state government. The City of Houston, for example, lobbied state officials to reform the city's pension obligations, which the state, not the city, controls.[27]

 TEXAS TAKEAWAYS

6.3.1 Which type of interest group serves the interests of a group of specific industries?

6.3.2 What is the primary characteristic of single-issue groups?

6.3.3 Explain the differences between government interest groups and public interest groups.

6.4 WHAT INTEREST GROUPS DO

Interest groups have a range of resources and strategies available to them. Political scientist Amitai Etzioni calls interest groups that represent a broad base of individuals and address a wide range of issues constituency-representing organizations. Their size alone can make these organizations powerful players on the policymaking scene. Other interest groups are small but have access to significant funding. However, interest groups access many resources—membership, funding, leadership, skills—to pursue a menu of tactics to achieve their goals. Political scientists Frank Baumgartner and Bryan Jones argue that interest groups engage in "venue shopping,"[28] looking for opportunities and tactics that will be most persuasive. In this section, we examine many of these tactics.

> **6.4** Describe the types of activities interest groups engage in to pursue their agendas.

EDUCATION

Ever pick up a voter information pamphlet at a laundromat or coffee shop? You might have noticed a logo with the words "The League of Women Voters of Texas." The League provides details about current elections, researches issues important to Texans, and lets you know where candidates stand on issues—without endorsing a party or candidate. Interest groups often reach out and educate their members or the public at large. They also develop policy and research expertise that makes them useful partners in understanding specific issues.

CITIZEN CAMPAIGNS

When Republican Governor Greg Abbott issued orders requiring Texans to stay at home amidst the outbreak of COVID-19, dozens of people took to the streets of Austin—some with red Trump hats but few with masks—to protest what they called an overreaction of fear and an overreach of government power[29]. Interest groups like the "You Can't Close America" rally often use people power to get their message across. **Grassroots lobbying** involves getting members of the general public who are interested in an issue to contact elected officials in order to persuade them on an issue. On most any day you visit the Texas Capitol, you will see an individual or groups outside protesting a government decision or proclaiming their positions on a range of issues. Group members may also call, e-mail, or meet with members of the legislature. For example, if a funding issue jeopardizes a popular school program in a small town in the middle of the state, the Texas State Teachers' Association can have hundreds of activated residents, upon command, flood the legislature with angry letters or show up at lawmakers' offices in Austin.[30]

Not all grass in the grassroots is real, however. Savvy public relations experts can make issue advocacy appear as though it originated from the bottom up when in reality it masks corporate interests. This is referred to as **AstroTurf lobbying**, named after the artificial grass used in Houston's Astrodome. AstroTurf lobbying often takes the form of an "inspired" letter or social media campaign that is in fact manufactured by an organized interest. Texas Senator Lloyd Bentsen coined the term in response to an outpouring of similarly worded letters favoring the insurance

grassroots lobbying: getting members of the general public who are interested in an issue to contact elected officials in order to persuade them on an issue

AstroTurf lobbying: manufacturing public support and making it appear as though it was inspired organically by a swell of public opinion

Members of a disability rights group rally outside the office of Governor Greg Abbott in support of raising the minimum wage for home care attendants. The proposed budget boosted their wage, but only by 10 cents.

industry. Bentsen noted, "A fellow from Texas can tell the difference between grass roots and AstroTurf."[31]

An AstroTurf lobbying campaign is only as effective as it is stealthy. In 2017, State Representative Drew Springer became suspicious when his office fielded 520 constituent letters from his rural district advocating for school vouchers, a policy most of his district opposed. All of the letters had an unknown Austin address, far from his district home in Muenster, and had the name of the constituent at the bottom. Several other legislators received the letters as well. Representative Springer's office started making calls to these letter writers—no one seemed to know where the letters originated, and none agreed with the positions. One letter was from a former state legislator who indicated, "I don't believe in vouchers of any kind. It ought to be illegal . . . representing me for something I have no interest in supporting or helping."[32] An organization called Texans for Education Opportunity claimed credit and argued they followed the rules, but several legislators have asked local district attorneys to investigate.[33]

ELECTIONEERING

Interest groups also promote their agenda through **electioneering**. Generally, electioneering involves advertising (radio, mail, Internet, or television) for or against issues or candidates, granting endorsements, and raising funds. Endorsements from influential groups serve as a cue for voters about where candidates stand on issues (see Figure 6.2).

electioneering: advertising (radio, mail, Internet, or television) for or against issues or candidates, granting endorsements, and raising funds

Interest groups often donate to a politician's campaign by hosting a fundraiser, bundling contributions from several individuals, or "buying a table" at an event where ticket purchases are funneled into candidate fundraising accounts. Interest groups contribute funds by setting up political action committees (or PACs). Interest groups also vet candidates to determine whether they support or oppose the issues of the group. As one veteran lobbyist representing the powerful Wholesale Beer Distributors of Texas explained, when someone becomes a candidate, the question the lobbyist asks is "Does he drink an occasional beer or is he high tenor in the Baptist Church choir who denounces demon rum every Sunday?"[35] Frequently, however, interest groups give funds to candidates from both parties to "hedge their bets," particularly in close electoral races.

Most scholars find mixed results with respect to spending by interest groups in campaigns, but the consensus is that electioneering can lead to positive outcomes under certain conditions. Campaign donations facilitate access for lobbyists to legislators.[36] As predicted by pluralist theory, however, and as with any interest group tactic, electioneering becomes less effective when more interest groups with opposing interests become involved in the political process or when the private issues an interest group is concerned with attract public attention.

According to former Democratic House Speaker Bill Clayton, "If you give $100 to a candidate running for office and somebody else gives $50,000, who's going to have that open door policy a little better?"[37] Yet, this access does not always mean members of the legislature will vote the way of the special

FIGURE 6.2 Endorsement Success in 2020 Republican Primaries

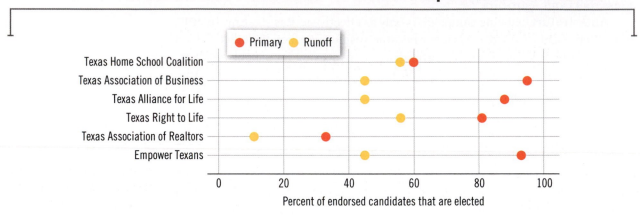

Source: Author-compiled data

COMMUNICATION:

Which groups endorsed best?[34]

- In the primary, the groups with the highest rate of successful endorsements were the Texas Right to Life, the Empower Texans, the Texas Association of Business, and the Texas Alliance for Life.

- Some groups, such as Empower Texans, the Texas Right to Life, and the Texas Association of Business, were somewhat effective in the primary but were less successful in the runoff.

CRITICAL THINKING:

Why the variation in success rates?

- The most broadly conservative (religiously oriented and Tea Party-based or business groups) groups appear to had the most sway with Republican voters. The broad ideological signal of these groups was influential for Republican primary voters.

- Groups with narrower political interests, such as the Texas Home School Coalition, had stronger endorsement success in the runoff because they had a focused set of issues to target supportive legislators and mobilize Republican voters.

interest. Former Democratic Texas House Representative Robert Early noted that a lobbyist for "the Texas Chemical Council helped me when I first got elected, and later sent a message that I wasn't doing very well for him once I was in office. And I sent a message back that I couldn't care less. I found that to be kind of bold and brazen. S—t, I was going to do what I wanted."[38]

LOBBYING THE COURTS, THE LEGISLATURE, AND THE EXECUTIVE BRANCH

Interest groups directly lobby all three branches of government, including the courts, which are also part of the policymaking process. Interest groups may file lawsuits or briefs to challenge policies that impact their members. The Institute for Justice, joined by three Texas craft brewers, claimed that the Texas Alcoholic Beverage Commission was "stifling the Texas craft beer renaissance." They filed a suit against the commission for prohibiting brewers from charging beer distributors a fee for the right to sell their beer.[39] The beer industry won the case in 2016 when a state judge struck down the law.

Interest groups also file **amicus curiae briefs**—literally, "friend of the court" briefs—when they have relevant opinions or information pertinent to a case that affects their interests, even if they are not directly part of the case. In 2018, for example, the Supreme Court of Texas met to consider whether or not the city of Laredo could ban single-use plastic bags. Several organizations filed briefs in favor and against the restriction. The conservative economic-focused Texas Public Policy Foundation argued that state law cannot prohibit retailers from providing such bags. The Turtle Island Restoration Network supported the city due to environmental hazards the bags pose to native sea turtles.[40] The court found that the bag ban conflicted with state law and struck it down.

Interest groups can also hire lobbyists to communicate directly with the Texas legislature or the executive branch to influence policy. We discuss this strategy in-depth in the next section.

> **amicus curiae briefs:** a legal filing with relevant opinions or information pertinent to a case that affects a group's interests, even if the group is not directly part of the case

★ TEXAS TAKEAWAYS

6.4.1 What is AstroTurf lobbying?

6.4.2 What types of activities characterize electioneering?

> **lobbying:** direct communications with members of the legislative or executive branch of government to influence legislation or administrative action

6.5 LOBBYING: THE THIRD HOUSE

When Andrew Jackson, "the people's president," first took office, Americans who were not allowed in the U.S. House or Senate chamber poured into the lobby of the White House to ply the president with their requests, hence the term **lobbying**. Lobbying is pervasive in Texas. During a single legislative session alone, 1.8 million pieces of unique communication flow into the Capitol—enough to fill more than 22 Dallas Cowboy football stadiums.[41] Lobbyists in Texas are often called the "Third House," the other two being the state house and state senate. In the

> **6.5** Explain what lobbying is and how lobbyists serve the interests of those involved.

1930s, the legislature considered requiring lobbyists to wear uniforms so that they could be easily spotted, but the measure was laughed down.[42]

THE ROLE OF LOBBYISTS

As the Texas economy grows and lawmakers deal with increasingly complicated and diverse issues, more and more lobbyists file into Austin to meet with government agencies, state senators and representatives, and their staff (see Figure 6.3).

FIGURE 6.3   Number of Lobbyists in Texas

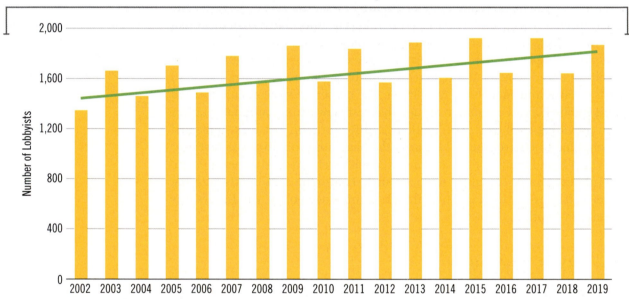

Source: Texas Ethics Commission annual reports. Line represents a predicted linear fit of the trend.

 COMMUNICATION:

How many lobbyists are there in Texas?

- The number of registered lobbyists has increased steadily over the past decade and a half.
- The number of lobbyists grew from 1,560 in 1999 to 1,928 in 2017, dropped back down to 1,644 in 2018, and rose again in 2019 to 1,870.

 CRITICAL THINKING:

Why have these numbers increased?

- Years in which the legislature is in session (every odd-numbered year) generate more lobbying and more lobbyists. The number of registered lobbyists is higher in those years.
- The growth in the Texas economy, the expansion of the bureaucracy, and the regulation of industry in the state produce more issues on which groups may wish to lobby.

Lobbying doesn't stop in the state's capital city. When Texas A&M played Prairie View A&M, Governor Abbott, Representative Dennis Bonnen, and State Senator Juan "Chuy" Hinjosa were invited to witness the Aggie's spectacular 67–0 win. Institutions of higher education host alumni, legislators, and community leaders. "We're proud to have them," according to Texas A&M Chancellor John Sharp, himself a former legislator. These suites showcase autographed helmets, socializing with donors and decision makers, and a buffet-style catering including a "12th man dip" made with jalapeno bacon.

Individual lobbyists or organizations that employ lobbyists (law firms or other interest groups) must file reports specifying the type of lobbying in which they engage. In 2019, more lobbyists worked on behalf of economic interests than on social issues (see Figure 6.4). To better understand the role lobbyists play in economic and social policymaking, we now look at what they do and how they work with government to influence policies.

WHAT LOBBYISTS DO

With the crack of the gavel convening the new legislative session, lobbyists begin the endless round of gratuities. They chat up the staff, offer to buy senators or representatives lunch or drinks, backslap those who respond to flattery, and keep a respectful distance from fiercely independent legislators.[43] Lobbyists make themselves essential to legislators by seeing to their needs, whether it is to run messages, obtain legal expertise, or just tell a good joke on a gloomy morning.

Shape Legislation. Lobbyists help shape legislation by bringing issues and possible solutions to the attention of legislators and by providing research, technical knowledge, legal expertise, and ideas. The American Legislative Exchange Council, a conservative pro-business group, has contributed ideas to dozens of bill in Texas, such as voter ID laws and "loser pays" rules to put limits on frivolous lawsuits.[44] Lobbyists may also encourage legislators to water down enforcement mechanisms and design rules that favor the group's interests. Self-described "mad moms in minivans" formed Texans for Vaccine Choice to advocate for the right to opt out of vaccinations, which they view as linked to autism despite research the Centers for Disease Control and Prevention has presented to the contrary. The group didn't score many major legislative wins, but it did get legislators to back off legislation that made it harder to opt out of vaccinations.[45]

Testify at Hearings. Lobbyists (or those they coach) often testify at hearings on legislation as a way to advocate for or against an issue. Testimony at hearings rarely changes votes, but it does allow a group's position to attract media attention, transmit information to legislators, and—importantly—impress the group's membership.[46]

In the 2017 legislative session, a bill was introduced to require Texas vineyards to make sure that 100 percent of the grapes used for winemaking

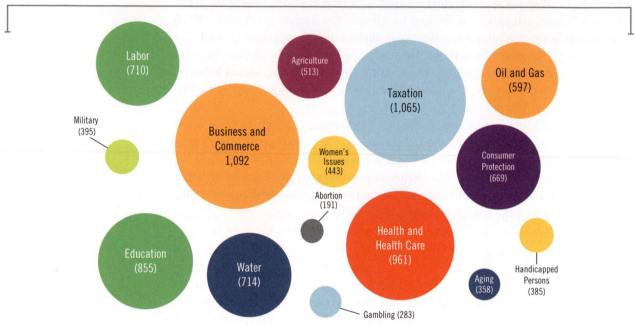

FIGURE 6.4 **Number of Lobbyists per Issue in 2019**

Source: Texas Ethics Commission annual reports.

 COMMUNICATION:

On what issues do lobbyists work?

- Almost 2,000 lobbyists work on issues of business, commerce, and taxes.
- Other profession-related groups, including education and health and health care, also were frequent lobbyers.
- Social issues like abortion and gambling or issues involving handicapped persons were lobbied on less frequently than economic issues.

 CRITICAL THINKING:

Why are some issues lobbied on more than others?

- Issues for which a financial outcome is at stake are likely to have more lobbyists on the payroll.
- Issues involving more technical know-how or specific (sometimes minor) regulations require more lobbyists to communicate with legislators.

were grown in Texas, mirroring laws in California, New York, and Oregon.[47] The founder of the Texas Wine Grape Growers Association testified that environmental factors may cause growers to lose fruit because some varietals of grape are hard to grow in Texas climates and winemakers may need to supplement with grapes grown outside the Lone Star State. The testimony suggested that the state's wineries could not compete with other states. The bill never made it out of committee.

Educate Members. While most members of the state legislature are well informed about many issues, they often lack knowledge of the nitty-gritty details (such as the capacity of existing oil refineries) needed to write or form an opinion about a bill. Lobbyists are experts in their fields or can access experts, and although often tilted toward a specific outcome, they can provide statistics, legal language, and technical specifications. Thus, legislation is often an outcome of a symbiotic exchange: Legislators receive valued information, and lobbyists have a chance to make their case.

Lobbyists, however, must earn legislators' trust. Former Democratic Representative Mike Martin remarked that lobbyists "who are trustworthy and who are good at communicating their position, as well as being fair in their communication about an issue" become valuable to legislators.[48] Austin lobbyists are keenly aware of the "one lie rule"—that is, furnishing false information to or about a legislator will damage the lobbyists' credibility, and that lobbyist will not be trusted again. Lobbyists also never ask a legislator to vote for or against a bill; this is considered bad form. They explain their position on the bill, answer questions, and suggest how it might hurt or help the legislator back home in the next election.[49]

Comment on Rule-Making. Agencies are required to publicly post proposed rule changes for public comment, and although most members of the public don't notice these potential rule changes, lobbyists often do, and they can press for or against it. In 2015, when the State Board for Educator Certification made a preliminary decision to change its rules and remove teaching experience as a requirement for serving as a school superintendent, lobbyist Kate Kuhlmann made sure the public knew about it. Speaking to the press, she quoted a report that showed superintendents needed more teaching experience, not less. The state board shifted course and voted to keep the teaching requirements.[50]

Build Coalitions. Interest groups build coalitions to push their mutual agendas forward. When San Antonio denied Chick-fil-A a concessions contract at the San Antonio International Airport because of the company president's history of hostility to LGBTQ issues, a coalition of socially conservative nonprofits like San Antonio Family Association, the Texas Values Coalition, and the Texas Justice Foundation banded together to back a "Save Chick-fil-A" bill (Senate Bill 1978), which prohibits Texas cities from discriminating against any individuals or businesses based on membership of or support to religious groups.[51] The groups then sued the city, claiming the denial of the contract to sell chicken to travelers was motivated by the company's charitable support of Christian organizations.[52] The bill passed and a lawsuit against the city led to a settlement where Chick-fil-A was allowed the chance to open at the airport.

Andrea McWilliams, co-founder of McWilliams Government Affairs Consultants

What makes some lobbyists more effective than others?

There are three key elements to successful lobbying: telling the truth, being present, and persevering despite the circumstances. In my business, your reputation determines your ability to be effective. Elected officials must know that you will tell them the truth about an issue, always. Without a reputation for honesty, it is extremely difficult to be effective. Given Texas's 140-day biennial session, decisions are made very quickly at the Capitol and at all times of the day and night. It is critical to always be "present" at the Capitol during session to ensure you do not miss a moment that could potentially impact your cause.

PERSONAL RESPONSIBILITY: **On what issue would you lobby, and how would you go about it?**

Monitor Programs. After legislation is passed and a law is put into effect, interest groups then work with the bureaucracy to monitor the program for compliance and efficiency. The process, called program monitoring, is time consuming and often requires significant technical skills or training. As the legislature is swamped with pressing work, interest groups often fill this oversight role.

IRON TRIANGLES IN TEXAS

Like legislators, bureaucrats in state agencies also rely on lobbyists to provide the detailed information they need to implement their programs effectively. An **iron triangle** describes the cozy relationship that forms between interest groups (lobbyists), the legislature (staffers), and executive agency regulators in the policy formation and implementation process. When iron triangles develop around a single issue, the relationship is often called an **issue network**. These working relationships generally produce policy decisions that are mutually agreeable.

Critics complain that iron triangles and issue networks put public policy into the hands of corporate interests. In 2015, for example, Texas Railroad Commission Chairman David Porter sent a letter to the Federal Communications Commission urging the federal agency to process applications for certain Texas pipeline companies. The letter, however, wasn't written by the chairman but by lawyers for Enbridge, one of the pipeline companies stuck in the application muck. A Houston-based government affairs specialist

iron triangle: the relationship that forms between interest groups, the legislature, and executive agency regulators in the policy formation and implementation process

issue network: a single-issue iron triangle

TABLE 6.1	**Spinning and Spinning: Legislators Working in the Lobby**	
HOUSE MEMBER	CLIENTS	LEADERSHIP OR COMMITTEE POST
Jim Keffer (R)	Southwest Business Corporation, Coalition for Affordable Responsible Insuring	Natural Resources Chair, House Committee on Energy Resources
Marisa Marquez (D)	Texas PACE Association	House Administration Vice Chair
Florence Shapiro (R)	Lifelong Learning Administration, Texas Association of Community Colleges	Senate State Affairs, Education
Craig Eiland (D)	AT&T, Texas Trial Lawyers Association	House Appropriations, Insurance
Kenneth Armbrister (D)	Hewlett Packard, Industrial Sand Producers of Texas	Joint Committee on Oversight of the Edwards Aquifer; State Affairs, Natural Resources

Source: Texas Ethics Commission. Former legislators can also contribute unused campaign donations to other candidates, making themselves even more powerful.

intervened, writing, "if you guys could put your letterhead on it and sign it and return to me electronically, our DC guys can add it to the docket for you. Does this work?"[53]

Another cause for concern is the **revolving door**, which occurs regularly when bureaucrats and legislators leave their jobs to become lobbyists, or vice versa (see Table 6.1). Retired members of the legislature who have leftover funds in their campaign accounts can donate that money to other politicians or to charities. Two of the legislators who retired in 2013 donated more than $500,000 to current members.

The legislature is the perfect training ground for lobbyists—former members have intimate knowledge of the rules and procedures of the legislature, have established relationships with key political figures, and are known figures around the statehouse. About 5 percent of registered lobbyists include former Texas legislators.[54] Former U.S. legislators or federal executive branch officials are banned from lobbying for one year after leaving office; this is termed the "cooling off period." No ban exists in Texas for former elected officials (see Figure 6.5). However, former agency heads are prohibited for 2 years from formally communicating with the agency they ran.[55] Similarly, Texas bars state employees who work on procurement or contract negotiations from working for that vendor for 2 years after leaving the agency.

Companies have also made it a habit to hire well-connected legislators—or their law firms—to work for them in the private sector. For instance, in 2002, two Republican lawmakers, State Senator Jeff Wentworth and State Representative Rick Green, worked to persuade the state health

SOCIAL RESPONSIBILITY:

Is it ethical to have former members of the legislature lobby? What kinds of rules should be in place to restrict this practice, if any?

revolving door: when agency bureaucrats and legislators leave their jobs to become lobbyists, or vice versa

IS IT BIGGER IN TEXAS?

FIGURE 6.5 **Number of Years Elected Officials Must Wait before Becoming Lobbyists**

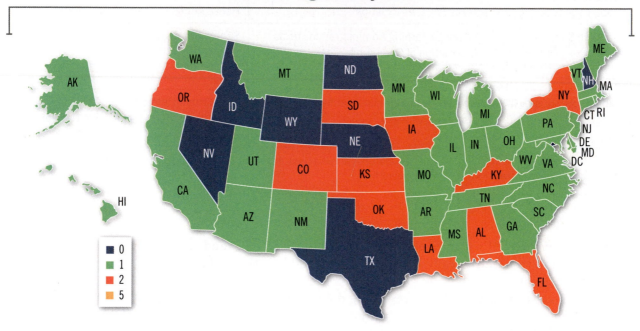

■	0
■	1
■	2
■	5

Source: National Council of State Legislatures.

 COMMUNICATION:

Which states ban "revolving door" practices?

- Only a handful of states (12), including Texas, do not ban revolving door practices.

- Most states (37) have a 1- to 2-year ban on former state officials lobbying the state legislature.

- Attempts to pass laws to slow the revolving door in other states have succeeded recently. Illinois, Kansas, North Carolina, and Vermont passed legislation to ban postemployment lobbying for state officials.

 CRITICAL THINKING:

Why do some states have stricter laws?

- States with a history of prominent scandals involving former legislators or high-profile ethics issues prompt more laws banning lobbying after leaving office.

- Western states with a small government ethos or part-time legislatures are less likely to have bans.

department not to require prescriptions for taking Metabolife International's weight-loss products that include ephedrine, a stimulant linked to various medical issues, including addiction, strokes, and seizures.[56] Metabolife was a client of both representatives' law firm. The department ruled that the Metabolife supplement would not require a prescription, only strong warning labels.[57]

Government agencies established to regulate an industry sometimes end up being "controlled" by the very industry that agency was designed to regulate. Political scientists call this **agency capture**. The Texas Railroad Commission (TRC) is a classic example. The oil and gas industries pay serious attention to the work of the commission because the TRC sets rules regarding the production of natural resources, well drilling, and physical conservation and also referees ownership of petroleum.[58] In addition, members of the TRC are elected rather than appointed to office. In 2016, oil and petroleum industry groups contributed more than $11 million to candidates for the TRC—60 percent of the total funds raised—providing a strong motivation for TRC commissioners to be attentive to industry needs.[59] Railroad Commission Chair Christi Craddick has deep family ties and investments in Texas oil, which some feel should disqualify her from acting as chief regulator.[60]

agency capture: government agencies "controlled" by the industries the agencies were designed to regulate

⭐ TEXAS TAKEAWAYS

6.5.1 What is lobbying?

6.5.2 What type of activities do lobbyists generally engage in?

6.5.3 How is the concept of a revolving door related to agency capture?

🔄 6.6 SCANDALS AND REFORMS

Iron triangles, the revolving door, and agency capture reinforce the public's perception of collusion between government and industry groups and diminish confidence in government. But do these institutions necessarily lead to corruption and the undue influence of wealthy industries? The sordid history of ethics scandals in Texas has highlighted some high-profile wrongdoing but has also led to significant political reform. In this section, we examine several of those scandals and the resulting reforms.

6.6 Illustrate the role of scandals in shaping interest group politics and reform efforts.

SHARPSTOWN SCANDAL

In 1971, Houston businessman and bank owner Frank Sharp pressed powerful state legislators to pass new state bank deposit insurance legislation that would benefit his banks. However, the media leaked a major scandal: to convince Governor Preston Smith, House Speaker Gus Mutscher Jr., and several legislators to support the legislation, Sharp had promised to grant loans of more than $600,000 from his Sharpstown State Bank to the state officials. The officials denied the charges, but Speaker Mutscher, Representative Tommy Shannon, and another staff member were tried in Abilene, convicted, and sentenced to 5 years' probation.

The Sharpstown affair sparked a call for reform. A group of legislators originally called the "Dirty Thirty" by a lobbyist in the house gallery pressed for an internal investigation of Speaker Mutscher.[61] The Dirty Thirty brought legislation to a halt by voting "no" on any bill and then leaving for Scholz Beer Garden for a long lunch. The Dirty Thirty thus blocked all bills the chamber considered until ethics legislation was passed.[62] Key among the changes were disclosures of the income of elected officials, public access to donor information, and regulation of lobbyists. Voters also backed a drive to "throw the rascals" out in the 1972 elections. The Sharpstown scandal was the first of its kind in Texas—but not the last—to lead to lasting political reform (see Table 6.2).

TABLE 6.2 **Scandals and Effects**

SCANDAL	YEAR	PERSONNEL	REFORM
Frank Sharp, in exchange for passage of favorable banking bills, helped politically connected friends get loans to buy stock in his insurance company for a quick profit.	1971	Governor Preston Smith, Speaker of the House Gus Mutscher Jr., and several members of the legislature	Passage of freedom of information law, open meetings legislation, lobbyist registration, and financial disclosure statements
Speaker Billy Clayton was indicted but acquitted for taking a bribe on behalf of a company. The speaker claimed that he had planned to return the money left in a credenza at the Capitol.	1980	Speaker Billy Clayton	Legislation to limit cash donations to $100
Speaker Gibson "Gib" Lewis was accused of accepting an illegal gift (a lobbyist paid for delinquent property taxes) and not reporting it.	1990	Speaker Gib Lewis	Creation of Texas Ethics Commission, ban on donations inside the Capitol, requirements for lawmakers to reveal business dealings
Texas Health and Human Services Department inappropriately awarded contract to Austin-based company with ties to agency staff.	2014	HHSC Commissioner Kyle Janek	Tightened requirements on local government contracting, disclosure requirements for agency personnel with financial interest in contracts

Source: Jay Root, "Long Haul Taking on a History of Scandal." *New York Times,* January 31, 2013.

THE 1991 REFORMS

Two specific incidents provoked major changes to campaign finance in Texas: Bo Pilgrim passed out checks on the floor of the Texas Senate, as described in the opening paragraphs of this chapter, and Speaker Gib Lewis, whom columnist Molly Ivins said had the "ethical sensitivity of a walnut," accepted illegal and unreported gifts in the form of travel expenses and payment of his tax bills from a law firm.[63] Many in Texas government realized something had to change.

The 1991 legislative session produced impressive reforms, including a gift reporting law, restrictions on lobbying expenditures, and establishment of the Texas Ethics Commission. Although the session was a success for ethics, Lieutenant Governor Bob Bullock used the opportunity to rib the ethics bill sponsor, Senator Bob Glasgow, who played golf with lobbyists. The gift limit had been set

Some of the key players in the Sharpstown financial scandal that ripped through Texas politics in 1971 were well connected. Pictured here are Speaker of the Texas House Gus Mutscher Jr., Governor Preston Smith, former President Lyndon Johnson, and Lieutenant Governor Ben Barnes.

to $50, some argued, so that the golf greens fees would not exceed it. Indeed, when Bullock gaveled the ethics bill to passage in 1991, he did so with a golf club.[64] Such is the trend in ethics reform: Every step toward greater disclosure opens new holes and workarounds for those seeking to beat the new system.

CURRENT ETHICS LEGISLATION

Concerns about "no bid" contracts given out by state agencies and failures in the 2015 legislative session at meaningful reform prompted Governor Abbott, in his 2017 State-of-the-State Address, to call on legislators to "shore up the cracks in our democratic process."[65] However, there is an old saying in Texas politics that the only way you'll find bipartisanship in Austin is through unity against ethics reform. The governor did sign a few reforms, including a bill that would snatch pensions away from officials convicted of felonies and one requiring lobbyists to disclose more of their wining and dining of lawmakers. But the governor balked at legislation that would have prohibited anyone donating more than $2,500 to the governor from serving as an appointee and required online posting of financial disclosure statements that are filed on paper with the Texas Ethics Commission.[66] Veteran journalist David Montgomery noted that the "paltry body of work" on ethics reforms cemented Texas's reputation as a place where "lip service on ethics trumps actual results."[67]

Due to unwillingness from legislators and resistance from interest groups, the state still lags behind many other states in passing responsible laws to provide answerability to the public, earning Texas a rank of 39th in the nation on public integrity.[68] This places the ability of the system to check the influence of interest groups on shaky ground.

⭐ TEXAS TAKEAWAYS

6.6.1 Why is ethics reform so difficult to pass?

6.7 OVERSIGHT OF INTEREST GROUPS

6.7 Outline the ways the state oversees the interactions of interest groups and state officials.

U.S. constitutional architect James Madison noted that the best counterweight to the influence of a powerful interest group is other powerful interest groups. Yet government oversight and laws supervising members of the legislature also have a role in regulating and overseeing the impact of interest groups.

TEXAS ETHICS COMMISSION

Since 1991, the Texas Ethics Commission (TEC) has served as the primary agency for regulating and enforcing laws related to interest group lobbying and campaign disclosure. The TEC has eight commissioners who are appointed by the governor, lieutenant governor, and speaker of the Texas House. Each potential appointee is chosen from a list provided by Republican and Democratic legislators—partisan balance on the commission is required.

Among the TEC's primary duties are collecting and maintaining records related to political fundraising, campaign spending, political lobbying activity, and the personal financial disclosure statements by state elected officials and officers. In practice, anyone can consider himself or herself a lobbyist, but Texas law requires an individual who receives more than $1,000 in salary from an organization or who spends more than $500 in a calendar year for lobbying to register as a lobbyist. Lobbying expenditures include payments, loans, gifts, meals, awards, or other entertainment.

Lobbyists are also required to detail any expenditure on behalf of a state officer or employee, their spouses, and their children. If a lobbyist spends more than $114 for entertainment, food and beverages, lodging, or transportation,

TABLE 6.3	Interesting Gifts to Legislators, 2011–2019

LEGISLATOR	GIFT
Joe Farias	San Antonio Spurs tickets
John Zerwas	Wildflower seeds
Dawnna Dukes	$50 Gift Certificate to Gumbo's Restaurant
Four Price	Helicopter model
Kelly Hancock	Model bulldozer
Dwayne Bohac	Framed Ronald Reagan stamps

Source: Texas Ethics Commission.

SOCIAL RESPONSIBILITY:

Should legislators be allowed to accept gifts? What limits, if any, should be placed on gifts to legislators?

this information must be recorded.[69] Gifts are not to exceed $500 in a given year to any individual official, and any gift with a value over $50 must be reported (see Table 6.3). The state punishes violators through criminal penalties or civil sanctions. Depending on the nature of the infraction, the fines range from $4,000 to $10,000, and the criminal punishments are either misdemeanors or second-degree felonies.[70] The TEC hears complaints related to these disclosure requirements and has the authority to issue fines for violations. Yet because of poor enforcement, politicians have racked up more than $1.3 million in unpaid fines.[71] The TEC also issues advisory rulings. These rulings do not have the force of law but are influential in future court proceedings (see Figure 6.6).

Despite the laws requiring full disclosure, lobbyists have found loopholes. One way this happens is by splitting restaurant checks. After a pricy steak dinner with cocktails and expensive wine, lobbyists may skirt disclosure requirements by splitting the ticket and staying under the dollar limit that would require naming the specific lawmaker wined and dined. In one instance, at the end of the 2013 legislative session, a $2,241 dinner for the House Calendars Committee at a famed Austin steakhouse was paid for by 65 different credit cards. The bill indicated that 121 people were in attendance but did not detail how many were lawmakers.[72] Legislation to require disclosure of the state official's name whose tab was picked up if it totaled over $50 died in committee in 2015.

You, as a member of the public, also have a role in ethics oversight. New technology has enabled citizens and activists to have access to campaign finance and lobbying records. The number of complaints in which the TEC imposed a fine has increased in recent years—likely because Texans now have online access to complaints through the TEC website.

Because moving forward on an enforcement action is difficult for the TEC, observers of Texas government worry that it is a toothless

FIGURE 6.6   **Number of Texas Ethics Commission Advisory Rulings**

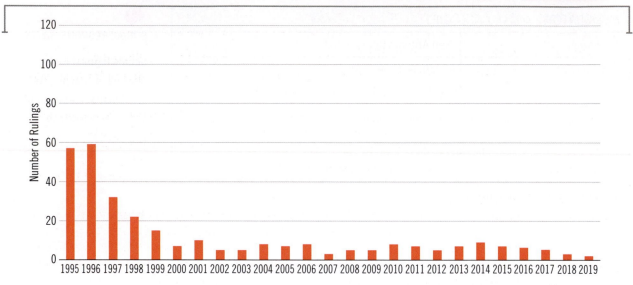

Source: Texas Ethics Commission.

 COMMUNICATION:

How many advisory rulings have been issued over time?

- Since the agency's inception in 1991, the number of rulings has decreased steadily.

- From a high of 112 in 1992 to a low of 2 in 2019, the commissioners have ruled on fewer and fewer cases per year.

 CRITICAL THINKING:

Why has the number of opinions declined?

- Fewer rulings are likely due to previous settlement of legal questions or greater legislative oversight of ethics and attention to disclosure issues.

- Frustrated with their inability to enforce their rulings, the commissioners may be issuing fewer of them.[73]

organization. Six of the eight members need to agree in order to fine or punish any individual thought to have violated the law. Because the members of the commission are appointed by the state's leading elected officials, these political interests have a significant say in how the rules are enforced.[74]

Even when the TEC fines an individual, however, the courts can reverse the decision. In response to a federal judge's dismissal of a fine against a lobbyist who had failed to register, TEC Commissioner Jim Clancy wrote to Paul

GREAT TEXAS POLITICAL DEBATES
Donations and Legal Defense Funds

Lone Star State politicians in ethical trouble are as Texan as chicken fried steak and the Alamo. But who pays for the legal defense of a politician in trouble? Ethics laws prevent elected officials from using campaign funds for legal defense if the criminal activity occurred before election. Ken Paxton, the state's embattled attorney general, is under criminal indictment for securities fraud and for failing to register as an investment adviser representative before acting as one. The Texas Ethics Commission considered what limits to place on Paxton and others in his position as they raised money for their defense. Only four of the eight members, however, agreed. As a result, the commission recommended, but did not approve, guidelines that required donors to have no connection to the jurisdiction in which the state's lawyers practice, which would ban political employee donations and mandate swift disclosure of donations over $250.[77]

SOCIAL RESPONSIBILITY: **Should public officials be allowed to raise money for their legal defense?**

YES: Everyone, including elected officials, has the right to adequate legal defense, which can cost hundreds of thousands of dollars. Defendants who don't have sufficient funds themselves should be allowed to reach out to their friends and supporters.

NO: Allowing fundraising for legal defense blurs the line between the public and private activities of an elected official. For many officials, their elected status is just another "permission slip" to generate donations from political allies.[78]

MAYBE: Adequate disclosure and clear rules allow everyone to see where donated funds come from and where they go.

Hobby, the chair of the TEC, to express his opinion that the agency must stop issuing orders if "those with extraordinary resources" can spend hundreds of thousands of dollars to challenge or delay paying a $10,000 fine.[75]

Yet the courts also broker settlements between the TEC and the individuals the commission fines. When the TEC fined Chief Justice Nathan L. Hecht of the Texas Supreme Court for failing to disclose that he had reduced his legal fee while working for U.S. Supreme Court nominee Harriet Miers, the courts eventually settled the case and forced Hecht to pay. However, while the TEC had fined him $29,000, the court-brokered settlement required the chief justice to pay only $1,000. Some argued that the commission let Hecht "off the hook" and that the fine was coming years late and "$28,000 light."[76]

RECUSAL

State lawmakers are not prohibited from authoring or voting on legislation that may benefit them as long as it benefits all others in the same way. After all, it is difficult for legislators to avoid participating in issues where they have some personal stake, sometimes on purpose and sometimes by accident. Representative Charlie Geren, Republican from Fort Worth, authored legislation

recuse: decide not to participate in legislative activity as an elected official

aimed at lowering the renewal fees for bars and restaurants. Geren, owner of Fort Worth's Railhead Smokehouse barbeque restaurant, stated that he was not sure whether the measure would have affected his restaurant (the measure passed but was vetoed by the governor).

Legislators, however, frequently **recuse** themselves—that is, elect not to participate in decisions—from issues in which they have a personal stake. They are not required to recuse themselves if they have a conflict of interest, however, and these conflicts abound. Representative Jim Murphy, who is on the state's powerful tax-writing committee and is the vice chair of the Republican Caucus, works as a consultant to the Westchase District, a government political subdivision of the state, with an annual salary of $312,000 and bonuses for securing funds for Westchase projects.[79] Representative Cecil Bell, a private contractor by profession, introduced legislation in 2017 to limit the financial liability of contractors who accidentally strike pipelines or telecommunication lines.[80] Those who argue against recusal suggest that legislators who have personal or business interests are uniquely situated to understand the ramifications of a particular policy issue and should be allowed to be directly involved.

DISCLOSURE

disclosure: the filing of a report that includes details about lawmakers' personal finances or business dealings

Texas has disclosure requirements for officials who have partial or total shares in a business entity. States are close to evenly divided on requirements for conflict of interest disclosures: 29 states (including the District of Columbia) have it, and 22 states do not. Although there may be some disagreement about recusal, Texans largely agree that **disclosure** of lawmakers' financial ties is critical for citizens to understand the possible financial conflicts of interest among legislators. Every year, lawmakers and appointed public officials are required to report details about their personal finances. Yet there are problems with the current disclosure laws. Texas does not require lawmakers' spouses to do the same, for example. Some senators, led by Senator Joan Huffman, led the charge to exempt spouses from reporting requirements after a complaint filed with the TEC alleged that she had filed "false" information by failing to list more than 35 nightclub businesses in which her husband had a stake.[81] Senator Huffman eventually updated her disclosure forms voluntarily to include her husband's businesses.

⭐ TEXAS TAKEAWAYS

6.7.1 What is the main function of the Texas Ethics Commission?

6.7.2 What is disclosure, and what kinds of disclosures does Texas law require?

THE INSIDER VIEW

An old Texas saying goes, "if you can't drink their [interest groups'] liquor, take their money, and vote against them in the morning, you don't belong in Austin." Yet in a state as large and complex as Texas, interest groups with all sorts of political and policy interests battle one other. Small ideological groups take on larger industry groups. Large business associations take on other large business associations. These interactions play out across all levels and points of government in Texas as powerful groups capture agencies and cajole lawmakers. In response, Texas has gone through several cycles of reform. Many of the most egregious problems have been addressed, and practices are in place to provide limits to and disclosure of lobbying activities. Yet the struggle of reformers against those who would like to work around the system is likely to continue—although as Molly Ivins wrote, our elected representatives may continue to "dance with the special interests what brung'em."[82]

 ## TEXAS TAKEAWAYS

6.1.1 Interest groups attempt to influence government for the benefit of their members through legislation, rules, or actions that are aligned with their cause

6.1.2 In a pluralist theory, powerful groups are kept in check, and no single group dominates. In elite theory, powerful groups with greater resources have more influence.

6.1.3 Transactional theory proposes that public policy is bought and sold like a commodity to the highest bidder

6.2.1 Free riders are people who obtain the benefits without paying the cost. Individuals who do not join groups still receive the benefits of groups that work for a collective good.

6.2.2 Selective benefits, such as material, solidarity, and purposive benefits, encourage people to join interest groups.

6.3.1 Trade associations serve the interests of a specific industry.

6.3.2 Single-issue interest groups are dedicated to addressing one specific issue, usually an ideological issue.

6.3.3 Public interest groups focus on providing quality collective goods, while government interest groups attempt to impact other local and state governments or the federal government.

6.4.1 AstroTurfing is advocacy that appears to have originated from the bottom up, but in reality it masks corporate interests.

6.4.2 Electioneering involves advertising (radio, mail, Internet, or television) for or against issues or candidates, granting endorsements, and raising funds.

6.5.1 According to Texas law, lobbying consists of "direct communications" with members of the legislative or executive branch of government to influence legislation or administrative action.

6.5.2 Lobbyists shape legislation by testifying at hearings, educating members of the legislature, commenting on rule-making, building coalitions for or against policies, monitoring enacted programs, and working with agencies.

6.5.3 A revolving door allows individuals to move between an agency and industry, leading to an agency being "controlled" by an industry.

6.6.1 Lawmakers dislike changing the rules of the game during the game.

6.7.1 The Texas Ethics Commission regulates and enforces laws related to interest group lobbying and campaign disclosure.

6.7.2 Disclosure is the filing of a report that includes details about lawmakers' personal finances or business dealings.

KEY TERMS

agency capture
amicus curiae briefs
AstroTurf lobbying
disclosure
electioneering
elite theory
free rider problem
grassroots lobbying
interest groups
iron triangle
issue network
lobbying
pluralist theory
private interest groups
public interest groups
recuse
revolving door
selective benefits
transactional theory

PRACTICE QUIZ

1. The theory that holds political power is distributed broadly among many organized interests who compete with each other for control of public policy is called . . .
   a. New institutionalism
   b. Separation of powers
   c. Pluralism
   d. Devolution

2. Individuals who obtain benefits from organized interests without paying the costs to get those benefits are called . . .
   a. Partisans
   b. Lobbyists
   c. Smoke-screeners
   d. Free riders

3. Which of the following is NOT a selective benefit?
   a. Monetary
   b. Material
   c. Solidary
   d. Emotional

4. Which of the following is NOT a type of interest group?
   a. Trade associations
   b. The presidential cabinet
   c. Identity groups
   d. Public interest groups

5. As of 2019, there are how many lobbyists in Texas?
   a. 253
   b. 786
   c. 1,389
   d. 1,870

6. The "iron triangle" consists of all of the following EXCEPT . . .
   a. Interest groups
   b. Legislators
   c. Political parties
   d. Agency regulators

7. Any formal organization or group that seeks to publicly or privately promote a common cause is called an interest group.

    a. True
    b. False

8. Lobbyists must record gift expenditures over $50.

    a. True
    b. False

9. A good lobbyist knows when to ask a legislator to vote for or against a bill.

    a. True
    b. False

10. Members of the legislature are required to recuse themselves if legislation considered presents a conflict of interest.

    a. True
    b. False

[Answers: C, D, A, B, D, C, A, A, B, B]

Learn more with this chapter's digital tools, including the Oxford Insight Study Guide, at www.oup.com/he/Rottinghaus3e.

THE LEGISLATURE

The ink was barely dry on most legislation when the Big Three—the governor, lieutenant governor, and speaker of the house—gathered for a picnic on the south lawn of the governor's mansion in celebration. Lieutenant Governor Dan Patrick deemed the 2019 legislative session the most successful in state history and labeled it the "Super Bowl of legislative sessions," delivering on promises to boost teacher pay, increase funds for public education, and cap property taxes.[1] Not all sessions end in bear hugs and congratulatory picnics.

Indeed, in 2017, the Texas House erupted in violence on the chamber floor. As hundreds of protesters carrying signs reading "I am illegal and here to stay" poured into the gallery to disrupt the last day of the regular session, Republican Representative Matt Rinaldi[2] turned to Democratic Representative Poncho Nevárez and chuffed, "F—k them, I called ICE."[3] Nevárez threatened to "get" Rinaldi, and Rinaldi threatened to shoot Nevárez in self-defense. Pushing and shoving ensued, and the scuffle was broken up by other members. This conflict is just the tip of the iceberg. In the past 100 years, Texas legislators have erupted into fistfights, the waving around of firearms (one member shooting off blanks at the ceiling), and passage of amusing resolutions to ridicule colleagues, such as one declaring a Hoverboard Safety Awareness Day after a representative broke his wrist while falling off a hoverboard.[4]

Legislative politics is not all fun and fighting, however. The legislature passes laws that affect every part of the lives of Texans, ranging from how much sales tax they pay to the quality of their

7.1 Identify the functions of the legislature and legislators.

7.2 Compare the strength of the Texas legislature to other state legislatures.

7.3 Describe the organizational structure and leadership of the legislature.

7.4 Outline the legislative process.

7.5 Assess how legislative tools are used to speed up or slow down legislation.

7.6 Explain how legislators represent their constituents demographically.

● Outgoing Speaker Dennis Bonnen attempts to get the attention of the chamber as Representative Dan Huberty bear hugs Senator Larry Taylor in celebration of passage of a massive education spending bill.

schools to the condition of their roads. With a budget that tops $250 billion every two years, everyone has a stake in the game.

To examine the unusual but important world of the Texas legislature, we first analyze its function and the tasks legislators carry out. We examine the structure of the legislature and compare it to that in other states. We outline the legislative process, paying special attention to the scramble to beat the calendar and to the way political struggles are resolved within this framework. Finally, we explore the demographics of the legislators.

7.1 THE FUNCTIONS OF THE LEGISLATURE AND LEGISLATORS

7.1 Identify the functions of the legislature and legislators.

The grand wings of the enormous Texas Capitol—which appears pink because of its "Sunset Red" limestone color—house the 181 members of the Texas legislature every odd-numbered spring in Austin. Like the federal Congress, the Texas legislature (called the "Lege" by observers) is a **bicameral legislature**, meaning it has two houses or chambers: the house of representatives and the senate. French political theorist Montesquieu first conceived of this division as a means of ensuring that the minority would have a voice in public affairs that could not be shouted down by the majority.

bicameral legislature: a legislative body with two houses or chambers

LAWMAKING

The Texas legislature's chief responsibility is to create and pass legislation. Laws establish and reinforce economic interactions, resolve disputes between individuals or groups, and protect rights and liberties. The legislature's laws dictate everything from the sales tax people pay on cars to the type of insurance they are required to carry to how many hours of training a hairstylist needs in order to be licensed.

The state legislature introduces bills on a wide variety of matters, some of which are serious and some of which are less so (see Table 7.1). Legislation considered by the legislature can be a **general law** if the bill potentially affects all Texans, a **local law** if it affects only units of government at the local level (often carried out by a legislator at the request of local government leaders), or a **special law** if it exempts businesses, organizations, or individuals from state laws. Three bills filed by El Paso Democratic Representative Mary González in the last legislative session illustrate these different types: a general law to

general law: law that potentially affects all Texans

local law: law that only affects units of government at the local level

special law: law that exempts businesses or individuals from state laws

TABLE 7.1	**Odd Laws and Resolutions Proposed in the 86th Legislature**

HB 37	Makes "porch pirates" (those stealing mail and packages from a porch) subject to state jail felony charge
HB 446	Makes brass knuckles legal
HB 2789	Establishes the sending of unsolicited nude photos as a Class C misdemeanor
SB 464	Bans ownership of "wild animals" such as baboons, jaguars, or gorillas
HB 234	Makes it illegal for local government to ban kids' (those under 18) lemonade stands
SB 1232	Allows "beer to go" sales at Texas breweries (letting consumers purchase packaged beer)
HB 410	Expands sale of fireworks to Juneteenth and Labor Day holidays
HB 3535	Designates the taco as the official state food, replacing chili
SCR 20	Makes the Bowie knife the official knife of Texas

Source: Texas Legislature Online

CRITICAL THINKING:

HBs are house bills and SBs are senate bills. Where do the oddest bills originate? Is this what you would expect given the difference between the two chambers?

require minimum education requirements for child protective services caseworkers; a local bill to establish a law school in El Paso County; and a special bill to exempt campus police from cooperating with federal immigration officers in deportation-related law enforcement.

In addition to bills that carry the force of law (after being signed into law by the governor), legislators debate and pass **resolutions** that convey the will of the chamber. These resolutions include:

resolutions: legislation that conveys the will of the chamber

- *Joint resolutions* are used to propose amendments to the Texas Constitution or to ratify proposed amendments to the U.S. Constitution.

- *Concurrent resolutions* are passed separately but simultaneously by both chambers and are used to direct state agencies on procedural issues such as legislative adjournment or special sessions initiation.

- *Simple resolutions* are passed by a single chamber and are used for adopting or changing rules of procedure or expressing congratulations or condolences. Simple resolutions are also used ceremonially to highlight Texas's history or to promote local tourism, such as declaring the state snack (chips and salsa), the state fruit (red grapefruit), or the wedding capital of Texas (Dripping Springs, a town located west of Austin).

The legislature often follows a similar procedure to pass each of these types of resolutions.

The legislature is also tasked with overseeing implementation of the laws passed in previous sessions to ensure that the programs and policies are operating effectively. Oversight may include program evaluation for executive agencies, periodic audits of legislative spending, or regulation of the rules implemented by executive agencies. The legislature can hold hearings to investigate abuse, mismanagement, or abuse of power, typically of executive agencies.[5] Lawmakers excoriated officials from the Texas Department of Family and Protective Services in 2016 for an unexpected increase in reported cases of abuse and for a shortage of foster care beds.[6] Heads roll when investigations lead to the removal or impeachment of officials. With the governor's consent, two-thirds of the Texas Senate can remove an appointed official. The Texas House can also initiate impeachment proceedings by bringing charges against an executive or judicial branch official, and the senate sits as the jury where a two-thirds majority is needed to convict. The legislature can also revise laws in later sessions if problems arise during implementation.

TEXAS HOUSE VERSUS SENATE

Although both chambers serve the same general function, important differences between them remain. The larger number of members and the shorter length of term, in theory, make the Texas House of Representatives a more representative and responsive body than the Texas Senate. Like the U.S. Constitution, the Texas Constitution designed the legislature with the idea that the house would be more accountable to the popular will and the senate would be more deliberative.

House. The Texas House is made up of 150 members. The entire membership is up for election every two years. The Texas Constitution requires members of the Texas House to be at least 21 years of age, a citizen of Texas for two years prior to election, and a resident of the district from which he or she is elected one year prior to election.

Senate. By contrast, the Texas Senate has 31 members who are elected for four-year terms from districts that carve up the state. Half of the membership is elected every two years, so the entire chamber is not up for reelection in any single cycle. As outlined in the Texas Constitution, a senator must be 26 years of age, a citizen of Texas five years prior to being elected, and a resident of the district from which he or she is elected one year prior to election.

Responsibilities. Similar to the U.S. Constitution, the Texas Constitution grants the house responsibilities that the framers believed belonged in the hands of the people, while the senate serves as the vehicle for protecting minority interests against the tyranny of the majority. So, for example, all revenue bills must originate in the house so that the power of the purse (funding policies) remains in the hands of the people. The house and senate take turns originating the budget bill every other session.

The senate is granted responsibilities that require more deliberation, such as confirming or rejecting all of the governor's appointments to state boards and commissions. The senate confirms a nominee through a two-thirds vote. Hometown senators (senators from the hometown of the nominee) are given some authority to reject a nominee, but this is usually not necessary because an astute governor will clear the nominee with the hometown senator before submitting his or her nomination. Most nominations are confirmed because problems are smoothed out early as part of the senate's more deliberative process, but trouble can flare as nominees wade into political waters. For example, David Whitley, the acting secretary of state and close aide to Governor Greg Abbott, had to answer tough questions from a senate hearing after a botched attempt to scour noncitizens from voter rolls that questioned the eligibility of 100,000 legitimate voters, although officials later did find the list chock full of noneligible voters as well. The senate did not confirm his nomination, forcing the governor to appoint someone else as secretary of state.[7]

CASEWORK

Legislators also have extra tasks outside the legislature that they must attend to if they are to succeed in future legislative sessions and win reelection. Between sessions, legislators and their staff spend time on **casework**, assisting constituents in their districts with specific requests and often acting as facilitators, go-betweens, or advocates. For instance, a constituent may request help applying for a state grant, obtaining a specific government benefit, or seeking relief from a state agency.[8] Legislators also meet with citizens, lobbyists, and organized groups to facilitate (or to stop) legislation of interest to the district. For example, early in the 2001 legislative session, Senator Leticia Van de Putte met with lobbyists representing teachers, prison guards demanding a pay raise, and leather-clad bikers who wanted to exempt alcohol carried in saddlebags from the state's open-container law.[9]

WINNING REELECTION

Legislators must engage in what political scientist David Mayhew identifies as position taking and credit claiming in order to win reelection.[10] Let's look at each of these terms in turn.

Briscoe Cain ✓
@BriscoeCain

It was a pleasure serving on the #txlege House Elections Committee.

8:51 PM · 5/23/19 from Austin, TX · Twitter for iPhone

Texas Representative Briscoe Cain (a Republican) jokingly strangles fellow Representative John Bucy (a Democrat).

SOCIAL RESPONSIBILITY: What makes a good legislator in your opinion? How might we judge a legislator's performance?

casework: legislators and their staff's assistance of constituents in their districts with specific requests

FIGURE 7.1 **Issues Tweeted before the 86th Legislature Using #txlege Hashtag by Party**

Source: Influence Opinions.

CRITICAL THINKING: **What issues did each party most tweet about before the 2019 session? Do the parties share any common concerns?**

Position Taking. Position taking involves members proclaiming where they stand on certain issues or policies. Former Speaker of the Texas House Pete Laney would say "Members vote your districts" before every vote as a reminder not to forget why the legislators were in Austin in the first place. He left office with a similar sentiment: "Pay attention to the process, pay attention to your constituents, and do what you think is right for the State of Texas. Sometimes you've got to weigh that: what's right for your constituents and what's good for the whole population."[11]

Indeed, some legislators act as **trustees** of their constituency, voting in accordance with their interpretation of what their district would want. Other legislators act as **delegates**, where members are simply a mouthpiece for the wishes of their constituency. Speaker Laney once noted, "The first time I ever voted in 1973 on a real controversial bill, I worried about it, and I finally said, 'This is not worth it. I'm going to vote for what I think is right for my constituents.' Thirty years later, I was still there. There's no way you can worry about getting reelected and do what's right."[12]

Legislators often craft a certain image to appeal to voters to gain their trust, which they then use to explain and justify decisions made in Austin. Political scientist Richard Fenno calls this development the "home style" of legislators. The way in which legislators are elected encourages a close relationship between the member and the citizens, fostering accountability.

Credit Claiming. Credit claiming occurs when legislators point out the positive things they have done while in office. Most members produce newsletters for their constituents and make frequent trips home for town hall-style meetings. This communication creates a pathway to accountability.

In recent years, legislators have begun utilizing social media to make sure their constituency follows their achievements. The #txlege hashtag has become a one-stop shop for breaking news and instant opinions from legislators and Capitol watchers, including journalists and lobbyists (see Figure 7.1).[13] Representative Wayne Christian notes, "The reason I got involved in social media then is because, back home—and I lived 300 miles away—while I was up in Austin working a ten-month session, my opponent is saying 'Hey, where's your rep? He's not working for you,' so I started posting pictures of where I was and what I was doing, so I could prove I was working hard for them in that ten-month session we had."[14] The number of tweets from legislators on Twitter rose 67 percent between the 2011 and 2019 legislative sessions: 27 legislators sent more than 1,000 Tweets in the 86th session, including Representative Poncho Navárez who sent 12,925 Tweets, averaging 49 tweets per day![15]

trustee: a legislator who votes in accordance with his or her interpretation of what the legislator's district would want

delegate: a legislator who is simply a mouthpiece for the wishes of his or her constituency

⭑ TEXAS TAKEAWAYS

7.1.1 What roles do legislators serve?

7.1.2 What are the main lawmaking functions of the Texas state legislature?

7.1.3 Compare and contrast general, local, and special laws.

7.1.4 How does the legislature oversee the implementation of laws?

7.1.5 Why is the Texas House considered to be more representative and responsive than the Texas Senate?

7.1.6 How do legislators act as caseworkers?

7.1.7 What two roles do legislators perform to help them establish credibility with their constituency and win reelection?

⚖️ 7.2 THE TEXAS LEGISLATURE IN CONTEXT

7.2 Compare the strength of the Texas legislature to that of other state legislatures.

Political scientists classify legislatures as "strong" or "weak" based on whether they have access to adequate resources to carry out their functions. Strong legislatures consist of full-time, professional, well-paid legislators, with year-round or annual sessions, plentiful legislative staff, and competitive elections. By many of these standards, Texas has a weak legislature—due to the length of its sessions, salary, staff, and boards that facilitate the legislative process.

THE LEGISLATIVE SESSION

The Texas legislature meets biennially (every two years) in the January of odd-numbered years. In maintaining this schedule, Texas is unique among large states. Just three other states (all smaller ones) have biennial legislative sessions. In the nineteenth century, when travel was more difficult and the public distrusted corrupt state legislatures, many states switched to a biennial system. However, between 1960 and 1970, as state budgets became larger and legislation more complicated, most legislatures switched back to annual sessions.[16]

Many watchers of Texas politics believe the state legislature should hold annual rather than biennial sessions. As the state's population has increased and the economy has diversified, the legislature must continually address a broader spectrum of issues. Indeed, the number of bills filed has risen sharply, yet the percentage of bills passed has declined; this suggests that the legislature may not be able to keep up with all the issues its members wish to address (see Figure 7.2). Between 1945 and 1975, however, Texas voters—wary of powerful government—rejected five constitutional amendments calling for a switch to an annual session.

regular session: legislative session meeting for 140 days in the January of odd-numbered years

special session: legislative session that can be called by the governor on any issue the governor decides requires attention

sine die: the end of a legislative session

Each **regular session** of the Texas legislature meets for 140 days, longer than most states with set lengths (see Figure 7.3). In addition, the governor can call a **special session** on any issue he or she would like the legislature to address. Special sessions are limited to 30 days. Special sessions are called roughly every other legislative session (as we will see in Chapter 8) and allow the legislature to address issues that were not taken up or settled during a regular session, emergencies, or legislative "bellyflops" on an important issue.[17] The end of the legislative session is called *sine die*, Latin for "without day," during which the body adjourns, accompanied by much rejoicing of weary legislators and exhausted staffers.

FIGURE 7.2 **Bills Passed by Session**

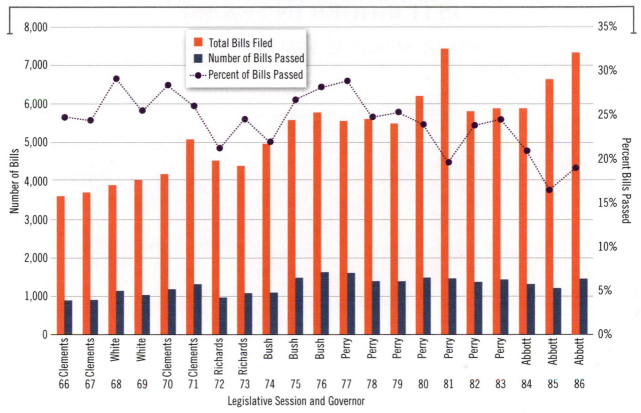

Source: Data taken from Legislative Reference Library. Bars represent total bills filed and passed by the Texas House and Senate. Line represents percentage passed of those filed.

 COMMUNICATION:

What are the trends in laws introduced and passed over time?

- The total number of bills filed has risen sharply since the 66th Legislature to the present, from 3,500 to more than 7,300.
- This growth (more than 108 percent) exceeded the growth in the state population during that time.

 CRITICAL THINKING:

Why the difference between legislation filed and legislation passed?

- The percentage of bills passed (out of bills filed) is lower now than it was a decade ago.
- More students in public schools and state universities, an expanding criminal justice system, booming populations, and a growing economy all create a rising need for new laws.
- Lower percentages of bills passed in the last few sessions reflect the increasing dominance of conservatives in the legislature, including the governor, who favor fewer laws and less regulation.

IS IT BIGGER IN TEXAS?

FIGURE 7.3 Length of Legislative Session

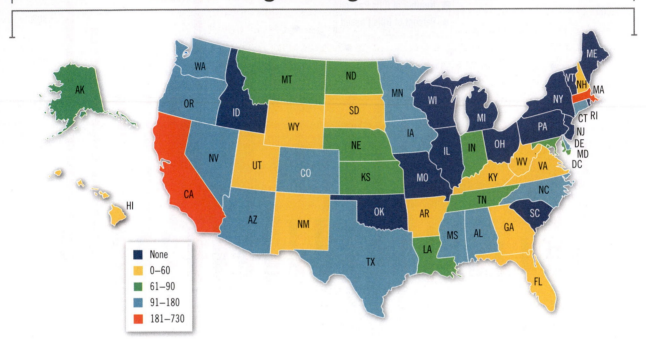

Legend:
- None (dark navy)
- 0–60 (yellow)
- 61–90 (green)
- 91–180 (blue)
- 181–730 (red)

Source: National Council of State Legislatures. Number indicates the maximum number of legislative days or, if the session had different lengths for different years, the longer of the two session dates. "None" signals that the chamber decides how long the session lasts.

 COMMUNICATION:

How long do legislative sessions last?

- Most states' legislative sessions last fewer than 100 days, especially in states with smaller populations.

- Texas has a long session compared to other states, but the Texas legislature only meets once every two years while most states meet annually.

- Fourteen states have no limit on the length of the session—legislators in these states agree on the length of the session instead of having it set by law.

 CRITICAL THINKING:

Why is Texas an outlier?

- Texans decided long ago that a shorter legislative session every two years should produce a smaller government footprint.

- While other states can extend their legislative sessions, the Texas Constitution limits the legislators' ability to run longer than the 140-day session.

LEGISLATIVE STAFF

Critics complain that the budget for legislative staff salaries is too low to hire an adequate number of people and to keep quality staffers from taking other opportunities. Senators are allotted $38,000 per month and house members $13,250 each month to run their offices. Legislators often use campaign funds to supplement staff salaries, but this too may indebt legislators to organized interests by forcing greater reliance on the groups that finance their campaign.[18] This insufficient staffing creates an opening for organized interest groups to step in to provide policy competency and persuade legislators to vote with them on legislation.

LEGISLATIVE BOARDS AND COUNCILS

As a way to compensate for a part-time legislature, some of the powers of the legislature are siphoned off to several boards and councils, all of which serve important roles. The Legislative Budget Board (LBB), for example, writes the first draft of the state budget, setting the stage for future debate. The lieutenant governor (who presides over the senate) and the speaker of the house co-chair the LBB. They also appoint the remaining eight members from their respective chambers. Because many legislators may not have the expertise necessary to draft bills, the Legislative Council assists in writing legislation, conducting research, and providing legal support services. The Legislative Council also provides the technical nuts-and-bolts evaluations of policy options in state government.

SALARY

Despite the size of its economy and population, Texans' belief in small government keeps legislators' annual salary at $7,200—the lowest set legislative salary in the nation. Legislators also receive a $221 per diem for meals and travel, a total of $31,000 for daily expenses during a regular session. The per diem pay also is fixed to the amount lobbyists can spend on lawmakers before they have to submit a detailed expense report; that threshold is $114 (60 percent of the per diem). Legislators are expected to have other jobs because lawmaking in Texas is not designed to be a full-time occupation. Professionalized legislatures (full-time, year-round sessions) in other states tend to pay legislators more. Texas members can use campaign accounts to supplement their lifestyles but not to pay themselves a salary. Former Republican Senator Troy Fraser, for example, spent more than $300,000 from his campaign account maintaining a personal airplane, paying country club fees, buying suits, and traveling to faraway locations like Hawaii and Buenos Aires.[19]

The relatively low pay makes serving in the legislature easier if a person is wealthy enough to self-finance. But the vast majority of legislators hold day jobs.

GREAT TEXAS POLITICAL DEBATES
Should Texas Have Annual Legislative Sessions?

A vestige of the Reconstruction Era's distrust of government, the Texas Constitution limits the length of the legislative session to minimize the scope of government. The state has grown immensely in the intervening 200 years, however. The population has exploded, with the economy now larger than that of all but 12 nations, and the needs of the state have diversified—all developments of a major modern state.

 SOCIAL RESPONSIBILITY: **Should Texas switch to an annual legislative session?**

NO: There is an old saying in Texas politics: "No man, woman, child, or their property is safe when the legislature is in session." With a limited window of time to meet and legislate, the legislature is less likely to expand government and intervene in the lives (and wallets) of Texans. Representative Donna Campbell argued, "It makes us look less like Washington [DC]."[20]

YES: In a massive, complex, and growing state like Texas, a biennial session of just over four months is not a sufficient amount of time to craft, consider, and confer on important legislation. Legislation may be hastily written, poorly researched, or insufficiently debated. This leads to consistently unfinished business and to lack of policy progress on a range of critical, long-standing issues such as the structure of the tax system, education financing, or border security. More frequent opportunities to legislate would lessen the partisan friction caused by short sessions.

MAYBE: Texas could hold shorter annual sessions with the possibility of extension if necessary.

INCUMBENCY AND TURNOVER

turnover: the process by which incumbents lose their seats or leave their seats and new members (freshmen) are voted into office

institutional memory: a collective understanding of the way an organization works held by those who run it

incumbent: an individual who currently holds a public office

Low salaries and a biennial session can lead to high **turnover** rates among legislators. Too much turnover can be a problem, leading to a loss of **institutional memory**—that is, an understanding of how a complex organization runs. Legislators without institutional memory may be less effective. Representative Garnet Coleman of Houston argues, "Your power comes from your knowledge of the subject matter. Ultimately, that's the thing with seniority: It's being around long enough to actually learn something."[21] The Texas legislature has strong continuity and institutional memory because most elections for Texas legislators are won by the **incumbent** (see Figure 7.4). In the 87th legislative session (2021), most legislators had between 1 and 10 years of legislative experience, and more than a dozen members had served for more than 20 years.[22] Lack of turnover, however, can mean that leadership positions are held by the same senior members and that frustrated younger members who want a turn in management are frozen out.

CONSEQUENCES OF THE TEXAS LEGISLATIVE STRUCTURE

The consequences of the part-time legislature—columnist Molly Ivins called it a "sometimes government"—may hinder representation and public policy

FIGURE 7.4 Incumbents' Reelection Rate

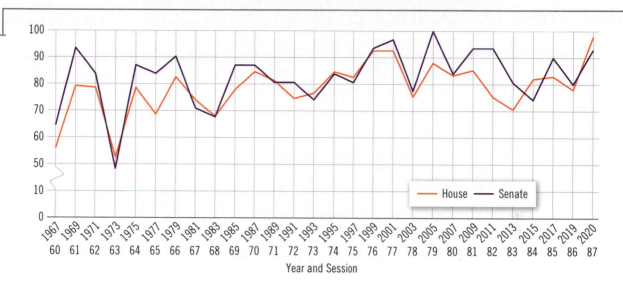

Source: Texas Legislature Online. Includes only races where an incumbent ran for reelection.

 COMMUNICATION:

What percentage of the Texas legislature is returned to office in each election?

- Generally, the incumbency advantage is high for legislators in Texas, although not as high as the 90 percent or higher for the U.S. Congress.

- The Texas House and Senate have similar rates of incumbents returning to office.

 CRITICAL THINKING:

Despite the strong incumbency advantage, what accounts for periods of decline?

- Certain years have seen fewer incumbents returned to office as a result of political scandals, such as the Sharpstown bribery scandal in 1973.

- Turnover is also larger where one party has made serious political gains in unseating incumbents, as occurred in 2003 when Republicans scored major victories over Democrats in the state. Redistricting in 2001 also contributed by making seats held by incumbent Democrats vulnerable.

- The incumbency advantage also diminishes when internal party fights lead to unseating incumbents. The incumbency rate fell to 70 percent in 2013 after several incumbent Republicans lost to conservative challengers in primary elections.

development.[23] Fewer resources, a shorter time span in which to meet, and lower salaries may put part-time Texas legislators at a disadvantage. Scholars of state politics have found that part-time legislators are less likely to have as much contact with their constituents, are less likely to be attentive to their concerns, and are more influenced by party leadership and the governor. In terms of public policy, part-time legislators are also less willing to take on government reforms and to enact the complex and innovative policies a state may need.[24]

TEXAS TAKEAWAYS

7.2.1 What characteristics define strong legislatures?

7.2.2 How does Texas rank in terms of legislative strength and why?

7.2.3 How do the length and frequency of Texas legislature sessions compare to those of other states?

7.2.4 What is the purpose of special sessions?

7.2.5 What are the advantages and disadvantages of legislative turnover?

7.2.6 What are the consequences of a part-time legislature?

7.3 HOW THE LEGISLATURE IS ORGANIZED

7.3 Describe the organizational structure and leadership of the legislature.

The legislature isn't just a collection of individual legislators. The organization of the legislature shapes how issues are introduced and how legislation is debated, and determines which laws are passed and which fail to pass.

THE COMMITTEE SYSTEM

committees: small groups of legislators who investigate, craft, assess, and take action on legislation before it is considered by the whole chamber

Most of the work of the two chambers is carried out through **committees**, small groups of legislators who investigate, craft, assess, and take action on legislation before it is considered by the whole body on the house or senate floor. Each member of the legislature sits on at least one committee but often more than one. Legislators specialize in policy topics and form legislation that addresses a particular problem. Membership on committees is usually determined by a combination of seniority and policy expertise, but politics plays a role as well. The 86th Legislature (2019 session) had 53 committees, including 1 select committee.[25]

Standing committees are permanent committees that deal with a specific issue or topic. The State Affairs Committee handles most of the senate's important legislation, acting as a clearinghouse for the lieutenant governor's bills and vetting controversial legislation. Important standing committees in the house are the appropriations committees (there are several, each devoted to a specific part of spending funds from the budget) and the House Ways and Means Committee, which monitors state revenue and taxes. All budget and funding items for the state flow through these powerful committees.

A **select committee** is a committee that is temporary and has a fixed issue to investigate or legislation to consider. In the 2019 session, for example, the Mass Violence Prevention and Community Safety Committee was tasked with investigating the causes of mass shootings, including incitement of racism and violent political culture.

Legislators compete to get onto the most influential committees and onto those that consider policy issues especially relevant to the districts they represent. Legislators ultimately hope to serve as chairs of committees so that they will be better able to direct and influence legislation. The leaders of each chamber, the speaker of the house and the lieutenant governor in the Texas Senate, determine which legislators to reward with these more powerful positions.

standing committees: permanent committees that deal with a specific issue or topic

select committee: a committee that is temporary and has a fixed issue to investigate or legislation to consider

SPEAKER OF THE HOUSE

The presiding officer in the Texas House, the speaker of the house, is elected by a simple majority of the house in a recorded vote at the beginning of every session. The speaker has several powers, one of which is to resolve all questions of process and procedure within the house. The speaker also decides which legislators become committee chairs and assigns most of the committee members—those not determined by **seniority**, which fixes half of all committee positions in the house—and therefore can stack committees with allies. This is an especially important power when it comes to assigning the Calendar Committee, which determines the order of bills considered. These powers make the speaker the most influential member of the chamber whose successes and failures give rise to achievements, reforms, and shifts in the policy process (see Table 7.2).

Because most action takes place in committees, positions on these committees are highly sought after. Members who aren't part of the speaker's "team" are often less influential in the session and may have a tougher time raising the funds and votes necessary to win reelection.

Speakers can use committee assignments to punish disloyalty. When Ben Barnes was a 22-year-old legislative freshman in 1961, he privately admitted to the newly elected speaker of the house that he had campaigned against him and thus didn't deserve a committee assignment. The speaker asked Barnes which committees he didn't want to be on. Barnes answered the Liquor Regulation Committee because "I come from a mostly dry district with about

seniority: having lengthier legislative service than others

PERSONAL RESPONSIBILITY:

What lessons should the next speaker learn from the frequent downfall of Texas speakers?

TABLE 7.2	Recent Speakers' Successes and Political Problems					
	BILL "BILLY" CLAYTON 1975–1983	GIB LEWIS 1983–1993	PETE LANEY 1993–2003	TOM CRADDICK 2003–2009	JOE STRAUS 2009–2019	DENNIS BONNEN 2019–2021
Greatest success	Worked to modernize legislature operations.	Ushered through public education reform. Appointed record number of women, African Americans, and Hispanics to leadership positions.	Fostered bipartisanship by appointing Republicans to key committees and other means.	Handled a serious $10 billion state budget deficit.	Balanced budgets while investing in higher education and keeping taxes low.	Unified Republicans and found consensus with Democrats on critical problems such as public education funding and tax reform
Political struggle	Urban legislators complained about the strong rural influence of "Billy's Boys," who had the ear of the speaker. Indicted on bribery allegations in 1980.	Pled guilty to campaign finance violations in 1983 and indicted in 1990 for skirting disclosure laws.	Failed to approve redistricting plan favored by Democrats in 2001 and reduced the number of his party's seats.	Ran the house in autocratic way, which led to a revolt by fellow Republicans against him.	Persistent calls that he wasn't conservative enough from his own party prompted frequent attempts to unseat him.	Private recordings with conservative group leader came out where the speaker passed a political "hit list" of members with whom he disagreed, leading to his resignation.

27 Baptist churches." The next week, when the committee lists came out, Ben Barnes was at the top of the list for the Liquor Regulation Committee.[29]

Committee Assignments and the Craddick D's. After taking over in 2003 as the first Republican speaker since Reconstruction, Tom Craddick had to contend with dwindling Republican support in the house. He doled out committee assignments that punished political foes and rewarded political friends, particularly Democrats who were willing to cross party lines and support Republican initiatives—a group that became known as the "Craddick D's."[30]

Eventually, however, Craddick's autocratic style even rubbed Republicans the wrong way. Eleven Republican members of the house—called the Polo Road Gang because they met at Representative Byron Cook's house on Polo Road in Austin—decided to join with Democrats to back Republican Joe Straus as speaker over Craddick.[31] Craddick's overthrow sent a clear message to future speakers that representatives would not be tyrannized by a speaker

ANGLES OF POWER
Choosing a Speaker

At the end of the 2017 legislative session, some Republicans accused outgoing Speaker Joe Straus (who had been elected in his first term as speaker with votes from Democrats) of blocking conservative priorities. Straus clashed with Lieutenant Governor Dan Patrick, whose background as a radio talk show host gave him an opportunity to listen to voters but also to side with them on more polarizing issues. During a battle about controversial legislation limiting local laws to protect transgender Texans, Straus complained that Patrick had "a different audience. I mean, literally an audience. . . . He's an entertainer, a talk show guy. . . . I'm not."[26] Patrick countered with the claim that if Straus had been at the Alamo, "He would have been the first one over the wall."[27]

With the hope of getting a more conservative leader, the House Freedom Caucus pushed the chamber's members to rewrite the rules for how speakers are chosen. The Texas House Republicans decided to pre-select a speaker by identifying a candidate who had the support of two-thirds of the Republican house members before submitting the proposal to a full floor vote. Advocates noted that a "Republican speaker of the house should first win the confidence of a majority of his or her fellow Republicans." Other Republicans opposed the rule change on the basis that votes for speaker could not be restricted in any way before the full floor vote and that this practice might allow legislators to "bribe" speakers to support their bills or ideological platform.[28] Dennis Bonnen, Republican from Angleton, however, did acquire the votes to become speaker of the house in 2019, but he announced his resignation after the session ended (see Table 7.2). Quickly after Republicans won a majority in the 2020 election Dade Phelan, Republican of Beaumont, announced he had enough votes to become speaker for the 2021 session.

SOCIAL RESPONSIBILITY: **Should most of the majority party approve of the speaker before the full house votes?**

who abused his or her power. Soon after assuming the position of speaker, Straus met with the committee chairs and told them that the pace of the session was up to them, that they would run their committees, and that if everyone followed the rules, he wouldn't call any fouls.[32]

Process and Procedures. Speakers decide all questions of process and procedure, and so they can indirectly influence the fate of specific legislation. For example, speakers assign legislation to committees. If a speaker sends a bill to a hostile committee, the committee can kill the bill. Conversely, if the speaker sends it to a friendly committee, the committee can enhance its chance of success. A similar procedural tool is the power of **recognition**, through which speakers call on house members, allowing them to speak during the discussion of a bill. Seemingly unimportant, the power of recognition allows speakers either to lengthen discussion or to end debate. In the 1971 session, Speaker Gus Mutscher Jr. presided over a house that was split between "wets," like Mutscher, who favored the sale of alcohol and "drys" who did not. At one point during the debate, the speaker looked up and saw that 100 (out of 150) legislators stood in favor of the measure, enough to pass the motion. He quickly announced that "[t]he gavel is coming down aye" to end the debate, and he had the sergeant at arms lock the door to the chamber so that those legislators who were present couldn't leave and change their minds.[33]

recognition: the power to call on a legislator and allow him or her to speak during debates

THE LIEUTENANT GOVERNOR

As we shall see in Chapter 9, the lieutenant governor (often referred to as the "lite" or "little" governor) is one of the most powerful elected officials in Texas government. Although not a member of the senate, the lieutenant governor acts as its presiding officer and is officially called the president of the senate. Thus, the lieutenant governor only casts a vote in the case of a tie. However, he or she enjoys other, more extensive powers. The lieutenant governor has full authority to assign senators to committees and appoint committee chairs. But unlike the speaker of the house, the lieutenant governor is not limited by seniority in assignments. Informally, senior senators get first pick at committee assignments until one-third of the committee is filled.

The lieutenant governor assigns legislation to specific committees, allowing him or her to influence the chances of a bill becoming law. For example, in 2015, Lieutenant Governor Dan Patrick sent a bill to ban in-state tuition for the children of undocumented immigrants to the Border Security Subcommittee instead of the Higher Education Committee or Senate Committee on State Affairs. Patrick knew that the Border Security Subcommittee was more likely to oppose the measure, and indeed, the subcommittee killed the bill.[34]

TEXAS TAKEAWAYS

7.3.1   Compare and contrast standing and select committees.

7.3.2   What are the speaker's powers?

7.3.3   What are the lieutenant governor's powers in the senate?

7.4 THE LEGISLATIVE PROCESS

> **7.4**   Outline the legislative process.

How a bill becomes a law in Texas echoes the federal legislative process in many ways: Bills pass from the committees to the floor of each chamber and require coordination between the chambers (see Figure 7.5). Legislators, often inspired by residents in the district, interest groups, or committee investigations, work up bills with the help of staff members and the Legislative Council. The multiple stages of the process and a short calendar, however, make passage of legislation even more challenging.

IN COMMITTEE

For a bill to become a law in Texas, each chamber has to hear it three times; these are referred to as the three readings. In the **first reading**, or the committee stage, the clerk in the house or senate reads the bill on the floor to introduce it, and then the speaker or lieutenant governor refers it to a committee.

first reading: legislation considered at the committee stage

FIGURE 7.5 **How A Bill Becomes a Law in Texas**

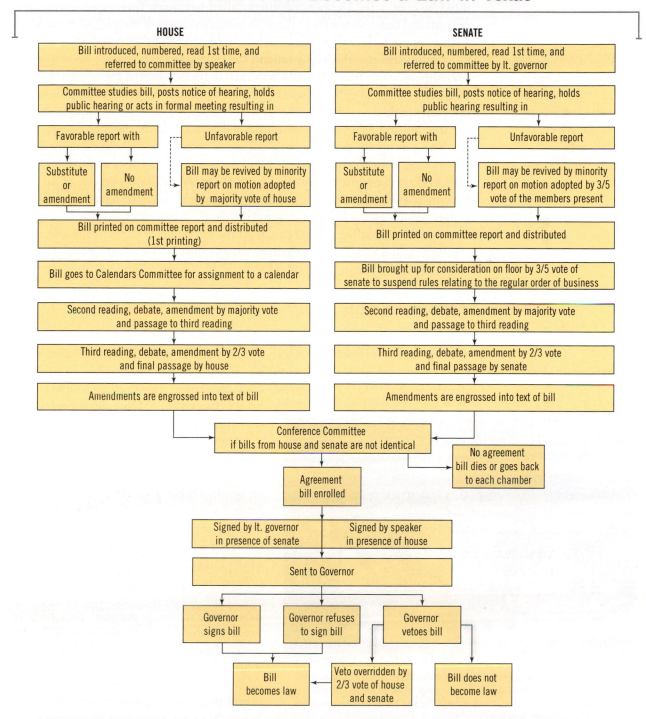

Source: Guide to Legislative Information (Revised). 2019. Texas Legislative Council for the 86th Legislature.

CRITICAL THINKING: **What role do the speaker, the lieutenant governor, committee chairs and members, interest groups, party leaders, the governor, and citizens play in each stage of the legislative process?**

amend: to mark up a bill

markup: the process whereby legislators add, subtract, or replace part of the original legislation so that it meets the preferences of the committee

All formal action taken by a committee in the Texas House and Senate must be conducted in open meetings called hearings. Interested parties not only attend but also testify at these hearings to shape or stop legislation. Most witnesses are lobbyists, partisan activists, or concerned bureaucrats.

Committee members may **amend** the legislation in a process known as bill **markup**, in which legislators add, subtract, or replace part of the original legislation. Committee members may also amend legislation by substituting the entire bill with another version of it. This process sometimes saves time of amending the original bill and offers a smooth transition to passage in the other chamber.

The committee can approve a bill, sending it to the full chamber, or it can do nothing with the bill, letting it wither and die for lack of attention. Many bills end up dying in committee. In 2019, more than 50 percent of all bills filed in 2019 died at this stage. For bills reported favorably, meaning the committee approves the bill, the committee drafts a report that includes recommendations regarding its placement on the calendar, the text of the bill, a bill analysis, and a fiscal note (reflecting the potential economic impact and consequences of balancing the budget).

ON THE FLOOR

second reading: legislation considered at the floor stage

third reading: the voting stage of legislation

In the **second reading**, or the floor stage, the full chamber debates the measure and amends it as desired through a simple majority vote. Effective legislators do their homework on the bills, cut deals, hustle for votes, and navigate the floor debate so that nothing goes wrong when legislation they favor or dislike comes up for discussion.[35] Most deals on legislation are made away from the floor.

During the second reading stage, members publicly debate the legislation being considered. Senators speak from their desks using a portable microphone. In the house chamber, which is much larger by comparison, the representatives speak either from the front microphone (where the defender of the bill speaks) or the back microphone (where members ask questions of those on the front microphone). Representatives have come up with unusual measures to limit debate. In 2015, one representative dangled a cookie on a string in front of another representative in an effort to lure him away from the back microphone so that he would stop asking questions and the chamber could move on to other legislation.[36]

The **third reading**, or the voting stage (called engrossment in the house), is the final

Senator Joan Huffman listens during a Senate State Affairs Committee hearing on legislation to raise the smoking age from 18 to 21. The bill passed out of the committee, was approved by the house and senate, and signed by the governor into law.

🔺 PERSONAL RESPONSIBILITY: **Is there an issue that riles you up enough to interrupt a legislative hearing in protest?**

stage. After the third reading, amendments can be offered, but a two-thirds majority is needed for approval of any amendment. This high voting hurdle makes amendments at this point infrequent. A simple majority is required to finally pass the legislation. The Texas Constitution requires bills to be read on three separate days, but the legislature can suspend the law with a four-fifths vote and conduct the second and third readings on the same day to speed things along.[37]

HOUSE AND SENATE AGREEMENT

Both chambers have to agree on legislation for it to arrive at the governor's desk. However, political agendas don't always match up. In the 2017 session, for example, tension between the chambers flared when one house member convinced the sergeant at arms to open the chamber doors as the full house membership shouted their protest over bottled-up bills in the senate. House Speaker Joe Straus and Lieutenant Governor Dan Patrick feuded over the budget, with the speaker calling out senate budget writers for "cooking the books" and using "Enron-esque" accounting gimmicks.[38] After an argument over property taxes led the house to adjourn a day early in the 2017 special session, Patrick lambasted the chamber: "With 27 hours to go, they walked off the job."[39]

Relations between the chambers are not always so contentious. When the two chambers are in agreement about a policy goal but disagree about specific aspects of the legislation, there are a few ways to reconcile house and senate bills. When a bill is still in committee in one of the chambers, a house bill can be amended by substituting it with a senate bill, and vice versa, which can save time because ultimately the legislature must reconcile house and senate bills to get a final version passed into law. If this swap does not occur and the house and senate versions of the bill differ, the bills are sent to a conference committee made up of lawmakers from both chambers.

IN CONFERENCE COMMITTEE

The speaker and lieutenant governor each appoint five members from their respective chambers to serve on a conference committee. Senate rules require that at least two of the conferees be members of the original committee that first heard the bill. The conference committee limits itself to the points of disagreement: It cannot add text or address areas of agreement.[40]

If the conference committee members hammer out differences and agree on a final version, a committee report is produced to summarize the changes. The house and senate must again vote to finalize the same version of the legislation. The report cannot be amended by either chamber; it must be accepted or rejected in its entirety. If no agreement is reached, the bill returns to the originating chamber and the process starts over. After the same version of the bill is agreed upon, it is sent to the governor for signature. The governor has 10 days (excluding Sundays) to sign the bill or the bill automatically becomes law. Alternatively, the governor can veto the bill. If, after a veto, the legislature decides to reconsider the legislation, two-thirds of the members of both chambers can override the veto.

Once a bill is approved by both chambers and signed by the governor, it takes effect as specified by the text of the passed legislation. If there is no specified "effective date," the act becomes effective on the 91st day following the final adjournment of the legislature. Bills that go into effect earlier than the 90 days or immediately upon the governor's signature require a two-thirds majority. More than a third of all bills passed in the 86th legislative session took effect immediately.

This process makes who gets on the conference committee important. Because the speaker and lieutenant governor want smooth passage of important legislation such as budget bills, they tend not to appoint members who have voted against a budget bill to the budget conference committee. This often leaves the minority party without a seat at the table.

THE REAL ENEMY: THE CALENDAR

The rules of the house and senate allow bills to be "pre-filed" from the Monday following the general election in November or to be filed within the first 60 days of a regular legislative session. "The first 60 days is like two-a-days for legislators," said former Republican Representative Cecil Bell of Magnolia, referring to grueling, twice-daily practices for football teams.[41]

After this 60-day deadline, only local bills (i.e., bills that deal with a fixed local entity), emergency appropriations, or emergency matters formally submitted by the governor can be considered. The 60-day deadline can also be waived if four-fifths of the members present vote to do so. After a certain point in the calendar, time runs short, and the political will to battle subsides. One member referred to these days as "bloody days," given that many bills die.[42]

Two calendar committees in the house, the Local and Consent Calendars Committee and the Calendars Committee, set the priorities and make the schedule for the legislative session. The Local and Consent Calendars Committee sets uncontested or local legislation on the agenda—for example, legislation concerning the fees of a local water district. The Calendars Committee prepares the daily calendar for all bills and, most importantly, determines the importance

Lawmakers confer and jockey for attention to their issues, pressured by the calendar, their party, interest groups, and voters.

SOCIAL RESPONSIBILITY: **Should legislators prioritize the needs of their districts, their party, or the state as a whole?**

of a bill by prioritizing some over others. In the senate, the secretary of the senate schedules most bills for floor debate, while the Senate Committee on Administration schedules noncontroversial legislation.

Given the short time for the full session, the fixed chamber deadlines by which legislation must pass, and the thousands of bills to sift through, any delay or distraction can kill a bill. In 2011, puppies temporarily bottlenecked legislation in the house. Long-time and much respected Representative Senfronia Thompson, Democrat of Houston and chair of the Local and Consent Calendar Committee, introduced legislation to regulate "puppy mills." First year lawmaker David Simpson opposed the bill and knocked it off the calendar. Thompson then put it back on again, and Simpson bumped it back off. The house eventually passed the bill, but it ate up significant legislative time in the process.[43] Similarly, important bills were stalled in 2005 when the legislature considered the "cheerleader booty bill," a measure regulating "overly sexual dance moves by school cheerleaders at sporting events."[44]

RULES RULE THE CHAMBERS

The Texas House and Texas Senate have both formal and informal rules that govern the chambers (see Table 7.3). When ethics legislation was voted on just before midnight the day the session was to end in 1991, most members had not even read the bill. Determined that this wouldn't happen again, Speaker Pete Laney pushed through new rules, setting deadlines by which bills are to clear committees, be passed by the full house and senate, and cleaned up. These rules compacted timelines and—in the words of columnist Dave McNeely—turned "a stock car race in the mud into a parade of septuagenarians showing off their walkers."[45]

The senate also has rules that govern when and if a bill can be brought to debate on the floor. By tradition, the senate considers bills in numerical order. So, bills with lower numbers are brought up first. Bills can, and frequently are, taken out of order, but three-fifths of the membership must agree to do so.[46] To counter the power of the lieutenant governor, who has absolute power to bring up legislation, senators pass a "blocker bill" each day the senate is in

TABLE 7.3	"Unwritten" Rules for Members of the Legislature
Always applaud when a fellow legislator recognizes constituents in the balcony.
Never launch a filibuster without informing the lieutenant governor and bill sponsor.
Don't knock bills off the uncontested calendar without first informing the author.
Never waste the chamber's time—this rule especially applies to freshmen.
Never act as though you know more than another member.

Source: Adapted from H. C. Pittman, Inside the Third House: A Veteran Lobbyist Takes a 50-Year Frolic through Texas Politics (Austin: Eakin Press, 1992).

session. It ensures that no other bill can be passed unless three-fifths of the senators agree to "suspend the regular order of business" and skip over the blocker bill.[47] This rule empowers the minority party, which could halt discussion on an issue with enough votes, and thus requires senators to build bridges to members of the other party.

⭐ TEXAS TAKEAWAYS

7.4.1 What are the main stages of the legislative process?

7.4.2 What happens during the committee stage?

7.4.3 What is the purpose of conference committees?

7.4.4 Why is the calendar the real enemy?

⚖ 7.5 WORKING TOGETHER

> **7.5** Assess how legislative tools are used to speed up or slow down legislation.

Each chamber has unique rules and traditions that contribute to the passage (or more often, stoppage) of legislation. Much as in the U.S. Congress, the process is purposely designed to slow down passage of legislation and thus ensure careful consideration of the laws that are passed. Such a process restricts the number of bills passed. However, with a short session and partisan politics at play, tension increases during the lawmaking process, making it difficult to accomplish important legislative goals.

Maintaining relationships and building bridges are more than professional courtesy—both are necessary to passage of legislation. In the 2001 legislative session, Senators Leticia Van de Putte and Royce West were debating legislation introduced by Van de Putte in committee that would stiffen penalties for grabbing a police officer's firearm. Long-time colleagues and allies, the two talked back and forth about the merits of the legislation, with West unsure the legislation was needed considering that fines for assaulting or killing police officers were already in place. As the questions became more damaging to her bill, Senator Van de Putte discreetly passed West a note, placing a kiss with her red lipstick at the bottom. West received the note, smiled, and stopped asking questions. When asked later what she wrote, Van de Putte responded that she had asked him to "knock it off—in unprintable language."[48]

Some legislators use **logrolling** (or favor trading) to get their preferred legislation passed. In the 2017 session, conservative Democrat Eddie Lucio of Brownsville joined Republicans pushing for a bill that restricted local governments from allowing transgender individuals to use the bathroom of their

logrolling: trading favors, votes, or influence for legislative actions

choice (called the "bathroom bill"), likely in exchange for a rider in the budget that provided $5 million in funding for an ecology center in his district.[49]

Some legislators base their success on maintaining good relationships. Lieutenant Governor Ben Barnes, one of two people elected as both speaker of the house and lieutenant governor, turned making (and keeping) allies into a "political crusade." Everyone got a chance to bend his ear, "Baptist or boozer, labor or management, bigot or Black."[50]

Tiffs, however, are common. Reacting to what they felt was house leadership obstruction on conservative priorities such as anti-abortion, Second Amendment, and property rights bills through "petty personal politics," 12 members of the House Freedom Caucus banded together to object to more than 100 bills on the Local and Consent Calendar just ahead of Mother's Day—dubbed the "Mother's Day Massacre."[51] The bills torpedoed included legislation to connect first-time pregnant women to Medicaid services and funding to study health care and pregnant African American women, prompting one representative who authored a killed bill to call it a "drive by shooting."[52] In these power struggles, legislators have access to an array of weapons that can slow down or speed up legislation.

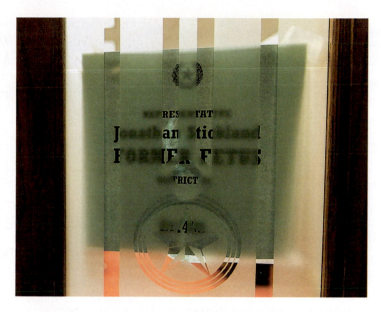

Republican Representative Jonathan Stickland changed the nameplate on his office door to "Representative Jonathan Stickland, FORMER FETUS, District 92, E1.402" to greet visitors on the day Planned Parenthood lobbied the Texas Capitol. The house's chief rule-enforcer promptly removed the sign, saying the State Preservation Board prohibits such displays. Underlying the skirmish was the presence of a growing lack of civility among the members of the chamber.*

PERSONAL RESPONSIBILITY: **How do civility and camaraderie (or lack thereof) influence the legislative process?**

SLOWING IT DOWN

Delay, distract, disrupt—these are all ways in which members of the legislature can interrupt or slow down the legislative process. This is an especially powerful tool when a party is in the minority and has less political muscle to force the chamber to a particular decision. The enemy of the majority is the clock—as delay is often the same as defeat. The following are a few effective tactics.

Taking a Walk. A legislator will leave the chamber so that not enough legislators are present to bring up a bill (the rules require the presence of a minimum number of legislators to proceed). Slowing down the senate was a specialty of the Killer Bees, a group of determined liberal Democrats who opposed Lieutenant Governor Bill Hobby in 1979. Hobby started calling them the Killer Bees because "no one knew when they would strike next." In one fateful episode, they opposed a bill that would set the Democratic and Republican primaries

After the Killer Bees incident, the group reunited to celebrate their anniversary at Scholz Beer Garten in Austin. Lieutenant Governor Hobby sent the Texas Rangers to bring the group to a reception in the Capitol. Clad in a beekeeper's hat, he jokingly greeted them from the dais.

PERSONAL RESPONSIBILITY: If you were a legislator, would you compromise on your principles to work together with fellow legislators to pass an important bill? On what issues?

point of order: a technical objection to an error in a bill

on different dates, enabling conservative Democrats to support former Governor John Connally, a former Democrat, who was running for president in the Republican primary in 1980. At the time, Texans could vote in either or both primaries. To prevent passage, 12 Killer Bees fled the Capitol to break the quorum, the minimum number needed to hold a vote. Texas Rangers were dispatched to round up the senators. Noting that the senators would have a State Official (S.O.) tag on their license plates, one senator rhymed: "The Texas Rangers hunt for them; Bill Hobby issues pleas, And says that on their license plates, It shows that they're S.O. Bees."[53]

The event was a fiasco. Lieutenant Governor Hobby lamented bringing up the bill, and attempting to catch the Killer Bees was a failure. One senator left the "hive" to see his granddaughter. A ranger came to her door only to arrest the senator's brother instead. The senator meanwhile jumped over the back fence and remained at large.

Point of Order. A **point of order** (POO) is a technical objection to an error in a bill. Once declared, a POO takes precedence on the floor, and the presiding officer (the speaker of the house, the lieutenant governor, or whoever is presiding in their place) must address the argument. A POO can hold up consideration of the legislation, send it back to the committee of origin for clarification, or kill it entirely (if the bill is missing a critical part like an enacting clause). Legislators often "scrub" a bill to look for rule violations.

For instance, in 2015, Democratic Senator Kirk Austin delayed a concealed firearms on campus bill by pointing out that the witness list on the bill was inaccurate—some of the witnesses listed as speaking "for" the legislation were only speaking "on" the legislation, making it subject to a POO on the technicality.[54] In 2019, Julie Johnson and a newly formed House LGBTQ Caucus conjured a POO to challenge the so-called Save Chick-fil-A bill that would have punished local governments for retaliating against businesses on religious grounds, as the city of San Antonio had done when it booted the popular chicken restaurant from the airport for making donations to anti-LBGTQ Christian organizations. As the parliamentarian sustained the POO on the grounds that the bill analysis was inaccurate, someone in the House chamber played a recording of "Taps."[55] Sometimes a POO can derail multiple bills. In the Democrat-controlled house during the 1997 session, Republican Representative Arlene Wohlgemuth called a POO that struck 52 bills from the house schedule in an episode that became known as "the Memorial Day Massacre."[56]

Stuffing the Box. Thousands of bills are filed each legislative session, making competition for attention and action significant. Opponents of a controversial bill may seek to debate noncontroversial bills in order to soak up time that would otherwise be spent on the controversial one. For instance, in 2015, the house discussed an uncontroversial bill relating to limiting the fees for the Velasco Drainage District, thereby delaying discussion of an "open carry" firearms bill that was next on the agenda. When fellow legislators called to end debate of the drainage bill, Democrat Terry Canales coyly remarked, "Why, do we need to move the bill?" to laughter in the chamber.[57]

Trey Martinez Fischer, Democrat of San Antonio, made his name in part with his frequent use of the point of order (POO). *Texas Monthly* crowned him the "prince of POO" in 2013.

Talk It to Death. For legislation on the Local and Consent Calendar in the house that is not expected to provoke disagreement, a representative can kill a bill simply by talking about it for 10 minutes in session and so stall a vote. House members can also hog the microphone in the chamber (from the "back mic," where members ask questions) for 10 minutes at a time.[58]

SOCIAL RESPONSIBILITY: **Should legislators cooperate and compromise, or should they stand on their principles and use POOs to sabotage bills they oppose?**

Party of Five. In the house, five representatives can kill a bill on the Local and Consent Calendar just by signaling their opposition to it.

Filibuster. Because debate is unlimited in the Texas Senate, a senator who objects to a bill or simply wants to slow the process down can hold the floor and talk until they are physically unable to do so. This is called a **filibuster**. During a filibuster, a senator who holds the floor cannot talk about issues not related to the legislation, eat or drink, leave the floor to use the bathroom, or lean on anything for physical support. Senators are allowed three warnings before the chamber can vote to end the filibuster by using a POO to point out a rules violation. If the POO is sustained by the chair, the senator must yield the floor.

filibuster: an action in which a senator holds the floor and restrains the chamber from moving forward on legislation

Donning her pink tennis shoes in the 2013 legislative session, Democratic Senator Wendy Davis took to the floor of the Texas State Senate at 11:18 A.M. on June 26 with the hopes of holding the floor long enough to run out the clock on the legislature's special session that ended at midnight. At issue was Senate Bill 5, which would institute a ban on abortions after 20 weeks of pregnancy, require clinics performing abortions to meet the same standards as other surgical clinics, and force doctors performing abortions to have admitting privileges at a nearby hospital. Senator Davis got her first warning at 5:30 P.M. for talking about funding cuts to women's health services. Her second strike came from

In one of the most noteworthy filibusters in Texas history, Democratic Senator Wendy Davis held the senate floor to delay a vote on a controversial abortion bill.

PERSONAL RESPONSIBILITY: **Thousands of citizens rallied behind Senator Wendy Davis in the Capitol during her filibuster of abortion legislation—so much so that the building literally shook. Critics complained about the lack of decorum. Do you agree or disagree? Why?**

a colleague providing her with a back brace. Her third strike came when she mentioned Texas's mandatory pre-abortion ultrasound law, which was ruled to be off-topic of the legislation. The jockeying about the rules on the third strike between legislative staff, the members, and the presiding officers, in addition to the rising crowd noise in the packed gallery, advanced the clock past the midnight deadline and ended the bill. The chaos surrounding the normally staid Capitol complex fell at the feet of the lieutenant governor. Leaving the dais after a ruling that time had expired, Lieutenant Governor David Dewhurst said, "It's been fun, but, um, see ya soon." Accusing Dewhurst of a "lack of leadership," Republican Dan Patrick succeeded in unseating Dewhurst in the subsequent 2014 election.[59]

The record for the longest filibuster in Texas history is held by Senator Bill Meier, Democrat from Hurst, who talked for 43 hours in 1977 against a bill that eventually passed anyway. He sipped water, ate lemon slices, and relieved himself in an "astronaut bag" attached to his leg under his pants.[60] Most filibusters, however, last about an hour or so and are used either to make a political point or to draw attention to an issue.[61]

The lieutenant governor can use his power of recognition to block a filibuster. Late in a legislative session, Democratic Senator Oscar Mauzy of Dallas filibustered a school finance appropriation, prompting a special session. Thereafter, Lieutenant Governor Hobby kept a reminder on his desk that read "Do not recognize Mauzy on the last day for ANY reason!"[62]

Chubbing. A generic term for delay, "chubbing," usually involves a combination of procedural tactics, such as raising technical questions and lengthy floor speeches, all designed to eat up more time. Late in 2019, House Democrats broke the dull and "humdrum" routine of the 2019 legislative session when they peppered Representative Candy Noble, the author of a bill that prohibited the partnering of local government and abortion providers, with so many questions that in exasperation she walked away from the front podium where legislative sponsors stand to take questions. One Democrat remarked on her "lack of professional courtesy," but across the rotunda, Lieutenant Governor Dan Patrick accused Democrats of chubbing to kill bills they didn't like by taking "five, six, seven hours for one bill."[63]

Tagging. In the Texas House and Senate, a lawmaker can "tag" a bill, informally putting it on hold for 24 hours. This tactic is effective used late in the session when deadlines for passing legislation are looming. Those who control the calendars are at their most powerful at this point. Senator Leticia Van de Putte, once fed up that her legislation was being restrained in this way, joked to her fellow senators that she was running a two-for-one special: She would tag two of their house bills for every one of her bills that got tagged. By the end of the day, she won almost every house bill she carried in the senate.[64]

SPEEDING IT UP

The party in the majority knows full well that the party in the minority wants to slow the process down, so the majority party attempts to counter these maneuvers with procedures of their own to speed the process up.

Suspending the 24-Hour Waiting Period. By the chamber rules, 24 hours must pass between readings of a bill. The chamber can suspend this rule with agreement of two-thirds of the members. For legislation concerning "campus carry," Republicans in the senate suspended the 24-hour waiting period, holding the vote on a Saturday and thus avoiding a Democratic filibuster.[65]

Discharge Petition. In 2005, proponents of the bill to limit third-party issue ads in primary and general elections appealed to House Speaker Tom Craddick. The bill had been bottled up in the Elections Committee for weeks. Proponents asked Craddick to pull out a "dusty" house discharge rule that allowed the full house to vote to yank a bill from committee to the full chamber for consideration. The effort wasn't needed, however, because legislators quickly killed the bill in committee before the full house could vote.[66]

Suspending Normal Business. On one occasion, the Texas Senate, while debating windstorm insurance, introduced a novel tactic. As the hands of the antique clock above the senate chamber's entry door approached midnight, the sergeant at arms, under orders from Lieutenant Governor David Dewhurst, opened a panel on the back of the clock, flipped a switch, and "froze" time at 11:58 P.M. Senators continued to debate and indeed actively played along with the charade of time. When asked what time it was about 40 minutes later, Senator Kel Seliger responded, "It's nighttime. Has been for several hours and will be several hours more."[67]

INCREASING PARTISANSHIP

One obstacle to cooperation within the state legislature is rising partisanship. The growing gap between liberals and conservatives has come to define politics not just nationally but also in Texas (see Figure 7.6). As we saw in Chapter 5, the rise the Republican Party precipitated an ideological split between conservatives and liberals. As individual voters' opinions on policy became more tightly linked to their identification with a political party, **political polarization** increased. As Stanford political scientist Morris Fiorina wrote, "Issues and ideology used to cross-cut the partisan distribution, now they reinforce it."[68]

political polarization: the stricter definition of voters' opinions on policy and political matters as a result of their identification with a political party

FIGURE 7.6   Increasing Polarization in the Texas Legislature

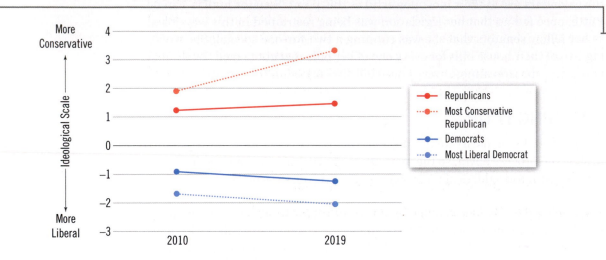

Source: State Ideologies Project, Boris Shor. Positive numbers designate conservative ideologies for median voter; negative numbers designate more liberal ideologies for median voter.

COMMUNICATION:

How polarized is the Texas House?

- The average ideology of the Republican Party has become more conservative, and the average ideology of the Democratic Party has become more liberal.

- The Democratic Party has become, on average, more liberal than the Republican Party, which has become more conservative.

- The most extreme liberal and conservative members of each party became more liberal and conservative from 2010 to 2019.

CRITICAL THINKING:

Why has polarization increased?

- Long-time Austin watchers claim that the extension of the Capitol in 1993 allowed members to spread out instead of being physically close together. The physical distance decreased personal contacts and hurt working relationships.

- The rise of social media has allowed members to communicate directly to constituents, often in partisan ways.

- Partisan activists on both sides have become more partisan.

- Too few voters vote in primary elections, allowing the most active (and extreme) ideological voters to have an outsized say in who is elected.

Polarization has profound consequences for governing the Lone Star State. Former Democratic Senator Pete Gallego, who went on to serve in the U.S. House of Representatives, said of politics in Austin: "In the old way of doing business, it was fine to disagree and then go to dinner. Now it's personal and more partisan, and a disagreement on one issue leads to a disagreement on another issue."[69]

As partisanship has increased, cooperation in both chambers has declined. For many decades, the majority party in the house voted as a bloc time after time. The senate, with a long-standing history of bipartisanship, deliberated and worked across party lines. No longer. Today, the senate acts more like the house, quashing any minority party input into the process.[70] These partisan conflicts limit the ability of the legislature to address many of the big problems the state faces and forces the two chambers to focus instead on temporary, incremental solutions.

TEXAS TAKEAWAYS

7.5.1 What are ways that legislators slow down and speed up the legislative process to block or pass legislation?

7.5.2 What are the disadvantages of increasing partisanship?

7.6 DEMOGRAPHIC REPRESENTATION

Just as the composition of the state has changed over the last century, so have the demographics and characteristics of the legislators sent to Austin to represent its people. Political scientists find that demographic representation has both symbolic and substantive value. Political representation by ethnic or racial minorities produces legislative outcomes that are more congruent with the needs of the racial and ethnic groups represented, may foster increased civic engagement among those groups, and can reduce the perception of racial discrimination broadly.[71]

> **7.6** Explain how legislators represent their constituents demographically.

Texas legislators are a diverse group and are growing even more diverse over time. Some demographic groups are overrepresented, however, and some are underrepresented. Although the legislature is still dominated by older white men, more women, African Americans, and Hispanics have been elected in the past two decades (see Figure 7.7). Let's take a closer look at some of these demographic trends.

WOMEN LEGISLATORS

Although women have made inroads regarding membership in both chambers, the perception that the legislature is a "boys' club" persists in the behavior of some legislators. Before the civil rights movement in the 1960s, legislative committees would meet in male-only clubs, prohibiting female members from attending.[72] The situation has improved since the 1990s, when then-Lieutenant Governor Bob Bullock said that if Senator Judith Zaffirini would "cut her skirt off about 6 inches and put on some high-heel shoes," she could pass whatever legislation she wanted. In 2011, however, when freshman Senator Wendy Davis raised a question about a male colleague's bill, she said

FIGURE 7.7 **Demographics of the Texas Legislature, 74th to 87th Sessions**

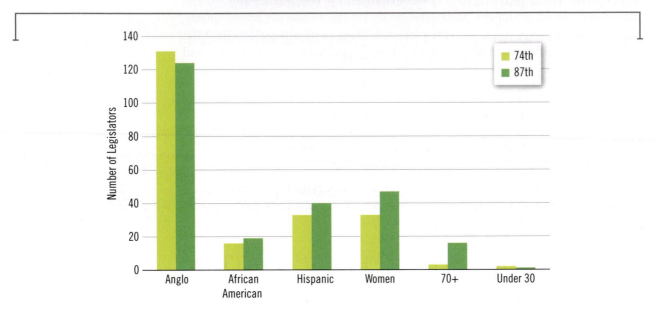

Source: Texas Legislative Council

 COMMUNICATION:

How has the makeup of the legislature changed?

- The number of women has increased.
- The legislature has aged, with more members in the 70-and-over category.
- The number of African Americans has stayed relatively stable, but the number of Hispanic representatives has increased slightly.

 CRITICAL THINKING:

Why has the makeup of the legislature become more inclusive of racial minorities and women?

- Districts have been geographically created to favor racial minorities, increasing the number of districts where racial minorities may win office.
- More women have taken leadership roles in parties and organizations, creating more opportunities for them to move into elected positions.

he growled "don't talk to me like that, little lady."[73] While the house and senate have policies to investigate misconduct, most view them as insufficient to deal with allegations because the incentive to investigate colleagues is low.[74] In 2019, however, the house voted unanimously on a new internal policy that would move investigations of inappropriate behavior complaints to a legislative committee with subpoena power.[75] With two members of the senate facing sexual harassment charges and dozens of unreported degrading comments, gestures, and unwanted advances, the senate adopted a policy to mandate in-person training for staff members, though not for the senators themselves.[76]

INSIDER INTERVIEW

Senfronia Thompson, State Representative, Houston, Texas

"Women are coming forward now to speak out about harassment. You did so your first term in 1973. Tell me about that experience."

I had a colleague from Cleburne [state Representative C. C. "Kit" Cooke]; it was [my first session], and he says, "Here comes my beautiful black mistress." It infuriated me. It was so insulting. I informed the speaker of the house that I wanted to give a personal privilege speech. I had people coming up telling me, "Don't do it. It's going to hurt you. You're not going to be able to pass legislation." I was just determined that I needed to set everybody on course, that I was duly elected.[77]

SOCIAL RESPONSIBILITY: **How can the legislature ensure members and staff are protected from sexual harassment and create an environment in which members interact in a civil and productive manner?**

AFRICAN AMERICANS

Providing African Americans with a pathway to the legislative process erupted in a major battle in Texas politics. Legislatures drew district boundaries to carve up the African American population into several districts so that no black representative served in a legislative chamber anywhere in the South from 1906 to 1966. Even in cities with a significant black population, candidates were forced to run in citywide or countywide multimember districts where Anglo voters refused to vote for black candidates.

The fight over civil rights turned into electoral combat in the 1960s. Curtis Graves's election in 1966, the first African American elected to the Texas House since Reconstruction, highlights this remarkable accomplishment. Just a few years earlier, he had had to take a literacy test in order to be eligible to vote. Barbara Jordan was the first African American woman to be elected to the clubbish Texas Senate (1967). Eddie Bernice Johnson (1973) and Senfronia Thompson (1972) were the first African American women to serve in the Texas House.[78]

HISPANICS

Despite significant population numbers, Texas Hispanics' fight for inclusion came only recently. The 1971 reapportionment in Texas made it practically impossible for Hispanics to be represented, as Hispanic populations were carved up and spread thinly across districts. Only 10 Hispanics served in the Texas House in 1971. However, court-mandated redistricting plans in the 1970s and 1980s increased that figure dramatically. By 1999, Texas led all other states in the number of Latino representatives. Irma Rangel was the first Latina elected to the Texas State House of Representatives in 1976.[79] Judith Zaffirini was the first Latina elected to the Texas Senate in 1986. Latinas are still less represented in the Texas legislature than Latinos, however, because traditional gender socialization may not encourage female participation in politics and women lack the support of party elites.[80]

RELIGION AND OTHER FACTORS

When not at the Capitol in Austin, the 181 members of the Texas legislature are cotton farmers, lawyers, realtors, or pharmacists, representing a diverse set of occupations and backgrounds.[81] As a group, however, the legislators are highly educated: most hold bachelor's or postgraduate degrees, and most are alumni of the University of Texas (see Figure 7.8). In this sense, they do not "look like" the average voter. Most legislators consider themselves Christian, and in this sense, they do "look like" most Texans.

 TEXAS TAKEAWAYS

7.6.1 Why is demographic representation important?

7.6.2 How did Texas prevent African Americans and Hispanics from holding seats in the legislature until the 1970s?

FIGURE 7.8 Education Attainment among Texas Legislators and Texans

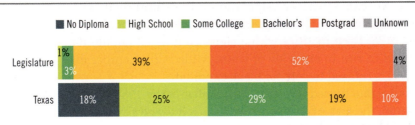

■ No Diploma ■ High School ■ Some College ■ Bachelor's ■ Postgrad ■ Unknown

Legislature	1% / 3% / 39% / 52% / 4%	
Texas	18% / 25% / 29% / 19% / 10%	

Source: U.S. Census Bureau, American Community Survey, 2015; Alexa Ura and Jolie McCullough, "Once Again, the Texas Legislature Is Mostly White, Male, Middle-Aged," *The Texas Tribune*, January 9, 2017.

COMMUNICATION:

What is the education level of the members of the Texas legislature?

- Most members of the legislature are well educated, receiving most frequently a postgraduate degree (52 percent) or at least a bachelor's degree (39 percent).
- Few in the Texas legislature have no diploma, but more than 18 percent of Texans do not. The same can be said for those without a high school diploma—25 percent of Texans but only 1 percent of legislators.

CRITICAL THINKING:

Why?

- Making laws and interpreting legislation require a breadth of education, often specialized in law or business.
- Individuals who have worked in an industry with well-connected or wealthy colleagues may be more likely to run for office as they will have an easier time fundraising.

THE INSIDER VIEW

A house member in the 1960s was quoted as saying that the state capitol "was built for giants and inhabited by pygmies."[82] Jokes aside, the power of the Texas legislature, though it meets infrequently, is significant. The volume of laws passed even in a short window of time affects nearly every aspect of the lives of Texans. Several pressure points in the Texas legislature determine whether or not legislation is passed—the short duration of the session, the desires of the speaker of the house and lieutenant governor, and partisan warfare. Colliding political rivalries shape the outcome of the legislative process, pitting the parties against each other with an arsenal of rules that speed up or slow down the process. Yet, cross-cutting these ideological rivalries, personal relationships and the need to claim credit for accomplishments have allowed legislators to work together for the good of the state, even if they don't always agree on what that is.

TEXAS TAKEAWAYS

7.1.1 Legislators pass laws and resolutions, oversee their implementation, perform casework, and take positions and claim credit in order to win reelection.

7.1.2 The main lawmaking functions of the Texas state legislature are to pass laws and resolutions, and to oversee the implementation of laws passed in previous sessions.

7.1.3 General laws affect all Texans, local laws are directed at specific local governments, and special laws exempt individuals or business from state law.

7.1.4 Oversight may include program evaluation for executive agencies, periodic audits of legislative spending, or regulation of the rules implemented by executive agencies. The legislature can hold hearings to investigate abuse, mismanagement, or abuse of power, typically of executive agencies. With the governor's consent, two-thirds of the Texas Senate can remove an appointed official.

7.1.5 The house has a larger number of members than the senate—150 compared to 31—that are elected for a shorter term—two years as compared to four years in the senate.

7.1.6 They and their staff act as caseworkers when they meet with constituents to help them obtain goals, such as obtaining a government benefit or changing a law.

7.1.7 Legislators establish credibility with their constituents by taking positions on major issues that their constituents claim and take credit for political achievements.

7.2.1 Strong legislatures have full-time, professional, well-paid legislators, with year-round or annual sessions, plentiful legislative staff, and competitive elections.

7.2.2 Texas has a weak legislature—due to the length of its sessions, salary, staff, and boards that facilitate the legislative process.

7.2.3 The Texas legislature meets biennially, a system shared with only three other states in the nation—all of them small states. Its legislative session is 140 days, longer than most states that set the length of sessions.

7.2.4 Thirty-day special sessions are called roughly every other legislative session to address issues that were not taken up or settled during a regular session, emergencies, or legislative "bellyflops" on an important issue.

7.2.5 Too much turnover can lead to loss of institutional memory, so that legislators may be less effective. Turnover, however, may allow for a more responsive body that is not dominated by senior members.

7.2.6 Part-time legislators may have less contact with their constituents, be more influenced by party leadership and the governor, and less willing to take on government reforms and to enact the complex and innovative policies a state may need.

7.3.1 Both committee types organize legislators to work on a policy topic or issue. Standing committees are permanent committees that deal with a specific issue or topic, whereas select committees are temporary committees that have a fixed issue to investigate or legislation to consider.

7.3.2 The speaker assigns members of the house to committees in half the cases, when seniority does not determine positions. The speaker also resolves all questions of process and procedure within the house, including sending bills to committees, recognizing legislators on floor debates, and lengthening or terminating debate on a bill.

7.3.3 The lieutenant governor only casts a vote in the case of a tie. However, he or she has full authority to assign senators to committees and appoint committee chairs. The lieutenant governor sends legislation to specific committees, influencing the chances of a bill becoming law.

7.4.1 The main stages of the legislative process are the first reading, when the clerk reads the bill on the floor, and the speaker or lieutenant governor refers it to a committee where it is amended and reports out favorably or unfavorably; the second reading in which legislators on the floor debate and amend the bill; and the third reading, after which the chamber votes.

7.4.2 Committees hold open meetings called hearings that lobbyists, bureaucrats, or other interested parties can attend or at which they can testify. Committee members mark up the bill and approve it or do nothing, letting it die.

7.4.3 Conference committees are convened to hammer out differences between the house and senate versions of a bill. If the committee can agree, each chamber must vote on the bill again before sending it to the governor.

7.4.4 Apart from local bills, emergency appropriations, and emergency matters submitted by the governor, all bills must be submitted within the first 60 days of the session. After a bill is submitted, its sponsors must contend with house and senate rules and leaders to ensure that it is referred to a receptive committee and placed on the calendar to be debated and voted upon before the session ends.

7.5.1 Legislators slow down the process by raising a point of order, talking bills to death, filibustering, chubbing, and leaving the chamber so that the minimum number of legislators needed to pass a bill is not present. Legislators speed up the process by suspending the 24-hour waiting period.

7.5.2 These partisan conflicts limit the legislature's ability to address big problems the state faces and forces the two chambers to focus instead on temporary, incremental solutions.

7.6.1 Political representation by ethnic or racial minorities produces legislative outcomes that are more congruent with the needs of the racial and ethnic groups represented; may foster increased civic engagement among those groups; and can reduce the perception of racial discrimination broadly.

7.6.2 In the past, the Texas legislatures carved up minority populations into several districts so that minority representative struggled to win elections.

KEY TERMS

amend
bicameral legislature
casework
committees

delegate
filibuster
first reading
general law
incumbent

institutional memory
local law
logrolling
markup
point of order
political polarization
recognition
regular session
resolutions
second reading
select committee
seniority
sine die
special law
special session
standing committees
third reading
trustee
turnover

PRACTICE QUIZ

1. Areas with fixed geographical boundaries that elect legislators are referred to as . . .

   a. Unitary actors
   b. Single-member districts
   c. Legislative zones
   d. Multimember districts

2. What is casework?

   a. Legislators work with the Legislative Council to craft legislation.
   b. Legislators hold hearings on specific legislation.
   c. Legislators and their staff assist constituents in their districts with specific requests.
   d. Legislators investigate claims by state agencies about fraud and waste.

3. A special session can only be called by . . .

   a. The speaker of the house
   b. The president of the senate
   c. The governor
   d. The chief justice of the Texas Supreme Court

4. The Latin phrase for the end of the legislative session, which means "without day," is . . .

   a. *Sine die*
   b. *Ceteris paribus*
   c. *Amicus curiae*
   d. *Sic semper tyrannis*

5. The Texas legislature is . . .

   a. Unicameral
   b. Bicameral
   c. Neither unicameral nor bicameral
   d. Both unicameral and bicameral, depending on the election year

6. The final stage of a bill in the Texas Legislature is called . . .

   a. Final reading
   b. *Sine die*
   c. Third reading
   d. Adjournment

7. If there are differences in legislation between the house and senate, the senate's version is always the one submitted to the governor.

   a. True
   b. False

8. The incumbency advantage is generally low for Texas legislators.

   a. True
   b. False

9. Resolutions convey the will of the chamber.

   a. True
   b. False

10. POO stands for a "point of order" and is a technical objection to an error in a bill.

    a. True
    b. False

[Answers: B, C, C, A, B, C, B, B, A, A]

Learn more with this chapter's digital tools, including the Oxford Insight Study Guide, at www.oup.com/he/Rottinghaus3e.

8 | GOVERNORS OF TEXAS

On June 17, 2001, the Texas state legislature faced down the "Father's Day Massacre." Nothing like it had ever happened before. In a single day, Texas Governor Rick Perry axed 82 bills. The vetoed legislation spanned a wide gamut of issues, ranging from the expansion of legal, charitable bingo games to the banning of the death penalty for convicted killers with mental disabilities.

Why did Perry do it? The state legislature had spent valuable time and taxpayer money crafting the legislation, some of which passed with overwhelming support. Yes, the majority of the bills had Democrats as sponsors (56 out of the 82)—and Perry was Republican—but bills from Republicans were also terminated. And many legislators didn't get courtesy calls that the governor was going to veto their bill, which was a long-standing tradition.[1] Charges of a power grab and political payback echoed throughout the state capitol.

Governor Perry's message was clear: He would be a strong and active governor. He intended to invigorate the Republican Party at a time when Democrats and Republicans were vying for control of the legislature. Perry was determined to cement the development of a strong Texas governor—even though historically the Texas executive branch has been weak and divided, as discussed in Chapter 9.

Fast forward almost 20 years. As reelected Governor Greg Abbott took the stage on January 15, 2019, through a line of crossed swords for his second inaugural address, he promised more bipartisanship. Abbott's conciliatory stance came in response to a bruising election for his party in 2018, with Democrats unseating 12 Republicans in the Texas House. He presented a blueprint for earnest work on issues Texans cared about: strengthening local schools, slashing the state's

8.1	Identify the eligibility requirements, term, succession process, and removal process for Texas governors.
8.2	Analyze how governors use their formal powers.
8.3	Evaluate the use of informal powers by the Texas governor to advance agendas.
8.4	Assess the strength of the Texas governor and proposals to modify gubernatorial power.

● The longest-serving governor in Texas history (by a large margin), Rick Perry established the precedent for a strong and active governor.

property tax burdens, and cracking down on human trafficking.[2] Then he used all the tools at his disposal and successfully pushed this agenda through.

Perry and Abbott, like governors before them, battled both the legislature and other powerful members of the executive branch. These struggles are a legacy from the past. Fearful of unchecked executives following Texans' unpleasant experience with Reconstruction Governor Edmund Davis, every state constitution since that time has maintained a plural executive and limited the governor's power. And yet, through political will, party strength, and personal relationships, modern Texas governors are more powerful today than at any time in the state's history.

In this chapter, we take an in-depth look at the roles and powers of the Texas governor. We first outline the rules of the office, including the eligibility to serve, succession in office, length of term, and removal from office. We then examine the formal and informal powers of the governor. We end by evaluating whether the Texas governor is weak or strong and examining the consequences for Texas government.

8.1 RULES OF THE OFFICE

8.1 Identify the eligibility requirements, term, succession process, and removal process for Texas governors

The Texas Constitution defines who can run for governor, how long the governor can stay in office, and under what conditions he or she serves. These rules also affect the power relationships between the governor and the rest of government in the Lone Star State. For example, the state legislature can use these rules to threaten the governor with impeachment. On the other hand, the length of the governor's term and the lack of term limits place a popular governor in a strong position relative to state legislators.

ELIGIBILITY

To serve as governor, an individual must be at least 30 years of age, a citizen of the United States, and a resident of Texas for at least 5 years immediately preceding his or her election. The governor cannot hold any other office (civil, military, or corporate) during the term and cannot accept any salary, reward, or compensation (or the promise of these) for any service rendered or performed. Interestingly, the governor need not be an eligible voter. Governor W. Lee "Pappy" O'Daniel was a registered voter but had not paid his poll tax (when a fee was required to vote) and could not even vote for himself in the 1938 election.

INFORMAL QUALIFICATIONS

Formal qualifications for governor are minimal, but informal qualifications, such as race, gender, profession, political experience, social network, charm, and charisma, also factor in. A 1962 *Houston Chronicle* editorial submitted that an ideal candidate for the office of governor needs "brilliance of mind," legal knowledge, political experience, and "sound knowledge of business and industry."[3] And one can add that almost all Texan governors have been white Protestant men with previous political experience. Texans have elected lawyers, bankers, baseball team owners, ranchers, and even a flour manufacturer to the highest office in the state. But the political environment has changed since 1962, as the media and online social networking have made politics more accessible. In 2006, Jewish country singer and satirist Kinky Friedman challenged Rick Perry for the governor's seat and received almost 13 percent of the vote. His campaign slogan was "How hard could it be?"

TERMS

Originally suspicious of executive power after their break with Mexico, the delegates at the Constitutional Convention of 1876 limited the governor's term to 2 years. In 1972, however, voters amended the Texas Constitution to extend the term to 4 years in order to reduce the frequency of elections and allow the governor to focus on governing rather than campaigning for reelection.

This expansion of time in office allows Texas governors to amass more power by leading the state for a longer term. This means more opportunities for appointments, more favors granted, and a more significant say on two (rather than one) legislative sessions. There are no **term limits**, so an individual can run for governor as often as he or she wishes. Traditionally, most governors have served only one term, so the average length of term since 1846 has been about 3.5 years. Governor Rick Perry broke that mold by serving as governor for more than twice as long as the 40 previous governors (see Figure 8.1).

REMOVAL FROM OFFICE

Impeachment is a legal process in which the legislative branch has the authority to indict and remove a public official. The state legislature can impeach

In 2006, Kinky Friedman presented himself not only as a singing cowboy, but also as a political outsider with a unique take on the power of the governor.

SOCIAL RESPONSIBILITY: **Should Texans take these kinds of candidates seriously?**

term limits: legal restrictions on the number of terms that an elected official can serve in a specific office

impeachment: the legal process in which the legislative branch has the authority to indict and remove a public official

FIGURE 8.1   Longest Serving Governors

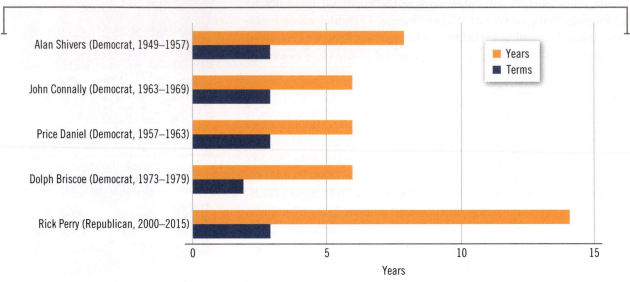

Source: Texas State Library and Archives.

COMMUNICATION:

Which governors have served longest?

- After Allan Shivers broke the long-standing Texas tradition by being elected for a third term, no governor won more than two terms in office for much of the 1970s to 2000.
- Rick Perry is tied with Allan Shivers (1949–1957), Price Daniel (1957–1963), and John Connally (1963–1969) for three consecutive elected terms in office, but Governor Perry alone holds the record for years served as governor, at 14.

CRITICAL THINKING:

Why did some governors serve longer than others?

- Longer serving governors cemented their powerful positions in their party.
- As the state became larger and the economy grew, the opportunity to leave a mark on state government required staying in office longer.

both elected and nonelected officials. It carries out this process in two stages. First, the Texas House of Representatives must cast a majority vote in favor of impeachment. Second, the Texas Senate sits as a jury, hearing and evaluating the evidence in a trial setting. To convict an individual who has been impeached by the house and remove that person from office, two-thirds of the senate must agree. Once removed, an individual is disqualified under the Texas Constitution from holding "any office of honor, trust or profit" in the state (Article 15, Section 4).

Unlike the U.S. Constitution, the Texas Constitution provides no specific grounds for impeachment. The charges are generally criminal in origin, but on occasion, they involve the misuse of public office. For instance, State District Judge O. P. Carrillo was impeached in 1976 for misuse of county funds, for which he later spent 3 years in prison.

Only one governor, James E. "Pa" Ferguson, has been impeached in Texas's history. After an unremarkable first term, Governor Ferguson raised the ire of the legislature when he vetoed the appropriation for the University of Texas because the University Board of Regents refused to remove certain faculty members whom

"Now sing us a little song"

Miriam A. "Ma" Ferguson was accused of being a puppet for her husband's ideas. However, she showed some independence in her political appointments and executive branch reorganization.

the governor found objectionable. The governor was indicted on nine criminal charges, including misapplication of public funds and embezzlement, nonenforcement of state banking laws, and receipt of a mysterious $156,500 (the source of which the governor refused to identify). The Texas House impeached him on 21 articles, and the Texas Senate convicted the governor on 10 of them.

Calling the process a "Kangaroo court," Governor Ferguson submitted his resignation one day before the senate rendered its final judgment.[4] When he ran again for governor in 1918, he argued that he could still hold the office, despite the impeachment, because he was never convicted. He was easily defeated by William P. Hobby in the Democratic Party primary. Then, in 1924, "Pa" Ferguson helped to elect his wife, Miriam A. "Ma" Ferguson, to the governor's office. The 1924 slogan went "Me for Ma, and I Ain't Got a Durned Thing Against Pa."

SUCCESSION

If the governor resigns, is removed, or dies in office, the lieutenant governor becomes the governor in what is called **political succession**. The lieutenant governor also serves as the acting governor when the governor is out of the state. Lieutenant Governor Preston Smith served as governor for 277 days during the term of John Connally, 5 weeks of which covered Connally's African safari.[5]

political succession: the sequential passing of authority from one person to another as the previous person is unable to serve

SALARY AND STAFF

The current annual salary of the governor is $150,000. This salary puts Texas governors in the middle of the income spectrum for governors nationally. In practice, many modern governors of Texas are wealthy before they enter office, often as a result of careers in real estate, ranching, or law. Taxpayers, however, pay large sums to ensure the governor's security when he travels. Governor Greg Abbott's annual security tab to the Department of Public Safety exceeds

IS IT BIGGER IN TEXAS?

FIGURE 8.2 Governor Staff Size

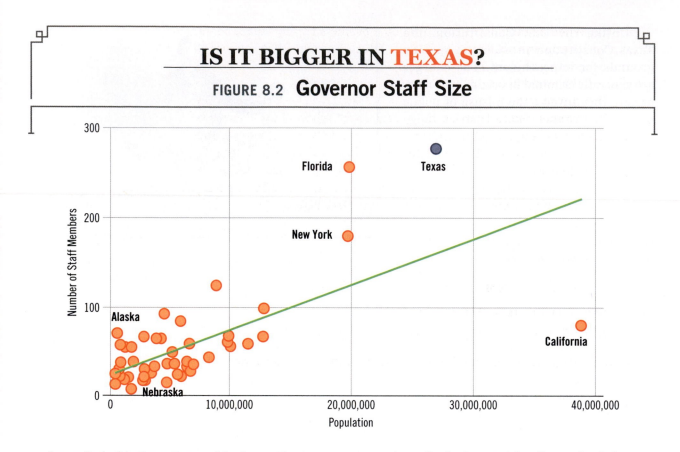

Source: Book of the States. Bureau of the Census. Figures represent executive staff and gubernatorial staff mapped with the population of the state. The line is a fitted prediction line: Points above the line are above average in staff size, while those below are below average.

 COMMUNICATION:

How does Texas compare on gubernatorial staff size?

- Texas leads the nation in the size of the executive staff. Other large states like New York and Florida also have large staffs. California is the exception to this trend.

- States with smaller populations tend to have a modest staff size.

 CRITICAL THINKING:

Why do some states have more staff?

- Larger states tend to have larger executive staff size and often also have a larger budget with which to grow staff size. California is the exception— budget cuts have driven the number of staff members down.

- The power of the governor in states with larger staff is greater, as governors seek a political advantage to establish their policies and communicate their messages.

- New York, Florida, and Texas are largely dominated by one party, so the legislatures in each state may allocate more funds to allow the governor's office to grow in size.

$1 million. When he rang in the New Year on a business trip to Japan, he insisted that his trip was not taxpayer funded—which was true—but the cost of the travel, meals, and lodging of the taxpayer-funded security staff that accompanied him amounted to $83,000.[6]

The Texas governor's office employs almost 300 staff members, who perform a range of services, including press relations, legal advice, scheduling and advance work, human resources, and expert policy advice (especially on the budget). Top advisers can earn as much as $265,000 per year.[7] These staffs work closely with the governor to create, sharpen, and support the governor's priorities as well as to protect the governor's image and govern the executive branch. The Texas governor has a large staff in comparison to his counterparts (see Figure 8.2).

 TEXAS TAKEAWAYS

8.1.1 What qualifications does a Texan need to run for governor?

8.1.2 How and why has the length governors have served changed?

8.1.3 How can the Texas legislature impeach a governor?

8.1.4 How does the size of the Texas governor's staff compare to that of other states?

8.2 FORMAL POWERS OF TEXAS GOVERNORS

The Texas Constitution outlines the formal powers granted to the governor. Governors use these formal powers to implement laws, manage the executive branch, push policies through the state legislature, check the judicial system, and protect Texans, particularly in the aftermath of natural disasters.

> **8.2** Analyze how governors use their formal powers.

EXECUTION OF LAWS

Like the U.S. Constitution, the Texas Constitution charges that the governor, as the state's chief executive, must "cause the laws to be faithfully executed." Although the 1876 Texas Constitution is vague with respect to carrying out this responsibility, governors over time have expanded their executive authority through executive orders and proclamations. Today, governors have wide latitude in controlling the operations of the state, especially state agencies.

Governors often issue unilateral **executive orders** to execute laws (see Figure 8.3). These orders have the force of law and often make use of powers

executive orders: legally binding orders from the governor that are used to direct government, especially state agencies, in the execution of law

FIGURE 8.3 **Unilateral Orders by Governor per Year**

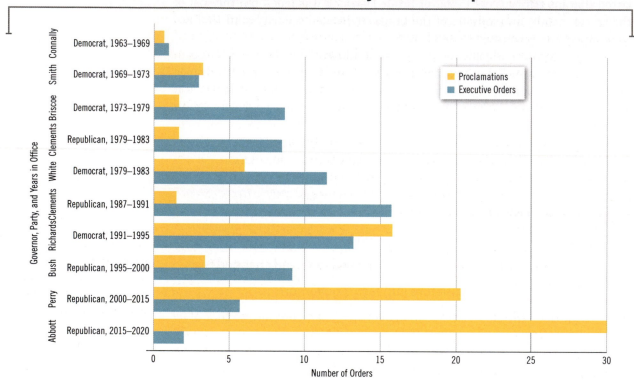

Source: Legislative Reference Library.

 COMMUNICATION:

How has the number of executive orders and proclamations changed over time?

- With a few exceptions, the number of executive orders and proclamations has increased over time, although the use of proclamations has increased more consistently.

- Governor Abbott has been stingy with executive orders compared to other governors.

 CRITICAL THINKING:

What explains the increases and decreases?

- The executive's power to act unilaterally expanded over this time as the legislature allowed the governor to do more by decree.

- Governors who serve when the opposition controls the state legislature (like Republican Bill Clements—first elected in 1978, then again in 1986—who confronted a Democratic legislative majority) have issued more orders than governors who enjoy majority support in the legislature. Democrat Ann Richards also dealt with a growing Republican tide in the legislature.

- Governors Richards and Perry used proclamations to appeal to groups inside and outside of their party: Richards to maintain a party losing support, and Perry to grow support.

granted to the governor by the legislature. Governors use executive orders for several purposes: to create task forces to assist with policy development, to respond to natural disasters and other emergencies, to fill interim political appointments, to call special sessions of the legislature, to issue "emergency" items for legislative consideration, and to hold special elections. For example, Governor Abbott suspended more than 200 laws or regulations, from vehicle registration and inspection requirements for victims of Hurricane Harvey to local hotel and motel occupancy taxes for the 14 days following the storm.[8]

Governors also use these orders to manage executive agencies and to push their political agenda, especially if they are up against opposition in the legislature (see Figure 8.4). To battle a rising state deficit, Republican Governor Bill Clements, who faced a majority Democratic legislature, directed each agency with an operating budget over $10 million to conduct an internal audit to find ways to save money.

Proclamations are similar to executive orders but are used to make factual determinations, such as to declare a state of emergency, and trigger other available powers, such as the ability to ask for disaster relief funds. These orders can also serve purely ceremonial purposes, allowing the governor to play a public role in the political culture of the state. Following the tragic 2019 mass shooting at a Walmart in El Paso, Governor Abbott proclaimed state flags to be flown at half-staff to honor those who lost their lives. After the Houston Astros won the World Series in 2017, Governor Abbott proclaimed November 3 to be Houston Astros Day, likening the team's spirit and resolve to that of Texas in the wake of Hurricane Harvey's devastation.

The use of unilateral power has been met with legislative backlash. In 2005, Governor Perry issued Executive Order 47, ordering the commissioner of education to establish a requirement that at least 65 percent of school districts' revenue be used for classroom instruction. In 2007, the governor issued an executive order mandating that all 11- and 12-year-old girls get an HPV (human papillomavirus) vaccine, which protects women and teens against a sexually transmitted disease that causes cervical cancer. In both instances, the legislature overturned the actions.

proclamations: gubernatorial orders that are used to make factual determinations to trigger other available powers

APPOINTMENT POWERS

Another way in which the governor manages the executive branch and implements laws is through the power of appointment. In all, a governor can make appointments to more than 3,000 positions in executive agencies, boards, and commissions (all nonlegislative offices). Most governors have the opportunity to fill about one-third of these positions in a 4-year term. Because of these appointees' political power and because appointments require senate approval, the selection is often contentious. Governor Connally once joked, "If you want to talk about real infighting, try making an appointment to the Board of Cosmetology."[9]

IS IT BIGGER IN TEXAS?

FIGURE 8.4 **Unilateral Executive Orders by Governor in Select States**

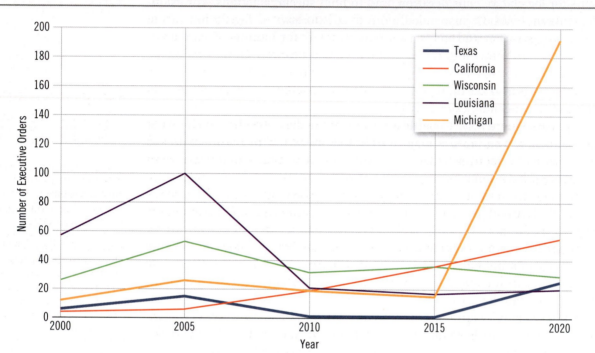

Source: Office of the Governor in each state.

 COMMUNICATION:

Where does Texas stack up against other states governors' use of executive orders?

- In recent years, Texas governors have used fewer executive orders, fewer than many states such as Wisconsin and California.

- Of the states listed in Figure 8.4, Texas is the only one with a session every 2 years rather than every year. Yet it is still the second lowest of the group listed, despite the likelihood that less frequent legislative sessions might encourage the governor to issue more orders.

 CRITICAL THINKING:

What explains this trend?

- The biggest driver of more orders issued is when a state's government is divided (where the legislature is controlled by one party and the executive by the other).

- The COVID-19 pandemic forced many governors to act quickly using executive orders.

- States with conservative governors during this time who embraced small government, such as Texas and Louisiana from 2010 on, have fewer executive orders.

Appointments can be political in function and appearance. During her single term as governor, Ann Richards made good on her campaign promise to make the government in Texas look like the people of Texas: 48 percent of her first 650 appointments were female, 12 percent were black, and 25 percent were Hispanic. This diversification did not sit particularly well with all segments of Texas. On one occasion, Richards appointed Democratic State Representative Guerrero to a vacancy left on the Texas Railroad Commission while John Sharp was serving as comptroller. On the day of the appointment, Sharp received a phone call from an angry oilman who demanded to know, "Who the hell is Leonard Guerrero?" Sharp answered, "It's worse than you think; it's *Lena* Guerrero."[10]

After Republicans won legislative majorities in the 2002 election, the state legislature surrendered much of its power to appoint and oversee boards and commissions to Republican Governor Perry—a move that seems contrary to Texans' long-held desire to restrict the power of the executive branch. Strong appointment powers raise the potential for cronyism as governors appoint influential political allies. For instance, in 2019 Governor Abbott appointed his longtime political ally Ruth Ruggero to secretary of state, an agency with a sprawling mandate that includes elections. As the former chair of the Texas Workforce Commission, Ruggero had been snared in a scandal over secretly coordinating with lobbyists for Handy, a company pushing for legislation to rewrite labor regulations.[11]

The governor's appointment powers are not absolute, however. The appointment power is shared with the Texas Senate, which must approve the appointee with a two-thirds majority. If the senate is in recess, the governor's appointee stays in office until the state senate votes on the nominee during the first 10 days in session. The legislature can also limit the term to be served by a person appointed by the governor should it wish to do so. Some boards and commissions also require by law that the representation be balanced by geography or professional background, thereby limiting the governor's discretion.

LEGISLATIVE POWERS

A major function of the governor is to work with the legislature. An effective governor focuses on two or three key goals to push through a sometimes friendly but more often hostile legislature.[12] The Texas political system splits policymaking power between the legislative and executive branches of government, making for tense political interactions. Policy agendas, election promises, different constituency demands, and divergent ideological approaches frame the skirmishes between the branches. Let's take a look at the powers governors employ during these skirmishes.

Recommending Legislation. By constitutional mandate, governors are allowed to suggest legislation to the legislature. Many governors take a direct role in

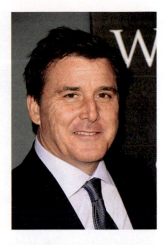

About one in three (29 percent) of Governor Greg Abbott's appointments in his first 4 years in office were campaign contributors. In 2015, Governor Abbott appointed billionaire T. Dan Friedkin chairman of the Parks and Wildlife Commission, where he still serves as chairman emeritus. The pick was criticized because Friedkin was a top donor to the governor and lobbied the legislature on his wildlife interests for his massive South Texas ranch.

PERSONAL RESPONSIBILITY: **Is it ethical to appoint political allies to important government posts? Why or why not?**

"I have a huge stack of bills to sign or veto. Decisions. Decisions." Governor Abbott wrote and posted this picture on his personal Twitter account.

the legislative arena. Governor Dolph Briscoe pledged to legislators that "the most persistent lobbyist you will see this session is the governor of Texas." Indeed, the introverted Briscoe successfully pushed through property protection laws, a streamlined penal code, and ethics reform legislation.[13]

Legislative "Emergencies." During the first 60 days of each legislative session, lawmakers are barred from passing legislation. Instead, they focus their time on organizing each chamber, holding hearings on legislation, and debating issues. Only the governor can break through this line. The Texas Constitution allows the governor to declare an "emergency" item and have it be prioritized in the first 60 days. These "emergencies" enable governors to highlight their pet issues and advance their political agenda. Governors often prioritize controversial matters to ensure that the legislature hears these issues first.

At the outset of the 2011 legislative session, just before the 2012 elections in which Governor Rick Perry was to run for president, the governor asked the legislature for two emergency items: to require a doctor to perform an ultrasound on a pregnant woman before an abortion and to require voters to present photo IDs before voting. Both issues were "red meat" to the conservative Republican base across the country, where he hoped to win points for his candidacy.[14] Governor Greg Abbott declared "emergencies" in 2019 that calmed the raging political storm and focused on issues voters cared about: reforming public school finance, beefing up responses to natural disasters, and improving mental health programs.

Special Sessions. After the biennial 140-day session is over, the governor has the power to call the legislature into special session, which can last up to 30 days. The governor sets the specific agenda for the session and can call as many as desired. For this reason, these sessions are often called the "governor's session." The legislature can only consider legislation related to that issue; no other issues can be discussed. However, the governor's ability to call the session does not extend to issues that are executive or judicial in character, such as appointments or impeachments.[15] Recent governors have been more

FIGURE 8.5 **Bills Introduced and Passed during Selected Special Sessions**

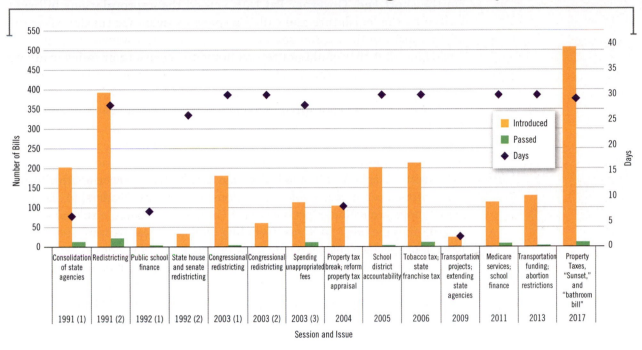

Source: Book of the States.

 COMMUNICATION:

What topics have special sessions addressed?

- The issues that most frequently called for a special session include education, redistricting electoral lines, reorganizing state agencies, and tax reforms.

- In recent sessions, legislators have also tackled transportation and moral issues.

 CRITICAL THINKING:

Is there a correlation between the length of a session and the number of bills enacted?

- Longer sessions tend to have more legislation enacted, while shorter sessions tend to have less.

- Longer sessions on contentious issues, such as redistricting, enact little or no legislation.

targeted in their calls, directing the legislature clearly on what issues they should discuss (see Figure 8.5). Historically, special sessions are more likely in times of war, depression, and financial crisis.[16] In modern Texas, special sessions are more likely to be called when the legislature is gridlocked over a specific issue or when an issue is politically challenging and cannot be solved in the regular 140-day legislative session.

Special sessions have ranged in duration from 30 seconds to 30 days. On the short end, Governor Pat Neff vetoed the appropriations bill sent to him by the legislature and called a special session for the day after the adjournment of the regular session. Incensed by the governor's tactics and frustrated that they could not return home to receive their mileage allowance, the legislature adjourned the special session without conducting any business.[17]

Governors can call a special session for any reason and at any time (outside of the biennial 140-day session). The governor's "call" (by executive proclamation) lets the legislature know what's on the menu for the session. Special sessions are politically risky for governors, however. The session can focus on the governor's agenda, but a failed session can hurt a governor politically and make him or her appear weak. Perceptions of ineffective leadership also hurt a governor's reelection effort. Governor Greg Abbott called a special session in 2017 that included 20 items, including one must-pass item to allow an extension of specific agencies. Opponents rallied behind the phrase "Sunset and *Sine Die*," meaning pass the must-pass bill and then adjourn. Supportive Republican legislators wore lapel buttons that read "Pass Them All." Ultimately, the legislature only passed half of his agenda and adjourned early, but the ideological tone of the special session allowed the governor to claim credit for pushing more conservative policies.[18]

Veto Powers. All constitutions in Texas have given the governor (or president under the Republic) the power of the **veto**. It is often called the "governor's gift" because it is such a valuable bargaining tool. A governor's veto must include a set of reasons for objection, which are sent to the chamber that introduced the original bill.

veto: formal, constitutional decision by the governor to formally reject a resolution or bill made by the legislature

The veto is the governor's strongest constitutional power in his or her struggle with the state legislature (see Figure 8.6). The governor has 10 days (excluding Sundays) to sign or veto the bill, or the bill automatically becomes law. Governors typically only let a few bills become law without their signature, but in 2019, Governor Abbott let 144 (or 11 percent of all bills taking effect) become law without his signature.[19]

If the legislature feels strongly enough about the legislation to reconsider it, two-thirds of the members of both chambers can override the veto. If the legislature adjourns after submitting a bill to the governor but before the normal 10-day period would have expired, the governor has 20 days from receipt to veto the legislation or the bill becomes law. During these periods when the legislature is adjourned, the governor can veto legislation without the threat of an override by the legislature.

Governors often use the veto to bring state policy in line with their political philosophy. Governor Ross Sterling, a businessman who lacked political experience and adopted the view that limited government was best, vetoed the fewest bills. Miserly with the state's finances, Governor Dan Moody vetoed 76 pieces of legislation and 4 specific budget items in 1929. He even went

FIGURE 8.6 **Number of Vetoed Bills, 1979–Present**

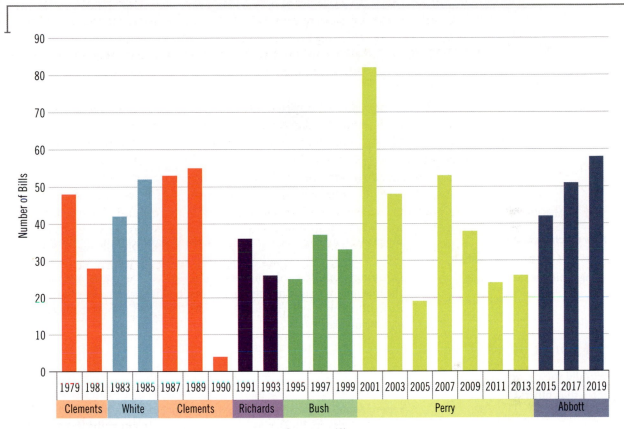

Source: Texas Reference Library.

 COMMUNICATION:

How frequently do governors use the veto?

- Since 1979, governors have vetoed, on average, approximately 30 pieces of legislation per session.
- Governor Clements vetoed more bills than those who preceded him in both of his terms of office, but Governor Perry vetoed the most legislation both in a single session and overall.

 CRITICAL THINKING:

Why more vetoes in some years than others?

- Greater political disagreement within a party, such as occurs when conservative and liberal factions fight over issues or when the legislature is of a different party than the governor, increases the use of the veto. This was especially true for Governor Clements, who as the first Republican-elected governor since the Civil War faced significant opposition in the Democratic legislature.
- Governor Perry, who sought to strengthen the office of the governor, frequently used the veto stamp to express his authority.

FIGURE 8.7   **First-Term Governor Line Item Veto Cuts**

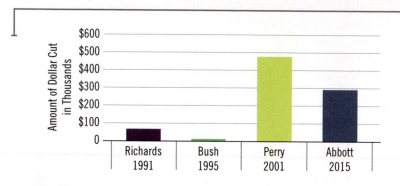

Source: Texas Reference Library.

 COMMUNICATION:

How much do first-term governors cut from the budget using their line item strategy?

- Since 2001, first-term governors have made significant use of the line item veto to cut funds from the budget.

- Governors Ann Richards and George W. Bush made modest use of the line item veto during their first years in office, cutting less than $100,000 combined, whereas Governors Perry and Abbott made more significant use.

 CRITICAL THINKING:

Why did some governors cut more than others?

- New governors with larger party majorities in the legislature, like Perry and Abbott, may be more willing to cut budgets with less fear of repercussions. Governors with smaller support in their majority party, like Richards and Bush, may be more reluctant to anger the legislature by cutting funds.

- Growing political pressure for slower state spending has contributed to more recent governors reducing budgets unilaterally.

so far as to veto legislation that would have authorized funds for members of the Texas legislature to travel to Washington, DC, to lobby for a new veterans hospital.

Unlike the president of the United States, Texas governors have a particularly effective defensive tool: the line item veto (see Figure 8.7). A **line item veto** allows the governor to reject a specific provision in a bill without rejecting the whole bill. The public (and to some degree the legislature) expect the governor to use the line item veto to hem in state spending. For instance, Governor Neff line item vetoed provisions amounting to more than $39 million. He used his veto to kill the proposed West Texas A&M College, stating that the

line item veto: a veto that allows the governor to reject a specific provision in a bill without rejecting the whole bill

appropriation was against the will of the state Democratic Party convention. Governor James V. Allred line item vetoed an $817,000 appropriation in 1937 for a hospital, noting that the state was already building one other hospital and didn't need a second.[20]

Vetoes are a powerful tool for Texas's chief executive, as they are rarely overridden—partly because the legislature is often not in session by the time governors veto bills. From 1876 to 1968, only 25 (out of 936) vetoes were overridden. Since the 1960s, only one veto has been overridden. In 1979, Governor Clements vetoed legislation to limit the ability of county governments to prohibit hunters from killing female deer. The governor claimed that a central authority like the Texas Parks and Wildlife Department, not local governments, should be in charge of this initiative. The legislature bristled, in part because of Governor Clements's approach to governing: He had declared that he was going to run Texas like a business and that "I'm the chief executive officer, and y'all can take it or leave it!"[21] The state legislature decided to "leave it" and overrode his veto.

Because of the difficulty in overturning a veto, even the threat of a veto from the governor is a highly effective weapon. Governors threaten to veto legislation on matters when they are certain they can coerce the legislature to alter proposed legislation to their liking. Amid legislative belt-tightening in 2017, house and senate budget negotiators planned to trim $300 million from Governor Abbott's prized pots of economic development funds, the Texas Enterprise Fund, his "high-quality" pre-kindergarten program, and a program for university scholar recruitment. The governor threatened to veto the budget, and the legislature abandoned their planned cuts.

MILITARY POWERS

Just as the president is the commander-in-chief of the U.S. military, the Texas governor serves as commander-in-chief of the Texas military forces (except when they are called into service of the United States). In practice, this means that the governor is in charge of the National Guard, appointing the adjutant general of the Guard and directing the Guard to protect lives and property. The Guard is most often used during natural disasters, such as Hurricane Harvey, the northern Texas wildfire, or the Marble Falls flooding.

The National Guard also protects the state in times of crisis. In 2019, Governor Abbott dispatched the National Guard to the border. He argued that he was forced to act because of a string of failures by the federal government in stemming the tide of undocumented immigration, including drug smugglers and unaccompanied minors from Central America. Abbott stated, "there is an escalating crisis at the border—a crisis Congress is refusing to fix." More than 133,000 migrants, mostly from Central America, illegally crossed the Texas border in 2019, a greater than 40 percent increase over the prior year.[22] Approximately 1,000 strong, the deployment cost $18 million per month in an effort to boost the law enforcement presence near the border.[23] Opponents claimed that the governor overreacted and that "deploying new troops to the border solves nothing."[24]

JUDICIAL POWERS: PARDON AND CLEMENCY

clemency: the power to reduce or delay punishment for a crime

pardon: the power to forgive a crime

In criminal cases except for treason and impeachment, the governor has the power to grant reprieves and commutations of punishment, remit any fines and forfeitures, and issue **clemency** (reduction or delay of a sentence) or **pardons** (forgiveness for a crime) with the written support of a majority of the Texas Prisons Board. In capital murder cases, the governor can grant a temporary "jailhouse reprieve" for 30 days on his own, without Board approval. In a 1925 case, for example, Governor Neff pardoned the famous bluesman Huddie William Ledbetter, better known as "Lead Belly," who was incarcerated in a Sugar Land prison for murder. In order to appear tough on crime, modern governors rarely use clemency or pardon powers.

The governor's ability to pardon is not absolute. Governor James E. "Pa" Ferguson exercised the power of the pardon so frequently that he was said to have an "open door policy" at the Texas Penitentiary. Ferguson issued 2,253 pardons in just 2 years, a state record! In one instance, coming to the office to discuss clemency, a man placed several bills in Governor Ferguson's palm when he shook hands. Governor Miriam "Ma" Ferguson (1925–1927, 1933–1935), wife to "Pa," was also criticized for abusing the pardon system, which led to legislative reforms. In 2 years, she granted 1,161 pardons, and rumors began circulating that pardons were being sold. Approaches were made to "practically all members of the Ferguson family," including a blatant offer to the Fergusons's daughter of $5,000 to use her influence to secure a pardon.[25] The legislature then passed a law to ensure that the governor must first receive majority support from the appointees of the Board of Pardons and Paroles before granting clemency or pardons or remitting fines.

🇨 TEXAS TAKEAWAYS

8.2.1 What formal powers do governors have?

8.2.2 How can governors use legislative "emergencies" to advance their agenda?

8.2.3 When and why do governors call special sessions?

8.2.4 Why are vetoes a highly effective weapon for the governor?

8.3 INFORMAL POWERS OF TEXAS GOVERNORS

The Texas Constitution gives governors a modestly sized toolbox of formal powers with which to work. Governors, however, have **informal powers** that derive from their experience, their natural ability to negotiate and lead, their popularity, and their relationship with the media. The prowess of governors to exploit their informal powers largely defines their legacy, enabling skillful governors to effectively bargain with the legislature, set the policy agenda, and serve as economic cheerleaders for the state.

> **8.3** Evaluate the use of informal powers by the Texas governor to advance agendas.

LEGISLATIVE BARGAINING

Governors are granted the formal power to recommend legislation, but they have to work well with members of the legislature to ensure passage of their agenda. Governors work with allies and enemies in the legislature to iron out policy differences. A savvy governor works both within the Capitol (through direct negotiation with members) and outside the pink dome (through indirect negotiation with the media).

informal powers: actions governors might take that are not formally written but are exercised through the activities of the governor

Meals and Midnight Visits. Being available and cordial can go a long way in legislative relations. On one occasion, Governor Price Daniel was called near midnight to the Capitol to break an impasse over the sales tax rate.

INSIDER INTERVIEW

Former Democratic Governor Mark White

Who are the governor's greatest allies while in office?

Think of it like a kaleidoscope—a combination of allies depending on the issues. As an example, I called a special session for education in 1984, not having great success on the issue. Working together with schoolteachers, highway contractors, and business leaders, we got it done. Working just with schoolteachers, we would not have had adequate ability to change.

SOCIAL RESPONSIBILITY: **In attempting to solve a complex problem facing the state, whom or what groups would you reach out to first? Why?**

The governor was already tucked in for the evening but arose, dressed, and sped across the street to the Capitol. Working into the early morning hours, the committee adopted a compromise sales tax bill with the governor's aid.

In contrast to the inaccessibility of Governor Ann Richards, Governor George W. Bush, clad in a ball cap and no shoes, would invite legislators late to his office with music playing. The governor and legislators hammered out many pieces of legislation over steaks and spirits, often at one of Austin's many locations frequented by the political elite, like Austin Land & Cattle or the Cloak Room.

Endorsements. Governors can lend their personal prestige to candidates for office with the presumption of reciprocal support. The 1980 elections saw huge gains for Republican candidates across the nation, with newly elected President Ronald Reagan leading the charge. Republican Governor Bill Clements came into the 1981 session riding high in the saddle after backing several winning Republican candidates in the 1980 election. These new Republican members of the Texas legislature, though outnumbered by Democrats at the time, owed their seats to Clements and returned the favor by supporting his proposed programs.

Working the Floor. The governor and his or her staff also coordinate and communicate with members of the legislature while the session is ongoing. This is known as "working the floor." Communication is key in making legislative deals, and staff with an eye toward legislative bargaining and the ear of the governor serve a vital role in a governor's success.

Keeping Score. Facing a tense special session and pushback from key house leadership in 2017, Governor Greg Abbott promised to keep a "naughty and nice" list of legislators who backed or opposed his priorities in order to "call people out." He also vowed to endorse and fundraise for supporters in the 2018 elections. Republican Representative Lyle Larson introduced legislation to restrict a governor's ability to appoint big donors to state boards, and in what Larson called retribution, Abbott vetoed nearly all the bills Larson passed in the 85th legislative session and kicked him off the Southwestern States Water Commission.[26] The two made up after the 86th session, however, with the governor endorsing Larson for reelection.

Going Public. Just as presidents take their case to the American people, Texas governors frequently speak directly to the citizens of the state. This persuasion technique is called "going public." The colorful radio personality and flour salesman Governor W. Lee "Pappy" O'Daniel in the 1940s made extensive use of his buoyant personality on the radio every Sunday from the "front room" of the executive mansion to discuss the business of Texas. A showman with little political experience, he had acquired the nickname "Pappy" from a song his band played, "Please Pass the Biscuits, Pappy." On one occasion, however, his tactics backfired. The governor bitterly attacked the legislature, which opposed his proposed sales tax amendment. He read a list of the specific senators who had supported his program, labeling this group the "honor roll" and threatening to "take the stump" to oppose the reelection of those who had worked against his program. Called a "Sabbath Caesar" for his coercive methods, O'Daniel failed to get his program passed by the Texas House.[27]

Dealing with the Media. The most dangerous place in Austin is the space between the governor and a television camera, or so goes an old saying about the importance of the media to modern governors. Governors have used the media platform to press their agenda, negotiate publicly with the legislature, brag about economic growth, and, most prominently, run for reelection. For instance, back in the 1940s, Governor Coke Stevenson used the Capitol press corps as his "kitchen cabinet," where he would solicit the advice of these reporters. Governor Mark White was often called "Media Mark" because of his affinity for talking with reporters about his administration's policies.

Governor Abbott brags about his marksmanship at a gun range after signing legislation to reduce the fees for a license to carry or to renew a license for a firearm. The governor joked, "I'm gonna carry this around in case I see any reporters." In fact, Abbott has stayed on relatively good terms with the media.

🏴 SOCIAL RESPONSIBILITY: **How does the governor's public image influence his or her ability to court legislators and to persuade the public?**

Governor Abbott has opted to communicate directly to supporters, bypassing the more traditional media press conference. In May 2017, the governor made an unannounced use of Facebook Live to sign a controversial "sanctuary cities" ban.[28]

AGENDA SETTING

Because of constitutional limitations, the power of the governor is only as strong as the governor makes it. Governor George W. Bush campaigned and then governed on four themes he constantly repeated to anyone who would listen: education reform, welfare reform, tort reform, and juvenile justice reform. When pressed for elaboration, he added a fifth item: "pass the first four things." This insistent attitude allowed him to overcome the traditional weakness of the office and led to an unusually impressive winning streak on his legislative items.

Agenda setting can backfire if governors fail to communicate effectively with key legislators. In 1997, the Texas budget was fat, with a sizeable $3 billion surplus. Governor Bush laid claim to some of that money, announcing that he wanted $1 billion of that surplus to go to reducing local school taxes. This proposition was

agenda setting: an informal power of governors to use their public platform to set the state's political and policy agenda

a surprise to Lieutenant Governor Bob Bullock and Speaker Pete Laney, who were central to passing Bush's agenda in the 1995 session. The three generally had good relations, but taking action without building consensus doomed the initiative. Speaker Laney told the governor to "stop listening to your political advisers and start listening to your legislative advisers,"[29] advice that Governor Bush followed religiously ever after. Recent governors have generally been successful in getting the initiatives that they lay out in their State-of-the-State Address passed in the legislature, especially when the legislature and the governor's mansion are controlled by members of the same party (see Figure 8.8).

Citizen Advisory Group. Governors can formally or informally assemble a citizen advisory group that studies policy issues and recommends actions. Prominent individuals on these committees help the governor or lieutenant governor understand the needs of the state, prioritize problems, and come up with innovative solutions. Governor Mark White, who made public education a priority during his term in office, appointed Dallas billionaire H. Ross Perot to chair the Select Committee on Public Education, which held hearings around the state on matters of school finance, teacher compensation, and secondary curriculum. Their fact-finding report led to passage of House Bill 72 in 1984, which raised teacher salaries but also tied them to teacher performance, instituted teacher certification programs, set strict attendance rules, and introduced "no-pass, no-play," a policy that prohibited students who were failing courses from participating in sports and extracurricular activities for 6 months.

Budget. The governor is required to submit a budget to the legislature, which the legislature is free to ignore. Historically, governors have only had a seat at the "kids' table" on budget issues. This is changing as recent governors have been more likely to use their power to line item veto legislation (see Great Texas Political Debates).

The governor, along with the LBB, does take the first step in the budget process—the preparation of a "mission statement" for the state in the fall before a legislative session. This statement sets out a framework for the development of strategic plans and constructs goals and principles to guide decision making. The Texas budget is required to include a list of appropriations for the current year and the amount requested by executive agencies for the 2-year budget. The Governor's Office of Budget, Planning, and Policy and the LBB issue instructions for developing agency-specific strategic plans to be reviewed and submitted.

As the chief executive in Texas, the governor also has the authority, shared with the LBB, to administer the budget. When necessary, the governor and the LBB have joint authority to transfer funds between programs within an agency or between agencies. This process, known as **budget execution**, allows changes to appropriations during the period in which the legislature is not in session. This power provides the governor with some flexibility to allocate budget funds to meet state goals. The public has some say, too: Any such transfers require that a public hearing be held and that input be received from citizens.

budget execution: the governor's implementation of the budget when the legislature is not in session

FIGURE 8.8 **Governor Legislative Success Rate**

Source: State-of-the-State Speeches. Legislative Reference Library. Bars represent the total requests in the governors' state-of-the-state addresses: Governor Perry from 2003 to 2013 and Governor Abbott from 2015 to 2019. Circles display the percentage passed (out of the total number of requests).

COMMUNICATION:

How successful are governors at pushing through their agenda items?

- The size of the governor's agenda (based on the number of requests) has decreased since 2007.

- Governors were successful in achieving more than 50 percent of their agenda items from the State-of-the-State Address, and in recent sessions, that percentage has increased to 85 percent.

CRITICAL THINKING:

Why have recent governors had more success?

- Governors are using the increasing number of tools at their disposal (described in this chapter) to enhance their ability to enact their political agenda. This was especially true of Governor Rick Perry beginning in 2001.

- The percentage of governors' initiatives passed rose from 2009 to 2015 because of the growing number of Republican legislators, dropped in 2017 due to Republican policy disagreements, but rose again in 2019 due to agreement from conservative leaders on policy initiatives.

GREAT TEXAS POLITICAL DEBATES
Budget Powers of the Governor

A governor's budget authority is generally limited, but changes in the line item veto authority have expanded Governor Abbott's budget veto powers. The tug of war began in 2015, when the legislature crafted a budget with "budget riders" or "informational items" that bundled fund appropriations with directions to state agencies. (The governor was barred by a 1911 Texas Supreme Court decision from erasing "language qualifying an appropriation or directing the method of its uses.") Governor Abbott line item vetoed several of these items, to the tune of about $300 million.[30] The director of the Legislative Budget Board (LBB) declared that the governor had strayed into the lawmakers' sandbox, erasing directions to agencies through a line item veto. Attorney General Ken Paxton legally backed the governor's actions, but a bipartisan group of budget writers raised concern about the precedent being set, warning that the legislature's authority was weakened. The courts have yet to rule definitively on this matter.

SOCIAL RESPONSIBILITY: **Should the governor be given more powers to control the budget?**

NO: The framers of the Texas Constitution gave the legislature the bulk of responsibility for crafting the state budget. The governor's powers to shape the budget should be limited. At the least, the legislature or the courts should approve the governor's actions.

YES: Legislators often overspend as they attempt to stream state revenue back into their own districts or fund programs and policies for which they can claim credit. Texans look to the governor to cut spending using the line item veto power.

When Governor Abbott faced a big decision about whether to extend the deployment of 1,000 National Guard troops from "Operation Strong Safety" who were protecting the Texas-Mexico border, he had three payment options. He could use an emergency rider, tap the governor's disaster funds, or utilize the traditional "budget execution" authority of the LBB. He opted to request $86 million in extending the National Guard deployment for another 11 months.[31] This action drew the scrutiny of lawmakers, including Republicans, who claimed that the governor and LBB should have pursued a legislative funding route to produce a more transparent process.

inaugural speech: an address that is not constitutionally required but is conventionally delivered at the beginning of a new gubernatorial term

Inaugural Speech. The governor's **inaugural speech** is not constitutionally required, but it is traditionally delivered with much pomp and circumstance at the beginning of a new gubernatorial term. The speech is generally more inclusive than partisan. It gives the governor, especially a new governor, a major platform from which to offer a strategic vision for the state.

Governor Greg Abbott's inaugural speech in 2019 was a departure from some of the fiery rhetoric heard during his 2018 campaign. His remarks on a sunny Tuesday in Austin in front of actor Chuck Norris and Apollo 8 astronaut Walter Cunningham played up the commonality of Texans and the importance of thinking about the future needs of the state, especially education and a strong economy.

FIGURE 8.9 **Word Cloud of Governor Abbott's Inaugural Address**

 CRITICAL THINKING:

What do the most commonly used words imply about the governor's agenda or his approach to governing?

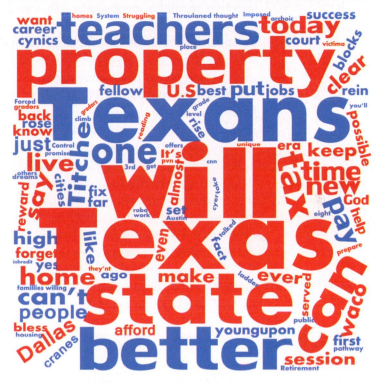

Source: Website of Governor Greg Abbott (2019).

State-of-the-State Address. Following the inaugural address, governors use the **State-of-the-State Address** to set a policy agenda. The Texas Constitution requires the governor to "give to the Legislature information, by message, of the condition of the State." This message is usually an outline of the governor's legislative priorities and policy agenda (see Figure 8.9). Before the 1960s, it was common for governors to submit their messages to the legislature in writing instead of in person.

State-of-the-State Address: address used by governors to set a policy agenda

Party Leader. The governor is often the most visible member of the state party, making him or her the natural choice to serve as ambassador of the party's message. Governor Bill Clements, the first Republican governor (first elected in 1978, then again in 1986) since Reconstruction, is considered the father of the modern Texas Republican Party for establishing a foothold in the state run exclusively by Democrats. His first budget called for reducing taxes, shrinking the bureaucracy, and improving education. Clements recruited new appointees, making them pledge to run in the future as Republicans. He also provided a new generation of young Republicans with opportunities in state politics they would not have gotten in the Democratic-led state.

Modern governors must balance the ideological wings of their party. Republican Governor Abbott's party, for example, has both moderate and conservative members, necessitating the careful calibration of a policy agenda.

Personal Outreach. Successful candidates are often the most personable, and when in office, Texas governors use these personal skills to court the electorate and develop powerful and important networks in state government. After her husband, Governor James "Pa" Ferguson, was impeached, the charming Miriam "Ma" Ferguson ran and won the gubernatorial election in 1924 and was elected again in 1932. Both Fergusons created a well-crafted image of being simple farmers and built their campaign around appealing to a rural constituency. One aide to Governor "Ma" Ferguson recalled that the reception room at the governor's mansion was continuously jammed with constituents waiting to see "one of the governors," referencing "Ma" and "Pa" Ferguson's campaign promise to elect "two governors for the price of one."[32] Similarly, Governor Preston Smith had breakfast every morning at the Driskill Hotel a few blocks away from the Governor's Mansion and would welcome members of the public to join him.

The primacy of personality can be a boom or a bust for governors. In the clubby world of Texas politics, sometimes personality outranks policy. Two political rivals who ran against each other two different times for governor had problems resulting from their personality: Bill Clements and Mark White. Clements was the model of a long series of wealthy oil men who entered Texas politics. His mean-spirited remarks, referring to members of the Texas Senate as "prairie chickens" and state employees as "parasitic bureaucrats," complicated his relationship with both elected and unelected state officials. White, on the other hand, was said to have good intentions, good ideas, and a good record but little ability to inspire loyalty. Slavishly listening to public opinion polls, walking back and forth between issue positions, and appearing weak on several positions, he lost his bid for reelection in 1986.

Governor Ann Richards on Election Night, 1990. Governors often use their big personalities to get elected and press their political agendas. Governor Richards once quipped, "I get a lot of cracks about my hair, mostly from men who don't have any."

PERSONAL RESPONSIBILITY: **How able are you to separate your personal feelings about a governor from your feelings about his or her legislative priorities? Do you think you tend to support candidates you "like" or candidates who align with your legislative goals?**

Economic Cheerleader. Recent Texas governors have spent a great deal of time on the road trying to lure jobs to the state. Governor Rick Perry spent months away from Austin recruiting companies to move to Texas, attracting Apple, Caterpillar, Facebook, and Toyota.[33] Governor Greg Abbott spent several weeks out of the country in the summer of 2019 touting energy, technology, and health care opportunities in Texas, declaring one trip to India as "a home run."[34] Texas led the nation in job growth during the economic downturn in the early 2000s, but the use of state funds to lure additional jobs has produced decidedly mixed outcomes, with several high-profile projects delivering less than promised.[35] Critics have complained that these economic incentives are little more than corporate welfare that provide little in return.

TEXAS TAKEAWAYS

8.3.1 What informal powers do governors use to pursue their agenda?

8.3.2 How do governors set their agenda?

(U) 8.4 WEAK AND STRONG GOVERNOR

The Texas governor is a "weak" governor on paper. The framers of the sections on gubernatorial power were so wary when they created the constitution in 1876, and the rule of former Governor Davis was so despised, that the framers divided the powers of the executive branch into multiple agencies to weaken the power of the governor. As one framer of the 1876 Constitution put it, "power is dangerous," and the only way to disarm the governor was to divide the powers.[36]

> **8.4** Assess the strength of the Texas governor and proposals to modify gubernatorial power.

The effect was a position with limited powers, short terms of office, and low pay. The strength of a governor's office depends on the extent to which the governor appoints other important members of the executive branch, oversees administrative functions of the bureaucracy, can veto legislation and the budget, and can remove officials from office. The Texas governor has few of these powers. In addition, the legislative branch significantly checks the authority of the governor on appointment matters, and the branches share power in several other functions.

Texas ranks comparatively low on a scale of gubernatorial power (see Figure 8.10). If used properly, however, the governor's powers allow significant expansion of executive authority. Governor Rick Perry's record-breaking number of vetoes in his first term was not the only way he strengthened the office. Let's consider a few ways Governor Perry and now Governor Abbott have strengthened the office.

SHEER LENGTH OF TERM

The position of governor is full-time, whereas the legislature is part-time, meeting only once every 2 years. This overlap of time gives the governor a natural

IS IT BIGGER IN TEXAS?

FIGURE 8.10 Map of Gubernatorial Power

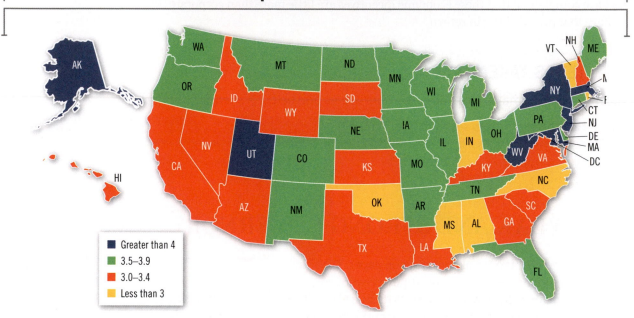

Greater than 4
3.5–3.9
3.0–3.4
Less than 3

Source: Governor Institutional Power Index (updated measures, based on Thad Beyle, "Governors." In Virginia Gray, Herbert Jacob, and Kennith N. Vines [Eds.], *Politics in the American States.* [Boston: Little, Brown, 1983]). Rankings are based on appointment powers, veto powers, term length and limits, and budgetary control.

 COMMUNICATION:

How does Texas compare to other states on executive power?

- Most states with large economies and significant industrial and manufacturing bases, such as New York, Pennsylvania, and Michigan, have strong governors.

- Even compared to smaller states with less robust economies, the Texas governor scores very low on executive power, practically near the bottom.

 CRITICAL THINKING:

What factors explain this trend?

- Many of the states in the original colonies (Massachusetts, New York, Maryland) had strong governors who were holdovers from an era of strong executives.

- The framers of the 1876 Texas Constitution made sure that the governor had minimal powers, at least on paper.

- Many southern states limited executive power following their experiences with overbearing governors during the Reconstruction Era.

advantage when it comes to policy expertise and political stamina. Governor Perry, as the longest-serving governor in the state's history, at 14 years, and Governor Abbott, now in his second term, have been able to make their mark on the politics of the state simply by holding the reins of government for so long.

APPOINTEES

By virtue of serving in office for so long, Governor Perry was able to appoint nearly every member of every state committee, commission, or panel. He served long enough to go through the entire cycle of 6-year executive appointments—twice. Perry appointed more than 8,000 individuals to head agencies, boards, and commissions during his terms as governor. Many of them were former staffers, aides, and allies. Governor Abbott has continued the tradition of strong use of appointments by not appointing new state officers after their terms expire. In this way, these appointees truly serve at the pleasure of the governor, who may more directly influence their actions. Critics claim that the appointment power of the governor is shared with the senate, and so this arrangement violates the constitution.[37]

PARTY POWER

The resurgence of the Republican Party in Texas didn't occur overnight. Whereas other Republican governors before him opened the door to Republican Party rule, Perry took the door off the hinges. Perry started off as a Democrat and switched parties, as many conservative Democrats did in the 1980s. He topped the ticket in 2002 when Republicans made historic gains at all levels, including a sweep of all statewide offices. As the state changes

ANGLES OF POWER
A "Power Grab" or Efficient Executive?

As of 2019, more than 400 state officers had overstayed their welcome by remaining in their positions beyond the legally allowed duration of service. Some "holdover" officials have served as many as 9 years without reappointment, as required by law, and every year that passes without additional appointment extends their "terms" longer and longer. Traditionally, officials are appointed by the governor, are confirmed by two-thirds of the Senate, and serve their 2- or 6-year terms. "Holdovers," on the other hand, serve at the governor's pleasure, have no set term, and can be removed by the governor at any time, expanding the governor's power.[38] The governor's office believes it has the legal authority, based on the Texas Constitution, to allow an existing officeholder to serve beyond his or her term until a qualified successor is found.

SOCIAL RESPONSIBILITY: **Is it right that the governor keep "holdovers" in office? Does this diminish the power of the senate? Should the governor be given more powers to control the executive branch?**

politically and becomes more competitive, Greg Abbott is attempting to keep more Republicans in office by creating "Abbott University" for training door-to-door canvassers and by record-breaking fundraising, raising more than $105 million since he first ran for governor.[39]

CRITICISMS AND REFORMS

Although individual governors have expanded the power of the office, not all governors have been as effective as Abbott. If efficiency and expedience of action are important in modern government, reformers point to several formal powers that should be expanded to ensure a more effective chief executive. Most of these reforms would require amending the Texas Constitution.

Appointment Powers

Problem: Governors have limited influence over other key executive decision makers because of Texas's plural executive system. Governors have no appointment powers over important executive offices, such as the state comptroller or attorney general, which are elected separately.

Context: One primary criticism in the 1960s was that after Governor Price Daniel's three terms in office, the bureaucracy in Texas, which was supposed to be independent of the executive, would be completely staffed by his loyalists. Opponents of Governor Daniel, who was eventually defeated after seeking an unprecedented fourth term, charged him with attempting to "control" the major agencies.[40]

Solution: Expand the appointment powers of the executive to other executive offices in state government. Limit the number of terms a governor can serve.

Cronyism

Problem: Because there are no term limits for governors, no restrictions on whom a governor can appoint to an office, and few limits on political contributions, political appointments to the state's many important positions are often used as political patronage.

Context: Twenty-nine percent of Governor Abbott's first-term appointees were donors, with contributions ranging from $25 to more than $1 million.[41] In 2018, one Lubbock developer admitted that he pledged $10,000 to the governor to be "eligible" for an appointment. The governor denied the "pay-to-play" allegation.[42]

Solution: Have the legislature submit a list of individuals the governor could consider to nominate. Improve the vetting process. Reduce the duration of time in office for appointees. Pass legislation banning donors from serving as appointees.

Removal Powers

Problem: The governor cannot remove appointed officials even if their performance declines or their support of the governor's program falters.

Context: With no formal removal powers, governors are forced to use alternative, often informal means to coerce most public officials to step down. In one instance, Governor "Pa" Ferguson threatened to make public an inappropriate relationship between an appointee and his subordinate if the appointee did not step down. The appointee quickly signed the letter of resignation.

Solution: Expand the governor's removal powers so that the governor, similar to the president, has the power to replace appointees.

Budget Powers

Problem: The governor is charged with setting the state's financial agenda and executing the budget (spending the money), but the governor is at the mercy of the legislature and other groups for the budget.

Context: Although past Texas constitutions required the governor to submit a budget, similar to the president, the current process requires agencies to report requests to the governor, and the governor reports these requests to the legislature. The governor's budget power is also shared with the LBB.

Solution: Extend the governor's budgetary responsibility to require the governor to submit a budget and require the legislature to formally accept or reject it. Because the legislature's first order of business is to pass a budget, the Texas Constitution could be altered to require a governor to propose, and the legislature to pass, a budget in the first 60 days of a session.

TEXAS TAKEAWAYS

8.4.1 Is the Texas governor weak or strong? Explain.

8.4.2 How have Texas's governors expanded their political powers?

 # THE INSIDER VIEW

Although the creators of the Texas Constitution intended to establish a weak governor, governors in the Lone Star State have expanded their power through aggressive use of the veto power, the appointment power, and the ability to call special sessions. Governors can also be highly effective when using their informal powers effectively. Ann Richards once said, "I'm not afraid to shake up the system, and government needs more shaking up than any other system I know." Like other governors, Richards attempted to leverage the "bully pulpit" and her standing with the legislature to set her political agenda. Still, governors need the legislature to be on their side in order to get things done—and in the absence of legislative success, governors become electorally vulnerable. Asked once what she might have done differently had she known she was going to be a one-term governor, Richards grinned, "Oh, I would probably have raised more hell."[43]

TEXAS TAKEAWAYS

8.1.1 To run for governor in Texas, a candidate must be at least 30 years of age, a citizen of the United States, and a resident of Texas for at least 5 years immediately preceding his or her election. Race, gender, profession, political experience, social network, charm, and charisma also factor in. Almost all Texan governors have been white Protestant men with previous political experience.

8.1.2 On average, governors are serving longer in office for two reasons. In 1972, Texans amended the constitution to lengthen a single term from 2 to 4 years. Governors have also broken with the tradition of serving only one term, and there are no term limits.

8.1.3 The Texas legislature impeaches a governor in a two-stage process. First, the Texas House of Representatives investigates charges and must cast a majority vote in favor of impeachment. Second, the Texas Senate sits as a jury, hearing and evaluating the evidence in a trial setting. To convict an individual who has been impeached by the house and remove that person from office, two-thirds of the senate must agree.

8.1.4 The Texas governor has a large staff in comparison to his counterparts, and top advisers can earn as much as $265,000 per year.

8.2.1 Governors routinely use executive orders, proclamations, political appointments, vetoes, line item vetoes, pardon powers, and military powers to run the executive branch. Governors also recommend legislation, declare legislative emergencies, call special sessions, and bargain with legislators.

8.2.2 During the first 60 days of each legislative session, lawmakers are barred from passing all legislation except for the governors' "emergency" items, which often address issues central to the governor's agenda.

8.2.3 Texas governors call the legislature into special session on any issue they choose, and sessions can last up to 30 days after the biennial 140-day session is over. Today, special sessions are more likely to be called when the legislature is gridlocked over a specific issue or when an important problem cannot be solved in the regular session.

8.2.4 Vetoes are hard to override both because two-thirds of each chamber must vote to override a veto and because the legislature is often not in session by the time governors veto bills. Moreover, the Texas governor has the line item veto, which allows the governor to reject a specific provision in a bill that governors often use to hem in state spending.

8.3.1 The governors' informal powers stem from their ability to bargain with legislators, set the agenda with their legislative powers and their role as representative of Texas governor, negotiate the budget, shape their party as its leader, and develop the economy.

8.3.2 The governors' annual State-of-the-State Address and inaugural speech are both used to set their political and legislative agenda. They can also use their role in budget preparation and execution, as well as their line item veto, to shape which programs and agencies are funded. The governor also plays a major role in business development and involves citizens in citizen advisory groups that advise on policy. They can further appeal to the press and the people to garner support for their policies.

8.4.1 The powers of the Texas governor are weak on paper. The constitution originally limited their powers and gave them short terms of office and low pay. Moreover, the legislature checks the authority of the governor. Texas ranks comparatively low on an index of executive power. In practice, however, stronger Texas governors exercise their powers more vigorously.

8.4.2 Texas governors have expanded their political powers through aggressive use of appointment powers, the veto, party building, and staying longer in office.

KEY TERMS

agenda setting
budget execution
clemency
executive orders
impeachment
inaugural speech
informal powers
line item veto
pardon
political succession
proclamations
State-of-the-State Address
term limits
veto

PRACTICE QUIZ

1. Who was the only Texas governor to be impeached?
   a. Allan Shivers
   b. James E. "Pa" Ferguson
   c. Mark White
   d. George W. Bush

2. Texas governors enjoy all of the following powers EXCEPT which of the following?
   a. Dispatch the National Guard
   b. Grant pardons
   c. Recommend legislation
   d. Submit a budget

3. Where does Texas rank on the Governor Power Index?
   a. In the top.
   b. In the middle.
   c. In the bottom.

4. To serve as Texas governor, a person must be at least how old (in years)?
   a. 30
   b. 35
   c. 37
   d. 40

5. The 1962 *Houston Chronicle* editorial submitted that an ideal person for the office of governor needs all of the "informal qualifications" EXCEPT which of the following?
   a. Brilliance of mind
   b. Legal knowledge
   c. Exceptional staffing
   d. Knowledge of business and industry

6. Texas governors use executive orders for several purposes but NOT which of the following?
   a. To create task forces to assist with policy development
   b. To appoint legislative committee chairs
   c. To respond to natural disasters and other emergencies
   d. To fill interim appointments

7. Which governor, since the 1960s, issued the greatest number of executive orders and proclamations per year on average?
   a. Abbott
   b. Bush
   c. White
   d. Smith

8. Governors can call a special session . . .
   a. Twelve days after the regular legislative session
   b. One month prior to the start of a legislative session
   c. Only during the summer, or the "off months"
   d. Any time outside of the biennial 140-day session

9. Which governor vetoed the fewest bills?
   a. Abbott
   b. White
   c. Sterling
   d. Clements

10. What tactic do governors often employ in the face of an obstinate legislature or to address an issue of special importance to the governor?
    a. "Going public"
    b. "Grandstanding"
    c. "Ignoring legislators"
    d. "Legislative debating"

[Answers: B, D, D, A, C, B, A, D, C, A]

OXFORD insight study guide
Active Engagement, Deeper Understanding

Learn more with this chapter's digital tools, including the Oxford Insight Study Guide, at www.oup.com/he/Rottinghaus3e.

THE PLURAL EXECUTIVE AND THE BUREAUCRACY

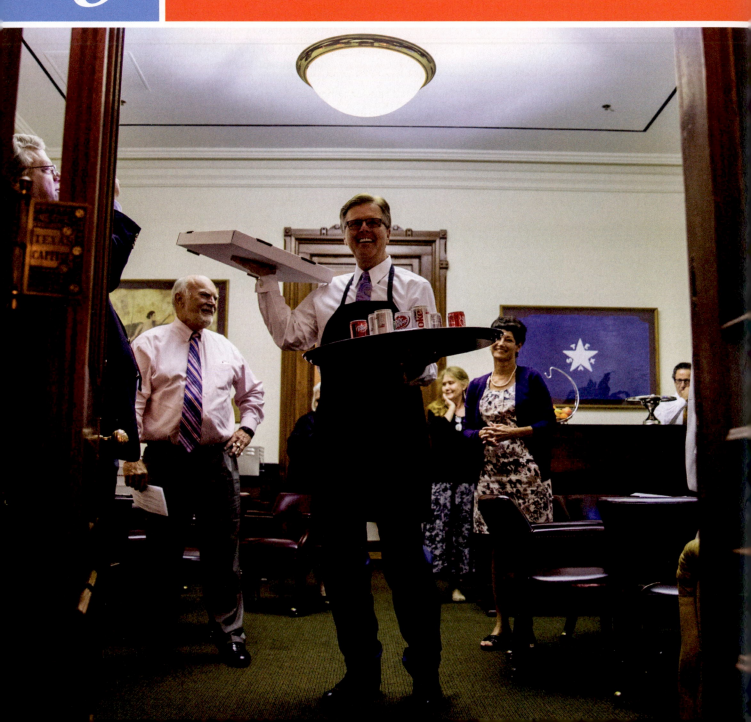

Rushed to the hospital during a heart attack, Drew Calver, Austin father of two, recovered only to be shocked again by the sticker price of his treatment: $108,951. Such "surprise" medical bills are not uncommon among those who find themselves out of their coverage network. Consumer advocates have been urging lawmakers to act for years.[1] In 2019, bipartisan supporters in the Texas Senate and the entire Texas House agreed on legislation that requires health care providers, like hospitals, and insurance companies to arbitrate excessive bills to arrive at a reasonable payment for the consumer. Such arbitration slashed Calver's bill to $332, making it one of the strongest protections in the country.

For Texans to take advantage of this law, the bureaucracy must write the rules that implement and enforce the new law. The Texas Medical Board, which is run by physicians and regulates doctors in the state, proposed rules to expand a narrow exception, which allowed for arbitration rights to be waived for scheduled surgeries with written notices to patients.[2] One provider charged that the rule "misinterprets the law's intent." An angry Lieutenant Governor Dan Patrick announced that he was "not happy" to learn that the bureaucracy had created a loophole in the law.[3]

Infighting weakens an already weak executive branch, but it is an inevitable result of the **plural executive**. The Texas Constitution deliberately fragments political power and policy management so that no single individual, group, or agency has the power to control government. The people elect the most powerful officers of the executive branch, including the lieutenant governor, the attorney general, the comptroller of public accounts, the land commissioner, and positions on dozens of boards and commissions that shape the

9.1 Describe the roles, functions, and structure of the bureaucracy in Texas.

9.2 Explain the roles of the elected members of the executive branch.

9.3 Identify the functions of important governor-appointed, single-headed agencies.

9.4 Describe the purposes that important multimember agencies serve.

9.5 Differentiate between multimember elected commissions and hybrid agencies.

9.6 Assess how the plural executive influences policy and the methods of holding the bureaucracy in check.

plural executive: the diffusion of authority and power throughout several entities in the executive branch and the bureaucracy

● Lieutenant Governor Dan Patrick delivers pizza at midnight as the Texas Senate gets a jump-start on legislative business in the 2017 special session. Like balancing pizza boxes, navigating the Texas bureaucracy is a delicate art.

policy direction of the state. The governor does not appoint most of them and has no direct authority over them.

Designed to prevent any one individual in the executive branch from acquiring too much power, the plural executive system can lead not only to slow, inefficient government but also to outright wastefulness as officials use their power to engage in infighting. How serious a problem is this? Is there a solution? To answer these questions, we must learn more about the executive branch, the plural executive, and the bureaucracy—the thousands of unelected individuals (bureaucrats) whom they oversee and who establish and enforce rules. In the sections that follow, we identify what a bureaucracy is, what it does, and how it is held accountable. The roles of the plural executive and the bureaucracy have changed as the state has grown, and we chart the political implications of this expansion.

9.1 BUREAUCRACY IN TEXAS

9.1 Describe the roles, functions, and structure of the bureaucracy in Texas.

The largest—but often most obscure—level of the executive branch in Texas is made up of the agencies and individuals who make and enforce the rules that govern us all. This branch of government directly touches all our lives, whether we know it or not. Take student financial aid: More than 855,000 Texas college and university students are on financial aid, and they received more than $9.7 billion in 2018 alone.[4] The Texas Higher Education Coordinating Board, part of the Texas bureaucracy, sets the rules for financial aid, and the Texas Education Agency, also part of the bureaucracy, collaborates with other agencies to use financial aid to increase enrollments, help students succeed, and achieve equality of opportunity. Even when you graduate, the Texas bureaucracy continues to touch your life. Did you graduate from a hair-styling school? Texas regulates health and safety standards for barber shops and establishes who can be certified to cut or shampoo hair or to own a salon.

The state agencies that administer financial assistance to college students and that regulate standards of the state's hair, nail, and beauty salons are all part of the **bureaucracy**. Bureaucracies set up a hierarchical chain of command: Employees at each level report to a single boss. The legislature or governor assigns each agency its own specialized mission, such as dispensing financial aid or regulating cosmetology standards. As a result, bureaucrats in

bureaucracy: a government organization that implements laws and provides services to individuals

these agencies have knowledge of or experience in a single area related to their mission.

THE SIZE OF THE TEXAS BUREAUCRACY

Bureaucracies need staff to operate. Because of the size of the land mass, the number of businesses, the number of people, and the enormity of the economy, the executive bureaucracy in Texas is necessarily huge. When compared to other states, however, Texas has fewer bureaucrats per person—approximately 1 bureaucrat for every 3,500 Texas residents (see Figure 9.1). Still, more than 7,800 people work for the Texas executive agencies, boards, and commissions that conduct most of the work in state government.[5]

Although it is comparatively smaller per person than most other states, the bureaucracy in Texas has expanded greatly since the early days of statehood. A growing population means more taxpayers, more driver's licenses, and more public school students. The bureaucracy administers to a growing population and must keep up with it. Likewise, Texas's economy has grown more diverse and larger; Texas now has more agricultural products, more types of energy production, more technology firms, and hundreds more industries. The bureaucracy keeps track of these industries and oversees compliance with rules and regulations. So, although Texans generally dislike big government, the size of the bureaucracy reflects the services required by a diverse, modern economy.

WHAT THE TEXAS BUREAUCRACY DOES

The bureaucracy often gets a bad rap. Politicians engage in "bureaucracy bashing" as a foil for their inability to make government work to their liking. Reporters often highlight the worst abuses, such as the denial of workers' compensation claims, to hold the government responsible, but these events may be isolated incidents. Texans complain about "red tape," or hassles of simple procedures such as renewing a driver's license or obtaining vehicle inspections. But in reality, the bureaucracy in Texas, while imperfect, performs a wide variety of vital tasks.

implementation: the execution by the bureaucracy of laws and decisions made by the legislative, executive, or judicial branch

Policy Implementation. Bureaucrats engage in **implementation** when they carry out laws and decisions made by the legislative, executive, or judicial branch. As of 2019, Texas has a new industry, oyster farming! With the near collapse of the oyster population after Hurricane Harvey, the legislature reversed its decision to restrict oyster harvesting to natural reefs. The

Where can I find all these rules? The *Texas Register*, the journal of state agency rule-making in Texas, keeps a record of rules proposed, adopted, and withdrawn. It can be accessed online.

IS IT BIGGER IN TEXAS?

FIGURE 9.1 **State Employees per 10,000 Residents**

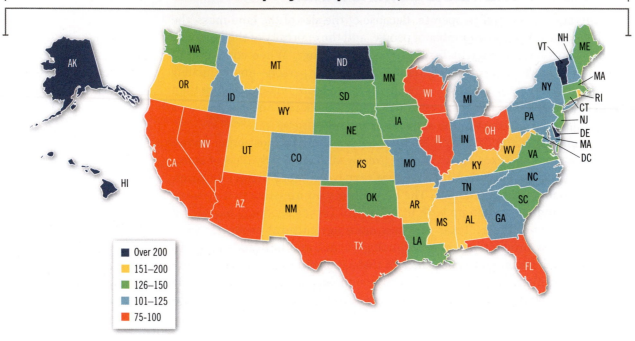

Legend:
- Over 200
- 151–200
- 126–150
- 101–125
- 75–100

Source: U.S. Census Bureau. Total includes noneducation (primary, secondary, or higher) employees per 10,000 in the 2018 estimated population.

 COMMUNICATION:

Which states have larger bureaucracies?

- Less populous states such as Alaska, Delaware, and Wyoming have more employees per 10,000 residents. Texas falls toward the bottom of the list.
- States with smaller populations tend to have a modest staff size.

 CRITICAL THINKING:

Why do some states have more employees per 10,000 residents than others?

- Even for small states, a certain minimum number of employees is necessary to run the government.
- States in fiscal trouble tend to reduce the number of employees.
- Conservative states, which prefer small government, like Texas, attempt to keep the number of bureaucrats low.

newly constructed farms are expected to help prevent coastal erosion, filter seawater, and protect wildlife. The Texas Parks and Wildlife Department is now implementing rules for these budding oyster farms and setting consumer safety standards.[6]

Rule-Making. The legislature or the governor may establish a broad policy with broad goals, but bureaucrats create **rules** to make sure that specific targets are met. For example, the Texas Racing Commission created its own rules when it tried to expand "historic racing" in Texas. Historic racing used video of past races with the dates and names removed and allowed individuals to gamble on the results. The Texas Racing Commission established rules that allowed the racing industry to make money from the practice. However, the ruling did not sit well with socially conservative Texans who oppose gambling. The legislature, led by prominent social conservatives Lieutenant Governor Dan Patrick and Senator Jane Nelson, objected that only the legislature could decide what was technically gambling. Under pressure from the legislature that included threatening to kill the agency's budget, the commission voted to repeal the rule.

rules: regulations designed to control government or the conduct of people and industries

Regulation. Bureaucrats regulate industry, business, individuals, and other parts of government. **Regulations** are often used to protect people; for example, the Texas Commission on Environmental Quality uses environmental regulations to minimize air pollution. Regulations also extend to projects that enrich communities, such as the guidelines for preservation of statewide historic sites issued by the Texas Historical Commission. Some Texans think the regulations are excessive and can hurt businesses and individuals. Case in point: Anita and Jim McHaney bought a small farm outside Hearne, Texas, as part of their retirement. They planned to harvest, pickle, and sell vegetables that grew well on their land, especially beets, carrots, and okra—until they learned of Texas Department of State Health Services regulations. These regulations narrowly defined "pickles" as pickled cucumbers. Producers of other pickled vegetables had to meet stricter regulations, installing a commercial kitchen, obtaining a license, and completing a course that cost hundreds of dollars. Legislators changed the law in 2019 to broaden the definition of the briny goodies. By that time, the McHaney farm had lain fallow for several years.[7]

regulations: standards that are established for the function and management of industry, business, individuals, and other parts of government

Texas's narrow definition of a "pickle" put an end to Anita and Jim McHaney's dreams of making and selling pickled vegetables.

🟥 SOCIAL RESPONSIBILITY: **How do regulations improve your life? How do they serve as obstacles for other Texans?**

licensing: the authorization process that gives a company, an individual, or an organization permission to carry out a specific task

Licensing. **Licensing** gives a company, an individual, or an organization permission to carry out a specific task. For instance, if you want to sell gasoline, market a Texas-made item, sell plants, or cut flowers in the Lone Star State, you'll need a license from the Texas Department of Agriculture. If you want to become a teacher in one of the more than 8,000 public schools in the state, the Texas Education Agency sets out a criterion to become a certified educator. Opponents of big government argue that licensing leads to overregulation; on average, Texans must complete 341 days of training, pass two exams, and pay $253 in fees to become licensed.[8] In 2017, Governor Abbott signed legislation to relax licensing requirements for shampooing and defined eyebrow threading as neither barbering nor cosmetology.

enforcement: the carrying out of rules by an agency or commission within the bureaucracy

Enforcement. The power of **enforcement** of rules falls to bureaucratic entities in the state. If rules are broken, the bureaucratic agents can investigate, issue warnings, levy fines, or even refer criminal activity to the court system. The Texas Department of Agriculture (TDA) launched Operation Maverick in 2015 to enforce the requirement that barbeque joint scales be certified and registered; this requirement ensures that a purchased pound of meat is in fact a pound of meat. Pushback from some of the state's most famous barbeque joints in 2017 resulted in the "Barbeque Bill," which exempted restaurants with "food sold for immediate consumption" from the regulation. The TDA interpreted the wording of the bill by adding "on the premises," which no longer exempted barbeque joints that sold food to go.[9] Despite legislative admonishment to leave these establishments (along with yogurt shops) alone, the agency continues to issue fines.[10]

THE STRUCTURE OF THE TEXAS BUREAUCRACY

There are four broad types of bureaucracies in Texas. All of these entities perform similar types of functions, but each is unique in how the key personnel are selected. These organizations provide the governor and other players in the state's plural executive a way to control (or not control) the actions of these bureaucratic organizations. These types of agencies are as follows:

- Agencies headed by officials appointed by the governor
- Agencies headed by officials independently elected by the people, outside of the governor's control
- Boards and commissions headed by a multimember, governor-appointed official
- Hybrid agencies with a mix of elected and appointed officials headed by an appointed or elected board or commission

The plural executive limits the governor's influence over the bureaucracy (see Figure 9.2). As mentioned, the governor appoints some employees

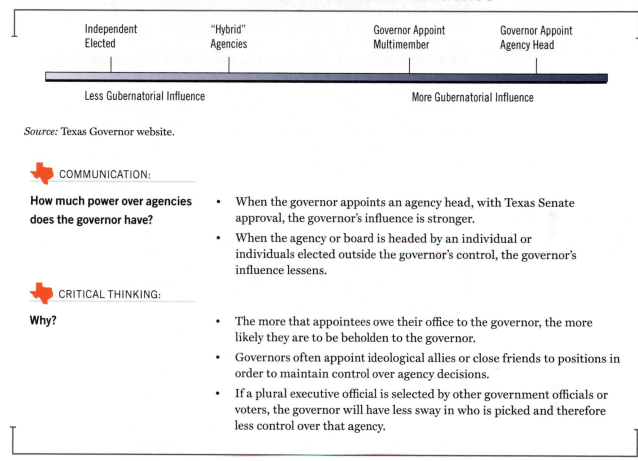

FIGURE 9.2 **Scale of Governor Influence**

Independent Elected · "Hybrid" Agencies · Governor Appoint Multimember · Governor Appoint Agency Head

Less Gubernatorial Influence ⟶ More Gubernatorial Influence

Source: Texas Governor website.

COMMUNICATION:

How much power over agencies does the governor have?

- When the governor appoints an agency head, with Texas Senate approval, the governor's influence is stronger.
- When the agency or board is headed by an individual or individuals elected outside the governor's control, the governor's influence lessens.

CRITICAL THINKING:

Why?

- The more that appointees owe their office to the governor, the more likely they are to be beholden to the governor.
- Governors often appoint ideological allies or close friends to positions in order to maintain control over agency decisions.
- If a plural executive official is selected by other government officials or voters, the governor will have less sway in who is picked and therefore less control over that agency.

within the bureaucracy, particularly upper-level management, but most of them are hired by management and perform administrative roles. Most positions are not politically appointed. These bureaucrats can remain in their posts even as political officials move in and out of office—although low pay and better benefits elsewhere led to 19.3 percent of state agency employees leaving their jobs in 2018.[11] The large number of hired bureaucrats, however, has led some to argue that the bureaucracy is the least responsive branch of government as the people vote for the governor and other leaders of the plural executive, but not the many bureaucrats who devise the rules and regulations.

Governors do influence agency action, however. Some governors require strict loyalty as repayment for appointment, while others are more hands off. The governor has the least influence over independently elected officers, and so we turn our discussion to these rivals for political power.

🏴 **TEXAS TAKEAWAYS**

9.1.1 What major characteristics define a bureaucracy?

9.1.2 How big is Texas's bureaucracy, and what factors contribute to its size?

9.1.3 What vital tasks does the Texas bureaucracy perform?

9.1.4 What type of agencies make up the Texas bureaucracy?

9.1.5 Why do some argue that the bureaucracy is the least representative branch of government?

Ⓤ 9.2 INDEPENDENTLY ELECTED OFFICERS

9.2 Explain the roles of the elected members of the executive branch.

Every 4 years, the citizens of Texas elect a range of important executive branch officials. The most powerful of these officers is the lieutenant governor, whose influence rivals the governor's. But neither the comptroller, attorney general, nor commissioners of agriculture and the General Land Office is beholden to the governor for their position, so they have a sizeable degree of autonomy and an ability to stir up trouble—like an armadillo in a garden—if they so desire.

LIEUTENANT GOVERNOR

Unlike lieutenant governors in other states, and unlike the U.S. vice president, the Texas lieutenant governor plays a formidable role within both the executive and legislative branches (see Figure 9.3). The duties are primarily managerial, but this responsibility makes the lieutenant governor the most powerful force in state government on paper. When Governor George W. Bush, a Republican, asked one of his consultants why he had a "Bob Bullock for Lieutenant Governor" bumper sticker on his car instead of a "Bush for Governor" sticker, the consultant noted, "You don't understand, governor, everyone in Texas works for Bullock."

Since the end of World War II, the lieutenant governor has had a significant say in the administration of the state and lawmaking in Texas. The lieutenant governor serves as the **presiding officer** of the Texas Senate and so is in charge of the administrative and procedural duties of the chamber. Lieutenant governors serve 4-year terms, with no term limits, and tend to

presiding officer: a role of the lieutenant governor who is in charge of the administrative and procedural duties of the Texas Senate

IS IT BIGGER IN TEXAS?

FIGURE 9.3 Lieutenant Governor Power Index

Legend:
- 0
- 1
- 2
- 3
- 4
- States that do not have a lieutenant governor

Source: Brandon Rottinghaus. Scale ranges from 0 (little power) to 4 (maximum power). The average score is 1.76 for the 45 states that have lieutenant governors.

COMMUNICATION

Which states have more powerful lieutenant governors?

- In general, southern and western states tend to have stronger lieutenant governors.
- Plains states and northeastern states typically have weaker lieutenant governors.

CRITICAL THINKING

Why is there such variation in the power states give to lieutenant governors?

- In the post-Reconstruction period, southern states tended to divest governors of their authority by granting more authority to other independently elected executive branch positions.
- The frontier legacy of western states encouraged more stable governing structures, including a strong lieutenant governor.
- Northeastern states have stronger governors and therefore weaken the positions of lieutenant governors (if they even have one).

TABLE 9.1	Lieutenant Governors and Their Controversies

LIEUTENANT GOVERNOR	CONTROVERSY
Ben Barnes (1969–1973)	Tainted by Sharpstown stock fraud scandal.
William "Bill" Hobby Jr. (1973–1991)	Ordered the arrest of senators who were purposely not attending floor debates.
Bob Bullock (1991–1999)	Hands-on management style and abusive behavior rubbed many the wrong way.
Bill Ratliff (2000–2003)	Broke with his party to join Democratic senators opposing redistricting proposals.
David Dewhurst (2003–2015)	Made embarrassing phone call to Allen, Texas, police regarding a jailed relative.
Dan Patrick (2015–present)	Responded to the COVID-19 outbreak saying "there are more important things than living" urging economic recovery over health concerns.

Source: Information is from the *Texas Almanac*. Beginning in 1974, the electoral term changed from 2 to 4 years.

PERSONAL RESPONSIBILITY:

Do Texas voters have the right to expect their elected officials to act in accordance with their moral values?

stay longer in office than other elected officers, increasing their influence. Since 1894, most lieutenant governors have served more than one term. Ben Ramsey holds the record at six consecutive terms. Lieutenant governors frequently have stepped down only after significant controversies (see Table 9.1).

The lieutenant governor must be at least 30 years old, a U.S. citizen, and a Texas resident for more than 5 years prior to the election. Because it is such an insider position, candidates for lieutenant governor tend to be politically connected and experienced. One exception was William Hobby Sr., who was elected in 1915. On being asked to run, a surprised Hobby—who had no political experience—replied, "Why, I can't tie a string cravat. I don't even own a swallow-tailed coat. And my hair just won't seem to grow down the back of my neck!"[12] Hobby would go on to be elected governor, his son would serve as lieutenant governor, and his grandson would serve as a member of the Texas Ethics Commission.

A closer look at the duties of the office shows how the lieutenant governor has a foot in both the legislative and executive branches, both making and executing the laws. This combination is why the position is so powerful.

Working with the Governor. As we saw in the previous chapter, governors often must rely on lieutenant governors to advance their agendas. Republican Governor George W. Bush made friends with the normally prickly Democratic Lieutenant Governor Bob Bullock, known to be as tough on subordinates as on fellow politicians. Bush's fondness for nicknames extended to the lieutenant governor, whom he called "Bully." During his first year as governor, and on his signature issue of tort reform, Bush looked to Bullock to govern over a fragile coalition of Democrats in the senate. Lobbyists tried to convince Bush to lower the ceiling on damages, but Bush stood by the compromise position that he and Bullock had reached. The governor could have threatened a veto, but he wisely chose not to turn his back on a key ally. When working together, jocular Bush would sometimes ask of Bullock, "You gonna get mad at me today, Bully?"[13]

Appointments to Senate Committees. The lieutenant governor is charged with appointing the legislative chairpersons and members of standing committees in the Texas Senate. This power, combined with the authority to dictate the flow of legislation, is a potent weapon in agenda control. Most lieutenant governors appoint sympathetic partisans to promote their party's agenda. However, Lieutenant Governor Ben Barnes, a bridge-builder across the liberal and conservative wings of the Democratic Party in the 1960s, did something no lieutenant governor had done before: He appointed a senator from the opposite wing of his party to serve on the powerful Senate Finance Committee. Conservative Democrats howled, "What the devil are you doing?" But the play was strategic. The appointed senator reported being "too busy" to make trouble.[14]

When necessary, the lieutenant governor can also set up a new standing committee or special committee to investigate or review issues or policies.

Managing the Senate. As the leader of the Texas Senate, the lieutenant governor has discretion in following the chamber's rules on proper parliamentary procedures, such as deciding when a bill will come up for a vote, when to allow a senator on the floor to speak, or how to deal with points of order (objections made to a bill).

One concern for the lieutenant governor is that contentious bills, with dozens of potential amendments, will stall senate business and eat up too much precious time in a legislative session that lasts only 140 days, potentially killing many other important but noncontroversial bills. While a freshman senator, David Sibley attended a session in which Lieutenant Governor Bullock was "machine-gun" gaveling one bill after another to passage in order to move the process along. Sibley asked to be recognized to complain that the senate had not had a chance to study or debate the legislation being approved. After several such attempts, Bullock resentfully relented: "The chair recognizes the crybaby from Waco," he bellowed.[16]

Lieutenant governors adopt different management styles. Bob Bullock represented the firm-hand method, using rewards, old-fashioned threats, and sometimes name-calling to get the job done. On the other hand, Bill Hobby embodied the light-touch method, pushing for nondramatic consensus on legislation. Dan Patrick followed Bullock's lead when he removed Republican senator Kel Seliger as chair of the Senate Higher Education committee. Seliger complained publicly that Patrick was punishing him for refusing to

ANGLES OF POWER
The Power of the Lieutenant Governor beyond Politics

The influence of the lieutenant governor can extend beyond legislative politics—even to the gridiron. In 1995, athletic conferences were negotiating directly with universities over television rights and revenue sharing. The Big Eight Conference was looking to expand to 10 teams, and the University of Texas and Texas A&M University were being courted away from the powerful Southwest Conference. This move would leave the remaining Southwest Conference universities (Texas Christian University, Houston, Rice, Southern Methodist University, Texas Tech, and Baylor) in a much weakened position.

Lieutenant Governor Bob Bullock, a graduate of both Texas Tech and Baylor, summoned the presidents of University of Texas and Texas A&M and, glaring at the two, said, "You're taking Tech and Baylor, or you're not taking anything. I'll cut your money off, and you can join privately if you want, but you won't get another nickel of state money." Calling his bluff, the presidents attempted to negotiate. "If you want to try me, go ahead." Observers reported that "at that moment, for all practical purposes, the Big 8 became the Big 12."[15] Although not a policy over which he had direct control, the lieutenant governor was able to exert political pressure to get his way.

PERSONAL RESPONSIBILITY: **Can a public official overstep his or her job description? In what circumstances do you think this is justified?**

embrace what the senator called "the lieutenant governor's pet projects of bathroom regulations and private school vouchers." When Patrick's spokeswoman Sherry Sylvester then threatened his chairmanship of the Agriculture committee, Seliger commented that he had a recommendation regarding "her lips and my backend." Patrick, referencing the lewd comment, made good on Sylvester's threat.[17] Later in the session, Patrick refused to recognize Seliger to bring up a vote on a bill that would save four nuclear waste facilities in Seliger's district.[18]

Directing the Flow of Legislation. As the presiding officer in the Texas Senate, the lieutenant governor has primary responsibility for where legislation goes, referring bills to one of the standing committees. In effect, the lieutenant governor is the traffic cop for moving legislation within and through the senate. Knowing which committees might favor or disfavor a certain kind of legislation, the lieutenant governor can promote or kill specific legislation by manipulating which committee takes first crack at a bill.

Lieutenant Governor Ben Ramsey had an encyclopedic memory for senate rules and a deep sense of tradition in the chamber. If he opposed a piece of legislation, Ramsey would often tell his chief aide to "lose a bill." When it came time for a senator's bill to be addressed, the bill would be missing (on purpose). In other instances, Ramsey referred a bill to the "Committee on S—it" by tossing it into his desk drawer, effectively killing the bill's chances to be heard.[19]

Lieutenant Governor Dan Patrick used priority bill preferences and procedural acumen to fast track his—and Governor Abbott's—agenda during the 2019 regular session: to advance reforms of the state's property tax and public education funding system.

Tiebreaking Vote in the Senate. Similar to the vice president of the United States, the lieutenant governor has the tiebreaking vote in the state senate if the chamber is evenly divided. In a close vote on the Tort Claim Act in 1969 waiving immunity for the government in civil lawsuits, the senate tied 15–15 (with one member skipping the vote). Lieutenant Governor Ben Barnes, a member of the moderate–conservative wing of the Democratic Party, unexpectedly voted for the act, shocking those in the gallery—including a lobbyist for the Texas Municipal League who, mouth wide open, dropped the pipe he was smoking onto the senate floor below, burning a hole in the carpet.

Membership on Key Legislative Boards. The lieutenant governor serves as chair, or as a member, of several key boards that govern the state, including the Legislative Budget Board, the Legislative Council, and the Legislative Redistricting Board. The lieutenant governor shares appointment power with the governor on most of these boards, making cooperation essential to efficient government.

Involving Texans in the Lawmaking Process. Like governors, lieutenant governors also form policy networks to help develop legislation. Lieutenant Governor Dan Patrick created six citizen committees (including 55 Texas business leaders) to advise him on legislation and policy matters affecting taxes, transportation, water, energy, and the economy.

David Dewhurst, Former Democratic Lieutenant Governor of Texas

How do all the power players balance competing interests in the legislative process?

It's been said that the legislature is a great teacher. I've learned a lot of patience. I've learned a lot of consensus-building. Because I respect everyone here. They all got elected. They're all loved by their constituents and/or their families, and they all have their point of view. I may disagree with them in certain areas, but I respect 'em, you know? And if you have that attitude, and you realize that everybody has something good to contribute—that even though the final product is going to be a Republican, conservative bill, everybody has things they can offer to improve it—then that buy-in will produce a better product, I think.[20]

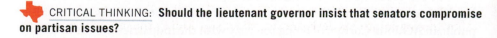

CRITICAL THINKING: **Should the lieutenant governor insist that senators compromise on partisan issues?**

ATTORNEY GENERAL

The attorney general (AG) is the state's lawyer, defending the laws and constitution of Texas by representing the state in court. The AG provides legal services to the governor, state agencies, and local and state government entities. The AG's actions and opinions can actively shape state policies. When requested, the AG's office files suit on behalf of state agencies in court. The Texas Constitution does not specify that the AG be a licensed attorney, only that the AG "represent the state" in various legal capacities.

In the 1970s, for instance, Texans found themselves vulnerable to every manner of consumer fraud: negligent nursing home owners, con artists selling phony oil investments, and retailers advertising everyday prices as "sale prices." After a series of banking scandals swept the state, AG John Hill sat down with his staff at a Tex-Mex restaurant in Austin and came up with a bill that would give legal recourse to swindled Texans with small dollar claims. As they scribbled guidelines for how to deal with deceptive practices, they spilled chile con queso and salsa picante onto their papers.[21] That "queso-stained plea for help for Texas's consumers" formed the basis of legislation that empowered consumers with courthouse access.[22]

The office's legal duties have spread into other areas as well. The AG's office enforces health, safety, and consumer regulations and protects the rights of the elderly and disabled. The AG's office investigates deceptive business practices, including car repair fraud, telemarketing scams, identity theft, "diploma mills," health care fraud, price gouging, and other consumer-related complaints. The AG is also responsible for enforcement of child support payments, including locating absent parents, establishing paternity, reviewing and adjusting child support payments, and collecting and distributing child support payments. The AG's office can also punish parents who are behind on their child support payments by blocking car registration renewal, revoking a driver's license, or stripping a professional license. The office collected a nationwide high $4.3 billion in child support in 2018.[23]

As a result of their constitutional role, lawyers from the AG's office spend a lot of time in court. These cases fall into three categories: antitrust, consumer protection, and environmental. Cases are often filed *against* the federal government to challenge or provoke a review of specific federal laws or regulations.

Another important function of the AG's office is to issue legal opinions to the governor, heads of state agencies, lawmakers, and local officials (see Figure 9.4). The courts view these opinions as so highly persuasive that the AG in effect makes policy by interpreting a statute, rule, or law that may serve as a basis for future legislative action (see Table 9.2). The power of the AG to interpret the constitution is second only to that of the Texas Supreme Court.

The AG often wades in tenuous, swampy water between the solid shore of legal representation and the murky marsh of politics. Journalists accused Republican AG John Cornyn of being too cozy with the industries he was litigating

FIGURE 9.4 **Attorney General Advisory Opinions**

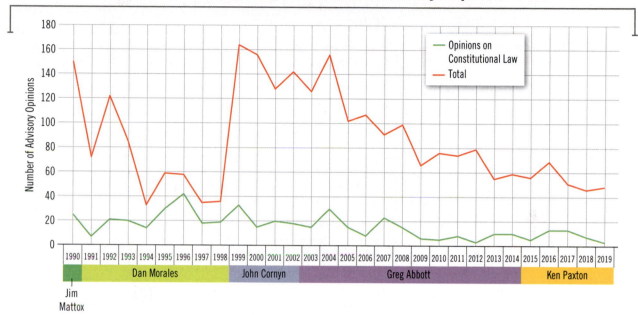

Source: Texas Attorney General's Office.

 COMMUNICATION:

How has the number of advisory opinions changed over time?

- The total number of advisory opinions decreased from 1999 to 2019, from 160 to around 50.
- The largest increase in advisory opinions occurred when John Cornyn (a Republican) took over as attorney general from Dan Morales (a Democrat).

 CRITICAL THINKING:

What factors have caused the attorney general to weigh in on a case?

- A change in the party controlling the office from Democrat to Republican may have prompted more legal inquiries from the new attorney general. Republicans had captured control of both the legislature and the governor's office at the time, and government entities were looking for the attorney general to provide favorable rulings for them.
- The attorney general is also asked to rule on more constitutional cases when major issues are being considered by the legislature, such as changes to tax policy or public school funding.

| TABLE 9.2 | **Key Attorney General Opinions** | |

YEAR	ATTORNEY GENERAL	OPINION
1990	Democrat Jim Mattox	Both "excused" and "unexcused" school absences count as absences for attendance counts.
1992	Democrat Dan Morales	Bingo games with monetary prizes are authorized only if conducted for charity.
1994	Democrat Dan Morales	School district-sponsored extracurricular activities may not take place at an athletic club that discriminates.
2001	Republican John Cornyn	Government body cannot prohibit the holder of a concealed handgun onto government property unless public notification is given.
2006	Republican Greg Abbott	State can deny driver's license renewal for failure to appear in municipal court or pay fines.
2017	Republican Ken Paxton	Licensed handgun owners can bring their weapons to church as long as the church does not prohibit it.

Source: Texas Attorney General's Office.

 CRITICAL THINKING:

How does the attorney general shape public policy? Does the political party of the attorney general influence his or her decisions?

- Democrats and Republicans tend to fall in line with their party's ideology.
- Democrat Dan Morales held that school extracurricular programs may not discriminate.
- Republicans, such as Greg Abbott and Ken Paxton, are tougher on crime and more supportive of gun rights.

against. Two years into Cornyn's tenure, journalist Paul Burka accused Cornyn of settling for less than expected on a water pollution suit against a pipeline company and of endorsing favorable settlements to health care providers.[24]

Because it is one of the most important and high-profile offices in the state, the AG has proven to be a good stepping stone to political advancement in recent years. The office has promoted Mark White (governor), John Cornyn (U.S. senator), and Greg Abbott (governor).

COMPTROLLER OF PUBLIC ACCOUNTS

Sometimes referred to as the "tooth fairy of public accounts" for his or her silent but authoritative approach to budgeting, the state comptroller is a powerful figure in Texas politics. The comptroller's role is to estimate revenue, certify budget funds, and chart state economic growth. The state's budget operates on a **pay-as-you-go system**: State funds spent must equal state funds received. The legislature must craft a budget that is only as big as the comptroller says it is allowed to be. The Texas Constitution requires that all appropriations bills (bills to allow spending) from the legislature be approved by the comptroller's office.

Bob Bullock reinvented the comptroller's office when he was first elected in 1975. When he arrived in the office, "Everything creaked: the procedures, the equipment, the employees."[25] Bullock established the comptroller's office as central in matters of taxes, school finance, and agency funding. He also jealously guarded state funds. One day, he walked into the store of a delinquent liquor distributor in San Antonio and confronted him: "I'm Bob Bullock. You owe me $236,000." The dealer said, "Say again?" And Bullock said, "I'm the state comptroller, and you owe the people of Texas $236,000 in sales taxes you haven't paid and I'm here to collect it." The dealer laughed and said he didn't have that kind of money. Bullock retorted, "I think you've got that kind of whiskey." Bullock then turned to one of his employees and ordered, "Start hauling this sh—t out of here." Bullock carried off two 18-wheelers full of whiskey. The media called the trucks Bullock's Raiders.[26]

The comptroller has an early say in the amount of money that Texas spends, giving the office significant control over the pot of money the legislature has to work with. After submitting the budget, the comptroller can still give the legislature the go-ahead to spend extra money. The comptroller also certifies that Texas's budget books are balanced.

The fiscal power of the comptroller also may extend into the political arena. Independent-minded Republican Comptroller Carole Keeton Strayhorn was a fiscal thorn in the side of Governor George W. Bush. Strayhorn reduced the previously plump revenue estimate by $700 million in 1999, forcing Governor Bush to slim down the property tax cut that he had promised voters.

Misestimating this revenue can have serious ramifications for both politics and policy. In 2011, Comptroller Susan Combs overestimated tax revenue by a whopping $11.3 billion, or 14 percent. Expecting economic bedlam, lawmakers cut more than $5 billion from public education, impacting the delivery of quality public education, laying off thousands of teachers, and prompting a constitutional challenge over educational quality in the state. Less disastrous

Texas Attorney General Ken Paxton was asked whether some online fantasy sports sites, where fans pay to assemble virtual teams and compete for advertised big payoffs, legally constitutes gambling. Like attorneys general in other states, Paxton held that because the "house" takes a cut of the pot, it is gambling and likely illegal under Texas law.

PERSONAL RESPONSIBILITY: If you were attorney general, how would you rule in this fantasy sports leagues case?

pay-as-you-go system: the system by which state funds spent must equal state funds received

errors are not uncommon (see Figure 9.5). Estimates are most frequently wrong due to unexpected recessions, overestimated tax collections, or precipitous declines in energy prices. Estimates are also required to project up to thirty-two months into the future, a difficult challenge for any economist.

FIGURE 9.5 ## Difference between Estimated and Actual Tax Collections

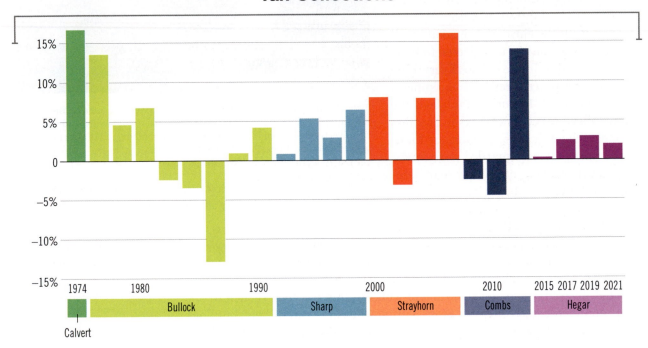

Source: Texas Comptroller's Office.

 COMMUNICATION:

When have revenue estimates been incorrect?

- Sharp decreases in the price of oil consistently put revenue estimates off-base. This occurred in the late 1980s.
- Booming population growth, such as in the late 1970s and from 2012 to the present, and increases in sales tax revenue have driven revenue higher than expected.

CRITICAL THINKING:

Why are some forecasts so wrong?

- Economic forecasts are based on assumptions. If these assumptions change, the forecasts change as well. Energy prices rise and fall, the housing market may be unpredictably weak in some areas of the state, or spending by Texans (and therefore sales taxes) may slow down.

COMMISSIONER OF THE GENERAL LAND OFFICE

The land commissioner, the oldest continuously elected position in Texas history, oversees state-owned land, including open beaches and submerged land off the coast of the Gulf of Mexico. When Texas agreed to enter the Union in 1845, it negotiated to keep its public debt but also its public lands. The land commissioner administers these lands by leasing them and generating funds from oil and gas production.

The General Land Office (GLO) pursues new revenue opportunities for the state. The GLO is investigating developing renewable offshore wind, solar, or geothermal energy on state lands. The GLO also oversees the Permanent School Fund, whose proceeds fund public schools, and the Veterans Land Board, which makes low-interest loans available to veterans and oversees state veterans' cemeteries and skilled-care facilities.

AGRICULTURE COMMISSIONER

The agriculture commissioner oversees the Department of Agriculture, which implements agricultural laws, promotes Texas's agriculture production and products, and administers school nutrition programs. The department also performs regulatory functions, such as protecting consumers from pesticides and certifying organic products. By the simple act of buying fruit at the grocery store, the consumer interacts with the Texas bureaucracy. The Department of Agriculture certifies Texas-grown produce. Because one in every seven working Texans (14 percent) works in an agriculture-related job and the economic impact of agriculture-related production exceeds $150 billion annually, the role of the department in managing agriculture issues is critical to the economic welfare of the state.

Like all agencies, the department's regulatory role is limited by available funds. Agriculture Commissioner Sid Miller reported in 2015 that Texas consumers are "getting screwed" by unscrupulous businesses because the Department of Agriculture has not been able to perform many of its regulatory functions—such as checking gas pumps for accuracy, verifying that grocery store scanners work properly, and inspecting taxicab meters to verify that people aren't being overcharged. Commissioner Miller briefed the legislature on the matter, requesting more funds to take care of the backlog. State Senator Paul Bettencourt, Republican

Agricultural Commissioner Sid Miller, in one of his first acts as agency head, granted full "amnesty" to cupcakes. Reminding Texans that the state had lifted the ban on selling cupcakes and other sugary treats, he delivered 181 cupcakes to the Capitol-enough for each member of the house and senate.

SOCIAL RESPONSIBILITY: **Should the government be in the business of banning unhealthy foods? Why or why not?**

of Houston, remarked that he had made a first-hand discovery of problems with the oversight of gasoline sales: "I learned about this when I drove my car in and filled up 27 gallons on a 19-gallon tank."[27]

PLURAL EXECUTIVE FEUDS

Internal feuding within the Texas executive branch harkens back to the first days of the state's constitution. Governor Pappy O'Daniel once labeled the Board of Control and the Game and Fish and Oyster Commission "giant oligarchies and juicy play-pretties of the professional politicians." The governor lamented that he was unable to meet public demand for reform because his office had been "stripped" of the power that was given to the bureaucrats. Today, both agencies are defunct, but the complicated arrangement between the most powerful offices within the executive branch remains.[28]

The governor and lieutenant governor should see eye to eye, especially if they are of the same party, but relations between them are not always cordial, making for diverging strategies. In 2019, after a racially motivated mass shooting at a Walmart in El Paso, Lieutenant Governor Patrick ticked off social media bullying, the lack of school prayer, and people not saluting the flag as possible factors in the spread of mass shootings, while Governor Abbott pointed to "mental health issues" and urged Texas officials to "do a better job" of handling these issues.[29]

Moreover, despite the strength of the office, the lieutenant governor does not always win internal fights with other executive officials. One heated exchange involved Attorney General Dan Morales's anger at Lieutenant Governor Bullock's office for hiring an outside attorney to consult on redistricting matters; this was a plum assignment because it involved the power to draw legislative district lines. Bullock became irritated by the attorney general's "incessant complaints" and physically challenged him by "bumping against him with his chest and lightly backhanding him."[30] The two were separated, and the attorney general was eventually allowed to handle the redistricting issue.[31]

🇹 TEXAS TAKEAWAYS

9.2.1 Who are the most important independently elected officers in the executive branch apart from the governor?

9.2.2 How long do lieutenant governors usually stay in office?

9.2.3 What are the key roles of the lieutenant governor?

9.2.4 What are the functions of the attorney general's office?

9.2.5 What are the chief powers of the state comptroller?

9.2.6 What are the roles of the commissioners of agriculture and the General Land Office?

9.3 GOVERNOR-APPOINTED, SINGLE-HEADED AGENCIES

The governor-appointed, single-headed agencies are more likely to be influenced by the governor's agenda because the governor has a direct say in who gets appointed. Of course, the Texas Senate must approve the individuals the governor selects, so the control is not absolute. Moreover, these agencies often pursue their own prerogatives, occasionally—as we shall see later—with politically damaging results.

9.3 Identify the functions of important governor-appointed, single-headed agencies.

SECRETARY OF STATE

Can dead people vote in Texas? After 239 "dead" people did just that in the May 2012 primaries,[32] Secretary of State Hope Andrade decided to purge the voter registration records of Texans she believed to be deceased. Unfortunately, four voters presumed dead (but not) sued Andrade, the first Latina secretary of state, for civil rights violations and for suppression of minority voters. Secretary Andrade suspended the purge.

More than a figurehead, the secretary of state serves as the chief elections administrator, the steward of all state records, and an ambassador of the state to other nations. First, the secretary assists county election officials, ensures the uniform application of election laws throughout the state, and maintains the registration records for more than 15 million voters and several voter education programs.[33] Second, as the chief recordkeeper, the secretary publishes government rules and regulations and thus is often referred to as the "State's Filing Cabinet." Third, the secretary serves as the lead liaison on issues involving the Texas–Mexico border and Texas's relations with Mexico.

COMMISSIONER FOR HEALTH AND HUMAN SERVICES

The Health and Human Services Commission (HHSC), headed by a commissioner selected by the governor, is responsible for the health and welfare of many needy Texans. Because of its wide-ranging responsibilities, the HHSC is massive and oversees the operations of most health-related programs, including the following:

- Medicaid
- Children's Health Insurance Program
- Texas Women's Health Program
- Temporary Assistance for Needy Families
- Supplemental Nutrition Assistance Program

A large and diverse state provides many options for governors looking to add diversity to the executive branch in Texas. The growth of the Hispanic and Asian populations in Texas makes this more important. Many governors seek representatives from underrepresented groups to serve in Texas government.

SOCIAL RESPONSIBILITY: **Does diversity matter in gubernatorial appointments? In what way?**

The HHSC is a mega-agency with four different departments, 58,000 employees, and a $30 billion budget. The size and number of policies the HHSC implements make it one of the toughest to run in state government. Languid leadership at the top of HHSC provoked a mass departure of senior employees, lowering staff morale low and hampering the state's ability to aid victims of natural disasters and those in need of health care assistance.[34]

DEPARTMENT OF INSURANCE

Think your neighbor can get away with a fraudulent insurance claim about damage caused by flooding from Hurricane Harvey? Think again. Insurance fraud costs Texans millions of dollars annually, and the Fraud Unit of the Texas Department of Insurance (TDI) investigates more than 500 cases each year.

The TDI also regulates the insurance industry and provides consumer protection. In one recent case, the TDI caught a former insurance agent who convinced more than 30 elderly customers to liquidate insurance plans and hand over the funds to him.[35] Consumers can also comparison shop for various types of insurance through the TDI and register complaints against insurance companies, health maintenance organizations, insurance agents, or claims adjusters. The TDI also oversees the allocation of workers' compensation benefits.

🏴 TEXAS TAKEAWAYS

9.3.1 What are some of the most powerful governor-appointed, single-headed agencies?

9.3.2 What does the secretary of state do?

9.3.3 Why is the Health and Human Services Commission so difficult to manage?

9.3.4 What are the responsibilities of the Department of Insurance?

9.4 GOVERNOR-APPOINTED, MULTIMEMBER AGENCIES

Multimember agencies whose members are appointed by the governor are certainly influenced by the governor's agenda and ideology. This influence is lessened, however, because there are many members of these organizations and the governor's reach may not grasp all of them all of the time. These groups largely operate independently of the other executive agencies but are accountable to the legislature through periodic review.

> **9.4** Describe the purposes that important multimember agencies serve.

multimember agencies: bureaucratic organizations staffed by a minimum of three individuals

PUBLIC UTILITY COMMISSION

If you get an electricity bill that is alarmingly high, contact the Public Utility Commission (PUC). Created in 1975 to provide statewide regulation of the rates and services of electric and telecommunications utilities, the PUC offers Texans assistance in resolving consumer complaints about electricity rates. Consumers can also use the "Power to Choose" website, www.powertochoose.org, to compare company prices, and if consumers feel exploited, they can file a complaint for PUC to investigate.[36]

DEPARTMENT OF TRANSPORTATION

Ever been stuck in traffic and wondered whom to blame? The Texas Department of Transportation (TxDOT), though not responsible for your immediate traffic delays, is in charge of operations and maintenance of the state's massive, 80,000-mile highway system in addition to overseeing aviation, railroads, and other public transportation systems in the state.

The TxDOT also awards state contracts for building and maintaining highways. With urbanization and a growing population, Texas has an all-time high number of vehicles on its roads and number of miles traveled. The state's current infrastructure is aging, with tens of thousands of lane miles in need of reconstruction. In the years ahead, the state will struggle to fund road construction. Texas voters passed a constitutional amendment to divert half of the general oil and gas revenue to the State Highway Fund, but this barely keeps up with growing needs.

TEXAS PARKS AND WILDLIFE DEPARTMENT

If you've ever wetted a fishing line, hunted a buck, paddled a canoe, or popped a tent in Texas, chances are you've encountered the Texas Parks and Wildlife Department (TPWD). The TPWD manages and protects wildlife and wildlife

Hunting from a helicopter ("aerial management") requires more than finding a buddy with a chopper and a rifle. To participate, hunters must file the proper paperwork with the Texas Parks and Wildlife Department. Aerial hunters must only hunt feral hogs and coyotes. It is otherwise illegal to sport hunt from aircraft.

PERSONAL RESPONSIBILITY: **Would you fish or hunt without a license? How much should the state regulate hunting?**

habitats and acquires and manages Texas's state parks and historic areas. Specifically, the TPWD sells hunting, fishing, and boating licenses; issues fees for service, such as state park entrance fees; and creates and enforces regulations to protect wildlife and stock fish. Buy a kayak or a baseball glove in Texas? Fees for sports equipment also go to the Parks Department after voters approved a constitutional amendment to funnel that money to TPWD. The TPWD's law enforcement, both game wardens and park police forces, makes the department the second-largest statewide law enforcement agency.

The TPWD is a traditionally rural agency that is attempting to serve an increasingly urban state. If an alligator shows up on your patio some summer afternoon, you can't simply shoot it. Getting an Alligator Nuisance Control Permit requires completing a course and passing two exams—one written exam and one "live alligator handling exam."[37] In 22 counties, hunters may secure a license but tag only one alligator per year, and they may only capture the creature with gigs and snares (although the alligator, once caught, can be "dispatched" with a firearm).

TEXAS COMMISSION ON ENVIRONMENTAL QUALITY

The Texas Commission on Environmental Quality (TCEQ) protects public health, preserves the natural resources of the state, maintains clean air and water, and assures the safe management of waste. The TCEQ is also responsible for licensing certain activities that have an environmental impact, such as wastewater operations, as well as for issuing permits to industry groups and creating and enforcing environmental rules. The TCEQ issues rules about responding to natural disasters, sets fees for environmental cleanups as necessary, and applies rules to industries.

The state clashes with both local and national actors on environmental protection. Governor Abbott has consistently argued against tightening national emissions limits on smog-forming pollution on the grounds that these changes would hurt the Texas economy. Governor Abbott temporarily suspended environmental rules in 2019 after both Hurricane Harvey and Tropical Storm Imelda caused power outages and equipment failures that resulted in the dumping of nearly 8 million pounds of cancer-causing chemicals and toxins into the air.[38] At the same time, TCEQ has invested $1.5 million to improve real-time air monitoring following these disasters and chemical fires along the Houston coast.[39]

🏴 **TEXAS TAKEAWAYS**

9.4.1 Compare governor-appointed agencies run by a single head or by more than one person.

9.4.2 What are the responsibilities of the Public Utility Commission, the Texas Parks and Wildlife Department, and the Texas Commission on Environmental Quality?

9.4.3 What major challenge does the Texas Department of Transportation face?

9.5 MULTIMEMBER ELECTED COMMISSIONS AND HYBRID AGENCIES

In some cases, voters themselves elect the members of a commission, giving the public a more direct say in the regulatory process. Elections to these multimember commissions are held either at the district or statewide level. In addition, some **hybrid agencies** comprise both elected and appointed officials.

> **9.5** Differentiate between multimember elected commissions and hybrid agencies.

TEXAS RAILROAD COMMISSION

Ironically, the Texas Railroad Commission (TRC) has almost no authority over railroads in Texas! Originally created in 1891 to regulate corruption and monopolies in the railroad industry, the TRC is Texas's oldest regulatory agency. In the late 1880s, to entice railroads to run their tracks through sparsely populated Texas, the legislature granted more than 24 million acres (38,000 square miles) to the railroads—an area larger than the state of Indiana—without oversight. The result was mayhem, fraud, and corruption. Public outcry and leadership from railroad-buster Governor James Hogg precipitated the creation of a regulatory agency to set rates, correct abuses, and enforce penalties.

Decades after its creation, the TRC's book of responsibility has expanded significantly. Currently, the TRC's primary functions are the regulation of the oil and gas industry. The TRC issues permits for drilling for or extracting natural resources, inspects oil and gas facilities, licenses waste haulers, assesses fees for environmental damage in oil fields, and ensures that oil and natural gas pipelines run safely. These dealings sometimes place the TRC in the center of a controversy. In 2014, citizens of Denton County voted to ban the practice

hybrid agencies: bureaucratic organizations whose leaders are selected by a mixture of appointments and elections

of hydraulic fracturing (fracking), a practice regulated by the TRC. The state legislature rejected local control of fracking and reaffirmed the TRC's central role in the commercial development of land. Local officials and other critics maintain that the TRC is protecting the industries it is supposed to regulate and that local control is needed to protect the health and safety of citizens.

TEXAS ETHICS COMMISSION

Which organizations are backing your elected officials? How much money do politicians spend to get reelected? How much money does the beer industry spend on lobbyists to persuade legislators to support a bill? The Texas Ethics Commission (TEC) keeps track of these figures by overseeing campaign contributions and regulating and enforcing lobbying activities. In terms of enforcement, the TEC hears complaints related to filing violations and can fine individuals.

STATE BOARD OF EDUCATION

How much should teachers in Texas focus on Thomas Jefferson's faith as part of his political beliefs? Should the study of important Confederate leaders be expanded on in the coverage of the Civil War in U.S. history classes? These questions are principally decided by the State Board of Education (SBOE). The SBOE is responsible for overseeing public primary and secondary education, setting curriculum standards, and establishing graduation requirements.

Because it has control over the curriculum taught in the state's public schools, SBOE is no stranger to controversy. Curriculum decisions—especially concerning the role of religion, the coverage of political figures, and the treatment of race—have sparked national debate. In 2010, the SBOE, led by conservative members, removed hip-hop from a list of influential cultural music because of complaints about inappropriate lyrics.[40] In 2018, the SBOE voted to keep defining the defenders of the Alamo as "heroic," as well as to reinsert Hillary Clinton and Helen Keller into curriculum standards. Motions to remove Moses as an influence on the country's Founding Fathers' and eliminate "states' rights" as a cause of the Civil War failed on a party line vote.[41] Although the governor appoints the Commission of Education and the head of the SBOE, the people elect all officials to the 15-member SBOE. So Texas voters can have a say in these controversial decisions.

🏴 TEXAS TAKEAWAYS

9.5.1 What is the difference between multimember elected commissions and hybrid agencies?

9.5.2 Name the primary functions of the Texas Railroad Commission.

9.5.3 What is the main goal of the Texas Ethics Commission?

9.5.4 Identify the primary responsibility of the State Board of Education.

9.6 CONTROLLING THE BUREAUCRACY

Is the Texas bureaucracy too closely aligned with business interests at the expense of ordinary Texas citizens? Does the structure of the plural executive contribute to sluggish policy innovation and slow responses to state problems? Does the diffusion of power among the governor, the lieutenant governor, the comptroller, and the other executive officers, agencies, and commissions mean that the people cannot hold the Texas government accountable? And has the weak structure of the executive, established to prevent the government from stamping out individual freedom, become too inefficient to meet the needs of a modernizing Texas? To begin answering these questions, we look at how the selection of the bureaucracy impacts policy, how the plural executive impacts efficiency, and what mechanism state representatives and the people can use to reform the bureaucracy.

9.6 Assess how the plural executive influences policy and the methods of holding the bureaucracy in check.

SELECTION OF THE BUREAUCRACY

How the bureaucracy is selected influences public policy in many ways. Texas voters influence public policy when they elect members of the bureaucracy. Governor appointees often shape policy in line with the governor's preferences. Governor Greg Abbott, for example, appointed Josh McGee, an advocate of cutting pension benefits, to head the Pension Review Board. One observer compared the choice to "appointing Godzilla to guard Tokyo."[42] Although the chair of the Pension Review has limited power to change pensions for all Texans, he has an influential voice in making changes to the pensions of state workers.

Often, the legislature introduces requirements for appointments that limit the governor. For example, although the nine individuals who head the TPWD are appointed by the governor (with senate approval), the governor is obligated by law to attempt to include persons with expertise in diverse fields, such as historical preservation, conservation, and outdoor recreation. This limits—but does not remove—the influence of outside agents and improves the ability of the agency to act in the best interests of the people of Texas. A game warden from the TPWD even filed state charges against Senate Majority Leader Lyndon Johnson in 1956 for shooting more than the legal limit of birds. The warden's charges were dismissed by a local justice of the peace who was politically friendly to Johnson.

Some agencies have appointees representing multiple interests across Texas government, attempting to balance the interests of all. The TEC's eight members are selected by three different officials: The governor appoints four members, the lieutenant governor appoints two members, and the speaker of the house appoints two members. As a result, no single part of the government has full authority to staff the TEC with its associates. Given that the tasks of the TEC are to serve as an enforcement agency on state ethics laws, this dispersion of power is important so that the commission is not beholden to any one individual. Governor Rick Perry himself was fined $1,500 for failing to report income from a rental house.

Voters also have a hand in selection, especially to agencies that make important policy decisions, such as the SBOE and the TRC. When voters don't like the policy created, they can vote officeholders out of these agencies. The SBOE's rewriting of history standards in 2010, including limiting discussion about race and gender issues and emphasizing gun rights and free markets, reflected the political values of the Texans who voted for the SBOE members at the time.[43] Voters rejected these educational policy choices in 2014 and 2018, however, when they elected more moderates to the board to replace several controversial members.[44] The board then toned down the rhetoric and looked to make more reasonable standards for textbooks.

Sometimes, agency officials are selected from industry groups that are regulated by that agency—even when voters elect these officials. These candidates have an advantage in that they have expertise in the field and often considerable campaign funds. The TRC provides a good example of how this can influence policy. Critics of the TRC suggest that the agency is too close to the industry it regulates and that the TRC's dual role of regulating industry and environmental stewardship creates conflicts of interest. In late 2013 and early 2014, a series of mysterious earthquakes rattled northern Texas along the Barnett Shale, home to gas-rich fields. Regulators worried that oil- and gas-related activities contributed to the seismic activities, as suggested from reports by energy experts and seismologists at Southern Methodist University. The TRC cleared two oil field companies of responsibility, arguing that the study was preliminary and that the link between extraction efforts and earthquakes is inconclusive. Environmental activists accused the TRC of siding with the industry and insisted that further investigations were warranted.

SLUGGISH POLICYMAKING

Much of the weakness in Texas government is due to the plural executive's diffusion of power and to bureaucratic policies that contribute to sluggish policy innovation and slow responses to state problems. Rules and regulations from a large bureaucracy choke government's ability to be agile. Proposed rules changes must be advertised for a specific period of time and open for public comment, after which they often face administrative delays. The legislature may use this formal process to slow down bureaucratic rule-making.

For example, the foster care system in Texas has let down the state's most vulnerable kids. The Department of Family and Protective Services overlooked dozens of cases of abuse, including one in which a young girl was killed by her foster family, prompting court challenges and federal intervention.

Because of complex rules, the amount of paperwork, deadlines, and family visits creates a pressure-filled environment that pushes away experienced employees. The Commissioner of the Department of Family and Protective Services says part of the problem is that there are too many policies and rules, making it "impossible for people to know what the policies are."[45]

OVERSIGHT AND CHANGE

An accountable bureaucracy is the key to ensuring that government is working properly and efficiently. With so many agency heads, staff, rules, and procedures, keeping tabs on the function of the bureaucracy in Texas is a massive task. Several players in government are in charge of reviewing agencies, monitoring their progress, evaluating their effectiveness, and altering or eliminating them.

As foster care providers lobbied the legislature to increase their reimbursements, Wilma David May explains how anyone who visits a foster home more than twice a month must be subjected to background checks. May explains how this can make it difficult to host friends from church who are a great source of support for foster parents.

PERSONAL RESPONSIBILITY: **What bureaucratic rules or regulations have you experienced that you believe need to be changed? How might the rules be changed?**

Sunset Process. The Sunset Advisory Commission is a 12-member panel established in 1977 with responsibility for reviewing more than 130 state agencies in order to evaluate their efficiency and effectiveness. Texas is one of only a few states that has this process (the federal government does not either).

The Sunset Commission asks a simple question: Does an agency's function continue to be needed by the state? For each state agency, the legislature sets a date for its abolishment on a 12-year calendar. The agency is set to be abolished unless legislation is passed to allow that agency to continue to function. The commission reviews agencies set to be "sunsetted" prior to that date, and the legislature decides whether to amend or abolish the agency based on the commission's recommendation. This process creates a unique opportunity for the legislature to establish rules and goals for agencies and to hold the bureaucracy accountable (see Table 9.3). Some boards or commissions are scheduled for periodic review, but not elimination, such as the Board of Pardons and Paroles. Between 20 and 30 agencies are reviewed every legislative session.

The good news for state agencies is that they are rarely given the death sentence (see Figure 9.6). Rather, specific functions are often transferred to another agency, or recommendations for improvements are made. For instance, in 2017, the Texas Veterinary Board came under scrutiny when a photograph of a dead cat shot through the head with an arrow by a veterinarian became public. The Sunset Commission investigated; found that the board

TABLE 9.3   ## Sunset Agency Review Process

SUNSET STAFF EVALUATION	SUNSET COMMISSION STAFF
Sunset staff performs extensive research and analysis to evaluate the need for, performance, and improvements to the agency under review.	• Reviews agency's Self-Evaluation Report • Receives input from interested parties • Evaluates agency and identifies problems • Develops recommendations • Publishes staff report
SUNSET PUBLISHES STAFF REPORT	
SUNSET COMMISSION DELIBERATION	PUBLIC HEARINGS
The Sunset Commission conducts a public hearing to take testimony on the staff report and the agency overall. Later, the Commission meets again to vote on which changes to recommend to the full legislature.	• Sunset staff presents its report and recommendations • Agency presents its response • Sunset Commission hears public testimony • Staff compiles all testimony for Commission consideration • Sunset Commission meets again to consider and vote on recommendations
SUNSET COMMISSION RECOMMENDS ACTION	
LEGISLATIVE ACTION	TEXAS LEGISLATURE
The full legislature considers Sunset recommendations and makes final determinations.	• Sunset bill on an agency is drafted and filed • Sunset bills go through normal bill processes • The senate and the house conduct committee hearings and debate the bill • Bill passes or fails adoption • Governor signs, vetoes, or allows bill to become law without signature
Agency continues with improvements. **OR** **Agency is abolished but may continue business for up to one year.**	

Source: Texas Sunset Advisory Commission.

 COMMUNICATION:

How does the Sunset Advisory Commission review agencies?

• First, the staff of the commission works with each agency to collect information, performing extensive research to analyze and review the agency's required self-evaluation. Outside parties, including the public, weigh in at this stage as well. This first stage ends with a report that details the efficiency of the agency, the agency's success in achieving their mission, and the agency's compliance with open government laws.

• In the second stage, the commission holds hearings on the preliminary report, receives a response from the agency, and votes on final recommendations to the legislature.

• The third stage involves the legislature, which turns the recommendations of the commission into legislation to be sent through the normal legislative process, including a full vote of the house and senate and the governor's signature.

FIGURE 9.6 Agencies Continued or Abolished

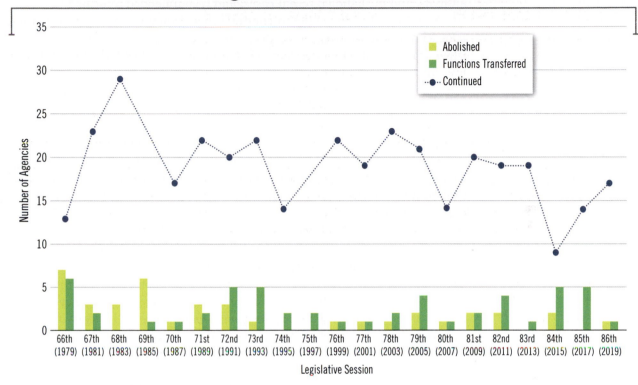

Source: Texas Sunset Advisory Commission.

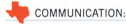

COMMUNICATION:

When are agencies continued, abolished, or transferred?

- Most agencies are continued after Sunset review, generally between 15 and 30 per year.

- Agencies are not very likely to be abolished. Abolishment was more likely to occur in the early days of the Sunset Commission's work—in 1979, 1981, and 1985.

- The Sunset Commission's recommendations are more likely to transfer functions to another agency than to abolish an agency. Beginning in the 1991 session, more agencies were asked to transfer functions rather than to dissolve.

CRITICAL THINKING:

Why are most agencies continued?

- Most agencies function well and efficiently, especially because Sunset regulations establish guidelines and benchmarks for success for agencies in the years they are not reviewed.

- The process of shutting down an agency is difficult and often enough to encourage agency officials and lawmakers to work together to reform a struggling agency.

had mismanaged funds, failed to track controlled substances prescribed for animals, and mishandled recent cases; and recommended reforms.[46]

Agencies that are abolished continue their function for one year as they transition into obscurity. Since 1977, a total of 80 agencies have been abolished or absorbed into other agencies. For example, in 2013, the Sunset Commission recommendations abolished the Office of Fire Fighters' Pension Commissioner and put the Pension Review Board in charge of overseeing local firefighter pensions. The Sunset Commission estimates that it has generated almost $1 billion in savings or increased revenue since 1982, and for every dollar spent on the commission, the state gets a return of approximately $23.[47]

The legislature has the authority to place some bodies that function like agencies under review, such as local transit agencies, the Port of Houston Authority, and the University Interscholastic League—which is important because the League sets rules for and administers Friday Night Football in the state, along with other athletic, music, and academic contests.

Legislative Oversight. The legislature is tasked with overseeing agency compliance with legislative polices. The legislature can transfer administration of a program to another agency, stripping a problematic agency or agency personnel out of the process. Standing and special committees in the legislature also investigate matters involving agency compliance. Republican Representative Giovanni Capriglione said, "During the interim, they don't go totally haywire. But sometimes, some do overstep their bounds."[48] In 2017, for example, state senate investigators discovered flyers showing the Texas Alcoholic Beverage Commission (TABC) agency director, licensing chief, and an agency analyst and contractor riding in a plane while holding or drinking bottles of Lone Star Beer. "Here we come California!" the caption proclaimed as passengers exclaimed "Woo Hoo!!!"[49] Although the photo had been doctored, house hearings discovered that TABC officials had taken personal vacation on state time, misreported the use of state vehicles, appropriated taxpayer funds to travel to conferences in Hawaii and San Diego, and attended lobbyist-funded gatherings with open bars and mariachi singers "where liquor flows and industry lobbyists abound." The legislature cut the agency's travel budget in 2017, and Sunset legislation in 2019 increased the number of commissioners from three to five members (adding rules prohibiting members from having a financial interest in an alcoholic beverage business), streamlined licensing, and strengthened the commission's ability to regulate the industry.[50]

Gubernatorial Oversight. The governor has several ways to oversee and manage agencies. The Governor's Office of Budget and Planning prepares biennial budget recommendations for the legislature to consider and regularly monitors state appropriations and operations between formal Sunset reviews. The governor also has the power to direct state agencies to implement specific rules. In the aftermath of a 2015 scandal involving improper contracts being awarded to close business associates of an agency head, Governor Abbott issued several rules

GREAT TEXAS POLITICAL DEBATES
Sunset Sunset?

At the close of the 2009 legislative session, Representative Carl Isett rose to give a personal privilege speech with dire warning: The state's Sunset system was broken and needed repair. Just before the house adjourned, on a pivotal day in the legislature, the Lubbock Republican, who served as the outgoing chairman of the Sunset Advisory Commission, leveled the charge that the system was "adulterated." He continued to say that instead of being used for realistic reform efforts, Sunset bills were seen by lobbyists, special interests, and legislators as "targets of opportunity" to eliminate provisions they disliked. Representative Isett concluded by saying that it was "time to sunset the Sunset process."[51] Despite the Sunset Commission's noble cause, the process has been compromised. Increasingly, interest group participation has shaped the Sunset process. In a review of the Department of Transportation, Speaker Joe Strauss, commenting on the 250 amendments in front of him, said that he "couldn't even see the parliamentarian" and that the lobbyists had taken control of the process.[52]

SOCIAL RESPONSIBILITY: **Should the state reform the Sunset laws?**

NO: Periodic review of individual agencies provides careful planning and oversight, and most agency reviews run smoothly. Any flaws are minor in comparison to achieving efficiency of government and mandatory review.

YES: With increasing power from lobbying interests in Austin and less oversight for the Sunset process, more transparency is needed with respect to participation in the process. Sunset Commission members should disclose potential conflicts of interest. Legislative rules must be changed to prohibit Sunset bills from being delayed or from having other legislation attached to them.

---

designed to hold agency contracting accountable. These rules require agencies to publicly disclose no-bid contracts, justify these contracts, and ensure that agency employees involved in a contract disclose any possible conflicts of interest. If all else fails, the governor can ask (but not force) the agency head to resign.

Other Agencies with Oversight. Other state agencies also provide oversight. The State Auditor reviews fiscal and management responsibilities and evaluates the efficiency, effectiveness, and legal compliance of state agencies. The state auditor may also monitor an agency's implementation of legislative or Sunset management recommendations. The Legislative Budget Board (LBB) prepares biennial appropriations bills, assesses performance reports from agencies, and reviews agency strategic plans. For example, in 2019, the LBB reported that over the course of 2 years, Texans spent over one million hours, the equivalent of 114 years, on the phone with eight major consumer-facing state agencies. The study found that callers waited 15.5 minutes on average to speak with representatives from the driver license division. One in five callers hung up before speaking with a representative. As a result, legislators considered transferring the driver's license division from the Department of Public Safety to the Department of Motor Vehicles, which had a more efficient track record.[53]

TEXAS TAKEAWAYS

9.6.1 How does the way Texas selects its bureaucrats allow Texans to influence the bureaucracy?

9.6.2 Describe the mission of the Sunset Commission.

9.6.3 How do the governor, the legislature, and agencies oversee the bureaucracy?

THE INSIDER VIEW

The dispersal of authority among several individuals, elected agency heads, and thousands of individual bureaucrats across state government often makes the bureaucracy feel remote from the public interest. Yet these bureaucratic organizations run Texas from the modest (regulating the operation of nursery floral businesses) to the immense (regulating environmental outcomes). Past internal conflicts, friction within the executive branch, and serious efforts to make government accountable have established checks on the actions of the plural executive and bureaucratic organizations in the state. These barriers do not allow any one person, branch of government, or agency to become too powerful and help government to stay limited in scope. However, the way the bureaucracy is selected plays a part in its power. Some agencies, such as the Railroad Commission, have close ties to the organizations they work with, whereas others, such as the Texas Ethics Commission, do not. Officials such as the lieutenant governor have significant sway in state policymaking. However, public policies are—at times—a product of the struggles between officers and agencies within the plural executive. The public can intervene in several ways, including tracking what government does and participating in reforms.

TEXAS TAKEAWAYS

9.1.1 As part of the executive branch, a bureaucracy is made up of agencies with a hierarchical organization and a specialized mission that make or implement rules that govern the people.

9.1.2 When compared to other states, however, Texas has fewer bureaucrats per person—approximately 1 bureaucrat for every 3,500 Texas residents. Still, more than 7,800 people work for the Texas executive agencies, boards, and commissions. The bureaucracy in Texas has expanded greatly to administer to a growing population and a large and diverse economy.

9.1.3 The bureaucracy implements laws and decisions made by the legislative, executive, or judicial branch. If rules are broken, the bureaucratic agents can investigate, issue warnings, levy fines, or even refer criminal activity to the court system. The legislature or the governor may establish a broad policy with broad goals, but the bureaucracy creates more specific rules, such as regulations, to make sure that specific targets are met. The bureaucracy also issues licenses.

9.1.4 The Texas bureaucracy includes agencies headed by officials appointed by the governor, agencies headed by officials independently elected by the people, agencies headed by a multimember, governor-appointed board or commission, and hybrid agencies with a mix of elected and appointed officials headed by an appointed board or commission.

9.1.5 Some argue that the bureaucracy is the least representative branch of government because most bureaucrats are hired by management rather than appointed by elected officials.

9.2.1 The most powerful of these officers is the lieutenant governor, whose influence rivals the governor's. But the comptroller, attorney general, the commissioners of agriculture, and the General Land Office are powerful as well.

9.2.2 Lieutenant governors serve 4-year terms, with no term limits, and tend to stay in office longer than other elected officers, thereby increasing their influence. Since 1894, most lieutenant governors have served more than one term.

9.2.3 The lieutenant governor serves as the presiding officer of the Texas Senate, assigning members to committees,

directing the flow of legislation by referring bills to committees, and managing the senate by deciding when a bill will come up for a vote and when to recognize a senator on the floor. On rare occasions, the lieutenant governor casts tiebreaking votes. The lieutenant governor also works with the governor to advance the agenda and serves on and appoints officials to key state boards and commissions.

9.2.4 The attorney general (AG) is the state's lawyer, representing the state in court. The AG provides legal services to the governor, state agencies, and local and state government entities. The AG's actions and opinions, interpreting law, can actively shape state policies. The AG's responsibilities have also extended to enforcement of health, safety, and consumer regulations and protection of the rights of the elderly and disabled.

9.2.5 The comptroller sets the revenue estimate and audits the budget.

9.2.6 The land commissioner oversees state-owned land leasing them and generating funds from oil, gas, and resource extraction. The Permanent School Fund helps finance public schools, and the Veterans Land Board uses revenue from public land to help veterans. The agriculture commissioner oversees the Department of Agriculture, which implements agricultural laws, promotes Texas's agriculture, and administers school nutrition programs. The department also performs regulatory functions, such as protecting consumers from pesticides and certifying organic products.

9.3.1 The secretary of state, the Health and Human Services Commission, and the Department of Insurance are three of the most powerful governor-appointed, single-headed agencies.

9.3.2 The secretary of state is the chief elections administrator, the steward of all state records, and an ambassador of the state to other nations.

9.3.3 The Health and Human Services Commission is so difficult to manage because it is a massive agency in charge of Medicaid, the Children's Health Insurance Program, the Texas Women's Health Program, Temporary Assistance for Needy Families, and the Supplemental Nutrition Assistance Program.

9.3.4 The Texas Department of Insurance investigates fraud, regulates the insurance industry, and provides consumer protection.

9.4.1 In a governor-appointed, single-headed agency, the appointee is often closer to the governor. Where there are more appointees on a larger commission, the governor may have less influence. Both groups largely operate independently of the other executive agencies but are accountable to the legislature through periodic review.

9.4.2 The Public Utility Commission regulates the rates and services of electric and telecommunications utilities. The Texas Parks and Wildlife Department manages and protects wildlife and manages Texas's state parks and historic areas. It sells hunting, fishing, and boating licenses. The department is also the second-largest statewide law enforcement agency. The Texas Commission on Environmental Quality deals with natural resources, maintains clean air and water, and protects the environment, among other functions.

9.4.3 The Texas Department of Transportation is in charge of operations and maintenance of the state's massive highway system and oversees other public transportation matters. With urbanization, a growing population, and the state's aging current infrastructure, the agency will struggle to fund road construction.

9.5.1 In some cases, voters themselves elect the members of a commission, giving the public a more direct say in the regulatory process. Hybrid agencies comprise both elected and appointed officials.

9.5.2 The Texas Railroad Commission's primary functions are the regulation of the oil and gas industry and environmental protection.

9.5.3 The main goal of the Texas Ethics Commission is to oversee, regulate, and enforce campaign finance and lobbying activities.

9.5.4 The State Board of Education oversees the curriculum standards for primary and secondary education.

9.6.1 Despite the fact that most bureaucrats are professionals who are hired by managers, Texas voters influence public policy when they elect key members of the bureaucracy as well as when they elect their governor. Governor appointees often shape policy in line with the governor's preferences.

9.6.2 The mission of the Sunset Commission is to periodically review the function and efficiency of agencies. The agency is abolished unless legislation is passed to allow that agency to continue to function. The legislature decides whether to amend or abolish the agency based on the Sunset Commission's recommendation. Agencies are rarely abolished, but specific functions are often transferred to another agency or recommendations for improvements are made.

9.6.3 The legislature can transfer administration of a program to another agency, stripping a problematic agency or agency personnel out of the process. The governor prepares biennial budget recommendations for the legislature to consider and regularly monitors state appropriations and operations. The governor also has the power to direct state agencies to implement specific rules. The governor can ask (but not force) the agency head to resign.

The State Auditor reviews fiscal and management responsibilities and evaluates the efficiency, effectiveness, and legal compliance of state agencies. The state auditor and the Legislative Budget Board may also monitor an agency's performance.

KEY TERMS

bureaucracy

enforcement

hybrid agencies

implementation

licensing

multimember agencies

pay-as-you-go system

plural executive

presiding officer

regulations

rules

PRACTICE QUIZ

1. The diffusion of power and authority throughout several entities in the executive branch is called . . .

    a. Delegation
    b. Reappraisal of agencies
    c. Reorganization planning
    d. Plural executive

2. Regarding power and political role, the lieutenant governor in Texas is . . .

    a. Strong
    b. Weak
    c. Nonexistent
    d. None of the above

3. _____ is when a government agency gives a company, an individual, or an organization permission to carry out a specific task.

    a. Regulation
    b. Licensing
    c. Enforcement
    d. Rule-making

4. If the senate is evenly split, which individual is responsible for being the "tiebreaking" vote?

    a. Governor
    b. Secretary of state
    c. Lieutenant governor
    d. Senate majority leader

5. What is the name of the complex, professional organization that administers government actions through routine tasks?

    a. The legislature
    b. The vote centers
    c. The Office of the Governor
    d. The bureaucracy

6. What is the name of the organization that periodically reviews executive agencies for efficiency?

    a. The Attorney General
    b. Sunset Commission
    c. Department of Licensing and Regulations
    d. Texas Legislative Council

7. The lieutenant governor is the presiding officer of the Texas Senate.

    a. True
    b. False

8. The Texas Railroad Commission's authority is limited to regulating railroads.

    a. True
    b. False

9. The Sunset Process is one of several ways that the state can hold the bureaucracy accountable.

    a. True
    b. False

10. The bureaucracy in Texas is made up of both independent agencies and agencies staffed by gubernatorial appointments.

    a. True
    b. False

[Answers: D, A, B, C, D, B, A, B, A, A]

Learn more with this chapter's digital tools, including the Oxford Insight Study Guide, at www.oup.com/he/Rottinghaus3e.

10 THE TEXAS JUDICIARY

In December 1992, Pamela Jean Johnson collapsed in tears as a Texas jury awarded her $25 million after her breast implant burst and forced her to endure a partial mastectomy. This vast sum was the largest award against a producer of silicone implants to date, and it served as a sign of things to come.[1] Over the next decade, Texas courts granted blockbuster damage awards, including the first multibillion-dollar settlement in Texas history.

Some Texans cried out for tort reform—that is, laws that would limit damages granted for negligence. This battle pitted the powerful trial lawyers associations against Texas business interests and their Republican supporters. Republicans claimed that outrageously large awards led to skyrocketing Texas medical malpractice insurance rates and that this was the reason Texas suffered from a shortage of physicians and medical specialists. Opponents of tort reform argued that victims harmed by negligence are entitled to fair compensation. The U.S. Chamber of Commerce had ranked Texas as among the five worst litigation states, however, and stated that several counties were "judicial hell holes," where "normal rules of balance and fair play under the law don't exist."[2] Houston-based mega-lawyer Joe Jamail, who made so many millions defending clients that he was dubbed the "King of Torts," objected and deemed reform initiatives as "tort deform, not tort reform."[3] Jamail and others argued that individuals who are harmed by companies or poor medical practices must be compensated properly. Coming off major electoral victories in 2002, Republicans secured passage of the 2003 Texas tort reform law with bipartisan support.

10.1 Outline the structure and functions of the Texas courts.

10.2 Describe the function of each of the trial courts in Texas.

10.3 Describe the function of the appellate courts in Texas.

10.4 Evaluate the quality of justice in Texas.

10.5 Identify problems associated with different methods of judicial selection.

10.6 Analyze the changes in the demographics of the Texas courts.

10.7 Evaluate proposals for reforming the selection of the judiciary.

● Judicial decisions in Texas affect and are affected by the political culture and shape Texas's values. Since the Republic was formed, Texas courts have ruled on murder and death penalty issues, the legality of pool halls, and the ownership of surface water.

The legislature's tort reform package profoundly impacted the legal process in state courts. It reduced the number of cases the courts had to handle and helped unclog the system. In the decade after Texas implemented tort reform, medical malpractice lawsuits plummeted 64 percent,[4] and civil lawsuits overall dropped by 17 percent.[5] As these events make clear, the judicial system crowns winners and losers. In theory, all Texans are equal before the law and judiciary. In practice, many fear that the system is strongly influenced by the powerful because they have greater resources. The most obvious culprit is the fact that judges are elected in Texas. Does this allow the people the ability to hold judges accountable, or does it give wealthy contributors to judicial campaigns an edge over others?

The power struggle between political, business, and public interests all collide in the elections of judges and rulings in the Texas courts. In this chapter, we explore the function, development, and impact of the judiciary in Texas. We examine how the power of the judiciary is constrained by the legislature, higher courts, and voters. Finally, we assess reform efforts that have followed political scandals and dysfunction within the courts.

10.1 THE ROLE OF THE COURTS

10.1 Outline the structure and functions of the Texas courts.

The judicial system's role is to interpret Texas laws in matters ranging from minor criminal offenses to those involving the Texas Constitution. Texans expect to have equal access to an efficient system that applies the law fairly and objectively and that protects their interests. Yet is this task even possible? Interests often conflict and can be weighted in favor of one group over another. And while Texans might expect impartiality from judges, political struggles make their way into the courtroom in many ways. In this section, we begin to evaluate the Texas judiciary by exploring its basic structure and functions.

DISPENSING JUSTICE

Texans did not always have ready access to the courts. Before the Texas Revolution, justice was a scarce commodity. The Mexican constitutions of 1824 and 1827 established state and local courts. In practice, however, ordinary

Texans could not appeal local decisions because higher courts were located several hundred miles away in the State Capitol.[6] After Reconstruction, resentment of central government swelled, and Texans reacted against the "interests" (corporations) and demanded accountability to the people. The current Texas Constitution's Article 5 divides the judiciary in Texas into many types of courts, allowing both local access and appeal to higher courts. The legislature has subsequently established additional courts to allow the state to handle a rising caseload as the economy and the population have boomed. As a result, the Texas judicial system has the greatest number of courts in the nation (see Figure 10.1). More courts means, in principle, more access to justice for Texans. However, in practice multiple layers of courts may increase the cost of a legal verdict for many Texans.

Judicial Hierarchy. The structure of the court system is hierarchical, meaning that cases start at the lowest level and funnel to the courts above as appropriate. The hierarchical nature of the court system also allows higher courts to check bad decisions or incorrect rulings by lower levels. This is one way in which the court system balances competing interests and provides access to all groups.

Legal Jurisdiction. The legislature helps the courts set **jurisdiction**, the official territory and types of cases over which a court exercises authority. Trial courts often have **original jurisdiction**; they are the court in which the case is first heard. If one is not satisfied with the outcome and the case meets the criteria for an appeal, it may advance to an appellate court. Higher courts can generally choose which cases to take from lower courts, making the appeals process something of a gamble. Higher courts with **appellate jurisdiction** review the decisions of lower courts. This appeals process can be lengthy, depending on the nature of the case and the efficiency of the court system.

Cases can be either criminal or civil in nature. In **criminal cases**, the government brings charges against a person (the defendant) who is accused of breaking a law, such as in cases of murder, robbery, larceny, or bribery. The government must prove the defendant is guilty beyond a reasonable doubt. **Civil cases** involve conflict between two parties (litigants), whether individuals, corporations, or the government. The standard of proof is lower in civil cases. The plaintiff, who is the party bringing suit against a defendant, who is the party being sued, must prove that the harm was done to them by a "preponderance of evidence." This standard emphasizes the convincing quality of the evidence rather than the amount. For instance, a witness with clearer details about an event has greater weight than several witnesses with hazier recollections.

Texas has many types of trial courts. So, how do you figure out which court hears a case? In civil cases, the amount of monetary damages helps determine which court will hear a case. The major factor that determines which court will hear a criminal case is the severity of the transgression. A **felony** is

jurisdiction: the official territory and types of cases over which a court exercises authority

original jurisdiction: the court in which the case is first heard

appellate jurisdiction: the authority of a court to review a case first heard by a lower court

criminal cases: cases in which the government brings suit against the defendant for violating the law and in which the defendant is guilty beyond a reasonable doubt

civil cases: cases involving a conflict between two parties (litigants), whether individuals, corporations, or the government

felony: the highest criminal offense under state or federal law

IS IT BIGGER IN TEXAS?

FIGURE 10.1 Total Trial Courts

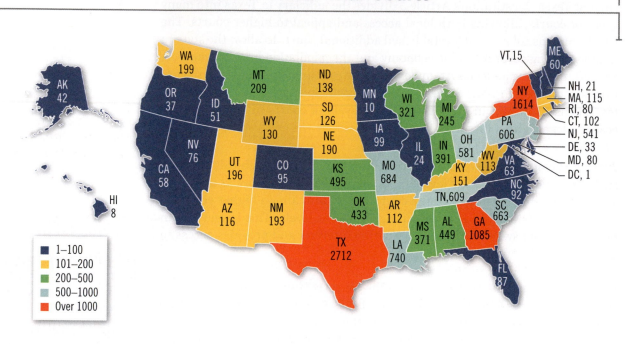

Source: Center for State Court. Figures include all trial courts.

 COMMUNICATION:

Where does Texas rank on the number of trial courts?

- Texas ranks number 1 in the total number of trial courts (2,712).

 CRITICAL THINKING:

Why so many courts?

- The Texas Constitution divides judicial power locally to prevent centralized power, increasing the number of courts.

- Southern states, such as Georgia and Louisiana, tend to have more courts than other states, as they have been historically distrustful of judicial oversight from the days of Reconstruction following the Civil War.

- Large states, such as New York and Pennsylvania, tend to have a greater number of courts. These states not only have large economies but also large populations, necessitating more courts to handle legal matters like divorce, contracts, and crime.

the highest stage of crime under state or federal law. These offenses are more severe in character than **misdemeanors**, which are minor wrongdoings. The judiciary classifies the severity of a crime based on factors such as the use of a weapon and whether the crime involved violence.

misdemeanors: a class of criminal offenses that are minor wrongdoings

INTERPRETING THE LAW

Texas courts interpret law by relying on legal traditions—the Texas Constitution, legislation, and **common law, or judge-made law**. These decisions then become binding as future courts consider similar cases. In making these decisions, the judicial branch not only delivers justice, but also acts as a check on the legislative and executive branches. Let's take a closer look at how this occurs.

common law: law that is established when judges apply past decisions by courts—called legal precedents—to the facts of a new case before them

Clarifying Laws. In their haste to make new laws and revise old ones in 140 days, the legislature often writes laws that are unclear, vague, misleading, or, on occasion, unconstitutional. The Texas Supreme Court sorts out contradictions or clarifies legislative meaning. In his 2015 state-of-the-judiciary address, Chief Justice Nathan Hecht remarked, "Ascertaining what is meant by what is said can be difficult. Try it with your spouse. Even when a statement is in writing, and has been carefully considered, its application in an unforeseen situation can be unclear."[7]

These clarifications are often minor but meaningful. For example, the court clarified the term *impounded* in 2016 when it ruled that the owner of a missing dog picked up by a private animal control shelter does not give up ownership rights to the shelter or foster family.

Checking the Legislature. The courts often take on political roles, acting to check or maintain legislative decisions by determining whether legislation is constitutional. For example, in 2015, a bipartisan effort in the Texas legislature passed a statute criminalizing "revenge porn" (sharing intimate images without the consent of the parties involved) and won a swift signature from the governor. In 2018, a legal challenge from the conviction of a Tyler man who was charged under the statute alleged that it violated free speech rights.[8] A state appeals court struck down the law as unconstitutionally broad, prompting the legislature to tweak the law to add language that the explicit images be posted with "the intent to harm" the person in the images.[9]

Tweet translation: "The Barbie Doll as Judge. And with Dark Hair. It's about Time." Despite the perception of judges as being out of touch, Justice Eva Guzman frequently takes to social media to describe her role as a judge. "I think [social media] helps the public and the bar to understand or at least know who the justices are; most people don't even know who we are."

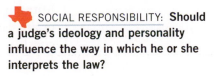 SOCIAL RESPONSIBILITY: **Should a judge's ideology and personality influence the way in which he or she interprets the law?**

Defining State Interests. When state interests clash with business or citizens' interests, the courts' job is often to sort out competing claims. For example, in the late nineteenth century, Texas

transitioned from an open frontier to land ownership. In 1888, famed cattle rancher Charles Goodnight fenced in large tracts of state land, much of which he did not actually own. The state had set aside the land to generate revenue for the public school system and sued Goodnight to remove the fences. When the "Grass Lease Fight" reached the high court, it ruled that the fences had to come down.[10]

Advancing the Rule of the People. The courts in Texas are not expressly designed to promote popular sovereignty. However, Texans have chucked out justices whom they feel don't represent their values. In a classic example, in 1874, Texans who hoped to restore antebellum practices after the Civil War elected Governor Richard Coke, who obliged his supporters by appointing Confederate sympathizers to the Texas Supreme Court in what came to be called the "Redeemer Court." Although the issues and cases were different, over a century later, when conservatives abandoned the Democratic Party and the Democrats ran more liberal judges, Texans swept in a new cast of conservative Republican judges to mirror the ideology of the voters.[11]

TEXAS TAKEAWAYS

10.1.1   What is the role of Texas courts?

10.1.2   How is the judicial system structured?

10.1.3   What factors determine the jurisdiction of Texas courts?

10.2 TRIAL COURTS

10.2   Describe the function of each of the trial courts in Texas.

Trial courts hear both criminal and civil cases. In these lowest level courts, witnesses are heard, evidence is presented in the form of exhibits, testimony is taken, and ultimately, a verdict is reached. Texas has several levels of trial courts: local, county, and state. Each type of trial and appellate court hears different types of cases (see Figure 10.2).

LOCAL COURTS

Municipal Courts. If you dump something in violation of city ordinances or are caught with alcohol as a minor, you'll end up in this court. Municipal courts in Texas have original and exclusive jurisdiction over violations of city

FIGURE 10.2 **The Structure of Texas Courts**

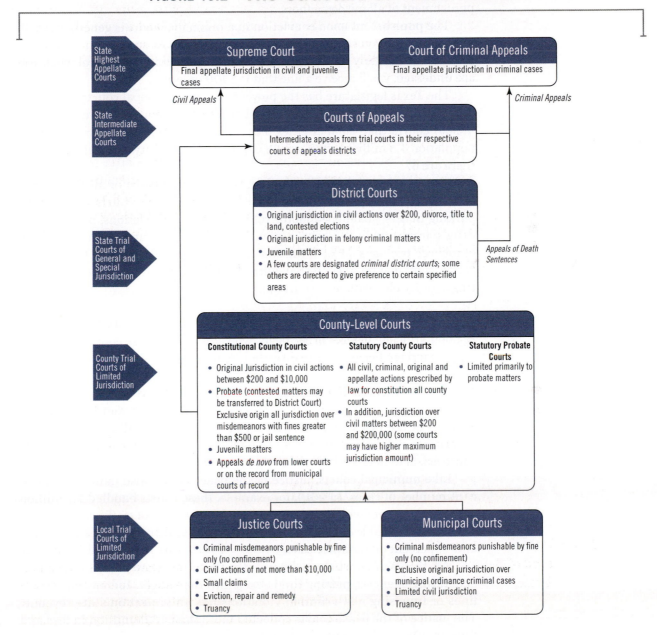

Source: The Texas Judicial Branch website.

SOCIAL RESPONSIBILITY: **There are many levels and types of Texas courts. Do all these judicial layers slow justice or promote efficient justice?**

ordinances and over Class C misdemeanors, which carry the lowest severity of punishment of all misdemeanors.

The punishment upon conviction in a municipal court is generally small. For example, if you steal property worth less than $50, speed, run a red light, engage in disorderly conduct, or are found in possession of alcohol when you are underage, you'll receive a fine that is $500 or less.

The Texas legislature has the power to create municipal courts to provide Texans with better access to justice. Larger cities generally have more municipal courts than smaller cities. For instance, in Houston (Harris County, population 4.5 million), there are 28 courts; in Hill County, population 34,855, there are 6.

Municipal courts handle the largest volume of cases of all the courts. This makes sense given the nature of the cases these courts deal with— parking tickets, abandoned motor vehicles, city code violations, possession of drug paraphernalia (like a bong with no drug), or a minor in possession of tobacco products. Most of the nontraffic cases (64 percent) and traffic cases (71 percent) end up uncontested, with the defendant paying a fine or submitting a guilty plea without a court appearance.[12]

Justice Courts. "Justice" courts are a specific type of local trial court. Contrary to popular belief, justices of the peace who administer these courts do not just issue marriage licenses. In reality, they hear cases that involve small claims, civil actions of $10,000 or less, and criminal offenses punishable by fine but not prison sentences. If your landlord refused to return your security deposit, you might appear before a justice of the peace to try to get your deposit back. Justices of the peace also serve as coroners in many small counties and as magistrate judges with authority to hold hearings to determine if probable cause exists to hold a criminal defendant in jail.

Like municipal courts, justice of the peace courts also handle a significant number of cases. In 2019, for example, these courts handled 2.7 million new cases, most of which were uncontested (87 percent of traffic cases and 88 percent of nontraffic cases) or dismissed (more than 43 percent of traffic cases and 41 percent of nontraffic cases).

We think of courts as arbiters of justice, but they are also revenue-generating agencies, putting funds back into the budget. Increasing certain fines or imposing new criminal violations has an impact on state revenue. The justice of the peace courts collected more than $324 million in fees and fines in 2018.

COUNTY TRIAL COURTS

Constitutional County Courts. Although constitutional county courts do not always deal with legal matters, they are part of the judicial structure. The Texas Constitution vests broad judicial and administrative powers in county judges who also oversee a five-member commissioner's court. This court has budgetary authority over county government operations. County judges also have wide authority over several administrative matters, including hearings for beer and wine license applications, admittance to state hospitals for the mentally ill, juvenile work permits, and temporary guardianships.[13]

County Courts at Law (Statutory). If you sue your roommate in justice court for ruining your laptop and she appeals the case, the case will end up in county court at law. These courts have original jurisdiction on civil matters between $200 and $200,000. County courts at law also have appellate jurisdiction in cases appealed from other local trial courts. In criminal appeals involving fines of $100 or less, the decision of the county courts at law is final.

The Texas Constitution limits each county to a single constitutional county court, so the legislature established the first county court at law in 1907 to relieve the county judge of some or all of the judicial duties of the office. Today, there are more than 240 of these courts.

Probate Courts. Probate courts, where they are created, hear primarily matters of **probate**—that is, the official recognition and registration of the validity of a person's last will and testament. These courts only exist in the state's largest counties (a total of 18 courts in 10 counties). If you don't live in these areas, you will need to settle these estates at a county court or a district court.

probate: the process by which there is official recognition and registration of the validity of a person's last will and testament

STATE DISTRICT COURTS

District courts are trial courts that handle most major criminal and civil cases, including murder, drug trafficking, contested elections, and civil cases involving high amounts of monetary damages—any amount over $200. The district courts are often the first rung on the ladder of the criminal justice system, so many criminal cases begin here. In 2018, most criminal cases were drug offenses. The district courts also have original jurisdiction in all divorce cases, land title cases, and any cases that do not fall under the jurisdiction of other courts. Most cases the courts deal with are family related (38 percent), followed by criminal cases (31 percent), civil cases (21 percent), and juvenile and other cases (2 percent). A growing population leads to more family cases—more divorces, more child custody issues, paternity issues, child support orders, and adoptions.

Texans charged with crimes heard by district courts can choose between a **bench trial**, in which a single judge presides and decides guilt or innocence and punishment, and a **jury trial**, in which a group of individuals picked at random decides on guilt or innocence. The advantages of one versus the other

bench trial: a trial in which a single judge presides and decides guilt or innocence and punishment

jury trial: a trial in which a group of individuals picked at random decides on guilt or innocence

depend on the details of the case (see Figure 10.3). In general, a defendant in Texas is convicted in more than half the cases, especially for felonies such as driving while intoxicated (95 percent), sexual assault (74 percent), and murder (85 percent).[14]

Prosecutors, however, dismiss many cases (22 percent) for lack of evidence or other reasons. In civil cases, more than a third of plaintiffs agree to dismiss their cases, while a little over 13 percent end in a mutually agreeable settlement. So, only about half of all cases filed actually go to trial.

⭐ TEXAS TAKEAWAYS

10.2.1 What are the types of local courts, and what is their general jurisdiction?

10.2.2 What are the types of county courts, and what is their general jurisdiction?

10.2.3 What are district courts?

⚘ 10.3 APPELLATE COURTS

10.3   Describe the function of the appellate courts in Texas.

What do appeals courts do differently from lower-level courts? **Appellate courts** do not hold trials but only review legal issues of cases decided by lower courts. An appellant (or petitioner) first files a notice of appeal and then submits a written set of arguments containing the appellant's view of the facts and the law (called a brief).

The justices in appellate courts may decide the case based on the brief alone, or they may hear oral arguments, during which attorneys for both sides present their cases in person to the justices.[15] Amicus curiae briefs (literally "friend of the court" in Latin) can be filed by interested parties that are not directly involved in the case, providing an avenue for outside groups to have a say in the judicial process. Interestingly, dissenting opinions also correlate to interest group participation. Amicus briefs allow interest groups to interject themselves into a case. They sometimes influence new judges but have little effect on veteran judges.[16]

After making a decision, the justices can either write an **opinion** to explain their reasoning or not. Justices often disagree on ideological or legal matters. In one recent case, the Texas Supreme Court limited the public's right to know about private groups that get government funds—three justices dissented.[17]

appellate courts: courts that review legal issues of cases decided by lower courts

opinion: a document that expresses the view of the judges and often takes the form of a majority opinion, when written by a justice representing the majority, but may also be a concurring or dissenting opinion

FIGURE 10.3 **Acquittals and Convictions at State District Court (Criminal Cases)**

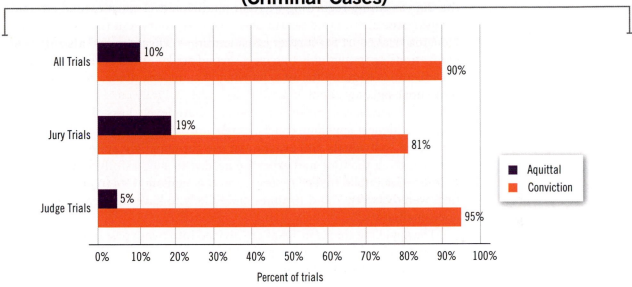

Source: Annual Statistical Report for the Texas Judiciary, 2018.

 COMMUNICATION:

What was the outcome for cases at the district court level by type of trial?

- For criminal jury trials, the defendant was convicted 81 percent of the time.
- For bench trials, the defendant was convicted 95 percent of the time.

 CRITICAL THINKING:

Why the differences in outcomes?

- Elected judges may be concerned about being perceived as "soft on crime" and may convict defendants more than juries.
- A jury of individuals may find a defendant sympathetic and be more likely to consider extenuating circumstances and less likely to convict.

If the appeals court affirms the lower court's judgment, the case ends (unless an appeal can be made to an even higher court). If the lower court's judgment is reversed, the higher court can remand (send) the case back to the lower court for further action, such as a new trial.[18] In 2019, the Texas Supreme Court reversed a lower court decision, ruling unanimously that while the U.S. Supreme Court had declared same-sex marriage legal, there is still room for state courts to explore the "reach and ramifications" of the Court's ruling regarding whether municipalities must extend city-paid spousal benefits to same sex couples. The high court sent the case back to a Houston trial court for further consideration.[19] These "redos" also allow organizations or individuals to have a second strike at the case—in this case, organizations arguing for an expansion of same-sex domestic benefits and those opposed.

Most cases never make it to the appellate level: Less than 10 percent reach the highest appellate courts. Often, only the wealthiest and most well-connected individuals and groups can use the appellate system to their advantage, given the time and expertise needed to successfully win cases here. A Texans for Public Justice report found that contributors to judges and justices were between 7 and 10 times more likely to have their case taken than noncontributors.[20]

The appellate courts in Texas are divided into two types: intermediate appellate courts and appellate courts of last resort. The creation of this tiered system reflects the suspicion of central authority stemming all the way back to the pre-Republic days, but the system is designed to promote the legal access and options available to Texans.

INTERMEDIATE APPELLATE COURTS

The first (lowest) level of appeals courts are the courts of appeals organized into 14 districts (see Figure 10.4). These courts agreed to review less than 10 percent of appealed cases in 2018.[21] However, many of the courts of appeals cases involve mandatory review, primarily felony convictions in cases without the death penalty.

en banc: a hearing in which all of the justices of the court hear and consider the case

Each court of appeals has a chief justice and at least two other justices. When cases are heard, three justices hear the case, unless an **en banc** hearing is ordered where all of the justices of the court hear and consider the case. In each case, a determination is made by a majority of the justices.

APPELLATE COURTS OF LAST RESORT

Sitting atop the appellate court structure are two supreme courts. Why two supreme courts? Appellants have one court for criminal matters and one court for civil matters. This creates a **dual structure** in which cases are sorted by the type of issue. The dual structure was designed for efficiency but was also based on mistrust. The framers of the Texas Constitution were suspicious of the centralizing power of legal decision making in any one court.

dual structure: Texas's two supreme court system

Texas Court of Criminal Appeals. The Texas Court of Criminal Appeals makes final determinations in all criminal matters, including applying (or not

FIGURE 10.4 **Court of Appeals Districts**

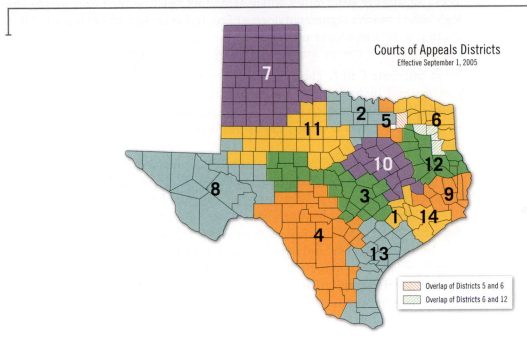

Courts of Appeals Districts
Effective September 1, 2005

Overlap of Districts 5 and 6
Overlap of Districts 6 and 12

Source: Texas Legislative Council.

 COMMUNICATION:

What are the geographic regions of the courts of appeals?

- The courts of appeals are organized into 14 geographic areas.
- More densely populated areas have a smaller geographic footprint for their district.

 CRITICAL THINKING:

Why are the districts carved like this?

- Districts reflect local political views and also help to distribute the caseload fairly.
- As regional populations grow, the legislature increases the number of justices in districts that serve those counties. In 1977, for instance, the first court of appeals (serving the Houston region) increased the size of the court to nine justices.

applying) the death penalty. This court is composed of nine justices: eight justices and a presiding judge. If four or more justices favor hearing a particular case, that case is scheduled for argument. However, most of the caseload of the Texas Court of Criminal Appeals—about 80 percent of its cases—consists

mandatory review: cases required to be heard by a specific court

of **mandatory review** of sentencing and direct death penalty appeals. The Texas legislature determines which sentences must be reviewed, giving the legislative branch a significant degree of control over the judicial branch. Most death penalty judgments are upheld by the court.

Texas Supreme Court. The Texas Supreme Court deals primarily with civil matters and juvenile justice and can order either monetary or equitable relief (directing the losing party to do something or not do something). In 2018, the court reversed about half (58 percent) of the lower courts' decisions.

The Texas Supreme Court is composed of nine justices: eight justices and a chief justice. Like the Texas Court of Criminal Appeals, if four or more justices favor hearing a particular case, that case is scheduled for argument. The likelihood of this court hearing a case is low, however. In most years, the Texas Supreme Court is selective about the cases it takes, as most appellate courts are. In 2018, the court only granted review in 12 percent of the cases filed, down from 15 percent in 2007. The system is designed to let lower courts handle much of the work; those cases that float up to the Texas Supreme Court are of statewide importance.

TEXAS TAKEAWAYS

10.3.1 What do appellate courts do differently from lower courts?

10.3.2 How many supreme courts does Texas have? Why?

10.4 QUALITY OF JUSTICE IN TEXAS

10.4 Evaluate the quality of justice in Texas.

Chief Justice Andrew Jackson "Jack" Pope came before the state legislature in 1983 to make an important request. The judiciary is inexpensive to run, he noted. Yet the courts were so overloaded that Texans had to wait months or even years to settle cases. If the legislature granted every judicial budget request, "It would be less than the utility and maintenance bill of the University of Texas at Austin."[22] The legislature agreed to appropriate more funds for the judiciary. But Pope's plea illustrates two points: first, the judiciary is dependent on the legislature for funding, and second, this funding is one factor that determines the quality of justice in Texas. Let's take a look at how well the judicial system is performing today.

ANGLES OF POWER
Two Supreme Courts?

By the time of the 1875 Constitutional Convention, the Texas Supreme Court had become overburdened with cases. To remedy this problem, "dual" Supreme Courts were proposed "so that when appeals in criminal charges come before them from criminal courts there should be a speedy response, so that the party might be either punished or released."[23] The two sets of supreme court justices would also be able to specialize in the law their courts heard. Currently, Texas and Oklahoma are the only two states with divided civil and criminal jurisdictions.

In 2013, a bill was introduced to merge the supreme courts. Representative Richard Peña Raymond, Democrat of Laredo, said, "The model is there for most of the country."[24] Those in favor also liked the efficiency of a single administration and the cost savings with fewer judges. Others disagreed. Efforts to merge the courts have failed six times since 1974. When Governor Bill Clements publicly announced support for the merger in 1987, Texas Supreme Court Justice James P. Wallace huffed, "There's only 24 hours in a day, and we deserve some sleep like everyone else."[25] Political parties also opposed the change because more courts give them more opportunity to influence the legal system.

SOCIAL RESPONSIBILITY: **Should Texas merge its two Supreme Courts into one? What are the pros and cons of doing so?**

CASELOAD: OVERWORKED JUDGES?

Caseload serves as an indicator of the efficiency of the judicial system and the speed of justice. Judges rushing to complete cases may make mistakes or be inconsistent. As case delays increase, witnesses' memories fade, those involved in cases may become financially bankrupt, companies might continue to lose revenue, and plaintiffs could remain in harmful situations. In 2018, Texas's 3,200 judges disposed of over 9 million cases, from not cleaning up dog poop on the sidewalk to traffic violations to capital murders. A case is **disposed** of when it is taken off the court's docket, generally by being heard or dismissed.

caseload: the workload (in cases) of the judiciary

disposed: when a case is taken off the court's docket, generally by being heard or dismissed

Even so, over the last several decades, the courts have become more efficient at handling the cases before them. For example, in 1984, the 80 justices on the courts of appeals disposed of 8,000 cases, while in 2018, with the same number of judges, the courts disposed of almost 10,000 cases.[26] Generally, the Texas courts are efficient at disposing of cases. The number of criminal filings in 2018 decreased at the Texas Supreme Court and Texas Court of Criminal Appeals as compared to 2006, allowing the justices to handle fewer cases and dispose of them more quickly.

LENGTH OF COURT CASES

The saying goes, "Justice delayed is justice denied." The length of time an individual's case takes to work through the system is another measure of the efficiency of the judiciary system. Overall, except for death penalty cases, the number of days until a final verdict was reached decreased in 2017 (see Figure 10.5).

FIGURE 10.5 **Average Number of Days between Filing and Disposition**

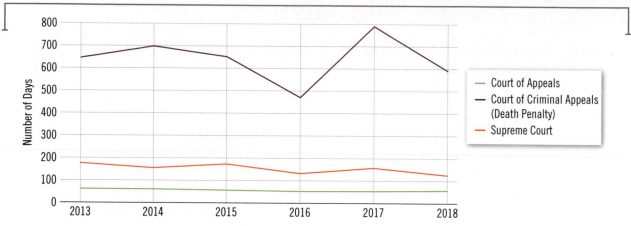

Source: Annual Statistical Report of the Texas Judiciary, 2018.

 COMMUNICATION:

How many days does it take for each Texas court to finish a case?

- Except for the Texas Court of Criminal Appeals, the appellate courts in the state have reduced the total days it takes to receive a final verdict.
- The courts of appeals were the quickest of the Texas appellate courts in 2018, at 57 days.
- Death penalty cases at the Texas Court of Criminal Appeals take longer from start to finish (almost 600 days) than other types of cases.

 CRITICAL THINKING:

Why the longer wait for some courts than others?

- Texas Appeals Courts cases involve matters of legal interpretation, allowing the cases to be decided more quickly.
- Criminal cases often take longer because the rules are more expansive, making the number of possible delays greater in those courts. Criminal cases take more lawyers, more experts, and therefore, more time.

SALARY: UNDERPAID JUDGES?

Because most judges could make high salaries in private practice, the state must offer a reasonable salary to keep quality lawyers on the bench. In the Republic's early days, judges received low pay ($1,750 a year), and when times were bad, sometimes the state didn't pay the justices at all.[27] Financial times are better for modern judges (see Figure 10.6), but judicial salaries in Texas still lag behind those in other large states. Current salaries are less than they

IS IT BIGGER IN TEXAS?

FIGURE 10.6 Salaries of Judges in the Five Most Populous States

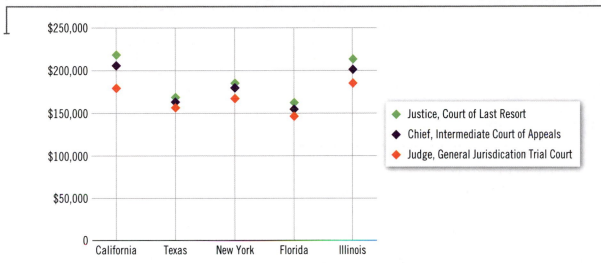

Legend:
- ♦ Justice, Court of Last Resort
- ♦ Chief, Intermediate Court of Appeals
- ♦ Judge, General Jurisdiction Trial Court

Source: 2018 Annual Texas Judicial Statistical Report. Average statewide salary, including supplements paid.

 COMMUNICATION:

How well are Texas justices paid?

- On average, New York pays judges and justices $30,000 more, Illinois $40,000 more, and California $50,000 more than Texas.

- Of the five largest states, only Florida pays less on average than Texas. The Texas legislature considered raising judges' pay by 21 percent in 2013 but ended up increasing it by only 12 percent.

 CRITICAL THINKING:

Why does Texas rank so low?

- Texas favors a lean government. Raising the pay for judges is not high on the state's list of funding priorities.

- Texas generally pays elected officials low salaries, especially legislators, who only receive $7,200 per year.

were in 1991 adjusted for inflation, according to Chief Justice Hecht's state of the judiciary in 2019.[28] Chief Justice of the Texas Supreme Court Wallace Jefferson cited having a child in college and two in high school as a reason he stepped down from the bench in 2013.[29] These low salaries may impact the ability of the state to attract quality judges.

In 2019, a video of a young woman removing the lid of a carton of Blue Bell ice cream, licking it, and putting it back in the freezer of a Walmart in Lufkin, Texas, went viral. The video spurred a series of copycat crimes by young people. The police identified her as a San Antonio juvenile. As a result, she was not charged as an adult, and the case was referred to the Texas Juvenile Justice Department.

PERSONAL RESPONSIBILITY:
How should the Blue Bell licker be punished? Should juvenile pranksters be treated differently than the young adults who copycatted her misdeed?

TURNOVER OF JUDGES

Because of the prestige, reasonable salary, job security, and snappy wardrobe associated with the judiciary, judges generally stay in their positions. Stability in the tenure of judges is a welcome advantage for a system that must handle so many cases as quickly as possible. Newer judges may have less experience, and replacing justices who leave may take time. For those judges quitting the judiciary in recent years, many identify the "judicial election" process as a major factor in their leaving. One judge called this process "random and unreliable" as she refused to run for reelection in 2016.[30] Others cite the low salary as a factor "to some extent."[31] Not surprisingly, most judges choose to leave office before the mandatory retirement age.

ACCESS TO JUSTICE

Many argue that the wealthy are at an advantage in the court system. Ethan Couch, a teenager from North Texas who drove drunk, killed four people, and injured two, was able to avoid jail time purportedly because of "affluenza," a legal defense that argued the defendant's upbringing was so wealthy and pampered that he could not understand the ramifications of his actions. Fearing that the terms of his 10-year probation might change once he turned 19, Couch fled to Mexico. He was returned to Texas and ordered to serve 2 years behind bars. Couch was released in 2018 under conditions that included wearing an ankle monitor and adhering to a 9 p.m. curfew.[32]

Wealthy groups and individuals do have significantly better access to the legal system than others. This "justice gap" acutely affects the lower and middle classes, the elderly, and veterans.[33] In 2015, a third-generation U.S. Army veteran escaped with her two young children from an abusive home. She sought help from a legal clinic, who got her and her boys court protection so that they could get back on their feet.[34] This veteran was one of the lucky ones. While more than 5.6 million Texans qualify for legal aid, just 150,000 cases were handled in 2019.[35]

The Texas Access to Justice Commission has identified several ways to increase Texans' access to the court system. These include removing the cost barriers, ensuring legal aid providers have the resources to meet the needs of low-income individuals seeking legal representation, and increasing pro bono services in the legal community.

 TEXAS TAKEAWAYS

10.4.1 What are some of the problems that limit the quality of justice in Texas?

10.4.2 What is the justice gap, and how might it be addressed?

10.5 JUDICIAL SELECTION AND REMOVAL

One way to mitigate the influence of wealth on judicial outcome is to change the way judges are selected. In this section, we look at different methods of judicial selection and their advantages and disadvantages.

10.5 Identify problems associated with different methods of judicial selection.

Judges may be appointed or elected to office. In some states, governors or legislatures appoint judges. Many states, however, have a **merit selection** system, in which a nonpartisan committee vets qualified candidates based on their qualifications and offers these selections to the governor. After selection, judges typically stand for reappointment ("retention") by voters. Merit selection has been found to reduce the partisanship of judicial candidates and to promote diversity on the bench. Judges can also be selected through partisan elections, in which the party of the judge is listed on the ballot, or through nonpartisan elections, in which the party is not listed.

Judicial selection methods often reflect a state's political culture (see Figure 10.7). In states that are more concerned about access to justice and popular control over judicial matters, judges are more likely to be elected. Only a handful of states have partisan elections, however. States more concerned with establishing an independent judiciary shielded from public opinion tend to appoint judges, often using a merit system.

merit selection: a nonpartisan way to select judges in which a commission selected by state officials sends recommendations to the governor and the governor selects the nominees from that list

JUDICIAL SELECTION IN TEXAS

During Texas's long judicial history, the state has tried different methods of selecting judges: election of judges by the legislature, appointment by the executive branch, and election by the people. The election of judges gained popularity in the 1820s with the emergence of egalitarian democratic ideals and the belief that justices, like other public officials, should be accountable to the voting public.[37]

Today, there are two ways to become a judge or a justice in Texas: appointment or partisan election. Election to office is the standard method of selection in Texas, and most obtain their seats in this manner. If there is an unexpected vacancy on a court at the district level or higher, however, the Texas Constitution allows the governor to make a temporary judicial appointment until the next general election, at which time the appointee must run as a candidate.

The justices (courts of appeals, Texas Court of Criminal Appeals, and Texas Supreme Court) are elected statewide to 6-year terms, which are staggered so that not all of the justices are up for reelection at the same time. Judges to lower-level trial courts are elected to 4-year terms (or 2-year terms for some municipal courts). The frequency of the election of trial court judges holds them strongly accountable to the public.

IS IT BIGGER IN TEXAS?

FIGURE 10.7 **Primary Judicial Selection Process at the State Supreme Court Level**

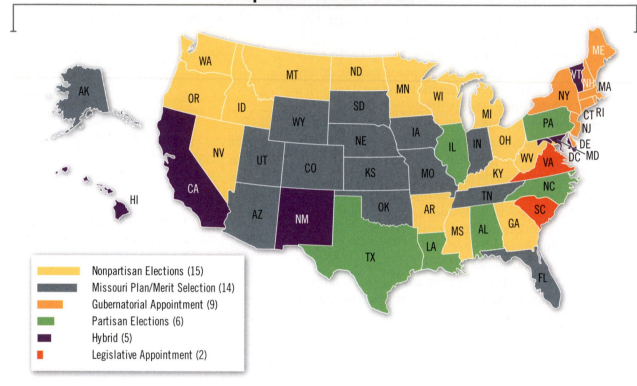

Nonpartisan Elections (15)
Missouri Plan/Merit Selection (14)
Gubernatorial Appointment (9)
Partisan Elections (6)
Hybrid (5)
Legislative Appointment (2)

Source: American Judicature Society.

 COMMUNICATION:

How do states select their judges?

- Many states (21) still use the popular election method to select judges.
- Only six states, including Texas, use the partisan method, while the others use nonpartisan elections.
- In nine states, the governor appoints the judges, usually based on recommendations from a nonpartisan commission.[36]

 CRITICAL THINKING:

Why is there so much variation by state?

- States that have elections (either partisan or nonpartisan) desire voters to have the final say in judicial selection in order to maintain the democratic value of the judiciary.
- This reflects Texas's political culture, which emphasizes a hierarchical political structure that meets the needs of the electorate.

Clearly, politics is part of the process as judges must campaign to win votes. However, they campaign under a more specific code of conduct than candidates for other offices. The Texas Code of Judicial Conduct warns judicial candidates to refrain from inappropriate political activity and prohibits them from making pledges or promises about pending cases or knowingly misrepresenting the identity, qualifications, or position of an opponent.[38] To violate this code of conduct is to risk sanction by the courts, fines, or possible disbarment by the Texas Bar Association, the organization that authorizes an attorney to practice law. Candidates for judicial office are also subject to the same campaign finance-reporting requirements as other elected officials.

Campaign signs outside a polling location.

PERSONAL RESPONSIBILITY: **What kinds of promises might you make if you ran for judge? What would you avoid discussing? Why?**

Politics and ethics clash in elections for judges: Judicial candidates must walk a fine line between not violating the ethics of their position and still communicating a partisan message to voters. In one instance, for example, a judge authorized campaign ads that noted, "I'm very tough on crimes where the victims have been physically harmed. . . . I have no feelings for the criminal." Observers fear that judges who make such promises are put in an ethical bind: They promise to dole out harsh sentences, yet they must be impartial.[39]

INSIDER INTERVIEW

Justice Rebeca Aizpuru Huddle, Texas Supreme Court

How do you like running for election?

The best part about running for office as a judge is meeting civic-minded Texans on the campaign trail. The jurisdiction of the Houston Courts of Appeals is incredibly diverse, including Houston, in Harris County, and nine surrounding counties, from Galveston to Grimes and Waller to Washington. Each area has well-organized groups with dedicated and inspiring volunteers who volunteer their time and other resources to preserve our democracy. The biggest challenge in running for office as a judge is getting information about one's qualifications and judicial philosophy to the more than 3 million registered voters in the jurisdiction. Voters can easily get fatigued educating themselves about the dozens of judicial candidates on the ballot.

SOCIAL RESPONSIBILITY: **How would you change the campaign process to provide more information about judicial candidates?**

CENSURE AND REMOVAL FROM OFFICE

Judges who violate the standards of conduct described previously face discipline, censure, or removal from office. Judges and justices can be suspended or removed in three primary ways in Texas: by the State Commission on Judicial Conduct (by recommendation of suspension); by the Texas Supreme Court (by recommendation of removal); and by the legislature (by impeachment). These avenues provide multiple ways to limit unethical or illegal behavior by judges, giving power to the legislature and fellow justices to check the integrity of the judiciary.

State Commission on Judicial Conduct. The State Commission on Judicial Conduct, which is made up of 13 commission members who include judges, attorneys, and citizens appointed by the governor, can investigate and prosecute allegations of misconduct by Texas judges. Justices can be removed from office for incompetence, for violation of the official Code of Judicial Conduct, or for conduct that is clearly inconsistent with the proper performance of judicial duties. The penalties include warning or reprimand, such as in the case of a judge who consumed too much alcohol at a social gathering and urinated into a garbage receptacle in sight of guests, or additional education, such as in the case of a justice of the peace who asked another judge hearing a case involving his son to let the son take a driving safety course in lieu of a fine.[40]

Texas Supreme Court. The judiciary has to protect its own reputation, and the recommendation of removal provision allows the Texas Supreme Court to police the lower courts. The court may sanction or remove district court judges, although it rarely does so. In 2019, a state district court judge received a public warning after he told a jury to keep deliberating over a defendant they convicted because God had told him the defendant was innocent.[41] The high court also suspended a Harris County justice of the peace based on allegations that she illegally abused prescription drugs, sent sexually explicit texts to a bailiff while on the bench, and hired prostitutes.[42]

Legislative Impeachment. The other branches of government have considerable say in the removal of judges. The Texas legislature can, but rarely does, impeach judges (at the district court and above) "for willful neglect of duty, incompetency, habitual drunkenness, oppression in office, or other reasonable cause."[43]

JUDICIAL QUALIFICATIONS

Each level of the court system specifies unique qualifications for being elected as a judge (see Table 10.1). Lower courts have shorter terms in office, allow younger attorneys to run for office, and have fewer restrictive residency or legal practice requirements. City governments determine the requirements for municipal court judges. The only legal qualification for county judges is that they "shall be well informed in the law of the State." A Texan whose knowledge

TABLE 10.1	Judicial Qualifications	
COURT	AGE	LEGAL PRACTICE
County Court at Law	25 or older	A practicing lawyer or judge, or both, for at least 4 years
District Court	25–74	A practicing lawyer or judge, or both, for at least 4 years
Appellate and Supreme Courts	35–74	A practicing lawyer or judge, or both, for at least 10 years

Source: Texas Constitution.

SOCIAL RESPONSIBILITY:

Given their responsibility, are the age and work requirements sufficient?

of the judiciary is based only on watching reruns of *Walker, Texas Ranger* can serve. As a result, justices of the peace are significantly less likely to hold law degrees than other justices. In 2018, only 8 percent were licensed to practice law.[44] These judges, however, have enormous responsibility as they oversee county government operations, manage responses to emergency management, and hear criminal trials for misdemeanors that are punishable by a year in jail. Of course, as elected officials, they are pressed by the public and businesses to do a good job keeping the streets safe and the roads in good shape.

The higher courts alter the age and experience requirements for justices. Justices for the appellate and two supreme courts must be over 35 years of age but are forced to retire at 74. Justices on these courts must also have 10 years of legal experience instead of 4 for the lower courts.

PROBLEMS WITH PARTISAN ELECTIONS

In a state that is most often dominated by one party (the Democrats until the 1980s, then the Republicans through the present), judicial contests are often one-sided, and the primary is where the real battle for the office takes place. Party labels provide some basic information about the attitudes and values of judges and hints at the way they may decide matters of public policy. Party labels, however, become crutches for voters who have little information about the judicial candidates and often scant knowledge about the judiciary or the issues at stake. Furthermore, judicial partisan elections in Texas suffer from low turnout, low interest, and conflicts of interest that arise when judicial candidates must rely on individuals and groups for campaign contributions.

Low Turnout. Voters are often less well informed about judicial races, which often are perceived to be less important and therefore are not as frequently discussed in the media. In fact, many voters simply do not complete their ballots all the way to the end, where the judicial candidates are generally listed. The number of drop-off votes (called "undervotes") for the judicial electoral races is high (see Table 10.2).

TABLE 10.2	"Undervote" for Judicial Elections, 2020		
COUNTY	TOTAL VOTES	SUPREME COURT	LOWER COURT
Harris	1,633,671	1,591,939	1,545,240
Dallas	918,088	909,890	711,625
El Paso	254,576	244,837	240,975
Bexar	757,821	733,471	725,247
Hidalgo	219,939	203,727	199,699

Source: Texas Secretary of State. Lower court is first competitive district or county court listed on the ballot.

COMMUNICATION:

What is the "undervote" for county judicial elections?

- Most counties in Texas had an undervote in the 2020 elections, some larger than others.
- The two counties with the biggest differences between the total vote and the vote for lower court positions were Dallas (206,463) and Harris (88,431).
- Most other large and small counties had relatively equal numbers of total votes and votes for judicial positions.

CRITICAL THINKING:

Why is there a drop-off?

- There are a large number of positions to vote for (up to 40 in some locations), the positions are generally at the end of a long ballot, and most members of the public are unaware of what the court at each level does.
- The number of total judicial positions may affect the vote drop-off—Dallas has many, and El Paso has fewer.

Reliance on Name Recognition. In low-interest and low-turnout judicial elections, voters often rely on name recognition to decide which candidate to select. As a result of mistakes in name identification, voters can elect a candidate they may not have intended to support.

In 1976, Don B. Yarbrough, an unknown Republican with modest legal experience, drew on the name recognition of the famous Yarborough family in Texas. Donald H. *Yarborough* had been a three-time candidate for governor (without winning), and Ralph *Yarborough* had served as a U.S. senator. The lesser-known Yarbrough emphasized his youth and religiosity, running against the establishment "good-ole boys" from the big law firms and pledging to decide cases based on the laws of God, not man. After winning the primary, Yarbrough admitted that there were 11 lawsuits pending against him for fraud and negligence in his legal practice, illegal stock selling, dealing in unauthorized loans, and other offenses. The legal community mounted a write-in campaign against the now-indicted Yarbrough, making every effort to inform voters what they were getting into. However, it was to no avail. With voter confusion as the likely cause, Justice Yarbrough won the election and took his seat on January 2, 1977. Six months later, Justice Yarbrough was indicted for forging a car title and lying in court. Facing legislative proceedings to impeach him, he resigned from the court.

The disinterest in and low turnout for judicial elections weaken the ability of Texans to hold judges accountable to the people, with random factors like a candidate's name—or the support of an interest group—factoring into who takes office.

Conflicts of Interest. Because candidates for judicial office must raise money to campaign and because donors may become the litigants in court, some people have argued that justice is "for sale" in Texas. In 1983, Justice C. L. Ray ruled in favor of attorney Pat Maloney Sr. and millionaire plaintiff Clinton Manges, who was accused of mismanaging mineral leases. Both were major contributors to the judge's election campaign.[45] The media also reported that Judge Ray had told another major donor (and litigant in front of the court) that his case was a "tough one" and that if the millionaire didn't "win this one, he would win the next."[46] Shining the national spotlight on the case, a *New York Times* editorial decried Texas courts as dispensing "what passes for justice in small countries run by colonels in mirrored sunglasses."[47]

The Republican Party used such conflict of interest claims to launch a "Clean Slate in '88" effort, going into districts held by Democrats to convince them to support Republican candidates who embraced reform and appeared to be, according to political adviser Karl Rove, "champions of the little man and not the big boys."[48] The strategy worked: Republican candidates won five of the six vacant Texas Supreme Courts seats.

Compromising Judicial Experience. In partisan elections, studies show candidate quality matters less than party affiliation.[49] Voters choose party over individual qualifications. In 2010, Republicans won every judicial office in Bexar County. In 2012, Democrats won every judicial office in Bexar County. This lurching from party to party—and the resulting chaos in staffing the judiciary—lead to frequent turnover and courts staffed by individuals with little or no judicial experience.

The Influence of Money. With billions of dollars at stake in the outcomes of judicial matters, interest groups embracing all political and financial interests pour millions into judicial races across Texas. Spending on state judicial races is increasing nationally as well. National interest groups and their affiliates spent an estimated $28 million on state supreme court races in 2016.[50] Candidates need on average more than $1.5 million to win election to the Texas Supreme Court or Texas Court of Criminal Appeals. In total, Texas ranked in the top ten of states with elected judges in total funds spent in 2018 (almost $3 million).[51] Much of these funds come from trial lawyers and law firms, most of whom do business in front of the courts. On average, almost 50 cents of every dollar raised for the highest courts in Texas comes from these groups (see Figure 10.8).[52]

When major initiatives like tort reform gain momentum, big spending floods the political system. For example, when the legislature tried to limit the funds from the Texas Windstorm Insurance Association that could be awarded to Texans suffering after storms, Steve Mostyn, a trial lawyer and major donor to Democrats, gave $10 million to unseat Republicans who voted in favor of the measure.[53]

Those opposed to judicial fundraising are concerned that a judge who takes money from a donor will rule in that donor's favor. One academic study found that campaign contributions to a state supreme court were correlated with judges' decisions.[54] The media have exposed instances in which this has happened, although it certainly does not happen all the time. Still, public perception remains that justice is for sale. The gap between the high ideals of fairness and transparency set for the courts and the practice of judicial politics in Texas seems to be widening.

Harsher Criminal Sentencing. Nonpartisan organizations have found that trial judges are more likely to sentence defendants convicted of serious felonies to longer sentences the closer the judges are to reelection. Judges in partisan elections are also less likely to reverse death sentences than judges selected by merit or by retention election.[55] These outcomes suggest that the partisan election system encourages a certain type of ruling and may compromise justice for Texans.

★ TEXAS TAKEAWAYS

10.5.1   How are judges selected in Texas?

10.5.2   How can judges and justices be removed?

10.5.3   What are some of the problems with partisan elections for judges?

⊍ 10.6 WHO ARE THE JUSTICES?

10.6   Analyze the changes in the demographics of the Texas courts.

In the first days of the Republic, many justices' careers were cut short. Some judges died from yellow fever, others were killed, and still others dared outlaws to do their worst. While we no longer face the challenges of the frontier in administering justice, the new challenge to Texas is to provide justice to a diverse and

FIGURE 10.8 **Donations to Judicial Candidates from Lawyers**

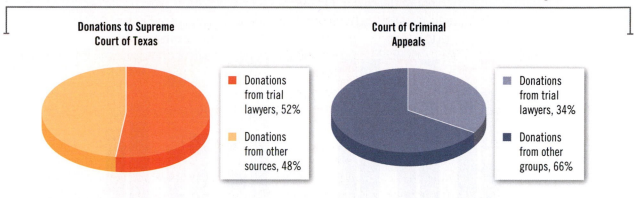

Source: Texas Ethics Commission, Data include the reporting periods of 2019–2020 (through July) for all justices. Includes both lawyers as individual donors (under occupation) and law firm PACs.

 COMMUNICATION:

From what sources do judicial campaign funds come?

- Most of the funds for the Texas Supreme Court come from lawyers and law firms (52 percent). In contrast, most funds for candidates for the Texas Court of Criminal Appeals come from sources other than lawyers or law firms (66 percent).

 CRITICAL THINKING:

Why the difference in donation patterns?

- The Texas Supreme Court deals with civil matters that are often connected to large financial issues, making those justices the logical target of more funds from lawyers and law firms.

- Lawyers are the most attentive to these elections and have the greatest stake in the outcome of elections of Supreme Court justices. The ideology and ruling habits of justices may mean winning or losing (and how much) in court.

growing population. Texas has rapidly become more diverse both racially and ethnically, and the justices on the bench need to reflect the population in order to develop trust in the legal system across racial groups. Greater judicial diversity can reduce racial resentment and enhance sensitivity to cultural issues in legal outcomes.[56] Increasingly, politicians, civil rights organizations, and the Texas Bar Association have taken notice and have encouraged greater diversity in the judiciary (see Figure 10.9). Still, a former justice recently noted that the high court is "not just a little unbalanced, it's a lot unbalanced."[57]

This diversity is a result of gubernatorial appointment of minority candidates and the centralization of racial and ethnic voters in geographic

FIGURE 10.9 **Demographic Changes of Texas Courts, 2007–2018**

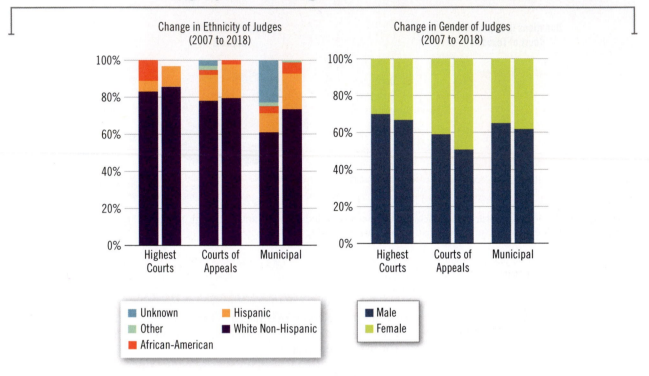

Source: Annual Texas Judicial Statistical Report.

 COMMUNICATION:

What are the changes in the demographics of Texas courts?

- Women make up about 36 percent of the total judicial seats in Texas state courts.[58] The percentage has grown from less than 30 percent to 33 percent on the highest courts and from 34 percent to 38 percent on municipal courts.

- There are currently no African Americans on the highest courts, falling from 10 percent of the total in 2007.

- Hispanic judges made the biggest gains on the state's highest courts and municipal courts and women in courts of appeals following gains in 2018.

 CRITICAL THINKING:

Why are some groups over- or underrepresented?

- Recent governors have sought ways to diversify the bench as a way to improve the judiciary's racial tolerance and to present candidates who are more appealing to minority voters. This is especially true for Hispanic jurists.

- Courts of appeals are more diverse than other courts because the district lines are often drawn in a way that allows racial groups to form a larger voting bloc.

Justices on the Texas Supreme Court made history by conducting the first virtual oral arguments during the COVID-19 outbreak. Although most justices on the highest courts are white men, the trend is changing.

SOCIAL RESPONSIBILITY: **What does diversity in the Texas judicial system mean to legal outcomes for diverse groups and minorities?**

areas, which promote voting for racial minorities to judicial offices. This electoral characteristic, however, limits the ascendancy of racial and ethnic minorities to the bench in some districts. The federal courts considered the case of *United Latin American Citizens et al. v. Mattox* (1993), in which the plaintiffs argued that the countywide voting (instead of districts assembled from common geographic neighborhoods) for judges diluted the power of minority voting. No changes were made, but the issue spurred debate. Lawsuits filed in 2016 by seven Latino voters argued that the voting system disenfranchised them and that a district-based election should be used instead.[59] The argument was rejected in 2018 by U.S. District Judge Nelva Gonzales Ramos. With statewide elections dominated by Republicans since 1996, "partisanship rather than race better explains Hispanic defeat at the polls," she ruled.[60]

WOMEN

The first, and to date only, Texas Supreme Court made up entirely of women heard a case in 1925. All three male Supreme Court justices (the total at the time) had to recuse themselves on a case, and Governor Pat Neff appointed three women to (temporarily) make up the bench. The first woman to serve on a district court in Texas was Sarah Hughes, appointed in 1935. It took another 50 years for the number of women on the bench to expand significantly. Today, women make up 36 percent of the State Bar and about 38 percent of the judicial seats in Texas state courts.[61] Indeed, Texas is in the top 10 states with the highest percentage of women judges.

AFRICAN AMERICANS

African Americans make up 6 percent of the State Bar and approximately 5 percent of state courts. Chief Justice Wallace Jefferson was the first African American to be appointed, then elected and reelected, to the position. Governor Rick Perry appointed him in 2001, and he was reelected in 2006 by a large margin (76 percent of the total vote).

HISPANICS

Hispanics make up 10 percent of the State Bar and about 17 percent of state courts. Hispanics are the only racial or ethnic minority that holds a significantly higher percentage of judicial positions than the percentage of their representation of the State Bar. Raul A. Gonzales was the first Hispanic to join the Texas Supreme Court when he was appointed by Democratic Governor Mark White in 1984.

ASIANS

Asians make up 4 percent of the State Bar and less than 1 percent of the judicial positions on state courts. As a percentage of judicial positions, they are the most underrepresented group in the judiciary. Judge R. K. "Ravi" Sandill was the first South Asian to run for any statewide court in 2018.

TEXAS TAKEAWAYS

10.6.1 Which groups are overrepresented and which are underrepresented on the Texas bench?

10.6.2 How might the method of judicial selection influence diversity on the bench?

10.7 REFORMING THE SYSTEM

10.7 Evaluate proposals for reforming the selection of the judiciary.

Concerns about the injection of partisan politics into the judiciary and the vast sums of money being spent on judicial elections have observers worried. In 2019, the legislature created a new Texas Commission on Judicial Selection tasked with evaluating alternative methods for judicial selection before the 2021 session. Indeed, advocates of reform of the judicial system in Texas have considered several imperfect options over the years.

NONPARTISAN ELECTIONS

Some judicial advocates have recommended keeping the election of judges but removing the partisan label. Former Chief Justice Wallace Jefferson lamented the partisan process of elections. He commented, "It is an irrational way of selecting judges. Just because you have an 'R' or a 'D' by your name does not mean you are more qualified to be a judge."[62] Both political parties dislike nonpartisan elections because it reduces their influence in the system.

MERIT SELECTION

Often called the "Missouri Plan" (after Missouri's innovation of the plan in 1940), merit selection of judges is a nonpartisan way to select qualified judges from a vetted list of possible candidates. After being appointed to a fixed period of service (often a year), the judge must stand for reelection in a "retention" election. If a majority of voters vote against retention, the judge is removed, and the process begins again. In theory, this system allows the governor to ensure that judges have sufficient experience. However, it also gives the governor greater sway over the judicial branch. Texas has not tried merit selection.

PUBLIC FINANCING OF ELECTIONS

Elections for the Texas high courts have become some of the costliest in the country, potentially allowing donors to have a larger say in who is elected. A pool of funds could be set aside (from taxpayer monies) to give each candidate a fixed sum with which to campaign. Democratic Representative Rafael Anchia of Dallas filed a bill in 2015 to start public financing of campaigns for appellate judges in Texas. It was sent to the House Elections Committee—and was never heard from again.[63]

LIMITING FUNDRAISING TOTALS

In the wake of fundraising scandals, the state legislature passed the Judicial Campaign Finance Act in 1995, which capped contributions from each individual donor to judicial candidates. Contribution limits change depending on the type of judicial race and the population of the district (see Table 10.3). To ensure the integrity of the system, the state uses its authority to regulate these funds, making the process more transparent and less able to be influenced by campaign funds. This also allows potential challengers who may have a

PERSONAL RESPONSIBILITY:

If you donated money to a judicial candidate, would you expect favorable treatment in court?

TABLE 10.3	**Funding Limits on Judicial Candidates**		
Population of the judicial district	Less than 250,000	Between 250,000 and 1 million	Statewide judicial offices
Funding limit from each donor	$1,000	$2,500	$5,000

*Source: T*exas Ethics Commission, Campaign Finance Guide for Judicial Candidates and Officeholders.

smaller fundraising base to compete with incumbent justices by limiting the amount of money that can be raised.

There are also limits on how much a law firm, the primary contributors to judicial candidates, can contribute to an individual candidate. The rules allow a maximum of a $30,000 contribution for a firm's associates for statewide courts, courts of appeals, and district courts. The legislature can decide to raise or lower these limits. If the Texas legislature wanted to take fundraising limits a step further, the U.S. Supreme Court ruled in 2015 that states could prohibit judicial candidates from personally asking supporters for campaign contributions.[64]

GREAT TEXAS POLITICAL DEBATES
The"Geezer Amendment" and Age Limits

Two Democrats crisscrossed the expansive Texas landscape, eating a lot of Tex Mex, fried catfish, and chicken-fried steak, all with the hope of gaining support to win the Democratic nomination to take on incumbent Republican Michael Keasler on the Texas Court of Criminal Appeals.[65] The problem, other than indigestion? It wasn't clear that there would be an election at all. Keasler turned 77 in 2019. However, according to what Keasler calls the "geezer amendment," state law mandates retirement for judges at 74 but allows a judge to serve out the term during which he or she turns 74.[66] Given his age and the dates he was elected, his seat would not be vacant until December of 2020, after the November 2020 elections, allowing the governor, not the voters, to decide on his replacement.

 SOCIAL RESPONSIBILITY: **Should the state have mandatory retirement for judges over 74 years of age?**

YES: Mandatory retirement allows for new voices in the Texas judiciary and avoids burnout on the bench resulting from new laws that increase demands on reading and updating. More senior judges are also expensive: The longer they serve, the larger the pension bill paid by Texas taxpayers.

NO: "70 is the new 50," according to one lawmaker, so an arbitrary retirement age might force good judges from the bench when they are "in their prime."[67] Ultimately, the matter of when jurists should retire should be decided by the voters rather than by a blanket retirement age clause. In fact, there are no age limits at all for the governor or legislators.

TEXAS TAKEAWAYS

10.7.1   How has Texas reformed the Texas judicial system in recent years?

10.7.2   What is the merit system, and what are its advantages and disadvantages?

THE INSIDER VIEW

Distrust of an overbearing centralized government put the Texas judiciary squarely in the hands of the people and led to the design of an ordered system in which judicial branch power checks, but is also checked by, the other branches. However, the participatory neglect of people in judicial elections and the injection of political parties and interest groups into the process foster the perception that justice can be purchased by the highest bidder. Reform efforts have minimized these potential problems by limiting the role of money in politics, expanding the size of the court, and ensuring continued public access to the courts for all Texans. Yet interest groups and political parties still play a leading role in judicial elections. As Texans attempt to improve the quality of justice in the state, they may look to greater legislative participation (especially through funding), an internal check on judicial power by higher courts, and the will of the people through elections.

TEXAS TAKEAWAYS

10.1.1   The judicial system's role is to interpret Texas laws and the Texas Constitution and to provide Texans with equal access to an efficient system that applies the law fairly and objectively and that protects their interests. Texas courts clarify the laws, check the legislature's power, check the executive's power, and advance the rule of the people.

10.1.2   The structure of the court system is hierarchical. Cases start at the lowest level trial courts, which review facts and make rulings, and may be funneled to higher appellate courts that can check bad decisions or incorrect rulings. Appellate courts also interpret legislative statutes, sort out policy contradictions, and advance public opinion.

10.1.3   The official territory and types of cases over which a court exercises authority are factors that determine the jurisdiction of a court. Trial courts often have original jurisdiction. Higher courts can generally choose which cases to take from lower courts. Cases can be either criminal or civil. In civil cases, the amount of monetary damages helps determine which court will hear a case. The major factor that determines which court will hear a criminal case is the severity of the transgression.

10.2.1   Local courts include municipal courts and justice courts. Municipal courts have original and exclusive jurisdiction over violations of city ordinances and over Class C misdemeanors. Justice courts hear cases that involve small claims, civil actions of $10,000 or less, and criminal offenses punishable by fine but not prison sentences.

10.2.2 County courts include constitutional county courts, county courts at law, and probate (last will and testament) courts. The Texas Constitution vests not only judicial, but also broad administrative powers in constitutional county courts judges who also oversee a five-member commissioner's court with budgetary authority over county government operations. County courts at law have original jurisdiction on civil matters between $200 and $200,000 and appellate jurisdiction in cases appealed from other local trial courts.

10.2.3 District courts are trial courts that handle most major criminal and civil cases, including murder, drug trafficking, contested elections, and civil cases involving high amounts of monetary damages (any amount over $200), as well as all divorce and support cases, land title cases, and any cases that do not fall under the jurisdiction of other lower courts.

10.3.1 An appellant (or petitioner) first files a notice of appeal and then submits a brief. The justices in appellate courts choose which cases to hear and may decide the case based on the brief alone, or they may hear oral arguments. Amicus curiae briefs can be filed by interested parties that are not directly involved in the case.

10.3.2 Texas has two supreme courts: one for criminal and one for civil matters. The dual structure allows judicial specialization and, in principle, quicker case resolution.

10.4.1 Some of the problems that limit the quality of justice are overworked judges, delays in court cases, low judicial salaries, turnover of justices, and underfunded or nonaccessed legal aid.

10.4.2 Many argue that the wealthy are at an advantage in the court system. The "justice gap" refers to the greater access to justice enjoyed by the wealthy as compared to the lower and middle classes, the elderly, and veterans. The gap might be addressed by removing cost barriers, ensuring legal aid to low-income individuals, and increasing pro bono legal services.

10.5.1 There are currently two ways to become a judge or a justice in Texas: appointment or partisan election.

10.5.2 Judges and justices can be removed in three ways in Texas: by the State Commission on Judicial Conduct (by suspension), by the Texas Supreme Court (by removal), and by the legislature (by impeachment).

10.5.3 Low voter turnout, overreliance on name recognition, and voting based on party without regard to judicial quality are some of the problems associated with partisan elections. Many Texans also fear that the high cost of running for election may make judges more likely to ruling in favor of large donors. Just prior to elections, judges also dole out harsher sentences.

10.6.1 White males are overrepresented, while females, African Americans, Hispanics, and Asian Americans are underrepresented on the Texas bench.

10.6.2 Governors can choose or not choose to appoint a greater number of women or minorities to the bench to increase diversity. Countywide elections dilute the power of minority votes and so may cause minorities to become underrepresented.

10.7.1 The Texas legislature has limited private fundraising for judicial elections, and legislators have tried but failed to establish public financing of elections.

10.7.2 In a merit selection system, the governor appoints judges, and after a certain period, the citizens vote on whether or not to retain them. This, in theory, allows the governor to ensure that judges have sufficient experience. However, it also gives the governor greater sway over the judicial branch.

KEY TERMS

appellate courts

appellate jurisdiction

bench trial

caseload

civil cases

common law

criminal cases

disposed

dual structure

en banc

felony

jurisdiction

jury trial

mandatory review

merit selection

misdemeanors

opinion

original jurisdiction

probate

PRACTICE QUIZ

1. The standard of evidence in a civil case is . . .
   a. Beyond a reasonable doubt
   b. Within the range of reason
   c. A preponderance of the evidence
   d. Beyond the shadow of a doubt

2. Which court has budgetary and administrative authority over county government operations?
   a. Constitutional county courts
   b. County courts at law
   c. Municipal courts
   d. Probate courts

3. Texas has _____ court(s) of last resort (e.g., Supreme Court[s]).
   a. Zero
   b. One

c. Two
d. Three

4. In comparison to past years regarding the handling of cases before it, the Texas Courts of Appeals . . .
   a. Are becoming less efficient
   b. Are becoming more efficient
   c. Have about the same amount of efficiency
   d. Not enough data to substantiate either way

5. Which Texas Supreme Court Justice has a popular Twitter account?
   a. Justice Sondock
   b. Chief Justice Hecht
   c. Justice Scalia
   d. Justice Guzman

6. Voter turnout is often high in judicial races.
   a. True
   b. False

7. Most cases in Texas are handled at the most local levels.
   a. True
   b. False

8. Merit selection of judges is a partisan way to select judges.
   a. True
   b. False

9. A defendant in a criminal case is the individual who is bringing the suit against another individual.
   a. True
   b. False

10. Amicus curiae are briefs submitted by interest groups to appellate courts.
    a. True
    b. False

[Answers: C, A, C, B, D, B, A, B, B, A]

OXFORD insight study guide
Active Engagement, Deeper Understanding

Learn more with this chapter's digital tools, including the Oxford Insight Study Guide, at www.oup.com/he/Rottinghaus3e.

11 CRIMINAL JUSTICE

Noticing the broken lock, off duty Dallas police officer Amber Guyger swung the door open and stepped into an apartment she believed was hers. Still in uniform, she confronted a strange man, unarmed 26-year-old Botham Jean, sitting on the couch eating ice cream and watching television in white shorts. Reacting quickly, she shot Jean in the heart before realizing that she was one floor above her own apartment and that Jean was not a burglar.[1]

Guyger was subsequently fired from the Dallas Police Department and sentenced to 10 years in prison for murder. The jury found that she had acted unreasonably by failing to notice clear signals the apartment was not hers (such as the red doormat outside), she did not follow proper police procedure to retreat if her life was not in danger, and she did not attempt to administer CPR. Guyger's defense argued that she was bleary after a 14-hour shift, had no malice toward Jean (having never met him), and made an innocent but grave "mistake of fact," a legal term used by police defense when an officer reasonably believed he or she saw something like a weapon even if one was not present.

During the 911 call, Guyger texted her police partner, Martin Rivera, twice: "I need you . . . hurry up" and "I [expletive] up."[2] Gugyer testified that it was fear, not racism, that led her to pull the trigger. However, the prosecution introduced other text messages in which Guyger joked about Martin Luther King Jr.'s death and mocked her black colleagues.[3] Some felt the 10- year sentence was just a "slap in the face."[4]

11.1 Identify the rights of the accused and of victims.

11.2 Distinguish the types of crimes and punishments in Texas criminal law.

11.3 Explain the stages of the criminal justice process in Texas.

11.4 Evaluate the consequences of postconviction punishment in Texas.

11.5 Assess reforms to the Texas criminal justice process.

● The case of a white police officer who shot and killed an unarmed black man sparked outrage and passionate questions about race in America. After Amber Guyger was sentenced, Botham Jean's brother told her he loved and forgave her, wished she would not end up in prison, and asked the judge for permission to give her a hug. Botham Jean's mother was not in a forgiving mood: She referred to Guyger as "the devil."

Several high-profile shootings by police officers or at police officers have heightened tensions across the racial and ideological divide: the assault arrest and suicide of Sandra Bland in a Waller County Jail in 2015 following a traffic stop; the murder of five police officers in Dallas during a protest against police violence in 2016; the fatal shooting of an unarmed black high school freshman Jordan Edwards by a white former Balch Springs, Texas, police officer in 2017; the shooting of Atatiana Jefferson in 2019 in her Fort Worth home during a routine welfare check; and the death in police custody of George Floyd (a Houston native) in Minneapolis, Minnesota, in 2020, which sparked protests all over Texas and the nation.[5]

Criminal justice in Texas occurs at the tense intersection of politics, personal freedom, and concerns about law and order. The authority granted to the state by the U.S. Constitution to investigate criminal violations and punish those convicted places it in the center of controversy. In this chapter, we examine the strain between maintaining law and order and using a fair and bias-free approach to these issues. We start by exploring the norms and laws surrounding crime and punishment in Texas. We next paint a picture of the state's criminal justice process, incarceration and other types of punishment, and the obstacles felons face upon release from prison. In the final section, we examine reforms put into place to remedy flaws in the system.

🔵 11.1 TEXAN JUSTICE

11.1 Identify the rights of the accused and of victims.

Political columnist Molly Ivins remarked that a "favorite thing" of Texas politicians is to "git tuff" on crime.[6] It's a historical legacy that runs deep. The Texas Rangers, the state's oldest law enforcement agency, traces its roots back to Stephen F. Austin's call for a league to defend the Texas frontier against attacks by Native Americans in 1823. In the days of the Wild West, Judge Roy Bean, a saloonkeeper and justice of the peace in the dusty town of Langtry along the Rio Grande, was said to have fined a corpse $40 for carrying concealed weapons.[7]

Texans generally revere their law enforcement officers, believing them to be a critical front line of defense against crime. However, racial groups divide on opinions of law enforcement. Some racial groups are more likely than others to have a negative view of police, driven by personal interactions and exacerbated by high-profile incidents (see Figure 11.1). Texans also vary in their attitudes toward victims and those accused of crime, and so they battle over victims' rights and the rights of the accused.

RIGHTS OF THE ACCUSED

Cases involving police shootings raise questions about how the rights of an accused are violated. Accused individuals are informed by law enforcement agents, just as they are in every television police show, that they have the right to remain silent, to consult with an attorney, and to have that attorney present when being questioned. Police officers are required to have **probable cause** to question a suspect. This requirement ensures that the accused is protected from an unreasonable **search and seizure**. The Texas Indigent Defense Commission works with counties to provide lawyers for **indigent defendants** (those who cannot afford a lawyer). Most of these rights of the accused are guaranteed by both the U.S. Constitution and the Texas Constitution. Texas has tripled the funding for indigent defense cases since 2001 but still ranks low on per capita defense spending, overloading the number of cases for defense attorneys by double or triple the recommended caseload.[8]

The murder of Deputy Darren Goforth in Harris County in 2015 by a repeat offender with a history of mental illness spawned the "Blue Lives Matter" sentiment that has been contrasted with the "Black Lives Matter" movement by some.

🔺 PERSONAL RESPONSIBILITY: **What does this and the chapter-opening case tell us about race relations, crime, forgiveness, and punishment in Texas?**

probable cause: the legal grounds law enforcement uses to make an arrest or conduct a search

search and seizure: procedure whereby law enforcement agents search an accused's property and collect any evidence relevant to the alleged crime

indigent defendants: accused individuals who, lacking resources to hire an attorney, are entitled to have a lawyer hired for them

VICTIM RIGHTS

The Texas Constitution guarantees several rights to crime victims and their families. Victims of crimes such as sexual assault, kidnapping, aggravated robbery, or other criminal bodily harm are entitled to protection by law enforcement, have the right to be informed about the progress of a case at various points, and also have the right to have the court take their safety into account when considering release of their attacker from a correctional facility. The legislature also created the Crime Victim's Compensation Act to provide funds to victims for loss of property, personal injury, or death.

FIGURE 11.1 **Attitudes toward Police, by Race**

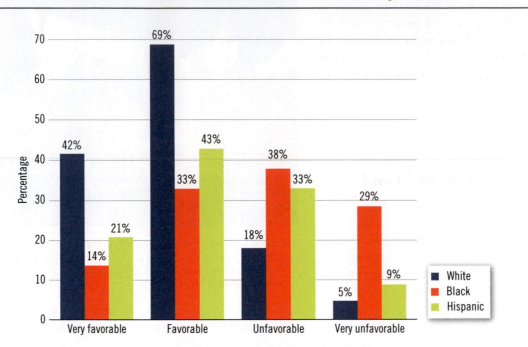

Source: UT/*Texas Tribune* poll, October 2020.

 COMMUNICATION:

How do the major racial and ethnic groups feel about law enforcement?

- Anglo residents feel most favorable toward law enforcement, followed by Latinos.

- African Americans are less likely to have a very favorable opinion of law enforcement and are much more likely to have an unfavorable opinion than any other racial group.

 CRITICAL THINKING:

Why are there different responses across races and ethnicities?

- African Americans generally have a disproportionate amount of negative interactions with law enforcement, leading to diminished trust between the groups.

- Highly publicized tragedies involving African Americans and law enforcement officers contribute to a widening gap in approval of law enforcement between African Americans and other racial groups in Texas.

⭐ **TEXAS TAKEAWAYS**

11.1.1 What are the specific rights the U.S. and Texas constitutions grant the accused upon police interrogation?

11.1.2 What are the rights of victims in Texas?

11.2 TYPES OF CRIMES

As described in Chapter 10, felonies are more serious offenses that elicit harsher punishments than misdemeanors. There are three classes of misdemeanors and five types of felonies in Texas, each associated with a range of penalties (see Table 11.1).

> **11.2** Distinguish the types of crimes and punishments in Texas criminal law.

MISDEMEANORS

As Table 11.1 illustrates, misdemeanors can range from Class A, the most severe, to Class C, the least severe. The most common Class C misdemeanor is a traffic offense (speeding). Other Class C misdemeanors are minor theft (usually shoplifting), a minor in possession of alcohol, or leaving a child unattended in a vehicle. In 2015, Houston Rockets point guard Patrick Beverley was arrested on a Class C misdemeanor warrant for an outstanding unpaid toll, which he attributed to an expired EZ TAG account. He was taken to a police substation and paid the $321 fine on his warrant. Although late to practice, Beverley played in the game that evening.[9]

Penalties increase for repeat offenders. For example, the most common misdemeanor in Texas is Driving While Intoxicated (DWI). The first conviction is a Class B misdemeanor punishable by up to 6 months in jail or a $2,000 fine, and a second offense (or if the defendant's blood alcohol level is greater than 0.15) is considered a Class A misdemeanor.

FELONIES

Felonies in Texas range from failure to pay child support to murder, and their punishment varies from short prison sentences to death by lethal injection. The circumstances of the crime also play a part in sentencing. If a defendant is convicted of a state jail felony, a judge can bump up the punishment to a third-degree felony if the defendant used or exhibited a deadly weapon during the crime or had been convicted of a felony in the past.

Although Texans have a reputation for being tougher than rawhide on crime and criminals, the criminal justice system—and the public—at times do have a soft spot for some offenders. Bernie Tiede, a 38-year-old mortician, befriended the gruff, wealthy, 81-year-old widow Marjorie Nugent, and the two became close companions, living, traveling, and shopping together. After Nugent's disappearance, Tiede continued to spend the widow's considerable fortune, giving much of it away as charitable contributions in the community. After months of questions about Nugent's whereabouts, police eventually discovered her body in a freezer in the garage, hidden under frozen food.[10] Although a cruel act, the town was sympathetic to the soft-spoken and well-liked Tiede. "From the day that deep freeze was opened, you haven't been able to

Galveston police came under fire for the arrest of Donald Neely for criminal trespass after photos were taken showing two mounted officers leading him down the street roped to their horses. 'This is gonna look really bad," said one of the officers. The Department admitted that the officers showed poor judgment and immediately changed its policy to prevent use of the technique, but concerns about prisoner treatment remained.

TABLE 11.1   **Misdemeanors and Felonies in Texas**

MISDEMEANORS		
CATEGORY	PUNISHMENT	EXAMPLE
Class A	Up to one year in jail and/or a fine up to $4,000	Assault, harassment, burglary of a vehicle, theft/criminal mischief of $500 or more
Class B	Up to 180 days in county jail and/or a fine up to $2,000	Indecent exposure, disorderly conduct, DWI (first offense), theft/criminal mischief of $50 or more
Class C	Fine only, not to exceed $500	Possession of alcoholic beverage in motor vehicle, theft/criminal mischief of $50 or less
FELONY		
CATEGORY	PUNISHMENT	EXAMPLE
Capital	Death by lethal injection (only if 18 years or older) or life in prison without parole	Murder
First Degree	5 to 99 years or life in prison, and/or fine up to $10,000	Murder; aggravated sexual assault; injury to child, elderly, or disabled individual; aggravated robbery; arson
Second Degree	2 to 20 years in prison, and/or fine up to $10,000	Murder (including sudden passion), manslaughter, indecency with a child, robbery, burglary of habitation
Third Degree	2 to 10 years in prison and/or fine up to $10,000	Intoxication assault, kidnapping, stalking (first offense), DWI (with two prior convictions only), theft/criminal mischief of $20,000 or more
State Jail	180 days to 2 years in state jail and/or fine up to $10,000	Criminally negligent homicide, burglary of a building, failure to pay child support, theft/criminal mischief of less than $1,500 to a habitation with a firearm, forgery

Source: State Bar of Texas, Criminal Justice Section.

find anyone in town saying, 'Poor Mrs. Nugent,'" said city councilman Olin Joffrion. "People here are saying, 'Poor Bernie.'"[11] Tiede was sentenced to life in prison in 2016.

DRUG CRIMES

Drug offenses are based on the type and amount of drug in question, how the drug was concealed, and whether the defendant manufactured, delivered, or possessed the drug. Since 1999, arrests for drug crimes have skyrocketed, although most arrests are for possession rather than distribution. Even trace amounts of drugs (1/100th the amount of a packet of Splenda) can lead to prosecution, often as a way to meet a political conviction goal for prosecutors.[12]

In a famous example, Willie Nelson was traveling on Honeysuckle Rose, his tour bus, in Hudspeth County. The road was on a border checkpoint, and border patrol agents stopped the bus and searched it. The agents found enough marijuana to charge the Texas icon with a Class B misdemeanor. Hudspeth County Attorney C. R. "Kit" Bramblett joked that the legendary country artist played his 1975 hit "Blue Eyes Crying in the Rain" in the courtroom as community service.[13] The judge ultimately fined him $500.[14]

Some local district attorneys in Texas are decriminalizing small amounts of marijuana, which they argue saves money and is good public policy. Critics charge these district attorneys with creating "sanctuary cities" for drugs.[15]

Willie Nelson, a notorious connoisseur of marijuana, pled guilty to lessened charges after his tour bus was stopped south of El Paso. Although it was reported that the bust was "not a holiday" for Nelson, the ordeal inspired a new song: "I'll Never Smoke Weed with Willie Again."

 SOCIAL RESPONSIBILITY: **Are punishments for drug crimes too harsh? What might be done alternatively to address drug problems in Texas?**

JUVENILE CRIME

The Texas Juvenile Justice Department is responsible for the supervision and rehabilitation of juveniles (10- to 16-year-olds) in the criminal justice system. At age 17, a defendant may be tried as an adult, and Texas is one of only four states to do so. Studies show that 90 percent of juvenile justice system kids have experienced trauma through confinement or inability to pay fines.[16] In 2019, legislators from both parties, with the support of the Texas Criminal Justice Coalition, introduced bills to raise the age but to no avail. Although high-profile cases, such as the 2019 murder of a San Antonio boxer, John Duane VanMeter, by a 12-year-old bring home the seriousness of the harm juveniles can do, approximately 95 percent of juvenile offenses are drug-related.[17]

Juvenile justice is administered locally, with the hearings, terms of detention, and probation determined at the county level. The state has established different procedures for police interrogations and confessions, and juveniles also have separate case managers, detention facilities, courts (for some offenses), and punishments. Juveniles may be designated to a "first offender" program as an alternative to jail or to programs for substance abuse, life skills, parenting, or animal therapy. Juveniles are not alone in this process: They are entitled to a lawyer, and if a parent or guardian cannot be located, a

SOCIAL RESPONSIBILITY:

Where would you draw the line between a misdemeanor and a felony? What kind of crimes and circumstances should shift the scale from minor to major?

guardian ad litem: a person appointed to represent the best interests of a child if a parent will not or cannot fulfill the responsibility

guardian ad litem is appointed.[18] Once sentenced, however, these offenders are transferred to adult facilities at the age of 19. More than 2,000 of these offenders are currently serving time in adult prisons for crimes they committed as juveniles.[19]

 TEXAS TAKEAWAYS

11.2.1 What are the differences between misdemeanors and felonies?

11.2.2 What is the age range for a juvenile defendant?

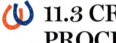 11.3 CRIMINAL JUSTICE PROCESS IN TEXAS

11.3 Explain the stages of the criminal justice process in Texas.

Texans look to state and municipal governments to handle criminal justice, and the state has created a bureaucracy to administer justice before, during, and after the trial. Let's take a look at the specifics of each.

PRETRIAL

So you've been arrested on charges that you violated the law—what's next? The first step is an appearance before a judge. Within 48 hours after an arrest, a suspect must have a hearing before a judge to be informed of the charges.[20] The judge must also advise the accused that he or she can retain counsel, remain silent, and have an attorney present during interviews with law enforcement officers or attorneys representing the state.

bail: a contract whereby the accused is temporarily released from prison on the condition that he or she pay a sum of money to guarantee an appearance in court

To get out of jail, the accused needs to post **bail**. Bail is a contract whereby the accused agrees to give something up (usually money) to ensure that he or she will appear when the court so orders. After a specific bail amount is set, a bond can be acquired to facilitate bail. A bond can be a cash bond, in which the defendant pays the full amount of the bond immediately; a bail bond, in which the defendant uses a bonding company to borrow the collateral; or "personal recognizance," in which a defendant is not required to put up anything. When defendants use a bondsperson to secure bail, they pay a fee—10 percent of the set bail amount—and pledge collateral, usually property or automobiles, for the remaining amount. If the defendant doesn't show up for court, the bondsperson must either pay the entire amount or finally produce the defendant.

If the accused is not in custody, the **prosecutor**—the state's lawyer who is responsible for bringing charges against the accused lawbreaker—has up to 2 years from the date of the offense to file misdemeanor charges and between 5 and 10 years to file felony charges.[21] Prosecutors have different titles depending on where they work. Both district and county attorneys represent the state in criminal cases and work with law enforcement to investigate criminal cases in their jurisdiction. Once the prosecutor files the charges, the accused must make an initial appearance or **arraignment**. The charges are read in open court, and the defendant enters a plea.

A **grand jury**, in conjunction with the prosecutor, determines whether there is sufficient evidence to bring criminal charges in serious cases against a defendant. The prosecutor presents evidence in the form of physical items, such as an alleged murder weapon, and witnesses. These meetings are not public, and so they protect the reputation of a defendant and allow witnesses to speak freely without fear of retaliation. Less serious felony charges can be brought in other ways, usually by a charging document.[22]

If the defendant wants to argue that law enforcement engaged in improper search, seizure, or statement, he or she engages in a suppression hearing to ask the judge to suppress the evidence by claiming it was collected illegally. Both sides in the case also take discovery, a process of collecting information, during this period. Texas does not have automatic discovery, so the defendant's lawyers must request that the prosecution disclose specific items, such as witness statements, audio or video of the event, and physical objects such as firearms or drugs. The accused may also plead guilty to reduced charges through a **plea bargain,** in which the defendant waives his or her right to a trial and the prosecutor recommends a punishment that the judge accepts or rejects. Almost all criminal cases are finalized with a plea bargain.[23]

TRIAL

If the case doesn't end in a plea, it will likely go to trial. For jury trials, a jury must be selected through **voir dire**, a French term meaning "to see to speak." During voir dire, jurors are questioned by attorneys and judges in court to determine if a potential juror is biased, cannot deal with the issues fairly, or knows a party to the case. Some jurors may be dismissed for a legal reason, such as knowing the defendant. Other jurors may be dismissed through a "preemptory challenge" by one of the attorneys because of a perceived bias against the defendant, predispositions about the crime, or other reasons.[24]

A defendant must enter a plea in response to the charges. The plea can be guilty, not guilty, or **no contest**; in the last-named plea, the defendant does not admit guilt but is not contesting the underlying facts. No contest pleas allow the defendant to accept punishment from the court but avoid admitting

prosecutor: the state's lawyer who is responsible for bringing charges against accused lawbreakers

arraignment: the initial appearance of the accused in court

grand jury: a legal body charged with the task of conducting official proceedings to investigate potential criminal conduct

plea bargain: the process by which the defendant agrees to a lesser set of charges than initially charged by the prosecutors

voir dire: the questioning of jurors by attorneys and judges in court to determine if a potential juror is biased, cannot deal with the issues fairly, or knows a party to the case

no contest: a plea whereby a defendant does not admit guilt but is not contesting the underlying facts

Jury duty is often seen as an important but cumbersome chore. Here, Senator Ted Cruz takes the juror oath in 2015. Most counties in Texas pay between $5 and $10 a day for jury duty—usually not enough to cover parking. Political science research, however, shows that even increasing that pay shows no positive effect on compliance with a jury duty summons.

PERSONAL RESPONSIBILITY: Should juror payment be increased, or is the civic responsibility important enough that the amount of pay is not important?

guilt. The defendant who does not plead to the charge can request a jury trial with 6 jurors in misdemeanor cases and 12 jurors in felony trials.

If a defendant wants a trial but waives his or her right to a jury trial, and if the state agrees, the defendant can receive a bench trial. Misdemeanor defendants who are found guilty usually are sentenced by the judge immediately. In felony cases, judges consider factors such as the nature of the crime, remorse expressed by the defendant, the defendant's criminal history and personal circumstances, and the wishes of the victim. Sentencing could include jail, probation, fines, restitution, and community service.[25]

PUNISHMENT

In the 1840s, the criminal justice apparatus in the Republic of Texas was ineffective by almost any standard. Many residents of the early ramshackle Texas towns, now beaming silvery metropolises, were shiftless, rowdy, and sometimes vicious loafers who had to be corralled by corrupt sheriffs into musty jails. In 1842, the legislature, seeking some control over the system, voted to provide funds for the construction of a state penitentiary to improve local law and order. Over the years since then, the corrections system has adopted new solutions and adapted to new trends, sparked by a mixture of state-based experimentation, evolving political values, and civil rights concerns.

Physical Labor. Originally, prisons were largely expected to be self-sufficient by growing or manufacturing items to generate revenue.[28] They relied on the physical labor of convicts to generate revenue. Even the State Capitol was built in part by 300 convicts from local prisons who earned 65 cents per day for breaking boulders of almost metallic density.[29] Prisoners produced millions of pounds of cast-iron works, including the dome and ornamentation for the inside of the Capitol building—much of which still stands today.[30] Currently, young, first-time offenders are sometimes sentenced to a type of "boot camp" modeled after the military's basic training—a sentencing sometimes called "shock probation." In addition, in adult prisons, some of the convicted work on "hoe squads," where they plant and pick produce and carry rocks.[31]

ANGLES OF POWER
Race and Finances in the Texas Prison System

By 1911, the Texas prison system was low on funds. Prisoners who were supposed to be compensated for their grueling work in the fields were not. Wages were paltry, short-lived, and infrequently paid. Prison commissioners were often forced to suspend pay (except Sunday overtime pay). Convict mutinies, called "bucks," broke out in which convicts refused to work.

Governor Oscar Branch Colquitt—and the state legislature—passed reforms to invest more than $2 million in prison funding, but they also required a return to producing profitable "money crops" and the closing of other prison industries like iron works. Regulators required a strict separation of the races, with African Americans and Hispanics sent to the fields and Anglos to prison factories working on farm equipment.[26] The racial segregation perpetuated society's Jim Crow legal and race-based class distinctions as it provided job skills—which would be useful after release—to whites only and relegated the Latinos and African Americans to work in the fields.[27]

SOCIAL RESPONSIBILITY: **How would you create a race-blind punishment and incarceration policy?**

Probation. Community supervision, or probation, is an alternative to incarceration that allows offenders to live and work outside of prison while they serve their sentence. The basic conditions require the defendant to commit no criminal offense while on probation, report to a supervision officer periodically, maintain employment to support dependents, and pay restitution to victims. Maximum periods are set at 10 years for a felony conviction and 2 years for a misdemeanor case. The length of supervision depends on the offense, the use of a deadly weapon, and prior convictions. A judge can assign additional supervision for 10 years if the case involves indecency with a child, sexual assault, or aggravated assault.[32] Texas ranks comparatively high nationwide (number 7 in 2018) on the state lists of defendants in community supervision (see Figure 11.2).

Other forms of community supervision allow flexibility in treating defendants. In **deferred adjudication** community supervision, a defendant pleads guilty, but the judge delays a final verdict until the time the defendant

community supervision: an alternative to incarceration whereby a defendant is released and allowed to live in the community under conditions set by the court

deferred adjudication: a type of supervision through which a defendant pleads guilty but the judge delays a final verdict until the time the defendant successfully completes the supervision period

FIGURE 11.2   Comparing State Community Supervision Populations

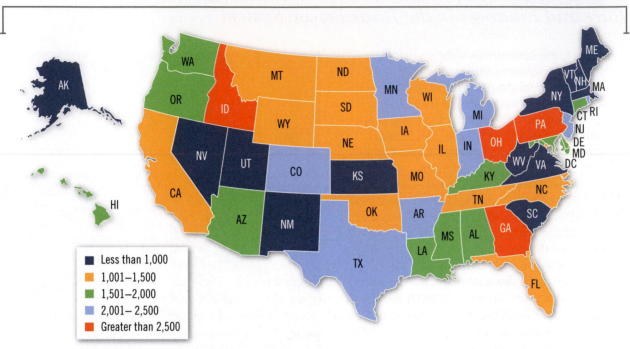

Source: Columbia University Justice Lab, 2020. Rates per 100,000 adult residents.

 COMMUNICATION:

How many defendants are on community supervision?

- Georgia leads the nation in community supervision population size.
- Texas ranks in the top 10 but is behind other large states like Pennsylvania and Ohio.

 CRITICAL THINKING:

Why do some states have more individuals on community supervision?

- Community supervision is often less costly, so states experiencing economic downturns, such as Ohio and Pennsylvania, may take this approach to keep costs low.
- Tougher sentencing laws in states like Georgia and Idaho drive the size of the community supervision population.
- Texas has increased the use of community supervision as a way to reduce the jail population, which can be expensive to maintain.

successfully completes the supervision period. If the conditions are met, the judge dismisses the proceedings and discharges the defendant. If the defendant violates a condition, however, the defendant may not appeal, and the punishment for the verdict will stand.

Community service can be a condition of probation. The service can range from picking up trash to volunteering for the Society for the Prevention of Cruelty to Animals to providing skilled labor at a construction site.[33]

INCARCERATION

Local, state, and federal governments maintain correctional facilities in Texas. Municipal (city) jails hold those arrested until either bail is made or they are transferred to county jails. County jails hold defendants awaiting trial or transfer to prison, community correctional facilities such as "boot camps," or substance abuse treatment facilities. The Texas Department of Criminal Justice oversees more than 100 state facilities of various types, including transfer facilities, state jail facilities, psychiatric units, and private prisons. Federal penitentiaries house convicts who have violated federal law. There are 106 correctional facilities in Texas, including federal correctional institutions, private correctional institutions, and residential reentry centers (halfway houses to provide assistance to inmates nearing release).[34] It costs the state approximately $62.34 a day to incarcerate an adult inmate and $479.56 to incarcerate a juvenile inmate.[35]

Overcrowding. During the 1980s, Texas—and the nation as a whole— experienced a sharp spike in the crime rate. By 1991, Texas significantly outpaced the nation in crimes committed, with the murder rate 56 percent higher than the national average, rape 26 percent higher, aggravated assault 19 percent, and burglary 44 percent.[36] From the 1980s to the 1990s, dangerous youth crime nearly doubled, while crimes committed by adults rose 25 percent.

Prison populations exploded in the 1980s as the U.S. Congress and state legislatures began to pass "tough on crime" legislation to appeal to a growing conservative voter base and to stem rising crime rates (see Figure 11.3). The overcrowding in Texas prisons instigated a seemingly unending series of lawsuits involving Texas prisoners, the federal government, and the Texas Department of Corrections.

Following federal court mandates to end prison overcrowding and Texans' concerns about rising crime rates in the 1990s, the state nearly tripled the number of prison beds in that decade to 150,000.[37] One criminal justice observer noted that the ramping up was like "mobilizing for a world war."[38] Rather than significantly reducing overcrowding, however, the incarceration rate shot up. Texas became an icon for states that wanted to get tough on crime. State court judges began handing out longer sentences for criminal defendants. State laws were passed that mandated convicts serve a minimum of 50 percent of their sentences.[39] The prison population ballooned from 290

IS IT BIGGER IN TEXAS?

FIGURE 11.3 State and Federal Prisoners under Jurisdiction of Correctional Authorities

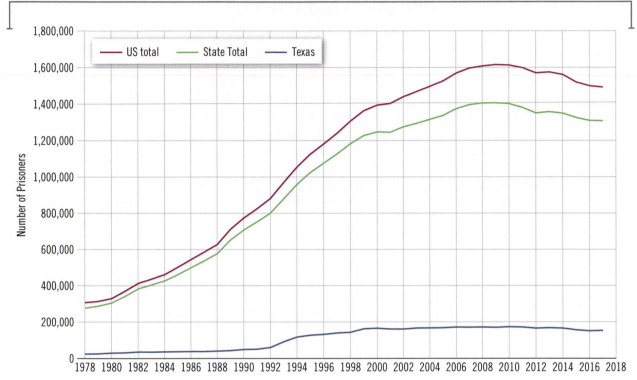

Source: Bureau of Justice Statistics, National Prisoner Statistics Program.

 COMMUNICATION:

How does the prison population in Texas compare to that in the rest of the states and the nation?

 CRITICAL THINKING:

Why did the prison population increase, then level off?

- State prison populations drove overall growth beginning in the 1980s.
- Texas's prison population rose in the 1990s, then plateaued as other state prison populations continued to rise.
- Federal prison populations also rose in the 1980s, but gradually and only by about 200,000 prisoners.
- Much of the growth in prison population was escalated by states, especially the southern states, whose prison populations collectively doubled in the decade between 1990 and 2000.
- Conservative southern states are more likely to have higher penalties and stricter enforcement of laws than other states.
- Texas's history of being tough on crime created incentives to fund more law enforcement and more prisons beginning in the 1990s. As the state sought to reduce the prison population after crime rates fell in the 2000s, the number incarcerated leveled off and then decreased.

FIGURE 11.4 **Demographic Makeup of Texas Prisons**

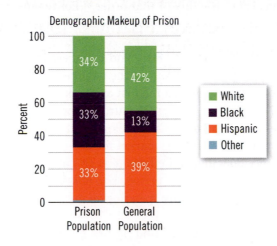

Source: Texas Department of Criminal Justice, "Statistical Report Fiscal Year 2019," both male and female prisoners included, *www.bjs.gov/content/pub/pdf/p17.pdf*. Figures rounded up. "Other" category = 1 percent. Population figures from the U.S. Census Bureau.

 COMMUNICATION:

What is the racial makeup of prisons in Texas?

- The percentage of the total prison population from each racial group is roughly equal, at about one-third each. Although the percentage of the prison population is similar, the representation by each group in prison is not balanced.

- African Americans and Latinos are overrepresented in the prison population, while Anglos are underrepresented.

 CRITICAL THINKING:

Why the racial imbalance?

- Statewide figures may mask the degree to which certain groups are in prison for certain crimes (drug crimes versus property crimes versus murder). African Americans are more likely to be in prison for drug crimes than other racial groups, and these crimes have longer sentences than other crimes.

- Racial profiling, through which racial minorities are targeted by police, may also be increasing arrest and conviction rates among African Americans and Latinos.

prisoners per 100,000 in 1990 to 704 prisoners per 100,000 in 1999. In addition, the average sentence served in prison tripled for violent crimes and burglary between 1991 and 1999, and the number of prisoners paroled decreased by 60 percent during this time period. Punitive sentences targeted defendants who were disproportionately racial minorities (see Figure 11.4).

Several states copied elements of what prison experts called the "Texas Control Model," which emphasized inmate obedience, discipline, work, and education—roughly in that order.[40] Politicians who believed longer sentences were best for rehabilitation took credit for getting tough on crime.[41]

Recent Fall in Crime Rate and Incarceration. The prison population in Texas has slowly declined during the twenty-first century, partially driven by a falling crime rate, which fell just as quickly as it rose during the 1990s. Between 1994 and 2000, arrests for murder dropped 68 percent, and arrests for robbery declined 51 percent. Criminologists attribute the decline in crime to a strong economy, a shrinking market for drugs, new police strategies involving community policing, and efforts to keep guns out of the hands of juveniles.[42] Even so, Texas spending on prisons and jails is the highest in the nation, growing five times faster than state spending on public schools over the past three decades.[43]

Drug Court Reform. Funding has been an issue as well. Republicans, while tough on crime, are also fiscally conservative, and prisons are expensive to maintain and run. Spending on incarceration increased by 205 percent during the 1990s.[44] Texas Republicans also responded by establishing drug courts to provide treatment for drug-addicted offenders rather than prison time. In addition, they diverted funds from prison construction to alternative approaches. Governor Rick Perry signed legislation to allow police officers to issue citations for misdemeanor possession of marijuana in place of arrests. He also supported legislation that mandated probation for first-time drug offenders who were caught with small amounts of drugs. The state poured significant funds into drug prevention programs and probation programs.[45] As a result, the state closed three prisons from 2000 to 2010.[46]

The public supports reasonable measures that reduce incarceration rates. Polling from the Texas Public Policy Foundation, a conservative-leaning think tank in Austin, found that most Texas voters favor making penalties more proportionate to the crime. Sixty-one percent support drug treatment over prison, 57 percent support raising the standard for a drug felony, and 57 percent support community supervision over prison for some crimes.[47]

Privatization. Privatization of prisons, whereby maintenance of a prison facility is outsourced to a private firm, saves money but also creates controversy. In 2015, some 2,800 inmates rioted by starting fires and taking control of the privately owned Willacy County Correctional Center in Raymondville. Their purpose: protesting the rough conditions of the prison as imposed by the Utah-based company operating the facility, including insect infestation, exposure to raw sewage, substandard medical care, and excessive solitary confinement.[50] The U.S. Bureau of Prisons canceled the contract, the prison closed, and the inmates were transferred. Private prisons are filling up to capacity, however, and Texas is building new facilities, such as one in Conroe, as the federal government cracks down on undocumented immigrants.[51] Texas private prisons hold about one-third of Immigration and Customs Enforcement (ICE) detainees.[52]

GREAT TEXAS POLITICAL DEBATES

Prison Conditions in Texas

The period from the 1950s to the 1970s was a particularly brutal time for convicts in Texas prisons. Prisoners who "bad-eyed" a guard or picked "dirty cotton" in the field might be ordered to balance for 3 hours on an elevated two-by-four called "the Rail." They might be forced to stay up all night shelling peanuts. Abuse by guards was frequent—prisoners were whipped, beaten, or flogged with a curved wooden stick called "the bat."

Responding to these conditions in 1980, the appropriately named federal judge William Wayne Justice held that the prisons in Texas violated the Eighth Amendment of the U.S. Constitution prohibiting "cruel and unusual punishment." In *Ruiz v. Estelle*, the courts prohibited the state from housing more than two prisoners per cell, ordered a 1:6 staffing ratio for guards to inmates, and ordered the prison to reduce its population to 95 percent of capacity.[48] After the agreement went into effect, conditions improved. However, 75 percent of prisons don't have air conditioning, and nearly two dozen inmates have died from heat stroke in the past two decades during Texas's sweltering summers. In 2017, a U.S. district court judge ruled that these conditions are inhumane and that the state must install air conditioning. When prison officials had not done so by 2020, the same judge allowed attorneys to investigate who in the Texas Department of Criminal Justice was responsible.[49]

SOCIAL RESPONSIBILITY: **Should Texas take more stringent measures to protect prisoner rights?**

NO: Prisoners have broken the social contract and violated civil norms. Prison officials tasked with their care and possessing limited financial resources need to be given a wide variety of tools to manage the convicts. Basic care is all the state can afford and all the prisoners have earned.

YES: Convicts are human beings who should be granted access to basic social services and who have the dignity of human rights. If the goal is to rehabilitate, not just punish, prisoners, they should be allowed to live as normal a life as possible.

MAYBE: Extending some privileges for good behavior at the discretion of the prison officials is a reasonable way to rehabilitate those in the prison population. Punishment for bad behavior while incarcerated should also be handled by prison officials.

DEATH PENALTY

Texas has a long history of issuing and implementing the **death penalty** for capital offenses. Prior to 1923, individual counties were responsible for executing their own prisoners. After 1924, fears of overzealous sheriffs, in conjunction with alleged abuse by county juries, led the legislature to mandate that all prisoner executions be carried out by the state at the Walls Unit (named because of the tall walls surrounding the unit) in Huntsville.[53] Texas carried out executions by hanging from 1819 to 1923 and through electrocution from 1924 on. "Old Sparky," as the electric chair was familiarly known, was constructed by inmates out of an oak chair.[54] The chair was the means of executing 361 men between February 1924 and July 1964.[55] Texas temporarily stopped executing prisoners after the U.S. Supreme Court banned capital punishment in the United States as a violation of the Eighth Amendment "cruel and unusual" prohibition in the case *Furman v. Georgia* (1972).

death penalty: the sentence of a convicted individual to death (capital punishment)

Once the death penalty was again permitted by the U.S. Supreme Court in 1977, Texas adopted the practice of lethal injection, carrying out the first such execution in 1982.[56] Tough-talking Governor Ann Richards approved 50 executions in her term as governor. On the campaign trail in 1994, Richards, a Democrat, bragged about being as tough on crime as any Republican. Gubernatorial candidate George W. Bush responded that if elected, he would shorten the time spent on death row appeals. The *Houston Chronicle* scolded them both in an editorial: "It is unseemly for political candidates to compete with one another over who would be the most enthusiastic and cheerful executioner."[57] After winning the election, Governor Bush signed off on 135 executions after approving legislation that expedited execution and limited capital appeals. "We're a death penalty state," he declared.[58]

Governor Rick Perry sanctioned more executions than any modern governor in U.S. history and was stingy with pardons. Despite talking tough, the governor also supported legislation to allow juries in capital murder trials to consider life without parole instead of death, which has greatly decreased the number of people sentenced to death. This legislation—signed in 2005—dropped the number of executions from 37 to 9 in slightly more than a decade (see Figure 11.5).[59]

Several crimes in Texas are eligible for the death penalty. These include hiring someone to murder someone else, murdering a judge or correctional officer, and murder committed during the act of specified felonies, such as kidnapping, burglary, and rape. When considering whether or not to apply a death sentence, a jury may weigh the circumstances of the crime and whether a defendant demonstrated remorse about the crime. Unanimous agreement that a defendant is likely to commit future criminal acts is required to sentence an offender to death.

Race is a significant factor in application of the death penalty. For instance, between December 2004 and 2016, every death sentence handed down in Harris County was to an African American or Hispanic man. The current membership on death row is 44 percent African American, 26 percent Hispanic, and 27 percent Anglo. The rate of prosecutors asking for the death penalty has slowed due to concern over racial and mental health issues raised by cases recently reviewed by the U.S. Supreme Court. Texas has reached historic lows in the number of individuals on death row.[61]

The first case under Court review involved Bobby Moore, who shot 73-year-old James McCarble in the head at point-blank range while

The Court of Criminal Appeals in Texas suspended Rodney Reed's death sentence indefinitely following an outcry by celebrities, politicians, and the public. Evidence had emerged that the fiancé of the woman Reed had been accused of murdering might be responsible for her death.

PERSONAL RESPONSIBILITY: **Does Rodney Reed's case provide evidence for or against the death penalty and the manner in which it is implemented?**

FIGURE 11.5 **Number of New Death Sentences and Prisoners Executed**

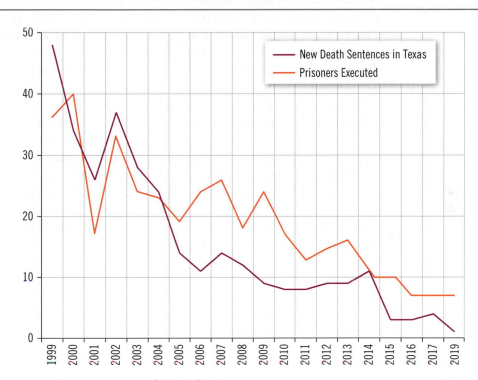

Source: Texas Department of Criminal Justice, 2019.

 COMMUNICATION:

How many prisoners are on death row or executed by year in Texas?

- The number of prisoners executed declined from a high of 40 in 2000 to 7 in 2019.
- The number of new sentences fell markedly after 1999, from 48 to 1 in 2019.

 CRITICAL THINKING:

Why have the numbers executed or scheduled to be executed fallen?

- The homicide rate in the state fell during the 2000s, reducing the need to use the death penalty.
- Prosecutors in the state have more flexibility when pursuing the death penalty than in the past.[60] Problems with the fairness of the death penalty also have reduced the likelihood of asking for it.
- Texans still support the death penalty but may be hesitant to use it unless the circumstances are extreme or the evidence in the case is very clear.

robbing the Birdsall Super Market with two others in 1980. Moore's lawyers claimed that he had "profound mental and social difficulty" from a young age and was unable to spell, tell time, or understand the days of the week. At age 14, Moore's father threw him out of his house for being "too dumb to stay at home."[62] Lawyers for the state of Texas argued that Moore's IQ test scores in the upper 70s were not evidence of mental deficiency, especially since he was able to show leadership, hold a job by mowing lawns, lie, act rationally, and respond to stimuli—all the standards used in a prior case by the Texas Criminal Court of Appeals. In 2016, however, the U.S. Supreme Court held that since Moore had a mild disability, executing him would be a violation of the Eighth Amendment to the U.S. Constitution's prohibition on cruel and unusual punishment.[63] In 2017, the Court additionally held that Texas's process for determining whether a convicted murderer was a future danger was racially tainted because experts testified that African Americans were more prone to violence.[64]

In 1999, death row was moved to a modern unit, called the Polunsky Unit, deep in the lonely, piney woods near Livingston, Texas. Today, Texas relies on lethal injection to carry out death sentences. Many lethal injection drugs, however, are in short supply, so the state relies on a single drug (pentobarbital, a drug used in animal euthanasia). The scarcity of this drug prompted more than 3,300 citizens to write to Governor Abbott between January and September of 2015 to suggest alternative means to swiftly carry out the death penalty. The public's creative methods included blood draining, carbon monoxide poisoning, and a firing squad.[65]

Support for use of the death penalty for capital cases is high in Texas. In a 2015 survey, 75 percent of respondents favored the death penalty as a sentence in capital cases, compared to 19 percent who did not support it and 6 percent who were not sure. In a national 2017 survey, only 55 percent supported use of the death penalty, a low not seen since 1972.[66] In Texas, however, even liberals, who have been classically opposed to the death penalty, are split on its use but generally they lean toward not supporting it (see Table 11.2).

TEXAS TAKEAWAYS

11.3.1 What procedures take place prior to the trial?

11.3.2 Who determines guilt in a criminal case?

11.3.3 What are some alternatives to incarceration?

11.3.4 How did Texas respond to federal court mandates to end prison overcrowding?

11.3.5 What change in policy precipitated a drop in the number of death penalty executions in Texas?

TABLE 11.2	Support for Death Penalty, by Ideology	
IDEOLOGY	**OPPOSE**	
Liberal	27%	
Moderate	7%	
Conservative	3%	

 COMMUNICATION:

How do Texans feel about the death penalty?

- Conservatives overwhelmingly support use of the death penalty in capital crimes (65 percent), followed closely by moderates (41 percent).
- Liberals in Texas are split but tend to oppose it, but a plurality oppose it (27 percent).

 CRITICAL THINKING:

Why the split in support among ideologies?

- Traditionalist political culture, dominant in Texas, holds that law and order is one of the main purposes of government. Most Texans, especially conservatives and moderates, embrace this function of government.
- Liberals disapprove more because of concerns about racial fairness of the penalty, denial of due process of law, and a belief that it is inhumane.

11.4 LIFE AFTER PRISON

After their release, persons with felony convictions may face **collateral consequences** by being banned from certain employment, access to benefits, and eligibility for specific programs.

> **11.4** Evaluate the consequences of postconviction punishment in Texas.

RESTRICTED LICENSING, EMPLOYMENT, AND ACCESS TO PROGRAMS

State law restricts felons from serving in many state positions, including as a railroad commissioner, a primary election judge, and several hospital district boards. Felons are also ineligible for food stamp benefits, selected Medicaid programs, and higher-education scholarships. Almost 200 certificates, permits, or specific types of employment are not available to felons. These include a license to sell alcoholic beverages, to serve as director at a child care center, and to conduct charitable bingo games.[67]

collateral consequences: additional civil punishments of criminal convictions

VOTING RIGHTS

criminal disenfranchisement: the loss of voting rights for felons during incarceration and after they have served their sentence

Another significant collateral consequence is the loss of voting rights, called **criminal disenfranchisement**. Close to 6 million Americans are unable to vote due to felony disenfranchisement policies.[68] States may suspend voting rights while the felon is in prison only, during parole and probation as well, or even for years after the sentence has been served (see Figure 11.6). There is a racial disparity in the voters who are disenfranchised. Nationally, 1 out of 13 African Americans has lost voting rights compared to 1 out of 56 non-African Americans.[69]

PAROLE

parole: a system in which a prisoner is released from prison prior to completing his or her full sentence

As the famous country musician Merle Haggard wrote in his hit song "Momma Tried," some Texans turn "21 in prison doing life without parole." A prisoner earns **parole** through good conduct while being locked up. Points are assigned based on effectively carrying out assignments, attempting to rehabilitate, and generally exhibiting good behavior[70] (see Table 11.3). Except in cases where prisoners are not eligible for parole, such as those on death row, parole becomes an option when their calendar time served plus good conduct time equals one-fourth of the maximum sentence or 15 years—whichever is less.[71] Depending on the case, the standard for parole may be higher.

At the high point of parole granting in the 1980s, inmates served approximately 22 days for each year of their sentences.[72] Jail overcrowding spurred the state to release convicts like Kenneth McDuff, who served only 20 years for a violent triple homicide. While on parole, McDuff kidnapped and killed a Waco woman.[73] In response to this and other heinous crimes committed on parole, the state instituted minimum time-served requirements before parole could be granted. The parole rate came down dramatically from 80 percent in 1991 to 50 percent in 1992 and to 20 percent in 1994.[74] The parole approval rate for 2018 was 33 percent for the state overall.[75] Still, two-thirds of the Texas Pardons and Parole Board members must vote "yes" to grant parole in capital offenses, making it difficult to achieve.

SOCIAL RESPONSIBILITY:

Does the risk assessment rubric seem fair to you? Should there be different risk levels for male and female prisoners? Why?

| TABLE 11.3 | **Risk Scores for Parole Justification** |

SCORE ASSIGNED RISK LEVEL (RISK LEVEL TO ASSIGNED INDIVIDUAL)	MALE POINTS	FEMALE POINTS
Low Risk	3 or less	3 or less
Moderate Risk	4–8	4–9
High Risk	9–15	10+
Highest Risk	16+	N/A

Source: Bureau of Pardons and Paroles.

IS IT BIGGER IN TEXAS?

FIGURE 11.6 Restrictions on Voting Post-Felony, by State

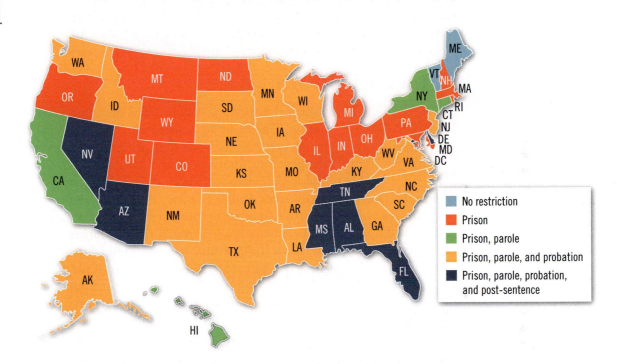

Legend:
- No restriction
- Prison
- Prison, parole
- Prison, parole, and probation
- Prison, parole, probation, and post-sentence

Source: The Sentencing Project, National Council of State Legislatures.

 COMMUNICATION:

Which states restrict voting rights for prisoners or released felons?

- Most states have a ban on voting rights for the duration of a felon's prison sentence, while on probation, or on parole (or all three). Texas is in this category.

- Fourteen states extend the voting restriction to the period after the offender has completed his or her sentence.

 CRITICAL THINKING:

Why are some states less likely to grant voting rights?

- The harshest postincarceration voting restrictions tend to be in the South (Florida, Mississippi, and Alabama), likely due to a traditionalistic political culture that is tough on crime.

TEXAS TAKEAWAYS

11.4.1 What are the collateral consequences persons with felony convictions face after their release?

11.4.2 How have parole policies changed?

11.5 REFORMS

11.5 Assess reforms to the Texas criminal justice process.

Criminal justice reforms in Texas are often punitive in nature. One observer joked that when the legislature meets every 2 years, the first thing they do is increase the penalties for everything.[76] Historically, Democrats and Republicans have been equally hard on crime and criminals. Democratic Governor Dolph Briscoe (1973–1979) railed against "long-haired weirdoes," made vigorous enforcement of crime a major issue, and pushed a hulking anticrime package through the legislature.[77] Republican Governor George W. Bush (1995–2000) increased punishment for juvenile offenders and pushed "truth in sentencing" laws to limit parole options. The question is how to balance the generally tough on crime approach with the requirements for a just system and controlling costs. The "lock-them-up-and-throw-away-the-key" crowd has given way to bipartisan efforts to come up with creative solutions to reform the criminal justice system in Texas.[78]

ALTERNATIVES TO INCARCERATION

On an average day, Texas county jails house about 65,000 individuals. Many of these incarcerated individuals are low-level, nonviolent offenders, especially those with mental illness or substance abuse problems. Both state and local governments have implemented strategies to provide alternative solutions for these specialized jail populations. One county sheriff rewarded positive inmate behavior with "good time" credits.[79] A legislative pilot program for offenders with mental health issues was initiated in 2013 to reduce repeat criminal behavior, limit time spent in jail, and expand clinical mental health and social support services through rehabilitation programs and residential housing opportunities.[80] However, overcrowding and inmate deaths have remained a problem.

BAIL REFORMS

Most prisoners in Texas and across the United States have not been convicted of any crime but remain in jail because they cannot afford to pay bail. In 2001, 39 percent of inmates in Texas were pretrial detainees. In Travis County (Austin), that figure was 75 percent in 2017.[81] Each prisoner costs taxpayers about 51 dollars a day.[82] Posting bail is especially burdensome for low-income defendants who cannot go back to work, support their families, and aid in their own defense.[83] The rigid, predetermined bail schedule does not provide enough flexibility, reformers argue, to ensure that the bail is fair. Reformers also argue that the court system can use statistical tools to improve the manner used to determine the risk of flight[84] (which bail is supposed to reduce), rely less on financial bonds, and ensure that defendants have a bail hearing within 24 hours of their arrest. In 2019, following a U.S. District Court judge review of a Harris County case, a landmark agreement was reached establishing an automatic, no-cash pretrial release for about 85 percent of low-level defendants, more funds for overworked indigent defense attorneys, and better access to social workers.[85] Dallas and Galveston counties have similar lawsuits in the works.

ADDRESSING PRISON SUICIDES

Even as prison populations are falling, Texas prisons witnessed a 140 percent increase in suicides from 2013 to 2018, with 40 suicides occurring in 2017 alone.[86] More than 150 inmates attempted suicide per month in 2017.[87] As one tool to prevent suicides, the Texas Department of Criminal Justice has increased the training of prison officer cadets to spot a mental health crisis in a distressed inmate. Criminal justice reform advocates also stress the need for access to services and more prison staff in general.

GRAND JURY REFORM

Until 2015, a district judge would personally select citizens to be jury commissioners, and those commissioners would then choose 15 to 20 citizens to serve as the grand jury pool.[88] Critics believed this process encouraged the selection of grand jurors who were more likely to bring charges against a suspect. Indeed, one *Houston Chronicle* reporter uncovered an instance in which grand jurors actively collaborated with prosecutors to intimidate witnesses.[89] In 2015, Texas passed legislation to outlaw the "pick a pal" grand jury system. The new system institutes a random process for drawing jurors from a broader pool of potential applicants.[90]

DEATH PENALTY REFORM

While Texans overwhelmingly support the death penalty, 49 percent of Texans believe that people are wrongly convicted of the death penalty "occasionally," and 13 percent feel this happens "a great deal of the time."[91] This sentiment is backed by concrete evidence. The Innocence Project, a national organization dedicated to exonerating individuals wrongly convicted using DNA testing, reports that 52 individuals in Texas (and 362 nationally) were exonerated as of 2018, more than any other state.[92]

In 2015, Sandra Bland committed suicide after being charged with assaulting a state trooper who stopped her for failing to signal a lane change.

Kerry Max Cook's fight is one example. Arrested in 1977 for the rape, mutilation, and murder of a woman who lived in his apartment complex, Cook endured a 40-year ordeal, including conviction for murder, three trials, two death sentences overturned, and freedom from death row in 1997. While in prison, he was repeatedly raped and stabbed—abuses that led him to attempt suicide twice.[93] In 1999, DNA tests revealed that none of the evidence collected at the scene of the gruesome murder belonged to Cook. Another man—the victim's lover, a married man—was linked to the evidence at the scene. Cook agreed to a plea deal that dropped the murder charges and allowed him to get out of jail but not be legally exonerated.[94] Even after four decades, Cook is still fighting to clear his name—winning could mean compensation of up to $2 million from the state, including health and education benefits. In the last 25 years, the state has paid wrongfully convicted men and women $93.6 million.[95]

DNA testing of evidence in criminal trials holds great promise to identify persons responsible for crimes, yet it is not always reliable. The Texas Forensic Science Commission introduced new standards on "mixed DNA" evidence (when more than one individual's DNA is found on evidence).[97]

Other procedural safeguards can also be employed to make the system less fallible. Civil rights organizations have outlined dozens of recommendations to reform the death penalty in the United States.[98] First, states should require review of credible claims of innocence even after conviction. Second, all evidence should be preserved for an extended time after a conviction and DNA databanks established to keep records, to which defendants should have access. Third, parameters should be established to ensure reliable testimony from eyewitnesses, including in jury instructions. Fourth, states should create an independent authority to screen and train defense attorneys representing clients charged with capital crimes. Finally, because the death penalty is disproportionately applied to racial minorities, states should pass legislation to ensure racial and ethnic diversity among the judges, lawyers, and jurors so that racial discrimination plays no role in capital punishment.

INSIDER INTERVIEW

Former Court of Criminal Appeals Judge Cathy Cochran

How is it that Texas, home to law and order, has enacted groundbreaking reforms to the death penalty?

I think that when you come right down to it, Texas is a pretty open-minded place. People listen and pay attention and acknowledge issues if you bring them to their attention in an appropriate sort of way. And all those DNA exonerations woke a lot of people up. I was as surprised as anybody.[96]

SOCIAL RESPONSIBILITY: Is the criminal justice system fair? How would you design a system that protects the innocent, punishes the guilty, and upholds basic human rights?

Although Texas is undeniably aggressive in using the death penalty as a sentence for capital crimes, the state has also led the nation in efforts to improve procedures in such cases relating to police practices, forensic evidence, and prosecutorial procedures. Legislation was passed in 2017 to improve law enforcement lineups, require that any testimony of jailhouse informants be corroborated, and guarantee a defendant's right to DNA testing after conviction.[99]

 TEXAS TAKEAWAYS

11.5.1 How did Texas reform its grand jury system in 2015?

11.5.2 What step has the Texas Department of Criminal Justice taken to address prison suicides?

11.5.3 What reform has Texas advanced to prevent juries from convicting the wrong person?

THE INSIDER VIEW

Historically, state political officials, often responding to public outcry for retribution against criminals, have been punitive and harsh. These efforts have trickled down into prison policy, sentencing policies, and punishment, but they are often countered by voters who have grown weary of spending funds on prisoners. In response, public officials have implemented reforms that have reduced the state's incarceration rate, dropped the state's crime rate to pre-1968 levels, decreased the number of repeat offenders, closed eight prisons over the last 7 years, and cut the number of death sentences and executions in half over two decades.[100] Many problems still remain, however, such as prison overcrowding, racial disparity in sentencing and incarceration, and treatment of prisoners.

TEXAS TAKEAWAYS

11.1.1 The accused has the right to remain silent, to consult with an attorney, to have an attorney present during questioning, and to be protected from unreasonable search and seizure.

11.1.2 Victims have the right to be informed about the progress of a case and to have the court take their safety into account when considering release of their attacker from a correctional facility.

11.2.1 Misdemeanors are less serious than felonies. They range from Class C for theft of property $50 or less to Class B for a first DWI to Class C for assault. The maximum penalty for a misdemeanor is up to a year in jail and/or a $4,000 fine. Felonies range from state jail for a crime such as burglary of a building that might receive up to 2 years in state jail to Third Degree for crimes such as kidnapping or third DWI, to Second Degree and First Degree for crimes such as murder and aggravated sexual assault to capital offenses. The maximum penalty for a capital felony is the death penalty.

11.2.2 The age range for a juvenile in Texas is 10 to 16 years; at age 17 defendants can be tried as adults.

11.3.1 Within 48 hours after an arrest, a suspect must have a hearing before a judge to be informed of the charges. To get out of jail, the accused needs to post bail. Once the charges are filed by the prosecutor, the accused must make an initial appearance or arraignment, and the defendant enters a plea. The accused may also plead guilty to reduced charges through a plea bargain. In serious cases, a grand jury and the prosecutor determine whether there is sufficient evidence to bring criminal charges. The defendant can initiate a suppression hearing to ask the judge to suppress evidence improperly seized.

11.3.2 A judge decides in bench trials. Otherwise, a jury with 6 jurors decides in misdemeanor cases and 12 jurors in felony trials.

11.3.3 Probation and deferred adjudication are two alternatives to incarceration.

11.3.4 In the 1990s, the state nearly tripled the number of prison beds and continued to be tough on crime. Due to overcrowding and expense, Texas also developed alternatives, such as treatment for drug-addicted offenders rather than prison time, and looked to private companies to build and manage prison facilities.

11.3.5 In 2005, Texas legislation was passed allowing juries in capital murder

trials to consider life without parole instead of death, which has greatly decreased the number of people sentenced to death.

11.4.1 Persons with felony convictions may face collateral consequences by being banned from certain kinds of employment, such as directing a child care center, and from obtaining permits or certificates needed for jobs. They also cannot have access to benefits such as food stamps. In many states, these persons also are not allowed to vote.

11.4.2 At the high point of parole granting in the 1980s, inmates served approximately 22 days for each year of their sentences. After a person convicted of triple homicide killed a Waco woman while on parole, the parole rate dropped dramatically from 80 to 20 percent in two years. Today it stands at about 33 percent.

11.5.1 The old system allowed grand jury commissioners to pick the grand jury pool. The new system institutes a random process for drawing jurors from a broader pool of potential applicants.

11.5.2 The Texas Department of Criminal Justice has increased the training of prison officer cadets to spot a mental health crisis in a distressed inmate as one tool to prevent suicides.

11.5.3 Legislation was passed in 2017 to improve law enforcement lineups, require that any testimony of jailhouse informants be corroborated, and guarantee a defendant's right to DNA testing after conviction.

KEY TERMS

arraignment
bail
collateral consequences
community supervision
criminal disenfranchisement
death penalty

deferred adjudication
grand jury
guardian ad litem
indigent defendants
no contest
parole
plea bargain

probable cause
prosecutor
search and seizure
voir dire

PRACTICE QUIZ

1. The oldest law enforcement agency in the state of Texas is . . .

   a. The Department of Public Safety
   b. The Criminal Justice Division
   c. The Texas Rangers
   d. The Texas Lawmen

2. Which of the following is the CORRECT order of the classification of penalties associated with the following felonies, ranked from most severe to least severe?

   a. State Jail, Capital, First Degree, Second Degree
   b. Capital, First Degree, Second Degree, Third Degree
   c. First Degree, Second Degree, Third Degree, Capital
   d. First Degree, Second Degree, Third Degree, State Jail

3. Which of the following is the CORRECT order of the criminal justice process in Texas?

   a. Pretrial, Trial, Punishment
   b. Trial, Posttrial, Punishment
   c. Amicus Curiae, Trial, Punishment
   d. None of the above is correct

4. Where does Texas rank in relation to other states in terms of prison population?

   a. Among the lowest
   b. Fourth
   c. Thirtieth
   d. Among the highest

5. From 1819 to 1923, the means of execution in Texas was _____ until it switched to electrocution in 1923.

   a. Firing squad
   b. Hanging
   c. Beheading
   d. Lethal injection

6. The number of Texas prisoners executed in 2014 was . . .

   a. 1
   b. 4
   c. 10
   d. 35

7. Grand jury reforms in Texas now allow district judges and jury commissioners to select the individuals to serve on a grand jury.

   a. True
   b. False

8. Texas has a history of being "tough on crime."

   a. True
   b. False

9. Felony disenfranchisement (or criminal disenfranchisement) is the loss of voting rights for those currently incarcerated and also for felons who have been released.

   a. True
   b. False

10. The standard for parole is the same for all cases, no matter what crime the prisoner committed.

    a. True
    b. False

[Answers: C, B, A, D, B, C, B, A, A, B]

Learn more with this chapter's digital tools, including the Oxford Insight Study Guide, at www.oup.com/he/Rottinghaus3e.

12 | LOCAL GOVERNMENT

One hot, June afternoon in Overton, Texas, 7- and 8-year-old Zoey and Andria Green set up a lemonade stand, hoping to raise money for a Father's Day gift. Police Chief Clyde Carter paid them a visit and shut down the operation because the girls lacked a $150 peddler's permit from the city.[1] The incident made headlines, and Governor Abbott pointed to this regulation as a classic example of government overreach when he set out to axe this local regulation and more in the 2019 legislative session.[2] Calling it a "common-sense" law, he tweeted on signing the legislation, "Capitalism is for kids!"[3]

Hoping to encourage businesses to operate across city and county lines, Governor Abbott critiqued the "multiple rifle shot" approach legislators were taking to override local regulations and instead suggested a broad law to prevent local regulations from exceeding a standard set by the state.[4] The tension centered on disagreements about "local control"—which level of government should have it and when.[5] Not all of the governor's suggested legislation passed, but limitations on local authority, such as the bill legalizing lemonade stands, did.

Legislation in recent years has aimed to roll back or limit local government's power to ban fees on tree removal, hike local property taxes, issue ordinances banning plastic bags, fingerprint drivers of ride-sharing companies (like Uber), designate historic landmarks, and ban short-term rentals like Airbnb.[6] These **preemption** laws are becoming more common in statehouses across the country, especially as Republican legislatures attempt to control local municipal governments that are run by Democrats.[7] Preemption hinges on the supremacy of state laws that control the actions of local government

12.1	Compare the functions and powers of local and state governments.
12.2	Outline the powers held by county government offices.
12.3	Explain the forms under which cities can incorporate.
12.4	Classify the types of city government.
12.5	Analyze the benefits and challenges of special districts.
12.6	Describe the process and challenges of local government elections.
12.7	Identify problems facing local government and possible solutions.

preemption: the supremacy of rules and laws handed down at the state level

● After the city shut down the lemonade stand, the Green girls set up again offering the lemonade for free. Customers gave the girls tips.

and restrain local flexibility. Not all of these efforts pass, but the long-fought feud between state and local leaders quickly turns into open warfare.[8]

A central struggle of modern government is the battle between state and local authorities over social policy and financial autonomy. Cities are given some autonomy to act but are still tethered to the laws of the state and are dependent on state and federal funds to operate. In this chapter, we examine the powers and types of local government. We then explore the role of smaller governments in local politics. Finally, we examine the problems facing local government. Pressures on city government to provide resources to residents and to promote economic growth may collide as modern cities confront tight fiscal times, minimal state aid, and a public that demands low taxes but robust services.

12.1 THE POWERS AND FUNCTIONS OF LOCAL GOVERNMENT

> **12.1** Compare the functions and powers of local and state governments.

Local governments are often considered less powerful than state or national governments, and yet the actions taken by local governments have some of the most profound impacts on the daily lives of Texans. Local governments provide an extensive range of services, most often related to public safety (fire and police), sanitation, planning for future development, maintenance of roads, incentives for local economic development, and access to recreational facilities. Yet local governments struggle with state government, businesses, interest groups, and even their own citizens in providing these services.

DILLON'S RULE

Dillon's rule: a ruling that established state governments can place restrictions on municipalities as long as these rules do not violate the state's constitution

Although the state and federal governments share power across a range of policy issues, local government is often fenced in by state authority. The U.S. Constitution does not mention local government. However, state leaders have interpreted the Tenth Amendment as giving states authority over local entities. In 1868, **Dillon's rule**, named after the Iowa justice, John Foster Dillon, whose legal rulings founded the principle, established that state governments can place restrictions on municipalities as long as these rules do not violate

GREAT TEXAS POLITICAL DEBATES
Paid Sick Leave

In 2018, the City of San Antonio voted to require all private employers with more than 15 workers in the city to provide employees at least 6 to 8 days of paid sick leave. A number of other cities like Austin and Dallas have passed similar measures to mandate paid sick leave. Several studies have found the impact on local businesses to be minimal and activists called it "a basic right," but opponents responded that the free market should determine these types of policies, not a government mandate.[9] Legislation was introduced in 2019 to ban cities from requiring paid sick leave, and while it did not pass, Texas courts stepped in and ruled that local paid sick leave ordinances conflict with state law.

SOCIAL RESPONSIBILITY: **Should the state have broad control over city issues?**

YES: The state has an overarching obligation to look out for interests of the whole state. Texans have a right to be able to operate small businesses that are not stifled by local regulations. Moreover, small businesses are the economic backbone of the state, so local governments should not be allowed to tax or regulate them "out of business."

NO: If the city isn't violating any other laws or running afoul of the state constitution, they should have the right to self-governance. Localities should have the ability to fit the rules and procedures to their local problems. City and county governments do a better job than state government on such issues.

MAYBE: Some issues are best handled from a statewide perspective, while others are best handled locally. State oversight on all local issues creates inflexibility, but adequate controls and oversight are needed to ensure that laws are not broken and that local laws are not inconsistent with state priorities.

---

the state's constitution. Furthermore, unless the state directly grants a local government a specific power, local governments must assume they do *not* have that power. Texas grants local governments the power to choose the form of government, the fiscal role of local government, and which offices can be filled by election or appointment. Local governments spend considerable time lobbying state governments for expanded power or fewer restrictions, and states have delegated more authority to cities in the last half century. Today, state power still rules the yard, but power struggles do erupt when city and state needs periodically diverge.

LOCAL REGULATION

City governments "legislate" by using **ordinances**, the local laws of a municipal area, passed by a city council. In providing services and dealing more directly with the people, local governments often grapple with policy issues that are not addressed at the state or national level. Everybody loves spring break, for example, but when the city council on South Padre Island, a popular beach spot for spring breakers, grew worried about underage drinking and emergency services capacity during peak vacation times, they passed an ordinance in 2017 to require permits for organizers of events over 1,000 people.[10]

ordinances: the local laws of a municipal area, passed by a city council

I BELIEVE IN "LOCAL CONTROL"...

MEANING, I CONTROL YOU LOCALLY...

ABBOTT

NICKANDERSON
HOUSTON CHRONICLE

MUNICIPALITIES

SOCIAL RESPONSIBILITY: **Should statewide officials be responsible for governing local areas?**

The Fort Worth City Council ruffled some feathers when it passed an ordinance to limit residents to 12 hens if they lived on an acre of land or less.[11] And the San Antonio City Council considered an ordinance to add new fines for drivers who illegally pass stopped school buses, authorizing school districts to install cameras on buses to capture violators.[12]

⬣ TEXAS TAKEAWAYS

12.1.1 How does Dillon's rule relegate state and local authority?

12.1.2 What functions do local governments fulfill?

⬣ 12.2 COUNTY GOVERNMENT

12.2 Outline the powers held by county government offices.

Texas—and much of the United States—witnessed an explosion of local governments as rural expanses converted to urban centers during the nineteenth and twentieth centuries. The number of current local governments in the United States totals just over 89,000, many in Texas (see Figure 12.1). The illusion of a small government ethos in Texas is shattered by the sheer number and impact of local governments. Texas has several different types of local government—counties, cities, and special districts—that scramble to fulfill the growing needs of the people.

The state legislature approves the creation of new counties. During the Republic of Texas, the state had a modest 23 counties. When Texas became a state, that number increased to 36. By 1931, and continuing to the present, the number became fixed at 254. This rise in the number of counties multiplied the number of elected officials and gave residents a more direct relationship with county officials.

Counties are the local arm of state government, carrying out state laws because they cannot enact their own ordinances. Counties serve dual purposes: they provide government services for residents and administrative services on behalf of the state.[13] Counties' responsibilities include public safety, property tax collection, jails, transportation and roads, elections, and environmental protection.

IS IT BIGGER IN TEXAS?

FIGURE 12.1 Number of Local Governments

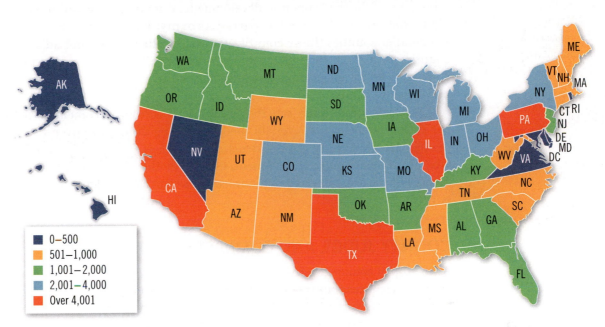

0–500
501–1,000
1,001–2,000
2,001–4,000
Over 4,001

Source: U.S. Census Bureau.

COMMUNICATION:

Which states have the most local government entities?

- Illinois stands out with almost 7,000 localities, which is 2,000 more than Pennsylvania, the state with the next most governments.

- Texas is in the top three with 4,856 total governments, behind Pennsylvania but ahead of California.

CRITICAL THINKING:

Why do some states have more local governments?

- States with large populations have more local governments.

- In some states, like Illinois, localities have increased the number of municipalities to thwart limits on debt and taxes.

- Some states, like California, grant authority to local government to handle water and other issues.

- In some states, responsibility for policy issues is shifted to local government entities. For instance, Nevada administers public libraries at the county level where Texas has smaller library districts.

Some counties are small: Rockwall County, east of Dallas, is only 148 square miles. Some counties are huge: Brewster County, home to the Terlingua Chili Cookoff, is more than 6,000 square miles, three times the size of Delaware. Size impacts governance, with larger counties having few restrictions. In larger counties, for example, county government leaders play a bigger role in the economic development of **unincorporated areas**, regions that are administered as part of a county but not a city. By contrast, 173 smaller counties (those counties that do not have or are not adjacent to counties with 250,000 residents or fewer) are not allowed by state law to have a fire code that would establish regulations on fire prevention and the storage of dangerous goods.

unincorporated areas: regions that are administered as part of a county but not a city

The legislature rigidly sets the structure of county governments, whether the county includes just over 100 people (Loving County) or over 4 million people (Harris County).[14] This structure comprises dozens of local officials who administer county government, elected by the county voters. Only the Texas legislature can—and sometimes does—authorize changes to county government structure.

COUNTY JUDGE AND COMMISSIONER'S COURT

At the top of county government are the county judge and the commissioner's court. Each Texas county is run by a county judge, and a commissioner's court is made up of four county commissioners. These commissioners serve 4-year terms and represent districts that must have equal populations, as decided by the U.S. Supreme Court in *Avery v. Midland County* (1968).

County judges are frequently called on to manage crises that occur in their jurisdictions, as they are responsible for homeland security and emergency management in their counties. County commissioners adopt a tax rate for the county, oversee a budget that they use to establish public works projects, and maintain county buildings and facilities. The largest expenditures are infrastructure (roads or bridges) and maintenance of the county jail.

Like cities, counties often engage in regulation. By Texas law, game rooms—businesses that operate popular "eight-liner" slot machines that cannot pay out more than $5—can legally operate. However, it is an open secret that payouts and prizes worth more are doled out to winning

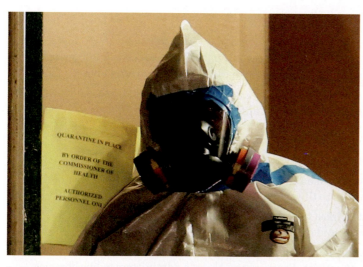

In Dallas, County, Judge Clay Jenkins was confronted with a public health crisis: the first U.S. case of the Ebola virus in 2014. Judge Jenkins led the efforts to contain the spread of the virus, working with the Dallas County Health Department, the Texas Department of State Health Services, and the Centers for Disease Control and Prevention.

customers. Tarrant County approved a laundry list of requirements for booming game rooms, including limited operating hours, restrictions on locations next to schools or churches, and mandating clear signage signaling it is a "game room."[15]

County commissioners allocate funds for projects and make strategic decisions for the county. For instance, the Grimes County Commissioner's Court voted unanimously in 2016 to require the developers of a high-speed rail connecting Dallas and Houston to obtain homeowner approval to build the line and maintain access to county roads. The purpose of the requirement was to protect the farms and ranches that dotted the central Texas county. When county commissioners misuse their budget power, however, they can get into legal trouble. After Dallas County Commissioner John Wiley Price was indicted on allegations a lobbyist paid almost $1 million in bribes in cash, cars, and land in exchange for actions that benefited corporate clients, cities like Dallas and Austin passed mandatory lobbying regulations laws.[16]

COUNTY SHERIFF

The county sheriff—part administrator, part politician, and full-time law enforcement officer—is often referred to as the "lord of the county line."[17] Sheriffs are charged with enforcing state laws, managing and operating the county jail, serving warrants and civil papers to residents, seizing property after court judgments, enforcing traffic laws on county roads, and providing security for the courts. In rural areas, the sheriff is often an all-around diplomat, troubleshooter, master of the county courthouse, and the last person teenagers want to see while drinking beer with their friends on remote county roads.[18] In larger urban areas, sheriffs and their many deputies patrol county roads and oversee the county jail. The number of inmates in any given month can reach several thousand. Careful management is critical as these jails functionally serve as the largest mental health facility in each county because those arrested and awaiting bail or trial often have mental health issues.

COUNTY PROSECUTORS

The county attorney and district attorney are the chief prosecutors for criminal cases in Texas counties. The county attorney operates at the county court level, and the district attorney handles the district court level. These officials often make policy as well. In a controversial move, Harris County District Attorney Kim Ogg announced in 2017 that people caught with less than 4 ounces of marijuana had the option of taking a drug education course.[19] The objective was to give nonviolent drug users a chance to avoid conviction, save space in jails, and reserve court administrative resources. Opponents of the move challenged the ruling, stressing that the district attorney needed to get tougher, not more lenient, on drug abusers.

Illegal massage parlors, often fronts for prostitution and sex trafficking, are found within 1,000 feet of more than 35,000 public school children. Texas county officials, from the district clerks who license businesses to the district attorneys who prosecute offenders, work together to shut down these operations. "This is a tremendous battle," said one county district attorney because of the sheer number of operations.

SOCIAL RESPONSIBILITY: **Is county government too complex to deal with a problem that spans several bureaucratic areas?**

COUNTY ADMINISTRATORS

Several positions are purely administrative and have little influence on policy. A district clerk, if a county has one, is predominately a legal recordkeeper, administering child support payments, processing court fees, and recording all proceedings of the district courts. If you want to run a felony background check on your future spouse, the district clerk keeps these records. A county clerk maintains county records (like birth certificates), issues vital documents (like marriage licenses), and serves as the chief elections officer.

Although primarily administrators, clerks can find themselves in the middle of state or national political battles. Following the U.S. Supreme Court's 2015 ruling that states could not restrict same-sex couples from marrying, Texas Attorney General Ken Paxton issued a statement encouraging clerks to follow their own religious beliefs and not issue marriage licenses to same-sex couples, but also to expect lawsuits for violating the law. The attorney general's advice proved confusing to many clerks. Brewster County Clerk Berta Rios Martinez e-mailed colleagues: "I just had my first gay couple come in for a marriage license and I ran them off!! . . . Did I do right? HELP!!!"[20] Ultimately, clerks were required to issue licenses, and those who refused were reassigned to a different job responsibility.

COUNTY FINANCE OFFICIALS

Several elected officials handle the county finances. The county tax assessor-collector collects revenue for both the state and the county and, in some counties, maintains the county voter rolls. The county auditor oversees the distribution of county funds. The county treasurer receives, manages, and pays out county funds for both general revenue (through property taxes, controlled by the commissioner's court) and special revenue (from fees or other dedicated revenue, controlled by other governments such as special districts).

TEXAS TAKEAWAYS

12.2.1 Why has the number of local governments grown?

12.2.2 What are the responsibilities of county governments?

12.2.3 Who runs the county government, and what is their role?

12.3 CITY GOVERNMENTS

From the end of the Republic in 1845 until 1858, the only way to incorporate a city in Texas was by special act of the state legislature.[21] In the state's early days, most cities were general law cities, operating under laws created by the legislature. Today, as city populations and responsibilities have grown, most large cities are home rule cities, giving them greater autonomy. Texas has approximately 1,200 incorporated cities.

> **12.3** Explain the forms under which cities can incorporate.

GENERAL LAW CITIES

In the nineteenth century, the Texas legislature passed general laws that define the structure and powers of general law cities. If a **general law city** has not been specifically granted authority to act by the legislature, it may not undertake the action. General law cities, for example, may not add mandatory fees to utility bills without permission of the state.[22]

State law officials may also step in when local ordinances conflict with state laws. This happened in 2016 when a group called Texas Voices for Reason and Justice sent a letter to 45 Texas general law cities demanding they repeal residency restrictions for sex offenders. The group argued that towns that passed these restrictions were in violation of the state constitution because the legislature had not granted them express permission to pass such laws.[23] The state agreed, and the restrictions were lifted.

general law city: a city that is only allowed to operate under laws the state provides

HOME RULE CITIES

By the early twentieth century, the state was growing rapidly enough to outstrip the legislature's ability to routinely deal with local matters. The number of cities grew by about 10 per year.[24] By 1913, the state allowed municipalities to become home rule cities, giving them the authority to choose the structure of their government (such as size and method used to elect the city council), annex land adjacent to the city, set property tax rates, create boards and commissions to handle city issues, and enact policies and rules for the city as long as they were not prohibited by state or federal law.[25] Unlike general law cities, a **home rule city** is permitted to do anything unless *prohibited* by state law. This is referred to as "inherent power" and has been sanctioned by the Texas Supreme Court. Any city in Texas with more than 5,000 people can become a home rule city. Most large cities in Texas have home rule (only 19 of the 309 cities with more than 5,000 Texans do not have home rule status).

A home rule city **charter** serves as the municipality's organizational plan, similar to a state or national constitution. A city charter establishes the form of government, sets the rules for operation and amendment, and establishes procedures for taxing and spending city finances. City government may

home rule city: a city that is allowed self-governance independent of state law

charter: a city's governing document

The City of Austin changed the rules of the road for electric scooters in 2019, banning multiple riders and requiring riders to wear helmets if they are under 18 and to avoid blocking sidewalks or building entrances when they park. El Paso and San Antonio issued similar regulations, banning riding the devices on sidewalks. Other local ordinances examples include banning specific dog breeds (like pit bulls), banning cell phones while driving, and restricting residency for registered sex offenders.

www.kut.org/post/austin-now-has-rules-dockless-scooter-riders

PERSONAL RESPONSIBILITY: **What sort of ordinance do you think your city should pass to address a substantive local problem? Is this better handled at the local or state level?**

Initiative, Referendum, and Recall. Citizens of home rule cities have the power to initiate policy issues or recall local public officials. What are these powers?

initiative: a process through which local voters can directly propose ordinances to city charters

referendum: a procedure through which local voters can repeal existing ordinances that a city council won't rescind

recall: a process through which voters can oust sitting members of the city government before their terms are up

amend the charter as needed. Citizens can force lawmakers on the city council to call an election and amend a city charter by filling out a petition signed by 5 percent of qualified voters or 20,000 qualified voters (whichever is less). Indeed, one of the main advantages of home rule cities over general law cities is the mechanism of direct democracy.

An **initiative** is a process through which local voters can directly propose ordinances to city charters. If the proper number of signatures is obtained (the number is set by the city), the initiative is placed on the ballot in an election, and if a majority of voters agree, the initiative becomes law. For example, voters in Texarkana used an initiative to approve beer and wine sales in 2014, allowing them to keep pace with their alcohol-selling kin on the Arkansas side of the border.[26]

A **referendum** enables voters to repeal existing ordinances that a city council won't rescind. Once citizens gather a sufficient number of signatures, the ordinance is put before the city council to repeal on its own or is put to all voters for repeal. College Station, for example, used a referendum to submit to voters a plan to ban the use of red light cameras (unmanned digital cameras that photograph a vehicle running a red light). College Station citizens then voted to remove red light cameras by a slim 51 percent.[27]

A **recall** enables voters to oust sitting members of the city government before their terms are up. Most cities only allow recalls after a council member has served for a set period and limit the number of recall attempts of the same councilperson. In each case, these powers are designed to give citizens greater control over local government. Although few of these recalls are successful in removing the public officials in question, the cities have to front the cost of these elections.[28] Over 4,400 Plano residents signed a recall petition against Plano City Council member Tom Harrison after he posted an inflammatory and seemingly anti-Islam Facebook post in 2018 after a group.[29] A Texas Court of Appeals ruled the city used the wrong number to certify the petition, ending the recall effort.

Annexation. In the past, the strongest power of a home rule city was **annexation**, the joining of land into the boundary of an existing city. It is through annexation authority that big Texas cities became gigantic. A larger city could not annex incorporated land—land that is unified as part of a city—but rather targeted *unincorporated* areas, which are often developing or ripe for development.

Annexation provided a larger tax base, thus enabling cities to benefit from the financial growth of outlying, usually suburban areas. These growing cities pulled in more taxpayers and became wealthier. In fact, if San Antonio had the same boundaries today as in 1945, it would have the highest poverty and unemployment rate of any city in the nation. Annexation of more territory expanded that city's revenue.

In the past, unincorporated areas or cities were generally powerless to stop a larger city from annexing it into their territory because cities did not need the permission of the residents of an area to annex it. Beginning in 1994, for example, the City of Houston announced plans to annex an affluent suburb called Kingwood with over 50,000 residents. Protesters showed up in busloads in Austin asking the legislature to halt Houston's expansion and carrying banners that read "Free Kingwood." Residents offered $4 million to the City of Houston in exchange for the community's independence. Kingwood residents also filed a lawsuit charging that annexation laws amounted to taxation without representation, echoing the familiar rallying cry of the American Revolution. All efforts failed, and Kingwood was absorbed into Houston's city limits.[30]

In 2019, however, the legislature passed and Governor Greg Abbott signed a bill to end "forced annexation" for Texas's 10 largest counties, protecting the property rights of those in rural parts of Texas according to advocates.[31] Opponents argue that the law will kill the ability of larger cities to manage growth and development as populations in large counties continue to boom.

annexation: the joining of unincorporated land into the boundary of an existing city

---

INSIDER INTERVIEW

Local activist Barry Klein, Texas Property Rights Association

How can citizens use the initiative and referendum process to make a difference?

Micro-politics holds the prospect of genuine and ever-renewing reform in the American political system. Currently, the United States has in excess of 5,400 home rule cities. Most are small enough that five-person teams of grassroots reformers can quickly gather sufficient signatures to put propositions on a city ballot that amend the local charter. This can occur hundreds of times a year across the country, creating new norms of governance that would inevitably shape the policy discussions at higher levels of government.

SOCIAL RESPONSIBILITY: **Some municipalities have attempted to increase the number of signatures required to amend a city charter to give government more control over policy. Should the public have more or less direct control over city policy? Why?**

Cities, however, can also tax and regulate unincorporated areas without fully annexing them. Under the 1999 reforms, cities were allowed to create agreements with local utility districts to charge a 1 percent sales tax in locations outside the proper city limits.[32] With city budgets more difficult to balance and outlying areas wary of full annexation, this regulation served as a backdoor solution to the annexation quagmire. Cities also use extraterritorial jurisdiction laws to control subdivision practices in unincorporated bordering territory.[33] Businesses or developers seeking to build in those areas are subject to city rules and regulations.

🇹🇽 TEXAS TAKEAWAYS

12.3.1 How are general law cities different from home rule cities?

12.3.2 How do home rule cities allow for a more direct democracy?

12.4 TYPES OF CITY GOVERNMENT

12.4 Classify the types of city government.

Today, cities govern themselves in different ways: a mayor–council form, a commission form, and a council–manager form. Let's look at each type.

MAYOR–COUNCIL SYSTEM

mayor–council system: a system of local government headed by an elected mayor and a city council

In the **mayor–council system**, a mayor acts as an executive, and a city council acts as a legislative body, enacting ordinances and adopting rules. There are strong and weak mayor–council systems.

In a weak-mayor system, the mayor has no formal authority to act outside of the council. The mayor lacks veto power, and other important city officers, such as the treasurer or department heads, are elected by the people.

In strong-mayor systems, the mayor has legislative powers (voting on many matters and presiding over city council meetings) and often exercises executive powers unilaterally. The mayor also can often take a wide range of independent actions, with little input from the council or the public. The mayor appoints the city judiciary, major boards and commissions, and department heads. The mayor also prepares the annual budget for the city. The city council must vote on the budget, and the city controller usually has an important say. However, the mayor is the first and the last to act as he or she also executes the budget. Perhaps most importantly, the mayor sets the agenda for city council meetings.

Irving mayor Beth Van Duyne sparked a controversy when she placed an item on the agenda to have the council back a bill in the state legislature that

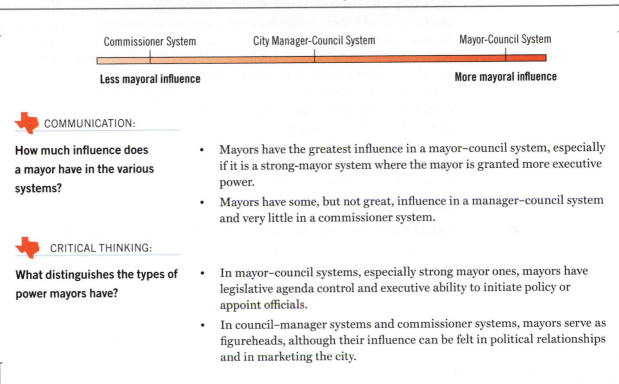

FIGURE 12.2 **Scale of Mayoral Influence**

Commissioner System   City Manager-Council System   Mayor-Council System

Less mayoral influence   **More mayoral influence**

COMMUNICATION:

How much influence does a mayor have in the various systems?

- Mayors have the greatest influence in a mayor–council system, especially if it is a strong-mayor system where the mayor is granted more executive power.
- Mayors have some, but not great, influence in a manager–council system and very little in a commissioner system.

CRITICAL THINKING:

What distinguishes the types of power mayors have?

- In mayor–council systems, especially strong mayor ones, mayors have legislative agenda control and executive ability to initiate policy or appoint officials.
- In council–manager systems and commissioner systems, mayors serve as figureheads, although their influence can be felt in political relationships and in marketing the city.

would forbid judges from using foreign law in their rulings. Several council members felt that the agenda item targeted a local Islamic Center that was using the Islamic code to settle disputes in a nonbinding way. The mayor argued that Islamic leaders were "bypassing Americans courts."[34] Several council members disputed the need for such a measure and argued that it only served to increase religious tension. However, the council passed the resolution by a 5-to-4 vote.

Mayors' power to implement their agenda is limited by the city council and their own budgets. The city council must approve the annual budget, sign off on appointments of department heads, and certify significant reallocations of budget funds during a year. The mayor must have the majority of support on the city council, in both the mayor–council system and other systems of local government (see Figure 12.2). Hostility between the players can halt a city's agenda, like in 2020 when tension between Dallas Mayor Eric Johnson and City Manager T.C. Brodnax seeped into a council meeting: "I am the city manager. I run this city," said the City Manager. "It's my job to maintain order in this meeting, and that's a fact," responded the Mayor.[35] Months later, the Mayor proposed cutting "bloated" city hall salaries, including the $400,000 salary of City Manager T.C. Brodnax. The city council rejected the cuts.[36]

Most mayors typically act in a nonpartisan fashion, often because they are elected as nonpartisans. Most city officials function as pragmatic problem solvers. One official noted, "A road is a road, and it doesn't care if you're a socialist or pro-life."[37] Often, however, they become ensnared in nonpartisan conflicts. City controllers (often called comptrollers) oversee and audit government finances, monitor compliance with laws, and serve vital efforts at transparency and credibility. In a high-profile instance, Houston City Controller Chris Brown became concerned when a $37 million recycling deal lacked transparency in the procurement process and its proposed subcontractor was named as a defendant in employment lawsuits. In 2017, Brown blocked the city council vote authorizing the project by not certifying city funds to fulfill the contracts.[38]

COMMISSION GOVERNMENT

Called the "Galveston Plan," the commission form of government resulted from the catastrophic Galveston hurricane of 1900 that claimed more than 6,000 lives and caused millions of dollars in property damage. Community leaders feared the fragile island city might never recover its prosperity under the leadership of the city council at the time, and so they persuaded the governor to appoint a commission during the rebuilding period. The commission served as the legislative and executive body for the city, handling taxation, appropriations, ordinances, and other functions.[39]

The commission form of government became popular in the early 1900s for its simplicity, nonpartisan approach, and merit selection. These features, however, also made it susceptible to corruption. Progressive reformers viewed the commission as a way to disenfranchise working-class citizens and to promote a business-friendly agenda by selecting commissioners cordial to industry. This government type was also highly influenced by political elites, became inefficient, and neglected basic city services.[40] As a result, no true commission form of government exists in Texas today. Rather, most Texas cities that switched to a commission government early in the 1900s changed to a more professional council–manager system later in the century.

COUNCIL–MANAGER SYSTEM

If you want to run a government like a corporation, a council–manager system is the best fit. In a **council–manager system**, the board of directors (the city council), acting on behalf of the stockholders (the people), appoints a chief executive officer (the city manager) to run city business. The **city manager** runs the day-to-day operations in the city and serves as the chief administrator and budget officer for the city. The city manager's primary role is to enforce city regulations, supervise municipal employees and programs, execute the city budget, and prepare the agenda of the city council.

In a council–manager system, the mayor and council members have no administrative duties. This does not mean they are unimportant. The city council

council–manager system: a system of local government in which the city council appoints a city manager to run city business

city manager: an administrator hired to run the day-to-day operations of a city

sets all city policies, rules, and the budget. Mayors serve an important but largely symbolic role. They have only one vote as a member of the council and no veto power, but they can use their personality and popularity to push their agenda. Fort Worth Mayor Betsy Price rode her bicycle to "rolling town hall meetings" at different venues across the city to encourage other city residents to do the same—that is, participate politically and stay fit at the same time.[41]

Dallas, the largest city to use the council–manager system of government, relies on its mayor as chief salesperson for the business community, agenda setter for political issues, and advocate for the values of city residents. In 2016, for example, Mayor Mike Rawlings tried to prevent Exxxotica, a pornography exhibition, from appearing at the Kay Bailey Hutchinson Convention Center in downtown Dallas. The mayor requested that the city attorney draft a resolution to direct the city manager not to enter into a contract with the organization to lease the space. The city's attorneys indicated that such a move would be an unconstitutional violation of free speech.[42] So, the mayor put public pressure on the city council to ban the convention, which the city council did in an 8-to-7 vote.[43] The city paid the legal bills to the tune of $650,000 for Exxxotica's parent corporation to settle a lawsuit in 2019.[44]

Studies show that growing cities often move from a mayor–council system to a council–manager arrangement.[45] This system is argued to provide a higher level of professionalism, continuity, and stability. In fact, about 90 percent of Texas home rule cities have a council–manager system.

One downside of the council–manager system is that it gives more power to the unelected officials than to the elected officials, allowing the city manager to set the agenda and enforce rules even over the objections of the elected city council. Cities, however, are at liberty to decrease the power of the city manager or even fire him or her. As a result, many city council members prefer the manager system because it gives them greater control over city priorities and finances and prevents mayors from becoming too dictatorial.

Although the council–manager system is designed to get the politics out of government, it can invite corruption. One Dallas city manager approved a deal to sell land worth $1.7 million to major real estate developer Ray Hunt for just $2,000. Hunt also did not want to pay property taxes on the land, so the city manager placed an item on the agenda to exempt the property from 90 percent of those taxes for 10 years. The council approved this by a vote of 10 to 5.[46]

Scholars have found that failures to govern ethically may result in calls to move away from council–manager systems.[47] As a result, larger cities outside of Texas frequently change to strong-mayor systems. Dallas, however, overwhelmingly voted not to "take off the training wheels" and maintained its council–manager system.[48]

El Paso City Manager Tommy Gonzales was sanctioned for violating the city's ethics ordinance for his role in several city projects, including street repaving and other mobility projects.

PERSONAL RESPONSIBILITY: **Should the standard for removal from office be the same for an elected official as for an unelected manager?**

⭐ **TEXAS TAKEAWAYS**

12.4.1 What are the differences between a strong-mayor system and a weak-mayor system?

12.4.2 How are powers and responsibilities allocated in a council–manager government?

⚓ 12.5 SPECIAL DISTRICTS

12.5 Analyze the benefits and challenges of special districts.

special districts: a single-purpose government that performs a specialized function

County and city governments cover only a small fraction of the governments in Texas. **Special districts** make up the bulk of the local government in the state. These are single-purpose governments performing a specialized function, such as education, water supply, economic development, or hospital care.[49] These districts originated during the New Deal in the 1930s as a way to generate revenue and govern locally without having to sort through layers of state or local government. Special districts raise their funds from property taxes, giving way to concern about the rising tax burden from citizens. These governments operate in a set geographic area and are created because of an inability by other governments to provide a particular service. As Texas expands in population and through urban growth, the battle to keep government small will be fought at the level of special districts, which is where government is growing rapidly.

One advantage of these districts is that they specialize in a single issue or set of issues and allow residents to have input into local decisions. Another advantage is that these districts do not require state funds, but rather can raise revenue on their own. A disadvantage is that they operate outside the view of most citizens. These special districts are often referred to as "invisible governments" because they are less visible, but no less important, than city or county government.[50] Another disadvantage is possible inefficiency of overlapping services provided by city or county governments.

Nationwide, there are more than 50,000 such districts. Texas relies heavily on them (see Figure 12.3). Several types of special districts are highlighted and discussed here.

SCHOOL DISTRICTS

Texans interact most frequently with a special district we know as our local school district. As smaller, rural systems have been consolidated with larger ones, the number of school districts in Texas has declined to the current 1,021. School boards of trustees oversee the school districts, managing schools and

IS IT BIGGER IN TEXAS?

FIGURE 12.3 Special-Purpose Districts Nationwide

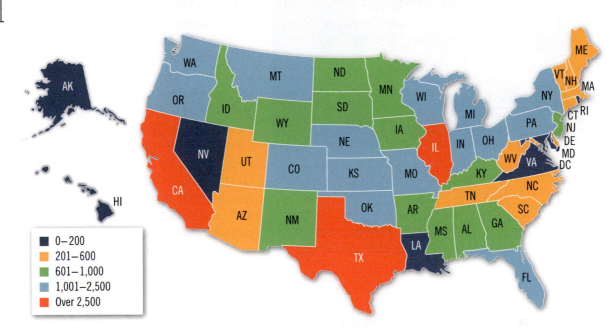

0–200
201–600
601–1,000
1,001–2,500
Over 2,500

Source: U.S. Census Bureau. Excludes school districts.

 COMMUNICATION:

How many special districts are there in each state?

- Texas is second only to Illinois and California in the number of special districts.
- Pennsylvania, Missouri, and Colorado follow Texas in the top six states with the most special districts.

 CRITICAL THINKING:

Why do some states have more special districts?

- Decentralized government allows patronage at the local level, which is preferred by politicians in states with a larger urban population.
- Fast-growing states (especially those having large suburban populations) with diverse local needs have expanded special districts for services like fire protection, sanitation, and public utilities.
- In Texas, local governments have taxing authority. As the state budget is less generous to local governments, special districts proliferate and raise money for local needs.

School board members are elected by the community and make important decisions about the local school system. Three Rivers Independent School District in southern Texas, for example, approved "paddling" at public schools for misbehavior. Parents can opt in or opt out.

SOCIAL RESPONSIBILITY: **Should school board members bend to national pressure, or should they reflect local values that they were elected to represent?**

selecting superintendents. They make final decisions on district policies, personnel, textbooks, and budgets. Board members have exclusive power to govern and tax residents within the district and are chosen through nonpartisan elections, usually to 3- to 4-year terms.

School district authority extends to all aspects of education, and they have exclusive control over what can be assigned to students within them. In 2019, the Lake Travis school district, outside of Austin, banned *1984* by George Orwell for not being age appropriate; the Blum Independent School District (ISD), outside of Hillsboro, banned Malcom X's biography, arguing that it was offensive on religious and racial grounds; and the Franklin ISD banned *Drama* by Raina Telgemeier, a graphic novel about friendship, crushes, and middle school drama, citing inappropriate material.[51]

SPECIAL IMPROVEMENT DISTRICTS

Special (or public) improvement districts allow an area to levy and collect special assessments on properties for a limited range of services, including landscaping, construction, parking facilities, and improving streets and sidewalks. The Woodlands, Texas, north of Houston, has 110,000 residents. It is classified as a district, not a city, to the consternation of its residents. "It frustrates the hell out of me," said a board member, complaining that these districts have "no power to do anything." Another resident expressed a desire for an incorporated city with a charter "rather than a book of covenants that only tell you how far up the driveway your kid's in-ground basketball goal must be." State law, however, was amended to allow the township board, a special improvement district that oversees city operations, to issue **municipal bonds** (like a bank loan paid back at a future date) and avoid annexation by Houston or Conroe until 2057.[52]

municipal bonds: debt securities where a municipality takes out a loan to spend funds and agrees to pay the funds back, generally with interest

JUNIOR/COMMUNITY COLLEGE DISTRICTS

Texas has more than 50 locally governed community college or junior college districts (or boards) for institutions that offer vocational and academic courses for certification, continuing education, or associate degrees. The board sets district policy, the cost of tuition and fees, the budget, and the school calendar.

A president or chancellor is hired by the board to govern day-to-day activities at the college.

LIBRARY DISTRICTS

In 1987, the Texas legislature allowed the creation of districts to enhance community and economic development through various means. Library districts are designed to establish and maintain public libraries for public use. Like other special districts, library districts may request voter approval for a sales and use tax.

MUNICIPAL UTILITY DISTRICTS

A Municipal utility district (MUD) provides water, sewage, drainage, and other services within a fixed boundary. These districts deal primarily with the supply of water, including protection, conservation, and storage. A MUD can be created by the Texas Commission on Environmental Quality or by the legislature. Since a MUD is the only government in many unincorporated areas, they have significant influence. MUDs are popular among developers because they can exclusively enter into cozy contracts with vendors or issue bonds related to district activities to cover the cost of development.[53] This may include solid waste disposal, parks, or swimming pools. The relative invisibility of MUDs, however, may harm accountability: Residents may not know who is in charge, board members are not required to live in the communities they represent, and board meetings may not be held in the districts. Voters in these districts may also be unsure what they are being asked to approve; one bond request asked for the creation of a "defined area" that was not explained in the ballot language.[54]

No one likes being bothered by the buzzing of mosquitoes. Mosquito Control Districts, an example of a special district, are permitted to tax residents to squish out these insects.

SOCIAL RESPONSIBILITY: **Does the proliferation of districts to deal with smaller, targeted issues justify the considerable tax funds they are allowed to raise? Or should other, larger government entities be responsible for these issues?**

HOSPITAL DISTRICTS

Hospital districts provide for the creation, maintenance, and operation of hospitals. These districts have considerable financial power, including the ability to issue bonds and impose taxes, which cannot exceed 75 cents per $100 valuation on taxable property in the district. Hospital districts also have a considerable charge to implement and enforce state laws relating to access to health care, interpreting whether an individual qualifies for health care, and establishing mental health facilities.

HOMEOWNERS' ASSOCIATIONS

Though not technically a special district, homeowners' associations (HOAs) are one of the largest types of government in the state. Nearly 5 million people reside in HOAs statewide.[55] HOAs have government-like power to issue fines and foreclose on homes. Residents who live within the boundary of a HOA agree to a covenant of rules and pay a fee for community maintenance. Membership is not optional: If you live within the boundary, you play by their rules. HOAs are free to choose ancillary service companies and vendors, and they are often strongly encouraged to use those partnered with the parent management company.[56]

State regulations control much of what HOAs are allowed to govern. Sweeping changes to laws passed in 2012 now require HOAs to maintain open public records and hold meetings, post notices of board meetings, strengthen residents' voting rights, and allow greater public expression of opinion. Want to fly your Navy flag on Army–Navy football game day? Want to display your religious beliefs with symbols on your house? The law now allows displaying of flags and religious symbols and exhibits, and it was changed partly in response to an incident where "a Jewish couple was threatened with a recurring fine for displaying a mezuzah, a parchment with Hebrew verses enclosed in a case affixed to the door post."[57] The new laws also established provisions to make sure those serving in the military don't unwittingly lose their homes while deployed, as happened in 2010 to an Army National Guard officer from Frisco.[58]

 TEXAS TAKEAWAYS

12.5.1 Why have special districts grown?

12.5.2 Which special districts are more visible and which are less so?

12.6 ELECTIONS

12.6 Describe the process and challenges of local government elections.

City and county elections can be either partisan or nonpartisan elections. Voters tend to have little interest in these elections, and voter turnout is typically low—even though Texans interact closely with these governments. The outcome of these elections can vary widely as different electoral systems—countywide, citywide, or districtwide—have a significant effect on who gets elected and, in turn, who is represented.

COUNTY ELECTIONS

The county judge and commissioners are elected for 4-year terms in partisan elections. Commissioners are elected to districts that divide the county into four geographic regions. County judges are elected countywide. Once county commissioners are elected, they often serve for a long period of time, being frequently reelected. Each county also elects a county sheriff every 4 years countywide. The positions of county attorney and district attorney are filled by partisan elections held every 4 years, as are positions for most administrative offices.

CITY ELECTIONS

Texas cities elect representatives in one of two ways. At-large elections are citywide and frequently the method used to select mayors, city comptrollers, and district attorneys. City council members, as well as some other offices, are often elected through a **place system** that carves the city into districts (referred to as "positions" or "places"). At-large elections tend to favor candidates who appeal to the majority of electors and who have the money to fund a citywide campaign. The place system tends to result in the election of representatives who are more concerned with voters' concerns in districts that council members represent.

Although most municipal city elections are nonpartisan, both political parties have gotten involved in local elections.[59] The Democratic Party formed Project LIFT (Local Investment in the Future of Texas) to recruit and train Democrats for local nonpartisan offices, and the Texas Republican Party endorses local candidates.[60] Elected officials have also gotten into the game. Governor Abbott endorsed several candidates in contentious local elections in Plano in 2019.

MINORITY REPRESENTATION IN MUNICIPAL GOVERNMENTS

Changing from one type of electoral system to another can create controversy. Beginning in the 1970s, a "gentlemen's agreement" in Austin allotted two seats to racial minorities, but this arrangement did not yield a diversity that reflected the city's makeup. By 2014, half the city council and 15 of the last 17 mayors had been elected from only four zip codes—out of 78 total zip codes in the city.[61] As a result, Austin switched to a place system to elect the city council. The switch to a single-member district place system increased the diversity of candidates and of those elected to the city council, in terms of race and gender, and the public felt more involved in municipal government. Dallas

place system: an electoral system that carves a citywide area into separate district seats for which voters elect council members also reduced the number of at-large seats to one after the courts ruled the eight-three system (eight district and three citywide seats) unconstitutional.

Other localities are moving from district representation to at-large representation, though with much resistance. Pasadena, east of Houston, former home to the honky-tonk Gilley's of the movie *Urban Cowboy* fame, voted to replace two of its eight council seats with at-large seats. Hispanic leaders objected that the move would negate the clout of rising population numbers (the city is more than 60 percent Hispanic). Because Hispanic turnout is low in city elections, Anglos could outvote them in every election in a citywide race.[62]

cumulative voting: system whereby voters cast multiple votes (usually equal to the number of positions in an election)

Some localities have experimented with **cumulative voting** to help boost minority representation. Cumulative voting allows voters to cast as many votes as there are positions, so that if a board or commission had seven seats, voters would have seven ballots to cast. African American and Latino residents sued the City of Amarillo in 1995, claiming that the at-large system for electing school board and college board members unfairly diluted minority influence. The groups settled out of court, and Amarillo agreed to implement a cumulative voting system that ultimately increased minority representation on the boards. An African American and Latino candidate both won in the subsequent election. More recently, in 2016, Carrollton-Farmers Branch ISD adopted cumulative voting in response to a legal challenge. Still, fewer than 50 municipalities conduct elections this way.

LOW-TURNOUT IN MUNICIPAL ELECTIONS

Most Texans don't vote in general, and even those who do vote regularly don't vote in local elections (see Figure 12.4). These elections are often held in May, separate from presidential and congressional elections that attract media attention. As a result, voters are often unfamiliar with the candidates and the issues and skip these elections altogether.

People's age influences whether they vote in local elections. One study found that people over 65 years of age were 19 times more likely to vote in primary elections and 14 times more likely to vote in the general election than people ages 18 to 34.[63] Younger people are more transient, moving frequently, whereas older voters are more likely to live in their homes much longer, establishing roots.

In many cases, only 10 to 15 percent of a city electorate selects leaders and votes on changes to local law. Low turnout can give those who do vote an outsized influence in local finances. A modest turnout of 150,000 voters in Harris County—fewer than 6 percent of registered voters—approved $2.5 billion in county flood projects!

VOTING AND CORRUPTION

In 2016, the federal government arrested all but one of the Crystal City, Texas, council members, including the mayor, city manager, city attorney, and mayor pro temp, for allegedly accepting bribes from contractors who wanted to do

FIGURE 12.4 **Turnout in Local Mayoral Elections in Selected Major Cities**

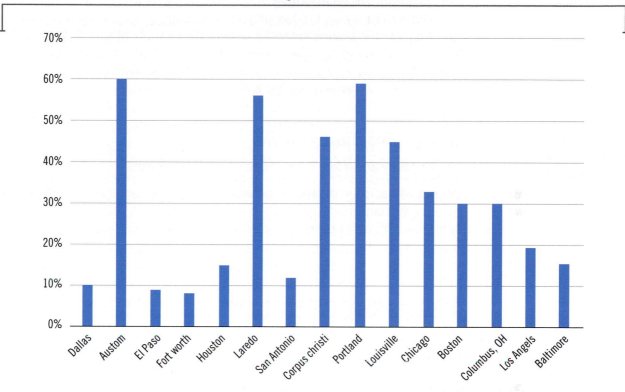

Source: County election websites. Portland State University *(www.whovotesformayor.org). Turnout is the percentage of registered voters.*

 COMMUNICATION:

What percentage of Texans turn out to vote in local elections?

- Turnout is generally low in Texas: Fewer than a third, and usually no more than a quarter, of the electorate vote in local elections.

- Comparatively, cities like Portland, Louisville, and Chicago have higher turnout than most Texas cities.

 CRITICAL THINKING:

Why is turnout in local elections so low?

- Municipal elections often feature candidates who are less familiar to voters than statewide or federal candidates.

- Partisan elections in Louisville and strong mayor systems like Chicago or Boston encourage higher turnout. Portland votes by mail, increasing voter participation.

- Local elections are often held during "off-years" (non-presidential election years) except in Laredo, Corpus Christi, and Austin; therefore, many voters don't show up to vote.

business with the city.[64] Referring to the self-made mess of city government, the executive of the Texas Municipal League said, "There's no state agency that monitors this type of thing."[65]

Ultimately, voters are key players in keeping local government honest. In 2016, Denton County voters kicked out the incumbent sheriff, William B. Travis, after an investigation revealed that in the 1990s, as a Drug Enforcement Agency agent, he had fabricated evidence for a search warrant and had an affair with a high school-aged girl.[66]

★ TEXAS TAKEAWAYS

12.6.1 Why do so few Texans vote in local elections?

12.6.2 What is the difference between at-large elections and the place system?

 # 12.7 ISSUES IN LOCAL GOVERNMENT

12.7 Identify problems facing local government and possible solutions.

Low turnout in local elections is just one of many challenges facing local government in Texas. Let's explore a few more.

LOCAL GOVERNMENTS SHORT ON CASH

The size and functions of local government generally require it to have access to large budgets (see Figure 12.5). City and county operating budgets can run into the tens of millions of dollars to pay for all the services needed within their jurisdictions. Texas cities and counties can levy both property taxes and sales taxes. Most sales tax revenues go to the state, but about 1 to 2 percent is remitted to cities if they charge extra above the state's base tax rate. Home rule cities can also charge residents fees for various projects or businesses' franchise fees.

Property taxes have long been a source of contention in Texas, especially because they are the single largest revenue generator in the state. Property tax receipts in 2017 totaled more than $59.2 billion from owners of everything from houses to commercial real estate. Special- purpose districts had the fastest growing tax rate, increasing 74.3 percent over the past decade.[67] Because the state is not allowed to have a statewide property tax, or anything that resembles one, some residents have argued that the high property tax rate charged by school districts amounts to an unconstitutional de facto state-mandated property tax (as we discuss in Chapter 13). During the 2019 session, the Texas legislature slashed billions of dollars from homeowners'

FIGURE 12.5 **County Expenditures**

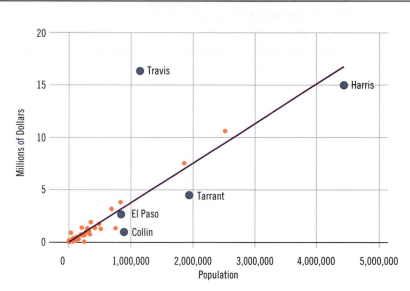

Source: Texas State Expenditures, Texas Comptroller of Public Accounts, 2019. The figure graphs expenditures and population. The fitted line is a linear representation of the two figures. Those counties above the line spent more than their population; those below the line spent less.

 COMMUNICATION:

Where do Texas counties rank on expenditures and population?

- Most counties are close to the line, showing a close correlation between expenditure and population. This means that they spend similar amounts per resident.
- Travis (Austin), Tarrant (Fort Worth), Collin (Plano) and Harris County (Houston) are outliers.

 CRITICAL THINKING:

Why are some counties higher or lower than others?

- A booming Travis County spends considerable funds on public assistance and public employee salaries and benefits, and so it spends more than average.
- Republican-controlled counties in Tarrant and Collin tend to keep budgets small for ideological reasons.

taxes by lowering the "rollback rate" from 8 to 3.5percent. This has reduced revenue for local government.

Tax Increment Reinvestment Zones (or TIRZs) provide one common way to generate additional revenue in city finances. These are special zones created to attract business and develop the economy within a defined geographic area. Taxes collected in these zones, however, are set aside to

Tax Increment Reinvestment Zones: special zones created to attract business and develop the economy within the defined geographic area

finance improvements within the boundaries of that zone, so the city may not collect a penny from the property tax revenue. As a result, these zones become private fiefdoms for trapping money for redevelopment in wealthy areas, often at the expense of poorer areas, and oversight is lax. Indeed, although the intent of the law was to help declining inner-city areas rehabilitate, TIRZs have quietly become a honeypot for developers to gain lucrative city subsidies.

RISING DEBT

In Texas, governments cannot spend more money than they receive in revenue, but they can accrue debt to fund activities. Texas cities and counties frequently issue debt to fund projects if they don't have the funds in the cookie jar. State and local governments that are short on cash can sell bonds to private investors with the promise to pay it back later with interest. Exploding population, the desire to keep taxes low, and the consequent tight budgets have caused local debt to skyrocket in recent years. Bonds typically fund capital projects and long-term programs, including highway construction, technology upgrades, water development, improvements to facilities, and even service of existing debt. Overall, in 2019, Texas local governments owed more than $230 billion in debt.[71] The average debt per capita for Texans is about $8,126.[72]

ANGLES OF POWER
The Stadiums That Ate Texas

Texas's esteemed Friday night lights that illuminate high school football also shine a light on local bond debt and raise questions about who should pay for high-priced football stadiums. School districts around the state appear to be in another competition: to build the most expensive high school football stadium. Under state law, each school district has the power to raise bond money with voter approval, but are these Texas-sized projects busting budgets? McKinney ISD in northern Texas spent some $80 million in voter-approved bond money for a new football stadium, the most expensive nonacademic public school facility in the United States.[68] Neighboring rival Allen ISD built a $72 million stadium with 18,000 seats—the size of an NBA arena—years before and within just a few miles of the McKinney stadium.[69] Twelve of the 48 measures on the ballot in 2017 came from

districts where enrollment had dropped, some by double digits. Floydada ISD in western Texas has lost 22 percent of its student body since 2005 but asked voters to approve $44.7 million in athletic facilities and other upgrades.[70] Critics question the need for such lavish facilities that are only used a few months each year and greatly increase local government debt, while proponents point to projected student growth and the need for a "wow" factor in municipalities to attract businesses and residents. In 2020, when stadium bonds were separated from campus construction or technology bonds, voters often rejected pricey stadiums.

SOCIAL RESPONSIBILITY: **Should school districts ask voters to pay for new or upgraded stadiums?**

Voters must approve bond financing, but they do not always know what they are voting on. One solution is to require ballot propositions to include specific details about the project to be financed. An attentive public can halt debt for undesirable projects. Indeed, this recently occurred in Montgomery County when voters rejected road bond proposals on two separate occasions (in 2014 and 2015). These proposals included a project that would have extended the Woodlands Parkway through undeveloped land, which would have worsened traffic conditions. Only after the bond proposal dropped the controversial parkway extension did it pass in late 2015.[73] City councils can also cap the total amount of debt available, although most have not: It is difficult to curb politicians' appetite for bond-financed revenue (see Table 12.1).

Eventually, the state may be forced to pick up the tab for the interest on the debt, local government may have to raise taxes to pay for some debt, and cities may face a reduced credit rating for large debt financing, making it harder to borrow funds in the future. "This is a pervasive problem at every single level," former State Comptroller Susan Combs insisted. "Nobody gets off scot-free on this."[75]

COOPERATION ACROSS GOVERNMENTS

Cooperation between local governments is challenging. The overlapping and interconnected elements of local governments may create duplicated efforts to address some needs or not enough attention to others as one government assumes another is handling the issue. For instance, Fort Bend County alone has 14 different levee improvement districts that aren't connected to each other, and 2 of these cover a single real estate district. Cooperation can be challenging, considering competing interests and the struggle for scarce budget resources. Conflict and poor communication may hinder planning efforts across these thousands of special districts, county governments, and city governments. For instance, the City of San Antonio pockets $40 million in annual revenue from energy fees in unincorporated city areas that it does not share with Bexar County.[76] The city benefits to the detriment of the county.

Cooperation does occur, but it often is program specific rather than issue specific. Harris County Judge Ed Emmett called for a summit of county and city leaders to address the "outrageous" problem with stray animals, prompted by the refusal of county officials to pick up a dog that lay dying from a gunshot across the street from a shelter facility because it was inside the city's jurisdiction but not the county's.[77] The City of Houston and Harris County have worked on a joint library project, a pauper's cemetery, a spaying and neutering program for stray dogs, and a voter-approved, city–county inmate processing center.[78] Teaming up to solve homelessness or access to health care facilities is less likely because of the cost and expansiveness of the problems involved.

One solution to this lack of coordination is to establish **councils of governments (COGs)**. A COG is a regional planning commission made up of area-wide local governments. Unlike city government, they do not have the

councils of governments (COGs): regional planning commissions made up of area-wide local governments

TABLE 12.1	Debt in Selected Texas Cities, 2019

CITY	PER CAPITA DEBT
Houston	$1,618
Denton	$5,413
San Antonio	$1,266
El Paso	$1,754
Austin	$1,560
Fort Worth	$837
Frisco	$4,394
Corpus Christi	$1,474

Source: Texas Bond Review Board, Bond Finance Office.

COMMUNICATION:

Which cities have higher debt?

- Denton ranks highest in public debt, followed by Frisco, El Paso, and Houston.

- Although smaller than many large cities, booming Denton has a significant debt per capita rate.

CRITICAL THINKING:

Why do some cities have higher debts than others?

- El Paso has undertaken several "quality-of-life" improvements financed by debt, including improving streets, building a children's hospital, and moving city hall to make room for a new baseball stadium.[74] Corpus Christi has also spent funds on infrastructure improvement projects.

- Austin's population has exploded in the past 20 years, and debt is being used to finance construction of new roads and maintenance on old ones, renovation to libraries, and construction of a new fire station.

- Houston has a massive pension debt that needs to be funded, a booming car population hungry for more roads, and strict limits on revenue receipts (from property taxes), requiring significant debt financing.

- Suburbs like Frisco and Denton are taking on new debt to develop infrastructure for an exploding number of residents.

power to tax, collect fees, establish ordinances, or take on debt. Rather, COGs work with local governments, the private sector, and state and federal agencies to address specific challenges, such as solid waste disposal, services for the elderly, specialized transit systems, regional 911 systems, as well as more general goals like economic development. Texas has 24 COGs, each covering a different region of the state. One that is critical to the Gulf Coast region in the Gulf Coast Community Protection and Recovery District is tasked with helping communities coordinate responses, reimbursement, and rebuilding after major storms such as Hurricanes Ike and Harvey.

SPRAWL

Thanks to permissive annexation laws, Texas cities are expanding rapidly. Suburban residents who have moved out of the immediate metropolitan area to escape the city are "clawed back into it—and often compelled to pay higher property taxes."[79] This **sprawl** creates several problems. For one, it makes commuting difficult as people begin to live farther from the city center. More congestion on the roads leads to more cars and fossil fuel emissions. Growth of residential and commercial properties edges out nature, forcing wildlife to seek refuge in manicured yards and crawl spaces and tempting them with leftovers scrounged from trash cans. Habitat destruction has even shooed off bumblebees, which are crucial to pollinating native and commercial plants and so is responsible for $15 billion in crop pollination.[80] Development reduces open green space and may contribute to flooding in some areas.

There has been pushback to creeping sprawl. Developers are finding older areas to develop closer to the city core. Cities are encouraging pedestrian-friendly developments closer to the city. Cities like Waco are creating plans to improve city infrastructure, revitalize its downtown area, and create a positive image for the city. Cities are turning to mass transit, even in car-loving Dallas and Houston.

sprawl: rapid growth of urban and suburban areas spreading into the undeveloped land surrounding it

Sprawl in San Antonio has accompanied tremendous population growth, almost a million people in 20 years. Photo dates: June 16, 1991, and June 4, 2010.

SOCIAL RESPONSIBILITY: **Do cities and counties have a responsibility to manage sprawl? What is the proper balance between growth and management of the problems of sprawl?**

TO ZONE OR NOT TO ZONE

City governments control and regulate the development of land through zoning. Zoning rules, for example, prohibit the erection of oil derricks next to multimillion-dollar mansions—and massage parlors next to churches. Zoning regulations exist in every major Texas city except Houston. In a mix of vibrancy, can-do spirit, unbridled capitalism, and a distrust of government oversight, Houston is the only major city in Texas—and in the United States—without a formal zoning code.[81] Proponents of no zoning argue that economic forces, rather than arbitrary rules, should govern development. Those opposed, including homeowners and many in the business community, argue that the aesthetics of development require some government oversight. Houston instead relies on a mash of city regulations, "buffering" ordinances that restrict tall buildings next to major activity centers, and deed restrictions that create a net of control over development.[82]

PENSIONS

One benefit to working for a local government is a pension when you retire. Local government employees, such as police, firefighters, municipal workers, and teachers, pay into a fund while employed by a city and receive benefits upon retirement. But with city budgets financially strapped, meeting obligations to pensions can be a challenge. Some pension plans are paying out more than they take in because those receiving pensions are living longer and extracting more funds.

Major Texas cities like Dallas, San Antonio, and Austin face a "Texas size threat of bankruptcy" over unfunded pension and retiree health care benefits, owing $110 billion, a debt burden of $10,000 for each Texan if the state paid off these liabilities today.[83] Cities are stuck: Voters grouse about approving tax hikes to pay for pension costs because paying more into pensions means less for police, fire, and road repair; beneficiaries currently in the funds don't want to make changes to their future benefits or pay more; and credit raters lambast city mayors for bad economic practice.

Complicating the problem is the fact that cities don't have full control over the pensions—they share this power with the state legislature. In the previous four sessions, attempts by the Texas legislators to yield more local control on pension issues was met with opposition, primarily by Democrats funded by the powerful unions who are the primary recipients.

Some cities have avoided "walking into the fan blades" of bankruptcy. Houston worked out a deal with the blessing of the legislature to restructure the city's pension obligations to police, fire, and municipal employees and to cap the city's risk by limiting contributions in hard times, accomplished by a voter-approved $1 billion bond. Dallas's Police and Fire Pension System was saved from insolvency by increasing the retirement age, increasing employee contributions, and reducing benefits. The plans will take decades to reach pension solvency, but both Dallas and Houston received better credit ratings in the wake of the reforms, making it easier to borrow funds in the future.[84]

TEXAS TAKEAWAYS

12.7.1   Why are local governments short on funds?

12.7.2   How do local governments cooperate?

THE INSIDER VIEW

Local governments are "creatures" of state government and frequently grapple with restrictive state laws and oversight. The state has eased its domineering ways over local governments as home rule gives cities more authority, but the friction between state and local government remains. Beyond their clash with state government, local governments also confront other problems and are often handicapped by powerful forces beyond their control. Local governments are hemmed in by tight budgets, a public that disapproves of high taxes but demands quality services, interest groups (especially business groups), and the bureaucracy that enforces city rules. Local governments expand their authority while seeking new revenue sources as state funds shrivel and resident demands grow. The resulting issues, such as sprawl, annexation, and the growth of smaller subgovernments, manufacture more friction as cities battle rising demand for services with cries from taxpayers about the strain on their pocketbooks. Cities criticize the state for keeping their funding ability on a leash. Cooperation across cities, coordination between governments, and increasing voter participation could help remedy the growing pains of the urban state that Texas is rapidly becoming.

 TEXAS TAKEAWAYS

12.1.1   Dillon's rule establishes that state governments can place restrictions on municipalities as long as these rules do not violate the state's constitution. Furthermore, unless the state directly grants a local government a specific power, local governments must assume they do not have that power.

12.1.2   Local governments provide an extensive range of services to the community spanning the social, economic, environmental, recreational, and cultural. These services usually relate to streets, sanitation, and safety.

12.2.1   The number of local governments, counties, cities, and special districts, has exploded over the past two centuries due to urbanization and population growth.

12.2.2   Counties carry out state laws since they cannot enact their own ordinances. Counties provide government services for residents and administrative services on behalf of the state. Counties' responsibilities include public safety, property tax collection, jails, transportation and roads, elections, and environmental protection.

12.2.3 Each Texas county is run by a county judge, and a commissioner's court is made up of four county commissioners. They are responsible for homeland security and emergency management, allocate funds for projects, and make strategic decisions. County commissioners adopt a tax rate for the county, oversee a budget, and maintain county buildings and facilities. The largest expenditures are infrastructure (roads or bridges) and maintenance of the county jail.

12.3.1 General law cities may not undertake the action unless the state legislature grants them that authority. choose the structure of their government, tax land adjacent to the city, set property tax rates, create boards and commissions to handle city issues, and enact policies and rules for the city as long as they are not prohibited by state or federal law.

12.3.2 Home rule cities allow citizens to launch initiatives, referendums, and recalls.

12.4.1 A weak mayor has no formal authority to act outside of the council. A strong mayor has legislative powers, setting the agenda, voting, and presiding over city council meeting, prepares the budget, and often exercises executive powers unilaterally. The mayor appoints the city judiciary, major boards and commissions, and department heads.

12.4.2 The city manager runs the day-to-day operations enforcing city regulations, supervising municipal employees and programs, executing the city budget, and preparing the agenda of the city council. The mayor and council members have no administrative duties. The city council sets all city policies, rules, and the budget. Mayors serve a symbolic role.

12.5.1 Special districts have grown because local government has passed off many of these functions to special districts, which are free to generate their own tax revenue.

12.5.2 School, junior/community college, hospital, and library districts are most visible. Municipal utilities districts, which deal with the supply of water, including protection, conservation, storage, irrigation, and drainage, are often less visible because residents may not know who is in charge, board members are not required to live in the districts, and board meetings may not be held in the districts.

12.6.1 Local elections often receive little media attention, include unfamiliar candidates or issues, and are usually held in years that are not presidential election years.

12.6.2 Holders of at-large offices are elected by all the voters citywide or countywide. At-large elections tend to favor candidates who appeal to the majority of electors and who have the money to fund a citywide campaign. City council members are often elected through a place system that carves the city into districts or places. The place system tends to result in the election of representatives who are more concerned with voters' concerns in districts that council members represent and are thought to increase diversity.

12.7.1 Local governments are short on funds because the state has reduced local property taxes but has not provided additional funds to make up these losses. Rising debt and pension payments are also eating up local government budgets.

12.7.2 Teaming up on specific projects and councils of governments are two ways that local governments may cooperate.

KEY TERMS

annexation
charter
city manager
council–manager system
councils of governments
cumulative voting
Dillon's rule

general law city
home rule city
initiative
mayor–council system
municipal bonds
ordinances
place system
preemption
recall
referendum
special districts
sprawl
Tax Increment Reinvestment Zones
unincorporated areas

PRACTICE QUIZ

1. Where does Texas rank compared to other states regarding the number of local governments?

   a. Lower than most
   b. About the same as most
   c. A little higher than most
   d. A lot higher than most

2. What are the two administrative entities in each Texas county?

   a. County judge; commissioner's court
   b. Mayor; board of directors
   c. City councillors; town councillors
   d. Administrative judge; county judge

3. Which of the following is the city-level equivalent to a constitution?

   a. "Play Book"
   b. "Book of Local Laws and Ordinances"
   c. "City Constitution"
   d. "Charter"

4. What is the process called whereby a home rule city joins unincorporated land into the boundary of an existing city?

   a. Annexation
   b. Zoning
   c. Reconfiguring
   d. Redistricting

5. All of the following are exclusive powers of home rule cities, compared to general law cities EXCEPT . . .

   a. Considering and passing initiatives
   b. Amending the state constitution
   c. Considering referenda
   d. Recalling city councillors

6. The system in which mayors have the least amount of influence is the . . .

   a. Council–manager system
   b. Mayor–council system
   c. Commissioner system
   d. None of the above

7. Special districts make up little of the local government in the state.

   a. True
   b. False

8. At-large city council members are elected citywide.

   a. True
   b. False

9. County sheriffs are elected.

   a. True
   b. False

10. For Texas, more local governments are created to deal with specific problems or issues.

    a. True
    b. False

[Answers: D, A, D, A, B, C, B, A, A, A]

Learn more with this chapter's digital tools, including the Oxford Insight Study Guide and a simulation activity, "True Texas Tales: Banning Cans in New Braunfels," at www.oup.com/he/Rottinghaus3e.

13

BUDGET, FINANCES, AND POLICY

13.1 Distinguish the types of taxes and revenue sources.

13.2 Identify alternative sources of revenue and funds.

13.3 Outline the state budget cycle.

Flush with cash from sales tax revenue and profits from natural resources, Texas passed a $250 billion budget for the 2020–2021 session, the largest in the state's history. This 15 percent increase from the prior budget came after "ranting and raving" about state spending and amidst fights about where to pump up or slice the budget. Two teenage girl scouts from Plano lobbied the legislature to exempt tampons and other feminine hygiene products from the sales tax to make them affordable to low-income women. The Comptroller's Office reported that eliminating this tax could cost up to $40 million in lost revenue over the 2- year budget. Opponents also feared such a measure would open a Pandora's box for other Texans to demand other exceptions.[1] The girl scouts' bill died in committee. The Texas legislature decided instead to cap sales tax on yachts. Yacht sales in Texas were down since Florida capped its sales tax at $18,000, and legislators argued that Texas needed to compete to keep this business in the Lone Star State.[2]

Should yacht buyers be given tax breaks? If light bulbs, Texas flags, and other items are tax exempt, how can the legislature justify taxing an essential item, like tampons? This is why budgets matter. They determine the scope of taxes Texans pay and shape public policy. The battle over the budget is a war over policy priorities. The state legislature can pass any bill it wants, but if that bill doesn't get signed by the governor or does not get funded, then the executive branch has no way to carry it out. According to journalists Gregory

● Texas exempts items such as Texas flags, light bulbs, and other items from sales taxes but even after attempts were made in 2017 and 2019 to exempt feminine hygiene products, Texas would not join a dozen other states in allowing such products to be tax exempt.

Curtis and Paul Burka, the art of crafting a budget lies in "plucking the goose so as to get the most feathers with the least hissing."[3]

In this chapter, we examine the nuts and bolts of state finance to uncover the political struggle involved in who, what, and how to tax—and how to spend the revenue collected from taxes and other sources. The confrontations on these issues divide along familiar battlefronts: partisanship, geography, and economic interests.

13.1 TAXES AND OTHER REVENUE SOURCES

> **13.1** Distinguish the types of taxes and revenue sources.

revenue: the income a state receives from taxes, fees, and other sources

Nobody likes paying taxes, especially Texans. Yet taxes are essential because they provide most of the funds the state and local governments use to operate. The state's **revenue** is primarily tax-funded (approximately 46 percent in 2019), although other funds are drawn from fees levied on the public, proceeds from the state lottery, and—as we saw in Chapter 3—receipts from the federal government.[4] Texas has hundreds of types of taxes, including unusual ones like a use tax for moving a boat from another state and using it in Texas. Unlike many other states, however, Texas does not have an income tax. As a result, Texas is primarily a two-tax state (see Figure 13.1): property taxes and sales taxes. Property taxes are assessed locally and stay local for use by school boards, counties, and cities. Sales taxes are sent to the state government for use in the state budget, although cities are allowed to assess and keep additional sales tax revenue. These two major taxes, along with other assorted taxes and fees, form the state's tax base.

SALES TAX

Since 1967, the sales tax has served as the state's largest single source of tax income (58 percent of all taxes collected).[5] The state sets the base rate at 6.25 percent, and local governments can add up to 2 percent to this (and most do). The extra 2 percent rate is generally shared across several areas (city, county, and transit authority). The base funds are collected for use by the state, while the extra sales tax funds are returned to cities by the comptroller for city projects and programs. Some cities impose other dedicated sales taxes for specific purposes such as mass transit, economic development, or new sports venues.

FIGURE 13.1 Texas: A Two-Tax State: Property and Sales Taxes

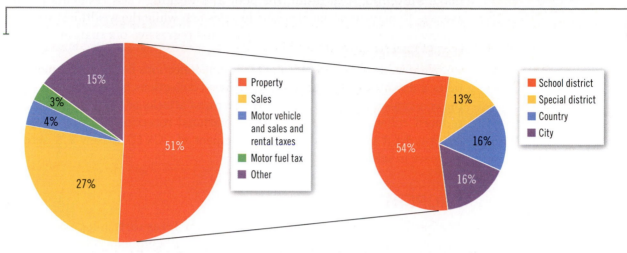

Source: Texas Comptroller of Public Accounts.

COMMUNICATION:

Where does tax revenue come from in Texas?

- Texas is a two-tax state: Most revenue comes from property taxes (51 percent), which funds local governments, followed by sales taxes (27 percent) used by the state.

- Property taxes are collected primarily by school districts (54 percent), but cities, counties, and special districts also levy small amounts.

CRITICAL THINKING:

Why these sources?

- A tax on overall income is prohibited by the Texas Constitution and is politically unsavory to politicians in the current no-tax-increase climate.

- Property taxes have historically driven tax revenues for local governments. As the state's needs have expanded, the number and amount of these taxes have multiplied.

Every local taxing jurisdiction with a local sales tax also has a local use tax. When a state use tax is levied on a taxable item, the local use tax is also due. For instance, when you buy an item online, the local use tax is due based on the ship-to address.[6] Consumers pay most of these sales taxes (58 percent) while businesses pay the balance (42 percent).[7]

The sales tax is a **regressive tax;** that is, the tax rate is the same for everyone. This tax gobbles up a larger percentage of the income of the poor and working class than it does of the wealthiest Texans' income. Let's say you make $10,000 and spend $3 on the sales tax at the grocery store. That

regressive tax: a tax that exacts a larger percentage of the earnings of low-income than of high-income individuals

$3 is going to be a larger portion of your total income ($10,000) than if you make $100,000. As a result, the poor and working-class residents pay on average 12 percent of their income in sales tax, while the wealthiest pay just 3 percent. Texas relies more heavily on this regressive tax than most other states (see Figure 13.2).

Another downside to the sales tax is that collections fall when the economy takes a downturn. Falling oil prices reduced collections by 5 percent in 1983; the economic slide in the wake of the terrorist attacks of September 11, 2001, reduced collections by 2 percent; the national recession in 2009 dropped receipts by 3 percent; the economic impact of COVID-19 saw a 5 percent decrease in sales taxes.[9]

PROPERTY TAX

The battle over the property tax is older than Texas dirt, going back to the days when the Mexican government's decision to eliminate property tax exemptions—previously used to attract Anglo settlers—sparked the Texas Revolution.[10] From the period of the Civil War to the Great Depression, properties were undervalued, and tax collection was sporadic due to corruption among local tax collectors and inaccurate recordkeeping. Even so, property taxes in the past supplied between 50 and 75 percent of tax revenue.

Property taxes (called *ad valorem*, meaning "according to value") are assessed based on the value of the property the taxpayer owns. Although Texas outlawed state-based property taxes in 1982, local governments use property tax revenue to fund schools, utility systems, fire and police protection, public libraries, parks, and other services. Most of the revenue from property taxes supports public schools, and the state kicks in the rest. Property tax revenue is collected locally and—for the most part—stays local.

Property tax burdens are high today primarily because Texas has no statewide income tax that could be shared with local governments, which consequently use the property tax revenue for projects and services. The largest jump in the source of revenue collected from taxpayers has been in the collection of property taxes, which increased from $15 billion in 1994 to $59.3 billion in 2019.[11] Why? A growing economy pushes up property values, and the proliferation of special-purpose districts means more entities are allowed to tax residents (see Chapter 12).

The state constitution provides a **homestead exemption**, a portion of the property value on which Texans don't have to pay taxes. Every Texan homeowner receives an exemption of $25,000 on their homes. Districts provide a $10,000 exemption for those over age 65 and for veterans. Local governments may also offer an additional exemption of $3,000 (or more) exemption for disabled individuals.

Think your property taxes are too high? Protest it! Local governments appraise, or estimate, the value of property, whether it be a home, a commercial property, a ranch, or an oil refinery. Appraisal districts at the county level

homestead exemption: a portion of property value on which Texans don't have to pay taxes

IS IT BIGGER IN TEXAS?

FIGURE 13.2 **State and Local Sales Taxes, 2019**

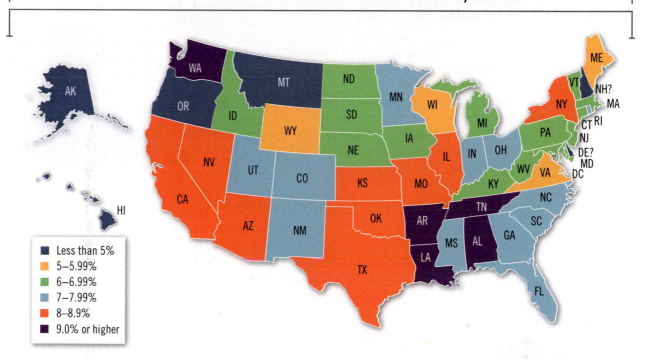

Less than 5%
5–5.99%
6–6.99%
7–7.99%
8–8.9%
9.0% or higher

Source: Tax Foundation. Figures represent combined sales tax for state and local levels.

 COMMUNICATION:

Where does Texas rank on sales tax rates?

- States with the largest sales tax include Washington, Kansas, Illinois, New York, Alabama, Louisiana, Oklahoma, Tennessee, Arkansas, and California. Texas's sales tax is almost as high as the sales tax of these states.

 CRITICAL THINKING:

Why is the sales tax rate high in some states and lower in others?

- Texas has no income tax, so sales taxes are higher in order to generate revenue. This is also true for other states with no income tax like Tennessee and Washington.

- Sales taxes have gone up most in states where governors have made a push to reduce income taxes, such as Arkansas.[8]

- States in economic distress have increased reliance on sales taxes, such as Louisiana and Illinois.

- Sales taxes are higher in states that rely more heavily on tourism, including California and Florida.

INSIDER INTERVIEW

Dale Craymer, President of the Texas Taxpayers and Research Association

How do we make the tax system fair?

Tax systems are never popular, and "fair" ones perhaps even less so. At best, they are a necessary evil that minimally interfere with economic decision making. From a policy perspective, the best and most stable tax systems are those that are balanced or diversified across a number of revenue sources. Taxes should apply as broadly as possible so that everyone has a stake and allow rates to be as low as possible. Ideally, everyone should feel some discomfort, but no one group should feel actual pain. Politics, though, often pulls tax systems in the opposite direction—focusing on as few as possible so that a greater majority may benefit. Or as the late Senator Russell Long, Democrat senator from Louisiana, noted, "Don't tax you. Don't tax me. Tax that fellow behind the tree."

 SOCIAL RESPONSIBILITY: **Are you satisfied with Texas's tax system? How would you change it?**

Over 100 taxpayers sued the Travis County Appraisal Review Board for failing to notify them of the time and place of their hearing during which they planned to protest the property value and tax the county had set for their homes. Chief Appraiser Marya Crigler, pictured here, insisted that the property owners did receive notification but that their agent did not show up at the Saturday hearings.

SOCIAL RESPONSIBILITY: **Should there be limits on housing appraisals for individuals or groups who are less able to pay? For the elderly? For veterans?**

establish a review board that sets appraisal rates and hears property owner protests. The county tax assessor calculates the taxes, prepares the tax rolls, and generates bills, while the county tax collector facilitates payment. Every county has a process whereby taxpayers can challenge a property estimate, either online or in person. An appraiser will reassess and issue a new evaluation.

Property value is at the heart of rising property taxes. In 2013, Philip Dominguez bought a less-than-800-square-foot, rundown old house for $6,000 in Big Spring. In 2015, the county appraised the house at $25,000, a 316 percent jump in price that tripled the property tax. An economic downturn in rural Texas kept wages down but taxes high. "If I could sell my home for what the property's valued at," said one Big Spring resident, "I'd get the hell out of here."[12] Across the state, low-income families and older Texans are worried about being taxed out of their homes.

The homestead exemption highlights the often tense relationship between local authority and state oversight. The legislature can only raise the homestead exemption and set limits for property value appraisal, but it is required to appraise property. This is politically frustrating for state representatives because efforts to reduce taxes require local counties to limit rising appraisals. In the past decade, housing evaluations have increased by 10 percent in some areas of Texas. In Grayson County in north Texas, for example, appraised value has shot up 57 percent since 2008.[13] The state legislature took a big bite out of the local property taxpayers' bills by increasing the homestead exemption from $15,000 to the current $25,000. But rising evaluations at the local level meant that taxpayers saw only small tax cuts—between $125 and $150 on average. The cuts provided a windfall for homeowners in rural and South Texas, but only mild relief to those with rapidly rising home values in suburban areas.[14]

When property values fall, however, local governments suffer economically. Local governments where the governor has declared a disaster area may request a reappraisal, although they are not required to do so. Hurricane Harvey sent property values for flooded or wind-destroyed houses spiraling downward in the 60 counties affected, creating a $1 billion drop in property tax collections due to damaged homes.[15]

FRANCHISE (BUSINESS) TAXES

The franchise tax (or "margins" tax) is the state's main business tax that flows to its coffers, amounting to about 6.6 percent of total tax receipts in 2019. This tax is the fourth-largest source of state revenue. Corporations, partnerships, business trusts, limited liability companies, and other businesses pay this tax, which amounts to 0.5 percent to 1 percent of their total revenue. Most small businesses and nonprofits are not subject to this tax, however, since the intent is to generate revenue from larger corporations. The legislature is constantly tinkering with this tax, often using the tax as a way to increase revenue so that it can cut other taxes or balance budgets. In prosperous economic times, the state legislature often reduces the tax to keep Texas competitive. In 2015, the legislature cut the rate by a massive 25 percent. Governor Greg Abbott, who in his 2017 State-of-the-State Address had vowed that "[w]e must continue to cut the business franchise tax until it fits in a coffin," backed legislation to phase out the tax altogether by 2020, but the bill did not pass.[17]

ANGLES OF POWER

Putting a Lid on Property Taxes

Skirmishes between city and state government are about more than policy; they are often about money. Local governments justify their increase of property taxes by pointing out that the state's share of funding for public schools has been declining and that the state issues many unfunded mandates, such as court-appointed attorneys for poor defendants.

State leaders have little control over local property taxes because a Texas constitutional amendment not only prevents them from creating a statewide property tax system, it also bars the legislature from setting the rates for local school districts and government—no matter how much

constituents complain to them.[16] Still, lawmakers have recently attempted to restrict the amount by which local government can raise property taxes. In 2019, the legislature capped the rate of property tax growth to 2.5 percent on school district taxes or 3.5 percent on other local property taxes. Local governments can only raise taxes higher than that amount if they obtain voter permission.

SOCIAL RESPONSIBILITY: **Who should set property tax rates? If these rates trend too high, should the state step in to limit them?**

OIL AND NATURAL GAS TAXES

Taxes on oil and natural gas (called "severance" taxes for the removal of oil from Texas land) come in two forms: oil regulation tax and oil production tax.[18] Together, these taxes amounted to 6.1 percent of tax revenue and just over $3.3 billion in 2019, up $1 billion from 2017! The state has kept the oil tax rate unchanged since 1951, a reflection of the friendly relationship between the oil and energy industries and Texas politicians.[19]

The amount of revenue Texas receives from severance taxes is connected to international events, technology, and natural occurrences. International events such as price spikes, threats from oil-rich countries, or increasing demand cause price fluctuations. In 2005, Hurricane Katrina devastated the industry's pipelines, platforms, and other facilities, leading to significant production losses and less tax revenue. The technological innovation of hydraulic fracturing (or "fracking"), however, increased production greatly in western Texas, increasing tax intake for the state.

CAR TAXES: MOTOR FUEL TAX ("GAS" TAX) AND MOTOR VEHICLE TAXES

The state imposes a gas tax on gasoline, diesel fuel, and liquefied gas. The more you drive, the more gas tax you pay. Currently, the state charges 20 cents per gallon. Five cents go to public education, and the rest goes to road-related projects. The gas tax has remained unchanged since 1991, and the revenue it has generated has been flat since 2016, at about $3.6 billion. During this time, however, construction materials (like pavement) and labor costs have increased for building roads, while cars are more fuel efficient, so Texans are buying less gas. Realistically, these taxes need to keep pace with the cost of building and maintaining roads, but as a former Republican state senator noted, "Nobody has the stomach to raise taxes."[20] In fact, in 2014, after Republican State Senator John Carona pushed to allow local governments to increase the tax, he lost his seat.

You also pay a motor vehicle tax when you buy a car, rent a car, or buy a manufactured (mobile) home. This amounted to about 6.6 percent of state revenue in 2019.

Texas has taxed liquor since the Great Depression (1935), the only tax revenue that didn't decline in the economic calamity during that time. Today, the tax on liquor is 6.7 percent. The legislature has repealed alcohol taxes for adult beverages sold on trains and airplanes.

SOCIAL RESPONSIBILITY: **Is it fair to levy taxes on certain products that a select few deem to be more harmful to society? Why?**

SIN TAXES

"Sin" taxes are imposed on the sale of alcohol and tobacco and on some forms of gambling, and fees are imposed on "sexually oriented" businesses (charging $5 for patrons of live nude shows). These taxes accounted for only 4.7 percent of total revenue in 2019, but they are also levied as a deterrent to what lawmakers consider harmful behavior.[21] The tax is often factored into the cost of liquor, beer, or cigarettes, so customers are not always aware they are paying it. State lawmakers see the "sin" tax as politically easier to swallow than other forms of taxes, especially in tough budget times. Between 2008 and 2017, as states legalized sports betting and recreational marijuana, and as e-cigarette sales took off, state revenue from sin taxes grew as fast as state sales or income taxes.[22]

> **"sin" taxes:** taxes imposed on the sale of alcohol and tobacco and on some forms of gambling, and fees imposed on "sexually oriented" businesses

 TEXAS TAKEAWAYS

13.1.1   What are the Texas state government's main sources of revenue?

13.1.2   How are sales taxes divided between state and local governments?

13.1.3   Why are property taxes so high?

13.1.4   What is a regressive tax?

13.1.5   What is the homestead exemption?

 ## 13.2 ALTERNATIVE SOURCES OF FUNDS

Taxes are not the only source of funds collected in Texas. Let's explore a few other ways the state's coffers are being filled.

> **13.2**   Identify alternative sources of revenue and funds.

FEES AND FINES

Every time you turn around, you're paying a **fee** in Texas. The state has hundreds of fees—vehicle registration, state park admission, permission to sell fireworks, and even licensing fees for certain professions. The state also assesses fees for business, such as air pollution control fees, oil and gas regulation and cleanup fees, and waste treatment inspection fees. The fees themselves are generally small, but they add up to big revenue. In fiscal year 2019, fees collected amounted to more than $6.4 billion, up from $4 billion in 1996, but down from $11 billion

> **fee:** a payment for a service rendered

fines: financial punishments for offenses

in 2017.[23] Fees go either to general revenue or to recoup the cost of a service provided by a program or agency.

Fines also flow into the state's coffers. Fines that Texans pay for violating certain traffic laws have climbed higher, especially for speeding, driving while intoxicated (DWI), or driving without a license. For instance, El Paso made $11 million each year between 2011 and 2014 on fines for traffic violations.[24] Some Texans, however, just can't or won't pay. Of the $3.4 billion in fees that have been levied over the last decade, less than half that amount has been collected. Nearly 1.3 million Texas drivers have an invalid license due to spiraling penalties from past infractions.[25] If these fees are not paid, the penalties get worse. In one well-publicized event, a 67-year-old woman paid nearly $25,000, spent 4 weeks in jail, and lost her driver's license because of a DWI in 2004.[26] The City of Amarillo has jailed people, including the elderly and disabled, for not paying city fines.[27] Bipartisan critics argue that this is unfair to poor Texans. The legislature passed legislation to allow judges to waive court filing fees for indigent Texans. However, this law currently only applies to a small fraction of Texans who opt to try their case in open court rather than plea bargain. [28]

THE "RAINY DAY" AND OTHER FUNDS

A small percentage of revenue is generated through several state funds. Ever sock away a little extra payday cash for the future? Texas does. In 1988, after emerging from a major recession in 1983 that rocked the Texas economy, the state's voters approved the establishment of the Economic Stabilization Fund, almost always referred to as the "Rainy Day Fund." The fund is drawn from oil and natural gas production tax revenue. Leftover (surplus) unspent funds at the end of each year and interest on the balance of the fund are also pooled back into the Rainy Day Fund.[33] Texas funnels a greater percentage of per capita state expenditure into its rainy day fund than any state except Wyoming and Alaska. Currently, the fund is flush, with north of $14 billion.

Hoarding the money in the Rainy Day Fund has become a badge of political honor, and spending funds from the "sacred" fund may provoke an outcry from budget-conscious primary voters. Many argue that the state has underfunded transportation and education in the name of fiscal conservatism and should use these funds to better address the state's fast-growing needs.[34] Legislators are reluctant to spend the money for fear of political retribution, but they are comfortable asking voters to approve changes to the distribution of funds. In 2019, voters approved a constitutional amendment diverting $800 million of the funds that would normally go to the Rainy Day Fund to a state flood infrastructure fund for flood control and mitigation projects.

GREAT TEXAS POLITICAL DEBATES
A "Poor Tax"?

Have you ever paid a fine for running a stop sign, public intoxication, or having a dog off leash? Local and state governments rely on that revenue. In 2019, these fees amounted to $3 million of Dallas County's general revenue.[29] In the Lone Star State, 95 percent of warrants were for outstanding fines, and these charges put more than 600,000 people in jail.[30]

Fines include court or filing fees. These fees increase significantly when unpaid. Some Texans are forced to choose between paying rent and paying fines. The result is a *de facto* debtor's prison, though debtor's prisons were outlawed in the nineteenth century. Those who go to prison may lose their jobs as they await trial.

In 2017, Texas implemented a new law that offered low-income individuals the opportunity of performing community service in lieu of paying these court or filing fees and that give judges the option of reducing or waiving them altogether. Unfortunately, the 2017 legislation only applies to indigent Texans who appear in open court, not the 90 percent who take plea deals. In 2019, legislation that would abolish court and filing fees for indigent Texans altogether failed to pass.[31] Some counties are experimenting with temporary amnesty for these fines but limit the program to violations not involving parking tickets or bond forfeitures.[32] However, in the meantime, poor Texans who can't pay these fines and fees represent about 75 percent of the local jail population.

SOCIAL RESPONSIBILITY: **Should fines for nonpayment of fees accumulate?**

YES: Texans must act responsibly and pay their fine promptly. By abolishing the fee, Texas would be reducing the punishment and letting low-income Texans off almost scot free. These fines deter Texans from committing infractions. Moreover, all Texans should be treated equally under the law, which would not be the case if fees were to be waived for indigent Texans.

NO: Since these Texans still pay a fine for the infraction, they are being punished. Moreover, charging court fees that accrue interest for indigent Texans is tantamount to debtor's prison. It prevents low-income individuals who make the same mistakes as other Texans from holding down jobs, keeping their homes, or paying child care expenses.

Other state funds include the Texas Mobility Fund, the Property Tax Relief Fund, individual trust funds from past budget funds squirreled away, bond proceeds, interagency contracts, and certain revenue held in higher education accounts.[35]

WHY NO INCOME TAX?

When Democrats floated the idea of establishing an income tax in 1993, Lieutenant Governor Bob Bullock declared that Texas would get an income tax when a Russian submarine sailed up the Houston Ship Channel.[36] The concept of an income tax runs against the grain of the individualistic

The state lottery brought in almost $2.2 billion in 2019, which went to support public education and programs benefiting Texas veterans. Critics claim that the lottery preys on financially vulnerable Texans; others oppose it on religious grounds.

🔺 PERSONAL RESPONSIBILITY: **Should the state limit individual lottery purchases to protect people from themselves? What rules might it use?**

progressive tax: a tax with a rate that increases as the amount that is taxed rises

political culture that most Texans embrace. It is a **progressive tax**: The more a person earns, the more a person pays. Theoretically, a progressive tax takes a larger percentage of income from someone earning more money than from someone earning less money, so from one perspective, income taxes punish those who make more money. Others argue that an income tax is fairer to low-salary earners since they would pay a lower tax rate on their comparatively smaller salaries. This would make the tax proportional to an individual's ability to pay. Polling suggests that the public is almost uniformly against a state income tax—94 percent oppose.[37]

Fiscal conservatives also argue that avoiding a state income tax maintains the state's economic edge. Texas, however, is one of only seven states with no income tax. And income taxes do provide a more stable funding source than sales taxes, particularly in sour economic times when consumers tighten their grip on their pocketbooks.

DEBATES OVER TAXES

The ongoing mission to set low taxes and provide modest services butts up against legal constitutional requirements for state financing of education and persistent demands for governmental assistance on health care or social welfare programs. With sizable chunks of the population wanting to cut every type of tax (see Figure 13.3), deciding which taxes to cut creates political problems. In 2019, Texas's "big three" (the governor, lieutenant governor, and speaker of the house) came together to hatch a "completely unprecedented" idea: cap the rate of property tax growth on other local property taxes that local governments could raise without an automatic rollback election.[38] Penny-pinching local governments warned that this restriction could prevent cities from paying for first responders, filling potholes, or keeping recreation centers or libraries open.[39]

Some tax cuts have long-term budgetary effects that are not easily undone. For example, when Governor George W. Bush made good on his pledge to cut property taxes in 1999, the state eventually had to balance out the loss of revenue by adding more items to the list of sales-taxable goods and by raising taxes on cigarettes, alcohol, and utilities.[40] Any reduction in revenue (through a tax cut) requires the legislature to make up the funds elsewhere—which, as we are about to see—is not an easy task.

FIGURE 13.3 **Tax Attitudes in Texas (Percent Dissatisfied by Party Affiliation)**

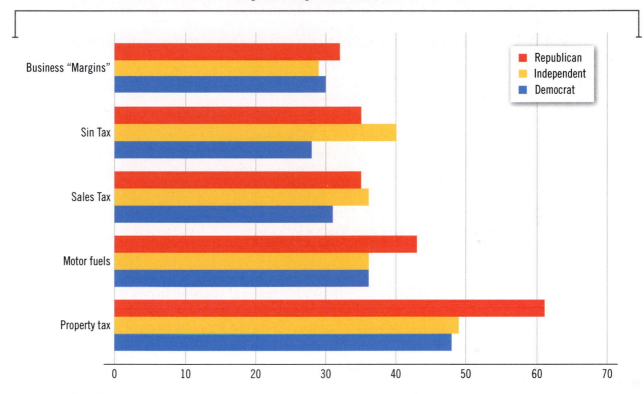

Source: Texas Politics Polling, February 2015.

 COMMUNICATION:

What taxes do Texans want cut?

- Property taxes are the taxes most Texans across the ideological spectrum want cut.

- In general, Republicans are more likely to desire tax cuts than other groups. Democrats are less likely than Republicans or independents to desire to cut specific taxes.

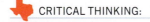 CRITICAL THINKING:

Why are property taxes the villain, especially for Republicans?

- Rising housing valuations and spiking property taxes grew to a fevered pitch in 2015 and have continued through the present day, with Texans looking for relief.

- Republicans believe in smaller government, so tax cuts fit naturally into that ideology. Republican political leaders have also made cutting taxes a major part of their appeal to voters, and Republicans in the state have followed.

- Democrats look for ways for the state to invest in key services such as roads, education, and health care. They would rather pay more in taxes than see essential state services cut.

🏴 **TEXAS TAKEAWAYS**

13.2.1 Where does the money from fees collected from individuals and businesses go?

13.2.1 Fees go either to general revenue or to recoup the cost of a service provided by a program or agency.

13.2.2 Why are penalties on unpaid fees a problem in Texas?

13.2.3 What is the Economic Stabilization Fund and when is it used?

13.2.4 Why is the income tax progressive?

🔵 13.3 THE BUDGET

13.3 Outline the state budget cycle.

general revenue funds: state funds that include revenue from all sources (even federal funds)

Most state taxes, fees, and other revenue are first banked in **general revenue funds** that are channeled into the all-funds budget, which also includes federal funding. Then the Texas legislature allocates—that is, divvies up—the funds, which is not an easy job. Former Lieutenant Governor Bill Hobby famously stated, "The main business of the legislature is passing the budget; the rest is poetry."[41] The budget process is complicated, constrained by limits on spending, and rife with conflicts between groups, parties, and branches of government.

BUDGET CYCLE

Each session, lawmakers pass a budget that is implemented in the following two fiscal years. Before 1942, budgets were approved for programs and departments without regard to the state's total biennial budget, leading to fiscal chaos.[42] Today, budget rules structure the budget process, but budgeting for 2 years is a challenge since the economy may tank, programs may fail, state priorities may change, or revenue may fall.

BUDGET LIMITATIONS

Although candidates for the state legislature may make lofty promises of reducing property taxes or drawing additional funds for underfunded public schools, once elected they are significantly constrained by the Texas Constitution and state laws.

"pay as you go": budget rule that Texas cannot spend more money than it receives in revenue

Pay as You Go. Texas is constitutionally required to balance its budget. This is because Texas is a **"pay as you go"** state, meaning the government cannot spend more money than it receives in revenue. The Texas Constitution also sets limits on debt (capping it at 5 percent of the general revenue fund), welfare spending (requiring that it cannot exceed 1 percent of the budget), and total spending.[43] As *The Texas Tribune*'s Ross Ramsey puts it, the budget is "a dog already dragging four leashes."[44] The state comptroller must check the budget to make sure it meets these requirements.

The Spending Cap. The most significant restraining rule is the spending cap, which restricts budget growth from the previous biennial budget to the estimated growth of the Texas economy. For the 2020–2021 budget, the Legislative Budget Board (LBB) estimated the growth in the prior 2 years as 9.8 percent, giving legislators $102 billion to work with, about $10 billion more than in the 2018–2019 budget.[45] Texas legislators can bust the cap by a simple majority vote in both chambers, but the political repercussions in a state that values small, efficient government are so high that this has only happened once (in 2006, in order to lower property taxes in school districts that had reached record highs).

Dedicated and Nondedicated Revenue. Legislators are further limited because they do not have discretion over all state **expenditures**. Almost one-third of the funds in the state budget are dedicated revenue, linked to a specific purpose either by constitution or by statute. For instance, revenue from hunting and fishing licenses is dedicated to conservation efforts, and a portion of marriage license fees is used to fund child abuse and neglect prevention programs.[46] Legislators do have discretion over how to spend general revenue funds, which in 2020–2021 amounted to about 40 percent of state funds (see Table 13.1).[47] Why is so much of the budget already fixed? Constitutional requirements, such as public education and federal programs, including Medicaid, are the culprits. However, Texas receives federal funds that provide 33 percent of its budget for these programs (see Figure 13.4).

expenditures: the total amount of funds that the state government can spend, as established by the spending cap

SOCIAL RESPONSIBILITY:

Should the state require that so much of the budget be dedicated to specific programs or purposes? Why?

| TABLE 13.1 | General Revenue, Dedicated Funds, 2020–2021 |

TYPE OF GENERAL REVENUE	PERCENT OF BUDGET (AMOUNT)	LARGEST EXPENDITURES
Appropriations restricted by constitutional provisions	9.6 percent ($11.6 billion)	Teachers retirement system ($4 billion), public education (textbooks) ($1 billion), foundation school program ($3 billion)
Appropriations restricted by statutory provisions	30.9 percent ($37 billion)	Public education ($29 billion), bond debt service ($1 billion), retiree health insurance ($879 million)

Source: Legislative Budget Board.

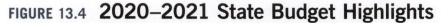

FIGURE 13.4 2020–2021 State Budget Highlights

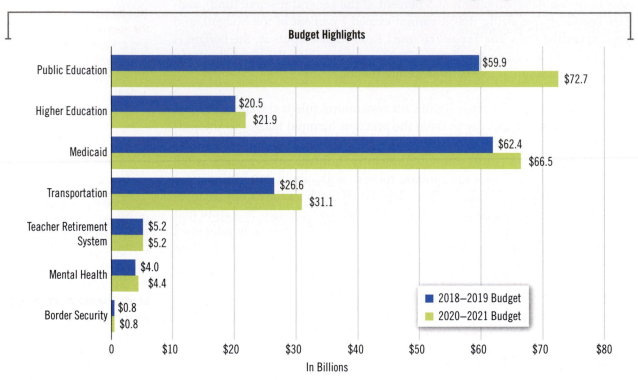

Budget Highlights

	2018–2019 Budget	2020–2021 Budget
Public Education	$59.9	$72.7
Higher Education	$20.5	$21.9
Medicaid	$62.4	$66.5
Transportation	$26.6	$31.1
Teacher Retirement System	$5.2	$5.2
Mental Health	$4.0	$4.4
Border Security	$0.8	$0.8

In Billions

Source: Texas Comptroller of Public Accounts.

COMMUNICATION:

What does the Texas budget look like?

- The state's 2020–2021 budget increased spending for many of the big-ticket items, including $12 billion for public education and $4 billion for Medicaid.

- Many Republican candidates also promised spending for border security, which they did to the tune of about $800 million.

CRITICAL THINKING:

Why does spending increase for some programs but not for others?

- The state's Republican leadership promised more attention to meat and potato issues affecting Texans' pocketbooks like transportation and a major increase in public education.

- Texas's flush financial bank account allowed additional expansion of key budget items.

BUDGET PLAYERS AND PROCESS

Texas uses a **dual budgeting process** in which the legislative branch and the executive branch coordinate to propose, shape, and pass a biennial budget (see Figure 13.5). Although most every other state requires their governor to submit a budget, Texans' fear of a strong executive has driven the state to distribute the important task of budget making across the two branches. In this section, we explore the stages of this process.

Can We Afford This? The state comptroller leads the parade by providing a biennial revenue estimate (BRE) at the beginning of each regular session. The BRE is used to make sure the state does not spend more money than it takes in. In addition, all bills submitted later during the legislative session must include a **fiscal note**, an overview of the estimated financial impact if the bill passes. The LBB adopts a constitutional spending limit in this early phase. The comptroller independently but concurrently prepares a statement about the financial condition of the state that estimates the revenue the state is to have in the upcoming biennium. The comptroller also lets the legislature know if there is any unspent money in the piggy bank. Before the 2019 legislative session, Comptroller Glenn Hegar reminded the legislature that about $883 million from the 2016–2017 budget was unspent.

What Is Our Vision? Since 1949, the LBB has been the most influential and active player in the budget, working with the governor to prepare a mission statement, set goals, adopt a spending limit, craft an **appropriation bill**, and review agency strategic plans. This early budget proposal is not binding, but it does provide a starting point for negotiations. Conflicts frequently occur because of differences in opinion, however. In 1997, Governor George W. Bush announced that he wanted $1 billion of a $3 billion budget surplus to go to reducing local school taxes,[48] and surprisingly, the LBB immediately threw up roadblocks. When the governor called Speaker of the House Pete Laney and said, "I won't make that mistake again," Laney responded, "That's a good idea, governor."[49]

Who Has Input? Executive branch agencies create long-term strategic plans and make budget requests. The LLB routinely—in boom times or bust times—asks state agencies to provide evidence to justify their expenditures and to propose methods of cutting their budgets. If the revenue estimates go sour and don't show as much funds as expected, the state then already has a plan in place to make cuts. If the estimates show that the state has sufficient revenue, the cuts don't occur. In 2016, the LBB asked agencies to submit budget requests that would include a 10 percent reduction, or what one observer called an "emergency warning signal test."[50]

dual budgeting process: the legislative branch and the executive branch coordinate to propose, shape, and pass a biennial budget

fiscal note: an overview of the estimated financial impact, including cost of the proposed changes, revenue generated, and staffing impacts to the bureaucracy that will result if the bill passes

appropriation bill: legislation that specifies what spending the state will undertake

FIGURE 13.5 **Roadmap of the Budget Process**

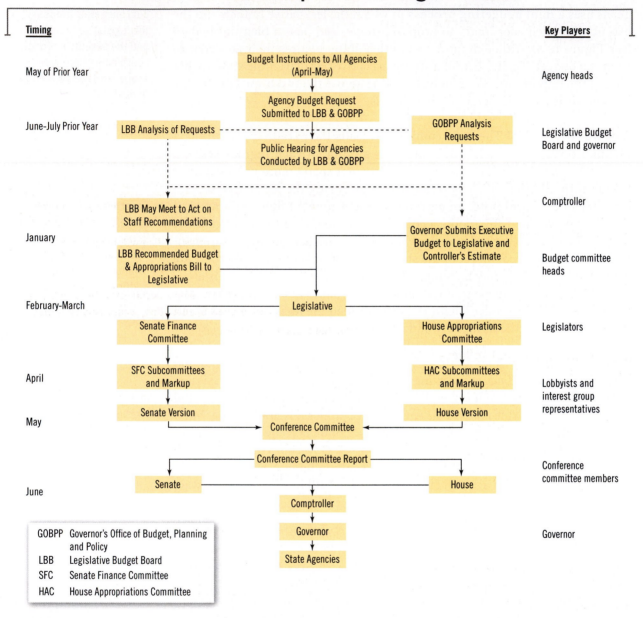

Timing		Key Players
May of Prior Year	Budget Instructions to All Agencies (April-May)	Agency heads
	Agency Budget Request Submitted to LBB & GOBPP	
June-July Prior Year	LBB Analysis of Requests — GOBPP Analysis Requests	Legislative Budget Board and governor
	Public Hearing for Agencies Conducted by LBB & GOBPP	
		Comptroller
	LBB May Meet to Act on Staff Recommendations	
January	Governor Submits Executive Budget to Legislative and Controller's Estimate	
	LBB Recommended Budget & Appropriations Bill to Legislative	Budget committee heads
February-March	Legislative	
	Senate Finance Committee — House Appropriations Committee	Legislators
April	SFC Subcommittees and Markup — HAC Subcommittees and Markup	Lobbyists and interest group representatives
May	Senate Version — House Version	
	Conference Committee	
	Conference Committee Report	Conference committee members
June	Senate — House	
	Comptroller	
	Governor	Governor
	State Agencies	

GOBPP	Governor's Office of Budget, Planning and Policy
LBB	Legislative Budget Board
SFC	Senate Finance Committee
HAC	House Appropriations Committee

Source: Adapted from Senate Research Center, "Budget 101: A Guide to the Budget Process in Texas," January 2011.

 SOCIAL RESPONSIBILITY:

At what point do you think citizen input is likely to have the most effect on the budget?

How Are Requests Evaluated? Because the state cannot spend more funds than it has, competition for budget menu items is fierce. The LBB submits appropriation bills to the House Appropriations Committee and the Senate Finance Committee. Both chambers' committees hold hearings, mark up legislation, and alter the budget bill, with input from fellow legislators. The legislature often provides the governor with budget funds for their pet projects to smooth over any objections from the governor. According to one observer, the three "big lies" legislators often tell as they evaluate requests while writing up the package are "We're already cut to the bone, Senator," "This program actually makes money for the state," and "This is one of the most important things the state does."[51]

State Senator Jane Nelson, Republican of Flower Mound, chairs Senate Finance Committee hearings on the budget. The 2-year, $250.7 billion spending plan is lengthy, complicated, and detailed.

SOCIAL RESPONSIBILITY: Beyond protecting the health and safety of Texans and promoting education, what responsibilities does the state have in the budget?

Because the process has multiple points of access in this phase, interest groups have significant influence. Lobbyists are not allowed on the floor of the Texas House or Senate, but electronic devices can allow lobbyists to communicate with legislators on the floor without physically being there. During one 12-hour budget debate later in the 2013 session, lawmakers were frantic to reconsider a vote that would have expanded the negotiating power of the state's chief health officer with the federal government on Medicaid. Why the sudden reversal? An e-mail "alert" sent from a conservative organization apparently prompted a change of heart for many lawmakers worried about political consequences.[52]

Can the Package Pass? After the conference committee hammers out differences between the house and senate budget bills, both chambers vote on the final budget, and the governor signs it, vetoes it, or uses the line item veto authority to trim it. A clash of budget titans put partners at odds in 2015. The legislature combined several items, including new state buildings in San Antonio and Austin, into a single $1 billion line item for the Facilities Commission. Governor Abbott broke precedent and vetoed the funds for a few of the projects but not the full $1 billion line. Ursula Parks, the director of the LBB, wrote a letter of concern to Comptroller Glenn Hegar that the governor had misused the line item veto.[53] Until the Texas Supreme Court weighs in on the matter, the governor's interpretation of his budget veto authority holds.

Does the Budget Square with Available Funds? "Is the sky falling in Texas?" State Senator Royce West asked Texas Comptroller Glenn Hegar in 2015,

certify: to confirm that the Texas government has enough money to cover the budget items as reported by the state controller

who had lowered his revenue projection by $2.6 billion because of slumping fossil fuel prices.[54] The state comptroller reviews the budget to **certify** that the anticipated revenue will be sufficient to cover the appropriations. The comptroller is essentially the budget enforcer.[55] This is usually a smooth process, but in 2003, for the first time in Texas history, Comptroller Carole Keeton Strayhorn informed state lawmakers that they were close but no cigar—and the governor was forced to "cap the well" and use his veto powers to trim down the budget. In 2019, Texas experienced a boom in natural resources and in the economy, more generally, driving up sales tax revenue, while the state also collected sales taxes on Internet purchases for the first time. As a result, the comptroller noted there was a whopping $518 million extra in general-purpose spending available late in the 2020–2021 budget crafting process, setting an amicable tone for the session.[56]

How Is the Budget Executed? The governor and the LBB typically have joint authority to execute the budget—to prohibit or allow a state agency to spend budget funds, to transfer budget funds, or to repurpose budget funds within an agency for a different purpose than that stated by the legislature. There are limitations on this authority, however: Public hearings may be held on an issue, especially if the legislature objects to a decision; elected officials' salaries cannot be reduced or eliminated; and funds appropriated by the legislature for a specific purpose cannot be reduced or eliminated.

riders: specific policy directives that convey instructions on how agency funds can be collected or spent

Budget rules are also found in legislative **riders**, which are specific policy directives that convey instructions on how agency funds can be collected or spent. Riders express legislative intent to direct spending preferences and are carried over from budget to budget unless changed. For one lawmaker who represented the tiny town of Abbott, Texas (home of Willie Nelson), a rider for the exact position of an exit ramp sign off of I-35 was written into the state budget. Republican State Representative Jim Pitts argued that the sign needed to be there so that road trippers would stop at the service station. It represented a significant source of sales tax revenue for this town of fewer than 400 people.[57]

The LBB and the governor may do battle at this point of the budget process as well. In 2014, Governor Rick Perry declared a state of emergency so that he could bypass the legislature to deploy the National Guard to the U.S.– Mexico border as more than 50,000 unaccompanied minors—primarily from Honduras, El Salvador, and Guatemala—flooded across. The governor argued that the emergency situation justified tapping a budget rule that allowed him to use earmarked funds without going to the legislature. The LBB dug in their heels, arguing that the move would set a bad precedent: Essentially, the governor could declare virtually any event an "emergency." The comptroller dove into the budget to find $38 million from another source to deploy the National Guard.[58]

BUDGET TRICKS

During the tense writing of the 2018–2019 budget, then Speaker of the Texas House Joe Straus noted, "There aren't any simple solutions when you've got a serious budget shortfall."[59] But the legislature has certainly tried over the years using **deferrals** to delay payments and so "make room" for increased spending—a practice that many would describe as an "accounting trick." One veteran journalist likened this strategy to those used by Texans who come up a little short at bill-paying time: Delay a payment by a day or two to get by without bouncing a check.[60] One way is for the state comptroller to grant wiggle room to state budget writers by temporarily delaying payments from the last day of one budget to the first day of the next, a "trick" that set off the verbal sparring described in the chapter opener. The state may also leave a hole in the budget with an IOU to pay it back in the next budget cycle, as they did for the state's Medicaid program in 2016–2017.[61] Some groups, like the conservative Texas Taxpayers and Research Association, claim this budget "magic" ends up costing the state double. Deferring $1 today ends up costing $2 tomorrow since the state will have to pay itself back in the next budget and add pay for the same policy for that current year.[62] Deferrals in recent budgets are like "kicking the can down the road," choking off funds without regard for future fiscal needs. As a result, Texans had to pay itself back billions of dollars in the 2020–2021 state supplemental budget. Legislative support for remedying the risky overuse of deferrals has both Republicans and Democrats calling for faithful budgeting.

deferrals: delaying guaranteed payments in one budget cycle to another budget cycle

🏴 TEXAS TAKEAWAYS

13.3.1 What are some of the limitations on budget funding?

13.3.2 What is the dual budgeting process?

13.3.3 Who has authority to execute the budget?

13.3.4 How do deferrals work?

THE INSIDER VIEW

Former Governor Rick Perry spelled out his philosophy on Texas's budget and policy: low taxes, low regulation, tort reform, and "don't spend all the money."[63] This recipe has put the state in fiscal health, but the state's booming population, aging citizenry, exploding diversity, and battles over natural resources mean that the economic fitness doesn't reach all Texans. The skirmishes over the budget, taxes, and public policy often center on party politics (Republicans versus Democrats), but just as often, urban interests are pitted against rural interests and organized interests (environmental, health care) are pitted against industry interests. The balance of power of any one group at any one time determines the type of policy and often policy change. These changes are usually gradual but shift as the state adapts to new circumstances.

TEXAS TAKEAWAYS

13.1.1 The Texas state's revenue is primarily tax-funded (approximately 46 percent in 2019), although other funds are drawn from fees levied on the public, proceeds from the state lottery, and receipts from the federal government. The sales tax is the state's largest single source of tax income.

13.1.2 The state sets the base rate at 6.25 percent, and local governments can add up to 2 percent to this (and most do). The base funds are collected for use by the state, while the extra sales tax funds are returned to cities by the comptroller.

13.1.3 Property tax burdens are high today primarily because Texas has no statewide income tax that could be shared with local governments. Consequently, local governments collect property taxes to fund schools, utility systems, fire and police protection, public libraries, parks, and other services.

13.1.4 A regressive tax, like the state's sales tax, is a tax rate that is the same for everyone.

13.1.5 The homestead exemption is that part of a property's value on which Texas homeowners don't have to pay taxes.

13.2.1 Fees go either to add to general revenue or to recoup the cost of a service provided by a program or agency.

13.2.2 Nearly 1.3 million Texas drivers have an invalid license due to spiraling penalties from unpaid fees. Additionally, Texans who can't afford to pay the fees on fines may be jailed.

13.2.3 Also known as the "Rainy Day Fund," this fund is drawn from oil and natural gas production tax revenue and leftover (surplus) unspent funds at the end of each year and interest on the balance of the fund. Because legislators are reluctant to spend the money and appear fiscally irresponsible, they ask voters to approve spending from this fund, as they did in 2019 in order to pay for state flood control and mitigation projects.

13.2.4 The income tax is progressive because the more a person earns, the more a person pays. So low-income Texans would pay less than higher-income Texans. Texas is one of seven states that does not have an income tax.

13.3.1 Pay as you go, the spending caps on debt spending and total spending, and revenue already dedicated to a specific policy (dedicated revenue) are all budget limitations.

13.3.2 The dual budgeting process refers to coordination of the legislative and executive branches to propose, shape, and pass a biennial budget.

13.3.3 The governor and the Legislative Budget Board typically have joint authority to execute the budget.

13.3.4 State budget writers delay an approved payment in the current budget cycle to balance the budget with the expectation that they can pay it back in the subsequent cycle. These deferrals double the amount the state has to pay during the next budget cycle.

KEY TERMS

appropriation bill
certify
deferrals
dual budgeting process
expenditures

fee
fines
fiscal note
general revenue funds
homestead exemption
"pay as you go"

progressive tax
regressive tax
revenue
riders
"sin" taxes

PRACTICE QUIZ

1. What is the current homestead exemption for most Texans?

   a. $5,000
   b. $10,000
   c. $25,000
   d. $35,000

2. What percentage of total tax receipts in 2019 were franchise (business) taxes?

   a. 4 percent
   b. 6.6 percent
   c. 9.5 percent
   d. 12 percent

3. On which of the following items does the state NOT include a gas tax?

   a. Gasoline
   b. Propane
   c. Liquefied gas
   d. Diesel fuel

4. What is the duration of the state's budget?

   a. 1 year
   b. 2 years
   c. 3 years
   d. 4 years

5. Which organization is responsible for preparing and executing the state's budget?

   a. Executive Finance Organization
   b. Legislative Redistricting Board
   c. Legislative Budget Board
   d. Texas Comptroller

6. What two taxes account for most of the state's tax revenue?

   a. Property tax and income tax
   b. Income tax and sales tax
   c. Sales tax and property tax
   d. Service fees and property tax

7. The largest jump in tax revenue in recent years was a result of rising . . .

   a. Property taxes
   b. Income taxes
   c. Sales taxes
   d. Service fees

8. The legislature's ability to provide tax relief for homeowners is limited by the fact that local governments . . .

   a. Collect a large, one-time tax for building new homes
   b. Appraise and raise the values of homes
   c. Charge fees for services that the state government delivers
   d. All of the above

9. Sales taxes provide a stable, steady source of state revenue year in and year out.

   a. True
   b. False

10. If you object to the appraisal of your house's value, you can appeal it.

    a. True
    b. False.

[Answers: C, B, B, B, C, C, A, B, B, A]

Learn more with this chapter's digital tools, including the Oxford Insight Study Guide, at www.oup.com/he/Rottinghaus3e.

14 PUBLIC POLICY IN TEXAS

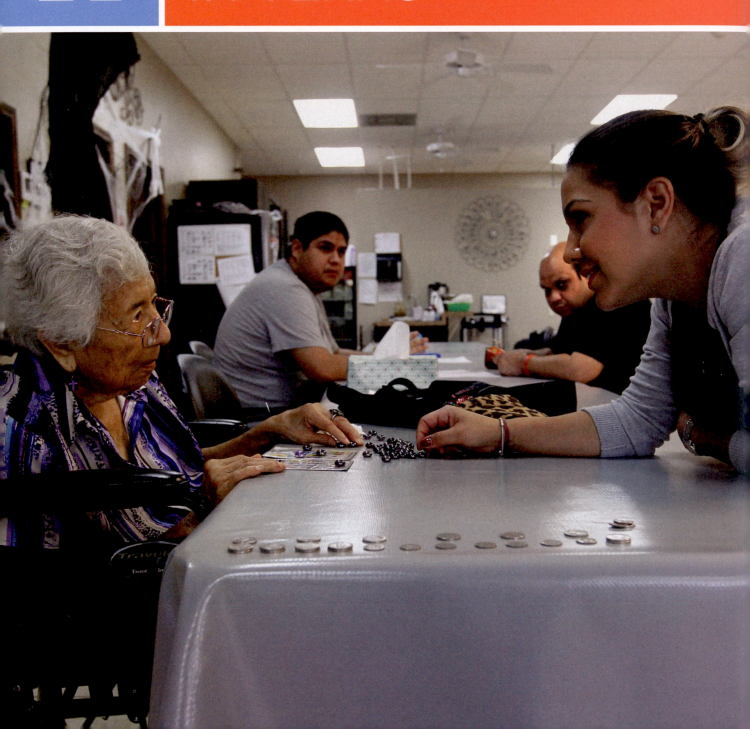

Some have called it the "silver tsunami."[1] By 2030, almost 20 percent of the state of Texas will be over 64 years old, and currently, about 10 percent (almost 3.5 million) live in poverty—a number that is expected to grow.[2] Low income makes seniors vulnerable to hunger and abuse in shady assisted living facilities, conditions exacerbated by the spread of infectious diseases. Hidalgo County, with its more than 86,000 Latinos over the age of 64, is home to Lindos Momentos Adult Day Care in McAllen. "It's like our second house," says one guest who joins others to gossip, eat, and listen to telenovelas. The group is part of an estimated 34,200 elderly Texans statewide who utilize Day Activity and Health Services, the name state officials give to adult day care.[3] Most access these facilities using joint state–federal social service programs like Medicaid. As the cost of elder care and the health needs of Texans rise, state and federal policymakers will need to find ways to meet the demands of a changing population.

In this chapter, we outline the policymaking process that builds concrete solutions for problems or concerns that face aging—and all other—Texans. We then take a close look at the dozens of policies created and administered by the state and examine where Texans stand on health care, welfare, education, transportation, energy, and environmental policy. Confrontations over these issues divide along familiar battlefronts: partisanship, geography, and economic interests.

14.1	Identify the phases of the policy process in Texas.
14.2	Describe the social welfare programs Texas administers.
14.3	Analyze the role of the state in border issues and immigration.
14.4	Evaluate the challenges facing Texas's education system.
14.5	Assess funding, affirmative action, and other issues in higher education.
14.6	Outline Texas's transportation policy and future challenges.
14.7	Explain the state's environmental and energy policies.

● An employee at the Lindos Momentos Adult Day Care helps a 91-year-old Texan with her card in *chalupa*, a bingo-like game featuring iconographic Mexican drawings.

(W) 14.1 PUBLIC POLICY PRIORITIES AND PROCESS

> **14.1** Identify the phases of the policy process in Texas.

Texas has a long history of being a "low-tax, low-service" state. With no income tax, Texas's support for social programs is generally low. Texas consistently spends less per capita—about $4,024 per person in 2018—than 49 out of the 50 states.[4]

Expenditures are an indicator of state priorities. The result of the pull and struggle of competing interests, however, produces a budget that reflects not only what Texans want to spend money on, but also what Texans *must* spend money on. These obligations are as plentiful as tumbleweeds in western Texas or taco trucks in Austin, and they involve all Texans—the elderly, the young, the disabled, the sick, the impoverished, and even those stuck in traffic. Because the responsibilities of education and public safety are delegated to the state, Texas spends most of its revenue on those policies and programs.

Like debates over the best Texas barbeque, the policymaking process is a cycle that never ends (see Figure 14.1). A triggering factor puts an issue on the agenda, the problem is studied, and solutions are proposed and implemented—but that's only the beginning. Texans then begin to argue over where the policy is working and where it is failing. Using research and feedback, lawmakers revise the policy. Let's take a closer look at the four prominent moments in this complex process, using the recent open carry debate as an example.

Everyday needs of the people as well as sudden crises, such as an economic shock, a natural disaster, or a massive policy failure, trigger the policymaking process. Citizens who have problems, interest groups, or political parties often identify issues they would like to place on the agenda. These individuals or groups frame the problem by identifying the causes and consequences and by attempting to control the narrative on the issue. In one case, at the dawn of the 2015 legislative session, Second Amendment supporters held a rally at the State Capitol advocating for "open carry," a provision that allows properly licensed individuals to display a firearm openly rather than concealing it. In Texas, one murder occurs every 7 minutes, and in 2014, 63 percent of these homicides involved firearms.[5] Some Texans argued that open carry deters crime. Texas was, at the time, one of only six states that did not allow it.[6] Advocates for open carry also claimed that concealed carry restricts their right to bear arms and that given recent mass shootings like those that have taken place in schools and movie theaters, Texans should be allowed to carry weapons openly. Organizations like Open Carry Tarrant County pressed lawmakers for support, who in turn confronted other reluctant lawmakers in their offices.[7]

agenda setting: the placement of an issue onto the public agenda

During the **agenda-setting** phase, policymakers ask, "Is this problem important enough for government to get involved?" Lieutenant Governor Dan

FIGURE 14.1 **The Policymaking Process**

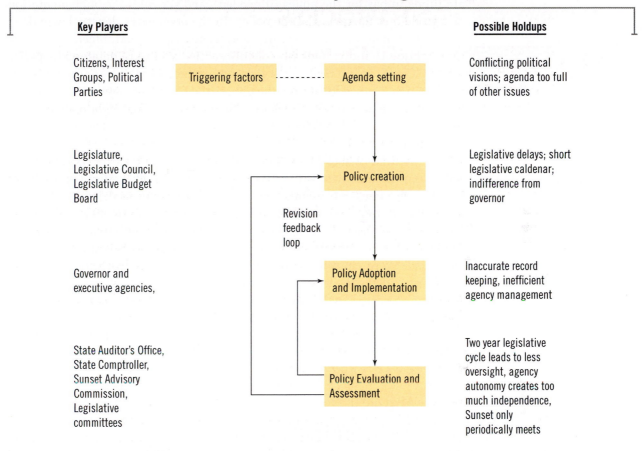

Key Players		Possible Holdups
Citizens, Interest Groups, Political Parties	Triggering factors - - - - - - Agenda setting	Conflicting political visions; agenda too full of other issues
Legislature, Legislative Council, Legislative Budget Board	Policy creation	Legislative delays; short legislative caldenar; indifference from governor
	Revision feedback loop	
Governor and executive agencies,	Policy Adoption and Implementation	Inaccurate record keeping, inefficient agency management
State Auditor's Office, State Comptroller, Sunset Advisory Commission, Legislative committees	Policy Evaluation and Assessment	Two year legislative cycle leads to less oversight, agency autonomy creates too much independence, Sunset only periodically meets

SOCIAL RESPONSIBILITY: **Think about a major policy issue debated in the news. What was the triggering event?**

Patrick had pledged support for the open carry issue, but when the early days of the legislative session passed without action, Republican Representative Jonathan Stickland stated, "If Dan hasn't had anyone bring this issue up to him, let me make it clear, I am bringing it up to him now."[8]

Policymakers then examine the problem to understand whether and how government can offer a solution. They gather information, meet with experts and Texans who are connected to the problem, and consider alternatives. In the policy creation stage, stakeholders from around the state shape legislation. For the open carry debate, municipal and public safety employees weighed in on where "gun-free zones" would begin and end. Private corporations expressed concern about negative consequences for tourism and retail.[9]

In the policy adoption phase, lawmakers adopt the policy, appropriate funds to pay for the policy (if needed), and set rules for implementation and guidelines for review of the policy. In the open carry debate, lawmakers grappled with how to protect search and seizure rights guaranteed by the U.S. Constitution to individuals who openly carried and were detained by police (called "Cop Stop"). The Texas legislature opted to strip those measures describing police procedures from the bill. As the bill passed, law enforcement in San Antonio had to develop policies to handle those who might open carry at Fiesta, the annual citywide event with parades, rides, and attended by more than 3 million people.[10]

In the final phase, evaluation, lawmakers and other experts review the policy and its outcomes. This final phase comes later, in the form of oversight hearings, guidance documents, and if needed, revisions to the policy creation or implementation. Six months after open carry went into effect, gun rights advocates complained that guns were still being banned in places where the law should protect the right to open carry—including jails.[11] Many questions remained. Were churches and other private, religious institutions also required to abide by the new law? Attorney General Ken Paxton penned a clarifying, nonbinding legal opinion that it is legal to carry a loaded gun into a church as long as there are no signs banning weapons.[12]

 TEXAS TAKEAWAYS

14.1.1 What are the four phases of the policymaking process?

14.1.2 How does agenda setting work?

14.2 HEALTH CARE AND WELFARE

14.2 Describe the social welfare programs Texas administers.

Many Texans are just "one crisis away" from financial disaster, and nearly a quarter of Texas children live in poverty.[13] Poverty rates for African Americans and Hispanics are nearly three times higher than those for Anglos or Asians. Geography matters as well: Although poverty rates in Texas have fallen, Texans along the border are more likely to be in poverty than the rest of the state—more than 40 percent versus 15 percent statewide.[14] One in seven Texas families is food "insecure," facing hunger or engaging in coping mechanisms to avoid it.[15] On health care issues, Texas has the biggest share of uninsured of any state in the union, both as a percentage (18 percent) and in number (more than 5 million residents in 2018), surpassing even California, and well above the national average of 9 percent.[16]

How does Texas address these issues? One path is **redistributive policies** that transfer wealth from those who have more to those who have less. Generally, social welfare programs pull taxes from working Texans to return them if and when Texans need assistance in the future. Like other Americans, Texans can receive health insurance as a benefit through their employer, purchase private plans, or qualify for government health care programs. These programs include Medicare, Medicaid, Social Security, and the Children's Health Insurance Program.

Federal and state governments fund these programs jointly, which allows each level to have input in determining the scope of the program—and illustrates how federalism, discussed in Chapter 3, works today. As federal funds are freed up (either through a reduction in need or stricter state rules), state lawmakers can shift funds to other programs like facilities, mental health hospitals, or child protective services.

> **redistributive policies:** policies that transfer wealth from those who have more to those who have less

MEDICARE

When you hit 65, you'll be eligible for **Medicare**, a national social insurance program for older Americans funded by a payroll tax, premiums, and surtaxes and administered exclusively by the federal government. Medicare only partially covers health care expenses, depending on the specific plan, and so it leaves some Texans to pay the remaining costs. As of 2019, more than 59 million Americans, and about 4.2 million Texans, were beneficiaries of Medicare.[17] Although Medicare is a wholly federal program, federal law does require the state to pay deductibles and premiums for low-income Medicare beneficiaries.[18]

> **Medicare:** a national social insurance program for older Americans funded by a payroll tax, premiums, and surtaxes and administered by the federal government

---

INSIDER INTERVIEW

Eva DeLuna Castro, State Budget Analyst, Center for Public Policy Priorities

How does the budget process set priorities and impact Texas social welfare?

Because of the requirement that the general revenue part of the Texas state budget has to balance, legislators and interest groups wield the most power when they change the revenue side of the equation. Proposals to cut state taxes and other revenue that supports public and higher education, social services, and public safety sailed through the 2013 and 2015 legislative sessions. The 2015 session also saw a significant diversion of existing sales tax revenue from these areas of the budget to state highways, in what many Capitol observers have described as "robbing Peter to pay Paul." Most lobbyists and public interest groups focus their time and powers of persuasion on the appropriations bill drafts that move through the House and Senate, but proposals that affect state revenue merit just as much attention—if not more.

SOCIAL RESPONSIBILITY: **Should the state have a limit on lobbyist influence in the budget process? Why or why not?**

Critics charge that Medicare is inefficiently managed, gives inadequate access to medical providers, and is wrought with fraud. The government routinely tracks down and prosecutes fraud. The largest Medicare fraud enforcement action in history netted 35 doctors, psychologists, and nurses charged with stealing more than $1.3 billion in 2017.[19]

MEDICAID

Medicaid: medical coverage for low-income Texans provided by the federal government

Medicaid covers more than 4 million Texans who have low income.[20] Established in 1967, it is administered by the Texas Health and Human Services Commission. Medicaid is a basic health insurance program that covers both acute care, such as visits to doctors, and chronic care or long-term services. This program increases the role of the national government in the states, especially Texas, because of the state's large low-income population. The federal government determines specific eligibility rules and picks up most of the tab, while the state must administer the program and can expand eligibility. Essentially, the federal government sets the table and cooks the meal, but the states must serve it. Federal law requires the state to cover certain population groups, such as the disabled, low-income families, and children based on income levels, but it gives the state the choice of whether to cover other population groups, such as pregnant women or infants up to 198 percent above the poverty level. The state also gets to decide what services to provide to these populations. Should it give mosquito repellent to pregnant mothers to prevent the Zika virus from infecting the child? Texas covers home health, lab and X-ray, well-baby, and well-child care. Optional coverage includes eye care, podiatry, hearing aids, mental health counseling, and hospice care.

The number of Medicaid recipients is double today what it was in 2000 as the number of poor Texans has expanded, covering 14 percent of Texans in 2019 and growing by 35 percent from the prior year. People enrolled in other low-income programs automatically qualify for coverage. The current Medicaid caseload is composed primarily of pregnant women (69 percent of total clients) and Texans under 21 years of age (77 percent). Families with nondisabled children make up 69 percent of program participants.[21] Texans with disabilities make up more than half of total Medicaid spending.[22] Statewide in 2019, 50 percent of Medicaid clients were Hispanic, 18 percent were Anglo, and 15 percent were African American.

Because a large percentage of individuals in Texas are in need of coverage, and because federal and state laws do not limit those eligible, Medicaid in Texas is on an "unsustainable budget trajectory" as rising health care costs and growing enrollment consume an ever larger portion of the state budget.[23] Texas also spends more on Medicaid than on any other program. However, most of the funds are provided by the federal government. The federal government funded almost 60 percent of the Medicaid program in 2019, and Texas the other 40 percent.[24] Texas's spending on Medicaid in the 2020–2021 budget—making up more than 29 percent of the budget—surpassed education spending. The state is allowed to add (but not subtract) individuals with specific needs to Medicaid, but this is less likely as the budget grows larger.

CHILDREN'S HEALTH INSURANCE PROGRAM

Children can also get special health coverage through the Texas **Children's Health Insurance Program (CHIP)**, a federal program that is run by the states to provide health (including dental) coverage to children whose families make too much to qualify for Medicaid but not enough to buy private insurance. Like Medicare, the federal and state governments share costs for the program: The federal government picked up 70 percent in 2019 to the state's 30 percent.[25] The state has more than half a million children in CHIP. Medicaid, combined with CHIP, covers more than half of all children in the state and two-thirds of people in nursing homes.[26] Funding for the 2020–2021 budget allocates about $200 per child per month to the approximately 425,000 eligible Texans.[27]

States have flexibility in designing their CHIP program. Texas's program expanded health coverage to children and families that earn up to 200 percent of the poverty line. Eligibility rules also require a child to be a Texas resident, under age 19, and uninsured for at least 90 days. Immigrant children were formerly ineligible for CHIP. However, rule changes in 2010 enabled the state to receive matching funds from the federal government, and so Texas extended coverage to some of these children. The Patient Protection and Affordable Care Act broadened federal funding for CHIP, prevented states from reducing certain eligibility standards, and required states to continue current levels of coverage.

Children's Health Insurance Program: a federal program run by the states to provide health coverage to children whose families make too much to qualify for Medicaid but not enough to buy private insurance

THE AFFORDABLE CARE ACT

The Patient Protection and Affordable Care Act, commonly referred to as the Affordable Care Act (ACA) or "Obamacare" (after President Barack Obama, who championed the program), allows states to expand Medicaid coverage to families with incomes up to 133 percent of the federal poverty level and provides insurance subsidies for families with incomes between 100 percent and 400 percent of the federal poverty level. The catch is that every individual who was not covered by their employer's plan must buy insurance or pay a fine. After the ACA was implemented, the national uninsured rate fell to 11 percent in 2015, the lowest recorded percentage since 2008.[28] More than 1 million Texans enrolled through the national exchange and received subsidies averaging $333 per month to help pay for their premiums in 2018.[29]

Approximately 1.7 million Texans could purchase subsidized policies under the ACA, Medicaid, or CHIP but aren't doing so. Many Texans don't understand that they are eligible, which researchers chalk up to confusion that could be solved through outreach and education. Because Texas did not expand Medicaid under Obamacare, however, the state has 638,000 adults who fall into a coverage "gap." These "gappers" earn too much to qualify for Medicaid but not enough to qualify for marketplace tax credits.[30]

The struggle between the federal government and Texas continues over future health care funding. The federal government encouraged states to join the ACA, but Texas has been reluctant to do so. The state was able to secure a waiver (called a Section 1115 waiver) until 2022 to help Texas privatize its managed care health insurance system for Medicaid patients and tamp down the exploding cost of uncompensated care.[31] Texas agreed under the temporary waiver to develop a Medicaid expansion program.[32] Meanwhile, during the first 2 years of the Trump administration, Congress attempted but failed to repeal or replace the ACA. President Trump rolled out a series of actions to cut the enrollment period and reduce funds for those eligible for coverage.[33]

SOCIAL SECURITY

A rising urban population, the fragmentation of Americans' extended families, and an increase in life expectancy, combined with the crippling effects of the Great Depression, prompted President Franklin Roosevelt and Congress to enact the Social Security program in 1935, run by the federal government and administered through the Social Security Administration. Working Texans pay Social Security taxes, and the federal government sets aside funds to help the blind and disabled and those with little income. In return, Texans receive Social Security payments when they reach the age of retirement (a sliding scale from 62 to 66) or Supplemental Security Income (SSI) if they become unemployed or disabled (and are age 65 or older). The federal government sets eligibility caps and benefit rates and determines eligibility.

Currently, about one in seven retired Texas residents receives benefits from Social Security, about $1,290 a month.[34] Social Security is especially important for retired Hispanics. Almost three-fourths of Hispanic beneficiaries nationwide rely on payments from Social Security for at least half their retirement income. In contrast, Social Security payments make up only about one-third of the retirement income for non-Hispanic Americans. This is because elderly Hispanics are more likely to live below the poverty line (18 percent) than other groups (17 percent of African Americans, 9 percent of Asians and Pacific Islanders, and 7 percent of Anglos).[35] Through SSI, blind, disabled, or low-income aged Texans received $750 per month per individual in 2019 to meet basic needs like food, clothes, and shelter.[36] Many states supplement SSI. Texas does not, but it does require a smaller percentage of one's income to automatically go to health care costs compared to other states.

TEMPORARY ASSISTANCE TO NEEDY FAMILIES

means-tested programs: income-measured programs that provide aid to individuals and families with low incomes

Several joint state and federal programs help Texans make ends meet. **Means-tested programs** are income-measured programs that provide aid to Texans or communities with low incomes, usually headed by a single-parent

GREAT TEXAS POLITICAL DEBATES
Drug Testing for Benefits

In 2015, the Texas legislature passed a bill to subject people seeking cash assistance from Temporary Assistance to Needy Families to drug tests. Failure to screen clean would make the recipient ineligible for financial assistance temporarily or permanently, depending on the number of positive tests recorded. Texas is not alone in this requirement: 12 other states have instituted drug-testing measures. Democrats and advocates for low-income families have pushed back, arguing that the tests unnecessarily single out poor Texans. They maintain that such drug tests are not cost effective, and they have even filed cases in court to determine if this measure is constitutional.[37]

SOCIAL RESPONSIBILITY: **Should a drug test be required to receive benefits?**

YES: If a recipient is receiving the public's money, he or she needs to live drug-free and receive proper medical attention. Drug addicts are more likely to use cash assistance to purchase drugs. Moreover, individuals free of drugs are more likely to seek employment and be productive in their jobs.

NO: It is too costly to administer these tests to all welfare recipients, especially for minor violations. Furthermore, these tests may lead to false positives. Drug testing also violates beneficiaries' rights to privacy and subjects them to humiliation.

household. The federal government pays for these welfare programs, and any Texans who qualify can access them. These programs consumed $1 trillion of the federal budget in 2019.

The largest welfare program is **Temporary Assistance to Needy Families** (**TANF**), a block grant to states. The federal government sets the basic rules, but the states develop the specifics of the programs, including eligibility limits and benefit levels. TANF provides financial and medical assistance to needy children and their parents or the relatives with whom the children live. TANF also offers "one-time" assistance payments of $1,000 to families in need to help solve a short-term crisis. To be eligible in Texas, the head of the family must receive job training or seek employment, follow child support rules, not quit a job while receiving funds, not abuse alcohol or drugs, take parenting classes, and get vaccines for their child. The number of families receiving TANF in April 2020 was 16,647, down from more than 50,000 in 2008.[38]

It is difficult to get these benefits in Texas because the state has placed caps on how long a family can obtain benefits and has instituted strict income eligibility rules. To qualify for a maximum $290 in monthly cash aid, a family of three cannot make more income than $188 a month—a rate that has been frozen for 20 years; thus, only the most destitute families qualify.[39] For every 100 poor families in Texas in 2016, only 4 received TANF (compared to 23 nationally).[40] In the past 20 years, TANF subsidies have dropped significantly in every state, leaving families who receive TANF well below the poverty line (Figure 14.2).[41]

Temporary Assistance to Needy Families: a program that provides financial and medical assistance to needy children and their parents or relatives

IS IT BIGGER IN TEXAS?

FIGURE 14.2 Maximum TANF Benefit as a Percentage of the Poverty Line

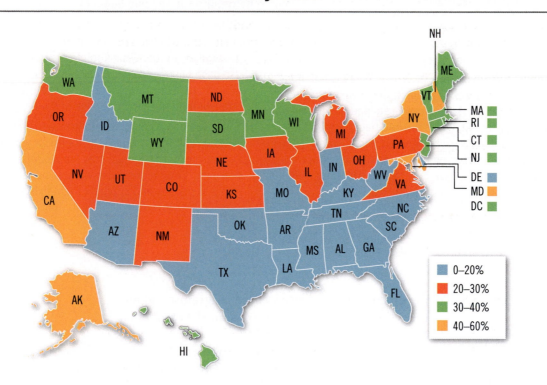

Legend:
- 0–20%
- 20–30%
- 30–40%
- 40–60%

Source: Ife Floyd, "TANF Cash Benefits Have Fallen by More Than 20 Percent in Most States and Continue to Erode," Center on Budget and Policy Priorities, October 13, 2017.

 COMMUNICATION:

Which states provide the lowest and highest TANF subsidies?

Are there regional patterns?

- Texas and other southern and southwestern states tend to offer lower subsidies.
- The northeastern and Pacific northwestern states tend to offer higher subsidies.

 CRITICAL THINKING:

What explains this variation?

- Southern states, like Texas, Louisiana, and Florida, tend to be politically conservative and are less likely to support funds for social welfare support.
- States like California and New York have larger social safety nets due to more support for progressive policy issues.

The "one-time TANF for grandparents" program offers $1,000 to grandparents if they have grandchildren on TANF and don't have significant assets or make more than twice the poverty level.

UNEMPLOYMENT BENEFITS

Texans who are temporarily out of work through no fault of their own may quality for unemployment benefits. But no one should just quit his or her job and hope for benefits. Only those who were laid off, who were "downsized," or who lost a job due to a reduction in force meet the requirements for benefits. Individuals fired for work-related misconduct or inadequate performance also do not qualify. The Texas Workforce Commission bases the weekly unemployment benefit amount on the individual's highest past quarterly earnings, up to $465 per week maximum.[42] Recipients are eligible for benefits for 52 weeks. The COVID-19 pandemic greatly accelerated the number of Texans seeking unemployment benefits, and as a result, the state temporarily expanded the duration of coverage an extra 13 weeks as long as the recipient is actively looking for work. Legislation passed in 2017 also renders anyone who fails a drug test ineligible for benefits, for a month, until the person passes another drug test (see Great Texas Political Debates).

WORKERS' COMPENSATION

If you are injured on the job, you are likely entitled to paid medical care, and you have the right to keep income and medical benefits. If you are killed on the job, your beneficiaries may be entitled to death and burial benefits.[43] These benefits are called workers' compensation. Texas leads the nation in worker fatalities. At the top of the list receiving these benefits are truck drivers, many in the oil patch in west Texas and construction trades: 534 in 2017, followed by California at 376.[44] The Texas Division of Workers' Compensation is responsible for the distribution of these benefits. The agency denies nearly half of all claims when they are first filed, however, and even when the claims are brought to trial, workers lose most of the time. "They throw these workers away like tissue paper. They're nothing more than a used Kleenex," said one employment attorney.[45] Although the state has fined businesses for failing to report injuries, the fines are generally small.[46]

⭐ TEXAS TAKEAWAYS

14.2.1 What is the difference between Medicare and Medicaid?

14.2.2 Who is covered under the Affordable Care Act?

14.3 IMMIGRATION AND BORDER SECURITY

14.3 Analyze the role of the state in border issues and immigration.

Texas, settled by wave after wave of immigrants, shares a longer contiguous border with another country than any other state in the union. The first undocumented immigration to Texas was Anglo immigration from the United States into what was then Mexico. In 1830, a Mexican colonel encountered several immigrants, checked them for passports, and finding no proper documentation, ordered them to leave.[47]

Immigration is driving Texas's population growth, as more than 786,000 legal immigrants arrived in Texas between 2010 and 2018, second only to Florida but ahead of California—17 percent of the state's total population.[48] As of 2019, Texas had just over 4.6 million foreign-born residents, up from 2.9 million in 2000.[49] Most (68 percent) were from Mexico and Central America, but a sizable group from Asia (22 percent) has driven much of the growth. More than one-third have become naturalized citizens.[50] Texas also has the second-largest undocumented immigrant population—about 1.8 million—second only to California. Most of these immigrants come from Mexico, followed by other Central American countries. Approximately 200,000 were under 17, and 834,000 Texas kids live with one or more parents who is undocumented.[51] Half of the incoming undocumented immigrants are 25–45 years old, and more than half are male.

ECONOMIC IMPACT

The effect of undocumented immigrants on the economy brings up a contentious point, but most agree that immigrants do displace workers for low-wage jobs while also creating new jobs by buying goods and services. According to the Federation for American Immigration Reform, undocumented immigrants cost Texas taxpayers $12.1 billion in 2018 for education, health care costs, and policing but contributed $1.27 billion to economic output in wages, salary, and business earnings.[52] Other figures from 2020 show that for every $1 the state spends on undocumented immigrants, it brings in $1.21, generating $427 million more than they cost the state (excluding health care costs).[53]

Undocumented immigrants may also pay taxes for services they can never use (especially Social Security or Medicare taxes). They often live in the shadows and neglect proper health care or educational opportunities, hoping not to get stopped by police or get turned in by neighbors.[54] They may face abuse or exploitation as they are hired under the table for wages that are lower than those of other workers. This is especially the case in labor-intensive industries like construction. They may be forced to live in segregated, substandard housing because they do not want to risk obtaining official documentation for a bank loan.

Children of undocumented immigrants cannot be denied access to public schools by federal law, regardless of the immigration status of the parents, as held by the U.S. Supreme Court in *Plyler v. Doe* (1982).[55] Twenty percent of undocumented immigrants speak English "very well," but more than half speak the language "not well" or "not at all."[56] Difficulties with English may increase the cost of educating those students who need expanded translation assistance or instruction in English.

PUBLIC OPINION AND STATE LAWS

Texans ranked undocumented immigration (19 percent) and border security (145percent) as the two most important problems facing the state in 2019, with Republicans (30 percent for immigration and 27 percent for border security) believing both to be more important than Democrats (9 percent and 3 percent, respectively).[57] While legal immigrants are screened prior to entering the country, undocumented immigrants of course bypass federal screening, raising concerns that criminals may penetrate the long border. In 2005, Victor Reyes assaulted, shot, and killed a 25-year-old Houston man at random who had stopped at a red light. Reyes was an undocumented immigrant who had been deported four times between 2003 and 2010 and had a criminal record that included burglary and illegal entry into the country. During a violent shootout, Reyes then killed two people and wounded another three before sheriff's deputies shot him.[58] This senseless killing rallied Republicans who passed legislation (known as Senate Bill 4). This law prohibits local government from creating safe havens for undocumented immigrants (known as sanctuary cities where local governments choose not to comply with federal requests to detain suspected illegal immigrants in local jails) and allows law enforcement to ask about the immigration status of detained individuals (called the "show me your papers" provision).[59] Opponents of the law argue that it unfairly targets racial minorities and cripples the relationship between law enforcement and immigrant communities.

Tough talk on illegal immigration does not always translate to all sectors in Texas. Business interests have partnered with immigration activists to limit Texas's enforcement of laws that prevent industries from hiring undocumented workers through programs like E-Verify.[60] An executive order signed by Governor Rick Perry places the Texas Workforce Commission in charge of enforcing a rule that bans undocumented immigrants from working directly for the state through its agencies or universities. Workers live "in the shadows" in this underground labor market, where a "don't ask, don't tell" system allows employers to hire these immigrants without fear of punishment and most employers are screened with E-Verify. (Only 32 percent of hires were screened with E-Verify in 2017.)[61] Still, anyone who hires an undocumented immigrant faces potential civil fines, although generally only businesses with multiple violations are fined.

DEPORTATIONS AND BORDER SECURITY

Although immigration and border security issues fall under federal authority, aggressive politics and the practical need for solutions have led the state to step in frequently. Led by Republican Governor Greg Abbott, lawmakers have annually added $800 million to border security efforts, including new equipment, facilities, and law enforcement officers.[62] Critics claim that this is a blank check for further increases in funds and that the funds are not needed because they reflect an overreaction to the problems along the Texas border. The governor also agreed to commit at least 1,000 National Guard troops to the border with Mexico in response to a call from President Trump to clamp down on illegal immigration, at a cost of approximately $12 million a month. Critics claim this is wasteful since border crossings are at a 40-year low, and some further charge that all this action is nothing but a publicity stunt.

Deportations are on the rise in major Texas cities after President Trump signed an executive order expanding the Immigration and Customs Enforcement (ICE) focus on any immigrant in the United States. In contrast, earlier efforts more narrowly prioritized arrests of those convicted of serious crimes. ICE arrests have ramped up across Texas, which leads the nation in arrests (128,000 compared to 71,000 in second-place California), including more than

The story of Texas is a story of immigration and two nations intertwined. Texas has always been a crucible for incorporating newcomers, but struggles over equal education, voting rights, and poverty remain.

🔺 SOCIAL RESPONSIBILITY: **How can Texas balance a desire to welcome immigrants with the need for border security?**

280 employees of a north Texas telecommunications repair company—the largest in a decade.[63] From 2000 to 2018, less than 30 percent of immigrants facing removal from Texas had legal representation; 68 percent of those cases ended with a removal order, compared to lower percentages in states where immigrants were more likely to have an attorney.[64]

⭐ TEXAS TAKEAWAYS

14.3.1 What percentage of Texas's foreign-born population is from Mexico and Central America?

14.3.2 Approximately how many undocumented immigrants live in Texas?

ⓌⓊ 14.4 EDUCATION

The Texas Constitution requires the state to provide "efficient and adequate" funding for its public schools. School finance is the toughest political issue the state faces because historically it has been the most expensive service the state provides.[65] Students, parents, and school districts have fought the battle over education through the state legislature, the courts, and bureaucratic agencies.

14.4 Evaluate the challenges facing Texas's education system.

SOURCES OF K–12 FUNDING

Schools are funded by a combination of state general revenue, local property taxes, and some federal taxes. The **permanent school fund** contains money from a long-term investment the state made in 1854. The state initiated the fund with a $2 million appropriation and set aside land whose proceeds go expressly into public school funding. In addition, one-quarter of taxes on the production of fossil fuels and one-quarter of the gas, water, and electric utility taxes are constitutionally dedicated to public education. Much of the proceeds from the state lottery are also earmarked for education. The state provides extra funds for students who need more support. The **foundation school fund** is a briefcase for holding general revenue funds allocated by the legislature and appropriated to the Texas Education Agency to administer. The **available school fund** is the separate pool of revenue schools, allocated annually from the permanent school fund earnings and from one-quarter of the state's motor fuel tax revenue.

Individual schools receive money through a complicated formula that includes the number of students in class (attendance) plus extra funding for

permanent school fund: the fund that contains the money from the state's long-term investment and that pays for public education

foundation school fund: education funds from general revenue

available school fund: annual transfers from the permanent school fund to school districts

specific students like those with learning disabilities, gifted and talented students, low-income students, or those learning English.[66] Districts can also increase their pool of available funds locally by holding a bond referendum election that, if approved, can fund the districts' construction projects, repairs, or technology upgrades. Critics of this system argue that it creates two districts: rich and poor.

SCHOOL FINANCE

Despite attempts to identify additional funds to increase spending on public education, the issue of school finance is perpetually on the table. In the landmark U.S. Supreme Court case *San Antonio Independent School District v. Rodriguez* (1973), the Court found that the school finance system relied too heavily on property taxes, which produced considerable inequities in state aid to education. As the fundamental right to a quality public education only existed in the Texas Constitution, however, and not the U.S. Constitution, the Court found no violation of federal law.

Since 1984, school districts have sued the state seven times over perceived inadequate funding.[67] Overreliance on property taxes to fund education and unequal distribution of education funds prompted the Texas Supreme Court to proclaim the state's school finance system unconstitutional in 1989 in *Edgewood Independent School District v. Kirby*. The court determined that the system "enabled rich districts to raise and spend far more money than poor districts."[68] Lawyers for the Mexican American Legal Defense Fund, representing Demitrio Rodriguez of San Antonio and his family, argued that there was a $500,000 difference in the property value taxed per student between the poorest and the richest district. Lawmakers in 1991 created a new system which they believed would fix the problem. First dubbed "recapture," then the "Fair Share Plan," and finally "Robin Hood," the current school finance structure redistributes tax money from wealthy school districts to poorer ones. The plan is the first constitutionally permissible school funding formula in 30 years. However, the Robin Hood plan is disliked by many districts, especially the wealthier ones that have to send extra funds to the state.

School districts are guaranteed a formula-driven funding amount dictated by a statutorily determined set amount per student (the "basic allotment"), enrollment in special programs (special education, English as a second language [ESL], gifted and talented), and a "cost of education" index since costs are higher in some areas of the state than in others. This is called Tier 1 money. Tier 2 funds depend on how high the tax rate is for a school district—the first 6 cents of the tax rate above the minimum rate (called pennies) are "golden" (not subject to recapture), but the tax rate above those "golden pennies" from 7 to 17 ("copper pennies") are subject to recapture to distribute to school districts with less revenue.

Equalizing spending across a giant state with wildly different local revenue, from rich suburbs to poor inner cities, is difficult. The state is forced to use some general revenue from sales taxes to pay for schools, making school funding subject to uncertain budgets and political infighting. A reform effort in 2003 (to replace the Robin Hood plan), which included a payroll tax, a restructuring of the franchise tax, and increased taxes on gambling, failed when Republicans howled about higher taxes and Democrats complained about education being paid for with gambling, an unstable source of revenue.

Two-thirds of state school districts, again charging that the system was underfunded, filed another suit that landed in Texas courts in 2014. The Texas Supreme Court in 2016 found that the state's school finance system was "imperfect," and while it had "immense room for improvement," it did meet constitutional requirements. The court urged the legislature to make transformational changes rather than just apply a temporary band-aid.[69] Texans "deserve transformation, top-to-bottom reforms that amount to more than Band-Aid on top of Band-Aid" and a revamped system "fit for the 21st Century."[70] This is a challenging issue because over the years the state has outlined three broad tests to ensure that the system is constitutional: suitability, efficiency, and adequacy (see Figure 14.4).

Major spending cuts to education in 2011 totaled $5 billion in Texas, forcing local cuts of up to 10 percent, which meant laying off teachers, increasing class sizes, and reducing other staff, such as tutors and instructional specialists. After critics charged that the state share of funding was "frozen in time," and former education-focused legislators called out "yellowbelly politicians" to save Texas public schools, state lawmakers agreed to let rising local property tax revenues fill the gap in state spending on public education. This decision frustrated taxpayers and robbed school kids.[71] State lawmakers returned much of that money as they passed a sweeping bill to dramatically increase the state's share of public school funding per student by 20 percent in the 2020 biennial budget.[72] Average state spending on education rose from 2008 to 2019 (a $1,486 per pupil increase; see Figure 14.3). State law limits class size to 22 students, although more than 6,000 waivers were granted to allow school districts to exceed this amount.[73]

School districts also may lose sources of funding because industries can take advantage of tax breaks that enable them to reduce their property tax obligations. This "deal-closing" program allows local governments to cut deals for companies to move to an area and pay fewer property taxes, the major source of school funding. These deals have cost $7 billion in tax revenue in the past 17 years.[74] The mayor of Texas City, Texas, claimed that Valero Energy Corporation, through its tax break–receiving refinery, was "robbing" millions of dollars from local school kids.[75] In response, proponents argue that such incentives keep local economies thriving and attract new business to an area.

TEACHER, STUDENT, AND SCHOOL PERFORMANCE

In 1984, the Texas legislature passed a major reform bill that raised teacher salaries but tied them to teacher performance. The reforms also introduced more stringent teacher certifications, limited elementary school classrooms to

FIGURE 14.3 **Selected States and Public Education Funding**

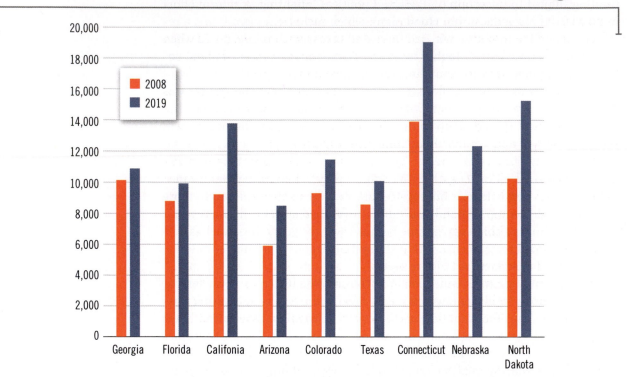

Source: National Education Association Rankings and Estimates. Calculations per pupil of elementary and secondary spending, 2008 and 2019 data.

 COMMUNICATION:

How has public education changed since 2008?

- Several southern states, including Georgia and Florida, increased spending per pupil or were flat. Eastern states like Connecticut increased spending by several thousand per pupil.
- Texas was on the small end of increases, slightly increasing spending by about $1,500 per pupil over the decade.
- California and North Dakota significantly increased spending per pupil.

 CRITICAL THINKING:

Why does Texas rank so low?

- Conservative leaders in states like Texas, Georgia, and Florida pushed for budget caps and less funding to public education in their states. Liberal politics in coastal states like California and Connecticut pressed for even more spending.
- Flush fiscal coffers in Nebraska and North Dakota, after a boom in funds from natural resources, provided more funds for spending on public education.

22 students, began competency testing for educators, initiated stricter attendance standards, and adopted a "no-pass, no-play" rule that prohibited students with failing grades from participating in extracurricular activities.

Governor Mark White, who initiated the efforts with the help of Dallas billionaire H. Ross Perot, took the credit—and then the blame—for the reforms. Anger was directed especially at the "no-pass, no-play" restrictions, upheld by the Texas Supreme Court, which ruled that students had no constitutional right to participate in sports. High school coaches were not the only ones upset: Even though the legislation included pay raises, teachers were also angered over the provision that required them to pass a competency test to keep their jobs. Mock tests circulated at the time asked the following sample questions: *"What comedy team had the greatest success in Texas since 1984?* (a) Laurel and Hardy, (b) Amos and Andy, (c) Tarzan and Cheeta, or (d) White and Perot" and *"Which of the following best describes "an educational expert" in Texas?* [here only one answer was offered]: a billionaire with a burr in his ass."[76]

Lieutenant Governor Bill Hobby became so irate that he called in the teachers groups to have it out with them. A state senator who attended the meeting characterized the situation as being "like the Alamo, but without the blood." In the 1986 election, the Texas State Teachers Association lined

A group of teachers, parents, and school administrators march up Congress Avenue toward the Capitol. These groups can exert significant pressure on legislators to reform education and can hold lawmakers accountable for their actions. In response to pressure from teachers groups and parents, the legislature in 2019 increased teacher pay, giving school districts flexibility to reward high-rated teachers, and added incentives for teachers to work in high-needs or rural districts.

PERSONAL RESPONSIBILITY: Think about your high school. Would the challenges facing your school be fixed with more money or greater teacher accountability?

up against Governor White, despite the fact that 97 percent of the teachers passed the competency provisions, which, according to *Texas Monthly*, were "so easy that only people who have trouble reading and understanding English are likely to fail."[77] Combined with a slumping economy and unpopular tax increases, the governor lost his reelection bid, but many of the reforms from 1984 remain in place.[78]

Parents are another major interest group in the education process. Reforms in 1995 cemented local control of schools by limiting the state's Texas Education Agency to broad education goal planning, managing the school fund accounts, and administering the accountability system. A decade later, beginning with the class of 2005, the state mandated that Texas students pass exit-level tests to meet graduation requirements, currently called the State of Texas Assessments of Academic Readiness tests, or STAAR. The percentage of students passing the test declined or remained flat from 2016 to 2017, with 75 percent of third through eighth graders statewide meeting the grade level.[79] Why does this matter? The results carry significant weight for fifth and eighth graders, who must pass the tests to move to the next grade. Backlash over exit-level testing peaked in 2015 as parents complained that the state put too much emphasis on the test. The legislature softened the test requirement and allowed graduates who passed two of their five end-of-course exams to graduate.[80]

Rating schools is difficult because there are many ways to do so. Since 1993, Texas has rated its schools in one way or another. The most recent incarnation, beginning in the 2017–2018 school year, assigns letter grades (A, B, C, D, or F) rather than the "met standard" or "improvement required" labels used before this system was established.

ANGLES OF POWER
Standardized Tests and Education Accountability

Texas students often want to drop an F-bomb while taking the STAAR standardized tests, but they rarely confront the word in the test itself. As it turns out, however, a fifth grader from Lumberton Independent School District (ISD) spotted an expletive in an image of a graffiti park on a reading comprehension exercise.[81] Expletives aren't the only problems with the test. One poet whose two works are included in the seventh and eighth grade STAAR tests admitted that she couldn't answer the confusing questions about her own poetry.[82] Proponents of standardized testing argue that it is a solid metric for evaluating learning and pinpointing areas for improvements. Opponents charge that teachers are encouraged to "teach to the test," but the scores don't measure a student's true abilities. Modern debates about standardized tests center on how to deploy them and on how much weight to put on them when considering teacher pay or school funding.

SOCIAL RESPONSIBILITY: **How would you design a system to evaluate Texas's public education system? What criteria and considerations would you use?**

In 2016, the Texas Supreme Court held that Texans "deserve transformation, top-to-bottom reforms that amount to more than Band-Aid on top of Band-Aid" and a revamped system "fit for the 21st Century."[83] This is a challenging dilemma because over the years the state has outlined three broad tests to ensure the system is constitutional: suitability, efficiency, and adequacy (see Figure 14.4).

Nationally, Texas's education consistently ranks lower than that of most other states. *Education Week* gave Texas a C– overall, a C– for K–12 student achievement, a C for students' future success in life, and a D+ for school finance. This put Texas in 41st place nationally. Texas was not alone in getting low grades: North Carolina, Nevada, and Oregon all scored a C– overall or worse.[84]

DIVERSITY IN PUBLIC EDUCATION

The makeup of state schools has grown increasingly diverse as the state matures and changes demographically. In recent decades, Texas schools have grown larger (now at 5.2 million public school kids), less white due to a rise in the state's Hispanic and Asian populations, and poorer.[85] Many Texas public schools remain as segregated (either almost all Anglo, African American, or Hispanic) as they were in the 1970s when landmark legislation sought to end racial segregation in schools.[86] This presents challenges as well as opportunities.

Texas schools are allowed to file misdemeanor charges against students who skip school, and the fines can range up to $500 plus court costs.[87] Race may play a role in determining who gets charged, however. Ashley

FIGURE 14.4 Three Tests for Texas Public Education

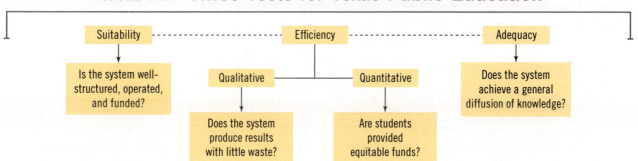

Source: Texas Public Policy Foundation, "Texas School Finance: Basics and Reform," March 2016.

SOCIAL RESPONSIBILITY: **Are these goals adequate to achieving a quality education for Texas's public school students? Can you think of any others?**

Brown, a 16-year-old African American sophomore from South Oak Cliff High School in Dallas, missed 4 days of school after her grandmother died of cancer. The school mistakenly charged her with more absences, and she had to appear in court.[88] The court ultimately dismissed the charges, but Ashley's case is not uncommon in Texas. African Americans are more likely than Latinos or Anglos to be suspended from school: 35 percent of suspensions in pre-K through second grade were African American students, compared to Anglo students at 27 percent and Latino students at 34 percent.[89] The legislature has now banned out-of-school suspensions of kindergarten through second grade, and some districts have increased resources to help teachers with students who need emotional or behavioral support.[90]

Another complication is the growing dropout rate among the state's poorer and Hispanic students. African Americans had the highest dropout rates (8.3 percent), followed by Hispanics (6.9 percent), multiracial (4.6 percent), and Anglo students (3.3 percent).[91] Such problems put many students on the "school-to-prison" pipeline and contribute to an undereducated Texas.[92] The solutions applied include identifying "dropout factory" schools that graduate less than 60 percent of their students and intervening early for students at risk of dropping out.[93] In recent years, because of these strategies, the performance gap between Anglo students and African American and Hispanic students has narrowed (see Table 14.1). Low-income and minority students were also hit harder than peers as school districts across the state scrambled to move instruction online during the COVID outbreak. Teachers planted "My teachers miss me" signs in the yards of missing students, but tens of thousands did not participate in online instruction.[94]

One reason Hispanic students have lagged behind is language. The state has been under legal scrutiny since the 1970s for failing to adequately fund English-language learner education.[98] Texas public schools had almost 1 million English as a Second Language (ESL) students in 2019.[99] Some school districts have begun more rigorously tracking the amount of time ESL students spend learning English, using periodic testing to make sure students understand academic concepts in English and furnishing the "Ferrari" of bilingual education programs where all students learn in both English and Spanish.

If a district has even one school campus that chronically fails to meet the state's standards for 5 or more years, "no excuses" legislation passed in 2015 allows the education commissioner to close campuses, replace the district's elected officials, or take over the district itself.[100] In three takeovers—El Paso ISD (59,400 students), Beaumont ISD (19,200 students), and Houston ISD (209,772 students)—the Texas Education Commissioner dismissed the elected school board and replaced its members with local community leaders.[101] The results of these takeovers have been mixed: Budgets have been balanced and leadership fissures have been repaired, but few changes have significantly raised student achievement rates.[102]

TABLE 14.1   ## Graduation Rates and Test Performance by Race

	ANGLO 1995/2018	HISPANIC 1995/2018	AFRICAN AMERICAN 1995/2018	ASIAN 1995/2018
Student population	47%/28%	36%/52%	14%/13%	3%/4%
Graduation rate[95]	91%/94%	80%/88%	80%/87%	90%/96%
Standardized Tests (TAAS/ STARR) "Approaches Grade Level or above" (2018)	75%/86%	46%/73%	38%/66%	78%/93%

Source: TEA Snapshots of Public Schools. Including Charter Schools. TEA Completion Reports. Texas Academic Performance Report (2018).

COMMUNICATION:

What are the makeup and success of school kids in Texas?

- Overall, Texas's graduation rates are very high, outpaced only by Iowa, New Jersey, West Virginia, and Nebraska in 2017.[96]
- Anglo and Asian students have the highest graduation rates and standardized test grades.
- Most gains between 1995 and 2017 have been among minority students.

CRITICAL THINKING:

Why is there variation in dropout rates?

- Testing standards may have produced more prepared students and made teachers accountable.
- The measurement may also be to blame: districts can avoid counting students who left for a variety of reasons, including taking the GED instead of graduating.[97] This may be artificially inflating the graduation rate.
- Poverty, racially segregated schools, and language issues may limit educational success for Hispanic and African American students.

VOUCHERS

One approach to public education is to make private schools more accessible through **vouchers** ("school choice," or where the "dollars follow the child").[103] Voucher programs provide a student with authorization for government funding to be used at a private school. Opponents argue that vouchers divert funding and therefore hurt public schools while aiding just a small number of private school students. Proponents claim that vouchers make schools work harder to attract students. On several occasions in the past few sessions, the legislature has attempted—but failed—to pass tax credits, a form of voucher, for Texans who send their children to private school to get a rebate.

vouchers: programs to provide a student with authorization for government funding to be used at a private school

Teachers play a major role in shaping public education in Texas, especially when the state threatens to take over underperforming public schools. Protests flared up when the state moved to take over the Houston Independent School District.

SPECIAL EDUCATION

Across the country, 13 percent of students on average are identified as needing special education, and every student eligible for special ed has a right to receive it under federal law. Federal courts have charged that in placing an "arbitrary" 8.5 percent cap (of total enrollment) on the number of students who could receive special education services, Texas had failed to fulfill its "child find" responsibility to locate children with disabilities entitled to these services. That cap, put into place in 2004. punished districts that went over it.[104] The Texas Education Agency reversed course and required local school districts to find and help the thousands of students who had been left out of special education. Still, administrators are concerned that the $65 million provided to accomplish this objective will not keep up with demand for services.[105]

BULLYING

In 2018, a businessman strode to the lectern at a public forum during a board meeting of the Katy ISD and accused Superintendent Lance Hindt of bullying him while in middle school 40 years earlier by taunting him about his last name (Gay, which he later changed to Barrett) and shoving his head in a urinal. Superintendent Hindt denied these allegations, but the incident highlighted the lingering effects of bullying on young Texans.[106]

Texas has taken a get-tough approach to bullying in public school classrooms. Indeed, the climate surrounding bullying, once thought to be just part of "growing up," has changed dramatically. Each school district is required to have a policy that prohibits bullying or harassment and to ensure that district employees enforce those provisions. Legislation passed in 2017 called David's Law, named after a 16-year-old student from San Antonio who took his own life after being cyberbullied, makes it a crime to cyberbully someone in Texas if it leads to injury or suicide of a minor. It also allows teachers to discipline students who bully other students off campus or online, thereby acknowledging the reach of this problem beyond the classroom.

 TEXAS TAKEAWAYS

14.4.1 How many times has the state been sued for inadequate funding since 1984?

14.4.2 What are vouchers?

14.5 HIGHER EDUCATION

Texas also funds and sets standards for higher-education institutions. Mirabeau B. Lamar, known as the "father of Texas education," is credited with the idea of establishing state support for higher education. In 1839, he outlined his vision for a public university system and professed, "A cultivated mind is the guardian genius of democracy."[107]

> **14.5** Assess funding, affirmative action, and other issues in higher education.

FUNDING

The permanent university fund (PUF) was established in 1839, even before Texas had universities. The scrubland the state set aside wasn't worth much until oil was struck. Proceeds from natural resources (oil, gas, sulfur, water), mineral leases, and grazing rights generated income for the fund and for permanent members: campuses of the University of Texas (UT) and Texas A&M University. The fund was set up in 1931 to provide two-thirds of its income to the UT and one-third to A&M.[108] With a boom in oil revenue pumping more than $1 billion a year into the PUF, the universities are flush with funds and have seen their endowments grow by 70 percent since 2014.[109] The fund is currently worth more than an estimated $19 billion, although that number is expected to flatline as oil prices plateau due to a dip in demand during the COVID-19 outbreak.[110]

The substantial wealth benefiting some of the state's universities has the rest of the universities calling foul. "Texas is not just driven by UT and A&M," State Representative Sylvester Turner, Democrat of Houston, opined during a hearing of the House Committee on Appropriations.[111] Representative Turner filed legislation to open up the PUF to state schools other than UT and A&M, which routinely receive double or triple the amount of funding other schools receive. Opponents argue that the state established the PUF to fund the state's flagship universities only. This creates a system that advantages only two state universities, despite broad resources. Defenders of the current system argue that the state has expanded the institutions allowed to access the PUF (like additional UT campuses and A&M research centers) for the good of the state. Texas only has eight Tier 1 universities, four of which became Tier 1 in 2016, compared to nine in California.

Tuition at public universities was set by the legislature until 2003, when a law was passed to allow individual universities to raise or lower tuition (called deregulation). As tuition has risen at all public schools, legislators have grumbled that they need to be regulated again. Yet the rate of tuition increase in the years since deregulation has been lower than the rate of increase in the decade before deregulation.[112] Higher tuition can contribute to growing student debt. The class of 2019 graduated college with $26,824 in student loan debt on average.[113] However, the problem is not just a problem for recent graduates: More than 222,000 Texans older than 60 years of age had student debt in 2017.[114]

COMMUNITY COLLEGES

The most explosive growth in higher education has come from community colleges in Texas. Enrollment in these 2-year institutions has risen 98 percent since 1990, totaling 685,831 students in 2018. These colleges educate many students (more than 50 percent of students enrolled in public higher education are in a community college).[115] As discussed in Chapter 12, these institutions are funded by taxes from locally elected Community College Boards (about $2.1 billion in 2018) but are supplemented with funds from the legislature for operations and instructional programs (about $1.8 billion in the 2020–2021 biennium).[116] A portion of the legislative funds are tied to "student success points" that assign point values for student-specific objectives, such as passing a math course the first time, being awarded a degree in a critical field, and transferring to a 4-year university.

STANDARDS

With growing demand for a college-educated workforce and the sprouting of colleges and universities across the Lone Star State, the Texas Commission on Higher Education was created in 1953, followed by establishment of the Texas Higher Education Coordinating Board (THECB) in 1965 to coordinate, develop, and evaluate Texas higher education. The THECB primarily approves construction of facilities, reviews and coordinates degree programs, and assists institutions of higher education with student retention and success issues. Does the state need more nurses, veterinarians, or big data scientists? The THECB is responsible for assessing the need for additional programs and for funneling students into them.[117] Institutions, driven by local concerns and alumni, may have different objectives than the state, increasing enrollment or degrees for their own sake. Powerful university lobbyists often circumvent the THECB by going to the legislature directly for funding help, increasing tensions between state resources, the THECB, and institutions of higher education.

AFFIRMATIVE ACTION

Abigail Fisher, a Sugar Land, Texas, student, dreamed of attending UT like her father and sister had before her. Her high school grades, test scores, volunteer efforts, and cello playing were not enough, however, as the university, she argues, rejected her application because of the "top 10 percent rule." This rule opens up educational opportunities by giving all racial and ethnic minority students who graduate in the top 10 percent at any Texas school, regardless of its rank or performance, automatic admission into a Texas public university. Arguing that her rejection was discriminatory based on race, Fisher sued the university.

The University of Texas as well as other schools have used **affirmative action**—a series of rules and procedures designed to give minorities a leg up by offering advantages in education or employment to specific groups to redress historic discrimination. The U.S. Supreme Court upheld the university's affirmative action program in 2016 in *Fisher v. University of Texas*, allowing UT to continue considering a prospective student's race as one factor among many to ensure a diverse student body. Even so, Latino enrollment has nearly tripled in Texas, but only about half of these students end up earning a bachelor's degree.[118]

affirmative action: a policy that provides additional benefits or opportunities to minorities who have suffered historically from discrimination

★ TEXAS TAKEAWAYS

14.5.1 What is the funding source of the University of Texas and Texas A&M University?

14.5.2 What are two funding sources for community colleges?

14.6 TRANSPORTATION

14.6 Outline Texas's transportation policy and future challenges.

Tired of sitting in traffic? You're not alone. Road conditions and traffic issues affect all Texans in one way or another. Several Texas cities are ranked near the top for worst commutes. And more than a million Texans living in and around major metropolitan cities commute annually.[119]

Transportation is often cited as the number 1 issue of concern for Texans, especially in big cities. The Texas Department of Transportation argues that it needs an additional $5 billion annually to maintain the current roads. Highway funds come mainly from motor vehicle registration fees, federal highway funds, the sales tax on motor oils, and some part of the motor fuel (gas) taxes: These make up the State Highway Fund.

With a small appetite to spend funds on transportation, lawmakers use toll roads as a way to develop and maintain road projects. For large projects like the expansion of the LBJ Expressway in Dallas, toll revenue is critical to funding the project's completion. But while Texans want more funding for roads, they don't want to pay for it with tolls. Opposition from fellow Republicans was enough to stop one of Governor Rick Perry's 2001 solutions to the state's transportation woes: the Trans–Texas Corridor, a new, 4,000-mile nexus of privately operated toll roads that would have crisscrossed the state. The price tag was to be $175 billion.[120] A 2014 constitutional amendment kicks in $1.7 billion yearly, although this is subject to economic variability because these funds are related to taxes on oil and natural gas production. Until funding shortages are resolved and congestion subsides, Texas drivers are going to be stuck behind the wheel in traffic.

Even with all this money, experts still point to Texas "transportation deserts"—areas where people who are too young, too old, too poor, or disabled cannot drive and live with unreliable public transportation (see Figure 14.5). Dependence on public transportation limits job opportunity and upward economic mobility in Texas. To improve the options of these tens of thousands of transit-dependent Texans, analysts recommend redesigning bus services by adding new lines, expanding service hours, and integrating bicycling with other transit services.[121] That expansion comes with a cost: Texas has not had a death-free day on its roads in 20 years. In an effort to reduce fatalities, cities have improved sidewalk and street design, more strictly enforced traffic laws, and provided education about roadway safety.[122]

TEXAS TAKEAWAYS

14.6.1 Where do state highway funds come from?

IS IT BIGGER IN TEXAS?

FIGURE 14.5 **Unmet Demand for Transportation (Percentage of Population)**

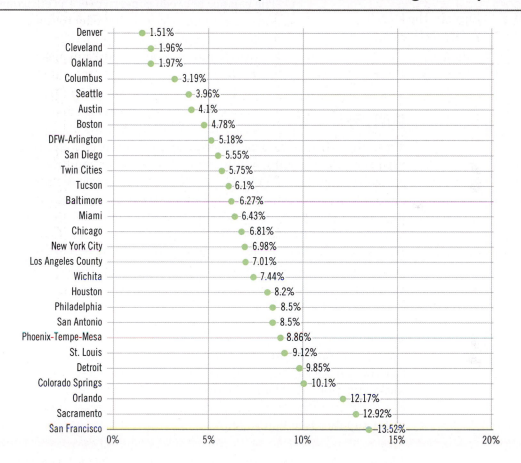

Source: *Smithsonian Magazine.*

 COMMUNICATION:

Which Texas cities have the highest and lowest percentage of unserved populations? How do these cities compare to other major cities?

- Denver, Cleveland, and Oakland have the lowest unmet demand for transportation.
- Sun Belt cities like Phoenix, San Antonio, and Orlando have more than 8 percent of demand unmet.

 CRITICAL THINKING:

What explains this variation?

- Cities that have invested in infrastructure are more likely to meet enough transportation demands.
- Sprawling and booming cities have a more difficult time keeping up with demand due to an influx of potential riders.

14.7 ENERGY AND THE ENVIRONMENT

| 14.7 | Explain the state's environmental and energy policies. |

The balance between concern over the environment and the promotion and regulation of energy sources reaches back generations. The political struggle between urban and rural interests also plays into regulating Texas's environment.

WATER

Since 2010, Texas has experienced drought conditions, draining reservoirs used for water, fueling wildfires and dust storms, and limiting water for agricultural use. At the height of the drought, cattle feed prices skyrocketed, rice farm output (water is used to soak the crop) tumbled, corn output fell 40 percent, and peanut production dropped.[123] Less water in the Rio Grande closed the tap on fast-growing border areas around El Paso that rely on the river for water, resulting in fewer healthy pastures and loss of livestock. More than 1,000 areas in Texas enacted water restrictions since the amount of water a single-family household uses to water its yard could fill 590,000 football fields with one foot of water.[124] Arlington banned watering between 10 a.m. and 6 p.m. year-round, and San Angelo reduced watering to once a week. A report from the organization Water Conservation by the Yard found that Texas could cut municipal water use by almost 9 percent if all its municipalities adopted these year-round outdoor watering restrictions.[125] The real danger facing Texas, however, lies not in the present but in the future as water demand surpasses dwindling existing water supplies (see Figure 14.6).

The Texas Water Development Board. In 1957, after a 7-year dry spell, the legislature founded an agency that would become the Texas Water Development Board (TWDB) to provide loans to local governments for water projects, administer water funds, and facilitate the transfer and sale of water and water rights throughout the state. The TWDB has promoted more efficient irrigation practices and the use of natural rainfall, with the result that irrigation water demands are projected to fall by almost 18 percent between 2020 and 2070. Unfortunately, population growth is likely to increase the demand on municipal water for drinking, bathing, and other purposes by 62 percent.[126]

Cities and suburbs are thirsty for more water. Parched rural agricultural land needs water for irrigation. It's no surprise then that instead of reflecting the polarized Republican versus Democrat politics, the water politics divide is between rural and urban or suburban interests. Rural

FIGURE 14.6 Thirsty Texas: Water Supply and Demand

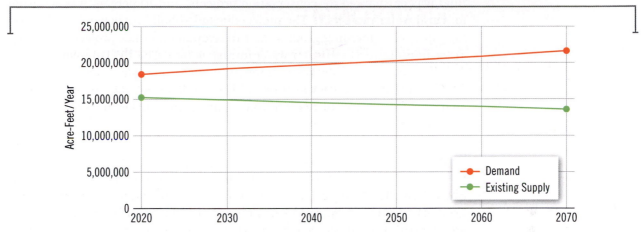

Source: The Texas Water Development Board.

 COMMUNICATION:

What are the trends in the supply of and demand for water?

- Demand for water is already outpacing supply, and the next 50 years will see demand rising much faster than supply.

 CRITICAL THINKING:

Why is demand rising but supply is falling?

- A growing population, especially in suburban areas, has raised demand for water to historic highs.

- Irrigation need for agriculture, including cattle, is increasing. Manufacturing and steam electric power needs are also predicted to increase over time.

- The number of new water projects funded by the state is not keeping up with the demand for more water.

representatives worry that cities will pay more for water and leave rural areas dry.[127] Republican Representative Drew Darby, arguing for rural Texas's fair share of the state's evaporating water supply, pointed out that "they don't grow cotton at Men's Wearhouse in San Antonio. They don't feed beef at the H-E-B in San Antonio. . . . The food, the fiber, the natural resources are produced in rural Texas."[128]

The rain quells the water problem in more ways than one. In 2015, voters overwhelmingly approved allocating $2 billion from the state Rainy Day Fund to a water fund for projects approved by the TWDB. Twenty percent of the fund was earmarked for conservation projects, and 10 percent was set aside for rural water projects.[129] The projects included building new reservoirs, fixing pipes, and pursuing groundwater development. Other projects may help Texas improve its D rating for water infrastructure. The TWDB financed over $1 billion in projects identified in the State Water Plan, including new reservoirs in northern and central Texas. El Paso built a desalination plan and created a facility to turn wastewater into drinking water as less water flowed into the Rio Grande River.[130]

Water Control and Ownership. A second environmental battlefront is the citizens versus the state over ownership of surface versus groundwater. Surface water is subject to control and management by the state, but groundwater is owned by the landowner of the property above it, known as the right of **capture**. Yet, as the reach of the state grew and water districts popped up around the thirsty state, landowners' use of this subsurface water was threatened. When local groundwater districts attempted to regulate how much water local property owners could pump, the cases ended up in court. The Texas Supreme Court in 2012 sided with landowners, certifying that the state could only issue rules that were "reasonable." The lack of clarity about what "reasonable" means, however, vexes water politics to this day.

capture: the right by which groundwater is owned by the landowner of the property above it

WATER AND AIR POLLUTION

Federal and state agencies track and monitor pollution in Texas. Congress has passed legislation, such as the Clean Air Act and Clean Water Act, setting standards for state and local governments that are implemented by the U.S. Environmental Protection Agency (EPA). Texas elected officials and state agencies have worked to meet these standards but have often battled the EPA and federal restrictions since the 1970s. At the state level, the Texas Commission on Environmental Quality (TCEQ) tracks air and water quality, water supply, and waste management and penalizes violators of state and local regulations.

Texas has met national standards for most pollutants with some notable exceptions. Vehicles, oil refineries, power plants, factories, and other industrial facilities have placed Texas far ahead of every other state in its greenhouse gas emissions, particularly ozone (smog) and carbon dioxide. Ozone levels have plagued the Dallas–Fort Worth and Houston metropolitan areas. Houston has dropped from the number 1 to the number 12 spot on the list of top ozone producers, but the city still experienced 21 days of unhealthy smog in 2017—taking its toll on children with asthma and older Texans with respiratory diseases.[131]

Environmental groups have filed suits against both Texas and the federal government, alleging that both have allowed Texas industries to violate federal regulations. A report from Environment Texas called "Troubled Waters" finds more than 900 instances of industrial facilities releasing pollution at levels beyond federal limits.[132] TCEQ issues fines in excess of a billion dollars a year, but a recent analysis carried out by environmental groups shows that, while the agency could issue fines as high as $2.3 billion for violations, the agency only levied a total of $1.2 million in fines, or two cents per pound of pollution.[133] Environmental groups charge that the TCEQ fails to hold polluters responsible and that in recent years, the EPA, which hears complaints against the TCEQ, has not challenged the TCEQ effectively.

Pollution is not just an urban problem. The state's most contaminated sources of drinking water can be found around farming communities, where a "hodgepodge" of chemicals mix to create a carcinogenic water supply and crop duster pilots release toxic chemicals in high winds, wafting them into animals and people as well.[134] In one of the windiest places on the planet, West Texas, DNA from antibiotic-resistant bacteria in cattle feedlots is airborne. Fecal material from the cow pen floor dries and then is released into the air, carrying with it antibiotic-resistant bacteria that limits doctors' ability to treat life-threatening infections.[135] One resident from Hale Center, who noted the smell from the lots, asked, "But even if I am not happy about the feed yard, what am I supposed to do? I live here."[136]

The economically vulnerable and racial minorities are also susceptible to pollution. In the Charlton–Pollard neighborhood of Beaumont, residents' eyes watered with the intense rotten-egg smell from the ExxonMobil refinery. Lawsuits initiated in 2000 alleged racial discrimination from the TCEQ, which they claimed allowed the plant to release an unsafe amount of emissions into the air. The EPA agreed to install an air monitor but did not agree to a half-mile greenbelt between the community and the refinery or to help in relocation or medical monitoring.[137]

ENERGY SOURCES

Texas is the largest consumer of electricity in the United States, using more than one-tenth of the country's total energy. As the state's population has grown, electricity demand has grown with it. The need for air conditioning most of the year, a growing energy-intensive industrial sector, and longer commutes to work all contribute to significant consumption. How will Texas meet these needs?

Texas's power needs can be partially satisfied from homegrown natural sources. The state is and has been a leading producer of energy, chiefly from crude oil, natural gas, and wind power (see Table 14.2).[138] Coal use, however, is still part of the energy consumed, accounting for 21 percent of the state's energy use in 2019 but lower than by wind energy by one percent.[139] In fact, Texas has its own electrical grid, which covers most of the state. This makes Texas unique because it has one of only three grids in the entire United States. The grid is run by the Electrical Reliability Council of Texas and is separate,

SOCIAL RESPONSIBILITY:

Should the Texas legislature provide incentives for energy companies to develop solar power? Why, or why not?

TABLE 14.2	**Innovations in Energy Production**
1955	Half of the energy generated in Texas comes from natural gas-fired power plants, while coal-fired power plants account for about one-third.
1988	Texas's two nuclear reactors account for 10 percent of the state's energy.
2014	Texas takes the lead nationally in wind-power generation, producing more than one-third of the nation's total.
2017	Texas is ranked number 1 in solar energy potential, but number 10 in solar energy production.

Source: "The State of Nuclear Energy in Texas," National Public Radio.

in part, to avoid interference from the federal government, which sets rates for transmission service and wholesale power.[140]

Much of the state's energy independence has resulted from a boom in hydraulic fracturing (or "fracking") in 2012 and 2013 continuing to today, with more than 50 percent of energy created in natural gas. In 2005, the state legislature passed legislation requiring that 5 percent of the state's electricity come from renewable sources by 2015. The state has exceeded these goals, with renewable sources accounting for about 10 percent by 2014, largely because of early investment in wind energy, the turbines of which dot the West Texas plains. Today, Texas leads the nation in wind-power capacity, with three times more than any other state and wind energy accounting for one-fourth of power generated by wind in the nation.[141]

The role of tax incentives in encouraging development of alternative energy is often hotly contested. In 2014, the state comptroller provoked controversy when she said that the wind energy industry in the state "should stand on its own two feet."[142] Citing a job already completed, an unfair market advantage, and cheap natural gas, the comptroller advocated for stripping the state's role in boosting wind power. In 2015, the Texas legislature considered and rejected a bill to end subsidies for alternative energy and the creation of transmission lines to deliver the electricity generated by the turbines. Despite the state's reputation for oil and gas, Texas is projected to utilize wind turbines to generate up to 37 percent of its total energy by 2030.[143]

TEXAS TAKEAWAYS

14.7.1 What does the Texas Water Development Board do?

14.7.2 What is capture?

THE INSIDER VIEW

State governments are often referred to as "laboratories for democracy," with the expectation that unique circumstances, problems, and events in individual states will encourage tailored policy innovation. A state the size of Texas, with its diverse and unique problems, demands a range of policy approaches. The development and maintenance of the thousands of policies in the Lone Star State illustrate the constantly changing economics, demographics, and preferences of the state. By design, Texas spends less than other states on social services and assistance. Those who support minimal government like it that way, but those who hope for a larger safety net, a better-funded educational system, and greater regulation of polluters are frustrated. The policy process helps the state find solutions to the problems it confronts, even as debate rages about how to handle these policies.

TEXAS TAKEAWAYS

14.1.1 The four phases of the policymaking process are agenda setting, examination, policy adoption, and evaluation.

14.1.2 Agenda setting refers to policymakers' questioning of whether or not a problem is important enough to address.

14.2.1 Medicare is a national social insurance program for older Americans funded by a payroll tax, premiums, and surtaxes and administered by the federal government. Medicaid is medical coverage for low-income Texans provided by the federal government.

14.2.2 The Affordable Care Act (or "Obamacare") covers families with incomes up to 133 percent of the federal poverty level and provides insurance subsidies for families with incomes between 100 and 400 percent of that level. All individuals are required to have health insurance or pay a fine.

14.3.1 Seventy percent of Texas's foreign-born population are from Latin America.

14.3.2 Texas has approximately 1.5 million undocumented immigrants.

14.4.1 Since 1984, school districts have sued the state seven times over perceived inadequate funding.

14.4.2 Vouchers are programs that provide a student with authorization for government funding to be used at a private school.

14.5.1 Funding for campuses of the University of Texas and Texas A&M University comes from the permanent university fund.

14.5.2 Local taxes and the state legislature stream funds into Texas community colleges.

14.6.1 The main sources of highway funds are motor vehicle registration fees, federal highway funds from the national government, the sales tax on motor oils, and some part of the motor fuels (gas) taxes.

14.7.1 The Texas Water Development Board provides loans to local governments for water projects, administers water funds, and facilitates the transfer and sale of water and water rights throughout the state.

14.7.2 Capture is water above the ground that is owned by the landowner of the property.

KEY TERMS

affirmative action
agenda setting
available school fund
capture
Children's Health Insurance Program
foundation school fund
means-tested programs
Medicaid
Medicare
permanent school fund
redistributive policies
Temporary Assistance to Needy Families
vouchers

PRACTICE QUIZ

1. Which is not a phase of policymaking process?
   a. Problem attribution
   b. Agenda setting
   c. Implementation
   d. Policy adoption

2. Policies that transfer wealth from those who have more to those who have less are called . . .
   a. Transformational policies
   b. Transferable policies
   c. Redistributive policies
   d. Conveyance policies

3. Which program is designed to exclusively cover children's health care?
   a. Medicare
   b. Social Security
   c. Temporary Assistance to Needy Families
   d. Children's Health Insurance Program

4. You lose your unemployment benefits for failing a drug test.
   a. True
   b. False

5. Which state leads the nation in legal immigration?
   a. Florida
   b. New York
   c. Texas
   d. California

6. What is another term for the state's "Robin Hood" plan?
   a. Redistributive
   b. Recapture
   c. Reorganization
   d. Restructuring

7. Dropout rates are currently higher for Hispanic students than for African Americans.
   a. True.
   b. False.

8. The state exceeded its self-imposed goal of 5 percent renewable energy earlier than anticipated.
   a. True.
   b. False.

9. Only the Texas A&M University system and the University of Texas system schools are eligible for funds from the permanent university fund.
   a. True
   b. False

10. Medicaid is a joint federal–state program.
    a. True
    b. False

[Answers: A, C, D, A, D, B, B, A, A, A]

Learn more with this chapter's digital tools, including the Oxford Insight Study Guide, at www.oup.com/he/Rottinghaus3e.

GLOSSARY

affirmative action: a policy that provides additional benefits or opportunities to minorities who have suffered historically from discrimination

agency capture: government agencies "controlled" by the industries the agencies were designed to regulate

agenda setting: an informal power of governors to use their public platform to set the state's political and policy agenda

agenda setting: the placement of an issue onto the public agenda

amend: to mark up a bill

amicus curiae briefs: a legal filing with relevant opinions or information pertinent to a case that affects a group's interests, even if the group is not directly part of the case

annexation: the joining of unincorporated land into the boundary of an existing city

appellate courts: courts that review legal issues of cases decided by lower courts

appellate jurisdiction: the authority of a court to review a case first heard by a lower court

appropriation bill: legislation that specifies what spending the state will undertake

arraignment: the initial appearance of the accused in court

AstroTurf lobbying: manufacturing public support and making it appear as though it was inspired organically by a swell of public opinion

at-large: an electoral unit in which all citizens in a county can vote

available school fund: annual transfers from the permanent school fund to school districts

bail: a contract whereby the accused is temporarily released from prison on the condition that he or she pay a sum of money to guarantee an appearance in court

bench trial: a trial in which a single judge presides and decides guilt or innocence and punishment

bicameral legislature: a legislative body with two houses or chambers

bill of rights: a formal declaration of the rights of citizens

block grants: fixed funds that are transferred to states for implementation of a policy or program

budget execution: the governor's implementation of the budget when the legislature is not in session

bureaucracy: a government organization that implements laws and provides services to individuals

capture: the right by which groundwater is owned by the landowner of the property above it

caseload: the workload (in cases) of the judiciary

casework: legislators and their staff's assistance of constituents in their districts with specific requests

categorical grants: funds distributed to state or local governments for programs that require those governments to meet conditions established by the federal government

certify: to confirm that the Texas government has enough money to cover the budget items as reported by the state controller

charter: a city's governing document

Children's Health Insurance Program: a federal program run by the states to provide health coverage to children whose families make too much to qualify for Medicaid but not enough to buy private insurance

city manager: an administrator hired to run the day-to-day operations of a city

civil cases: cases involving a conflict between two parties (litigants), whether individuals, corporations, or the government

clemency: the power to reduce or delay punishment for a crime

closed primary: an election in which only voters registered with a party may vote for the party's candidates

coercive federalism: a system in which the federal government establishes guidelines for the states and may punish the states for not participating

collateral consequences: additional civil punishments of criminal convictions

commerce clause: the clause in the U.S. Constitution that gives Congress the power to regulate commerce with foreign nations and among the states

committees: small groups of legislators who investigate, craft, assess, and take action on legislation before it is considered by the whole chamber

common law: law that is established when judges apply past decisions by courts—called legal precedents—to the facts of a new case before them

community supervision: an alternative to incarceration whereby a defendant is released and allowed to live in the community under conditions set by the court

concurrent powers: powers shared between the state and federal governments

confederal system: a power-sharing arrangement in which a central government's authority is granted by the individual political units

conservative: one who believes in a political philosophy that emphasizes limited government, free markets, and individual entrepreneurship

constitution: a document that establishes principles, powers, and responsibilities of government

cooperative federalism: a federalist system in which each level of government has overlapping and intertwined authority over shared issues

councils of governments (COGs): regional planning commissions made up of area-wide local governments

council–manager system: a system of local government in which the city council appoints a city manager to run city business

criminal cases: cases in which the government brings suit against the defendant for violating the law and in which the defendant is guilty beyond a reasonable doubt

criminal disenfranchisement: the loss of voting rights for felons during incarceration and after they have served their sentence

cumulative voting: system whereby voters cast multiple votes (usually equal to the number of positions in an election)

death penalty: the sentence of a convicted individual to death (capital punishment)

decentralization: the distribution of authority between national, state, and local party organizations so that each level exercises a degree of independent authority

deferrals: delaying guaranteed payments in one budget cycle to another budget cycle

deferred adjudication: a type of supervision through which a defendant pleads guilty but the judge delays a final verdict until the time the defendant successfully completes the supervision period

delegate: a legislator who is simply a mouthpiece for the wishes of his or her constituency

Dillon's rule: a ruling that established state governments can place restrictions on municipalities as long as these rules do not violate the state's constitution

disclosure: the filing of a report that includes details about lawmakers' personal finances or business dealings

disenfranchise: to deprive individuals of the right to vote

disposed: when a case is taken off the court's docket, generally by being heard or dismissed

dual budgeting process: the legislative branch and the executive branch coordinate to propose, shape, and pass a biennial budget

dual federalism: a federalist system in which the government, whether federal, state, or local, has exclusive powers that are reserved to it alone

dual structure: Texas's two supreme court system

Duverger's law: a winner-take-all electoral system generally leads to a two-party system

early voting: the ability to cast a ballot in Texas up to 2 weeks before Election Day

elite theory: groups with greater resources are in a better position to accomplish their goals

en banc: a hearing in which all of the justices of the court hear and consider the case

enforcement: the carrying out of rules by an agency or commission within the bureaucracy

enumerated powers: powers that are expressly identified as those on which the federal government alone can act

executive orders: legally binding orders from the governor that are used to direct government, especially state agencies, in the execution of law

expenditures: the total amount of funds that the state government can spend, as established by the spending cap

federal system: a power-sharing arrangement between the central governing authority and individual political units

fee: a payment for a service rendered

felony: the highest criminal offense under state or federal law

Fifteenth Amendment: the 1870 amendment to the U.S. Constitution, which prohibited the denial of voting rights on the basis of race

filibuster: an action in which a senator holds the floor and restrains the chamber from moving forward on legislation

fines: financial punishments for offenses

first reading: legislation considered at the committee stage

fiscal note: an overview of the estimated financial impact, including cost of the proposed changes, revenue generated, and staffing impacts to the bureaucracy that will result if the bill passes

foundation school fund: education funds from general revenue

free rider problem: a situation in which individuals benefit from a publicly provided good or service without paying for it and actively supporting its acquisition

full faith and credit clause: Article IV, Section 1, of the U.S. Constitution, which requires that each state respect the rights and proceedings of other states

general law: law that potentially affects all Texans

general law city: a city that is only allowed to operate under laws the state provides

general revenue funds: state funds that include revenue from all sources (even federal funds)

gerrymander: a process of manipulating district boundaries to benefit a single group

"get out the vote": a tactic to get friendly voters to the polls

grand jury: a legal body charged with the task of conducting official proceedings to investigate potential criminal conduct

grassroots lobbying: getting members of the general public who are interested in an issue to contact elected officials in order to persuade them on an issue

guardian ad litem: a person appointed to represent the best interests of a child if a parent will not or cannot fulfill the responsibility

home rule city: a city that is allowed self-governance independent of state law

homestead exemption: a portion of property value on which Texans don't have to pay taxes

homestead law: a law that prevents Texans from losing their homes in the event of bankruptcy or other financial problems

hybrid agencies: bureaucratic organizations whose leaders are selected by a mixture of appointments and elections

impeachment: the legal process in which the legislative branch has the authority to indict and remove a public official

implementation: the execution by the bureaucracy of laws and decisions made by the legislative, executive, or judicial branch

implied powers: powers that the federal government is not expressly granted but is assumed to possess so that Congress can carry out its duties

inaugural speech: an address that is not constitutionally required but is conventionally delivered at the beginning of a new gubernatorial term

incumbent: an individual who currently holds a public office

incumbents: candidates who are also the current officeholders

indigent defendants: accused individuals who, lacking resources to hire an attorney, are entitled to have a lawyer hired for them

individualistic political culture: emphasizes personal achievement, individual freedoms, individual enterprise, and loyalty to self instead of others

informal powers: actions governors might take that are not formally written but are exercised through the activities of the governor

Initiative, Referendum, and Recall: Citizens of home rule cities have the power to initiate policy issues or recall local public officials. What are these powers?

initiative: a process through which local voters can directly propose ordinances to city charters

institutional memory: a collective understanding of the way an organization works held by those who run it

interest groups: formal organizations of individuals or groups that seek to influence government to promote their common cause

iron triangle: the relationship that forms between interest groups, the legislature, and executive agency regulators in the policy formation and implementation process

issue network: a single-issue iron triangle

jurisdiction: the official territory and types of cases over which a court exercises authority

jury trial: a trial in which a group of individuals picked at random decides on guilt or innocence

law and order: a dimension of Texas political culture that demands strict adherence to a fair and adequate criminal justice system and swift enforcement of laws

Legislative Redistricting Board: the group of officials who draw the district lines if the legislature is not able to agree

liberal: one who believes in a political philosophy that emphasizes social equality and a large role for government to protect liberties and alleviate social problems

licensing: the authorization process that gives a company, an individual, or an organization permission to carry out a specific task

limited government: a political system in which the government's functions and powers are restricted to protect individual liberty

line item veto: a veto that allows the governor to reject a specific provision in a bill without rejecting the whole bill

lobbying: direct communications with members of the legislative or executive branch of government to influence legislation or administrative action

local law: law that only affects units of government at the local level

logrolling: trading favors, votes, or influence for legislative actions

mandatory review: cases required to be heard by a specific court

markup: the process whereby legislators add, subtract, or replace part of the original legislation so that it meets the preferences of the committee

matching grants: funds the state adds to supplement specific federal government programs

mayor–council system: a system of local government headed by an elected mayor and a city council

means-tested programs: income-measured programs that provide aid to individuals and families with low incomes

Medicaid: medical coverage for low-income Texans provided by the federal government

Medicare: a national social insurance program for older Americans funded by a payroll tax, premiums, and surtaxes and administered by the federal government

merit selection: a nonpartisan way to select judges in which a commission selected by state officials sends recommendations to the governor and the governor selects the nominees from that list

microtargeting: identifying potential subgroups of supporters for customizable messages; also known as narrowcasting

minimal government: a government that provides minimal services and interferes as little as possible in the transactions of individuals and institutions

misdemeanors: a class of criminal offenses that are minor wrongdoings

monarchy: a government run by a single individual, often a king or a queen, until death or abdication

motor voter law: a statute mandating that state governments provide voter registration opportunities to individuals applying for or renewing their driver's license

multimember agencies: bureaucratic organizations staffed by a minimum of three individuals

municipal bonds: debt securities where a municipality takes out a loan to spend funds and agrees to pay the funds back, generally with interest

name identification: familiarity with a candidate's name

necessary and proper clause: Article 1, Section 8, of the U.S. Constitution, which specifies that Congress is allowed to assume additional powers needed to carry out its function

negative campaigning: a campaign that highlights the negative of the opponent over the positive of its own candidate

New Deal: a federal economic recovery program in response to the Great Depression that stabilized the banking industry, created jobs, promoted fair labor standards, and produced a social welfare network

new federalism: a federal system that returns greater responsibilities, duties, and funding to the states

no contest: a plea whereby a defendant does not admit guilt but is not contesting the underlying facts

open primary: an election in which any registered voter can vote for a party's candidates

opinion: a document that expresses the view of the judges and often takes the form of a majority opinion, when written by a justice representing the majority, but may also be a concurring or dissenting opinion

ordinances: the local laws of a municipal area, passed by a city council

original jurisdiction: the court in which the case is first heard

pardon: the power to forgive a crime

parole: a system in which a prisoner is released from prison prior to completing his or her full sentence

partisans: strongly committed members of a party

party competition: electoral conflict that signals how successful one party is over another

party platform: a list of values, beliefs, and policy issues that are endorsed and supported by a political party

"pay as you go": budget rule that Texas cannot spend more money than it receives in revenue

pay-as-you-go system: the system by which state funds spent must equal state funds received

permanent school fund: the fund that contains the money from the state's long-term investment and that pays for public education

place system: an electoral system that carves a citywide area into separate district seats for which voters elect council members

plea bargain: the process by which the defendant agrees to a lesser set of charges than initially charged by the prosecutors

plural executive: diffusion of authority and power throughout several entities in the executive branch

plural executive: the diffusion of authority and power throughout several entities in the executive branch and the bureaucracy

pluralist theory: the theory that competition keeps powerful interest groups in check and that no single group dominates

point of order: a technical objection to an error in a bill

political action committees (PACs): organizations that collect donations and use these funds to donate to candidates, parties, or other political causes

political culture: a set of shared values and practices held by people that informs their expectations of government and their vision of a just society

political efficacy: the belief that a person's participation can influence the political system

political polarization: the stricter definition of voters' opinions on policy and political matters as a result of their identification with a political party

political socialization: the process by which individuals acquire political values and behaviors that have a strong influence on future voting behavior

political succession: the sequential passing of authority from one person to another as the previous person is unable to serve

poll tax: an unconstitutional tax that required those registering to vote to pay a fee

popular sovereignty: rule by the people.

preemption: the supremacy of rules and laws handed down at the state level

preemptions: when the federal government grants states permission and funding to implement federal regulations in policy areas, but only if the states comply with a host of conditions

presiding officer: a role of the lieutenant governor who is in charge of the administrative and procedural duties of the Texas Senate

primary election: an election in which each party selects its nominees for office

private interest groups: groups that advocate for the benefit of their members

probable cause: the legal grounds law enforcement uses to make an arrest or conduct a search

probate: the process by which there is official recognition and registration of the validity of a person's last will and testament

proclamations: gubernatorial orders that are used to make factual determinations to trigger other available powers

progressive tax: a tax with a rate that increases as the amount that is taxed rises

progressive tax: a tax with a rate that increases as the amount that is taxed rises

prosecutor: the state's lawyer who is responsible for bringing charges against accused lawbreakers

public interest groups: groups that benefit the public in general

public opinion polling: a battery of survey questions asked of a representative sample of individuals

reapportionment: redistribution of representation based on decennial recounting of residents

recall: a process through which voters can oust sitting members of the city government before their terms are up

recognition: the power to call on a legislator and allow him or her to speak during debates

recuse: decide not to participate in legislative activity as an elected official

redistributive policies: policies that transfer wealth from those who have more to those who have less

redistricting: the redrawing of legislative districts to meet federal and state requirements

referendum: a procedure through which local voters can repeal existing ordinances that a city council won't rescind

register: sign up to vote in elections

regressive tax: a tax that exacts a larger percentage of the earnings of low-income than of high-income individuals

regular session: legislative session meeting for 140 days in the January of odd-numbered years

regulations: standards that are established for the function and management of industry, business, individuals, and other parts of government

religiosity: the belief, practice, and activity of organized religion

republic: a form of government in which people rule indirectly through elected representatives

reserve clause: the Tenth Amendment to the U.S. Constitution, which states that powers not delegated to the federal government are reserved for the states

resolutions: legislation that conveys the will of the chamber

revenue: the income a state receives from taxes, fees, and other sources

revolving door: when agency bureaucrats and legislators leave their jobs to become lobbyists, or vice versa

riders: specific policy directives that convey instructions on how agency funds can be collected or spent

rules: regulations designed to control government or the conduct of people and industries

runoff election: an election in which, if no candidate receives a majority of the votes, the two-top vote getters run again

search and seizure: procedure whereby law enforcement agents search an accused's property and collect any evidence relevant to the alleged crime

second reading: legislation considered at the floor stage

segregation: enforced or de facto separation of different racial groups

select committee: a committee that is temporary and has a fixed issue to investigate or legislation to consider

selective benefits: private goods made available to people who organize for a collective good

seniority: having lengthier legislative service than others

separation of powers: a system that vests political, judicial, and policymaking authority across different branches of government

sine die: the end of a legislative session

"sin" taxes: taxes imposed on the sale of alcohol and tobacco and on some forms of gambling, and fees imposed on "sexually oriented" businesses

single-member districts: an electoral unit that elects only one member of a political body, such as a legislature, and through which smaller communities can gain representation on that body

social contract: an agreement in which the governed give up certain freedoms in return for government protection

sovereignty: authority over a political entity, such as a province or a state

special districts: a single-purpose government that performs a specialized function

special election: an election held as needed to fill vacancies created by death, resignation, or removal from office

special law: law that exempts businesses or individuals from state laws

special session: legislative session that can be called by the governor on any issue the governor decides requires attention

split-ticket voting: choosing candidates from different parties for different offices

sprawl: rapid growth of urban and suburban areas spreading into the undeveloped land surrounding it

standing committees: permanent committees that deal with a specific issue or topic

State-of-the-State Address: address used by governors to set a policy agenda

straight-ticket voting: checking one box to vote for every candidate that a specific party has on the ballot

suburbanization: population shifts from urban and rural areas to suburban areas adjacent to major cities

suffrage: the right to participate in the electoral process by voting

super PACs: independent expenditure committees that are legally permitted to raise and spend unlimited funds from individuals, corporations, unions, or other groups to advocate on behalf of their causes but are not permitted to give to candidates directly

supremacy clause: Article VI, Section 2, of the U.S. Constitution, which states that the U.S. Constitution and federal laws "shall be the supreme law of the land"

Tax Increment Reinvestment Zones: special zones created to attract business and develop the economy within the defined geographic area

Tejanos: Mexican Texans during the time of the Texas Revolution

Temporary Assistance to Needy Families: a program that provides financial and medical assistance to needy children and their parents or relatives

term limits: legal restrictions on the number of terms that an elected official can serve in a specific office

Texas Miracle: the economic good fortune the state experienced from 2001 to 2008

third reading: the voting stage of legislation

traditionalistic political culture: the goal of the political system is to maintain order, and a hierarchical set of political elites largely determines public policy

transactional theory: the theory that public policy is bought and sold like a commodity to the highest bidder

trustee: a legislator who votes in accordance with his or her interpretation of what the legislator's district would want

turnover: the process by which incumbents lose their seats or leave their seats and new members (freshmen) are voted into office

unfunded mandate: federal or state legislation that requires states to implement a policy but does not supply funding necessary for implementation

unincorporated areas: regions that are administered as part of a county but not a city

unitary system: a central government that has complete authority over all levels of government

veto: formal, constitutional decision by the governor to formally reject a resolution or bill made by the legislature

voir dire: the questioning of jurors by attorneys and judges in court to determine if a potential juror is biased, cannot deal with the issues fairly, or knows a party to the case

Voting Rights Act of 1965: landmark federal legislation that established practices to overcome racial discrimination in voting at the state and local levels

vouchers: programs to provide a student with authorization for government funding to be used at a private school

winner-take-all election: whichever candidate wins the most votes wins the seat

NOTES

Chapter 1 The Struggle for Texas: Demographics, Culture, and Political Power

1. Office of the Texas Governor, "Governor Abbott Delivers State of the State Address," January 31, 2017, *https://gov.texas.gov/news/post/governor_abbott_delivers_state_of_the_state_address*.
2. 13-year-old Texan takes out 400-pound feral hog wreaking havoc on ranch, Mary Claire Patton, KSAT.com, March 10, 2020, *www.ksat.com/news/local/2020/03/10/13-year-old-texan-takes-out-400-pound-feral-hog-wreaking-havoc-on-ranch*.
3. John Morthland, "A Plague of Pigs in Texas," *Smithsonian Magazine*, January 2011, *www.smithson-ianmag.com/science-nature/a-plague-of-pigs-in-texas-73769069*; Craig Hlavaty, "East Texas Man Takes Down 416-Pound Wild Hog in Backyard," HoustonChronicle.com, October 17, 2017, *www.chron.com/news/houston-texas/texas/article/East-Texas-man-takes-down-416-pound-wild-hog-in-12284271.php*; Bill Hanna, "In North Arlington's 'Wild Kingdom,' Hogs Roam, Root—Then Get Trapped," *Star-Telegram*, January 10, 2018, *www.star-telegram.com/news/local/community/arlington/article193938354.html*; Art Young, "Texas Must Get a Grip on the Wild Hog Problem, and Here's How," *Dallas Morning News*, January 9, 2018, *www.dallasnews.com/opinion/commentary/2018/01/09/texas-must-get-grip-wild-hog-problem*.
4. *www.texastribune.org/2016/08/02/eagle-ford-tiny-nordheim-keeps-battling-drilling-w*
5. Randolph B. Campbell, *Gone to Texas: A History of the Lone Star State* (New York: Oxford University Press, 2003); Stephen Harrigan, *They Came from the Sky: The Spanish Arrive in Texas* (Austin: University of Texas Press, 2017).
6. Robert Rickliss, *The Karankawa Indians of Texas* (Austin: University of Texas Press, 1996).
7. George Klos, "Indians," *Handbook of Texas Online*, June 15, 2010, *https://tshaonline.org/handbook/online/articles/bzi04*.
8. Marquis James, *The Raven: A Biography of Sam Houston* (Austin: University of Texas Press, 1929).
9. Harrigan, *They Came from the Sky*, 12.
10. Robert A. Calvert, Arnoldo de Leon, and Gregg Cantrell, *The History of Texas* (Wheeling, IL: Harlan Davidson, 2002).
11. A. Ray Stephens, *Texas: A Historical Atlas* (Norman: University of Oklahoma Press, 2010).
12. "Tejano Origins," *Sons of DeWitt Colony Texas*, 2000, *www.tamu.edu/faculty/ccbn/dewitt/tejanoorigins.htm*; Andres Tijerina, *Tejanos and Texas under the Mexican Flag, 1821–1836* (College Station: Texas A&M Press, 1994), 5.
13. Tijerina, *Tejanos and Texas*, x.
14. Andres Tijerina, "Tejano Origins," May 4, 1998, *www.tamu.edu/faculty/ccbn/dewitt/tejanoorigins.htm*.
15. *www.texasmonthly.com/the-culture/high-school-football-el-paso-plano-game*
16. W. Marvin Dulaney, "African Americans," *Handbook of Texas Online*, June 9, 2010, *https://tshaonline.org/handbook/online/articles/pkaan*.
17. Ibid.
18. Samuel Stebbins and Grant Suneson, "Does Texas or Russia Have the Larger GDP? Here's How US States Compare to Other Countries," *USA Today*, April 17, 2019, *www.usatoday.com/story/money/2019/04/17/how-gdp-of-us-states-compares-to-countries-around-the-world/39295197/* and International Money Fund.
19. Sheehy, *Texas Big Rich*, 17.
20. *https://tshaonline.org/handbook/online/articles/ama01*
21. Henry C. Dethloff and Garry L. Nall, "Agriculture," *Handbook of Texas Online*, June 9, 2010, *https://tshaonline.org/handbook/online/articles/ama01*.
22. *https://www.farmflavor.com/texas-agriculture*
23. Judith Walker Linsley, Ellen Walker Rienstra, and Jo Ann Stiles, *Giant under the Hill* (Austin: Texas State Historical Association, 2002), 89.
24. *https://comptroller.texas.gov/transparency/reports/revenue-by-source*
25. Anne Dingus, "Texas Primer: Barbed Wire," *Texas Monthly*, March 1984.
26. Caroline Gleaton and John Robinson, Texas A&M AgriLife Extension Service, "Facts about Texas and U.S. Agriculture," August 2018, *https://agecoext.tamu.edu/wp-content/uploads/2018/09/AgFacts2018-CoversAndIntro.pdf*; *www.texasagriculture.gov/About/TexasAgStats.aspx*.
27. Ben H. Procter, "World War II," *Handbook of Texas Online*, June 15, 2010, *tshaonline.org/handbook/online/articles/npwnj*.
28. U.S. Census Bureau, Texas Workforce Commission, Bureau of Economic Analysis, Bureau of Labor Statistics, *www.nam.org/state-manufacturing-data/2019-texas-manufacturing-facts*.
29. Campbell, *Gone to Texas*, 401.
30. Sheehy, *Texas Big Rich*.
31. *www.travelstats.com/dashboard?ucode=4300; www.bizjournals.com/austin/news/2019/05/02/tourisms-economic-impact-in-texas-164-billion.html*
32. Mitchell Ferman, "Canales Bill Would Allow Accents on State Documents," *The Monitor*, May 14, 2017, *www.themonitor.com/news/local/*

article_96736bf0-0925-11e7-a6b2-0b9abc3598oc.html.

33. Erica Grieder, *Big, Hot, Cheap and Right: What America Can Learn from the Strange Genius of Texas* (New York: PublicAffairs Books, 2013), 13.

34. Max Ehrenfreund, "The Facts about Rick Perry and the 'Texas Miracle,'" *Wonkblog*, June 8, 2015*www.washingtonpost.com/blogs/wonkblog/wp/2015/06/08/the-facts-about-rick-perry-and-the-texas-miracle*; and Jim Tankersley, "The 'Texas Miracle' Missed Most of Texas," *New York Times*, July 7, 2019, *www.nytimes.com/2019/07/07/business/texas-economy-jobs-cities.html.*

35. Fernando Ramirez, "Texas' '1 percent' earn 24 times more than the average Texan," Houston Chronicle, July 30, 2018. https://www.chron.com/politics/texas/article/texas-1-percent-richest-99-percent-income-study-13101062.php

36. *www.houstonpublicmedia.org/articles/news/2018/11/02/310352/the-latina-wage-gap-is-bigger-in-texas.*

37. Lawrence Wright, "Dark Bounty," January 1, 2018; *www.statesman.com/business/20180310/mix-of-startups-incoming-firms-keeps-austin-job-growth-buzzing; https://www.usnews.com/news/best-states/articles/2019-07-30/texas-expected-to-see-the-most-cybersecurity-growth-report-says.*

38. Lauren Etter, "Texas Has a Great, and Most Unusual, Economic Stimulus Package," *Bloomberg*, June 23, 2015, *www.bloomberg.com/news/articles/2015-06-23/texas-has-a-great-and-most-unusual-economic-stimulus-package*; Dave Fehling, "Drop in Oil Tax Revenue 'Not Going to Be Pretty' for Texas," *Houston Public Media*, January 26, 2016, *www.hous-tonpublicmedia.org/articles/news/2016/01/26/135115/drop-in-oil-tax-revenue-not-going-to-be-pretty-for-texas.*

39. Alexa Ura and Ryan Murphy, "Texas Population Grew to 28.3 Million in 2017," *The Texas Tribune*, December 20, 2017, *www.texastribune.org/2017/12/20/texas-population-grew-283-million-2017.*

40. Skip Hollandsworth, "Dispatch from Higgins: Little Town on the Prairie," *Texas Monthly*, May 2017, *www.texasmonthly.com/the-edge/dispatch-from-higgins-little-town-on-the-prairie.*

41. *www.census.gov/newsroom/press-releases/2020/pop-estimates-county-metro.html*

42. Campbell, *Gone to Texas*, 327.

43. *www.census.gov/newsroom/press-releases/2019/estimates-county-metro.html*

44. Brandon Formby, Chris Essig, and Annie Daniel, "Despite 'Texas Miracle,' Affordable Housing Difficult for Many Urban Dwellers," *The Texas Tribune*, June 16, 2017, *www.texastribune.org/2017/06/16/search-affordable-home-urban-texas-getting-more-difficult.*

45. Timmy Huynh and Lauren Kent, "In Greater Dallas Area, Segregation by Income and Race," *Fact Tank*, June 29, 2015, *www.pewre-search.org/fact-tank/2015/06/29/in-greater-dallas-area-segregation-by-income-and-race.*

46. Sarah Mervosh and Julieta Chiquillo, "Why the Top Program to Help Poor Dallas Families Make Rent Is Failing," *Dallas Morning News*, September 13, 2017, *www.dallasnews.com/news/investigations/2017/09/13/top-program-help-poor-dallas-families-make-rent-failing-section-8.*

47. David G. McComb, "Urbanization," *Handbook of Texas Online*, June 15, 2010, *https://tshaonline.org/handbook/online/articles/hyunw.*

48. Sarah Champagne, "Texas has the highest uninsured rate in the US.," *The Texas Tribune*, July 14 2020, *https://www.texastribune.org/2020/07/14/texans-health-insurance-jobs-pandemic/.*

49. National Poverty Center, "The Colors of Poverty: Why Racial and Ethnic Disparities Persist," *Policy Brief 16*, January 2009, *www.npc.umich.edu/publications/policy_briefs/brief16/PolicyBrief16.pdf.*

50. "Larger Percentage of Texas Hispanics Have Enrolled in Health Insurance Marketplace Plans," *Science Daily*, May 9, 2014, *.www.sciencedaily.com/releases/2014/05/140509130038.*

htm;www.kut.org/post/fewer-latinos-central-texas-are-enrolling-obamacare-marketplace-year.

51. Alexa Ura and Lindsay Carbonell, "Young Texans Make Up Most Diverse Generation," *The Texas Tribune*, June 23, 2016, *www.texastribune.org/2016/06/23/texas-children-make-most-diverse-generation.*

52. Alexa Ura and Annie Daniel, "See Demographic Shift by Texas County," *The Texas Tribune*, June 25, 2015, *www.texastribune.org/2015/06/25/see-demographic-shift-tx-counties-2010–2014.*

53. Ann Beeson, "Texas Undocumented Immigrants Pay at Least $1.5 Billion in Taxes," *Center for Public Policy Priorities*, February 24, 2016, *bettertexasblog.org/2016/02/texas-undocumented-immigrants-pay-at-least-1-5-billion-in-taxes/;https://www.thoughtco.com/illegal-immigrants-and-tax-estimates-3321604.*

54. "Immigrants Drive the Texas Economy," *Center for Public Policy Priorities*, March 2017, *http://forabet-tertexas.org/images/EO_2017_02_ImmigrantsInTexas.pdf.*

55. Texas Education Agency, "Enrollment in Texas Public Schools, 2013–2014," November 2014, *tea.texas.gov/acctres/Enroll_2013-14.pdf.*

56. David Montejano, *Anglos and Mexicans in the Making of Texas, 1836–1986* (Austin: University of Texas Press, 1987).

57. Chris McNary, "Texas Leaders, Educators and Courts Grapple with Segregated Public Schools," *Dallas Morning News*, May 2013, *www.dallasnews.com/news/education/headlines/20130503-texas-leaders-educators-and-courts-grapple-with-segregated-public-schools.ece.*

58. Texas Education Agency, Completion, Graduation, and Dropouts, *https://tea.texas.gov/reports-and-data/school-performance/accountability-research/completion-graduation-and-dropouts#reports.*

59. "State of Student Aid and Higher Education in Texas," Carla Fletcher and Kasey Klepfer, Trellis Research, January 2019, p. 75, *https://files.eric.ed.gov/fulltext/ED594869.pdf.*

60. *https://statisticalatlas.com/state/Texas/Household-Income*

61. Alexander T. Abraham and Amy Jordan, "Rising Education Helps Explain Hispanic Household Income Growth in Texas," *Federal Reserve Bank of Dallas*, Fourth Quarter 2017, *www.dallasfed.org/~/media/documents/research/swe/2017/swe1704f.pdf*.

62. Jamelle Bouie, "White Out," *Slate*, May 15, 2015, *www.slate.com/articles/news_and_politics/politics/2015/05/whites_prefer_to_live_with_whites_why_integrating_america_s_neighborhoods.html*.

63. "Immigrants Drive the Texas Economy"; Alexa Ura, "Report: Texas Population to Double by 2050," *The Texas Tribune*, March 5, 2015, *www.texastribune.org/2015/03/05/report-texas-population-double-2050*.

64. Texas Health and Human Services, Data & Statistics, *https://hhs.texas.gov/about-hhs/records-statistics/data-statistics*.

65. William A. Vega, Kyriakos S. Markides, Jacqueline L. Angel, and Fernando M. Torres, eds., *Challenges of Latino Aging in the Americas* (New York: Springer, 2015).

66. Chuck Lindell, "Appeals Court Tosses Lawsuit Blocking Texas Medicaid Cuts," *MyStatesman.com*, April 21, 2016, *www.mystatesman.com/news/news/appeals-court-tosses-lawsuit-blocking-texas-medica/nq8tC*.

67. Terri Langford, "Charting a Better Exit Strategy for Fragile Populations," *The Texas Tribune*, September 19, 2015, *https://apps.texastribune.org/road-from-rita/aiding-fragile-populations*.

68. John Steinbeck, *Travels with Charley* (New York: Viking Press, 1962).

69. Lucian Pye, "Political Culture," *International Encyclopedia of the Social Sciences*, vol. 12 (New York: Crowell, Collier and Macmillan, 1968), 218.

70. Daniel J. Elazar, *American Federalism: A View from the States*, 3rd ed. (New York: Harper and Row, 1984).

71. Samuel Bazzi, Martin Fiszbein, and Mesay Gabresilasse, "Frontier Culture: The Roots and Persistence of 'Rugged Individualism' in the United States," NBER Working Paper 23997, November 2017, *www.nber.org/papers/w23997#fromrss*.

72. James R. Dickenson, "The Best Little Statehouse in Texas," *The Washington Post*, August 26, 1981, *www.washingtonpost.com/archive/lifestyle/1981/08/26/the-best-little-statehouse-in-texas/8f556914-ad18-4bd0-8b0d-dd853aef51f9/?utm_term=.8b995504334d*.

73. James McCandless, "The Rise and Fall of the 'Freest Little City in Texas,'" *Texas Observer*, July 31, 2017, *www.texasobserver.org/the-rise-and-fall-of-the-freest-little-city-in-texas*.

74. Kevin Sullivan and Peter Holley, "Texans' Do-It-Ourselves Rescue Effort Defines Hurricane Harvey," *The Washington Post*, September 2, 2017, *www.washingtonpost.com/amphtml/national/texans-do-it-ourselves-rescue-effort-defines-hurricane-harvey/2017/09/02/f41bb8ee-8f2f-11e7-8df5-c2e-5cf46c1e2_story.html*.

75. Texas Politics Project/University of Texas Poll, July 2008.

76. Texas Politics Project/University of Texas Poll, July 2009. Question asked: "Some people think the country needs leaders who have experience and knowledge about how businesses, politics, and special interests work in the United States. Suppose these people are at one end of a 1–7 scale, at point 1. Others think things in government are so broken that we need to bring in people from outside politics who might be able to reform the way things are done. Suppose these people are at the other end of the scale, at point 7. People who are exactly in-between are at point 4, and of course other people have opinions at other points between 1 and 7. Where would you place yourself on this scale, or wouldn't you have any opinion about that?"

77. Ross Ramsey, "UT/TT Poll: Texans Distrust Big Institutions on Privacy," *The Texas Tribune*, November 8, 2013.

78. 2010 U.S. Religion Census, Church Membership Figures for Texas, *www.usreligioncensus.org*.

79. Mary Lasswell, *I'll Take Texas* (Boston: Houghton Mifflin, 1958).

Chapter 2 The Texas Constitution

1. Beauford Chambless, *The Birth of Texas: The Ad-Interim Government of The Republic of Texas March, 1836–October, 1836* (Waco, TX: Printed by Author, 1992), 10.

2. Ibid., 16.

3. William C. Binkley. *The Texas Revolution* (Austin: Texas State Historical Association, 1952).

4. Manuel Mier y Teran's Letter to President Guadalupe Victoria, June 30, 1828. From Alleine Howren, "Causes and Origin of the Decree of April 6, 1830," *The Southwestern Historical Quarterly* 16, no. 4 (April 1913): 395–398.

5. Ernest Wallace, David M. Vigness, and George B. Ward, eds., *Documents of Texas History* (Austin: State House Press, 1994), 85.

6. Eugene C. Barker, ed., *The Austin Papers*, vol. 3 (Austin: University of Texas, 1927), 116–119.

7. Wallace, Vigness, and Ward, *Documents of Texas History*, 118.

8. Jesús F. de la Teja, "Introduction," *Tejano Leadership in Mexican and Revolutionary Texas*, edited by Jesús F. de la Teja (College Station: Texas A&M Press, 2010), 7.

9. Lewis W. Newton and Herbert P. Gambrell, *Texas: Yesterday and Today with the Constitution of State of Texas* (Dallas: Turner Company, 1949), 144.

10. Frederic L. Paxson, "The Constitution of Texas, 1845," *Southwestern Historical Quarterly* 18, no. 4 (1915): 386–398.

11. James E. Crisp, "Navarro: Tejano Powerlessness," *Tejano Leadership in Mexican and Revolutionary Texas*, edited by Jesús F. de la Teja (College Station: Texas A&M Press, 2010), 156.

12. Richard Parker, "Sam Houston, We Have a Problem," *New York Times*, January 31, 2011, *http://opinionator.blogs.nytimes.com/2011/01/31/sam-houston-we-have-a-problem/?_r=0*.

13. Ibid.

14. Carl H. Moneyhon, "Reconstruction," *Handbook of Texas Online*, June 15, 2010, *https://tshaonline.org/handbook/online/articles/mzr01*.

15. Gary Cartwright, *Galveston: A History of the Island* (New York: Maxwell Macmillan, 1991), 132.

16. Alwyn Barr, *Black Texans* (Norman: University of Oklahoma Press, 1996), 48.

17. Moneyhon, "Reconstruction."

18. Seth Shepard McKay, ed., *Debates in the Texas Constitutional Convention of 1875* (Austin: University of Texas Press, 1930), 40.

19. Barry A. Crouch and Donaly E. Brice, *The Governor's Hounds: The Texas State Police, 1870–1873* (Austin: University of Texas Press, 2011), 1.

20. Seth Shepard McKay, *Seven Decades of the Texas Constitution of 1876* (Lubbock, TX: Printed by Author, 1941), 31.

21. Ibid., 89.

22. Robert A. Calvert, Arnoldo De León, and Gregg Cantrell, *The History of Texas*, 5th ed. (Chichester, West Sussex, UK: John Wiley, 2013), 175.

23. McKay, *Debates*, 147.

24. Ibid., 177.

25. Harold H. Bruff, "Separation of Powers under the Texas Constitution," *Texas Law Review* 68, no. 7 (1990): 1337–1367.

26. Nina Totenberg, "Is a Confederate Flag License Plate Free Speech?" NPR. org, March 23, 2015, *www.npr.org/2015/03/23/394308609/is-a-con-federate-flag-license-plate-free-speech.*

27. Research Division of the Texas Legislative Council, "Amendments to the Texas Constitution Since 1876: Current through the November 3, 2015, Constitutional Amendment Election," May 2018, *www.tlc.state.tx.us/docs/amendments/Consta-mend1876.pdf.*

28. Frank M. Stewart and Joseph L. Clark, *The Constitution and Government of Texas*, rev ed. (Boston: D. C. Heath, 1936), 27.

29. McKay, *Debates*, 135.

30. Ibid., 139.

31. Staff of the Office of Constitutional Research, Texas Legislative Council, "Constitutional Amendments Analyzed: Analysis of the Eight Proposed Amendments for Election— November 4, 1975," October 1975, *www.lrl.state.tx.us/scanned/Constitutional_Amendments/amendments64_tlc_1975-11-04.pdf.*

Chapter 3 Federalism

1. *www.gregabbott.com/state-of-the-state-2019*

2. *www.texastribune.org/2019/10/02/gov-greg-abbott-threatens-intervene-austins-homelessness-crisis/; www.texastribune.org/2019/10/18/greg-abbott-says-txdot-will-remove-austin-homeless-under-highways*

3. Sam Biddle, "'I DO NOT TRUST BARAK OBAMA': The Paranoid Emails of Jade Helm 15," *Gawker.com*, June 16, 2015, *http://gawker.com/i-do-not-trust-barak-obama-the-paranoid-emails-of-ja-1711669400.*

4. Dylan Baddour, "Texans Organize 'Operation Counter Jade Helm' to Keep an Eye on the Federal Troops," *Chron.com*, July 13, 2015, *www.chron.com/news/houston-texas/texas/article/Texans-organize-Opera-tion-Counter-Jade-Helm-to-6378017.php?mc_cid=46356c6a06&mc_eid=101a099a60.*

5. Office of the Texas Governor, "Governor Abbott Directs Texas State Guard to Monitor Operation Jade Helm 15," April 28, 2015, *http://gov.texas.gov/news/press-release/20805.*

6. Biddle, "Paranoid Emails."

7. Ross Ramsey, "UT/TT Poll: Texans Wary of Domestic Use of Military," *The Texas Tribune*, June 25, 2015, *www.texastribune.org/2015/06/25/uttt-poll-texans-wary-domestic-use-military.*

8. Caitlin M. Dunklee and Rebecca A. Larsen, "Examining the Texas Prison Reform Model: How Texas Is Maintaining Racial Disparity and Mass Incarceration," Institute for Urban Policy Research and Analysis, University of Texas at Austin, May 14, 2015, *www.utexas.edu/cola/iupra/_files/Criminal%20Justice%20Brief%20Final%20final.pdf.*

9. University of Texas/*Texas Tribune* Poll, June 2019.

10. Ibid., April 2020.

11. Ibid., February 2014.

12. *www.lbb.state.tx.us/Documents/Appropriations_Bills/86/Conference_Bills/5872_S12_Bill_Summary.pdf*, p. 7.

13. U.S. Census Bureau, U.S. Department of Commerce Bureau of Economic Analysis, *https://rockinst.org/wp-content/uploads/2019/01/1-7-19b-Balance-of-Payments.pdf*, p. 15.

14. "Legislative Budget Board Fiscal Size-Up: 2016–17 Biennium," Submitted to the 84th Texas Legislature, Prepared by Legislative Budget Board Staff, May 2016, p. 37, *www.lbb.state.tx.us/Documents/Publications/Fiscal_SizeUp/Fiscal_SizeUp.pdf.*

15. Andrew Reeves, "Political Disaster: Unilateral Powers, Electoral Incentives, and Presidential Disaster Declarations," *Journal of Politics* 73, no. 4 (2011): 1142–1151.

16. Fred Gantt Jr., *The Chief Executive in Texas: A Study in Gubernatorial Leadership* (Austin: University of Texas Press, 1964), 224.

17. Texas State Library and Archives Commission, "Texas Legislature, Joint Committee Investigating the Pink Bollworm Infestation in Texas: An Inventory of the Stenographic Report at the Texas State Archives, 1920," University of Texas Libraries, *www.lib.utexas.edu/taro/tslac/50061/tsl-50061.html.*

18. Ben H. Procter, "Great Depression," *Handbook of Texas Online*, June 15, 2010, *https://tshaonline.org/handbook/online/articles/npg01.*

19. "Reagan's 'New Federalism,'" *CQ Researcher*, April 3, 1981, *library.cqpress.com/cqresearcher/doc-ument.php?id=cqresrre1981040300.*

20. Republican Party of Texas, "Report of Permanent Committee on Platform and Resolutions as Amended and Adopted by the 2016 State Convention of the Republican Party of Texas," January 2016, *www.texasgop.org/wp-content/uploads/2016/01/PERM-PLATFORM.pdf.*

21. Texas Health and Human Services, "About Medicaid and CHIP," accessed July 27, 2018, *https://hhs.texas.gov/services/health/medicaid-chip/about-medicaid-chip.*

22. Robert Pear, "Reagan Modifies 'New Federalism' Plan," *New York Times*, January 26, 1983, *www.nytimes.com/1983/01/26/us/reagan-modifies-new-federalism-plan.html.*

23. Becca Aaronson, "Perry Directs HHSC to Pursue Medicaid Block Grant," *The Texas Tribune*, September 16, 2013, *www.texastribune.org/2013/09/16/*

perry-directs-hhsc-pursue-medicaid-block-grant.

24. John Kincaid, "From Cooperative to Coercive Federalism," *Annals of the American Academy of Political and Social Science* 509 (May 1990): 139–152.

25. Jess Bravin and Louise Radnofsky, "Court Backs Obama on Health Law," *Wall Street Journal*, June 29, 2012, *www.wsj.com/articles/SB10001424052702304898704577480371370927862.*

26. Will Weissert, "Could Texas Win Block Medicaid Grant from Feds?" *Dallas Morning News*, January 1, 2015, *www.dallasnews.com/news/state/headlines/20150101-could-texas-win-block-medicaid-grant-from-feds.ece.*

27. Neena Satija, "Texas May Refuse to Follow Climate Rules," *The Texas Tribune*, August 7, 2014, *www.texastribune.org/2014/08/07/texas-may-refuse-follow-climate-rules.*

28. Jennifer Hiller, "Texas Takes over Greenhouse Gas Permitting from EPA," *Houston Chronicle*, November 25, 2014, *http://fuelfix.com/blog/2014/11/25/texas-takes-over-greenhouse-gas-permitting-from-epa.*

29. *www.uschamber.com/litigation-update/texas-supreme-court-holds-texas-clean-air-act-preempts-houston-air-ordinance*

30. *Pollard's Lessee v. Hagan*, 44 U.S. 212 (1845).

31. Price Daniel, "Tidelands Controversy," *Handbook of Texas Online.* Accessed July 27, 2018, *https://tshaonline.org/handbook/online/articles/mgt02.*

32. Jim Malewitz, "Blurred Lines: Dispute Between Texas, BLM Has Complicated History," *The Texas Tribune*, April 28, 2014, *www.texastribune.org/2014/04/28/blurred-lines-texas-blm-spat-has-complicated-histo.*

33. *www.texastribune.org/2018/06/20/abbott-tells-texas-delegation-find-bipartisan-fix-family-separation*

34. *www.usatoday.com/in-depth/news/nation/2019/09/23/border-crisis-trump-administration-real-cost-tax-money/1739727001*

35. *www.americanprogress.org/issues/immigration/news/2019/07/25/472535/*

state-local-governments-opt-immigrant-detention

36. Abby Livingston and Julian Aguilár, "Congress to Vote on Sanctuary Cities," *The Texas Tribune*, July 22, 2015, *www.texastribune.org/2015/07/22/texas-congress-sanctuary-cities.*

37. Julian Aguilár, "Day 24: Stringent Voter ID Law Means Changes at Texas Polls," *The Texas Tribune*, August 24, 2011, *www.texastribune.org/2011/08/24/day-24-voter-id-law-means-changes-ballot-box.*

38. Mitch Mitchell, "Fort Worth Woman Admits Guilt in Voter Fraud Case as National Debate Continues," *Fort Worth Star-Telegram*, June 7, 2015, *www.star-telegram.com/news/local/community/fort-worth/article23415846.html#storylink=cpy.*

39. Wayne Slater, "Few Texas Voter-Fraud Cases Would Have Been Prevented by Photo ID Law, Review Shows," *Dallas Morning News*, September 8, 2013, *www.dallasnews.com/news/politics/headlines/20130908-few-texas-voter-fraud-cases-would-have-been-prevented-by-photo-id-law-review-shows.ece.*

40. Jeffrey Weiss, "What Texans Need to Know about Common Core Education Standards," *Dallas Morning News*, June 24, 2014, *www.dallasnews.com/news/education/headlines/20140623-what-texans-need-to-know-about-common-core-education-standards.ece.*

41. Andrew Ujifusa, "Days Apart, Two States Opt to Replace Common Core," *Education Week*, June 6, 2014, *www.edweek.org/ew/articles/2014/06/06/35commonore.h33.html.*

42. "Inauguration Day Remarks by Lt. Gov. Dan Patrick," *KSAT.com*, updated January 20, 2015, *www.ksat.com/news/inauguration-day-remarks-by-lt-gov-dan-patrick.*

43. Texas Constitution, Article 1, Section 1, *www.statutes.legis.state.tx.us/Docs/CN/htm/CN.1.htm.*

Chapter 4 Voting and Elections
1. Alex Samuels and Patrick Svitek, "State Rep. Rick Miller drops reelection bid after saying opponents were

challenging him because they're Asian," Texas Tribune, December 3, 2019, https://www.texastribune.org/2019/12/03/greg-abbott-rescinds-endorsement-texas-republican-rick-miller/

2. Zach Despart, "With two Jerry Garcias in Harris County constable race, one challenger sees a ploy," Houston Chronicle, December 20, 2019. https://www.houstonchronicle.com/news/houston-texas/houston/article/With-two-Jerry-Garcias-in-Harris-County-constable-14922524.php?utm_source=twitter.com&utm_medium=referral&utm_campaign=sftwitter

3. Jan E. Leighley and Jonathan Nagler, *Who Votes Now? Demographics, Issues, Inequality, and Turnout in the United States* (Princeton, NJ: Princeton University Press, 2014).

4. "Register to Vote," VoteTexas.gov, n.d., *www.votetexas.gov/register-to-vote.*

5. *www.kut.org/post/more-texas-schools-are-helping-students-register-vote-vast-majority-arent*

6. Stephen Knack and James Whit, "Did States' Motor Voter Programs Help the Democrats?" *American Politics Research* 26, no. 3 (1998): 344–365; Daniel P. Franklin and Eric E. Grier, "Effects of Motor Voter Legislation," *American Politics Research* 25, no. 1 (1997): 104–117.

7. Jacob R. Neiheisel and Barry C. Burden, "The Impact of Election Day Registration on Voter Turnout and Election Outcomes," *American Politics Research* 40, no. 4 (2012): 636–664.

8. *www.houstonchronicle.com/politics/texas/article/Record-number-of-candidates-running-for-Congress-14981404.php#.*

9. Ross Ramsey, "Analysis: What Happens When Texans' Presidential Primary Votes Matter," *The Texas Tribune*, April 20, 2015, *www.texastribune.org/2015/04/20/analysis-what-happens-when-texans-votes-matter.*

10. Elena Mejia Lutz, "Report: Texas Has Closed Most Polling Places Since Court Ruling," *The Texas Tribune*, November 4, 2016, *www.texastribune.org/2016/11/04/report-texas-holds-highest-number-polling-place-cl/;www.theguardian.*

com/us-news/2020/mar/02/ texas-polling-sites-closures-voting.

11.   www.eac.gov/crunching-the-numbers-to-help-voters-with-disabilities-and-election-officials

12.   www.texasobserver.org/the-death-of-mobile-polling-places-could-shrink-early-voting-in-texas

13.   Maurice Chammah, "They Weren't in the Running, but They Still Won Some Write-In Votes," *The Texas Tribune*, January 2, 2013, www.texastribune.org/2013/01/02/voting-mickey-mouse.

14.   The National Conference of State Legislatures, "Vote Centers," www.ncsl.org/research/elections-and-campaigns/vote-centers.aspx.

15.   www.houstonchronicle.com/news/politics/texas/article/Report-277-000-Texas-voters-vied-with-machine-13716992.php?utm_source=newsletter&utm_medium=email&utm_campaign=HC_TexasTake&utm_term=news&utm_content=briefing

16.   www.texasobserver.org/texas-counties-are-struggling-to-find-money-to-replace-antiquated-voting-machines

17.   www.texasmonthly.com/politics/can-hackers-mess-texass-elections/?utm_source=newsletter&utm_medium=email&utm_campaign=HoustonChronicle_TexasTake

18.   Quoted in Alan Greenblatt, "States Rolls Back Early Voting, Enforce Vote ID Laws," Governing.com, June 2011, www.governing.com/topics/politics/States-Roll-Back-Early-Voting-Enforce-Voter-ID-Laws.html.

19.   Donald Strong, "American Government and Politics: The Poll Tax: The Case of Texas," *American Political Science Review* 38, no. 4 (1944): 693–709.

20.   Arnoldo De León, *Mexican Americans in Texas: A Brief History*, 2nd ed. (Wheeling, IL: Harlan Davidson, 1990), 82.

21.   Ben H. Procter, "Great Depression," *Handbook of Texas Online*, June 15, 2010, https://tshaonline.org/handbook/online/articles/npg01.

22.   Conrey Bryson, *Dr. Lawrence A. Nixon and the White Primary* (El Paso: Texas Western Press, 1993).

23.   Darlene Clark Hine, *Black Victory: The Rise and Fall of the White Primary in Texas* (Millwood, NY: KTO Press, 1979), 25.

24.   De León, *Mexican Americans in Texas*, 82.

25.   Hine, *Black Victory*, 25.

26.   De León, *Mexican Americans in Texas*, 41.

27.   Henry Flores, *Latinos and the Voting Rights Act: The Search for Purpose* (Lanham, MD: Lexington Books, 2015), 121.

28.   www.dallasnews.com/news/2018/10/17/why-dont-more-texas-latinos-vote-many-are-cynical-about-politics-and-dont-trust-politicians-new-study-shows; https://latino.ucla.edu/wp-content/uploads/2018/12/LPPI_2018_vote.pdf

29.   Paul Burka, "El Gobernador," *Texas Monthly*, February 2008, www.texasmonthly.com/politics/el-gobernador.

30.   Martin Tolchin, "How Johnson Won Election He'd Lost," *New York Times*, February 11, 1990, www.nytimes.com/1990/02/11/us/how-johnson-won-election-he-d-lost.html.

31.   John E. Clark, *The Fall of the Duke of Duval* (Austin, TX: Eakin Press, 1995).

32.   David Montejano, *Anglos and Mexicans in the Making of Texas, 1836–1986* (Austin: University of Texas Press, 1987), 278.

33.   Ibid., 285.

34.   Suzanne Gamboa, "For Latinos, 1965 Voting Rights Act Impact Came a Decade Later," *NBCNews.com*, August 6, 2015, www.nbcnews.com/news/latino/latinos-1965-voting-rights-act-impact-came-decade-later-n404936.

35.   Burt A. Folkart, "Obituaries: Willie Velasquez; Leader of Latino Political Movement," *Los Angeles Times*, June 16, 1988, http://articles.latimes.com/1988-06-16/news/mn-6570_1_latino-political-power.

36.   www.houstonpublicmedia.org/articles/news/politics/2019/08/22/343602/harris-county-offers-first-ever-voter-registrar-training-in-vietnamese-and-chinese

37.   Robert Reinhold, "Los Angeles Board Is Said to Exercise Anti-Hispanic Bias," *New York Times*, June 5, 1990, www.nytimes.com/1990/06/05/us/los-angeles-board-is-said-to-exercise-anti-hispanic-bias.html.

38.   Benjamin Marquez, *Democratizing Texas Politics: Race, Identity, and Mexican American Empowerment, 1945–2002* (Austin: University of Texas Press, 2014), 1.

39.   Paul Burka, "Swept Away," *Texas Monthly*, December 2002, www.texasmonthly.com/articles/swept-away.

40.   Matt A. Bareto, Mario Villarreal, and Nathan D. Woods, "Metropolitan Latino Political Behavior: Voter Turnout and Candidate Preference in Los Angeles," *Journal of Urban Affairs* 27, no. 1 (2005): 71–91.

41.   Nate Cohn, "Why House Republicans Alienate Hispanics: They Don't Need Them," *New York Times*, October 21, 2014, www.nytimes.com/2014/10/21/upshot/why-house-republicans-alienate-his-panics-they-dont-need-them.html.

42.   Kenneth Bridges, *Twilight of the Texas Democrats: The 1978 Governor's Race* (College Station: Texas A&M University Press, 2008), 14.

43.   George Norris Greene, *The Establishment in Texas Politics: The Primitive Years, 1938–1957* (Norman: University of Oklahoma Press, 1984), 176.

44.   Alwin Barr, *Black Texans: A History of African Americans in Texas, 1528–1995* (Norman: University of Oklahoma Press, 1996), 78.

45.   Ibid., 232.

46.   Philip Bump, "When Did Black Americans Start Voting So Heavily Democratic?" *The Washington Post*, July 7, 2015, www.washingtonpost.com/news/the-fix/wp/2015/07/07/when-did-black-americans-start-voting-so-heavily-democratic.

47.   Elizabeth Taylor, "Woman Suffrage," *Handbook of Texas Online*, August 31, 2010, https://tshaonline.org/handbook/online/articles/viw01.

48.   Judith N. McArthur and Harold L. Smith, *Texas through Women's Eyes* (Austin: University of Texas Press, 2010), 162.

49.   Ibid.

50.   Texas Tribune/University of Texas poll, February 2020.

51.   www.nbcnews.com/politics/meet-the-press/parties-see-

big-demographic-changes-despite-overall-static-split-n1118521

52. Nancy E. Baker, "Focus on the Family: Twentieth Century Conservative Texas Women and the Lone Star Right," *The Texas Right: The Radical Roots of Lone Star Conservatism*, edited by David O'Donald Cullen, and Kyle G. Wilkison (College Station: Texas A&M University Press, 2014), 135.

53. Abby Livingston, "Historic Nature of Latina's Campaign Drew Attention but not Enough Support," *The Texas Tribune*, March 11, 2016, *www.texastribune.org/2016/03/11/texas-continues-dry-spell-among-congressional-wome*.

54. Ronald Schmidt, Sr., Yvette M. Alex-Assensoh, Andrew L. Aoki, and Rodney E. Hero, *Newcomers, Outsiders, and Insiders: Immigrants and American Racial Politics in the Early Twenty-First Century* (Ann Arbor: University of Michigan Press, 2009).

55. Edward J. M. Rhoads, "Chinese," *Handbook of Texas Online*, June 12, 2010, *https://tshaonline.org/handbook/online/articles/pjc01*.

56. Office of the Texas State Demographer.

57. Texas Demographer Office.

58. Janelle Wong, S. Karthick Ramakrishnan, Taeku Lee, and Jane Junn, *Asian American Political Participation: Emerging Constituents and Their Political Identities* (New York: Russell Sage, 2011).

59. Congressional Cooperative Election Study, 2018, Data compiled by the Author.

60. Alan S. Gerber, Donald P. Green, and Christopher W. Larimer, "Social Pressure and Voter Turnout: Evidence from a Large-Scale Field Experiment," *American Political Science Review* 102 (February 2008): 33–48.

61. Jimmy Banks, *Money, Marbles, and Chalk* (Austin: Texas Publishing Company, 1971), 180.

62. Wendy K. Tam Cho, "Naturalization, Socialization, Participation: Immigrants and (Non-)Voting," *Journal of Politics* 61, no. 4 (1999): 1140–1155.

63. R. Michael Alvarez and J. Andrew Sinclair, "Making Voting Easier: Convenience Voting in the 2008 Presidential Election," *Political Research Quarterly* 65, no. 2 (2011): 248–262.

64. R. Hans Miller, "Texas Mail-In Ballot Application Process Changes for 2018, Elections Official Says," *Community Impact Newspaper*, January 26, 1018, *https://com-munityimpact.com/houston/katy/news/2018/01/26/texas-mail-ballot-application-process-changes-2018*.

65. *https://texasmonitor.org/texas-vote-harvesters*

66. Abdurashid Solijonov, "Voter Turnout Trends around the World," International Institute for Democracy and Electoral Assistance (Stockholm, Sweden: December 31, 2016), *www.idea.int/publications/catalogue/voter-turnout-trends-around-world*.

67. Thomas M. Holbrook and Aaron C. Weinschenk, "Campaigns, Mobilization, and Turnout in Mayoral Elections," *Political Research Quarterly* 67, no. 1 (2014): 42–55.

68. Melissa R. Michelson, "How to Increase Voter Turnout in Communities Where People Have Not Usually Participated in Elections," *Scholars Strategy Network*, July 11, 2014, *http://journalistsresource.org/studies/politics/elections/increasing-voter-turnout-in-communities-where-people-have-not-usually-participated-in-elections#sthash.ywwlzgZQ.dpuf*.

69. *www.tandfonline.com/doi/abs/10.1080/10584609.2018.1548530*

70. Ibid.

71. Lisa García Bedolla and Melissa R. Michelson, *Mobilizing Inclusion: Transforming the Electorate through Get-Out-the-Vote Campaigns* (New Haven, CT: Yale University Press, 2012).

72. Costas Panagopolous, "Thank You for Voting: Gratitude Expression and Voter Mobilization," *Journal of Politics* 73, no. 3 (2011): 707–717.

73. Alan Gerber, Greg Huber, David Doherty, Conor Dowling, and Seth Hill, "Do Perceptions of Ballot Secrecy Influence Turnout? Results from a Field Experiment," *American Journal of Political Science* 57, no. 3 (2013): 537–551.

74. Marisa Abrajano and Costas Panagopoulos, "Does Language Matter? The Impact of Spanish versus English-Language GOTV Efforts on Latino Turnout," *American Politics Research* 39, no. 4 (2011): 643–663.

75. Tolchin, "How Johnson Won."

76. Demond Fernandez, "Voter Fraud Allegations under Investigation, Again, in Dallas County," *WFAA.com*, February 15, 2018, *www.wfaa.com/article/news/politics/voter-fraud-allegations-under-investigation-again-in-dallas-county/287-519427028*; Alex Samuels, "Carrollton mayoral candidate arrested on suspicion of fraudulently obtaining mail-in ballots," *Texas Tribune*, October 8, 2020, *www.texastribune.org/2020/10/08/voting-fraud-arrest-carrollton*.

77. Wayne Slater, "Few Texas Voter-Fraud Cases Would Have Been Prevented by Photo ID Law, Review Shows," *Dallas Morning News*, September 2013, *www.dallasnews.com/news/politics/headlines/20130908-few-texas-voter-fraud-cases-would-have-been-prevented-by-photo-id-law-review-shows.ece*.

78. W. Gardner Selby, "Light a Match to Greg Abbott's Ridiculous Claim About 'Rampant Voter Fraud,'" *Politifact.com*, March 17, 2016, *www.politifact.com/texas/statements/2016/mar/17/greg-abbott/light-match-greg-abbotts-claim-about-rampant-voter*.

79. Ross Ramsey, "Analysis: Scant Evidence for Abbott's 'Rampant' Voter Fraud," *The Texas Tribune*, March 3, 2015, *www.texastribune.org/2016/03/15/analysis-scant-evidence-abbott-rampant-voter-fraud*.

80. *www.dallasnews.com/news/2018-elections/2018/07/10/voter-fraud-investigation-deepens-dallas-county-targeting-grand-prairie-candidate*; Berenice Garcia, "Four Arrested on Charges of Illegal Voting in Starr County," *The Monitor*, February 20, 2018, *www.themonitor.com/news/local/article_9c6d3856-1699-11e8-9723-73e5e99326f5.html*; *www.star-telegram.com/news/local/community/fort-worth/article207176829.html*.

81. "In the United States Court of Appeals for the Fifth Circuit," April 27, 2018, *www.texasattorneygeneral.gov/files/epress/Veasey_-_CA5_opinion_4_27_2018.pdf?cachebuster:59*.

82. David Saleh Rauf, "AP Exclusive: Hundreds of Texans May Have Voted

Improperly," *APNews.com*, February 18, 2017, *https://apnews.com/b7b57fc61c5b462d871a942864c0afad*

83. *Texas Tribune Polling, June 2017.*

84. Banks, *Money, Marbles, and Chalk*, 36.

85. H. C. Pittman, *Inside the Third House* (Austin: Eakin Press, 1992), 83.

86. Jay Newton-Small, "Davis Campaign Seizes on 'Abortion Barbie' Posters," *Time*, May 28, 2014, *http://time.com/132067/wendy-davis-texas-abortion-barbie*.

87. Quoted in Molly Ivins, *Molly Ivins Can't Say That, Can She?* (New York: Vintage Books, 1991), 46.

88. Ted Oberg, "Dan Patrick Mental Health Detailed in Court Depositions," *ABC13.com*, May 21, 2014, *http://abc13.com/politics/dan-patrick-mental-health-records-leaked-in-last-days-of-lt-govs-race/63863*.

89. Richard R. Lau, Lee Sigelman, and Ivy Brown Rovner, "The Effects of Negative Political Campaigns: A Meta-Analytic Reassessment." *Journal of Politics* 69, no. 4 (2007): 1176–1209.

90. T. W. Farnam, "Study: Negative Campaign Ads Much More Frequent, Vicious Than in Primaries Past," *The Washington Post*, February 20, 2012, *www.washingtonpost.com/politics/study-negative-campaign-ads-much-more-frequent-vicious-than-in-primaries-past/2012/02/14/gIQAR7ifPR_story.html*.

91. Bill Hobby, *How Things Really Work: Lessons from a Life in Politics* (Austin: University of Texas Press, 2010), 52.

92. Jeffrey E. Cohen, *Going Local: Presidential Leadership in the Post-Broadcast Age* (New York: Cambridge University Press, 2010).

93. Gromer Jeffers Jr., "Greg Abbott, Wendy Davis Launching Extensive Voter Turnout Efforts, *Dallas Morning News*, October 2014, *www.dallasnews.com/news/politics/headlines/20141018-ab-bott-davis-launching-extensive-vot-er-turnout-efforts.ece*.

94. Allison Brennan, "Microtargeting: How Campaigns Know You Better Than You Know Yourself," *CNN.com*, November 5, 2012, *www.cnn.com/2012/11/05/politics/voters-microtargeting*.

95. Jonathan Berr, "Election 1026's Price Tag: $6.8 Billion," *CBSNews.com*, November 8, 2016, *www.cbsnews.com/news/election-2016s-price-tag-6-8-billion*.

96. Jay Root and Becca Aaronson, "Texas Governor's Race: Analyzing the Money," *The Texas Tribune*, July 30, 2014, *www.texastribune.org/2014/07/30/texas-governors-race-analyzing-money*.

97. David Saleh Rauf, "Abbott, Davis Combine to Spend $83 Million to Become Next Texas Governor," *Chron.com*, October 28, 2014, *http://blog.chron.com/texaspolitics/2014/10/abbott-davis-combine-to-spend-83-million-to-become-next-texas-governor*.

98. *www.expressnews.com/news/local/politics/article/Outgoing-House-Speaker-Straus-spends-big-to-12721137.php*

99. Associated Press, "Martin Pleads Guilty, Resign House Seat," *The Bonham Daily Favorite*, April 23, 1982, *https://news.google.com/newspapers?id=MTNfAAAAIBAJ&sjid=VU8NAAAAIBAJ&pg=6718,4614285*.

100. *https://txelects.com/by-the-numbers-money-and-open-seat-races*

101. Billy Monroe, Nathan K. Mitchell, and Lee Payne, "Texas Judicial Primary Elections: A Quantitative Analysis," *Journal of Political Science* 44 (2016): 109–134.

102. Edgar Walters and Alex Duner, "Farmers Insurance Company Gave a Lot of Money to Texas' Greg Abbott," *Governing.com*, July 22, 2014, *www.governing.com/news/headlines/the-farmers-insurance-company-is-giving-a-lot-of-money-to-the-gops-greg-abbott.html*.

103. Benjamin I. Page, Larry M. Bartels, and Jason Seawright, "Democracy and the Policy Preferences of Wealthy Americans," *Perspectives on Politics* 11, no. 1 (2013): 51–73.

104. Larry M. Bartels, *Unequal Democracy: The Political Economy of the New Gilded Age* (Princeton, NJ: Princeton University Press, 2008).

105. Christy Hoppe, "Texas' Republican Primaries Are Steeped in Tea Party Agenda," *Dallas Morning News*, May 2014, *www.dallasnews.com/news/politics/headlines/20140526-texas-gop-primaries-are-steeped-in-tea-party-agenda.ece*.

106. Robert Draper, "The Life and Death (and Life?) of the Party," *Texas Monthly*, August 2013, *www.texasmonthly.com/politics/the-life-and-death-and-life-of-the-party*.

107. Lynda W. Powell, *The Influence of Campaign Contributions in State Legislatures* (Ann Arbor: University of Michigan Press, 2012).

108. Stephen Ansolabehere, John M. De Figueiredo, and James M. Snyder, "Why Is There So Little Money in Politics?" *Economic Perspectives* 17, no. 1 (2003): 105–130.

109. Paul Burka, "Minority Report," *Texas Monthly*, January 2007, *www.texasmonthly.com/politics/minority-report*.

110. Wayne Thorburn, *Red State: An Insider's Story of How the GOP Came to Dominate Texas Politics* (Austin: University of Texas Press, 2014), 164.

111. National Conference of State Legislatures, "Straight Ticket Voting," May 31, 2017, *www.ncsl.org/research/elections-and-campaigns/straight-ticket-voting.aspx*.

112. DallasNews Administrator, "Editorial: Upgrade Texas Governing by Ending Single-Party Pull," *Dallas Morning News*, March 2013, *www.dallasnews.com/opinion/editorials/20130312-editorial-upgrade-texas-governing-by-ending-single-party-pull.ece*.

113. *www.washingtonpost.com/politics/2020/04/17/no-voting-by-mail-does-not-give-either-party-an-advantage-heres-how-we-know/?utm_campaign=wp_monkeycage&utm_medium=social&utm_source=twitter*

114. *www.texastribune.org/2020/04/13/voting-person-during-pandemic-best-we-can-do*

115. *https://thedailytexan.com/2020/05/05/texans-continue-debate-on-mail-in-ballots-before-summer-runoff-elections*

116. Ross Ramsey, "Analysis: When Apathy Becomes a Political Tactic," *The Texas Tribune*, November 23, 2015, *www.texastribune.org/2015/10/23/analysis-when-apathy-becomes-political-tactic*.

117. Alwin Barr, *Black Texans: A History of African Americans in Texas, 1528–1995* (Norman: University of Oklahoma Press, 1996), 232.

118. *www.vanityfair.com/news/2019/ 01/texas-2020-presidential-election ?mbid=social_twitter&utm_social- type=owned&utm_source= twitter&utm_brand=vf&utm_ medium=social&utm_source=Editori al%3A+Texas+Tribune+Master&utm_ campaign=05c875255e-trib-newsletters- the-brief&utm_medium=email&utm_ term=0_d9a68d8efc-05c875255e- 101290241&mc_cid=05c875255e&mc_ eid=101a099a60*

119. *www.vanityfair.com/news/ 2019/01/texas-2020-presidential- election?mbid=social_twitter&utm_so- cial-type=owned&utm_source= twitter&utm_brand=vf&utm_ medium=social&utm_source=Ed itorial%3A+Texas+Tribune+Mast er&utm_campaign=05c875255e- trib-newsletters-the-brief&utm_ medium=email&utm_term=0_d9a68 d8efc-05c875255e-101290241&mc_ cid=05c875255e&mc_eid=101a099a60*

120. Paul Taylor, Ana Gonzales- Barrera, Jeffrey S. Passel, and Mark Hugo Lopez, "An Awakened Giant: The Hispanic Electorate Is Likely to Double by 2030," *Pew Research Center,* November 14, 2012, *www.pewhispanic. org/2012/11/14/an-awakened-giant- the-hispanic-electorate-is-likely-to- double-by-2030.*

121. *www.texasmonthly.com/ politics/how-win-texas-2020/?utm_ campaign=The%20Armadillo%20 -%20Editorial&utm_source=hs_ email&utm_medium=email&utm_ content=79758004&_hsenc= p2ANqtz—MI56fYJ1-XEEw4GleCFn- qu0rseyVyfenI-s2K5MjGXUly- CPAw1k2k-6R3Tfg9sv-KVnx- s0QjZm2MDCazqS3ob9aEhQ&_ hsmi=79758006*

Chapter 5 Political Parties: Texas in Blue and Red

1. *www.newsweek.com/texas-repub- licans-accidentally-send-2020- strategy-email-democrats-attack-ads- mistake-1474168?utm_medium= Social&utm_source=Twitter&utm_ campaign=NewsweekTwitter*

2. Jan Reid, *Let the People In: The Life and Times of Ann Richards* (Austin: University of Texas Press, 2012), 399.

3. Corbett Smith, "How Bernie's People and the DNC Are Getting Involved in a Dallas Schools Elec- tion," DallasNews.com, May 28, 2017, *www.dallasnews.com/news/ education/2017/05/28/party-texas- democrats-getting-involved-local- school-board-elections.*

4. Mary Beth Rogers, *Turning Texas Blue* (New York: St. Martin's Press, 2016), 143.

5. Fred Gantt Jr., *The Chief Execu- tive in Texas: A Study in Gubernato- rial Leadership* (Austin: University of Texas Press, 1964).

6. Patrick Svitek, "A San Antonio Wake-Up Call for Democrats," *The Texas Tribune,* June 14, 2015, *www. texastribune.org/2015/06/14/taylors- triumph-new-day-or-another-fluke.*

7. Joseph Bafumi and Robert Y. Sha- piro, "A New Partisan Voter," *Journal of Politics* 71, no. 1 (2009): 1–24.

8. Geoffrey C. Layman, Thomas M. Carsey, John C. Green, Richard Hererra, and Rosalyn Cooperman, "Activists and Conflict Extension in American Party Politics," *American Political Science Review* 104, no. 2 (2010): 324–346; Michael A. Bailey, Jonathan Mummolo, and Hans Noel, "Tea Party Influence: A Story of Ac- tivists and Elites," *American Politics Research* 40, no. 5 (2012): 769–804.

9. Mike Ward and Peggy Fikac, "A Conservative Wave Swept the Texas Legislature, but It Wasn't Big Enough for the Tea Party," *Houston Chronicle,* May 30, 2015, *www.houstonchronicle. com/news/politics/texas/article/A- conservative-wave-swept-the-Texas- Legislature-6297070.php.*

10. *www.texasgop.org/wp-content/ uploads/2015/03/Precinct-Chair- Duties.pdf*

11. *https://therivardreport.com/ challengers-line-up-to-unseat-party- chairs-as-infighting-persists*

12. *www.houstonchronicle.com/ politics/houston/article/In-conser- vative-stronghold-of-Montgomery- County-15056241.php#*

13. Catherine Dominguez, "Mont- gomery County GOP in Turmoil after Longtime Chair Wilkerson's Powers Weakened," *The Courier,* June 28, 2018, *www.yourconroenews. com/neighborhood/moco/news/article/ Montgomery-County-GOP-in-turmoil- after-longtime-13035417.php.*

14. *www.houstonchronicle.com/ politics/houston/article/In-conser- vative-stronghold-of-Montgomery- County-15056241.php#*

15. *www.dallasnews.com/news/ politics/2020/06/04/texas-leaders- demand-resignation-of-bexar-county- gop-chairwoman-who-spread-george- floyd-conspiracy-theory*

16. *www.epbusinessjournal. com/2019/12/texas-democratic-party- chair-declares-ramsey-english-cantu- as-ineligible-candidate-for-texas- house-of-representative-district-74*

17. Morgan Smith, "Party Crashers," *The Texas Tribune,* May 7, 2010, *www. texastribune.org/2010/05/07/three- candidates-vying-to-lead-state-gop.*

18. Ibid.

19. Valeria Olivares, "From the Iraq War to representing Florida in Con- gress to Texas GOP Chair: Here's what you need to know about Allen West," *Texas Tribune,* July 20, 2020, https:// www.texastribune.org/2020/07/20/ allen-west-texas-gop-chair/

20. Dylan Baddour, "Texas GOP Re- jects Proposal for Vote on Secession," Chron.com, December 7, 2015, *www. chron.com/news/houston-texas/texas/ article/Texas-secession-resolu-tion- passes-GOP-committee-6676280.php.*

21. Patrick Svitek, "Texas GOP Votes Down Controversial Secession Proposal," *The Texas Tribune,* De- cember 5, 2015, *www.texastribune. org/2015/12/05/texas-gop-votes- down-controversial-secession-propo.*

22. Alan D. Monroe, "American Party Platforms and Public Opinion," *American Journal of Political Science* 27, no. 1 (1983): 27–42; Daniel J. Cof- fey, "More than a Dime's Worth: Using State Party Platforms to Assess the Degree of American Party Polariza- tion," *PS: Political Science and Politics* 44, no. 2 (2011): 331–337.

23. Coffey, "More than a Dime's Worth."

24. Sarah M. Morehouse and Malcolm E. Jewell, "The Future of Political Par- ties in the States," *CSG.org,* n.d., http:// www.csg.org/knowledgecenter/docs/ BOS2005-PoliticalParties.pdf.

25. James R. Soukup, Clifton McCleskey, and Harry Holloway, *Party and Factional Division in Texas* (Aus- tin: University of Texas Press, 1964), 22.

26. Lionel V. Patenaude, "Garner, John Nance," *Handbook of Texas Online*, June 15, 2010, *https://tshaonline. org/handbook/online/articles/fga24*.

27. Kenneth Bridges, *Twilight of the Texas Democrats: The 1978 Governor's Race* (College Station: Texas A&M University Press, 2008), 5.

28. Jimmy Banks, *Money, Marbles and Chalk* (Austin: Texas Publishing Company, 1971), 201.

29. Mickey Leland, July 10, 1981, "The Tumor in the Texas Delegation," in *Fifty Years of the Texas Observer*, edited by Char Miller (San Antonio, TX: Trinity University Press, 2004), 207.

30. Bridges, *Twilight of the Texas Democrats*, 15.

31. Char Miller, "The Political Tumult," *Fifty Years of the Texas Observer*, edited by Char Miller, (San Antonio, TX: Trinity University Press, 2004), 151.

32. Rogers, *Turning Texas Blue*, 85.

33. Gregory Curtis, "Who Killed the Texas Democratic Party?" *Texas Monthly*, January 1998, *www.texasmonthly.com/politics/who-killed-the-texas-democratic-party*.

34. John R. Knaggs, *Two-Party Texas: The John Tower Era, 1961–1984* (Austin: Eakin Press, 1986).

35. Wayne Thornburn, *Red State: An Insider's Story of How the GOP Came to Dominate Texas Politics* (Austin: University of Texas Press, 2014), 68.

36. Knaggs, *Two-Party Texas*, 13.

37. Ibid., 2.

38. Ibid., 5.

39. Jon Mecham, *Destiny and Power: The American Odyssey of George Herbert Walker Bush* (New York: Random House, 2015), 165.

40. Knaggs, *Two-Party Texas*, 137.

41. Edward H. Miller, *Nut Country: Right-Wing Dallas and the Birth of the Southern Strategy* (Chicago: University of Chicago Press, 2015), 140.

42. Knaggs, *Two-Party Texas*, 251.

43. Sam Kinch Jr., *Too Much Money Is Not Enough: Big Money and Political Power in Texas* (Austin: Campaign for People, 2000), 29.

44. Dubose and Reid, *The Hammer*, 44.

45. Miller, *Nut Country*.

46. Paul Burka, "The Elephants in the Room," *Texas Monthly*, January 2006, *www.texasmonthly.com/articles/the-elephants-in-the-room*.

47. Ibid.

48. Kate Zernicke, "Unlikely Activist Who Got to the Tea Party Early," *New York Times*, February 27, 2010, *www.nytimes.com/2010/02/28/us/politics/28keli.html?login=email&mtr ref=undefined*.

49. Martin Kaste, "Tea Party Star Leads Movement on Her Own Terms," NPR.org, February 2, 2010, *www.npr.org/templates/story/story. php?storyId=123229743*.

50. Jim Norman, "In US, Support for Tea Party Drops to New Low," *Gallup*, October 26, 2015, *www.gallup.com/poll/186338/support-tea-party-drops-new-low.aspx*.

51. Mark Binelli, "Lone Star Crazy: How Right-Wing Extremists Took over Texas," *Rolling Stone*, July 1, 2014, *www.rollingstone.com/politics/news/lone-star-crazy-how-right-wing-extremists-took-over-texas-20140701*.

52. R. G. Ratcliffe, "Former Republican Railroad Commissioner: Bathroom Bill Harms Teens and Republicans," *Texas Monthly*, July 28, 2017, *www.texasmonthly.com/burka-blog/former-republican-railroad-commissioner-bathroom-bill-harms-teens-republicans*.

53. Jeremy Wallace, "Republican Discontent Continues Despite the Party's Dominance in Texas," *Houston Chronicle*, September 30, 2017, *www.houstonchronicle.com/news/houston-texas/houston/article/Republican-discontent-continues-despite-the-12243640.php*.

54. Bobby Cervantes, "Texas GOP Chairman Quits, Warns Party Leaders to Broaden Diversity," *Houston Chronicle*, May 20, 2017, *www.houstonchronicle.com/news/houston-texas/houston/article/Texas-GOP-chairman-quits-warns-party-leaders-to-11161659.php*.

55. Curtiss, "Who Killed the Texas Democratic Party?"

56. Ibid.

57. Paul Burka, "More Power to Him," *Texas Monthly*, February 1995, *www.texasmonthly.com/politics/more-power-to-him*.

58. Jake Silverstein, "The Great Campaigner," *Texas Monthly*, September 2011, *www.texasmonthly.com/politics/the-great-campaigner-2*.

59. Morehouse and Jewell, "The Future of Political Parties."

60. Thornburn, *Red State*, ix.

61. Ibid., 51.

62. Jerusalem Demsas, "Democrats fail to make gains in state legislative races in advance of 2021 redistricting." *Vox*, November 5, 2020, *www.vox.com/2020/11/5/21551388/democrats-republicans-state-legislative-races-election-results-redistricting-gerrymandering-census*.

63. Victoria Loe, "The Deal That Didn't Work," *Texas Monthly*, August 1981.

64. *Reynolds v. Sims*, 377 U.S. 533 (1964).

65. Katy Vine, "The Agitator," *Texas Monthly*, August 2015, *www.texasmonthly.com/politics/the-agitator*.

66. Michael King, "Killer D's Come Home, but the Saga Goes On," *Austin Chronicle*, May 23, 2003, *www.austinchronicle.com/news/2003-05-23/161001*.

67. ABQJournal News Staff, "Quorum-Busting Texas Senator Who Fled to ABQ in 20032 Advises Wisconsin Dems to Hang Tough," *Albuquerque Journal*, February 23, 2011, *www.abqjournal.com/7348/remem-ber-the-texas-eleven.html*.

68. Ross Ramsey, "Redistricting Plan Set, but Legal Debate Isn't Over," *The Texas Tribune*, August 17, 2013, *www.texastribune.org/2013/08/17/legislators-volley-redistricting-back-courts*.

69. Ibid.

70. Ross Ramsey, "Judges: 2014 Primaries Can Use Maps Approved This Summer by Lege," *The Texas Tribune*, September 6, 3013, *www.texastribune.org/2013/09/06/2014-primaries-can-proceed-judges-rule*.

71. *www.texastribune.org/2018/06/25/us-supreme-ruling-court-texas-redistricting-case*

72. Michael Li, "Two Texas Cases Test the Boundaries of Redistricting Law," Brennan Center for Justice, February 17, 2015, *www.brennancenter.org/blog/two-texas-cases-test-boundaries-redistricting-law*.

73. Seth C. McKee and Antoine Yoshinaka, "Late to the Parade: Party Switchers in Contemporary US

Southern Legislatures," *Party Politics* 21, no. 6 (2015): 957–969.

74. *www.texasgop.org/wp-content/ uploads/2013/11/Party-Switchers-1. pptx*

75. Dan Wallach, "County Judge Switches to Republican; Will Run for Final Term in 2018 with GOP," *Beaumont Enterprise*, February 8, 2017, *www.beaumontenterprise.com/news/ article/County-judge-switches-to-Republican-will-run-for-10918388.php*.

76. Ross Ramsey, "Hopson's Choice," *The Texas Tribune*, November 6, 2009, *www.texastribune.org/2009/11/06/ hopson-switches-to-the-republicans*.

77. Melissa del Bosque, "Portrait of a Party Switcher," *Texas Observer*, May 14, 2012, *www.texasobserver.org/ portrait-of-a-party-switcher*.

78. Ibid.

79. *www.mrt.com/news/ar-ticle/In-Texas-politics-there-is-a-rich-history-of-7498862.php*

80. Timothy P. Nokken, "Party Switching and the Procedural Party Agenda in the U.S. House of Representatives," *Political Parties and Legislative Party Switching*, edited by William Heller and Carol Mershon (New York: Palgrave Macmillan, 2009), 81–108.

81. Christian R. Grose and Antoine Yoshinaka, "The Electoral Consequences of Party Switching by Incumbent Members of Congress, 1947–2000," *Legislative Studies Quarterly* 28, no. 1 (2003): 55–75.

82. Dubose and Reid, *The Hammer*, 46.

83. Ross Ramsey, "TribBlog: Ritter Confirms He's Switching Parties," *The Texas Tribune*, December 11, 2010, *www.texastribune.org/2010/12/11/ allan-ritter-confirms-hes-switching-parties*.

84. Peggy Fikac, "Democratic Party-Switchers Give GOP a House Supermajority," MySanAntonio. com, December 15, 2010, *www. mysanantonio.com/news/politics/ texas_legislature/article/Democratic-party-switchers-give-GOP-a-House-894784.php*.

85. "Bernard Erickson" Legislative Reference Library of Texas, n.d., *www. lrl.state.tx.us/lege-leaders/members/ memberdisplay.cfm?memberID=292*.

86. *www.dallasnews.com/news/ politics/2020/01/22/texas-new-ballot-requirements-have-libertarians-and-greens-confused-ahead-of-elections*

87. David Montejano, *Anglos and Mexicans in the Making of Texas, 1836–1986* (Austin: University of Texas Press, 1987), 289.

88. Ibid., 292.

89. Judith N. McArthur and Harold L. Smith, *Texas through Women's Eyes* (Austin: University of Texas Press, 2010), 208.

90. Ross Ramsey, "Analysis: Minor Parties Matter, Even If They Lose," *The Texas Tribune*, May 7, 2014, *www. texastribune.org/2014/05/07/analysis-minor-parties-still-matter-even-if-they-l*.

91. *www.houstonchronicle.com/ news/politics/texas/article/As-Texas-elections-get-tighter-more-third-party-14867024.php*

92. *www.texasmonthly.com/burka-blog/will-rap-4-weed-independent-candidates-texas-governor*

93. Michael Ennis, "All Shook Up," *Texas Monthly*, October 2006, *www.texasmonthly.com/politics/ all-shook-up*.

94. Dubose and Reid, *The Hammer*, 36.

Chapter 6 Interest Groups

1. Bill Hobby, *How Things Really Work: Lessons from a Life in Politics* (Austin: University of Texas Press, 2010).

2. AP, "Texas Businessman Hands Out $10,000 Checks in State Senate," *New York Times*, July 9, 1989, *www.nytimes.com/1989/07/09/ us/texas-businessman-hands-out-10000-checks-in-state-senate.html*.

3. Quoted in Erica Grieder, "The Private Sector's Influence on the Public Interests of Texas," *Texas Monthly*, January 14, 2013, *www.texasmonthly. com/politics/the-private-sectors-influence-on-the-public-interests-of-texas*.

4. Evan Smith, "Lobbying," *Texas Monthly*, February 2009, *www.texas-monthly.com/articles/lobbying*.

5. Mark A. Smith, "The Mobilization and Influence of Business Interests," *The Oxford Handbook of American Political Parties and Interest Groups* (New York: Oxford University Press, 2010).

6. James Drew, "Insurers, Plaintiff's Lawyers Square Off in Austin over Hail Storm Bill," *Houston Chronicle*, February 3, 2017, *www.houston-chronicle.com/news/houston-texas/houston/ article/Insurers-plaintiff-s-lawyers-square-off-in-10907598.php*.

7. Jay Root, "Even in Texas, Sometimes the Billionaires Lose," *The Texas Tribune*, May 17, 2017, *www.texastribune.org/2017/05/17/even-texas-sometimes-billionaires-lose*.

8. Quoted in Kay L. Schlozman, "Who Sings in the Heavenly Chorus? The Shape of the Organized Interest System," *The Oxford Handbook of American Political Parties and Interest Groups* (New York: Oxford University Press, 2010), 425–450.

9. Nathan Bernier, "Texas Environmentalists Mostly Disappointed with Legislative Session," *KUT.org*, June 1, 2011, *http://kut.org/post/texas-environmentalists-mostly-disappointed-legislative-session*.

10. Quoted in Sam Kinch Jr., *Too Much Money Is Not Enough: Big Money and Political Power in Texas* (Austin: Campaigns for People, 2000), 81.

11. *www.texasobserver.org/are-silicon-valley-giants-responsible-for-a-mysterious-new-texas-labor-rule*

12. *www.texasobserver.org/ texas-workforce-commission-labor-regulators-lobbyists-rewrite-rule-gig-economy*; *www.nytimes. com/2019/03/26/business/economy/ gig-economy-lobbying.html*

13. *www.houstonchronicle.com/business/article/Texas-adopts-rule-to-classify-digital-gig-economy-13754532. php*; *https://www.texasobserver.org/ handy-wanted-to-disrupt-texas-labor-laws-it-may-have-also-disrupted-texas-lobbying-laws*

14. Sam Best and Paul Teske, "Explaining State Internet Sales Taxation: New Economy, Old-Fashioned Interest Group Politics," *State Politics and Policy Quarterly* 2, no.1 (2000).

15. H. C. Pittman, *Inside the Third House: A Veteran Lobbyist Takes a 50-Year Frolic through Texas Politics* (Austin: Eakin Press, 1992).

16. David Saleh Rauf and Neal Morton, "Austin Braces for Tesla

Lobbying Blitz," *Houston Chronicle*, December 18, 2014.

17. Jim Malewitz, "Abbott Shuts Door on Tesla Loophole," *The Texas Tribune*, July 14, 2015, *www.texastri-bune. org/2015/07/14/abbott-tesla-dealership-model-works-just-fine.*

18. Mark Smith, *American Business and Political Power: Public Opinion, Elections, and Democracy* (Chicago: University of Chicago Press, 2001).

19. Frank R. Baumgartner, "Interest Groups and Agendas," *The Oxford Handbook of American Political Parties and Interest Groups* (New York: Oxford University Press, 2010), 519–533.

20. Dara Z. Strolovitch and M. David Forrest, "Social and Economic Justice Movements and Organizations," *The Oxford Handbook of American Political Parties and Interest Groups* (New York: Oxford University Press, 2010), 468–484.

21. Ibid.

22. Guadalupe San Miguel Jr., *"Let Them All Take Heed": Mexican Americans and the Campaign for Educational Equality in Texas, 1910–1981* (College Station: Texas A&M University Press, 1987).

23. Christy Hoppe, "Senate Panel Agrees to Change Corruption Investigations," *Dallas Morning News*, March 16, 2015.

24. Run out of a basement office in Austin by Craig McDonald, Texans for Public Justice adopted a "no frills" approach that underscores their interest in good government and public disclosure of political financial information. Says McDonald of his office, which has three employees, one intern, and a budget of $250,000: "Once a year, I bring in cookies, but that's about it."

25. *www.texastribune. org/2019/05/16/texas-born-alive-abortion-bill-likely-headed-greg-abbotts-desk.*

26. Schlozman, "Who Sings in the Heavenly Chorus?"

27. Municipal Finance Task Force, "The City of Houston's Finances: Let's Be Clear about Where We Are," Greater Houston Partnership, July 24, 2015, *www.houston.org/municipal-finance/pdf/Municipal%20Finance-FINAL.pdf.*

28. Frank R. Baumgartner and Bryan D. Jones, *Agendas and Instability in American Politics* (Chicago: University of Chicago Press, 1993).

29. *www.nytimes.com/2020/04/18/us/texas-protests-stay-at-home.html*

30. Richard West, "Inside the Lobby," *Texas Monthly*, July 1973, *www.texas-monthly.com/the-culture/inside-the-lobby/#sthash.MgnytzkU.dpuf.*

31. Ryan Sager, "Keep Off the Astroturf," *New York Times*, August 19, 2009, *www.nytimes.com/2009/08/19/opinion/19sager.html.*

32. Aliyya Swabby, "Watch Senate Education Committee Discuss School Choice Legislation," *The Texas Tribune*, March 21, 2017, *www. texastribune.org/2017/03/21/senate-public-ed-set-hear-amended-school-choice-bill.*

33. Eleanor Dearman and Scott Braddock, "Rural GOP House Lawmakers Alarmed by 'Fraudulent' Letters Promoting School Vouchers," *Houston Chronicle*, March 22, 2017, *www.houstonchronicle.com/local/texas-politics/quorum-report/article/Rural-GOP-House-lawmakers-alarmed-by-fraudulent-11020696.php.*

34. Taken from the website of each organization, usually in the form of a "voter guide," the average is calculated as the total number of successful (winning) candidates divided by the total number of endorsements. Although most of the endorsees were included on these lists, on occasion a group would endorse a candidate privately, in a newsletter (or listed elsewhere on their website), in a public event, or implicitly by saying good things about the candidate (for the analysis here, only the roster of endorsed candidates on each website was used since this is the most common way for voters to learn about the endorser preferences).

35. West, "Inside the Lobby."

36. Thomas Stratmann, "Are Contributors Rational? Untangling Strategies of Political Action Committees," *Journal of Political Economy* 100, no. 3 (1992): 647–664.

37. Quoted in Kinch, *Too Much Money Is Not Enough*, 43.

38. Ibid., 55.

39. Reeve Hamilton, "State Sued for 'Stifling the Texas Craft Beer Renaissance," *The Texas Tribune*, December 10, 2014, *www.texastri-bune.org/2014/12/10/state-sued-stifling-texas-craft-beer-renaissance.*

40. *www.texaspolicy.com/press/tppf-supreme-court-ruling-on-bag-ban-affirms-cities-are-not-above-the-law; https://law.utexas. edu/clinics/2018/03/21/filing-texas-supreme-court-amicus-brief-supporting-laredos-single-use-bag-ban*

41. Amanda Zamora, "How to Make Sure Your Voice Gets Heard at the Texas Capitol," *The Texas Tribune*, March 3, 2017, *www.texastri-bune. org/2017/03/24/how-make-sure-your-voice-gets-heard-texas-capitol.*

42. Byron C. Utech, *The Legislature and the People* (San Antonio: Naylor Company, 1937), 117.

43. West, "Inside the Lobby."

44. Aman Batheja, "Some Say Group Has Too Much Sway Over Legislation," *Fort Worth Star Telegram*, December 4, 2011.

45. Sophie Novack, "How 'Mad Moms in Minivans' Injected Themselves into Texas' Anti-Vaccine Debate," *Texas Observer*, August 2017, *www.texasobserver.org/mad-moms-minivans-injected-texas-anti-vaccine/amp.*

46. Alan Rosenthal, *The Third House: Lobbyists and Lobbying in the States* (Washington, DC: CQ Press, 2001).

47. Dagny Pruner, "Lawmakers Heart Testimony on Bill to Abolish 'Texa-Fornian Wine,'" *Dal-lasNews.com*, April 2017, *www.dallasnews.com/news/texas-legislature/2017/04/25/law-makers-hear-testimony-bill-abolish-texa-fornian-wine.*

48. Quoted in Kinch, *Too Much Money Is Not Enough*, 79.

49. West, "Inside the Lobby."

50. KCBD 11, "State Could Allow Superintendents Without Teaching Experience," *KCBD.com*, August 13, 2015, *www.kcbd.com/story/29785294/state-could-allow-superintendents-without-teaching-experience.*

51. *www.cnn.com/2019/06/12/politics/texas-save-chick-fil-a—bill-greg-abbott/index.html*

52. *https://therivardreport.com/group-sues-city-of-san-antonio-under-states-new-save-chick-fil-a-law*

53. Jim Malewitz, "Pipeline Company Ghost-Wrote Texas Regulator's Letter," *The Texas Tribune*, September 22, 2015.

54. Ross Ramsey, "Legislature Is a Training Ground for Lobbyists," *The Texas Tribune*, June 10, 2010.

55. "Representation by Former Officer or Employee of Regulatory Agency Restricted; Criminal Offense." Title 5 *Texas Government Code*, Sec. 572.054(a). Available at *https://statutes.capitol.texas.gov/Docs/GV/htm/GV.572.htm*.

56. Aman Batheja, "Despite Reforms, Some Elected Officials Still Lobby," *The Texas Tribune*, February 8, 2013.

57. Penni Crabtree, "$17 Billion Industry Largely Unregulated," *San Diego Union-Tribune*, August 25, 2002, *http://legacy.sandiegouniontribune.com/news/business/20020825-9999_1n25metabo.html*.

58. David Prindle, *Petroleum Political and the Texas Railroad Commission* (Austin: University of Texas Press, 1981).

59. Texans for Public Justice, Public Citizen's Texas Office, and Sierra Club Lone Star Chapter, "Conflicted!" March 2017, *http://info.tpj.org/reports/RRCpolice.pdf*.

60. *www.kxan.com/oil-empire*

61. Charles Deaton, *The Year They Threw the Rascals Out* (Austin: Shoal Creek Publishers, 1973).

62. Pittman, *Inside the Third House*, 202.

63. Ibid., 102.

64. Ibid., 237.

65. Office of the Texas Governor, "Governor Abbott Delivers State of the State Address," January 31, 2017, *https://gov.texas.gov/news/post/governor_abbott_delivers_state_of_the_state_address*.

66. Jay Root, "Texas Senate Passes Ethics Reform," *The Texas Tribune*, February 7, 2017, *www.texastribune.org/2017/02/07/texas-senate-passes-ethics-reform*.

67. David Montgomery, "Texas Gets D– Grade in 2015 State Integrity Investigation," Center for Public Integrity, November 9, 2015, *www.publicin-tegrity.org/2015/11/09/18532/texas-gets-d-grade-2015-state-integrity-investigation*.

68. Johnny Kampis, "House Critics: Where's the Ethics Reform?" *Texas Monitor*, August 3, 2017, *https://texasmonitor.org/house-critics-wheres-ethics-reform*.

69. Texas Ethics Commission, *Lobbying in Texas: A Guide to the Texas Law*. Revised. Austin, TX: Texas Ethics Commission, January 1, 2017. Available at *www.ethics.state.tx.us/guides/lobby_guide.pdf*.

70. Ibid.

71. *https://texasmonitor.org/in-texas-more-than-a-million-dollars-in-ethics-fines-have-gone-unpaid*.

72. Ross Ramsey, "Analysis: Lobbyists Can Split Tabs, Hide Names," *The Texas Tribune*, February 2, 2015, *www.texastribune.org/2015/02/02/analysis-splitting-tabs-and-hiding-names*.

73. John Reynolds, "Clancy: Ethics Commission Should Stop Enforcing Law," *The Texas Tribune*, March 24, 2015.

74. James Drew, "State Law Allows for Lobbying Deep in the Shadows of Texas," *Dallas Morning News*, September 9, 2015.

75. David Saleh Rauf, "Former Ethics Chief Says Agency Should Stop Enforcement Actions," *San Antonio News Express*, March 25, 2015, *www.expressnews.com/news/politics/texas_legislature/article*.

76. Jim Malewitz, "Texas Senator Calls State Ethics Commission 'Arrogant' and 'Haughty,'" *The Texas Tribune*, October 5, 2016, *www.texastribune.org/2016/10/05/texas-senator-calls-ethics-commission-arrogant-and*.

77. Ross Ramsey, "Analysis: Is Attorney General Ken Paxton Feeling Lucky?" *The Texas Tribune*, February 3, 2016, *www.texastribune.org/2016/02/03/analysis-attorney-general-ken-paxton-feeling-lucky*.

78. Nicole Cobler, "Ethics Commission: Paxton May Not Accept Out-of-State Donations to Pay for Legal Fees," *The Texas Tribune*, February 1, 2016, www.texastribune.org/2016/02/01/opinion-attorney-general-case-fails-pass.

79. *www.click2houston.com/news/investigates/channel-2-investigates-at-over-312000-a-year-who-does-this-state-representative-represent?utm_source=Texas+Tribune+Master&utm_campaign=7a48f6e083-trib-newsletters-the-brief&utm_medium=email&utm_term=0_d9a68d8efc-7a48f6e083-101290241&mc_cid=7a48f6e083&mc_eid=101a099a60*

80. Gus Bova, "Lawmaker on State Tax Committee Also Works for Texas' Corporate Welfare King," *The Texas Observer*, November 16, 2017, *www.texasobserver.org/drew-springer-tax-committee-lob-byist-corporate-welfare/amp*; Jim Malewitz, "Texas Rep Wants to Limit His Industry's Liability for Busting Pipes," *The Texas Tribune*, September 3, 2016, *www.texastribune.org/2016/09/03/texas-lawmaker-wants-curb-squabbles-over-utility-l*.

81. Jay Root, "Abbott Vetoes Spousal Loophole," *The Texas Tribune*, June 20, 2015, *www.texastribune.org/2015/06/20/abbott-vetoes-spous-al-loophole-davis-says*.

82. Quoted in Pittman, *Inside the Third House*, 234.

Chapter 7 The Legislature

1. *www.kxan.com/news/texas-politics/promises-and-results-from-the-super-bowl-of-legislative-sessions*

2. Matt Rinaldi, "A Statement Regarding Today," *Twitter*, May 29, 2017, https://twitter.com/MattRinaldiTX/status/869269896365998080

3. Matthew Watkins, Alexa Ura, and Julián Aguilar, "Republican Lawmaker: I Called Immigration Authorities on Capitol Protestors," *The Texas Tribune*, May 29, 2017, https://www.texastribune.org/2017/05/29/protesters-disrupt-house-proceedings-raise-opposition-sanctuary-cities/

4. 85th Legislative Session, HR 280 enrolled (2017).

5. Douglas L. Kriner and Eric Schickler, *Investigating the President* (Princeton, NJ: Princeton University Press, 2016).

6. Robert T. Garrett, "Lawmakers Lash Texas CPA for not Offering Big Solutions to Caseworker Turnover, Foster-Care Bed Shortages," *Dallas Morning News*, August 2016, *www.dallasnews.com/news/texas-legislature/2016/08/29/lawmakers-lash-texas-cps-offering-big-solutions-caseworker-turnover-foster-care-bed-shortages*.

7. *www.texastribune.org/2019/05/27/texas-secretary-state-david-whitley-forced-leave-office*

8. R. Eric Petersen and Sarah H. Eckman, "Casework in a Congressional Office: Background, Rules, Laws, and Resources," Congressional Research Service, January 3, 2017, *www.fas.org/sgp/crs/misc/RL33209.pdf.*

9. Patricia Hart, "Session Player," *Texas Monthly,* July 2001, *www.texasmonthly.com/politics/session-player.*

10. David Mayhew, *Congress: The Electoral Connection* (New Haven, CT: Yale University Press, 1974).

11. Texas Monthly and Brian D. Sweany, "The Wise Men: Peter Laney and Bill Ratliff," *Texas Monthly,* February 8, 2013, *www.texas-monthly.com/politics/the-wise-men-pete-laney-and-bill-ratliff.*

12. Ibid.

13. Joel Nihlean, "The History and Power of the Hashtag," *County,* December 16, 2014, *http://county.org/magazine/features/Pages/2015Jan/The-History-and-Power-of-the-Hashtag.aspx.*

14. Ibid.

15. Everything Is Bigger in #TX-LEGE: Analysis of the Online Conversation Leading up to the 86th Session. February 2019. Influence Opinions. *https://influenceopinions.com/reports.*

16. Kate Gailbraith, "Biennial Blues?" *The Texas Tribune,* December 31, 2010, *www.texastribune.org/2010/12/31/defying-national-trend-texas-clings-biennial-legis.*

17. Ross Ramsey, "Analysis: Legislative Overtime? Look to the Federal Courts," *The Texas Tribune,* April 27, 2015, *www.texastribune.org/2015/04/27/analysis-legislative-overtime-look-courts.*

18. Brandi Grissom, "Legislators Dip into Campaign Accounts to Boost Their Staff's Pay," *The Texas Tribune,* April 28, 2013, *www.texastribune.org/2013/04/18/cam-paign-funds-prop-lawmakers-capitol-operations.*

19. Emily Ramshaw, "Exotic Trips, Luxury Gifts Are Perks of Office," *The Texas Tribune,* April 14, 2013, *www.texastribune.org/2013/04/14/exotic-trips-luxury-gifts-are-perks-elective-offic.*

20. Will Weissert, "Texas' Every Two-Year Legislature Isn't So 'Part Time,'" *Dallas Morning News,* February 16, 2015.

21. Ross Ramsey, "Generation Next," *The Texas Tribune,* April 19, 2010, *www.texastribune.org/2010/05/19/at-the-lege-age-mat-ters-seniority-may-not.*

22. Alexa Urea and Jolie McCullough, "Meet Your 84th Texas Legislature: White. Male. Middle-Aged, Christian," *The Texas Tribune,* January 14, 2015, *www.texastribune.org/2015/01/14/demographics-2015-texas-legislature.*

23. Molly Ivins, *Molly Ivins Can't Say That Can She?* (New York: Random House, 1991).

24. Jeffrey J. Harden, "Multidimensional Responsiveness: The Determinants of Legislators' Representational Priorities," *Legislative Studies Quarterly* 38, no. 2 (2013): 155–184, *http://fivethirtyeight.com/features/how-much-should-state-legislators-get-paid.*

25. Texas Legislative Council for the 86th Legislature.

26. Patrick Svitek, "Straus Agrees with Patrick on Their Different Audiences," *The Texas Tribune,* March 23, 2017, *www.texastribune.org/2017/03/23/straus-agrees-pat-rick-their-different-audiences.*

27. Chuck Lindell, "A Fiery Dan Patrick Lashes Out at Speaker Straus," *Statesman,* August 16, 2017, *www.statesman.com/news/fiery-dan-patrick-lashes-out-speaker-straus/dRd9qq0ZDy1eSrfTYqbT7H.*

28. Morgan Smith and Patrick Svitek, "House Republicans to Caucus on Speaker Rules," *The Texas Tribune,* August 15, 2017, *www.texastri-bune.org/2017/08/15/house-republi-cans-caucus-speaker-rules.*

29. Ben Barnes, *Barn Burning, Barn Building* (Albany, NY: Bright Sky Press, 2006), 46.

30. Ross Ramsey, "Key Change: From Minor to Major," *The Texas Tribune,* February 3, 2003, *www.texastribune.org/2003/02/03/key-change-from-minor-to-major.*

31. Ross Ramsey, "Keffer, a Straus Lieutenant, Won't Seek Re-Election," *The Texas Tribune,* June 16, 2015, *www.texastribune.org/2015/06/16/keffer-straus-lieutenant-wont-seek-reelection.*

32. Ross Ramsey, "Now It Starts," *The Texas Tribune,* Texas Weekly, 26(6), February 16, 2009. *www.texastribune.org/2009/02/16/now-it-starts.*

33. Patricia L. Cox and Michael Philips, *The House Will Come to Order* (Austin: University of Texas Press, 2010), 97.

34. Bobby Cervantes, "A 'Bloody' Few Weeks in Austin," *Houston Chronicle,* March 31, 2015, *www.houston-chronicle.com/politics/texas-take/article/A-bloody-next-few-weeks-in-Austin-6171147.php.*

35. Paul Burka, Kaye Northcott, and Alison Cook, "The Ten Best and the Ten Worst Legislators," *Texas Monthly,* July 1983, *www.texasmonthly.com/politics/the-ten-best-and-the-ten-worst-legislators-3.*

36. Morgan Smith, "House Antagonist-in-Chief Faces His Foes," *The Texas Tribune,* May 3, 2015, *www.texastribune.org/2015/05/03/stickland-and-texas-house.*

37. Aziza Musa, "Texplainer: What's a Third Reading?" *The Texas Tribune,* April 4, 2017, *www.texastribune.org/2011/04/27/texplainer-whats-a-third-reading.*

38. Mike Ward and Nicole Cobler, "Rift Stalls State Bills," *Houston Chronicle,* May 2, 2017, *www.houstonchronicle.com/news/houston-texas/houston/article/Houston-news-11116351.php.*

39. Lindell, "A Fiery Dan Patrick."

40. Guide to Legislative Information (Revised).

41. Chris McNary, "Texas' Every-Two-Year Legislature Isn't So 'Part Time,'" *Dallas Morning News,* February 2015, *www.dallasnews.com/news/politics/state-politics/20150216-texas-every-two-year-legislature-isnt-so-part-time.ece.*

42. Cervantes, "A 'Bloody' Few Weeks."

43. Ross Ramsey, "Puppies, and the Legislative Power of Distraction," *The Texas Tribune,* May 5, 2011, *www.texastribune.org/2011/05/06/puppies-and-the-legislative-power-of-distraction.*

44. Ibid.

45. Dave McNeely, "Rules Curtail Chaos," *Victoria Advocate,* May 16, 1999.

46. Hobby, *How Things Really Work*, 133.

47. Maurice Chammah, "Texplainer: What Is the Blocker Bill?" *The Texas Tribune*, January 28, 2013, *www.texastribune.org/2013/01/28/what-blocker-bill*.

48. Hart, "Session Player."

49. Harvey Kronberg, "Kolk-horts Helped Slip $5 Million Project for Lucio into Budget after He Was Lone Dem to Support SB 6," *Quorum Report*, March 18, 2017, *http://quorumreport.com/quorum_report_daily_buzz_2017/kolkhorst_helped_slip_5_million_project_for_lucio__buzziid26396.html*.

50. Richard West, "Ben Barnes Is Still Running," *Texas Monthly*, June 1979, *www.texasmonthly.com/politics/ben-barnes-is-still-running*.

51. Morgan Smith, "Tears and Shouting on Texas House Floor as Freedom Caucus Delays Bills to Death," *The Texas Tribune*, May 11, 2017, *www.texastribune.org/2017/05/11/conservative-house-members-kill-more-100-bills-over-petty-personal-pol*.

52. Brandi Grissom and Lauren Mc-Gaughy, "What Happens When a Small Band of Angry Legislators Takes Control of the Texas House? We're about to Learn," *Dallas Morning News*, May 2017, *www.dallasnews.com/news/texas-legislature/2017/05/19/happens-small-band-angry-legislators-takes-control-texas-house-learn*.

53. Carolyn Barta, *Bill Clements: Texian to His Toenails* (Austin: Eakin Press, 1996), 226.

54. *www.dallasnews.com/news/politics/2019/05/10/dallas-lgbtq-lawmaker-torpedoes-save-chick-fil-a-bill*

55. *www.dallasnews.com/news/local-politics/2015/05/26/dizzying-moves-by-texas-house-dems-endanger-campus-carry-abortion-measures*

56. Ibid.

57. *www.salon.com/2013/06/26/wendy_davis_marathon_fili-buster_kills_texas_abortion_bill_for_now*

58. Manny Fernandez, "You Call that a Filibuster? Texas Still Claims Record," *New York Times*, July 4, 2013, *www.nytimes.com/2013/07/04/us/politics/you-call-that-a-filibuster-texas-still-claims-record.html*.

59. Dave Montgomery, "Senate Gives up on Budget Deal; Special Session Looms," *Fort Worth Star Telegram*, May 20, 2011.

60. Hobby, *How Things Really Work*, 64.

61. *www.texasmonthly.com/politics/culture-wars-texas-legislature-roaring-back*

62. Hart, "Session Player."

63. Lauren McGaughy, "Campus Carry Passes Senate," *Chron.com*, May 30, 2015, *www.chron.com/news/article/House-passage-is-final-hurdle-for-campus-carry-6296777.php*.

64. Ross Ramsey, "Hoist by Their Own Petard," *The Texas Tribune*, Texas Weekly, 21(44), May 2, 2005. *https://texasweekly.texastribune.org/texas-weekly/vol-21/no-44/hoist-by-their-own-petard*.

65. Ken Herman, "Senate Stops Clock to Finish Business," *Statesman*, November 13, 2009, *www.statesman.com/news/news/state-regional-govt-politics/senate-stops-clock-to-finish-business-1/nRRX3*.

66. Morris Fiorina, "Americans Have not Become More Politically Polarized," *The Washington Post*, June 23, 2014, *www.wash-ingtonpost.com/news/monkey-cage/wp/2014/06/23/americans-have-not-become-more-politically-polarized*.

67. Ramsey, "Generation Next."

68. Paul Burka, "Capitol Affair," *Texas Monthly*, July 2011.

69. John D. Griffin, "When and Why Minority Legislators Matter," *Annual Review of Political Science* 17, May (2014): 327–336.

70. Cox and Philips, *The House Will Come to Order*, 172, 174.

71. Emily Rimshaw, "Is There a Boys Club under the Pink Dome?" *The Texas Tribune*, May 28, 2011, *www.texastribune.org/2011/05/28/is-there-a-boys-club-under-the-pink-dome*.

72. Alexa Ura, Morgan Smith, Jolie, McCullough, and Edgar Walters, "At the Texas Capitol, Victims of Sexual Harassment Must Fend for Themselves," *The Texas Tribune*, November 13, 2017, *www.texastribune.org/2017/11/13/texas-capitol-victims-sexual-harassment-must-fend-them-selves*.

73. *www.texastribune.org/2019/01/09/texas-house-sexual-harassment-investigations*

74. *www.texastribune.org/2018/05/30/texas-senate-revises-anti-sexual-harassment-policy*

75. Sophie Novack, "Senfronia Thompson Says #MeToo: Texas Lawmaker of 45 Years on Sexism, Racism at the Capitol," *Texas Observer*, February 5, 2018, *www.texasobserver.org/interview-senfronia-thompson-texas-sexism-racism-metoo*.

76. Judith N. McArthur and Harold L. Smith, *Texas through Women's Eyes* (Austin: University of Texas Press, 2010).

77. Britney Jeffrey, "Rangel, Irma Lerma," *Handbook of Texas Online*, June 15, 2010, *https://tshaonline.org/handbook/online/articles/fra85*.

78. Sonia R. Garcia, Valeria Martines-Ebers, Irasema Cornado, Sharon Navarro, and Patricia A. Jaramillo, *Politicias: Latina Public Officials in Texas* (Austin: University of Texas Press, 2008).

79. Hart, "Session Player."

80. R. G. Ratcliffe, "The Worst Little Statehouse in Texas," *Texas Monthly*, August 18, 2017, *www.texasmonthly.com/burka-blog/worst-little-statehouse-texas*.

Chapter 8 Governors of Texas

1. Katrina Trinko, "The Vetoes of Rick Perry," *National Review Online*, September 6, 2011, http://www.nation-alreview.com/article/276264/

2. *www.elpasotimes.com/story/news/2019/01/15/inauguration-day-texas-gov-greg-abbott-and-lt-gov-dan-patrick/2584760002*

3. Quoted in Fred Gantt Jr., *The Chief Executive in Texas: A Study in Gubernatorial Leadership* (Austin: University of Texas Press, 1964), 13.

4. Ralph W. Steen, "Ferguson, James Edward," *Handbook of Texas Online*, June 12, 2010, *www.tshaonline.org/handbook/online/articles/ffe05*.

5. Brian McCall, *The Power of the Texas Governor: Connally to Bush* (Austin: University of Texas Press, 2009), 23.

6. *www.expressnews.com/news/politics/texas_legislature/article/Gov-Abbott-s-Japan-trip-cost-taxpayers-83-000-14038995.php*

7. *www.expressnews.com/news/ politics/texas_legislature/article/ Gov-Abbott-pays-executive-staff-top-dollar-13147430.php*

8. Brandi Grissom, "Laws? We Don't Need No Stinkin' Laws—If They Hamper Texas Hurricane Recovery," *Dallas Morning News*, October 5, 2017, *www.dallasnews.com/news/ politics/2017/10/05/laws-need-stinking-laws-hamper-texas-hurricane-recovery.*

9. James Reston Jr., *The Lone Star: The Life of John Connally* (New York: Harper and Row, 1989).

10. McCall, *Power of the Texas Governor*, 107.

11. *www.texasobserver.org/governor-abbott-swaps-one-scandal-scarred-secretary-of-state-for-another*

12. McCall, *Power of the Texas Governor*, 5.

13. Ibid., 42–43.

14. Ross Ramsey, "Legislative Emergencies, Real Ones and the Governor's," *New York Times*, January 29, 2011, *www.nytimes.com/2011/01/30/ us/30ttramsey.html.*

15. Quoted in Gantt, *Chief Executive in Texas*, 211.

16. Gantt, *Chief Executive in Texas*, 234.

17. Ibid., 222n.9.

18. Brandi Grissom, "Gov. Greg Abbott Gives Special Session Mixed Review, Blames Speaker Straus for Blocking Agenda Items, *Dallas Morning News*, August 16, 2017, *www.dallasnews.com/news/ texas-legislature/2017/08/16/ gov-greg-abbott-gives-special-session-mixed-review-blames-speaker-straus-blocking-agenda-items.*

19. https://cbsaustin.com/news/local/ governor-abbott-vetos-49-bills-more-go-unsigned

20. Quoted in Gantt, *Chief Executive in Texas*, 184.

21. McCall, *Power of the Texas Governor*, 52.

22. *www.texastribune. org/2019/06/21/texas-greg-abbott-national-guard-border-security*

23. Antonio Olivo, "Deployed by Governor Rick Perry, National Guard Adjusts to Its New Role on the Texas Border," *The Washington Post*, September 1, 2014.

24. *www.texastribune. org/2019/06/21/texas-greg-abbott-national-guard-border-security*

25. Gantt, *Chief Executive in Texas*, 152.

26. Peggy Fikac, "Rep. Lyle Larsen: 'No Governor's Ever Going to Scare Me,'" *San Antonio Express-News*, August 5, 2017, *www.ex-pressnews.com/ news/local/article/Rep-Lyle-Larson-No-governor-s-ever-going-11737044. php.*

27. Quoted in Gantt, *Chief Executive in Texas*, 250.

28. Kolten Parker, "Without Notice, Texas Gov. Greg Abbott Signs 'Sanctuary Cities' Ban on Facebook Live," *Texas Observer*, May 7, 2017, *www. texasobserver.org/without-notice-texas-governor-greg-abbott-signs-sanctuary-cities-ban-facebook-live.*

29. Paul Burka, "The Honeymoon Is Over," *Texas Monthly*, January 1997.

30. Robert T. Garrett, "Inside the Dispute about Gov. Greg Abbott's Budget Power," *Dallas Morning News*, July 22, 2015, *www.dallasnews.com/news/ local-politics/2015/07/22/inside-the-dispute-about-gov.-greg-abbotts-budget-power.*

31. *www.dallasnews.com/news/ politics/2015/02/19/abbott-straus-tiptoe-around-fraught-issue-of-troops-at-border*

32. Quoted in Gantt, *Chief Executive in Texas*, 86.

33. Aman Batheja, "'Deal Closer' Funds Draw Bipartisan Concerns," *The Texas Tribune*, December 28, 2014, *http://apps.texastribune.org/ perry-legacy/texas-enterprise-fund.*

34. Peggy Fikac, "Abbott to Travel World to Lure Business," *Houston Chronicle*, June 3, 2015.

35. Batheja, "'Deal Closer' Funds."

36. Quoted in Gantt, *Chief Executive in Texas*, 25.

37. *by-failing-to-appoint-state-officers-gov-abbott-is-making-an-unfair-power-grab*

38. *www.dallasnews.com/opinion/ commentary/2019/04/23/by-failing-to-appoint-state-officers-gov-abbott-is-making-an-unfair-power-grab*

39. *www.texasstandard.org/stories/ greg-abbott-has-raised-more-campaign-cash-than-any-governor-in-us-history*

40. Ibid., 131.

41. Peggy Fikac and Allie Miller-bernd, "Gov. Abbott's Appointees Have Given Him More Than $14 million," *Houston Chronicle*, January 5, 2018, *www.houstonchronicle.com/news/ article/Gov-Abbott-s-appoin-tees-have-given-him-more-12480023.php.*

42. *www.houstonchronicle.com/ news/houston-texas/houston/article/ Ahead-of-Abbott-fundraiser-a-Lubbock-developer-13180844.php*

43. "Quotes from Ann Richards," *New York Times*, September 14, 2006, *www.nytimes.com/2006/09/14/us/ richards_quotes.html.*

Chapter 9 The Plural Executive and the Bureaucracy

1. *www.npr.org/sections/health-shots/2019/06/18/733369370/ texas-is-latest-state-to-attack-surprise-medical-bills*

2. *www.dallasnews.com/business/ health-care/2019/11/26/texas-law-to-end-surprise-medical-bills-could-be-irrelevant-by-jan-1*

3. *twitter.com/RobertTGarrett/ status/1199525524567199744/photo/1*

4. Texas Higher Education Coordinating Board, *Report on Student Financial Aid in Texas Higher Education for Fiscal Year 2018*, September 2019, https://reportcenter.highered. texas.gov/reports/data/report-on-student-financial-aid-in-texas-higher-education-for-fy-2018/.

5. This excludes those individuals working for university systems.

6. Suzanne Freeman, "Texas Muscles in on Oyster Farming," Corpus Christie Business News, May 28, 2019, *www.ccbiznews.com/news/ texas-muscles-in-on-oyster-farming.*

7. Shannon Najmabadi, "'Somebody Had to Push': One Couple's Fight to Change How Texas Defines a Pickle," *The Texas Tribune*, May 31, 2018, *www.texastribune. org/2018/05/31/how-texas-definition-word-pickles-prompting-lawsuit-over-economic-libe*and "Texas Picklers Get a Victory from the Legislature," *The Texas Tribune*, May 23, 2019, *www.texastribune.org/2019/05/23/ texas-pickles-legislature.*

8. Anya Bidwell, "It's Time for Texas to Take a Long, Hard Look at

Its Licensing Regulations," *Dallas Morning News*, December 20, 2017, *www.dallasnews.com/opinion/commentary/2017/12/20/time-texas-take-long-hard-look-licensing-regu-lations*.

9. Daniel Vaugh, "With a Battle over Barbecue, the Ag Commissioner's Office Is Officially a Food Fight," *Texas Monthly*, December 19, 2017, *www.texasmonthly.com/bbq/texas_barbecue-gets-political*.

10. *www.houstonchronicle.com/news/politics/texas/article/War-on-BBQ-is-getting-messy-13044808.php?utm_campaign=twitter-premium&utm_source=CMS%20Sharing%20Button&utm_medium=social*

11. *www.texastribune.org/2019/01/08/state-auditor-texas-agencies-lost-nearly-29000-employ-ees-last-year*

12. James A. Clark and Weldon Hart, *The Tactful Texan: A Biography of Governor Will Hobby* (New York: Random House, 1958), 47.

13. Paul Burka, "Four for Four," *Texas Monthly*, June 1995, *www.texasmonthly.com/politics/four-for-four*.

14. Ben Barnes, *Barn Burning Barn Building: Tales of a Political Life, from LBJ to George W. Bush and Beyond* (Albany, TX: Bright Sky Press, 2006).

15. Dave McNeely and Jim Henderson, *Bob Bullock: God Bless Texas* (Austin: University of Texas Press, 2008), 235.

16. Ibid.

17. Rebekah Allen, "'Her Lips and My Back End' Comment Costs Texas State Senator His Committee Chairmanship," *The Dallas News*, January 22, 2019, *www.dallasnews.com/news/politics/2019/01/22/her-lips-and-my-back-end-comment-costs-texas-state-senator-his-committee-chairmanship*.

18. Emma Platoff, "'I'm Still Doing Penance': How Kel Seliger Gets by in the Texas Senate Dog House," *The Texas Tribune*, May 24, 2019, *www.texastribune.org/2019/05/24/kel-seliger-dan-patrick-texas-senate-dog-house*.

19. Bill Hobby and Saralee Tiede, *How Things Really Work: Lessons from a Life in Politics* (Austin: University of Texas at Austin, 2010).

20. Erica Grieder, "The David Dewhurst Exit Interview," *Texas Monthly*, December 2014, *www.texasmonthly.com/politics/the-david-dewhurst-exit-interview*.

21. John L. Hill Jr. and Ernie Stromberger, *John Hill for the State of Texas: My Years as Attorney General* (College Station: Texas A&M University Press, 2008), 25.

22. Ibid., 33.

23. *www.texasattorneygeneral.gov/news/releases/ag-paxtons-child-support-division-sets-new-nationwide-record-collecting-4378-billion-child-support*

24. Paul Burka, "The Case against John Cornyn," *Texas Monthly*, June 2000.

25. McNeely and Henderson, *Bob Bullock*, 96.

26. Patricia Kilday Hart, "25 Stories about Bob Bullock," *Texas Monthly*, July 2003.

27. Jay Root and Neena Satija, "Ag Commissioner Says Consumers Being 'Screwed,'" *Texas Tribune*, February 27, 2015.

28. Gantt, *Chief Executive*, 129.

29. *www.sacurrent.com/the-daily/archives/2019/08/05/surprise-sur-prise-texas-gop-lawmakers-blame-el-paso-shooting-on-everything-but-guns*

30. McNeely and Henderson, *Bob Bullock*, 214.

31. Lou Dubose, "So What's the Truth about Dan Morales and Tobacco?" *Texas Monthly*, March 2002, *www.texasmonthly.com/politics/so-whats-the-truth-about-dan-morales-and-tobacco*.

32. W. Gardner Selby, "Greg Abbott Says State Proved in Court that More than 200 Dead People Voted in the Latest Texas Elections," *POLITI-FACT Texas*, July 24, 2012, *www.politifact.com/texas/statements/2012/jul/24/greg-abbott/greg-abbott-dead-voters-Texas*.

33. Texas Secretary of State, "Turnout and Voter Registration Figures (1970–Current)," n.d., *www.sos.state.tx.us/elections/histori-cal/70-92.shtml*.

34. *www.texastribune.org/2017/10/02/texas-health-agency-disarray-amid-mass-departure-senior-staff*

35. "Texas Investigated More than 550 Insurance Fraud Cases in 2013," *Insurance Journal*, April 28, 2014, *www.insurance-journal.com/news/southcen-tral/2014/04/28/327471.htm*.

36. Jim Malewitz, "Report: Utility Regulators See Rise in Complaints," *The Texas Tribune*, October 14, 2014.

37. Casey Stinnett, "What Do You Do with a 'Nuisance Alligator'?" *Cleveland Advocate*, June 2, 2014, *www.chron.com/neighborhood/cleveland/news/article/What-do-you-do-with-a-nuisance-alligator-9684947.php*.

38. *www.houstonchronicle.com/opinion/editorials/article/Blame-Texas-bad-air-on-Abbott-and-the-TCEQ-14474284.php*

39. *www.houstonchronicle.com/news/houston-texas/houston/article/TCEQ-invests-more-than-1-5-million-to-to-improve-14551313.php*

40. *www.dallasnews.com/news/education/2010/05/22/20100521-Texas-State-Board-of-Education-approves-9206*

41. *www.texastribune.org/2018/11/13/hillary-clinton-helen-keller-state-board-education-texas*

42. Peggy Fikac, "Abbott Can Spark an Outcry with Appointments, by Design," *Houston Chronicle*, April 24, 2016, *www.houstonchronicle.com/news/news_columnists/peggy_fikac/article/Abbott-can-spark-an-outcry-with-appointments-by-7306569.php*.

43. Brian Thevenot, "Social Conservatives Rewrite History Standards," *The Texas Tribune*, March 12, 2010, *www.texastribune.org/2010/03/12/social-conservatives-rewrite-history-standards*.

44. Lauren McGaughy, "Dems Stay Steady on State Board of Education: Panel's 15 Members Equally Divided into Dems, Far-Right GOP, Centrists," *Houston Chronicle*, November 8, 2014, *www.houstonchronicle.com/news/politics/texas/article/Dems-stay-steady-on-State-Board-of-Educa-tion-5880898.php*.

45. Andrea Ball and Eric Dexheimer, "CPS Once Again Faces Overhaul, but Leaders Say This One Is Different," *Austin American-Statesman*, January 13, 2015, *http://projects.statesman.com/news/cps-missed-signs/overhaul-strategy.html*.

46. Rhonda Fanning, "The Texas Veterinary Board Was Scolded for

Mismanagement, Then a Third of Its Officials Resigned," *Texas Standard*, December 9, 2016, *www.texasstandard.org/stories/texas-veterinary-board-chastised-for-mismanagement-then-a-third-of-its-officials-resigned*.

47.   Texas Sunset Advisory Commission, "Frequently Asked Questions," *www.sunset.texas.gov/about-us/frequently-asked-questions*.

48.   Anna M. Tinsley, "Texas –Lawmakers Worry State Agencies Are Going Rogue," *Star-Telegram*, December 20, 2014, *www.star-telegram.com/news/politics-government/article4736820.html*.

49.   Jay Root, "Liquor Regulators Partying on Taxpayers' Tab," *The Texas Tribune*, March 24, 2017, *www.texastribune.org/2017/03/24/liquor-regulators-partying-taxpayers-tab*.

50.   Jay Root, "House Delivers Rebuke to TABC, Cuts Travel Budget," *The Texas Tribune*, April 6, 2017, *www.texastribune.org/2017/04/06/house-delivers-rebuke-tabc-cuts-travel-budget*; *www.sunset.texas.gov/public/uploads/files/reports/Final%20Results%20of%20Sunset%20Reviews.pdf*.

51.   Robert T. Garrett, "Taking Texas 'Sunset' Model Nationwide?" *Trail Blazers Blog*, The Dallas Morning News, June 2, 2009, *http://trailblazersblog.dallasnews.com/2009/06/taking-texas-sunset-model-nati.html*.

52.   Ross Ramsey, "Analysis: Texas Legislative Review Process Needs a Review," *The Texas Tribune*, April 25, 2016, *www.texastribune.org/2016/04/25/analysis-texas-legisla-tive-review-process-needs-re*.

53.   Allie Morris, "114 Years of Waiting: Callers Kept on Hold by Texas State Agencies," *Houston Chronicle*, March 20, 2019, *.www.houstonchronicle.com/news/politics/texas_legislature/article/114-years-of-waiting-Callers-kept-on-hold-by-13703605.php?utm_source=newsletter&utm_medium=email&utm_campaign=HC_TexasTake&utm_term=news&utm_content=briefing*.

Chapter 10 The Texas Judiciary

1.   Reuters, "Record $25 Million Awarded in Silicone-Gel Implants Case," *New York Times*, December 24, 1992, *www.nytimes.com/1992/12/24/us/record-25-million-awarded-in-silicone-gel-implants-case.html*.

2.   Governor Rick Perry speech transcript, October 2003, *www.tmltexposed.org/uploads/Manhat-tan_Institute_oct_8_2003.pdf*.

3.   Evan Smith, "Joe Jamail," *Texas Monthly*, December 2003; John Spong, "The Greatest Lawyer Who Ever Lived," *Texas Monthly*, January 2015.

4.   Brian Rosenthal, "How a Wayward Cow Could Change Texas' Tort Reform Law," *Houston Chronicle*, March 9, 2015.

5.   Angela Morris, "Why Are Filings Falling? Civil Lawsuits Down 17 Percent in 10 Years," *Texas Lawyer*, March 9, 2015.

6.   James L. Haley, *The Texas Supreme Court* (Austin: University of Texas Press, 2013).

7.   Nathan L. Hecht, "The State of the Judiciary in Texas," February 18, 2015, *www.txcourts.gov/media/857636/state-of-the-judiciary-2015.pdf*.

8.   *www.texastribune.org/2018/12/12/revenge-porn-free-speech-texas-court-criminal-appeals/?utm_source=Editorial%3A+Texas+Tribune+Master&utm_campaign=ce2312c0b2-trib-newsletters-the-brief&utm_medium=email&utm_term=0_d9a68d8efc-ce2312c0b2-101290241&mc_cid=ce2312c0b2&mc_eid=101a099a60*

9.   *www.chron.com/news/houston-texas/texas/article/Houston-State-Senator-key-to-new-revenge-porn-13798007.php*

10.   Haley, *The Texas Supreme Court*, 123.

11.   Ibid., 88.

12.   State of Texas Judicial Branch, Annual Statistical Report for the Texas Judiciary: Fiscal Year 2018, Austin, TX: Office of Court Administration, 49–50, *www.txcourts.gov/media/1308021/2015-ar-statistical-print.pdf*.

13.   Texas Association of Counties, Description of Office, County Judge, *https://county.org/texas-county-government/texas-county-officials/Pages/County-Judge.aspx*.

14.   State of Texas Judicial Branch, Annual Statistical Report for the Texas Judiciary: Fiscal Year 2018, Austin, TX: Office of Court Administration, 22, *www.txcourts.gov/media/1308021/2015-ar-statistical-print.pdf*.

15.   Texas Judicial Branch, "Oral Arguments," *Supreme Court*, *www.txcourts.gov/supreme/oral-arguments*.

16.   Ryan Rebe, "Amicus Curiae and Dissenting Votes at the Texas Supreme Court," *Justice System Journal* 34, no. 2 (2013): 171–188.

17.   Mark Collette, "Texas High Court Limits Open Government Law; GHP Can Keep Books Closed," *Houston Chronicle*, June 26, 2015, *www.houstonchronicle.com/news/houston-texas/houston/article/Texas-high-court-limits-open-government-law-GHP-6352311.php*.

18.   American Bar Association, "How Courts Work," *www.ameri-canbar.org/groups/public_education/resources/law_related_education_network/how_courts_work.html*.

19.   *www.houstonpublicmedia.org/articles/news/2019/02/22/322873/houston-judge-tosses-same-sex-marriage-benefits-challenge-but-plaintiffs-pledge-to-appeal*

20.   Texans for Public Justice, "Pay to Play: How Big Money Buys Access to the Texas Supreme Court," April 2001, *http://info.tpj.org/docs/pdf/paytoplay.pdf*.

21.   State of Texas Judicial Branch, Annual Statistical Report for the Texas Judiciary: Fiscal Year 2018, Austin, TX: Office of Court Administration, 22, *www.txcourts.gov/media/1308021/2015-ar-statistical-print.pdf*.

22.   State of the Texas Judiciary, 1983.

23.   Michael Massengale, "Dual Texas Supreme Courts," *Texas Constitution History*, January 7, 2015, *https://texconst.wordpress.com/2015/01/07/dual-texas-supreme-courts*.

24.   Maurice Chammah, "Bill Renews Debate on Merging Top Two Courts," *The Texas Tribune*, December 13, 2012, *www.texastribune.org/2012/12/13/bill-merge-highest-courts-brings-back-old-debate*.

25.   Ibid.

26.   Haley, *The Texas Supreme Court*, 214; State of Texas Judicial

Branch, Annual Statistical Report for the Texas Judiciary: Fiscal Year 2018, Austin, TX: Office of Court Administration, 17, *www.txcourts.gov/media/1308021/2015-ar-statistical-print.pdf*.

27. Haley, *The Texas Supreme Court*, 32.

28. *www.txcourts.gov/supreme/news/chief-justice-delivers-state-of-judiciary-to-texas-legislature*

29. *www.dallasnews.com/news/texas/2013/09/02/texas-chief-justice-wallace-jefferson-to-resign-oct.-1*

30. Jolie McCullough, "Texas Judge Who Questions Death Penalty Won't Seek Reelection," *The Texas Tribune*, December 29, 2016, *www.texastribune.org/2016/12/29/judge-known-criticizing-death-penalty-step-down-te*.

31. State of Texas Judicial Branch, *Annual Statistical Report for the Texas Judiciary, 2014*, *www.txcourts.gov/media/885306/Annual-Statistical-Report-FY-2014.pdf*.

32. Jake Harris, "Ethan Couch Released from Jail: These Were the Victims in the 'Affluenza' Case," *Austin American-Statesman*, April 3, 2018, *www.statesman.com/news/ethan-couch-released-from-jail-these-were-the-victims-the-affluenza-case/MDURaX4OXOLcC9o3VWXbtM*.

33. Dallas News Administration, "Editorial: Texas Must Expand Funding for Legal Aid," *Dallas Morning News*, May 2015, *www.dallasnews.com/opinion/editorials/20150503-editorial-texas-must-expand-funding-for-legal-aid.ece*.

34. Nathan L. Hecht and William H. McRaven, "Legal Aid for Our Veterans, Now It's Our Turn," Chron.com, November 9, 2015, *www.chron.com/opinion/outlook/article/Hecht-McRaven-Legal-aid-for-our-veterans-Now-6616182.php*.

35. Texas Access to Justice Foundation, *www.teajf.org/news/statistics.aspx*; Nathan L. Hecht, "The State of the Judiciary in Texas," February 1, 2017, *www.txcourts.gov/media/1437289/soj-2017.pdf*.

36. The following 10 states use merit plans only to fill midterm vacancies on some or all levels of court: Alabama, Georgia, Idaho, Kentucky, Minnesota, Montana, Nevada, New Mexico, North Dakota, and West Virginia.

37. Anthony Champagne and Kyle Cheek, "The Cycle of Judicial Elections: Texas as a Case Study," *Fordham Urban Law Journal* 29, no. 3 (2001): 907–940.

38. State of Texas Judicial Branch, *Texas Code of Judicial Conduct: As Amended by the Supreme Court of Texas through August 22, 2002*, *www.txcourts.gov/media/514728/TXCodeOfJudicialConduct_20020822.pdf*.

39. Joanna Cohn Weiss, "Tough on Crime: How Campaigns for State Judiciary Violate Criminal Defendants' Due Process Rights," *New York University Law Review* 81 (June 2006): 1101–1136.

40. *www.scjc.texas.gov/disciplinary-actions/?t=Private+Sanctions&stype=FY+2014&ptype=1182*

41. Fares Sabawi, "Texas Judge Disciplined after Claiming God Told Him Defendant Was Innocent," *Houston Chronicle*, March 6, 2019, *www.chron.com/news/local/crime/article/Texas-judge-disciplined-after-claiming-God-told-13664417.php?utm_source=twitter.com&utm_campaign=socialflow&utm_medium=referral*.

42. Lise Olsen, "Texas High Court Suspends Harris County Justice of Peace After Sex, Pill-Popping Admissions," *Chron.com*, July 7, 2017, *www.chron.com/houston/article/Jurist-who-admitted-to-sexting-and-popping-pills-11273782.php*.

43. Texas Government Code, "Causes for Removal," Sec. 665.052, *https://codes.findlaw.com/tx/government-code/gov-t-sect-665-052.html*.

44. State of Texas Judicial Branch, Annual Statistical Report for the Texas Judiciary: Fiscal Year 2018, Austin, TX: Office of Court Administration, p. 58, *www.txcourts.gov/media/1308021/2015-ar-statistical-print.pdf*.

45. Champagne and Cheek, "The Cycle of Judicial Elections," 912.

46. Ken Case, "Blind Justice," *Texas Monthly*, May 1987.

47. Champagne and Cheek "The Cycle of Judicial Elections."

48. Robert Swansborough, *Test by Fire* (New York: Palgrave, 2008), 42.

49. Morgan Smith, "Tipping the Scales," *The Texas Tribune*, April 12, 2010, *www.texastribune.org/2010/04/12/ethical-lapses-become-focus-in-court-campaign*.

50. Alicia Bannon, Cathleen Lisk, and Peter Hardin, "Who Pays for Judicial Races?" Brennan Center for Justice, n.d., *www.brennancenter.org/sites/default/files/publications/Politics_of_Judicial_Elections_Final.pdf*, 9.

51. Ibid., 5.

52. Scott Greytak, Alicia Bannon, Allyse Falce, and Linda Casey, "Bankrolling the Bench: The New Politics of Judicial Elections 2013–14," Laurie Kinney, ed., The Brennan Center and the National Institute for Money in State Politics. Available at *www.brennancenter.org/sites/default/files/publications/The_New_Politics_of_Judicial_Election_2013_2014.pdf*.

53. Brandi Grissom and Jay Root, "Perry TWIA Nemesis Loses Battle but Promises War Isn't Over," *The Texas Tribune*, July 6, 2011, *www.texastribune.org/2011/07/06/perrys-twia-nemesis-promises-to-continue-his-fight*.

54. Champagne and Cheek, "The Cycle of Judicial Elections," 912.

55. Kate Berry, "How Judicial Elections Impact Criminal Cases," Brennan Center for Justice, December 2, 2015, *www.brennancenter.org/publication/how-judicial-elec-tions-impact-criminal-cases*.

56. Ciara Torres-Spelliscy, Monique Chase, and Emma Greenman, "Improving Judicial Diversity," Brennan Center for Justice, 2010, *www.brennancenter.org/sites/default/files/legacy/Improving_Judicial_Diversity_2010.pdf*.

57. *www.texastribune.org/2019/08/05/texas-supreme-court-diversity-vacancy-abbott-appoint*

58. *www.txcourts.gov/media/1444865/judge-profile-sept-2019.pdf*

59. Jim Malewitz, "Latino Voters in Texas Sue to Bolster Influence on Electing Judges," *The Texas Tribune*, July 28, 2016, *www.texastri-bune.org/2016/07/28/latino-voters-take-texas-court-bolster-their-influ*.

60. Chuck Lindell, "Federal Judge Rejects Challenge to Texas Court

Elections," *Austin American-States-man*, September 13, 2018, *www.mystatesman.com/news/state—regional-govt—politics/federal-judge-rejects-challenge-texas-court-elections/Ik39YfVYlv5tYYwDgL37vM*.

61.   State Bar of Texas, "State Bar of Texas Membership: Attorney Statistical Profile (2017–18)," n.d., *www.texasbar.com/AM/Template.cfm?Section=Content_Folders&Template=/CM/Content-Dis-play.cfm&ContentID=38873*; Torres-Spelliscy, Chase, and Greenman, "Improving Judicial Diversity."

62.   Mark Curriden, "Texas Chief Justice Wallace Jefferson to Resign October 1," *Dallas Morning News*, September 3, 2013.

63.   Ross Ramsey, "Analysis: Should Judges Exit Fundraising Business?" *The Texas Tribune*, May 15, 2015, *www.texastribune.org/2015/05/15/analysis-distance-between-judges-and-politics*.

64.   Adam Liptak, "Supreme Court Upholds Limit on Judicial Fund-Raising," *New York Times*, April 29, 2015.

65.   *www.texastribune.org/2019/11/08/texas-democrats-campaigning-no-ballot-election-court*

66.   *www.dallasnews.com/news/crime/2010/04/13/mandatory-retirement-age-for-judges-varies-across-country*

67.   *www.ydr.com/story/news/local/2016/04/05/voters-to-decide-whether-mandatory-retirement-age-judges-in-pennsylvania-should-be-raised/82517938*

Chapter 11 Criminal Justice

1.   *www.texastribune.org/2019/10/01/amber-guyger-verdict-former-dallas-police-officer-found-guilty-murder/?utm_source=Editorial%3A+Texas+Tribune+Master&utm_campaign=b92a019f62-trib-newsletters-the-brief&utm_medium=email&utm_term=0_d9a68d8efc-b92a019f62-101290241&mc_cid=b92a019f62&mc_eid=101a099a60*

2.   *www.texastribune.org/2019/10/01/amber-guyger-verdict-former-dallas-police-officer-found-guilty-murder/?utm_source=Editorial%3A+Texas+Tribune+Maste*

r&utm_campaign=b92a019f62-trib-newsletters-the-brief&utm_medium=email&utm_term=0_d9a68d8efc-b92a019f62-101290241&mc_cid=b92a019f62&mc_eid=101a099a60*

3.   *www.texastribune.org/2019/10/02/amber-guyger-text-messages-emerge-sentencing-trial/?utm_source=Editorial%3A+Texas+Tribune+Master&utm_campaign=7604269c02-EMAIL_CAMPAIGN_2019_10_02_12_16&utm_medium=email&utm_term=0_d9a68d8efc-7604269c02-101290241&mc_cid=7604269c02&mc_eid=101a099a60*

4.   *www.houstonchronicle.com/news/article/Amber-Guyger-was-hugged-by-her-victim-s-brother-14488372.php?utm_source=newsletter&utm_medium=email&utm_campaign=HC_TexasTake&utm_term=news&utm_content=briefing*

5.   *Austin American–Statesman*, "Dan Patrick: Texans Should Call Police 'Sir and Ma'am,' Pay Their Meals," Updated September 2, 2015, *www.statesman.com/news/news/dan-patrick-texans-should-call-police-sir-and-maam/nnW8r*.

6.   Molly Ivins, *Shrub: The Short but Happy Political Life of George W. Bush* (New York: Vintage Books, 2000).

7.   C. L. Sonnichen, *Roy Bean: Law West of the Pecos* (Lincoln: University of Nebraska Press, 1991), 5.

8.   Neena Satija. "No Defense." *Texas Monthly*, September 2019.

9.   Calvin Watkins, "Patrick Beverley Misses Shootaround after Arrest for Toll Toad Violation," ESPN.com, November 11, 2015, *www.espn.com/nba/story/_/id/14107119/houston-rockets-guard-patrick-bev-erley-misses-shoot-around-arrest-toll-road-violation*.

10.   Craig Hlavaty, "Texas Killer Made Famous by Jack Black Movie Goes Free," Chron.com, May 7, 2014, *www.chron.com/news/houston-texas/article/Texas-killer-made-famous-by-Jack-Black-movie-goes-5456716.php*.

11.   Skip Hollandsworth, "Midnight in the Garden of East Texas," *Texas Monthly*, January 1998.

12.   William Martin, "The Policy and Politics of Drug Sentencing," *Texas Monthly*, May 5, 2013, *www.*

texasmonthly.com/politics/the-policy-and-politics-of-drug-sentencing.

13.   Alan Duke, "Willie Nelson Could Sing His Way Out of Pot Trouble, a Prosecutor Says," CNN. com, March 29, 2011, *www.cnn.com/2011/SHOWBIZ/celebrity.news.gossip/03/28/willie.nelson.pot.plea*.

14.   Alan Duke, "Plea Deal Ends Willie Nelson Pot Prosecution," CNN. com, June 7, 2011, *www.cnn.com/2011/SHOWBIZ/celeb-rity.news.gos-sip/06/07/willie.nelson.fine*.

15.   Sam DeGrave, "The Interview: Harris County District Attorney Kim Ogg," *Texas Observer*, July 26, 2017, *www.texasobserver.org/the-interviewkim-ogg*.

16.   *www.texascjc.org/system/files/publications/Seventeen%20in%20the%20Adult%20Justice%20System%20Report.pdf*

17.   *www.nbcnews.com/news/us-news/12-year-old-charged-capital-murder-spotlights-justice-system-ill-n962886*

18.   State of Texas, Office of the Attorney General, *2018 Juvenile Justice Handbook: A Practical Reference Guide Including Updates from the 85th Legislative Session* (Austin, TX, July 2018), 14–15, *www.texasat-torney-general.gov/files/cj/juvenile_justice.pdf*.

19.   Jennifer Emily and Diane Jennings, "Raised Behind Bars," *The Dallas Morning News*, August 27, 2015, *http://interactives.dallasnews.com/2015/kids-or-criminals/part1.html*.

20.   Texas Young Lawyers Association and the State Bar of Texas, *Criminal Law 101: Overview of the Texas Criminal Justice Process*, 2013, *www.texas-lawhelp.org*.

21.   Ibid.

22.   State Bar of Texas, Criminal Justice Section, *Texas Criminal Justice Procedure: A Citizen's Guide*. January 1, 1996, Revised 2005, *www.texasbar.com/Content/Naviga-tionMenu/ForThePublic/FreeLegalIn-formation/OurLegalSystem/TheTexasCriminalJusticeProcessACitizen'sGuide.pdf*.

23.   Ibid.

24.   Janet Portman, "Jury Selection in Criminal Cases in Texas," *Criminal Defense Lawyer*, n.d., *www.*

criminaldefenselawyer.com/resources/criminal-defense/criminal-defense-case/jury-selection-texas.htm.

25. State Bar of Texas, *Texas Criminal Justice Procedure.*

26. Robert Perkinson, *Texas Tough: The Rise of America's Prison Empire* (New York: Picador, 2010), 173.

27. Ibid., 172.

28. Ben M. Crouch and James W. Marquart, *An Appeal to Justice: Litigated Reform of Texas Prisons* (Austin: University of Texas Press, 1989), 13.

29. Gary Brown, *Singin' a Lonesome Song: Texas Prison Tales* (Plano: Republic of Texas Press, 2001), 39.

30. Ibid., 176.

31. Emily and Jennings, "Raised Behind Bars."

32. State Bar of Texas, *Texas Criminal Justice Procedure.*

33. SPCA of Texas, "Court Appointed Community Service Program," n.d., *www.spca.org/cacs.*

34. Texas Department of Criminal Justice, "Unit Directory," n.d., *http://tdcj.state.tx.us/unit_directory.*

35. Legislative Budget Board, TDCJ, p. 12, *https://twitter.com/Grits4Breakfast/status/1090027960160210946/photo/1.*

36. Morgan O. Reynolds, "Crime and Punishment in Texas in the 1990s," National Center for Policy Analysis, *www.ncpathinktank.org/pub/st237.*

37. Oliver Roeder, Lauren-Brooke Eisen, and Julia Bowling, "What Caused the Crime Decline?" Brennan Center for Justice, February 12, 2015, *www.brennancenter.org/publication/what-caused-crime-decline.*

38. Perkinson, *Texas Tough,* 7

39. Reynolds, "Crime and Punishment."

40. John J. Dilulio, *Governing Prisons* (New York: Macmillan, 1987), 105.

41. Perkinson, *Texas Tough.*

42. John Hubner, *Last Chance in Texas: The Redemption of Criminal Youth* (New York: Random House, 2005), xx.

43. Khorri Atkinson, "Rate of Texas Prison Spending Growth Outpaces Schools," *The Texas Tribune,* July 14, 2016, *www.texastribune.org/2016/07/14/texas-spending-prison-and-jails-higher-any-other-s.*

44. Roder, Eisen, and Bowling, "What Caused the Crime Decline?"

45. Krissah Thompson, "Prison Reform Advocates Press State to Shift Money Out of Corrections System," *The Washington Post,* April 5, 2011, *www.washingtonpost.com/politics/prison-reform-advocates-press-states-to-shift-money-out-of-corrections-system/2011/04/04/AFeCXolC_story.html.*

46. *Texas Monthly,* "The Rick Perry Report Card: Criminal Justice," *www.texasmonthly.com/list/the-rick-perry-report-card/criminal-justice.*

47. *Right on Crime,* "New Poll Shows Voters Strongly Support New Justice Reforms in Texas," March 9, 2015, *http://rightoncrime.com/2015/03/new-poll-shows-voters-strongly-support-new-justice-reforms-in-texas.*

48. Perkinson, *Texas Tough,* 269.

49. Jolie McCullough, "Texas Prison Officials Violated a Judge's Order to Provide Inmates With Air Conditioning. Now Prisoners' Lawyers Get to Investigate," *The Texas Tribune,* December 11, 2019, *www.texastribune.org/2019/12/11/texas-prison-temperatures-can-be-investigated-attorneys-judge-says.*

50. Matt Levin, "Controversy Abounds at Texas' Private Prisons," *Chron.com,* February 25, 2015, *www.chron.com/news/houston-texas/article/Controversy-abounds-at-Texas-many-private-prisons-6101496.php.*

51. Julián Aguilar, "White House Greenlights a New Immigration-Detention Center in Texas," *The Texas Tribune,* April 14, 2017, *www.texastribune.org/2017/04/14/white-house-green-lights-new-immigration-detention-center-texas.*

52. Lise Olsen, "Private Prisons Boom in Texas and Across America in Trump's Immigration Crackdown," *Houston Chronicle,* October 28, 2017, *www.houstonchronicle.com/news/houston-texas/houston/amp/Private-prisons-boom-in-Texas-and-across-America-11944652.php.*

53. Brown, *Singin' a Lonesome Song.*

54. Ibid., 15.

55. Ibid., 19.

56. Texas Department of Criminal Justice, "Death Row Information," n.d., *www.tdcj.state.tx.us/death_row/dr_facts.html.*

57. Erika Casriel, "Bush and the Texas Death Machine," *Rolling Stone,* August 3, 2000, *www.rolling-stone.com/politics/news/bush-the-texas-death-machine-20000803.*

58. Perkinson, *Texas Tough,* 341.

59. *Texas Monthly,* "The Rick Perry Report Card."

60. *The Economist,* "Capital Punishment: The Slow Death of the Death Penalty," April 26, 2014, *www.economist.com/news/united-states/21601270-america-falling-out-love-needle-slow-death-death-penalty.*

61. *www.texastribune.org/2018/12/13/texas-executed-more-people-any-other-state-2018/?utm_source=Editorial%3A+Texas+Tribune+Master&utm_campaign=eb3b103cc6-trib-newsletters-the-brief&utm_medium=email&utm_term=0_d9a68d8efc-eb3b103cc6-101290241&mc_cid=eb3b103cc6&mc_eid=101a099a60*

62. Thomas Johnson, "The Texas Death Penalty Is Dying," TribTalk. org, January 12, 2017, *www.tribtalk.org/2017/01/12/the-texas-death-penalty-is-dying.*

63. Jordan Rudner, "'Cruel and Unusual': Supreme Court Rejects How Texas Evaluates Mental Disability in Death-Row Inmates," Dallasnews.com, March 28, 2017, *www.dallasnews.com/news/courts/2017/03/28/supreme-court-rejects-texas-use-outdated-medical-standards-disabled-death-row-inmates.*

64. Jolie McCullough, "US Supreme Court Rules in Favor of Texas Death Row Inmate," *The Texas Tribune,* February 22, 2017, *www.texastribune.org/2017/02/22/su-preme-court-rules-in-favor-of-texas-death-row-inmate.*

65. Brandi Grissom, "Firing Squad, Blood Draining among Suggestions Sent to Gov. Greg Abbott to Continue Texas Death Penalty," *Dallas Morning News,* September 4. 2015, *http://trailblazersblog.dallasnews.com/2015/09/firing-squad-blood-draining-among-suggestions-sent-to-gov-greg-abbott-to-continue-texas-death-penalty.html.*

66. *Texas Tribune* Polling, February 2015; Keri Blakinger, "Conservatives' Distaste for Death Penalty Sends

Support to 45-Year Low," Chron. com, October 29, 2017, *www.chron. com/news/houston-texas/article/ Conservatives-help-drive-support-for-death-12315774.php.*

67. The Council of State Governments, Justice Center, "National Inventory of the Collateral Consequences of Conviction," *https://niccc.csgjusticecenter.org.*

68. Jeff Manza and Christopher Uggen, "Punishment and Democracy: Disenfranchisement of Nonincarcerated Felons in the United States," *Perspectives on Politics* 2, no. 3 (2004): 491–505.

69. Jean Chung, "Felony Disenfranchisement: A Primer," The Sentencing Project, July 17, 2018, *www. sentencingproject.org/publications/ felony-disenfranchisement-a-primer.*

70. State Bar of Texas, "Texas Criminal Justice Procedure."

71. Texas Board of Pardons and Paroles, "Revised Parole Guidelines," February 13, 2017, *www.tdcj.state. tx.us/bpp/parole_guidelines/parole_ guidelines.html.*

72. Ken Anderson, *Crime in Texas: Your Complete Guide to the Criminal Justice System* (Austin: University of Texas, 2005).

73. Ibid., 2.

74. Ibid., 4.

75. The Texas Board of Pardons and Paroles, "Parole Guidelines Annual Report FY 2018," (Austin, January 2018), *www.tdcj.texas.gov/bpp/publications/ FY%202018%20AnnualStatistical%20Report.pdf.*

76. Perkinson, *Texas Tough,* 306.

77. Ibid.

78. Ross Ramsey, "Analysis: Legislators Seeking a More Efficient Approach to Jail Policies," *The Texas Tribune,* January 25, 2016, *www.texastribune. org/2016/01/25/analysis-criminal-justice-reformers-take-police-an.*

79. Sarah R. Guidry, Elizabeth Hen-neke, Jay Jenkins, Sarah Pahl, Jessica Schleifer, Matthew Simpson, and Alycia Welch, "A Blueprint for Criminal Justice Policy Solutions in Harris County," Texas Criminal Justice Coalition, January 2015, *www. texascjc.org/system/files/publications/ Blueprint%20for%20Criminal%20 Justice%20Policy%20Solutions%20 2015.pdf.*

80. Ibid.

81. Dottie Carmichael, George Naufal, Steven Wood, Heather Caspers, and Miner P. Marchanks, III, "Liberty and Justice: Pretrial Practices in Texas," *Public Policy Research Institute,* March 2017, *https:// ppri.tamu.edu/wp-content/uploads/2017/04/170308_bond-study-report.pdf,* 7.

82. Texas Public Policy Foundation, "Corrections Budget and Prison Operations," n.d., *www.texaspolicy. com/library/doclib/Corrections%20 Budget%20and%20Prison%20Operations.pdf.*

83. Ibid.

84. *https://ppri.tamu.edu/wp-content/uploads/2017/04/170308_bond-study-report.pdf*

85. *www.texastribune. org/2019/07/31/harris-county-bail-settlement-dallas-texas*

86. *www.houstonchronicle.com/ opinion/editorials/article/Texas-prison-suicides-are-up-why-aren-t-state-14038257.php*

87. Keri Blakinger, "Suicide Attempts Have More than Doubled in Texas Prisons," Chron.com, February 5, 2018, *www.chron.com/news/houston-texas/ amp/Attempted-suicides-rise-sharply-in-Texas-prisons-12553728.php.*

88. Joseph W. McKnight, "Grand Jury," *Handbook of Texas Online,* June 15, 2010, *https://tshaonline.org/ handbook/online/articles/jlg01.*

89. Dan Solomon, "Is the Grand Jury System in Texas Broken?" *Texas Monthly,* July 29, 2014, *www.texas-monthly.com/the-daily-post/is-the-grand-jury-system-in-texas-broken.*

90. Patrick Svitek, "Abbott Signs Grand Jury Reform Legislation," *Texas Tribune,* June 19, 2015.

91. *Texas Tribune* Poll, February 2015.

92. Carlita Salazar, "Texas, Maryland, Rhode Island and Oregon Sign Measures to Fix DNA Testing Laws," *The Innocence Project in Print* 11, no. 1 (Fall 2015): 5, *www.innocenceproject. org/wp-content/uploads/2017/05/IP-Newsletter_17-FINAL.pdf.*

93. Michael Hall, "Four Decades, Three Trials, Two Death Sentences, One Exoneree. Almost," *Texas Monthly,* September 14, 2015, *www.*

texasmonthly.com/news/four-decades-three-trials-two-death-sen-tences-1-exoneree-almost.

94. Ibid.

95. Johnathan Silver and Lindsay Carbonell, "Wrongful Convictions Have Cost Texans More than $93 Million," *The Texas Tribune,* June 24, 2016, *www.texastribune. org/2016/06/24/wrongful-convictions-cost-texans-over-93-million.*

96. Michael Hall, "The Reformer," *Texas Monthly,* February 2015, 161.

97. Terri Langford, "Lawyers, Scientists Try to Unravel Thorny New DNA Standard," *The Texas Tribune,* September 18, 2015, *www.texastribune. org/2015/09/18/lawyers-scientists-try-unravel-thorny-new-dna-stan.*

98. The Constitution Project, "Death Penalty," n.d., *www. constitutionproject.org/issues/criminal-justice-reform/ death-penalty.*

99. Jolie McCullough and Justin Dehn, "How Some See Texas as the 'Gold Standard' Against Wrongful Convictions," *The Texas Tribune,* September 20, 2017, *www.texastribune. org/2017/09/20/texas-lawmakers-hope-prevent-wrongful-convictions.*

100. David W. Murray and Ryan Blake, "Why Texas' Criminal Justice Reforms Don't Translate to the Federal Level," *Hudson Institute,* May 6, 2016, *www.hudson.org/research/12476-why-texas-criminal-justice-reforms-don-t-translate-to-the-federal-level.*

Chapter 12 Local Government

1. Kenneth Dean, Overton Officials Shut Down Girls' Lemonade Stand, Saying They Lack Permit, *Tyler Morning Telegraph,* June 8, 2015, *https://tylerpaper.com/news/local/ overton-officials-shut-down-girls-lemonade-stand-saying-they-lack/ article_aee67f4f-3cdc-5238-9263-1d64fda6e0c0.html.*

2. *www.houstonchronicle.com/ news/politics/texas/article/Gov-Abbott-signs-bill-legalizing-lemonade-13968105.php*

3. *www.easttexasmatters.com/ news/texas-politics/governor-abbot-signs-bill-approving-lemonade-stands*

4. Patrick Svitek, "Abbott Wants 'Broad-Based' Law That Pre-Empts

Local Regulations," *The Texas Tribune*, March 21, 2017, *www.texastribune.org/2017/03/21/abbott-supports-broad-based-law-pre-empt-ing-local-regulations*.

5. Brandon Formby, "Mayors Say Texas, US Politics Increasingly Undermine City Needs," *The Texas Tribune*, March 13, 2017, *www.texastribune.org/2017/03/13/mayors-say-texas-us-politics-increasingly-undermine-city-needs*.

6. Jim Malewitz, "Amid Local Control Fight, a Proposal Cities Like," *The Texas Tribune*, May 2, 2015, *www.texastribune.org/2015/05/12/amid-local-control-fight-gop-pro-posal-cities*; Mike Ward, "Big City Mayors to Lege: Don't Mess with Taxes," *Houston Chronicle*, February 16, 2015, *www.houstonchron-icle.com/news/politics/texas/article/Big-city-mayors-to-Lege-Don-t-mess-with-taxes-6083909.php*; *www.kut.org/post/texas-lawmakers-tried-take-reins-cities-session-results-were-mixed*.

7. Shaila Dewan, "States Are Backing Local Regulations, Often at Industry's Behest," *New York Times*, February 24, 2015, *www.nytimes.com/2015/02/24/us/govern-yourselves-state-law-makers-tell-cities-but-not-too-much.html*; Wendy Hundley, "Bills Take Aim at LGBT Protections," *Dallas Morning News*, March 2015, *http://planoblog.dallas-news.com/2015/03/bills-take-aim-at-lgbt-protections.html*.

8. Tom Benning, "Texas Legislators Mostly Kept Hands Off Local Control," *Dallas Morning News*, June 2015, *www.dallasnews.com/news/politics/state-politics/20150602-texas-legisla-tors-mostly-kept-hands-off-local-control*.

9. *www.kut.org/post/austin-city-council-mandates-six-eight-paid-sick-days-all-private-employees*

10. Raul Garcia, "Island Beach Gatherings Face Tougher Rules," *The Monitor*, July 18, 2017, *www.themoni-tor.com/news/local/article_2f6e06b1-c09d-5264-8426-b5b168fe5f5e.html*.

11. Elvia Limón, "Irving City Council Votes on Ordnance Restricting Number of Chickens Residents Can Own," *Dallas Morning News*, April 2017, *www.dallasnews.com/news/irving/2017/04/06/irving-city-council-votes-ordinance-restricting-amount-chickens-residents-can*.

12. Fox San Antonio, "Passing a Stopped School Bus Will Cost Drivers Hundreds of Dollars," FoxSanAnto-nio.com, November 29, 2016, *http://foxsanantonio.com/news/local/pass-ing-a-stopped-school-bus-will-cost-drivers-hundreds-of-dollars*.

13. Texas Municipal League, "Local Government in Texas," n.d., *www.tml.org/Handbook-M&C/Chap-ter1.pdf*.

14. Randy Lee Loftis, "Texas Prohibits Nearly 70 Percent of Its Counties from Having a Fire Code," *Dallas Morning News*, May 2013, *www.dal-lasnews.com/news/news/2013/05/25/texas-prohibits-nearly-70-percent-of-its-counties-from-having-a-fire-code*.

15. *www.star-telegram.com/news/politics-government/arti-cle237251639.html*.

16. Kevin Krause, "John Wiley Price Bribery Trial Shines Light on Secret World of Lobbying within County Government," *Dallas Morning News*, March 2017, *www.dallas-news.com/news/crime/2017/03/17/john-wiley-price-bribery-trial-shines-light-secret-world-lobbying-county-government*.

17. Thad Sitton, *The Texas Sheriff* (Norman: University of Oklahoma Press, 2000), xii.

18. Ibid.

19. Tom Dart, "Houston's New District Attorney Stands by Her Bold Move to Decriminalize Marijuana," *The Guardian*, April 18, 2017, *www.theguardian.com/us-news/2017/apr/18/houston-district-attorney-kim-ogg-marijuana-decriminaliza-tion-texas*.

20. Bud Kennedy, "As Hood County's Clerk Preached, Others in Texas Just Fumed," *Star-Telegram*, June 30, 2015, *www.star-telegram.com/opinion/opn-columns-blogs/bud-ken-nedy/article25934896.html*.

21. Laura Mueller and Scott N. Houston, "Alphabet Soup: Types of Texas Cities," Texas Municipal League, n.d., *www.tml.org/p/docs/typesofci-ties.pdf*.

22. Ibid.

23. David Warren, "More than 20 Texas Towns Repeal Sex Offender Residency Law," Associated Press, February 7, 2016.

24. Texas Municipal League, "Local Government in Texas."

25. Terrell Blodgett, "Home Rule Charters," *Handbook of Texas Online*, June 15, 2010, *https://tshaonline.org/handbook/online/articles/mvhek*.

26. Field Walsh, "Texarkana, Texas Voters Approve Beer and Wine Sales," *TXK Today*, November 5, 2014, *http://txktoday.com/news/texarkana-texas-voters-approve-beer-wine-sales*;WorldAdmin, "Petition Circulates for Texarkana, Texas Alcohol Sales," KTBS.com, June 5, 2011, *www.ktbs.com/story/22312867/petition-cir-culates-for-texarkana-texas-alcohol-sales*.

27. Susan Schrock, "Arlington's Red-Light Camera Opponents Say They Can Force Election," *Star-Telegram*, January 7, 2015, *www.star-telegram.com/news/local/community/arling-ton/article5553912.html*.

28. "Recall Campaigns in Texas," Bal-lotPedia.org, n.d., *https://ballotpedia.org/Recall_campaigns_in_Texas*.

29. Stephen Young, "Plano City Council Signs Off on Recall Election for Tom Harrison over Anti-Muslim Face-book Posts," *Dallas Observer*, April 10, 2018, *www.dalla-sobserver.com/news/plano-schedules-recall-for-tom-harrison-10564927*.

30. Renée C. Lee, "Annexed King-wood Split on Effects," Chron.com, October 8, 2006, *www.chron.com/neighborhood/humble-news/article/Annexed-Kingwood-split-on-effects-1868661.php*.

31. *https://texasscorecard.com/state/success-story-texas-ends-forced-an-nexation*

32. Jayme Fraser, "Houston Plugs Budget Holes with Suburban Sales Tax Increase," *Houston Chronicle*, January 24, 2015, *www.houstonchroni-cle.com/news/houston-texas/houston/article/Houston-plugs-budget-holes-with-suburban-sales-tax-6038195.php*p.

33. Ann O'M. Bowman and Richard Kearney, *State and Local Government* (Boston: Wadsworth, 2013), 273.

34. Avi Selk, "Dispute over Islam Lands Irving Mayor Beth Van Duyne on National Stage, *Dallas Morning News*, March 2015, *www.dal-lasnews.com/news/metro/20150319-dispute-on-islam-roils-irving.ece*.

35. Robert Montoya, "Citizens Matter, Not City Hall Brawls," *The Texas Scorecard*, September 13, 2020, https://texasscorecard.com/commentary/montoya-citizens-matter-not-city-hall-brawls/

36. Kevin Krause, "Dallas Mayor says Council is Cutting 'Backroom' Budget Deals. But Some Say He Quit Communicating," *Dallas Morning News*, September 19, 2020, https://www.dallasnews.com/news/politics/2020/09/19/dallas-mayor-says-council-is-cutting-backroom-budget-deals-but-some-say-he-quit-communicating/

37. Rebecca Elliott, "City, County Leaders Talk Up Possibility for Increased Cooperation," *Houston Chronicle*, December 24, 2015, *www.houstonchronicle.com/news/politics/houston/article/City-county-leaders-talk-up-possibility-for-6720378.php.*

38. *www.chron.com/news/politics/houston/article/Controller-puts-Houston-recycling-deal-on-hold-12424322.php*

39. Bradley R. Rice, "Commission Form of City Government," *Handbook of Texas Online*, June 12, 2010, *https://tshaonline.org/handbook/online/articles/moc01.*

40. Richard Gambitta, "Bumpy Road to City's Current Form of Government," MySanAntonio.com, April 25, 2015, *www.mysanantonio.com/opinion/commentary/article/Bumpy-road-to-city-s-current-form-of-government-6223668.php.*

41. Michael Lee Stallard, "How Fort Worth's Bike Riding Mayor Steers the City," FoxBusiness.com, July 7, 2015, *www.foxbusiness.com/features/2015/07/07/how-fort-worths-bike-riding-mayor-steers-city.html.*

42. Robert Wilonsky, "Mayor Moves to Block Porn Expo," *Dallas Morning News*, February 7, 2016.

43. Robert Wilonsky, "Federal Judge Says Dallas Was Within Its Rights to Ban Exxxotica Sex Expo from Convention Center," *Dallas Morning News*, April 2016, *http://cityhallblog.dallasnews.com/2016/04/federal-judge-says-dallas-was-within-its-rights-to-ban-exxxotica-sex-expo-from-convention-center.html.*

44. *www.dallasnews.com/news/2019/06/07/dallas-city-hall-is-ready-to-settle-porn-expo-s-federal-lawsuit-for-650k*

45. "Growing Cities Swap Council-Manager, Mayor-Council Governments," Governing.com, June 26, 2012, *www.governing.com/blogs/by-the-numbers/government-mayor-council-manager-form-changes.html.*

46. Laura Miller, "How I Leaned to Hate the Media and Love Politics (Well, Sort Of)," *Texas Monthly*, March 2001, *www.texasmonthly.com/politics/how-i-learned-to-hate-the-media-and-love-politics-well-sort-of.*

47. James H. Svara and Douglas J. Watson, *More Than Mayor or Manager: Campaigns to Change Form of Government in America's Large Cities* (Washington, DC: Georgetown University Press, 2010).

48. Michael Ennis, "What's the Matter with Dallas?" *Texas Monthly*, July 2005, *www.texasmonthly.com/articles/whats-the-matter-with-dallas.*

49. Texas Municipal League, "Local Government in Texas."

50. Texas Senate Research Center, "Invisible Government: Special Purpose Districts in Texas," *Research SPOTLIGHT*, October 2008, *https://senate.texas.gov/_assets/srcpub/SL-SpPurposeDistricts.pdf.*

51. *www.aclutx.org/en/publications/banned-books-2016-2017*

52. John D. Harden, "Woodlands to Seek Legislative OK for More Authority," *Houston Chronicle*, January 27, 2015, *www.houstonchronicle.com/neighborhood/woodlands/news/article/Woodlands-to-seek-legislative-OK-for-more-6044387.php.*

53. James Drew, "Municipal Utility Districts in Texas Have Sweeping Power to Sell Bonds, Levy Taxes," *Houston Chronicle*, August 20, 2016, *www.houstonchronicle.com/news/houston-texas/houston/article/Municipal-Utility-Districts-in-Texas-have-9175418.php.*

54. James Drew, "MUD Measures on Tuesday's Ballot Anything but Clear," *Houston Chronicle*, November 7, 2017, *www.houstonchronicle.com/news/politics/election/amp/MUD-measures-on-Tuesday-s-ballot-anything-but-12331100.php.*

55. Cindy George, "Keys to Unlocking Your Rights with HAO," *Houston Chronicle*, May 24, 2013, *www.houstonchronicle.com/news/houston-texas/houston/article/Keys-to-unlocking-your-rights-with-HOA-4547900.php.*

56. Jay Root, "Growing Disillusioned with HOAs," *Texas Monthly*, May 20, 2013, *www.texasmonthly.com/politics/growing-disillusioned-with-hoas.*

57. Jennifer Hiller, "Laws Loosen HOA Grip on Homeowners," Chron.com, February 3, 2012, *www.chron.com/business/article/HOA-changes-in-effect-3004723.php.*

58. Valerie Wigglesworth & Erinn Connor, "Frisco Soldier Gets Home Back after HOA Foreclosure," NBCDFW.com, July 29, 2010, *www.nbcdfw.com/the-scene/real-estate/Frisco-Soldier-Gets-Home-Back-After-HOA-Foreclosure-99556729.html.*

59. R. G. Ratcliffe, "The Partisans Are Coming for Your Cities and Schools," *Texas Monthly*, May 5, 2017, *www.texasmonthly.com/burka-blog/partisans-coming-cities-schools.*

60. Gromer Jeffers Jr., "Taking Cue from Democrats, Texas Republicans Moving to Influence 'Nonpartisan' Elections," Dallasnews.com, July 2017, *www.dallasnews.com/news/texas-politics/2017/07/03/taking-cue-democrats-texas-republicans-moving-influence-nonpartisan-elections.*

61. The Annette Strauss Institute for Civic Life and Leadership Austin, "Civic Engagement in Austin," November 2015, *http://leadershipaustin.org/wp-content/uploads/2015/11/Civic-Engagement-in-Austin-Report_November-2015.pdf.*

62. DallasNews Administrator, "Voting Rights Fight Looms over Latino Clout in Texas City," *Dallas Morning News*, January 2015, *www.dallasnews.com/news/state/headlines/20150102-voting-rights-fight-looms-over-latino-clout-in-texas-city.ece.*

63. Kyle Bozentko, "Local Politics and the Malaise of the Millennials," Governing.com, October 12, 2015, *www.governing.com/gov-institute/voices/col-local-politics-voting-community-engagement-millennials.html.*

64. Ed Payne, "Crystal City: All but One Member of City Council

Indicted on Corruption Charges," CNN.com, February 5, 2016, *www.cnn.com/2016/02/05/us/crystal-city-texas-corruption.*

65. Jim Malewitz, "No State Help for Crystal City Council Meltdown," *The Texas Tribune*, February 13, 2016, *www.texastribune.org/2016/02/13/crystal-city-left-alone-rebuild-troubled-governmen.*

66. Christian McPhate, "Denton County Sheriff William Travis Is Losing Endorsements," *Dallas Observer*, February 26, 2016, *www.dallasobserver.com/news/denton-county-sheriff-william-travis-is-losing-endorsements-like-mad-8068237.*

67. Glenn Hegar, "A Field Guide to the Taxes of Texas," Office of the Texas Comptroller, March 2019, *https://comptroller.texas.gov/transparency/revenue/docs/96–1774.pdf.*

68. Marc Wortman, "The Stadiums that Ate Texas," CityLab, February 15, 2017, *www.citylab.com/design/2017/02/the-stadiums-that-ate-texas/516279.*

69. Ibid.

70. Steve Miller, "$5B in Debt Before Texas Voters; Some Asks Raise Questions," *Texas Monitor*, May 2, 2017, *https://texasmonitor.org/5b-debt-texas-isd-city-county-voters-week-asks-raising-questions.*

71. Texas Bond Review Board, 2017 Local Annual Report. Available at *www.brb.state.tx.us/publica-tions_state.aspx.*

72. Ibid., 4.

73. Matthew Tresaugue, "Road Bond OK'd on 3rd Try," *Houston Chronicle*, November 3, 2015, *www.houston-chronicle.com/politics/election/local/article/Road-bond-OK-d-on-3rd-try-6609206.php.*

74. David Crowder, "City CFO: How We'll Pay Off Big Bond Debt," El Paso Inc., September 30, 2012, *www.elpasoinc.com/news/local_news/article_d9e0e61c-0b21-11e2-834c-0019bb30f31a.html.*

75. Aman Batheja, "Local Debt Climbs as City Deals with Growth," *The Texas Tribune*, August 27, 2014, *www.texastribune.org/2014/08/27/local-debt-soaring-across-texas.*

76. Gilbert Garcia, "Helotes Just Might Win This Battle with S.A.,"

MySanAntonio.com, April 14, 2013, *www.mysanantonio.com/news/news_columnists/article/Helotes-vs-S-A-in-the-battle-for-ETJ-4432927.php.*

77. Craig Malisow, "Rather Than Fix the Problem, Houston Officials Ship Stray Animals Off to Other States," HoustonPress.com, February 17, 2015, *www.houstonpress.com/news/rather-than-fix-the-problem-houston-officials-ship-stray-animals-off-to-other-states-6717198.*

78. Elliott, "City, County Leaders."

79. "Texan Tug-of-War," *The Economist*, May 28, 2015, *www.economist.com/news/united-states/21652342-texas-poli-ticians-line-themselves-up-against-states-big-cities-texan-tug-war.*

80. Monic S. Nagy, "Is Urban Sprawl in Texas Swatting Out Bumblebees?" *Star-Telegram*, July 4, 2014, *www.star-telegram.com/news/local/education/article3864132.html.*

81. Peter Coy, "How Houston Gets Along Without Zoning," Bloom-berg.com, October 1, 2007, *www.bloomberg.com/news/ar-ticles/2007-09-30/how-houston-gets-along-without-zoning.*

82. Ryan Holeywell, "Houston: All the Burdens of Zoning, None of the Foresight," *Houston Chronicle*, September 10, 2015, *www.hous-tonchron-icle.com/local/gray-matters/article/Houston-All-the-burdens-of-zoning-but-none-of-6493863.php.*

83. Walsh, "Dallas Stares Down"; Stephen Young, "Sizing Up Dallas' Massive Pension Problem," *Dallas Observer*, November 6, 2015, *www.dallasobserver.com/news/sizing-up-dallas-massive-pension-problem-7752330*; Samantha Calimbahin, "City Committee to Tackle Pension Issues," *Forth Worth Business Press*, January 9, 2016, *www.fortworthbusiness.com/news/city-committee-to-tackle-pension-issues/article_a6816844-b660-11e5-b186-8befbbac14af.html*; *https://texasmonitor.org/financial-watchdog-texas-mired-in-unfunded-pension-debt.*

84. Kriston Capps, "The Great Texas Pension Fix," CityLab, January 18, 2017, *www.city-lab.com/solutions/2017/01/the-great-texas-pension-fix/512060.*

Chapter 13 Budget, Finances, and Policy

1. *www.dallasnews.com/opinion/commentary/2017/02/08/tampon-sales-tax-should-not-be-eliminated-in-texas*

2. *www.houstonchronicle.com/news/politics/texas/article/Luxury-yacht-buyers-in-Texas-get-big-tax-break-13999200.php*

3. Gregory Curtis and Paul Burka, "For an Income Tax," *Texas Monthly*, May 1997, *www.texasmonthly.com/politics/for-an-income-tax.*

4. Office of the Texas Comptroller, "Revenue by Source for Fiscal Year 2019," *https://comptroller.texas.gov/transparency/reports/revenue-by-source.*

5. Glenn Hegar, "A Field Guide to the Taxes of Texas," Texas Comptroller of Public Accounts, December 2017, *https://comptroller.texas.gov/trans-parency/revenue/docs/96–1774.pdf.*

6. Glenn Hegar, "Local Sales and Use Taxes," *Tax Topics*, June 2016, *https://comptroller.texas.gov/taxes/publications/94–105.pdf.*

7. Hegar, "A Field Guide," p. 4

8. Mike Maciag, "States' Shifting Reliance on Income Versus Sales Taxes," Governing.com, May 6, 2015, *www.governing.com/topics/finance/gov-state-tax-collection-bur-den-shifts.html.*

9. Ibid.

10. Josh Haney, "The (Long, Long) History of the Texas Property Tax: A Controversial Levy," *Fiscal Notes*, Office of the Texas Comptroller, *https://comptroller.texas.gov/economy/fiscal-notes/2015/october/proptax.php.*

11. Hegar, "A Field Guide."

12. Patrick Michaels, "Wrong Side of the Tax," *Texas Observer*, June 24, 2015, *www.texasobserver.org/big-spring-exposes-texas-broken-property-tax-system.*

13. *www.ksat.com/news/local/2019/12/19/how-property-taxes-have-changed-skyrocketed-in-san-antonio-neighborhoods/*; *www.heralddemocrat.com/news/20190315/taxes-paid-in-county-have-gone-up-57-percent-since-2008.*

14. R. G. Ratcliffe, "The Dark Lining in the Prosperity Tax-Cut Silver Cloud," *Texas Monthly*, February 24, 2015, *www.texasmonthly.com/*

burka-blog/the-dark-lining-in-the-property-tax-cut-silver-cloud.

15. Mike Morris, "City Plans Hearings on Harvey-Related Property Tax Rate Hike," *Houston Chronicle,* September 13, 2017, *www.houston-chroni-cle.com/news/politics/houston/article/City-plans-hearings-on-Har-vey-re-lated-property-12195951.php.*

16. Ross Ramsey, "Analysis: The Texas Legislature Giveth—and Taketh Away," *The Texas Tribune,* March 8, 2017, *www.texastribune. org/2017/03/08/analysis-texas-legis-lature-giveth-and-taketh-away.*

17. R. G. Ratcliffe, "John Shape, the State's Fixer in Chief, Comes to the Rescue after Harvey," *Texas Monthly,* September 7, 2017, *www. texasmonthly.com/burka-blog/john-sharp-the-states-fixer-in-chief-comes-to-the-rescue-after-harvey.*

18. Hegar, "A Field Guide."

19. Ibid.

20. Dug Begley, "State Shuffles Other Sources for Road Work as Gas Tax Stays Flat," *Houston Chronicle,* October 29, 2015, *www.houston-chronicle.com/news/local/article/State-shuffles-other-sources-for-road-work-as-gas-6577475.php.*

21. Lisa Minton, "How Texas Taxes 'Sin': Levies Play Dual Role," *Fiscal Notes,* Office of the Texas Comptroller, *https://comptroller.texas.gov/economy/fiscal-notes/2015/november/sintax.php.*

22. *www.taxpolicycenter.org/publications/are-states-betting-sin-murky-future-state-taxation/full*

23. "Revenue by Source—Fiscal 1996," Comptroller.Texas.Gov, n.d., *https:// comptroller.texas.gov/transparency/reports/revenue-by-source/history. php#1996.*

24. Leif Reigstad, "Texas Has a Debtors' Prison Problem," *Texas Monthly,* August 29, 2016, *www. texasmonthly.com/the-daily-post/texas-debtors-prisons-problem.*

25. Forrest Wilder, "The P.E.A. Party Strikes Back against the Driver Responsibility Program," *Texas Observer,* September 18, 2014, *www.texa-sobserver.org/p-e-party-strikes-back-driver-responsibility-program.*

26. Bobby Blanchard, "Texas Lawmakers Take Critical Look at Driver Responsibility Program," *Dallas Morning News,* January 2016, *http://trail-blazersblog.dallasnews. com/2016/01/lawmakers-take-criti-cal-look-at-driver-responsibility-pro-gram.html.*

27. Robert Stein, "City Sued over Municipal Fines Policy," *Amarillo Globe-News,* January 15, 2016, *http://amarillo.com/news/crime-and-courts/2016-01-15/city-sued-over-municipal-fines-policy.*

28. Johnathan Silver, "House Votes to End Jail Time for Being Too Poor to Pay Fines," *The Texas Tribune,* May 23, 2017, *www.texastribune. org/2017/05/23/texas-house-clears-bill-eliminating-jail-time-being-too-poor-pay-traff.*

29. *www.dallasnews.com/news/courts/2019/07/05/dallas-county-studying-whether-it-can-reduce-or-eliminate-criminal-fees-fines*

30. *www.theatlantic.com/politics/archive/2017/07/texas-court-fines/534363*

31. *www.texasobserver.org/texas-legislature-considers-bills-debtors-prison-cycle-court-costs-fines-fees-indigent*

32. *https://abc13.com/politics/houston-municipal-courts-kick-off-amnesty-program/5196966*

33. Texas Comptroller of Public Accounts, "Economic Stabilization Fund," July 2018, *https://comptroller.texas. gov/transparency/budget/docs/Eco-nomicStabilizationFund.pdf.*

34. R. G. Ratcliffe, "Budget Wizardly," *Texas Monthly,* March 25, 2015, *www.texasmonthly.com/burka-blog/budget-wizardry.*

35. Senate Research Center, "Budget 101: A Guide to the Budget Process in Texas," Senate.Texas.gov, January 2017, *https://senate.texas.gov/_assets/srcpub/85th_Budget_101.pdf.*

36. Jan Reid, *Let the People In: The Life and Times of Ann Richards* (Austin: University of Texas Press, 2012), 386.

37. Texas Politics Polling, "Support for Revenue Increases: Implement a State Income Tax," May 2011.

38. *www.texastri-bune.org/2019/01/31/*

texas-leaders-want-let-voters-cap-local-property-tax-revenues

39. *www.texastribune. org/2019/01/31/texas-leaders-want-let-voters-cap-local-property-tax-revenues*

40. Dan Balz, "Bush Puts His Brand on Texas Policies," *The Washington Post,* March 21, 1999, *www.washing-tonpost.com/wp-srv/politics/cam-paigns/wh2000/stories/bush032199. htm.*

41. Vicky Garza, "'Entertaining' Lege Sessions Ends This Month," *Dallas Business Journal,* May 6, 2011, *www.bizjournals.com/dallas/print-edition/2011/05/06/entertaining-lege-session-ends-this.html.*

42. Patricia L. Cox and Michael Phillips, *The House Will Come to Order* (Austin: University of Texas Press, 2010), 49.

43. Legislative Budget Board, "Constitutional Spending Limits," December 4, 2014, *www.lbb.state. tx.us/Documents/Publications/Pre-sentation/1987_HACSpendingLimi-tandOverview.pdf.*

44. Ross Ramsey, "Analysis: A Senate Trying to Regulate Its Own Spending Habits," *The Texas Tribune,* April 16, 2015, *www.texastribune. org/2015/04/16/analysis-senate-try-ing-regulate-its-own-spending.*

45. Jim Malewitz, "Texas Lawmakers Set a Spending Cap They Likely Won't Reach," *The Texas Tribune,* December 1, 2016, *www.texastribune. org/2016/12/01/texas-lawmakers-set-spending-cap-they-likely-wont-/; https://www.lbb.state.tx.us/Docu-ments/Appropriations_Bills/86/LBB_Recommended_House/5492_House_LBE_Bill_Summary.pdf,* p. 28.

46. Legislative Budget Board, "Constitutional Spending Limits."

47. Legislative Budget Board, "Summary of Conference Committee Report for Senate Bill 1: Appropriations for the 2018–2019 Biennium," 85th Texas Legislature, May 2017, *www.lbb.state. tx.us/Documents/Appropria-tions_Bills/85/Conference_Bills/4083_Sum-mary_CCR_SB1_2018-19.pdf;* and Legislative Budget Board, "General Appropriations Act for the 20182019 Biennium: Text of Conference

Committee Report on Senate Bill No. 1," 85th Texas Legislature Regular Session, 2017, *www.lbb.state.tx.us/Documents/GAA/General_Appropriations_Act_2018-2019.pdf*.

48. Paul Burka, "The Honeymoon Is Over," *Texas Monthly*, January 1997.

49. Brian McCall, *The Power of the Texas Governor: Connally to Bush* (Austin: University of Texas Press, 2009), 125.

50. Ross Ramsey, "Analysis: Cutting the Texas Budget, but Only Hypothetically," *The Texas Tribune*, July 13, 2016, *www.texastribune.org/2016/07/13/analysis-cutting-texas-budget-only-hypothetically*.

51. Paul Burka, "The Bloody Billion," *Texas Monthly*, March 1985, *www.texasmonthly.com/politics/the-bloody-billion*.

52. Patricia Kilday Hart, "Electronic Lobbying Changes Influence-Peddling," *Houston Chronicle*, April 13, 2013, *www.houstonchronicle.com/news/kilday-hart/article/Electronic-lobbying-changes-influence-peddling-4432727.php*.

53. Robert T. Garrett, "Inside the Dispute about Gov. Greg Abbott's Budget Power," *Dallas Morning News*, July 2015, *www.dallasnews.com/news/politics/state-politics/20150722-inside-the-dispute-about-gov.-greg-abbotts-budget-power.ece*.

54. Enrique Rangel, "Comptroller: Oil Bust Does Not Have Sky Falling in Texas," *Lubbock Avalanche-Journal*, February 20, 2016, *http://lubbockonline.com/filed-online/2016-02-20/comptroller-oil-bust-does-not-have-sky-falling-texas#.WDtVi2bruUk*.

55. Paul Burka, "Carole Keeton Strayhorn Has Guts. Carole Keeton Strayhorn Is Nuts. Discuss," *Texas Monthly*, June 2005, *www.texasmonthly.com/politics/carole-keeton-strayhorn-has-guts-carole-keeton-strayhorn-is-nuts-discuss*.

56. *https://comptroller.texas.gov/economy/fiscal-notes/2019/sep/highlights.php*; *www.texastribune.org/2019/05/14/texas-tax-collectors-predict-another-500-million-state-budget*

57. Aman Batheja, "Sales Taxes, an Exit Ramp, and the Texas Budget," *The Texas Tribune*, March 28, 2013, *www.texastribune.org/2013/03/28/budget-plans-riders-telling-numbers*.

58. Eli Okun, "Aide: Perry Chose Best Option on National Guard Funding," *The Texas Tribune*, August 5, 2014, *www.texastribune.org/2014/08/05/gov-office-defends-national-guard-deployment-fundi*.

59. Garrett and McGaughy, "Straus Hits Senate,"

60. Ross Ramsey, "Analysis: Is This Texas State Budget Trick Constitutional?" *The Texas Tribune*, March 24, 2017, *www.texastribune.org/2017/03/24/analysis-texas-state-budget-trick-constitutional*.

61. Robert T. Garrett, "Texas House to Ponder Easing Cuts with Rainy Day Money and Payment Delays, Budget Chief Says," *Dallas Morning News*, February 13, 2017, *www.dallasnews.com/news/texas-legislature/2017/02/13/texas-house-ponder-easing-cuts-rainy-day-money-payment-delays-says-budget-chief*.

62. Ross Ramsey, "Analysis: Texas State Budget Tricks Are Great—Until You Total Them Up," *The Texas Tribune*, August 11, 2017, *www.texastribune.org/2017/08/11/analysis-texas-state-budget-tricks-are-great-until-you-total-them*.

63. Erica Grieder, *Big, Hot, Cheap, and Right: What America Can Learn from the Strange Genius of Texas* (New York: Public Affairs Books, 2013), p. 23.

Chapter 14 Public Policy in Texas

1. Jeremy Schwartz, "Austin Not Ready for 'Silver Tsunami' of Poor Seniors, Experts Warm," *Statesman*, April 8, 2012, *www.statesman.com/news/local/austin-not-ready-for-silver-tsunami-poor-seniors-experts-warn/31VShdqtOgnymBqSAFPKxI*.

2. Juliette Cubanski, "How Many Seniors Are Living in Poverty? National and State Estimates Under the Official and Supplemental Poverty Measures in 2016," KFF.org, March 2, 2018, *www.kff.org/medicare/issue-brief/how-many-seniors-are-living-in-poverty-national-and-state-estimates-under-the-official-and-supplemental-poverty-measures-in-2016*.

3. Daniel Blue Tyx, "The Day Shift," *Texas Observer*, January 8, 2018, *www.texasobserver.org/the-day-shift*.

4. Kaiser Family Foundation, "Total State Expenditures per Capita," KFF.org, n.d., *www.kff.org/other/state-indicator/per-capita-state-spending*.

5. "Texas Crime Analysis," *www.dps.texas.gov/crimereports/14/citCh2.pdf*.

6. Kelsey Jukam, "Open Carry Activists Rally at Capitol," *Texas Observer*, n.d., *www.texasobserver.org/open-carry-activists-rally-capitol/amp*.

7. Morgan Smith, "Gun Rights Activists Cause Stir at Texas Capitol," *The Texas Tribune*, January 13, 2015, *www.texastribune.org/2015/01/13/gun-rights-activists-cause-stir-texas-capitol*.

8. Morgan Smith, "Patrick on Open Carry: The Votes Aren't There," *The Texas Tribune*, January 27, 2015, *www.texastribune.org/2015/01/27/lt-gov-patrick-open-carry-votes-arent-there*.

9. Morgan Smith, "As Open Carry Takes Effect, Local Officials Predict Lawsuits," *The Texas Tribune*, January 1, 2016, *www.texastribune.org/2016/01/01/new-open-carry-law-could-come-lawsuits*.

10. Camille Garcia, "San Antonio Police Prepare for First Fiesta with Open Carry," *The Rivard Report*, April 7, 2016, *https://therivardreport.com/police-preparing-for-first-open-carry-fiesta*.

11. Kirby Wilson, "Six Months In, Few Open Carry Complaints," *The Texas Tribune*, July 11, 2016, *www.texastribune.org/2016/07/11/open-carry-law-yields-few-complaints*.

12. Ibid.

13. Kate Weidaw, "Report: Nearly a Quarter of Texas Children Live in Poverty," KXAN.com, April 13, 2016, *http://kxan.com/2016/04/13/report-nearly-a-quarter-of-texas-children-live-in-poverty*.

14. *www.dallasfed.org/~/media/microsites/cd/colonias/econop.html*

15. *www.feedingtexas.org/learn/what-is-food-insecurity*

16. *www.expressnews.com/news/local/article/More-people-going-without-health-insurance-in-14428681.php*

17. Kaiser Family Foundation, "Total Number of Medicare Beneficiaries," KFF.org, n.d., *www.kff.org/medicare/state-indicator/total-medicare-beneficiaries.*

18. Texas Health and Human Services Commission, "Texas Medicaid and CHIP in Perspective, Eleventh Edition," February 2017, *hhs.texas.gov/sites/default/files/documents/laws-regulations/reports-presentations/2017/medicaid-chip-perspective-11th-edition/11th-edition-complete.pdf.*

19. Jesse Pound, "Austin, Houston Doctors Among 35 Texans Charged in $1.3 Billion Medicare Fraud Sting," *MySanAntonio.com*, July 13, 2017, *www.mysanantonio.com/business/national/article/Houston-doctor-among-25-Texans-charged-in-1-3-11286753.php.*

20. Texas Health and Human Services Commission, *Healthcare Statistics*, Accessed February 2016, *https://hhs.texas.gov/sites/default/files/documents/about-hhs/records-statistics/research-statistics/medicaid-chip/2018/monthly-enrollment-by-risk-group-may-2018.xlsx.*

21. P, 4.

22. Texas Health and Human Services Commission, *Texas Medicaid and CHIP in Perspective*, 12th ed. (Austin: Texas Health and Human Services Commission, 2018), *https://hhs.texas.gov/sites/default/files/documents/laws-regulations/reports-presentations/2018/medicaid-chip-perspective-12th-edition/12th-edition-complete.pdf.*

23. John Davidson and Vance Ginn, "Texas Medicaid Reform Model: A Market-Driven, Patient-Centered Approach," Texas Public Policy Foundation, September 28, 2015, *www.texaspolicy.com/content/detail/texas-medicaid-reform-model-a-mar-ket-driven-patient-centered-approach.*

24. Texas Health and Human Services Commission, *Texas Medicaid.*

25. Ibid.

26. Ibid.

27. Alex Samuels, "Hey, Texplainer: How Much Money Does Texas Spend per Child through CHIP?" *The Texas Tribune*, December 1, 2017, *www.texastribune.org/2017/12/01/hey-texplainer-how-much-money-does-texas-spend-child-through-chip*; *https://hhs.texas.gov/sites/default/files/documents/laws-regulations/reports-presentations/2018/medicaid-chip-perspective-12th-edition/12th-edition-complete.pdf*, p. 87.

28. Allegra Kirkland, "Survey: US Uninsured Rate Hits Record Low," *Talking Points Memo*, July 10, 2015, *http://talking-pointsmemo.com/livewire/survey-uninsured-rate-record-low.*

29. *www.dallasnews.com/business/health-care/2019/12/24/nearly-112-million-texans-sign-up-for-obamacare-this-year-up-25/?utm_content=buffer5dd25&utm_medium=social&utm_source=twitter.com&utm_campaign=buffer*

30. Louise Norris, "Texas and the ACA's Medicaid Expansion," *healthinsurance.org, November 11, 2019, www.healthinsurance.org/texas-medicaid.*

31. Mark Richardson, "Feds Grant Texas $25 Billion Extension of Medicaid Waiver," *Public News Service*, January 3, 2018, *www.publicnewsservice.org/2018-01-03/health-issues/feds-grant-texas-25-billion-extension-of-medicaid-waiver/a60873-1.*

32. Jenny Deam, "Number of Uninsured Americans on the Rise, Especially in Texas, New Study Finds," Chron.com, May 14, 2018, *www.chron.com/news/houston-texas/houston/amp/Number-of-uninsured-Americans-on-the-rise-12914114.php?*

33. Matt Goodman, "Texas Receives 15-Month Extension on Its $29 Billion Medicare 1115 Waiver," *HEALTHCARE*, May 2, 2016, *http://healthcare.dmagazine.com/2016/05/02/texas-receives-15-month-extension-on-its-29-billion-medicaid-1115-waiver.*

34. AARP, "Social Security: 2014 Texas Quick Facts," *www.aarp.org/content/dam/aarp/research/surveys_statistics/general/2014/ssqf/Social-Secu-rity-2014-Texas-Quick-Facts-AARP-res-gen.pdf*; Social Security Administration, "Monthly Statistical Snapshot, May 2018," June 2018, *www.ssa.gov/policy/docs/quickfacts/stat_snapshot.*

35. United Health Foundation, "Senior Report," AmericasHealth Rankings.org, n.d., *www.americashealthrankings.org/explore/2016-senior-report/measure/poverty_sr/state/TX.*

36. Social Security Administration, "SSI Recipients by State and County, 2018," November 2019, *www.ssa.gov/policy/docs/statcomps/ssi_sc/2018/tx.html;https://hhs.texas.gov/sites/default/files/documents/laws-regulations/reports-presentations/2017/medicaid-chip-perspective-11th-edition/11th-edition-complete.pdf.*

37. Alexa Ura, "Drug Testing for Welfare Benefits Back on the Table," *The Texas Tribune*, February 5, 2015, *www.texastribune.org/2015/02/05/drug-testing-welfare-benefits-back-table*; National Conference of State Legislatures, "Drug Testing for Welfare Recipients and Public Assistance," NCSL.org, March 24, 2017, *www.ncsl.org/re-search/human-services/drug-testing-and-public-assistance.aspx.*

38. Texas Health and Human Services Commission, *Healthcare Statistics.*

39. Alexa Ura, "How Texas Curtailed Traditional Welfare Without Ending Poverty," *The Texas Tribune*, November 30, 2017, *www.texastribune.org/2017/11/30/how-texas-curtailed-traditional-welfare-without-ending-poverty.*

40. Ife Floyd, Ladonna Pavetti, and Liz Schott, "TANF Reaching Few Poor Families," CBPP.org, December 13, 2017, *www.cbpp.org/research/family-income-support/tanf-reaching-few-poor-families.*

41. "State Temporary Assistance for Needy Families Programs Do Not Provide Adequate Safety Net for Poor Families," CBPP.org, n.d., *www.cbpp.org/state-temporary-assistance-for-needy-families-programs-do-not-provide-adequate-safety-net-for-poor.*

42. Lisa Guerin, "Collecting Unemployment Benefits in Texas," NOLO.com, n.d., *www.nolo.com/legal-ency-clopedia/collecting-unem-ployment-benefits-texas-32500.html.*

43. Office of Injured Employee Counsel, "Notice of Injured Employee Rights and Responsibilities in the Texas Worker's Compensation System," June 2012, *www.oiec.texas.gov/documents/ierightsrespeng.pdf.*

44. Bureau of Labor Statistics, "Fatal Occupational Injuries in California," n.d., *www.bls.gov/iif/oshwc/cfoi/tgs/2016/iiffw06.htm*.

45. Jay Root, "Best Insurance for Texas Workers? 'Don't Get Injured,'" *New York Times*, June 28, 2014, *www.nytimes.com/2014/06/29/us/the-state-has-a-record-of-high-worker-fatalities-and-of-weak-benefits.html*.

46. Jay Root, "Hurting for Work," *The Texas Tribune*, June 29, 2014, *https://apps.texastribune.org/hurting-for-work*.

47. Jay Root, "State Records Shed Light on Texas' Early 'Illegals,'" *The Texas Tribune*, December 14, 2012, *www.texastribune.org/2012/12/14/back-when-americans-were-illegals*.

48. Office of the State Demographer, "The Foreign Born Population in Texas: Sources of Growth," October 2015, *http://demographics.texas gov/Resources/Publications/2015/2015_10_07_ForeignBorn.pdf*.

49. American Immigration Council, "Immigrants in Texas," October 4, 2017, *www.americanimmigrationcouncil.org/research/immigrants-in-texas*.

50. Migration Policy Institute, "Texas," n.d., *www.migra-tionpolicy.org/data/state-profiles/state/demographics/TX*.

51. Center for Migration, Texas, November 2019, http://data.cmsny. org, Center for Public Policy Priorities, "Texas Children in Immigrant Families," March 2017, *https://forabettertexas.org/images/2017_TXkids_ImmigrantFamilies.pdf*.

52. Bloomberg View, "Editorial: How to Enrich Immigrants and Help the States," timesrecordnews. com, February 28, 2016, *www.timesrecordnews.com/story/opinion/editorials/2016/02/28/editorial-how-to-enrich-immigrants-and-help-the-states/92559698*; Federation for American Immigration Reform, "The Fiscal Burden of Illegal Immigration on Texans (2014)," January 2014, *www.fairus.org/issue/publications-resources/fiscal-burden-illegal-immigration-texans-2014*.

53. *www.houstonchronicle. com/politics/texas/article/Illegal-immigration-not-a-drain-on-Texas-economy-15278150. php?utm_campaign=CMS%20Sharing%20Tools%20(Premium)&utm_source=t.co&utm_medium=referral*

54. Damien Cave, "An American Life, Lived in Shadows," *New York Times*, June 8, 2014, *www.nytimes.com/2014/06/09/us/for-illegal-immigrants-american-life-lived-in-shadows.html*.

55. Jeff Salamon, "Everything You Ever Wanted to Know about Illegal Immigration (but Didn't Know Who to Ask)," *Texas Monthly*, November 2010, *www.texasmonthly.com/politics/everything-you-ever-wanted-to-know-about-illegal-immigration-but-didnt-know-who-to-ask*.

56. Migration Policy Institute, "Profile of the Unauthorized Population: Texas," n.d., *www.migrationpolicy.org/data/unauthorized-immigrant-population/state/TX*.

57. UT/*Texas Tribune* Poll, February 2018.

58. Jay Root, "Houston Slayings Fueled Border Security Debate," *The Texas Tribune*, January 31, 2016, *www.texastribune.org/2016/01/31/houston-slayings-ignited-immigration-debate*.

59. Enrique Rangel, "Immigration Debate Takes Center Stage," *Amarillo Globe News*, March 15, 2015.

60. Jay Root, "In Texas, Lawmakers Don't Mess with Employers of Undocumented Workers," *Texas Tribune*, December 14, 2016, *www.texastribune.org/2016/12/14/lawmakers-go-easy-employers-undocumented-workers*.

61. *www.athensreview.com/news/most-texas-employers-are-skipping-e-verify-when-hiring/article_fb455c86-4e58-11e8-9ceb-17c46afdbccb.html*

62. Paul J. Weber, "Texas Approves $800 Million for Border Security," PBS.org, June 16, 2015, *www.pbs.org/newshour/rundown/texas-approves-800-million-border-security*.

63. *www.usatoday.com/story/news/nation/2019/04/04/ice-arrests-texas-biggest-immigration-bust-decade-cve-technology-group/3362163002*

64. Julián Aguilar and Darla Cameron, "Immigrants in Texas Are among the Least Likely to Have a Lawyer, Most Likely to Get Deported," *The Texas Tribune*, April 12, 2018, *www.texastribune.org/2018/04/12/trump-charges-for-ward-immigration-enforcement-texas-detainees-are-leas*.

65. Paul Burka, "An F for Effort," *Texas Monthly*, June 2004, *www.texasmonthly.com/politics/an-f-for-effort-2*.

66. Laura Isensee, "Learn How Texas Funds Public Schools in 7 Easy Steps," HoustonPublicMedia. org, April 27, 2015, *www.houstonpublicmedia.org/articles/news/2015/04/27/59742/learn-how-texas-funds-public-schools-in-7-easy-steps-2*.

67. Kiah Collier, "State Urges Texas Supreme Court to Drop School Finance Lawsuit," *The Texas Tribune*, September 1, 2015, *www.texastribune.org/2015/09/01/one-year-later-school-finance-appeal-back-court*.

68. Paul Burka, "The Honeymoon Is Over," *Texas Monthly*, January 1997, *www.texasmonthly.com/politics/the-honeymoon-is-over*.

69. Kiah Collier, "Texas Supreme Court Rules School Funding System Is Constitutional," *The Texas Tribune*, May 13, 2016, *www.texastribune.org/2016/05/13/texas-supreme-court-issues-school-finance-ruling*.

70. Express-News Editorial Board, "The State's War on Public Education Hits Home," MySanAntonio.com, April 17, 2018, *www.mysanan-tonio.com/opinion/editorials/article/The-state-s-war-on-public-education-hits-home-12832922.php*.

71. Sally Beauvais, "Why Is the State's Share of Public School Funding Shrinking?' *Texas Standard*, May 1, 2017, *www.texasstandard.org/stories/why-is-the-states-share-of-public-school-funding-shrinking*; *www.wacotrib.com/opinion/interviews/fighting-yellowbelly-politicians-to-save-texas-public-schools-q-a/article_dcd608ae-c8be-568f-bde6-cf0e0f3b1b99.html?utm_source=Texas+Tribune+Master&utm_campaign=ff050f3acc-trib-newsletters-the-brief&utm_medium=email&utm_term=0_d9a68d8efc-ff050f3acc-101290241&mc_cid=ff050f3acc&mc_eid=101a099a60*.

72. www.texastribune. org/2019/05/24/texas-school-finance-bill-here-are-details

73. Kiah Collier, "2011 Budget Cuts Still Hampering Schools," *The Texas*

Tribune, August 31, 2015, *www.texas-tribune.org/2015/08/31/texas-schools-still-feeling-2011-budget-cuts*.

74. Patrick Michels, "Free Lunch," *Texas Observer*, n.d., *www.texasobserver.org/chapter-313-texas-tax-incentive*.

75. Mike Snyder, "Texas City– Mayor: Valero 'Robbing' Millions from School Kids," *Houston Chronicle*, August 1, 2017, *www.houston-chronicle.com/neighborhood/bayarea/amp/Texas-City-mayor-Valero-robbing-millions-from-11723280.php*.

76. Paul Burka, "Degrading Teachers," *Texas Monthly*, June 1986, 216.

77. Ibid.

78. Bill Hobby, *How Things Really Work: Lessons from a Life in Politics* (Austin: University of Texas Press, 2010), 107.

79. *https://tea.texas.gov/sites/default/files/comp_annual_biennial_2018.pdf*, 7.

80. "Recent Changes in Public Schools," *Texas Almanac*, n.d., *http://texasalmanac.com/topics/education/recent-changes-public-schools*.

81. *www.chron.com/houston/article/TEA-STAAR-Test-F-bomb-obscenity-13813449.php#photo-7487322*

82. *www.dallasnews.com/opinion/commentary/2017/01/06/i-can-t-answer-the-staar-test-questions-about-my-own-poem*

83. Express-News Editorial Board, "The State's War on Public Education Hits Home," MySanAntonio.com, April 17, 2018, *www.mysanan-tonio.com/opinion/editorials/article/The-state-s-war-on-public-education-hits-home-12832922.php*.

84. Laura Isensee, "Texas Ranked 43rd in Nation on 2016 Education Quality Report," *HoustonPublicMedia.org*, January 7, 2016, *www.houstonpublicmedia.org/articles/news/2016/01/07/133321/texas-ranked-43rd-in-nation-on-2016-education-quality-report*.

85. Kiah Collier and Alexa Ura, "Texas Public Schools Are Poorer, More Diverse," *The Texas Tribune*, December 9, 2015, *www.texastribune.org/2015/12/09/new-schools-explorer-shows-changing-face-schools*.

86. Chris McNary, "Texas Leaders, Educators and Courts Grapple with Segregated Public Schools," *Dallas Morning News*, May 3, 2013, *www.dallasnews.com/news/education/2013/05/03/texas-leaders-educators-and-courts-grapple-with-segregated-public-schools*.

87. Brennan Griffin, "Ending the Criminalization of Truancy," *Texas Appleseed*, November 28, 2016, *www.texasappleseed.org/ending-criminalization-truancy*.

88. Joaquin Sapien, "Time Out: Federal Complaint Alleges Rampant Abuse in Texas Truancy Program," *Pro Publica*, June 12, 2013, *www.propublica.org/article/federal-complaint-alleges-rampant-abuse-in-texas-truancy-program*.

89. Diane Ewing, Peter Clark, Stephanie Rubin, John Jacob Moreno, and Josette Saxton, "Keeping Kids in Class: Pre-K Through 2nd Grade Suspensions in Texas and a Better Way Forward," Texans Care for Children (Austin, TX, March 2018), *https://txchildren.org/s/keeping-kids-in-schools.pdf*.

90. *www.houstonchronicle.com/news/politics/texas/article/Texas-banned-out-of-school-suspensions-for-most-14398476.php*

91. Texas Education Agency, "Secondary School Completion and Dropouts in Texas Public Schools, 2017–2018," April 2018, *https://tea.texas.gov/sites/default/files/dropcomp_2017-18_v3.pdf*.

92. McNary, "Texas Leaders, Educators and Courts."

93. Morgan Smith, "Texas High School Graduation Rates among Top Nationally, but Why?" *The Texas Tribune*, November 29, 2012, *www.texastribune.org/2012/11/29/texas-high-school-graduation-rates-climb-why*.

94. *www.houstonchronicle.com/news/education/article/arae-students-school-missing-thousands-coronavirus-15261497.php*

95. Texas Education Agency, "1996–1997 Report on High School Completion Rates," August 1999, *https://tea.texas.gov/acctres/DropComp_completion_1996-97.pdf*; "Grade 9 Four-Year Longitudinal Graduation and Dropout Rates, by Race/Ethnicity, Economic Status, and Gender, Texas Public Schools, Class of 2014," August 2015, *https://rptsvr1.tea.texas.gov/acctres/completion/2014/state_demo_4yr.html*; "Secondary School Completion and Dropouts in Texas Public Schools, 2014–2015," August 2016, *https://tea.texas.gov/acctres/dropcomp_2014-15.pdf*.

96. *Education Week*, "Data: U.S. Graduation Rates by State and Student Demographics," December 7, 2017, *www.edweek.org/ew/section/multimedia/data-us-graduation-rates-by-state-and.html*.

97. Smith, "Texas High School Graduation Rates among Top Nationally."

98. Alana Semuels, "Can Texas Figure Out How to Teach English to Immigrant Children?" *The Atlantic*, March 7, 2016, *www.theatlantic.com/business/archive/2016/03/texas-experiments-with-teaching-english-language-learners/472401*.

99. Legislative Budget Board, "Texas State Government Effectiveness and Efficiency Report," January 2015, *www.lbb.state.tx.us/Documents/Publications/GEER/Government_Effectiveness_and_Efficiency_Report_2015.pdf*.

100. Laura Isensee, "Dozens of Texas Districts Must Improve Failing Schools—Or Outside Managers Could Take Over," *HoustonPublicMedia.org*, August 7, 2017, *www.houstonpublicmedia.org/articles/news/2017/08/07/228974/dozens-of-texas-districts-must-improve-failing-schools-or-outside-managers-could-take-over*.

101. Jacob Carpenter, "Close Schools? Take over Board? Give a Break? TEA Faces Big Choices on Houston ISD," *Houston Chronicle*, April 27, 2018, *www.houstonchronicle.com/news/houston-texas/houston/article/Close-schools-Take-over-board-Give-a-break-TEA-12870766.php*.

102. *www.houstonchronicle.com/news/houston-texas/houston/article/Mixed-results-follow-Texas-moves-to-replace-14297008.php?utm_source=newsletter&utm_medium=email&utm_campaign=HC_TexasTake&utm_term=news&utm_content=briefing*

103. Kiah Collier, "Texas Senate Debates School Voucher Legislation,"

Statesman, March 26, 2015, *www.statesman.com/news/news/state-regional-govt-politics/private-school-voucher-bills-face-backlash/nkf2q*.

104. Anya Kamenetz, "Department of Education Finds Texas Violated Special Education Law," NPR.org, January 11, 2018, *www.npr.org/sections/ed/2018/01/11/577400134/texas-violates-federal-law-education-department-finds*.

105. Aliyya Swaby, "Texas School Administrators Warn They Need Money for Likely Spike in Special Education," *The Texas Tribune*, April 16, 2018, *www.texastribune.org/2018/04/16/tea-richardson-special-education*.

106. Mike Glenn, "Man Levels 3-Decades-Old Bullying Charge against Katy ISD Superintendent at Public Session," Chron.com, March 26, 2018, *www.chron.com/neighborhood/katy-news/article/Katy-ISD-superintendent-accused-of-being-school-12768656.php*.

107. Herbert Gambrell, "Lamar, Mirabeau Buonaparte," *Handbook of Texas Online*, June 15, 2010, *https://tshaonline.org/handbook/online/articles/fla15*.

108. Vivian Elizabeth Smyrl, "Permanent University Fund," *Handbook of Texas Online*, June 15, 2010, *www.tshaonline.org/handbook/online/articles/khp02*.

109. *www.statesman.com/news/20180808/approval-of-record-1-billion-payout-from-endowment-on-regents-plate*

110. John Newton, "Available University Fund: Summary of Recommendations –Senate," State of Texas, Legislative Budget Board (Austin, TX: January 23, 2017), 4, *www.lbb.state.tx.us/documents/sfc_summary_recs/85r/agency_799.pdf*.

111. Lauren McGaughy, "Rep. Turner Wants to Give UH Access to Permanent University Fund," Chron.com, March 9, 2015, *www.chron.com/local/education/campus-chronicles/article/Houston-rep-UH-shouldn-t-take-back-seat-to-UT-6123579.php*.

112. Ryan McCrimmon and Bobby Blanchard, "Deregulating Tuition Slowed Increase, Universities Say," *The Texas Tribune*, March 17, 2015, *www.texastribune.org/2015/03/17/deregulating-tuition-slowed-increase-universities-*.

113. Rebecca Ayers, "Study: Here's Where Texas Ranks Among States with Most Student Debt," *Dallas Business Journal*, July 12, 2019, https://www.bizjournals.com/dallas/news/2019/07/12/texas-student-debt-wallethub.html

114. *www.texastribune.org/2019/10/23/student-debt-not-just-millennial-problem/?+Texas+Tribune+Master*

115. *Texas Association of Community Colleges*, "Community College Enrollment," n.d., *www.tacc.org/pages/data-and-info/community-college-enrollment*.

116. *tacc.org/sites/default/files/documents/2018-08/copy_of_tacc_fy_2018_tax_report_-_community_colleges.pdf*

117. Matthew Watkins, "Agency Staff: Texas Doesn't Need Any More Traditional Veterinary Schools," *The Texas Tribune*, July 20, 2016, *www.texastribune.org/2016/07/20/texas-new-veterinary-school-higher-education*.

118. *www.dallasnews.com/news/education/2017/12/31/only-half-of-latino-college-students-graduate-what-are-texas-schools-doing-to-help*

119. Jolie McCullough and Alexa Ura, "Long Way Home: Census Details Texas Commutes," *The Texas Tribune*, August 27, 2015, *www.texastribune.org/2015/08/27/where-suburban-texans-commute-work*.

120. Aman Batheja, "Tolling Texans: Impact of Trans-Texas Corridor Seen in Road Projects," *The Texas Tribune*, December 3, 2012, *www.texastribune.org/2012/12/03/tolling-texans-impact-trans-texas-corridor-lingers*.

121. Junfeng Jiao and Nicole McGrath, "Where Are the 'Transit Deserts' in Texas?" *Houston Chronicle*, July 26, 2017, *www.houstonchronicle.com/local/gray-matters/amp/Where-are-the-transit-deserts-in-Texas-11437081.php*.

122. *www.houstonchronicle.com/news/transportation/article/Texas-has-not-had-a-death-free-day-on-its-roads-14818569.php?utm_campaign=CMS%20Sharing%20Tools%20(Premium)&utm_source=t.co&utm_medium=referral*

123. StateImpact, "Everything You Need to Know about the Texas Drought," n.d., *https://stateimpact.npr.org/texas/tag/drought*.

124. Texas Commission on Environmental Quality, "List of Texas PWSs Limiting Water Use to Avoid Shortages," July 3, 2018, *www.tceq.texas.gov/drinkingwater/trot/droughtw.html*; Ross Ramsey, "What Drought? Just Don't Tread on Our Green Grass," *New York Times*, March 23, 2013, *www.nytimes.com/2013/03/24/us/in-texas-suburbs-water-restrictions-are-touchy-subject.html*; Jennifer Walker and Ruthie Redmond, "Securing Texas' Water Future, One Lawn at a Time," *TribTalk.com*, April 12, 2018, *www.tribtalk.org/2018/04/12/securing-texas-water-future-one-lawn-at-a-time*.

125. Walker and Redmond, "Securing Texas' Water Future."

126. Texas Water Development Board, "2017 Texas State Water Plan," n.d., *https://2017.texasstatewaterplan.org/statewide*.

127. Neena Satija, "Friday Night Football Returns to Water Politics," *The Texas Tribune*, January 30, 2015, *www.texastribune.org/2015/01/30/after-prop-6-water-politics-back-friday-night-foot*.

128. Ibid.

129. StateImpact, "Everything You Need to Know."

130. Mallory Falk, "For El Paso and Ciudad Juarez, Managing Scarce Water Is Critical," TPR.org, March 16, 2018, *http://tpr.org/post/el-paso-and-ciudad-juarez-managing-scarce-water-critical*.

131. Matt Tresaugue, "Air Pollution Is Still Harming Houstonians," *Houston Chronicle*, January 18, 2018, *www.houstonchronicle.com/opinion/outlook/article/Tresaugue-Air-pollution-is-still-harming-12508728.php*; Jamie Smith Hopkins, "In Texas, Environmental Officials Align with Polluters," *National Geographic*, March 17, 2015, *https://news.nationalgeographic.com/2015/03/20150317-ozone-air-pollution-clean-air-act-smog-texas-houston-dallas*; and U.S. Energy Information Administration,

"Energy-Related Carbon Dioxide Emissions by State, 2000–2015," January 2018, *www.eia.gov/environment/emissions/state/analysis/pdf/stateanalysis.pdf*.

132. Environment Texas Research and Policy Center, "Troubled Waters 2018: Industrial Pollution Still Threatens America's Waterways," *Environment Texas*, March 15, 2018, *https://environmenttexas.org/reports/txc/troubled-waters-2018*.

133. *https://environmenttexas.org/news/txe/polluters-spewed-63-million-pounds-unauthorized-air-pollution-2017-few-penalized*

134. Christopher Collins, "The 7 Most Pressing Issues Facing Rural Texas," *Texas Observer*, December 20, 2017, *www.texasobserver.org/7-pressing-issues-facing-rural-texas*.

135. Erin Schumaker, "Researchers Discover New Source of Airborne Antibiotic-Resistant Bacteria," *Huffington Post*, April 1, 2015, *www.huffingtonpost.com/2015/04/01/texas-scientists-find-ant_n_6972362.html*.

136. Eva Hershaw, "Texas Scientists Find Antibiotic Resistance Blowing in Wind," *The Texas Tribune*, March 29, 2015, *www.texastribune.org/2015/03/29/scientists-find-antibiotic-resistance-blowing-nort*.

137. Naveena Sadasivam, "After 17 Years, EPA Settles Racial Discrimination Case against TCEQ," *Texas Observer*, June 2, 2017, *www.texasobserver.org/after-17-years-epa-settles-racial-discrimination-case-against-tceq*.

138. U.S. Energy Information Administration, "Texas State Profile and Energy Estimates," Last updated January 18, 2018, *www.eia.gov/state/analysis.php?sid=TX*.

139. Vandana Ravikumar, "Not Blowing Smoke: Wind has Overtaken 'Risky' Coal for Energy Use in Texas for the First Time" *USA Today*, July 24, 2019, *https://www.usatoday.com/story/news/nation/2019/07/24/wind-beats-coal-energy-usage-texas-first-time-report/1822043001/*.

140. Kate Galbraith, "Texplainer: Why Does Texas Have Its Own Power Grid?" *The Texas Tribune*, February 8, 2011, *www.texastribune.org/2011/02/08/texplainer-why-does-texas-have-its-own-power-grid*.

141. Ryan Maye Handy, "Texas Wind Power Continues to Dominate," Chron.com, February 1, 2018, *www.chron.com/business/energy/article/Texas-wind-power-continues-to-dominate-12536484.php*; Dan Solomon, "Why Texas Uses More Energy Than Any Other State," *Texas Monthly*, August 2, 2017, *www.texasmonthly.com/energy/texas-uses-energy-state*; *https://www.eia.gov/state/?sid=TX*.

142. Jim Malewitz, "First Wind, Now Gas: Tax Breaks Face Scrutiny," *The Texas Tribune*, October 10, 2014, *www.texastribune.org/2014/10/20/big-tax-break-natural-gas-get-scrutiny*.

143. Denise Marquez, "Wind Energy Technology Booms, Increases Roles in Texas Electricity Power," *Lubbock Avalanche-Journal*, March 5, 2016, *http://lubbockonline.com/business/2016-03-05/wind-energy-technology-booms-increases-role-texas-electricity-power#0020*.

CREDITS

PHOTOS

Chapter 1
p. 2: Dirt Nap Outfitters; p. 8: The Lyda Hill Texas Collection of Photographs in Carol M. Highsmith's America Project, Library of Congress, Prints and Photographs Division; p. 16 Nathan Hunsinger/Dallas News; p. 23: Russell Lee Photograph Collection, The Dolph Briscoe Center for American History, The University of Texas at Austin; p. 31: Andrew D. Brosig/Tyler Morning Telegraph via AP

Chapter 2
p. 34 Texas Parks & Wildlife; p. 38: Wilson Special Collections Library, University of North Carolina at Chapel Hill; p. 41: Dolph Briscoe Center for American History; p. 43: John Anderson/The Austin Chronicle; p. 49: Bob Daemmrich; p. 52: By permission of Tom Phillips; p. 54: Nick Anderson Editorial Cartoon used with the permission of Nick Anderson, the Washington Post Writers Group and the Cartoonist Group. All rights reserved.

Chapter 3
p. 68: Stephen Spillman for The San Antonio Express-News; p. 71: Photo by Joe Raedle/Getty Images; p. 75: John Burnett/NPR; p. 76: Jay Janner/Austin American-Statesman via AP; p. 90: Stuart Borrett/flickr

Chapter 4
p. 98: Michael Ciaglo/©Houston Chronicle. Used with permission; p. 102: courtesy, Carmen Ayala; p.111: courtesy, Victor Morales; p. 116: FREDERIC J. BROWN/AFP via Getty Images; p. 122: Gary Varvel Editorial Cartoon used with the permission of Gary Varvel and Creators Syndicate. All rights reserved; p. 124: Marie D. DeJesus/©Houston Chronicle. Used with permission of Joyce Lee; p. 128: Texans for Greg Abbott

Chapter 5
p. 136: Bob Daemmrich for The Texas Tribune; p. 142: Photo by Dan Keshet; 147: Nick Anderson Editorial Cartoon used with the permission of Nick Anderson, the Washington Post Writers Group and the Cartoonist Group. All rights reserved; p. 153: © Robert Hughes/ZUMA Press/Alamy; p. 156: By permission of Jared Woodfill; p. 159: © 2012 The Atlantic Media Co., as first published in The Atlantic Magazine. All rights reserved. Distributed by Tribune Content Agency, LLC; p. 160: Photo by Rick Scibelli/Getty Images; p. 166: AP Photo/Ferd Kaufman

Chapter 6
p. 172: Farm and Ranch Freedom Alliance; p. 174: RoadsideAmerica.com; p. 176: Hunter L/Shutterstock; p. 178: Ralph Barrera/Austin American-Statesman via AP; p. 197: 1970/140–01, Courtesy of Texas State Library and Archives Commission

Chapter 7
p. 206: Bob Daemmrich; p. 226: Gabriel C. Pérez/KUT; p. 228: Deborah Cannon/Austin American-Statesman via AP; p. 231: Rodolfo Gonzalez/Austin American-Statesman via AP; p. 232: Texas Senate Media Services; p. 233: Jay Janner/Austin American-Statesman via AP; p. 234: AP Photo/Eric Gay; p. 239: AP Photo/Eric Gay

Chapter 8
p. 244: Eric Gay/AP/Shutterstock; p. 247: © Jeff Newman/Globe Photos/ZUMAPRESS.com/Alamy; p. 255: Photo by Frederick M. Brown/Getty Images; p. 263: Rod Aydelotte/Waco Tribune-Herald via AP; p. 265: Bob Daemmrich for The Texas Tribune; p. 270: Ann W. Richards Papers, The Dolph Briscoe Center for American History, The University of Texas at Austin

Chapter 9
p. 278: © Ashley Landis/Dallas News; p. 283: Laura Skelding for The Texas Tribune; p. 291: Bob Daemmrich/Alamy Stock Photo; p. 295: AP Photo/Stephan Savoia; p. 297: Reshma Kirpalani/Austin American-Statesman via AP; p. 300: AP Photo/Juan Carlos Llorca, File; p. 302: HeliBacon; p. 307: Robert T. Garrett/Dallas News

Chapter 10
p. 316: The Lyda Hill Texas Collection of Photographs in Carol M. Highsmith's America Project, Library of Congress, Prints and Photographs Division; p. 337: courtesy, Rebeca Huddle

Chapter 11
p. 352: Tom Fox/The Dallas Morning News via AP, Pool; p. 355 Jon Shapley/©Houston Chronicle. Used with permission; p. 359: Photo by Taylor Hill/Getty Images; p. 362: AP Photo/Houston Chronicle, Mayra Beltran; p. 363: Texas Prison Museum; p. 370: Ricardo B. Brazziell/Austin American-Statesman via AP; p. 377: Waller County Sheriff's Department via AP; p. 378: By permission of Cathy Cochran

Chapter 12
p. 382: Andrew D. Brosig/The Tyler Morning Telegraph via AP; p. 386: Nick Anderson Editorial Cartoon used with the permission of Nick Anderson, the Washington Post Writers Group and the Cartoonist Group. All rights reserved; p. 388: REUTERS/Jim Young; p. 390: iStockPhoto; p. 392 Thomas Jackson/StockimoNews/Alamy Live News; p. 393: courtesy, Barry Klein, Texas Property Rights Association; p. 400: Guiseppe Barranco/Beaumont Enterprise; p. 401: AP Photo/Wilfredo Lee; p. 411: PHOTO BY NASA

Chapter 13
p. 416: Photo by Ben Porter; p. 424: REX C CURRY/The New York Times/Redux; p. 428: Patric Schneider; p. 435: Bob Dammerich

Chapter 14
p. 440: Nathan Lambrecht; p. 445: courtesy, Eva DeLuna Castro; p. 454: Todd Heisler/The New York Times/Redux; p. 459: AP Photo/Eric Gay; Shelby Webb/©Houston Chronicle. Used with permission

FIGURES

Chapter 1
p. 5: University of Texas Libraries; p. 13: Texas Comptroller of Public Accounts; p. 18: US Census Bureau; p. 21: U.S. Census, Office of the State Demographer, Population Projections; p. 29: Texas Politics Project/University of Texas Polls 2020; p. 30: Texas Politics Project/University of Texas Poll, February 2019

Chapter 2
p. 46: Texas Almanac; p. 57: Texas Legislative Council; p. 58: Texas Legislative Council; p. 60: Texas Secretary of State, Election Returns; p. 62: Book of the States

Chapter 3
p. 78: Texas Tribune Polling, June 2019; p. 81: U.S. Census Bureau and Tax Foundation; p. 82: Legislative Budget Board; p. 83: Federal Emergency Management Administration

Chapter 4
p. 101: Texas Civil Rights Project; p. 104: Texas Secretary of State; p. 106: Texas Secretary of State website; p. 112: Texas Secretary of State, U.S. Census; p. 115: US Census; p. 119: US Elections Project; p. 130: National Institute on Money in State Politics

Chapter 5
p. 140: Texas Ethics Commission: p. 145: Republican Party of Texas and Texas State Democratic Party; p. 152: Legislative Reference Library of Texas; p. 154: Texas Politics Polling, 2016–2020; p. 158: Folded Ranney Index; p. 162: Texas Legislative Reference Library

Chapter 6
p. 181: US Bureau of Labor Statistics, 2018 annual averages; p. 186: Author-compiled data; p. 188: Texas Ethics Commission annual reports; p. 190: Texas Ethics Commission annual reports; p. 194: National Council of State Legislatures; p. 195: Texas Ethics Commission

Chapter 7
p. 212: Influence Opinions; p. 215; Data taken from Legislative Reference Library; p 216: National Council of State Legislatures; p. 219: Texas Legislature Online; p. 219: Guide to Legislative Information (Revised). 2019. Texas Legislative Council for the 86th Legislature; p. 236: State Ideologies Project, Boris Shor; p. 238: Texas Legislative Council; p. 240: U.S. Census Bureau, American Community Survey, 2015; Alexa Uru and Jolie McCullough,

"Once Again, the Texas Legislature is Mostly White, Male, and Middle-Aged," The Texas Tribune, January 9, 2017.

Chapter 8
p. 248: Texas State Library and Archives; p. 250; Book of the States, Bureau of the Census; p. 252: Legislative Reference Library; p. 254; Office of the Governor in each state; p. 257: Book of the States; p. 259: Texas Reference Library; p. 260: Texas Reference Library; p. 267: State of the State Speeches. Legislative Reference Library; p. 269: Website of the Governor Greg Abbott (2019); p. 272: Governor Institutional Power Index (updated measures, based on Thad Beyle, "Governors." In Virginia Gray, Herbert Jacob, and Kennith N. Vines [Eds.], *Politics in the American States*. [Boston: Little, Brown, 1983]).

Chapter 9
p. 282: US Census Bureau; p. 285: Texas Governor website; p. 287: Brandon Rottinghaus; p. 293: Texas Attorney General's Office; p. 296: Texas Comptroller's Office; p. 309: Texas Sunset Advisory Commission

Chapter 10
p. 320: Center for State Courts; p. 323: The Texas Judicial Branch website; p. 327: Annual Statistical Report for the Texas Judiciary, 2018; p. 329: Texas Legislative Council; p. 332: Annual Statistical Report of the Texas Judiciary, 2018; p. 333: 2018 Annual Texas Judicial Statistical Report; p. 336: American Judicature Society; p. 343: Texas Ethics Commission; p. 344: Annual Texas Judicial Statistical Report

Chapter 11
p. 356: Texas Tribune poll, February 2017; p. 364: Columbia University Justice Lab, 2020.; p. 366: Bureau of Justice Statistics, National Prisoner Statistics Program; p. 367: Texas Department of Criminal Justice, Statistical Report Fiscal Year 2017; p. 371: Texas Department of Criminal Justice, 2019; p. 375: The Sentencing Project. National Council of State Legislatures

Chapter 12
p. 387: US Census Bureau; p. 399: US Census Bureau; p. 405: County election websites;, Portland State University *(www.whovotesformayor.org)*; p. 407: Texas State Expenditures, Texas Comptroller of Public Accounts, 2019

Chapter 13
p. 419: Texas Comptroller of Public Accounts; p. 421: Tax Foundation; p. 429: Texas Politics Polling 2015; p. 432: Texas Comptroller of Public Accounts; p. 434: Adapted from Senate Research Center, "Budget 101: A Guide to the Budget Process in Texas," January 2011.

Chapter 14
p. 450: Ife Floyd, "TANF Cash Benefits Have Fallen by More Than 20 Percent in Most States and Continue to Erode," Center on Budget and Policy Priorities, October 13, 2017.; p. 458: National Education Association Rankings and Estimates; p. 461: Texas Public Policy Foundation, "Texas School Finance: Basics and Reform," March 2016; p. 469: *Smithsonian Magazine*; p. 471: The Texas Water Development Board

INDEX

Note: Page references followed by a *t* indicate table; *f* indicate figure; *italics* indicate photo.

Abbott, Greg, *68*
    legacy of, 3, 92, *93*, 129, 197, 252*f*,
        255, *255*, 267*f*, 268, 271, 273,
        284, 294*t*, 302, 372, 393,
        403, 435, 454
    reputation of, 69, 74–75, 77, 88,
        121, *125*, *128*, 179, 184, *184*,
        189, 245–46, 252, 253, 256,
        256, 258, 261, 264, *265*, 268,
        269*f*, 270, 274, 291, 298, 305,
        310–11, 383
abortion, 28–29, 30*f*, 182–83, 190*f*,
    233–34, *234*
ACA. *See* Affordable Care Act
accountability, 310–11
accused, rights of the, 355
acquittals, 327*f*
activism. *See also* lobbying
    by citizens, *76*, 76–77, *176*
    feminism, 184
    get out the vote, 125
    grassroots activism, 152–53, 156
    Institute for Justice, 187
    iron triangles for, 192–95, 193*t*, 194*f*
    lawsuits as, 392–94
    NRA in, *178*
    precinct chairs in, 142
    students in, 185
    taxes and, 422, *422*
    for Tejanos, 39–40
    for voting, 119*f*, 120–21, 140
Adler, Steve, 74, 75
administration, 107, 228–29, 390
ad valorem, 420
advisory groups, 266
aerial management, *302*
affiliation, in politics, 149*f*, *159*
affirmative action, 467
Affordable Care Act (ACA), 20, 87,
    447–48
affordable housing, 20
African Americans
    candidates, 153
    culture of, 9
    discrimination against, 47, 363, *363*
    economics for, 15
    history of, 44–45
    NAACP for, 182
    in politics, 238*f*, 239
    reconstruction for, 47–48

in Supreme Court (TX), 346
    voting for, 51–52, 112*f*, 113–14, 115*f*
AG. *See* attorney general
age, 23–24, 238*f*, 441, 448
agency capture, 195
agenda setting
    as informal powers, 265–71, 267*f*,
        269*f*, *270*
    policy for, 442–43, 443*f*
agriculture, 12, 84, 284, *297*, 297–98
air pollution, 472–73
alcohol, 357, 358*t*, *424*, 425–26
Allred, James V., 261
amendments, 226
    of Constitution (TX), 56–61, 57*f*,
        58*f*, 59*t*, 60*f*
    reform for, 61–64, 62*f*
America's Party, 165
amicus curiae briefs, 187, 326
Anchia, Rafael, 347
Andrade, Hope, 299
Anglos
    conflict for, 39
    culture of, 7–8, *8*
    politics for, 113–14
    voting by, 148
    Voting Rights Act (1965) for, 108
annexation, 41–42, 392–94
annual legislative sessions, 218
appellate courts, 319, 326–30, 327*f*, 329*f*
appointees, 273
appointment powers
    for governors, 252, 254*f*, 255, *255*,
        299–303, *300*, *302*
    psychology of, 274
apportionment, 157–58, 158*f*
appropriation bills, 433–36, *435*
Arizona v. United States, 73*t*
Armbrister, Kenneth, 193*t*
Armey, Dick, 153
arraignment, 361
Articles of Texas Constitution, 50–51, 51*t*
Asian Americans
    culture of, 21
    in politics, *300*
    in Supreme Court (TX), 346
    voting for, 116, *116*
AstroTurf lobbying, 184–85
at-large voting, 132
attorney general (AG)

in plural executive structure,
        292–94, *295*
    politics of, 293*f*, 294*t*
Austin (city), *43*, 74–75
Austin, Kirk, 232
Austin, Stephen F., 8, 37–38, *38*, 354
authority
    agencies and, 285*f*
    autonomy as, 86–87
    budget powers, 268, 275
    bureaucracy and, 61, 63
    for citizens, 58–59
    coercive federalism, 87
    concurrent powers, 74–75, *75*
    conflict with, 111
    of Constitution (TX), 246
    of Constitution (US), 47
    cooperative federalism, 85–86
    for courts, 63
    dual federalism, 84–85, *85*
    enumerated powers, 71–72
    of federalism, *76*, 76–80, 78*f*
    of government, 48
    for governors, 251, 252, 252*f*,
        254*f*, *255*, 255–56, 255–62, 257*f*,
        259*f*–60*f*
    implied powers, 72
    for judiciary, 43, 317–18
    law enforcement, 74–75, *75*
    of legislative redistricting board,
        159, 161
    of legislators, 208–11, 209*t*, *211*
    for lieutenant governors, 287*f*
    of local government, 53,
        384–86, *386*
    local politics and, 19*t*
    new federalism, 86–87
    pardons, 262
    policy for, 56
    of political parties, 273–74
    in politics, 15, 41
    preemptions, 89
    removal powers, 274–75
    Senate (TX) and, 289
    separation of powers, 42–43
    speaker of the house and, 223
    for Supreme Court (TX), 328, 331
    United States and, 88, 90, *90*,
        272*f*, 287*f*
    in voting, 63

autonomy, 86–87
available school fund, 455
Avery v. Midland County, 388
ayuntamiento, 7

Bafumi, Joseph, 140–41
bail, 360, 376–77
Bailey, Ken, 397
Baker v. Carr, 73*t*, 159
banking, 53
bankruptcy, 412
Barnes, Ben, 221–22, 231, 288*t*, 291
base identity, in politics, 125
Bean, Jack, 123
Bean, Roy, 354
Bell, Cecil, 202, 228
Bell, Chris, 168
Benavides, Plácido, 40
bench trials, 325
benefits, 175–79, *178*, 449
Bentsen, Lloyd, 148
Bettencourt, Paul, 297–98
Beverly, Patrick, 357
bicameral legislature, 208
biennial revenue estimate (BRE), 433
bill of rights, 36–37, 54–55, 61–63
bills. *See also* law; legislators;
    resolutions
    appropriation bills, 433–36, *435*
    calendars for, *228*, 228–29
    data for, 267*f*
    debates for, *226*, 226–27
    partisanship for, 227
    policy for, 229–30, 229*t*
    readings of, 224–27, 225*f*, *226*,
      235–37
    "Save Chick-fil-A" bill, 191, 232
    in special sessions, 214, 256–58, 257*f*
    vetoes of, 259*f*
black codes, 47
Bland, Sandra, *377*
block grants, 86–87
Blue Bell ice cream licker, *334*
Blue Lives Matter, *355*
boards, for legislators, 217
Bohac, Dwayne, 199*t*
bonds, 400, 408–9
Bonnen, Dennis, 189, *206*, 222*t*
border security. *See* immigration
Bramblett, C. R. "Kit," 359
Branick, Jeff, 163
BRE. *See* biennial revenue estimate
Brehm, Cynthia, 143
bribery, 173–74. *See also* ethics;
    scandals
Briscoe, Dolph, *124*, 248*f*, 256, 376
Brodnax, T. C., 395
Brown, Ashley, 461–62
Buckingham, Brad, *325*
Bucy, John, *211*
budgets
    budget execution, 266
    budget powers, 268, 275

certification for, 436
comptroller of public accounts,
    294–96, 296*f*
cycles for, 430
data for, 432*f*
dual budgeting process, 433
funding for, 425–28, *428*, 429*f*
LBB, 431, 433–36, 434*f*
learning objectives for, 417, 438
policy for, 430–37, 431*t*, 432*f*,
    434*f*, *435*
politics of, 266–68
practice quizzes for, 439
revenue and, 418–25, 419*f*, 421*f*, *422*
Buffett, Warren, 175
Bullock, Bob, 237, 266, 289, 295
    Bush, G. W., and, 288–89
    Hobby, W. P., Jr., *vs.*, 289
    legacy of, 288*t*, 289–90
    reputation of, 197, 286, 298, 427
bullying, 464–65
bureaucracy
    authority and, 61, 63
    for governors, 285*f*
    learning objectives for, 279, 312–14
    organization of, 284–86, 285*f*
    policy and, 281, *281*, *283*, 283–84,
      305–11, 308*t*, 309*f*
    practice quizzes for, 315
    revolving door theory of, 193
    theory of, 279–81
    in United States, 282*f*
Burka, Paul, 418
Bush, Barbara, 149–50
Bush, George H. W., 150
Bush, George P., 91
Bush, George W., 137, 153
    Bullock and, 288–89
    legacy of, 260*f*, 370, 376
    reputation of, 265–66, 286, 295, 428
business
    business groups, 179–80
    taxes, 423

Cabeza de Vaca, Álvar Núñez, 6
Cain, Briscoe, *211*
calendars, for bills, *228*, 228–29
California
    employment in, 12
    Garza v. County of Los Angeles, 111
    Hispanics in, 21
    workers' compensation in, 451
Calver, Drew, 279
Campaign Finance Act (1995), 347
campaigns
    citizens in, 129, 130*f*, 131, *184*,
      184–85
    economics of, 126–28, 127*t*, *128*
    for elections, 123–28, *124*, 127*t*, *128*
    Federal Election Campaign Act, 128
    industry in, 130*f*
    negative campaigning and, 124, *125*
Campbell, Donna, 218

Canales, Terry, 15
candidates
    African American, 153
    for citizens, 163–64
    funding for, 348*t*
    Hispanic, *166*, 166–67
    informal qualifications for, 247, *247*
    party switching for, 163–64
    recruitment of, 139, 140*f*
    women, 167
Canion, Rod, 14
Cantu, Ramsey, 143
Capriglione, Giovanni, 310
capture, 472
Carillo, O. P., 249
cars, 424. *See also* transportation
Carter, Clyde, 383
Carter, Jimmy, 126
caseload, 331
casework, 211
cash, 406–8
Castro, Eva DeLuna, 445, *445*
categorical grants, 86
cattle, 12
censure, for justices, 338
centralization, 39, *76*, 76–77
certification, 436
charters, 391
Chick-fil-A, 191, 232
Children's Health Insurance Program
    (CHIP), 447–48
Chinese Exclusion Act, 117–18
Christian, Wayne, 213
Christian Party, 165
chubbing, 234
cities
    city elections, 403
    debt in, 410*t*
    home rule cities, 391–94
    local government in, *390*, 391–98,
      395*f*, 397
    regulation and, 385–86, *386*
    sanctuary cities, 92
citizens, 225*f*
    activism by, *76*, 76–77, *176*
    advisory groups for, 266
    AstroTurf lobbying, 184–85
    authority for, 58–59
    in campaigns, 129–31, 130*f*, *184*,
      184–85
    candidates for, 163–64
    discrimination for, 353–54, *377*
    HHSC for, 299–300
    interest groups for, 180–82, 181*f*, *182*
    justice for, 322
    language for, 62*f*
    League of United Latin American
      Citizens v. Perry, 160
    opinions for, 454–55
    politics for, 59–61, 60*f*
    psychology of, 106*f*, 151–53
    public opinion polling, 123
    representation for, 77, 78*f*, 281, 282*f*

Citizens United v. Federal Election Commission, 126
city managers, 396–97, *397*
civil cases, 319, 321
Civil Rights Act, 150
Civil War, 44–45, *62f*
Clancy, Jim, 200
clauses
  commerce clause, 72
  full faith and credit clause, 75
  necessary and proper clause, 72
  reserve clause, 74
  supremacy clause, 71
Clayton, Billy, 185, *196t*, *222t*
clemency, 262
Clements, Bill, 150, 155, 166–67, 264, 331
  legacy of, 173, *252f*, *259f*
  reputation of, 252, 261, 269
  White and, 270
closed primaries, 102
coalitions, 191, 230–37, *231–34*, *236f*
Cochran, Cathy, 378, *378*
coercive federalism, 87
COGs. *See* councils of governments
Coke, Richard, 49–50, 322
Coleman, Garnet, 218
collateral consequences, 373
college, 29–31, 400–401, 466
colonialism, 38–39
Colorado, 12
Colquitt, Oscar Branch, *363*, *363*
Combs, Susan, 295–96, 409
commerce
  commerce clause, 72
  politics of, 179
commissions
  agriculture commissioner, *297*, 297–98
  Citizens United v. Federal Election Commission, 126
  commissioners, *297*, 297–98
  commission governments, *395f*, 396–97
  HHSC, 299–300, 446
  multimember elected commissions, 303–4
  PUC, 301
  State Commission on Judicial Conduct, 338
  Sunset Advisory Commission, 307–11, *308t*, *309f*
  TABC, 187, 310
  TCEQ, 89, 302, 472–73
  TEC, 198–201, *199t*, *200f*, 304–6
  Texas Commission on Judicial Selection, 346–47
  Texas Indigent Defense Commission, 355
  Texas Racing Commission, 283
  Texas Workforce Commission, 176–77, 255, 451, 453
  TRC, 195, 303–4, 306

committees, 220–21, 224–28, *225f*
common core standards, 94
common law, 321
communication
  for courts, *73t*
  for government, *62f*
  of ideology, 140–41
  inaugural speeches, 268
  language and, *145f*
  in leadership, 264
  lobbying as, 192
  party executive committees for, 143–44
  state-of-the-state address, 269
  Texas Register, 281
community
  community colleges, 400–401, 466
  community supervision, *363*, 363–64, *364f*
  government and, 71
  leadership in, 396
  neighborhood precincts, 105
compensation, 173, 451
competition, 156–65, *158f*, *159*, *160*, *162f*
comptroller of public accounts, 294–96, *296f*
concurrent powers, 74–75, *75*
concurrent resolutions, 209
conditional preemptions, 89
confederal system, 70–71
Confederate flags, 55
conflict
  for Anglos, 39
  with authority, 111
  in centralization, *76*, 76–77
  ethnicity-related, 6
  in federalism, 89–94, *90*, *93*
  history of, 29–31, *31*
  militias in, 76
  with Native Americans, 7
Connally, John, 231–32, *248f*, 249, 252
conservatives, 138–39, *147*, 157, *159*. *See also* Republican Party; Tea Party
Constitution (TX)
  1836 version, 40–42, *41*
  1845 version, 42–44, *43*
  1861 version, 45, *46f*
  1866 version, 45, 47
  1869 version, 47–49, *49*
  1876 version, 49–55, *51t*, *53f*, *54f*
  amendments of, 56–61, *57f*, *58f*, *59t*, *60f*
  Articles of Texas Constitution, 50–51, *51t*
  authority of, 246
  constitutional convention (1974), 61–63
  Declaration of Independence (TX) for, 37–40, *38*, *39t*
  dual structure in, 328
  for government, 36–37, *37*
  individualism in, 69–70, 94–95

law in, 110, 251, 252, *252f*
learning objectives for, 35, 65–66
policy in, 279–80
practice quizzes for, 66–67
reform for, 61–64, *62f*
United States and, *62f*
Constitution (US)
  authority of, 47
  commerce clause, 72
  discrimination and, 54–55
  enumerated powers, 71–72
  full faith and credit clause, 75
  implied powers, 72
  necessary and proper clause, 72
  reserve clause, 74
  supremacy clause, 71
Constitutional convention (1974), 61–63
constitutional county courts, 324–25
consumers, 64, 406, 418–20, *419f*, *421f*
controversies, 281, *288t*
convenience voting, 120
conventions, 147–48
convictions, *327f*
Cook, Byron, 222
Cook, Kerry Max, 378
Cooke, C. C. "Kit," 239
cooperation, 409–11
cooperative federalism, 85–86
Cornyn, John, 292–94, *294t*, 321–22
corporations, 14, 173–74, 283–84, 423
corruption, 404–6
cotton, 10, 85, *85*
Couch, Ethan, 334
councils
  council-manager system, 396–97, *397*
  Electrical Reliability Council of Texas, 473–74
  for legislators, 217
  mayor-council system, 394–96, *395f*
councils of governments (COGs), 409–10
counties
  Avery v. Midland County, 388
  county administrators, 390
  county elections, 403
  county party chairs, *142*, 142–43
  county trial courts, 324–25
  expenditures for, *407f*
  finance officials, 390
  Garza v. County of Los Angeles, 111
  local government in, *19t*, 386–90, *387f*, *388*, *390*
  sheriffs, 389
  single-member districts, 111
  slavery for, *46f*
courting, for votes, 125
courts, 339–41, *339t*. *See also specific courts*
  appellate courts, 319, 326–30, *327f*, *329f*
  authority of, 63

courts *(cont.)*
  civil cases in, 319, 321
  communication for, 73*t*
  criminal cases in, 319, 321
  drug court, 368
  economics of, 341–42
  filing fees, 426, 427
  grand juries, 361, 377
  jurisdiction of, 319
  jury trials, 361–62, *362*
  municipal courts, 322–24
  in politics, 161–63
  probate courts, 325
  systems for, 323*f*
  trial courts, 320*f*, 322–26, 323*f*
  TWIA in, 175, 342
COVID-19 pandemic, 16, 79, 184, 420,
    451, 462, 466
Craddick, Christi, 195
Craddick, Tom, 222, 222*t*, 235
Craymer, Dale, 422, *422*
credit claiming, 213
Crigler, Marya, *422*
Crime Victim's Compensation Act, 357
criminal justice. *See also* felons;
    judiciary
  criminal appeals, 328–30, 329*f*
  criminal cases, 319, 321
  criminal disenfranchisement, 374
  criminal sentencing, 342
  death penalty, 369–73, 371*f*, 373*t*,
    377–79
  DNA evidence, 377–79
  drug crimes, 358–59, *359*
  incarceration, 365–68, 366*f*–67*f*
  juvenile crime, 359
  learning objectives for, *353*,
    379–80
  misdemeanors, 321, 357, 358*t*
  policy for, 354–57, 356*f*
  practice quizzes for, 381
  pretrials in, 360–61
  punishment, *363*, 363–64, 364*f*
  reform and, 376–79
  sex offenders, *390*
  trial courts, 320*f*, 322–26, 323*f*
  trials, 361–62, *362*
  voter fraud, 121–23, *122*
critical thinking, 18
cronyism, 274
Cruz, Ted, 126, 132, 153, *362*
culture
  African American, 9
  Anglo, 7–8, *8*
  Asian American, 21
  convenience voting, 120
  of conventions, 147–48
  of cotton, 10
  Democratic Party, 140*f*, *160*, 160–61
  family values, 28–29, 30*f*
  Hispanic, 7, 133
  history of, 64–65
  of individualism, 37

individualistic political culture,
    26–28, 26*t*, 27*t*
  of labor, 63
  learning objectives for, 3, 32
  of legislators, 229*t*
  of militias, 48
  moralistic political culture, 26*t*, 31
  name identification in, 124
  Native American, 4–6, 5*f*
  pioneer, 24–25
  political culture, 3–4, 24–31, 26*t*,
    27*t*, 29*f*, 30*f*, 35
  of political parties, 60*f*, 131
  political socialization, 118
  practice quizzes for, 32–33
  principles and, 50–55, 51*t*, 52, 53*f*, *54*
  of recreation, 14
  of reform, 58*t*
  Republican Party, 137–38, 155
  The Right to Vote (Keyssar), 107
  of settlement, 46*f*
  Spanish settlers, 6–7
  Tejano, 7
  traditionalistic political culture,
    26*t*, 28–30, 29*f*, 30*f*
  tradition in, 64
  weather and, *16*
cumulative voting, 404
Cunningham, Walter, 268
Curtis, Gregory, 417–18
cycles, budget, 430

Daniel, Price, 248*f*, 285
Darby, Drew, 471
data
  abortion, 30*f*
  amendment, 57*f*, 58*f*, 60*f*
  on attorneys general, 293*f*
  on bills passed, 215*f*
  budget allocation, 432*f*
  campaign contribution, 130*f*, 343*f*
  community supervision, 364*f*
  on conviction rate, 327*f*
  correctional population, 366*f*, 367*f*
  county expenditure, 407*f*
  on court case length, 332*f*
  court demographic, 344*f*
  on death sentences, 371*f*
  district, 399*f*
  endorsement, 186*f*
  ethics, 200*f*
  executive order, 252*f*, 254*f*
  federal aid, 81*f*–83*f*
  government approval, 78*f*
  on governors, 248*f*, 250*f*, 267*f*, 272*f*
  judicial salary, 333*f*
  legislative, 236*f*, 238*f*, 240*f*
  on lieutenant governor, 287*f*
  lobbying, 188*f*, 190*f*, 194*f*
  local government, 387*f*
  mayoral election, 405*f*
  on police, 356*f*
  political party, 149*f*, 152*f*, 154*f*, 158*f*

political spending, 140*f*
  population, 18*f*, 21*f*
  public education funding, 458*f*
  on reelection rate, 219*f*
  registration, 101*f*
  on religion, 29*f*
  session length, 216*f*
  special-purpose district, 399*f*
  special session, 257*f*
  state constitution, 62*f*
  on state government size, 282*f*
  sunset agency, 309*f*
  tax, 296*f*, 419*f*, 421*f*, 429*f*
  transportation, 469*f*
  trial court, 320*f*
  on union membership, 181*f*
  on U.S. House of Representatives, 162*f*
  veto, 259*f*, 260*f*
  voting, 104*f*, 105*f*, 112*f*, 115*f*, 119*f*, 375*f*
  water supply and demand, 471*f*
  welfare benefit, 450*f*
David's Law, 465
Davis, Edmund J., 48–50, 54, 146, 271
Davis, Wendy, 124, 233–34, *234*
death penalty, 369–73, 371*f*
  ideology of, 373*t*
  reform and, *370*, 377–79
debates
  on abortion, 233–34, *234*
  on annual legislative sessions, 218
  for bills, *226*, 226–27
  on budget powers of governor, 268
  on drug testing for public
    benefits, 449
  on fees for unpaid fines, 427
  on free speech, 55
  in House of Representatives
    (TX), 223
  on legal defense funds, 201
  on mail-in voting, 132
  on mandatory retirement age for
    judges, 348
  on paid sick leave, 385
  on party switching, 164
  prisons in, *363*, 363–64, 369
  on sanctuary cities, 92
  on state documents, 15
  on sunset laws, 311
  on taxes, 428
debt, 408–9, 410*t*, 427
decentralization, 141–42
Declaration of Independence (TX)
  history of, 37–40, *38*, 39*t*
  politics of, 39–40, 39*t*
  psychology of, 35–36
dedicated revenue, 431, 431*t*
Deepwater Horizon, 84
defense industries, 12–13
Defense of Marriage Act, 75
deferrals, 437
deferred adjudication, 261
DeLay, Tom, 151, 160, 168–69
delegates, 35, 47, 63, 213

DeLeon, Martin, 8
Dell, Michael, 14
democracy, 35–36, 78–79, 475
Democratic Party. *See also* political
    parties
    culture of, 140*f*, *160*, 160–61
    Hispanics for, 166–67
    history of, 137–38, 146–48, *147*, 149*f*
    identification with, 154*f*
    ideology of, 161–63, 162*f*
    psychology of, 155
    recruiting by, 403
    Republican *vs.*, 143–44, 145*f*, 149*f*,
        152*f*, 168–69, 236*f*, 383
demographics
    of delegates, 47
    of early voters, 104*f*
    of employed persons, 4
    ethnolinguistic distribution, 5*f*
    and government, 16–24, 18*f*, 19*t*,
        21*f*, *23*
    of justices, 342–46, 344*f*, *345*
    learning objectives for, 3, 32
    of legislators, 237–40, 238*f*, 240*f*
    of lobbyists, 188*f*
    in politics, 168–69
    practice quizzes for, 32–33
    of prison population, 367*f*
    reapportionment for, 157
    and support for secession, 46*f*
    of union members, 181*f*
    of United States, 18*f*, 119*f*
Department of Family and Protective
        Services, 306–7
Department of Public Safety, 249–50
deportation, 454–55
Dewhurst, David, 234–35, 291, *291*
DeWitt, Green, 8
diacritical marks, 15
Diaz, Chris, 99
Dickey, James, 143
Dillon's rule, 384–85
disasters
    environmental quality after, 302
    Federal Emergency Relief Act,
        85–86
    funding for, 80, 82, 83*f*
    government in, 83*f*
    management of, *71*, 83*f*
    for United States, 84
discharge petitions, 236
disclosure, 176, 202
discrimination
    against African Americans, 47,
        363, *363*
    Constitution (US) and, 54–55
    Fifteenth Amendment, 112*f*,
        113–14, 115*f*
    against Hispanics, 161–63
    "Jim Crow" laws, 108
    against minorities, 161, 356*f*, 367*f*,
        370–72
    by police, 353–54, *377*

religion and, 392
Shelby County v. Holder, 90, 93
voter identification, 121–23, *122*
Voting Rights Act (1965), 90, 93
white primaries, 108–9
disenfranchisement, 107, 374
dismissals, of cases, 331
dispositions, 331, 332*f*
districts
    court of appeals districts, 329*f*
    hospital districts, 401–2
    legislative redistricting board,
        159, 161
    MUD, 401, *401*
    public improvement districts, 401
    redistricting, 159, 161–63, 162*f*
    single-member districts, 111
    special districts, 398–401, 399*f*,
        400–401
    for state district courts, 325–26, 327*f*
    unincorporated areas, 388, 393
    in United States, 399*f*
distrust, 27–28
diversity
    benefits and challenges of, 8
    in government, *300*, 342–46,
        344*f*, *345*
    policies to improve, 9
    in public education, 461–62, 463*t*
DNA evidence, 377–79
Dobie, Frank, 26
Dominguez, Philip, 422
driver's licenses, 311
Driving While Intoxicated (DWI), 357,
    358*t*, 426
drugs, 358–59, *359*, 368, 449
dual budgeting process, 433
dual federalism, 84–85, *85*
dual structure, 328
Dukes, Dawnna, 199*t*
Dunn, Tim, 131
Dunnam, Jim, 161
Duval, Duke of, 110
Duverger, Maurice, 165
Duverger's law, 165
Duyne, Beth Van, 394
DWI. *See* Driving While Intoxicated

Early, Robert, 186
early voting, 103–4, 104*f*
Ebola virus, *388*
economics. *See also* salaries
    ad valorem, 420
    bail, 360, 376–77
    bonds, 400, 408–9
    BRE, 433
    budget execution, 266
    of campaigns, 126–28, 127*t*, *128*
    cash, 406–8
    college funding, 29–31
    courts, 341–42
    education, 457
    elections, 129–33, 130*f*

employment, 181*f*
factories, 12
Federal Election Campaign Act, 128
and federalism, 80–84, 81*f*–83*f*
fees, 425–27
finance officials, 390
free markets, 28
government, 22, 48
health care, 20
HOAs, 402
immigration, 4, 452
industry, 3, 9–16, 11*f*, 13*f*, *16*
lawsuits, 189–91
lobbying, 193*t*
in Mexico, 7
money, 31
oil, 14
PACs, 123, 126–29, *128*
pay-as-you-go system, 295, 430–31
pensions, 412
policy in, 9, 41
population and, 17–19, 18*f*, 19*t*
of poverty, 15, 51–52
psychology and, 270–71
PUF, 465–66
race and, 363, *363*
rainy day funds, 58, 426–27
reporting law, 197
school finance, 456–57
taxes, 44, 296*f*
Texas Miracle, 14–16
in United States, 9–10, 81*f*
*Edgewood Independent School District
    v. Kirby*, 456
education, *49*. *See also* students
    available school fund, 455
    college funding, 29–31
    common core standards for, 94
    economics of, 457
    Fisher v. University of Texas, 467
    foundation school fund, 455
    funding for, 55, 63, 457–60, 458*f*,
        459, 461*f*, 465–66
    government and, 280–81
    higher education, 465–67
    ideology of, 184
    income and, 22–23
    language and, 456
    of legislators, 191
    for minorities, 22, 462
    No Child Left Behind Act for, 79
    permanent school fund, 455–56
    about policy, 191
    politics of, 88, 240, 240*f*
    poverty and, 82*f*
    public education, 458*f*, 461–62,
        461*f*, 463*t*
    public policy for, 455–67, 458*f*, *459*,
        461*f*, 463*t*
    PUF, 465–66
    SBOE, 304–6
    school districts, 398–400, *400*
    school finance, 456–57

education (cont.)
    special education, 464
    teachers, 457–60, 459
    testing, 460, 461f
    THECB, 467
    vouchers for, 463
Eiland, Craig, 193t
Eisenhower, Dwight D., 91, 114, 148
elections. See also voting
    campaigns for, 123–28, 124,
        127t, 128
    Citizens United v. Federal Election
        Commission, 126
    city elections, 403
    county elections, 403
    economics of, 129–33, 130f
    Election Day, 102–3, 105–6, 106f
    electioneering, 185–86
    electoral choices, 138–39
    electoral systems, 132
    Federal Election Campaign Act, 128
    funding for, 126–28, 127t, 128
    for governors, 43
    immigration in, 46f
    independents in, 168
    for justices, 43
    laws on, 93, 93, 100–107, 104f, 106f
    learning objectives for, 99, 134
    for legislators, 211–13, 212f
    in local government, 402–6, 405f
    for mayors, 392
    in municipalities, 403–6, 405f
    partisanship in, 339–43, 340t,
        343f, 347
    place systems for, 403
    political machines for, 110
    practice quizzes for, 135
    primary elections, 102–3
    psychology and, 60f, 117–23, 117t,
        119f, 122
    public financing for, 347–48, 348t
    reelections, 211–13, 219f
    runoff elections, 103
    special elections, 103
    suffrage and, 107–16, 112f, 115f, 116
    winner-take-all elections, 165
Electrical Reliability Council of Texas,
    473–74
electric scooters, 392
eligibility, 246–47
elitism, 176–77
El Paso, mass shooting in, 34, 253, 298
emergencies, 256
Emmett, Ed, 409
employment
    in California, 12
    compensation for, 173, 451
    demographics of, 4
    economics of, 181f
    for felons, 373–74
    in government, 14–15
    immigration and, 15, 16
    labor, 63, 147, 180, 181f, 362, 451, 453

of legislators, 43
    retirement, 14
    in United States, 282f
    urbanization and, 17
en banc hearings, 328
endorsements, 186f, 264
energy. See also oil
    Electrical Reliability Council of
        Texas, 473–74
    energy industry, 4, 10–12
    natural gas, 424
    public policy for, 473–74, 474t
    technology for, 474t
    use of, 20
enforcement, 284
enumerated powers, 71–72
environment
    public policy for, 470–74, 471f
    TCEQ, 89, 302, 472–73
Environmental Protection Agency
    (EPA), 89, 151, 472–73
Erickson, Bernard, 164
ethics. See also scandals
    amicus curiae briefs, 187, 326
    AstroTurf lobbying, 184–85
    black codes, 47
    culture conflicts over, 31
    data for, 200f
    in government, 41
    law and, 197–98
    in law and order culture, 28
    of leadership, 193t
    of lobbyists, 191, 199t
    moralistic political culture, 26t, 31
    and partisanship, 197–98
    public interest groups for, 177,
        182, 182
    public policy supporting, 192
    of punishment, 400
    in Republican Party, 153–55
    sin taxes, 424, 425
    State Commission on Judicial
        Conduct, 338
    TEC, 198–201, 199t, 200f, 304–6
ethnicity
    conflict-related to, 6
    in gerrymandering, 159–60
    politics of, 22–23, 23
    in redistricting, 159
    trends in, 20–22, 21f
Etzioni, Amitai, 183
Evans, Charlie, 163
Evenwel v. Abbot, 163
E-Verify, 453
executive orders, 251–52
expenditures, 407f, 431, 431t

factories, 12
family
    CHIP, 447–48
    Department of Family and
        Protective Services, 306–7
    family values, 28–29, 30f

foster care, 307
    TANF, 449, 450f
Farias, Gomez, 39
Farias, Joe, 199t
farming. See agriculture
Federal Election Campaign Act, 128
Federal Emergency Relief Act, 85–86
federal government, approval for, 78f
federalism
    authority of, 76, 76–80, 78f
    conflict in, 89–94, 90, 93
    economics of, 80–84, 81f–83f
    learning objectives for, 69, 95–96
    policy for, 70–75, 71, 73t, 75
    politics of, 84–89, 85, 88
    practice quizzes for, 96–97
Federalist Paper 10 (Madison), 175
fees, 425–27
felons, 373–74, 374t, 375f
    felonies, 321, 357–58, 358t
    probation for, 363, 363–64
feminine hygiene products, taxes on,
    416, 417
feminism, 184
Fenno, Richard, 213
Ferguson, James E. "Pa," 249, 249,
    262, 270, 275
Ferguson, Miriam A. "Ma," 249, 249,
    262, 270
fiber, 10
Fifteenth Amendment, 112f, 113–14, 115f
filibusters, 233–34, 234
filing, of cases, 332f, 426, 427
finance officials, 390
finances. See budgets
fines, 425–27
Fiorina, Morris, 235
first readings, 224
Fischer, Trey Martinez, 233
Fisher, Abigail, 467
Fisher v. University of Texas, 467
flags, 8
Fleming, JoAnn, 175
flooding. See disasters
Floyd, George, 143, 176
food, 10
Ford, Gerald, 150
formal powers. See also authority;
    policy
    appointment powers, 252, 254f,
        255, 255
    judicial powers, 262
    law and, 251, 252, 252f
    legislative powers, 255–61,
        256, 260f
    military powers, 261–62
foster care, 307
foundation school fund, 455
franchise taxes, 423
Franklin, Ben, 3
Fraser, Troy, 217
Freedom from Religion Foundation, 31
free markets, 28

free rider problem, 177–79, *178*
Free School Zone Act, 72–74
free speech, 55
Friedkin, T. Dan, *255*
Friedman, Richard "Kinky," 168, 247, *247*
fuel, 10–12, 11*f*, 424
funding
    available school fund, 455
    for budgets, 425–28, *428*, 429*f*
    for candidates, 348*t*
    for disasters, 80, 82, 83*f*
    for education, 55, 63, 457–60, 458*f*, *459*, 461*f*, 465–66
    for elections, 126–28, 127*t*, *128*
    expenditures and, 431, 431*t*
    foundation school fund, 455
    fundraising, 201, 347–48
    general revenue funds, 430
    for government, 80–84, 81*f*–83*f*
    for higher education, 465–67
    LBB, 431, 433–36, 434*f*
    municipal bonds, 400
    in pay-as-you-go system, 295, 430–31
    permanent school fund, 455–56
    PUF, 465–66
    riders on, 436
    school finance, 456–57
    for sports, 408
    for transportation, 82*f*
    unfunded mandates, 88
Furman v. Georgia, 369

Gallego, Pete, 236
gambling, *295*, 388–89
Garcia, Hector P., 109
Garcia, Jerry, 99
Garner, John Nance "Cactus Jack," 147
Garza v. County of Los Angeles, 111
"geezer amendment," 348
General Land Office (GLO), 286
general laws, 208–9, 209*t*, 391
general revenue funds, 430
Geren, Charlie, 201–2
gerrymandering, 159–60
get out the vote, 125
Gibbons v. Ogden, 73*t*
gifts, for legislators, 199*t*
Glasgow, Bob, 197
GLO. *See* General Land Office
Goforth, Darren, *355*
Goldwater, Barry, 113
Gomillion v. Lightfoot, 159
Gonzales, Henry B., 109
Gonzales, Raul A., 346
Gonzalez, Tommy, *397*
Goodnight, Charles, 322
government. *See also* local government
    agency capture by, 195
    authority of, 48
    centralization of, 39, *76*, 76–77
    certification by, 436

COGs, 409–10
commission governments, 395*f*, 396–97
communication for, 62*f*
community and, 71
comptroller of public accounts, 294–96, 296*f*
concurrent powers of, 74–75, *75*
Constitution (TX) for, 36–37, *37*
debt for, 408–9, 410*t*
deferrals used by, 437
delegates for, 35
democracy and, 475
demographics and, 16–24, 18*f*, 19*t*, 21*f*, *23*
diacritical marks on documents, 15
in disasters, 78*f*, 83*f*
diversity in, *300*, 342–46, 344*f*, *345*
economics of, 22, 48
education and, 280–81
employment in, 14–15
enumerated powers of, 71–72
ethics in, 41
Federalist Paper 10 (Madison), 175
full faith and credit clause, 75
funding for, 80–84, 81*f*–83*f*
government interest groups, 183
Hispanics in, 111
implied powers of, 72
limited government, 36, 52–53, 65
lobbying of, 185–87, 186*f*
in Mexico, 39*t*
minimal government, 27
monarchies, 37–38
municipal bonds issued by, 400
municipal governments, 403–4
networking in, 409–11
organization of, 141
plural executive structure for, 52
policy innovation in, 78–79
population shifts and, 17–19
psychology of, 298
republics, 37–38
reserve clause, 74
Secretary of State, 299
separation of powers in, 41, 53–54, 53*f*
social contract in, 36–37
social services provided by, 16–17
spending caps for, 431
supremacy clause, 71
taxes for, 44
of Tejanos, 7
voting for, 392
welfare for, 27*t*
governors
    appointment powers of, 252, 254*f*, 255, *255*, 299–303, *300*, *302*
    authority for, 251, 252, 252*f*, 254*f*, 255–56, *255*–62, 257*f*, 259*f*–60*f*
    budgetary powers of, 268
    bureaucracy for, 285*f*
    elections for, 43

    leadership for, 263–71, *265*, 267*f*, 269*f*, *270*
    learning objectives for, 245, 276
    lieutenant governors, 43, 224, 225*f*, 286–91, 287*f*, 288*t*
    policy for, 246–51, *247*, 248*f*, *249*, 250*f*
    practice quizzes for, 277
    psychology of, 271, 272*f*, 274–75
    scandals for, 249
    staff of, 250*f*
Gramm, Phil, 164
grand juries, 361, 377
Granger Movement, 51–52
Grant, Ulysses S., 49
grants, 86–87
grassroots, 152–53, 156, 184
Graves, Curtis, 239
Graves v. Barnes, 111
Green, Andria, *382*, 383
Green, Rick, 193
Green, Ronald, 396
Green, Zoey, *382*, 383
Green Party, 166–67
Grose, Christian, 164
groups. *See* interest groups
guardian ad litem, 360
Guerrero, Leonard, 255
guns, *159*, *176*, 442–44
Gutiérrez, José Ángel, 166
Guyger, Amber, *352*, 353
Guzman, Eva, *321*

Haggard, Merle, 374
Hamilton, Andrew Jackson, 47
Hancock, Kelly, 199*t*
Handy (company), 176–77
Hansen, Dale, 8
Hawkins (city), *31*
Health and Human Services Commission (HHSC), 299–300, 446
health care, 14, 20, 401–2
    excessive hospital bills, 279, *325*
    Medicaid, 24, 446–48
    public policy on, *388*, 444–48
hearings, 189–91
Hecht, Nathan L., 201, 321, 333
HHSC. *See* Health and Human Services Commission
higher education, 465–67
high school registration, 101*f*
Hightower, Jim, 124
Hill, John, 166, 292
Hill Country Rebellion, 48
Hindt, Lance, 464
Hinjosa, Juan "Chuy," 189
Hinojosa, Gilberto, 143
Hispanics, 21, 111, 131, 139, 448
    candidates, *166*, 166–67
    culture, 7, 133
    discrimination against, 161–63

Hispanics *(cont.)*
    health care for, 14
    *League of United Latin American
        Citizens v. Perry*, 160
    in politics, 238*f*, 239–40, 299, *300*
    in Supreme Court (TX), 346
    voting by, 109–12, 115*f*
history
    African American, 44–45
    of conflict, 29–31, *31*
    of culture, 64–65
    Declaration of Independence (TX),
        37–40, *38*, 39*t*
    Democratic Party, 137–38, 146–48,
        147, 149*f*
    Federalist Paper 10 (Madison), 175
    Furman v. Georgia, 369
    Granger Movement, 51–52
    "Jim Crow" laws, 108
    of judicial selection, 335, 337
    of justice, 318–19, 321
    Mexican, 6–7, 38–39
    of policy-making by attorney
        general, 294*t*
    of political parties, 146–56, *147*,
        149*f*, 152*f*
    Republican Party, 149–51
    segregation, 47–48
    settlement, 4–9, 5*f*
    Shays's Rebellion, 76
    social security, 448
    of taxes, 442
    Texas Miracle, 14–16
    United States, 7–9
    Voting Rights Act (1965), 103–4
    World War II, 85
HOAs. *See* homeowners' associations
Hobby, William, Sr., 85, 288
Hobby, William P., Jr., 200–201,
        459–60
    Bullock *vs.*, 289
    legacy of, 231–32, *232*, 288*t*
    reputation of, 125, 173–74
hog apocalypse, *2*, 3
Hogg, James, 303
holdover officials, 273
Holley, Joe, 25, *25*
homeowners' associations (HOAs), 402
home rule cities, 391–94
homestead exemption, 420, 422–23
homestead law, 43–44
hospital bills, excessive, 279, *325*
hospital districts, 401–2
House of Representatives (TX), 207,
        210, *211*, 223, 227
    filibusters, 233–34, *234*
    odd bills proposed, 209*t*
    speaker of the house, 221–23,
        222*t*, 225*f*
housing, 20, 23, 402
    homelessness, 74–75
    homestead exemption, 420, 422–23

property taxes, 58*f*, 406–7, 419*f*,
        420, *422*, 422–23
Houston (city), *43*
Houston, Sam, 26, 35, 45
Houston Independent School District,
        462, *464*
Huberty, Dan, *206*
Huddle, Rebeca Aizpuru, 337, *337*
Huffman, Joan, 202, *226*
Hughes, Sarah, 345
Hunt, Ray, 397
hunting, *2*, 3, *302*
hurricanes. *See* disasters
hybrid agencies, 303–4

ICE. *See* Immigration and Customs
        Enforcement
identity, 125, 147–48, 149*f*, 163–67, *166*
ideology
    of business groups, 179–80
    communicating, 140–41
    on death penalty, 373*t*
    of Democratic Party, 161–63, 162*f*
    on education, 184
    of government interest groups, 183
    on higher education, 465
    of identity groups, 180–82
    of interest groups, 177–79, *178*
    of judiciary, 318–22, 320*f*
    on justice, 378
    of labor unions, 180
    of lobbyists, 174, 188–89
    and partisanship, 169
    on policy, 312
    of private interest groups, 177–79
    of professional organizations, 180
    as propaganda, 156
    psychology of, *139*
    of public interest groups, 177, 182
    and representation, 152*f*
    of single-issue groups, 182–83
    of state party chairs, 143
    of trade associations, 180
    tradition in, 148
immigration, 15, 16, 452–55, *454*
    and elections, 46*f*
    National Guard at border,
        261–62, 268
    politics of, 91–93
Immigration and Customs
        Enforcement (ICE), 454
impeachment, 247–49, *249*, 338
implied powers, 72
inaugural speeches, 268
incarceration, 365–68, 366*f*–67*f*, 376
income, 22–24, 448–51
    identity and, 147–48, 149*f*
    income taxes, 427–28
incumbents, 124, 131–33, 218, 219*f*
independents, 168
indigent defendants, 355, 357, 377,
        426, 427

individualism, *8*, 37, 40–41, 79
    in Constitution (TX), 69–70, 94–95
    individualistic political culture,
        26–28, 26*t*, 27*t*
industry, 9–16, 11*f*, 13*f*, *16*, 130*f*
influence, 285*f*
informal powers
    and agenda setting, 265–71, 267*f*,
        269*f*, *270*
    legislative bargaining, 263–65, *265*
informal qualifications, 247, *247*
infrastructure, 19
initiatives, 392
Institute for Justice, 187
institutional memory, 218
interest groups, 175–79, *176*, *178*,
        203–4, 225*f*
    for citizens, 180–82, 181*f*, *182*
    learning objectives for, 173, 203–4
    lobbying by, 187–95, 188*f*, 190*f*,
        193*t*, 194*f*
    policy for, 173–74, *174*
    practice quizzes for, 204–5
    reform for, 195–98, 196*t*, *197*
    regulation of, 198–203, 199*t*, 200*f*
    theory of, 183–86, 186*f*, 187
intermediate appellate courts, 328
Internet, 120, *281*, *295*
iron triangles, 192–95, 193*t*, 194*f*
Isett, Carl, 311
Islam. *See* religion
issues, 182–83, 190*f*, 192. *See also*
        public policy
    in local government, 406–13, 407*f*,
        410*t*, *411*
    single-issue groups, 182–83
    on Twitter, 212*f*, 213
Iturbide, Augustín de, 38, 66
Ivins, Molly, 174, 197, 203, 218, 354

Jade Helm 15, 76–77
Jamail, Joe, 317
Janek, Kyle, 196*t*
Jean, Botham, *352*, 353
Jefferson, Wallace, 333, 346–47
Jenkins, Clay, *388*
"Jim Crow" laws, 108
Joffrion, Olin, 358
Johnson, Andrew, 47
Johnson, Eddie Bernice, 239
Johnson, Eric, 395
Johnson, Julie, 232
Johnson, Lyndon, 110, 147, 150, *197*, 305
Johnson, Pamela Jean, 317
Joiner, Columbus Marion "Dad," 11
joint resolutions, 209
Jones, Jerry, 8
Jordan, Barbara, 239
judiciary, *316*
    appellate courts, 326–30, 327*f*, 329*f*
    authority for, 43, 317–18
    ideology of, 318–22, 320*f*

judge-made law, 321
judicial hierarchy, 319
judicial powers, 262
justice and, 330–34, 332f–33f
justices in, 335–47, 336f, 339t–40t,
    343f, 344f, 345
learning objectives for, 317, 349–50
legal jurisdiction of, 319, 321
practice quizzes for, 351
reform for, 346–49, 348t
trial courts, 320f, 322–26, 323f
Junell, Rob, 64
junior colleges, 400–401, 466
juntas, 38
jurisdiction, 319, 321
jury trials, 325, 361–62, 362
justice, 322, 324, 328–34, 332f–33f
history of, 318–19, 321
ideology on, 378
technology for, 377–79
Justice, William Wayne, 369
justices, 43, 54, 322, 333f, 334
demographics of, 342–46, 344f, 345
policy for, 335–43, 336f, 339t–40t,
    343f
voting for, 339–43, 340t, 343f
juvenile crime, 359

Kansas, 12
Keffer, Jim, 193t
Kennedy, John F., 110, 150
Kessler, Michael, 348
Key, V. O., Jr., 138
Keyssar, Alex, 107
Killer Bees, 231–32, 232
Kirk, Ron, 111
Klein, Barry, 393, 393
Koehler, Kermit, 3
Kuhlmann, Kate, 191

labor. See employment
Lamar, Mirabeau B., 6, 465
Laney, Pete, 212–13, 222t, 229, 266
language, 5f, 61, 62f, 145f, 269f, 456
Larson, Lyle, 264
Laswell, Mary, 8
Latinos. See Hispanics
law(s)
on abortion, 182–83
ACA, 20, 87, 447–48
amicus curiae briefs, 187, 326
arraignment, 361
bail, 360, 376–77
Campaign Finance Act (1995), 347
Chinese Exclusion Act, 117–18
Civil Rights Act, 150
common law, 321
community supervision, 363,
    363–64, 364f
in Constitution (TX), 110, 251,
    252, 252f
Crime Victim's Compensation
    Act, 357

criminal cases, 319, 321
David's Law, 465
deferred adjudication, 261
DWI, 357, 358t
for elections, 93, 93, 100–107,
    104f, 106f
for eligibility, 246–47
en banc, 328
and ethics, 197–98
Federal Election Campaign Act, 128
Federal Emergency Relief Act, 85–86
felonies, 321, 357–58, 358t
as formal powers, 251, 252, 252f
Free School Zone Act, 72–74
general laws, 208–9, 209t, 391
grand juries, 361, 377
guardians ad litem, 360
homestead law, 43–44
on impeachment, 247–49, 249
indigent defendants, 355, 357, 377,
    426, 427
"Jim Crow" laws, 108
judge-made law, 321
law and order, 28
lawmaking, 208–10
on lobbying, 435
local laws, 208–9, 209t
martial law, 77
misdemeanors, 321, 357, 358t
motor voter law, 100
No Child Left Behind Act, 79
no contest pleas, 361–62
odd laws proposed by legislature, 209t
open carry law, 442–44
opinions in, 326
ordinances, 385–86, 390
parole, 374, 374t
plea bargains, 361
preemptions in, 89, 383
probable cause, 355
probation, 363, 363–64
prosecutors, 361, 389
religion and, 40, 41
reporting law, 197
resolutions, 209–10, 209t
rights of the accused, 355
sanctuary cities and, 92
search and seizure, 355
special laws, 208–9, 209t
for succession, 249
on suffrage, 50–51
sunset processes, 307–11, 308t, 309f
for Supreme Court (TX), 52
Texas Register record of, 281
Tort Claim Act (1969), 291
victim rights, 355–56
voir dire, 361–62, 362
on voting, 47–48
Voting Rights Act (1965), 90, 93
law enforcement, 389
lawsuits, 189–91, 392–94
lawyers, 343f
LBB. See Legislative Budget Board

leadership, 114, 193t, 286–88, 396, 397
by governors, 263–71, 265, 267f,
    269f, 270
in military, 45, 47
psychology of, 271
reform and, 274–75
by speaker of the house, 221–23,
    222t
in United States, 41
League of United Latin American
    Citizens v. Perry, 160
League of Women Voters of Texas, 184
legal defense funds, 201
legal jurisdiction, 319, 321
legislative bargaining, 263–65, 265
Legislative Budget Board (LBB), 431,
    433–36, 434f
legislative impeachment, 338
legislative powers, 255–61, 256, 260f
legislators. See also law
authority of, 208–11, 209t, 211
in bicameral legislature, 208
boards of, 217
casework for, 211
coalitions of, 230–37, 231–34, 236f
councils of, 217
culture of, 229t
demographics of, 237–40, 238f, 240f
disclosure for, 176, 202
education level of, 191
elections for, 211–13, 212f
employment of, 43
endorsements and, 186f
filibusters, 233–34, 234
gifts for, 199t
hearings by, 189–91
iron triangles for, 192–95, 193t, 194f
learning objectives for, 207, 241–42
legislative redistricting board,
    159, 161
networking with, 191, 290
organization for, 220–24, 222t
policy for, 189, 194f, 224–30, 225f,
    228, 229t
politics and, 214–18, 215f–16f, 219f
practice quizzes for, 243
recusal by, 201–2
resolutions of, 209–10, 209t
revolving door theory, 193
rule-making by, 191
salaries for, 217
sessions for, 214, 215f–16f
staff of, 217
sunset processes for, 307–11,
    308t, 309f
term limits for, 63
unfunded mandates for, 88
in United States, 216f
Leland, Mickey, 148
León, Martín de, 40
Lewis, Gib, 196t, 197, 222t
liberals, 139, 147. See also Democratic
    Party

Libertarian Party, 167
liberties, *54*, *54–55*
libraries, 401
licensing, 284
lieutenant governors. *See* governors
limited government, 36, 52–53, 65
Lincoln, Abraham, 44–45, 146
line item vetoes, 260–61, 260*f*, 268
literacy tests, 108
lobbying, *172*
    on abortion, 190*f*
    AstroTurf lobbying, 184–85
    as communication, 192
    demographics of lobbyists, 188*f*
    economics of, 193*t*
    and electioneering, 185
    ethics of, 191, 199*t*
    and gift reporting law, 197
    of government, 185–87, 186*f*
    grassroots lobbying, 184
    ideology of lobbyists, 174, 188–89
    by interest groups, 187–95, 188*f*,
        190*f*, 193*t*, 194*f*
    iron triangles for, 192–95, 193*t*, 194*f*
    issues lobbied for, 190*f*
    law on, 435
    policy on, 194*f*, 445
    regulation of, 389
    for Supreme Court (TX), 187
    and transactional theory, 176–77
    in transportation, 179
local government, 19*t*, 53, *98*, 383–84,
        386, 413–14
    approval of, 78*f*
    in cities, *390*, 391–98, 395*f*, *397*
    elections in, 402–6, 405*f*
    issues in, 406–13, 407*f*, 410*t*, *411*
    learning objectives for, 383, 413–14
    local laws, 208–9, 209*t*
    practice quizzes for, 415
    special districts, 398–401, 399*f*,
        400–401
    in United States, 387*f*
The Logic of Collective Action
        (Olson), 178
logrolling, 230–31
lottery, *428*
Lozano, J. M., 163
Lucio, Eddie, 230
Lundy, Benjamin, 39–40

Madison, James, 175, 198
mail-in voting, 132
Maloney, Pat, Sr., 341
management, *71*, 83*f*, 396–97, *397*
mandatory retirement, 348
mandatory review, 329–30
Manges, Clinton, 341
manufacturing, 12
marketing, 144
markups, 226
Marquez, Marisa, 193*t*
martial law, 77
Martin, Mike, 176, 191

Martinez, Berta Rios, 390
massage parlors, *390*
Massengale, Michael C., 88, *88*
mass shootings, 34, *176*, 253, 298
matching grants, 86
Mattox, Jim, 294*t*
Mauzy, Oscar, 234
May, Wilma David, *307*
Mayhew, David, 211
mayors, 392, 394–96, 395*f*, 405*f*
McCarble, James, 370–72
McCullough v. Maryland, 72, 73*t*
McDonald, Craig, *182*
McDuff, Kenneth, 374
McGee, Josh, 305
McHaney, Anita, 283, *283*
McHaney, Jim, 283, *283*
McNair, Bob, 189
McNeely, Dave, 229
McWilliams, Andrea, 192, *192*
means-tested programs, 448–49
media, 124, *124*, 265, *265*, 281
Medicaid, 24, 80, 95, 446–48
Medicare, 445–46
Meier, Bill, 234
merit selection, 335, 347
Mexican Americans. *See* Hispanics
Mexico, 6–8, 38–39, 39*t*, 42–43
Meyers, Larry, 164
microtargeting, 125
Miers, Harriet, 201
military, 12–13, 13*f*, 38–39, 261–62
    Jade Helm 15, 76–77
    leadership in, 45, 47
militias, 48, 50, 76
Miller, Rick, 99
Miller, Sid, 297, *297*
Mills, C. Wright, 176
minimal government, 27
minimum wage, *184*
minorities, 21*f*, 22–23, 161, 462
    discrimination against, 356*f*, 367*f*,
        370–72
    in municipal governments, 403–4
    in politics, 342–46, 344*f*, *345*
    voting and, 115*f*, 133
misdemeanors, 321, 357, 358*t*
mistakes of fact, 353
mobile voting, 105
monarchies, 37–38
money, 31
Montgomery, David, 197
Moody, Dan, 258
Moore, Bobby, 370–72
Morales, Dan, 148, 294*t*, 298
Morales, Victor, 111, *111*
moralistic political culture, 26*t*, 31
morality. *See* ethics
Morrow, Robert, *142*
Moscoso Alvarado, Luis de, 6–7
Mostyn, Amber, 131
Mostyn, Steve, 131, 342
motor vehicle taxes, 424
motor voter law, 100

MUD. *See* municipal utility districts
multimember agencies, 301–3, *302*
multimember elected commissions,
        303–4
municipal courts, 322–24
municipalities, 400, 403–6, 405*f*
municipal utility districts (MUD),
        401, *401*
Muñiz, Ramsey, 166, *166*
Mutscher, Gus, Jr., 196, 196*t*, *197*, 223
Múzquiz, Virginia, 167
name identification, 124
National Association for the
        Advancement of Colored People
        (NAACP), 182
National Guard, 261–62, 268
National Rifle Association (NRA), *178*
national trends, 125
Native Americans, 4–7, 5*f*
natural gas, 424
Navárez, Pancho, 213
Navarro, Jose Antonio, 40, 42–43
necessary and proper clause, 72
Neece, Scott, *2*, 3
Neely, Donald, *357*
Neff, Pat, 258, 260–61, 345
negative campaigning, 124, *125*
neighborhood precincts, 105
Nelson, Jane, *435*
Nelson, Willie, 359, *359*
networking, 178, 409–11
    with legislators, 191, 290
    in politics, 230–31, *231*
Nevárez, Poncho, 207
New Deal, 147
new federalism, 86–87
New Mexico, 21
New Spain. *See* Mexico
Nixon, Lawrence A., 108
Nixon, Richard, 114, 150
Noble, Candy, 234
no-cash pretrial release, 377
No Child Left Behind Act, 79
no contest pleas, 361–62
non-dedicated revenue, 431, 431*t*
None of the Above Party, 165
non-partisan elections, 347
Norris, Chuck, 268
North Cypress Medical Center, *325*
NRA. *See* National Rifle Association
Nugent, Marjorie, 357

Obamacare. *See* Affordable Care Act
Obergefell v. Hodges, 75
O'Daniel, Pappy, 108, 247, 264–65, 298
Ogg, Kim, 389
oil, 9–16, 84, 195, 424
Olson, Mancur, 178
online gambling, *295*
open carry law (guns), 442–44
open primaries, 102
opinions, 293*f*, 294*t*, 326, 454–55
ordinances, 385–86, *390*, 392
organization

of bureaucracy, 284–86, 285*f*
of legislature, 220–24, 222*t*
of political parties, 141–45, *142*, 145*f*
original jurisdiction, 319
O'Rourke, Beto, 126
overcrowding, 365–68, 366*f*
oversight. *See* regulation
oyster farming, 281, 283
PACs. *See* political action committees
paid sick leave, 385
pardons, 262
Parker, Anise, 114
parks, 301–2, *302*, 305
Parks, Ursula, 435
parole, 374, 374*t*
Parr, Archie, 110
Parr, George, 110
parties. *See* political parties
partisanship, 155–56
and bills, 227
in elections, 339–43, 340*t*, 343*f*
ethics of, 197–98
ideology and, 169
of justices, 322
merit selection and, 335
non-partisan elections, 347
politics and, 141, 236*f*, 237
psychology of, 156–57
for Republican Party, 162*f*
party chairs, *142*, 142–43
party platforms, 144–45, 145*f*
party switching, 163–64
Patrick, Dan, *278*
legacy of, *124*, 126, 153, 289–90
reputation of, 207, 223, 227, 234,
291, 298, 442–43
patrón system, 110
Patterson, Jerry, 124
Paxton, Ken
legacy of, 268, 294*t*, *295*, 444
reputation of, 201, 390
pay-as-you-go system, 295, 430–31
Peña, Aaron, 164
pensions, 412
Perez, Guillermo, 4
permanent school fund, 455–56
permanent university fund (PUF),
465–66
Perot, Ross, 266, 459
Perry, Rick, *244*, 252, 453, 468
legacy of, 151, 155, 160, 164, 248*f*,
252*f*, 256, 259*f*–60*f*,
261–62, 267*f*, 271–73, 346,
370, 436
reputation of, 55, 168, 245–46, 255,
270, 437
personal outreach, 270, *270*
personal rights, *54*, 54–55
Phillips, Tom, 52, *52*
physical labor, 362
Pilgrim, Bo, 173–74, *174*, 196*t*, 197
Pilgrim's Pride Corporation, 173–74
pioneers, 24–25
place systems, 403

Plano Independent School District
(PISD), 8
plea bargains, 361
plural executive structure, 52
AG in, 292–94, *295*
agriculture commissioner in, *297*,
297–98
bureaucracy and, 279–84, *281*, 282*f*,
283, 285*f*, 305–11, 308*t*, 309*f*
commissioner of the general land
office in, 297
comptroller of public accounts in,
294–96, 296*f*
data on, 293*f*, 294*t*
hybrid agencies in, 303–4
learning objectives for, 279, 312–14
lieutenant governor in, 286–91,
287*f*, 288*t*
multimember agencies in, 301–3, *302*
multimember elected commissions
in, 303–4
politics of, 298
practice quizzes for, 315
single-head agencies in,
299–300, *300*
pluralism, 175–77
Plyler v. Doe, 453
Poder Quince initiative, *102*
points of order (POOs), 232
polarization, in politics, 235–36, 236*f*
police, *352*, 353, 355, 356*f*
policy. *See also* public policy
abortion, 28–29, 30*f*
for ACA, 447–48
administration schedules, 228–29
affordable housing, 20
for agenda setting, 442–43, 443*f*
annexation, 392–94
and authority, 56
banking, 53
benefit, 175–79
for bills, 229–30, 229*t*
budget, 430–37, 431*t*, 432*f*,
434*f*, *435*
bureaucracy and, 281, *281*, *283*,
283–84, 305–11, 308*t*, 309*f*
centralization, 39
certification, 436
charter, 391
clemency, 262
in Constitution (TX), 279–80
criminal justice, 354–57, 356*f*
deportation, 454–55
on disclosure, 202
on diversity, 9
economic, 9, 41
education, 191, 398–400, *400*
Electrical Reliability Council of
Texas, 473–74
enforcement of, 284
for executive orders, 251–52
federalist, 70–75, *71*, 73*t*, *75*
free market, 28
fundraising, 201

for government, 17–18
for governors, 246–51, *247*, 248*f*,
249, 250*f*
grant, 86–87
history of, 294*t*
homestead exemption, 420, 422–23
ICE, 454
ideology and, 312
implementation of, 281, *281*, 283
individualist, 40–41
infrastructure, 19
innovation in, 78–79
for interest groups, 173–74, *174*
Internet, *281*
for justices, 335–43, 336*f*,
339*t*–40*t*, 343*f*
legislative redistricting board, 159
for legislators, 189, 194*f*, 224–30,
225*f*, 228, 229*t*
liberties and, *54*, 54–55
licensing, 284
lobbying, 194*f*, 445
for militias, 50
POOs, 232
recusal, 201–2
redistributive, 445
redistricting, 159
reform, 57*f*
regulatory, 283
retirement, 334
riders, 436
segregation, 20–22, *23*
sin taxes, *424*, 425
sprawl, 411, *411*
SSI, 448
for Supreme Court (TX), 43
TANF, 449, 450*f*
on term limits, 247, 248*f*
transportation, 183
veto, 258–61
water use, 470–73, 471*f*
zoning, 412
political action committees (PACs),
123, 126–29, *128*
political parties
authority of, 273–74
competition between, 156–65, 158*f*,
159, *160*, 162*f*
culture of, 60*f*, 131
history of, 146–56, *147*, 149*f*, 152*f*
identification with, 154*f*
learning objectives for, 137, 169–70
organization of, 141–45, *142*, 145*f*
polarization of, 235–36, 236*f*
practice quizzes for, 170–71
psychology of, 132–33
theory of, 138–41, 140*f*
third parties, 165–68, *166*
political power
and Constitutional amendments, 63
and diversity, 8
and financing for football
stadiums, 408
of holdover officials, 273

political power (cont.)
    in Jade Helm military training
        exercise, 77
    learning objectives for, 3, 32
    of lieutenant governor, 290
    of political machines, 110
    practice quizzes for, 32–33
    and prison system, 363
    for property tax control, 423
    redistricting for, 161
    of speaker of the house, 223
    and standardized testing, 460
    of Texas Supreme Court, 331
politics
    and ACA, 87
    administration schedules, 228–29
    affiliation in, 149f, 159
    African Americans in, 238f, 239
    of AG, 293f, 294t
    age and, 23–24, 238f, 441
    Anglos in, 113–14
    of appointees, 273
    appropriation bills, 433–36, 435
    Asian Americans in, 300
    authority in, 15, 41
    base identity in, 125
    of budget-making, 266–68
    chubbing, 234
    for citizens, 59, 60f, 61
    and Civil War, 62f
    coalitions in, 191
    COGs, 409–10
    of commerce, 179
    committees in, 220–21, 224–28, 225f
    controversies in, 288t
    of cotton, 85, 85
    courts in, 161–63
    credit-claiming in, 213
    cronyism in, 274
    debates in, 15
    decentralization of, 141–42
    and Declaration of Independence
        (TX), 39–40, 39t
    of deferrals, 437
    and democracy, 35–36
    and demographics, 168–69
    discharge petitions, 236
    disenfranchisement in, 107
    of education, 88, 240, 240f
    emergencies in, 256
    ethnicity and, 22–23, 23
    of federalism, 84–89, 85
    filibusters, 233–34, 234
    fundraising in, 347–48
    of gambling, 295
    of government, 3
    Hispanics in, 238f, 239–40,
        299, 300
    of immigration, 91–93
    independents in, 168
    of insurance, 285
    of integration, 150
    interest groups in, 175–77, 176
    Ivins on, 354

    of language, 61, 269f
    legislators and, 214–18, 215f–16f, 219f
    limited government in, 65
    logrolling in, 230–31
    marketing of, 144
    and media, 265, 265
    of Medicaid, 447–48
    minorities in, 342–46, 344f, 345
    MUD for, 401, 401
    networking in, 230–31, 231
    and New Deal, 147
    pardons, 262
    partisanship and, 141, 236f, 237
    in plural executive structure, 298
    political culture, 3–4, 24–31, 26t,
        27t, 29f, 30f, 35
    political efficacy, 117
    political machines, 110
    political polarization, 235–36, 236f
    political science, 183
    political socialization, 118
    politiqueras, 131
    and population, 19–20
    position taking in, 212–13
    of poverty, 15, 16
    proclamations, 252
    of property rights, 43–44
    psychology of, 133–34, 187, 409–11
    PUC, 301
    race in, 240
    rainy day funds, 426–27
    ratification, 51
    of Reagan, 86
    recommendations, 255–56
    redistricting, 161
    in Red River border dispute, 91
    and religion, 28, 29f, 65, 240
    of Republican Party, 146
    resolutions, 209–10, 209t
    riders in, 436
    salaries in, 217
    scandals in, 249
    seniority in, 221
    of slavery, 9
    of sports, 290
    stuffing the box, 233
    succession, 249
    suffrage, 42–43, 56
    tagging, 234–35
    taxes, 153
    Tea Party, 131
    tidelands controversy, 90–91
    of transportation, 82f, 388–89
    unilateral orders in, 252f
    vetoes, 245–46
    violence and, 49
    women in, 237–38, 238f
Polk, James, 42
poll taxes, 108
POOs. See points of order
Pope, Andrew Jackson "Jack," 330
popular sovereignty, 50–52
population, 19–20, 282f, 444, 452
    economics and, 17–19, 18f, 19t

    overcrowding, 365–68, 366f
    sprawls and, 411, 411
    position taking, 212–13
poverty, 15, 16, 20, 51–52, 82f. See also
        income; welfare
precinct chairs, 142
preemptions, 89, 383
presidents, 114, 146–47
presiding officers, 286
pretrials, 360–61
Price, Betsy, 397
primary elections, 102–3
principles, 50–55, 51t, 52, 53f, 54
prison. See punishment
private interest groups, 177–79
privatization, of prisons, 368
probable cause, 355
probate courts, 325
probation, 363, 363–64
proclamations, 252
professional organizations, 180
progressive taxes, 428
projections, 21f
propaganda, 110, 124, 124–26, 156
property, 91, 291, 317–18
    property rights, 43–44
    property taxes, 58f, 61, 406–7, 419f,
        420, 422, 422–23
prosecutors, 361, 389
prostitution, 390
psychology
    accountability, 310–11
    appointment powers, 274
    AstroTurf lobbying, 184–85
    bullying, 464–65
    of citizens, 106f, 151–53
    convenience voting, 120
    cooperation, 409–11
    death penalty, 369–73, 371f, 373t,
        377–79
    and Declaration of Independence
        (TX), 35–36
    of delegates, 63
    in democracy, 78–79
    of Democratic Party, 155
    Duverger's law, 165
    economics and, 270–71
    elections and, 60f, 117–23, 117t,
        119f, 122
    electoral choices, 138–39
    endorsements, 264
    government, 298
    of governors, 271, 272f, 274–75
    identity, 163–64
    and ideology, 139
    influence, 285f
    leadership, 271
    limited government, 52–53
    logrolling, 230–31
    negative campaigning, 124, 125
    networking, 178
    opinions, 293f, 294t
    partisanship, 156–57
    personal outreach, 270, 270

political efficacy, 117
of political parties, 132–33
politics, 133–34, 187, 409–11
rebellion, 37–40, *38*, *39t*
recognition, 223
reconstruction, 50
representation, 77, *78f*
suicide, 377
taxes and, 58, 76, 146, 422, *422*, 427–28, *429f*
tradition, 118
trust, 27–28, 79
violence, 54
voting, 57–59, *58f*
World War II, 85
public policy, 123, 192, 441, 475
benefits, 175–79, *178*, 449
education, 455–57, *458f*, *459*, 460–67, *461f*, *463t*
energy, 473–74, *474t*
environmental, 470–74, *471f*
financing, 347–48, *348t*
health care, 279, *388*, 444–48
immigration, 452–55, *454*
improvement districts, 401
interest groups, 177, 182, *182*
learning objectives for, 441, 475
practice quizzes for, 476
process for making, 442–44, *443f*
public education, *458f*, 461–62, *461f*, *463t*
transportation, 468, *469f*
welfare, 448–51, *450f*
Public Utility Commission (PUC), 301
PUF. *See* permanent university fund
punishment, *363*, 363–64, *364f*, 369, *400*
death penalty, 369–73, *371f*, *373t*, 377–79
parole, *374*, *374t*
qualifications, 338–39, *339t*

race, 150, 159, 240, *356f*, 467. *See also* ethnicity; minorities; *specific races*
death penalty and, 370–72
economics and, *363*, *363*
in gerrymandering, 159–60
identity and, *166*, 166–67
racing, 283
rainy day funds, 58, 426–27
Ramsey, Ben, 288, 290
Ramsey, Ross, 431
ranching, 12
Ranney, Austin, 156–57
ratification, 51, 56–57
rational voter theory, 117–18
Ratliff, Bill, 64
Rawlings, Mike, 397
Ray, C. L., 341
Rayburn, Sam, 147
Raymond, Richard Peña, 331
La Raza Unida Party, *166*, 166–67
readings, of bills, 224–27, *225f*, *226*, 235–37

Reagan, Ronald, 86, 114, 148, 150, 264
reapportionment, 157
rebellion, 37–40, *38*, *39t*, 48
recalls, 392
recognition, 223
recommendations, 255–56
reconstruction, 47–48, 50
recruitment, 139, *140f*, *142*, 142–43, 403
recusal, 201–2
redistributive policy, 445
redistricting, 159, 161–63, *162f*
Red River border dispute, 91
Red State (Thornburn), 157
red-tape, 281
Reed, Rodney, *370*
reelections, 211–13, *219f*
referendums, 392
reform, *57f*, *58f*, 61–64, *62f*, 376–79
death penalty, 377–79
drug court, 368
immigration policy, 452
for interest groups, 195–98, *196t*, *197*
judicial, 346–49, *348t*
leadership and, 274–75
tort reform, 317–18
voting for, *59t*, *60f*
registration, *100*, 100–102, *101f*, *102*
regressive taxes, 419–20. *See also* sales tax
regular sessions, 214
regulation, *130f*, 283, 385–86, *386*, 389
of interest groups, 198–203, *199t*, *200f*
TWDB, 470–72, *471f*
religion, 28–29, *29f*, *30f*, 55, 165, 185
discrimination and, 392
law and, 40, *41*
in politics, 65, 240
slavery and, *39*
removal powers, 274–75, 338
reporting law, 197
representation, *152f*, 403–4
apportionment and, 157–58, *158f*
for citizens, 77, *78f*, 281, *282f*
Republican Party, *136*, 137–39, 146, 149–51, 153–57. *See also* political parties
Democratic *vs.*, 143–44, *145f*, *149f*, *152f*, 168–69, *236f*, 383
identification with, *154f*
partisanship for, *162f*
republics, 37–38
reserve clause, 74
residential segregation, 21–22
resolutions, 209–10, *209t*
retirement, 14, 334, 348
revenge porn, 321
revenue, *296f*, 430–33, *431t*
budgets and, 418–25, *419f*, *421f*
lottery for, *428*
review, 329–30
revolving door theory, 193
Reyes, Victor, 453
Richards, Ann, 137, 153, 155, 275

legacy of, *252f*, *260f*
reputation of, 255, *270*, 275, 370
riders, 436
The Right to Vote (Keyssar), 107
Rinaldi, Matt, 207
Ritter, Allan, 164
Rivera, Martin, 353
Roberts, Crystal, *325*
Rodriguez, Demitrio, 456
Roosevelt, Franklin, 147, 448
Roosevelt, Theodore, 113
Rove, Karl, 341
Ruby, George Thompson, 47
Ruggero, Ruth, 255
Ruiz, Jose Francisco, 40
Ruiz v. Estelle, 369
rule-making, 191, 283
rules. *See* law; policy
runoff elections, 103
Rusk, Thomas Jefferson, 43

safety, 24, 74
salaries, 217, 249–51, *333f*
for legislators, 217
for teachers, 457–60, *459*
sales tax, 64, 406, *416*, 417–20, *419f*, *421f*
same-sex marriage, 75, 328. *See also* minorities
San Antonio Independent School District v. Rodriguez, 456
San Antonio International Airport, 191
Sanchez, Tony, 111, 126
sanctuary cities, 92
Sandill, R. K. "Ravi," 346
San Francisco, 92
Santa Anna, Antonio Lopez de, 26, 39, 40
"Save Chick-fil-A" bill, 191, 232
SBOE. *See* State Board of Education
scandals, 195–98, *196t*, *197*, 249, 406
Schlozman, Kay, 183
school finance, 456–57
scooters, electric, *392*
search and seizure, 355
secession, 44–45, *46f*
Secretary of State, 299
security, 23–24
segregation, 20–22, *23*, 47–48, 150
Seguin, Juan Nepomuceno, 40
select committees, 221
selective benefits, 178
Seliger, Kel, 235, 289–90
Senate (TX), 210–11, 224, *225f*, 227, 289
filibusters, 233–34, *234*
Killer Bees in, 231–32, *232*
odd bills proposed, *209t*
seniority, 221
sentencing. *See* punishment
separation of powers, 41–43, 53–54, *53f*
sessions, legislative, 214, *215f*–16*f*, 218
settlement, 4–9, *5f*, *46f*
sex offenders, *390*
sexual harassment, 237–38

Shapiro, Florence, 193*t*
Shapiro, Robert Y., 140–41
Sharp, Frank, 196, 196*t*, *197*
Sharp, John, 189, 255
Sharpstown scandal, 196, 196*t*, *197*
Shaw v. Reno, 159
Shays's Rebellion, 76
Shelby County v. Holder, 90, 93
sheriffs, 389
Shivers, Allan, *147*, 147–48, 248*f*
Sibley, David, 289
sick leave, paid, 385
Silicon Hills, 14
simple resolutions, 209
Simpson, David, 229
sine die, 214
single-head agencies, 299–300, *300*
single-issue groups, 182–83
single-member districts, 111
sin taxes, *424*, 425
skilled labor, 180
slavery, 9, 39, 41–45, 46*f*
Smith, Lonnie E., 109
Smith, Preston, 196, 196*t*, *197*, 249
Smith v. Allwright, 109
social contract, 36–37
social pressure, 118
social security, 448
social services, 16–17, 27*t*, 29, 444
social welfare, 27*t*, 444
sovereignty, 39
Spain, 7
Spanish settlers, 6–7
speaker of the house, 221–23, 222*t*, 225*f*
special districts, 398–401, 399*f*, *400–401*
special education, 464
special elections, 103
special laws, 208–9, 209*t*
special sessions, 214, 256–58, 257*f*
spending caps, 431
split ticket voting, 105
sports, 283, 290, *302*, 408
sprawls, 411, *411*
Springer, Drew, 185, 202
SSI. *See* Supplemental Security Income
STAAR standardized tests, 460
staff, 217, 249–51, 250*f*, 282*f*
standardized tests, 460
standing committees, 221
State Board of Education (SBOE), 304–6
State Commission on Judicial Conduct, 338
state district courts, 325–26, 327*f*
state documents, 15
state government, approval of, 78*f*
state-of-the-state address, 269
state party chairs, 143
statutory courts, 325
Steinbeck, John, 24
Sterling, Ross, 258
Stevenson, Adlai, 148
Stickland, Jonathan, *231*, 442–43

straight ticket voting, 131, 341
Straus, Joe, 155, 222*t*, 223, 311
    legacy of, 268
    reputation of, 227
Strayhorn, Carole "Grandma," 168, 295, 436
students, 185
stuffing the box, 233
suburbanization, 17
succession, 249
suffrage, 50–51
    elections and, 107–16, 112*f*, 115*f*, *116*
    politics of, 42–43
suicide, 377
Sunset Advisory Commission, 307–11, 308*t*, 309*f*
sunset agencies, 309*f*
sunset laws, 307–11, 308*t*, 309*f*
sunset processes, 307–11, 308*t*, 309*f*
Super PACs, 126. *See also* political action committees
Supplemental Security Income (SSI), 448
supremacy clause, 71
Supreme Court (TX), 338
    African Americans in, 346
    Asian Americans in, 346
    authority for, 328, 331
    Evenwel v. Abbot, 163
    Hispanics in, 346
    justices for, 54
    law for, 52
    League of United Latin American Citizens v. Perry, 160
    lobbying for, 187
    policy for, 43
    Ruiz v. Estelle, 369
    women in, 345–46
Supreme Court (US)
    ACA for, 87
    Arizona v. United States, 73*t*
    Avery v. Midland County, 388
    Baker v. Carr, 73*t*, 159
    Citizens United v. Federal Election Commission, 126
    Edgewood Independent School District v. Kirby, 456
    Fisher v. University of Texas, 467
    Furman v. Georgia, 369
    Garza v. County of Los Angeles, 111
    Gibbons v. Ogden, 73*t*
    Gomillion v. Lightfoot, 159
    Graves v. Barnes, 111
    McCullough v. Maryland, 72, 73*t*
    Obergefell v. Hodges, 75
    Plyler v. Doe, 453
    presidents and, 147
    San Antonio Independent School District v. Rodriguez, 456
    Shaw v. Reno, 159
    Shelby County v. Holder, 90, 93
    Smith v. Allwright, 109
    United States v. Lopez, 74
    White v. Regester, 111

Wickard v. Filburn, 72
surfing, of national trends, 125
Sylvester, Sherry, 290
systems. *See also* federalism
    commission governments, 395*f*, 396–97
    confederal system, 70–71
    council-manager system, 395*f*, 396–97, *397*
    for courts, 323*f*
    electoral systems, 132
    federal system, 71
    mayor-council system, 394–96, 395*f*
    patrón system, 110
    pay-as-you-go system, 295, 430–31
    place systems, 403
    unitary system, 70, 77

TABC. *See* Texas Alcohol Beverage Commission
tagging, 234–35
Talyor, Ivy, 140
TANF. *See* Temporary Assistance to Needy Families
taxes, *49*
    activism and, 422, *422*
    business taxes, 423
    for corporations, 423
    in debates, 428
    franchise taxes, 423
    for government, 44
    history of, 442
    income taxes, 427–28
    for natural gas, 424
    for oil, 424
    politics of, 153
    poll taxes, 108
    progressive taxes, 428
    property taxes, 58*f*, 61, 406–7, 419*f*, 420, *422*, 422–23
    psychology of, 58, 76, 146, 422, *422*, 427–28, 429*f*
    regressive taxes, 419–20
    salaries from, 249–51
    sales tax, 64, 406, *416*, 417–20, 419*f*, 421*f*
    sin taxes, *424*, 425
    tax collection, 296*f*
    for transportation, 424
Tax Increment Reinvestment Zones (TIRZs), 407–8
Taylor, Larry, *206*
TCEQ, 89, 302, 472–73
TDA. *See* Texas Department of Agriculture
TDI. *See* Texas Department of Insurance
teachers, 457–60, *459*, *464*
Tea Party, 131, 151–53, *153*
TEC. *See* Texas Ethics Commission
technology, 14, 474*t*
    for justice, 377–79
    mobile voting, 105
Tejanos, 7, 39–40

Temporary Assistance to Needy Families (TANF), 449, 450f
term limits, 63, 247, 248f
testing, 461f
Texas Alcohol Beverage Commission (TABC), 187, 310
Texas A&M, 189
Texas Commission on Environmental Quality (TCEQ), 89, 302, 472–73
Texas Commission on Judicial Selection, 346–47
Texas Criminal Justice Coalition, 359
Texas Department of Agriculture (TDA), 84, 284
Texas Department of Insurance (TDI), 300
Texas Department of State Health Services, 283
Texas Department of Transportation (TxDOT), 301, 468
Texas Ethics Commission (TEC), 198–201, 199t, 200f, 304–6
Texas Higher Education Coordinating Board (THECB), 467
Texas Historical Commission, 283
Texas Independence Convention, 34
Texas Indigent Defense Commission, 355
Texas judiciary. See judiciary
Texas Juvenile Justice Department, 334
Texas Medical Board, 279
Texas Miracle, 14–16
Texas Parks and Wildlife Department (TWPD), 255, 283, 301–2, 302, 305
Texas Public Policy Foundation, 187
Texas Racing Commission, 283
Texas Railroad Commission (TRC), 195, 303–4, 306
Texas Register, 281
Texas Water Development Board (TWDB), 470–72, 471f
Texas Windstorm Insurance Association (TWIA), 175, 342
Texas Workforce Commission, 176–77, 255, 451, 453
THECB. See Texas Higher Education Coordinating Board
third parties, 165–68, 166
Thompson, Laura, 168
Thompson, Senfronia, 229, 239, 239
Thornburn, Wayne, 157
Throckmorton, James W., 45
tidelands controversy, 90–91
tiebreaking, 291
Tiede, Bernie, 357
TIRZs. See Tax Increment Reinvestment Zones
tobacco, 425
Tort Claim Act (1969), 291
tort reform, 317–18
Tower, John, 114, 150, 156
trade associations, 180
tradition, 64, 79, 118

in ideology, 148
traditionalistic political culture, 26t, 28–30, 29f, 30f
transactional theory, 176–77
transportation
    commerce clause, 72
    data on, 469f
    DWI, 357, 358t
    funding for, 82f
    lobbying in, 179
    policy for, 183
    politics of, 82f, 388–89
    public policy for, 468, 469f
    taxes, 424
    Texas Racing Commission, 283
    TRC, 195, 303–4, 306
    TxDOT, 301, 468
Travis, William Barret, 35
TRC. See Texas Railroad Commission
trial courts, 320f, 322–26, 323f
trials, 361–62, 362
Truman, Harry, 113
Trump, Donald, 91, 454
trustees, 213
Turner, Sylvester, 93
Turtle Bayou Resolutions, 39
Turtle Island Restoration Network, 187
TWDB. See Texas Water Development Board
TWIA. See Texas Windstorm Insurance Association
Twitter, 212f, 213
TWPD. See Texas Parks and Wildlife Department
TxDOT, 301

unemployment. See employment
unfunded mandates, 88
unilateral orders, 252f, 254f
unincorporated areas, 388, 393
unions, 180, 181f
unitary system, 70, 77
United States (US). See also Supreme Court (US)
    authority in, 88, 90, 90f, 272f, 287f
    autonomy in, 86–87
    bill of rights, 54–55
    bureaucracy in, 282f
    CHIP, 447–48
    community supervision in, 364f
    Constitution (TX) and, 62f
    Constitution of, 47, 54–55, 71–72
    decentralization in, 141–42
    demographics of, 18f, 119f
    Department of Agriculture, 84
    Dillon's rule, 384–85
    disasters for, 84
    districts in, 399f
    economics in, 9–10, 81f
    employment in, 282f
    EPA, 89, 150, 472–73
    federal aid in, 81f
    full faith and credit clause, 75
    governor staff size, 250f

history of, 7–9
ICE, 454
judicial selection in, 336f
land seizure by federal government, 91
leadership in, 41
legislators in, 216f
local government in, 387f
Medicaid, 24
military, 12–14, 13f
parole in, 375f
reserve clause, 74
sales tax in, 421f
secession from, 44–45
Spain and, 7
state party platforms, 144
TANF, 449, 450f
trial courts, 320f
unilateral orders in, 254f
United States v. Lopez, 74
voting in, 119f
Urban Cowboy (film), 404
urbanization, 17
US. See United States
utilities, 401, 401

Van de Putte, Leticia, 140, 230
VanMeter, John Duane, 359
Vasquez de Coronado, Francisco, 6–7
Velasquez, Willie, 110
vetoes
    of bills, 259f
    line item vetoes, 260–61, 260f, 268
    for mayors, 394–96
    policy on, 258–61
    in politics, 245–46
victim rights, 355–56
violence, 49, 54
voir dire, 361–62, 362
voting
    activism for, 119f, 120–21, 140
    administration, 107
    by African Americans, 51–52, 112f, 113–14, 115f
    by Anglos, 148
    by Asian Americans, 116, 116
    at-large voting, 132
    authority in, 63
    on bonds, 408–9
    convenience voting, 120
    corruption and, 404–6
    courting voters, 125
    criminal disenfranchisement, 374, 375f
    cumulative voting, 404
    early voting, 103–4, 104f
    on Election Day, 105–6, 106f
    electoral systems for, 132
    by felons, 373–74
    by Hispanics, 109–12, 115f
    for incumbents, 131–33
    on initiatives, 392
    for justices, 339–43, 340t, 343f
    law regarding, 47–48

voting *(cont.)*
  learning objectives for, 99, 134
  literacy tests for, 108
  mail-in voting, 132
  microtargeting of voters, 125
  by minorities, 115*f*, 133
  mobile voting, 105
  motor voter law, 100
  national trends in, 126
  negative campaigning and, 124, *125*
  neighborhood precincts for, 105
  politics of, 56
  poll taxes for, 108
  practice quizzes for, 135
  psychology of, 57–59, 58*f*
  for ratification, 56–57
  recalls, 392
  on referendums, 392
  for reform, 59*t*, 60*f*
  registration for, 100–101, 101*f*
  The Right to Vote (Keyssar), 107
  Shelby County v. Holder, 90, 93
  social pressure related to, 118
  split ticket voting, 105
  straight ticket voting, 131, 341
  theory of, 117–18, 117*t*
  tiebreaking, 291
  in United States, 81*f*, 119*f*
  vote centers, 105, 106*f*
"vote harvesting," 120
voter fraud, 121–23, *122*
voter identification, 93, *93*, 121–23, *122*
Voting Rights Act (1965), 90, 93, 103–4, 108, 110
  in white primaries, 108–9
  by women, 114
vouchers, 463

Walker, Texas Ranger (TV show), 339
Wallace, James P., 331
Warren, Earl, 159
Washington, George, 76
water use, 20, 470–73, 471*f*
welfare
  CHIP, 447–48
  public policy for, 448–51, 450*f*
  social welfare, 27*t*, 444
  TANF, 449, 450*f*
Wentworth, Jeff, 193
West, Allen, 143
West, Royce, 55, 230, 435–36
White, Mark, 263, *263*, 265–66, 294, 346
  Clements and, 270
  legacy of, 459, 460
white primaries, 108–9
White v. Regester, 111
Whitley, David, 211

Whitmire, John, 161
Wickard v. Filburn, 72
wildlife, 301–2, *302*, 305
Wilkerson, Wally, 142, 143
Wilks, Farris, 131
Williams, Michael, 153
winner-take-all elections, 165
women. *See also* feminism
  as candidates, 167
  League of Women Voters of Texas, 184
  in politics, 237–38, 238*f*
  in Supreme Court (TX), 345–46
  voting by, 114
Woodfill, Jared, 156, *156*
World War II, 85

Yarborough, Donald H., 340–41
Yarborough, Don B., 340–41
Yarborough, Ralph, *147*, 148, 150, 340–41
  legacy of, 180
  reputation of, 113
Yoshinaka, Antoine, 164
"You Can't Close America" rally, 184

Zaffirini, Judith, 237
Zavala, Lorenzo de, 40
Zerwas, John, 199*t*
zoning, 412